ANALECTA ORIENTALIA
COMMENTATIONES SCIENTIFICAE DE REBUS ORIENTIS ANTIQUI
53

COPTIC GRAMMATICAL CATEGORIES

STRUCTURAL STUDIES IN THE SYNTAX
OF SHENOUTEAN SAHIDIC

1986

PONTIFICIUM INSTITUTUM BIBLICUM
I-00187 ROMA   PIAZZA PILOTTA 35

ARIEL SHISHA-HALEVY

COPTIC GRAMMATICAL CATEGORIES

STRUCTURAL STUDIES IN THE SYNTAX
OF SHENOUTEAN SAHIDIC

1986

PONTIFICIUM INSTITUTUM BIBLICUM
I-00187 ROMA   PIAZZA PILOTTA 35

ISBN 88-7653-255-2

IURA EDITIONIS ET VERSIONIS RESERVANTUR

PRINTED IN ITALY

TIPOGRAFIA POLIGLOTTA DELLA PONTIFICIA UNIVERSITÀ GREGORIANA
PIAZZA DELLA PILOTTA, 4 - ROMA

For Malca, with lots of love and gratitude

FOREWORD

This book is not a Coptic grammar, nor is it cast in the semblance of one: it is a series of studies of a fairly central area of Coptic syntax, a detailed systematic charting of a subsystem or more or less continuous range of grammatical phenomena.

It is with great pleasure and warmth of feeling that I wish to acknowledge the help and advice I have enjoyed for the last decade from my colleagues and close friends: N. Barri (Jerusalem), W.-P. Funk (Berlin–DDR), J. Horn (Göttingen), B. Layton (New Haven) and H. Quecke (Rome). To my teacher, Prof. H. B. Rosén of the Department of Linguistics, the Hebrew University, I owe my initiation into structural linguistics, and much more than that: a great many ideas in this book may be traced back to his brilliant lectures and stimulating classroom talks.

I am deeply thankful for the privilege of having been able to study under Prof. H. J. Polotsky since 1963 in the Departments of Linguistics and Egyptian, the Hebrew University. He has been an unfailing source of friendly encouragement, wise advice, constant inspiration — CBШ NAME EЧXHK EBOΛ. EPEOYA NAШXOOC ON XEOY NNA2PN-TEKMNTPEЧ†CBШ NAN EEIME EПШPX; OYXAI NAN, ПACA2 ANOK AYШ ПENMEPIT NCA2 THPN, EKKYBEPNA MMON 2N2ШB NIM.

My sincere thanks are extended to Mr. G. D. Myers, who spared no effort in improving my English style.

A. Shisha–Halevy

CONTENTS

PRELIMINARY CHAPTER

AIMS, SCOPE AND METHOD

" Das Koptische wird sobald keiner auslernen, und ich muss m ich
bescheiden, wenn der Weg, den ich zeige, der richtige ist "

L. Stern, *Koptische Grammatik,* xv

" Willst du dich am Ganzen erquicken,
So mußt du das Ganze im Kleinsten erblicken "

Goethe, *Sprüche*

" Die paritätische Verbindung von Mikroskopie und Makrosko pie
bildet das Ideal der wissenschaftlichen Arbeit; in Wirklichkeit kommt
meistens die eine gegen die andere zu kurz "

Schuchardt-Brevier, 410

0.0.1 RATIONALE. SELECTION OF PROBLEMS

This study or series of studies aims primarily at being a methodologically conscious account of several interrelated phenomena in the grammar of an important literary corpus of Coptic; namely, the application of the procedures of structural analysis to the linguistic data in the works of SHENOUTE, the fourth-

— 1 —

fifth century Archimandrite. Secondarily, it is meant as a detailed description of a Coptic grammatical system made with programmatic and consistent regard for procedural tenets — indeed beginning with the principle of strictly *corpus-based* statements, '' corpus '' meaning a homogenous set of data, as idiolectal and synchronic as possible, and reflecting an *état de langue* as closely as possible. The success of this work will be judged on both counts: its only *prima facie* merit lies in its being the first of its kind.

This is not a '' Grammar of Shenoutean Coptic '' in the traditional and still conventional sense. Indeed, I contend that writing a '' Grammar '' is the only unacceptable way of writing about (i.e. reporting on) grammar, unless it be for the purpose of tuition (that is, applied linguistics), a '' textbook ''. I envisage two radically different conceptions for tackling the syntax of a given text or texts: the first a descending, text-to-word scanning, class-and-member analysis of a linear structure (Hjelmslev's '' *deling* ''), the second — which I adopt here as being more profitable at the present stage of Coptic grammatical research — a *categorial* (still class-and-member) scanning of sub-systems (Hjelmslev's '' *leddeling* ''), valid for and verifiable within the said texts: a '' pattern grammar ''. The sub-system or set of categories I have chosen for description is that of the MODIFIER. A look at the Tables of Contents — which are also a synopsis of patterns — would show the scope of this hyper-category (§0.3). While it may at first impulse appear that an exaggerated edifice is here erected on what is perhaps the narrowest basis possible, namely the expansion-marker morpheme N‒, no one with a practical or theoretical acquaintance with the workings of Coptic grammar would deny the keynote standing of modifiers — adnominal, adverbal; verbal, non-verbal; adjunctal, predicative — in the overall picture of Coptic.

0.1 CORPUS; AUTHENTICITY

The statements made on the following pages will be strictly corpus-grammatical, based only on attested facts, with no extra- or interpolation, the '' corpus '' thus acquiring the additional sense of a '' predictive sample of the language '' (HARRIS 1951:§2.33). Whereas all Coptic grammars of general validity are in reality *mixing-grammars* and must be rejected in principle on the objection that they cannot claim to be descriptive of *any* single Coptic *état de langue*, but are, at best, overall, stereoscopic impressions of grammatical phenomena, it is my intention here to present systematically corpus-based facts in verifiable *Spezialgrammatik* statements. This objective constitutes a third facet of the *raison d'être* of the present study. Before proceeding to define my corpus, I feel I should defend, be it briefly, the choice of Shenoute's works as most suitable for the present purpose. While perhaps not many today would care to subscribe explicitly to Vergote's statement (*BiOr* 6:102 1949) that '' Sahidic is at its purest in the New Testament '' — whatever '' pure '' may here mean — the fact that this is implicitly accepted, without the least realization of its basic circularity, is reflected everywhere: in teaching policy and practice as well as in grammatical research, where almost all corpus-based monographs concern the Scriptures (e.g. WILSON 1970, KICKASOLA 1975) and yet claim general validity. I believe that this rooted bias is wrong, not merely from the theory-conscious descriptive linguist's point of view — who would of course reject at the outset any aprioristic evaluating preference for a given corpus — but, more fundamentally, since we badly need a formulation of authentic (in the sense of '' untranslated '') grammatical usage for Coptic before we can even begin to argue contrastively about the native-idiomatic *vs.* Greek components of Scripture Coptic, and the degree and quality of artificiality, of adherence to the *Vorlage* and of its influence on the system of the translation. Moreover, the monolithic nature of the Scripture corpus cannot be taken for granted, but must be established through independent description of its constituents. Thus, the precedence of the authentic (though later) source over the translated (albeit earlier, and, by dint of historical prestige, '' classical '') ought to be obvious. For a large, homogenous, untranslated literary corpus there is nothing in Coptic to compete with Shenoute's writings. It is, I am convinced, precisely this kind of source that is advisable as a *testo di lingua* for a grammatical treatise meant to depict grammatical usage as a system[1]. One may thus add a fourth element to the *raison d'être* of the present work, namely the need to find a way of representing the grammar of Coptic literary norm as realistically as possible.

As for the source material itself: the self-evident major problem here lies in the obvious necessity of basing the descriptive statements on a corpus the Shenouteanity of which is at least reasonably certain, by direct or indirect attribution: on the strength of internal extra-linguistic information, unambiguous linguistic (grammatical, phraseological, "stylistic") data, or — most difficult to formulate — the accumulation of factors of familiarity, the sense of norm and idiosyncrasy, the philologist's *Sprachgefühl*[2]. There is here an evident danger of circularity of applying to doubtful texts criteria of authenticity distilled from a collection including these self-same sources, or taking as Shenoutean and admitting as basis for critical statements material eligible solely on the strength of these doubtful texts. On the face of it, this pitfall may seem easy enough to avoid, yet in the actual process of selecting, sifting and describing the texts, with simultaneous isolation of critical characteristics, such slips are ever imminent. On the other hand, the highly selective approach is at odds with the pressing need for more complete documentation. My decision has been not to compromise in this matter, and accordingly texts of doubtful (yet possible) Shenouteanity, although certainly consulted and occasionally quoted, have been left outside the core of critical corpus: such sources are indicated by queries in the Appendix lists. Needless to say, such selection involves making subjective and in all probability provisional decisions, which may be contested on the basis of different judgement or independent contrary evidence (e.g. an explicitly attributed parallel turning up, a passage identified as non-Shenoutean by scholars more competent than myself in patristic lore, and so on). The actual procedure is in fact not circular but spiral: from a bona-fide core one works out, along ever-increasing radii, to a periphery of doubtful sources, always drawing upon the newly familiar territory for criteria. I have used all major, minor and minimal published editions of Shenoute and most of the unpublished manuscripts: it is especially with regard to the latter that the above reservation is made.

0.1.1 CRITERIA OF SHENOUTEANITY are too many and too various — even pending a systematic working-over of the corpus— to be enumerated here. A few have been suggested by the present writer (1975, 1976a); others (like ⲧⲱ ⲉⲧⲱ, ϢⲀⲚⲦⲈⲞⲨ Ϣⲱⲡⲉ, the notorious "Disiunctio Sinuthiana"[3], lexical favourites or monopolies — ϢⲞⲞⲨ "incense", (ⲌⲰϤⲦ)ⲌⲈϤⲦ- "eject", ϢⲰⲂ2 "be withered", ϢⲰⲔ2 "be/ dig deep", ⲔⲢⲞϤ, ⲀⲞⲒⲘⲞⲤ and so on[4]) are well known[5]; numerous others (like ⲈⲒⲭⲱ ⲘⲡⲀⲒ ⲭⲈ- "by

---

[1] An early lone advocate of Shenoute as a basis for a Coptic syntax was SPIEGELBERG (1909:440). In the Department of Linguistics, the Hebrew University of Jerusalem, first acquaintance with Coptic through Shenoute is characteristic of students approaching Coptic with a purely linguistic motivation: they testify to an entirely different impression of the language and, on the whole, get a better grasp of it, although this may be partly due to their training.

[2] See Lindroth, "Das Sprachgefühl, ein vernachlässigter Begriff", *IF* 55:1-16 (1937). KERN (1888:139), criticising (wrongly, I believe) H. Paul for using as argument (PAUL 1920:§258) the fact that the German *Sprachgefühl* does not distinguish between adverb and adjective in predicative status, says: "Wenn doch die gelehrten Grammatiker nicht so oft auf das Sprachgefühl sich da berufen wollten, wo es lediglich darauf ankommt, sprachliche Erscheinungen zu beurteilen! Gewiss weiss das Sprachgefühl hier von einem Unterschied nicht, weil es überhaupt über wissenschaftliche Dinge unwissend ist: dafür ist es eben Gefühl". What Kern here opposes to the "linguistic intuition" must be pre-analytic, aprioristic so-called "scientific informedness", a kind of praeter-factual intelligence which is the cardinal sin in descriptive misinterpretation, while Paul's *Sprachgefühl* is but a misnomer for "listener's model information".

[3] Ⲁ ⲠⲀⲌⲎⲦ ⲞⲨϢⲰⲤ Ⲏ ⲀϤⲞⲨϢⲰⲤ 2ⲢⲀⲒ Ⲛ2ⲎⲦ (*P* 130[5] 19 ⲢⲄ); see SHISHA-HALEVY 1976a:37ff.; cf. FEHLING 1969:216-8; this is a kind of "linguistic self-criticism" (Jespersen's term, in a 1935 article of that name), or compulsive "legalistic"-precisionist quirk. Other typical Shenoutean turns of phrase, constructions and figures will be pointed out in the course of the present work, without going into such difficult questions as how a "figure" is to be defined (cf. FEHLING 1969:7ff.), the degree of awareness in the use of a given construction, its functional charge and cotextual correlation.

[4] Cf. SHISHA-HALEVY 1976b:364ff.

[5] See AMÉLINEAU, *Oeuvres de Schenoudi* I (1907) xiii ff. The serious practical problem of distinguishing Shenoute's works

which I mean to say ", rhetoric-argumentative figures using ⲈϢⳤⲈ-, a " ⲠⲢⲰⳘⲈ ⲠⲈ ⲠⲀⲒ ⲈⲦ- " hyperbatic Nominal Sentence pattern, collocations of the " irreversible binomial " [6] type like ⲠⲀⲚ - ⲤⲬⲎⳘⲀ, ⲦⲈⳲⲢⲈ - ⲐⲂⲤⲰ, ⳤⲰⳲⳘ - ⳤⲒⲞⲨⲈ, ⲔⲢⳘⲢⳘ - ⳠⲚⲀⲠⲒⲔⲈ, are yet to be properly definied and statistically established in special studies; some have to do with peculiarities of dialectal admixture or " substratal " traces (SHISHA-HALEVY 1976b, cf. SPIEGELBERG 1909:441), others with a more or less fragmentated stylistic impression, yet others are definable in terms of subsystems of grammatical usage, such as the one under scrutiny here: this adds yet another motivation to this study, since the conclusions arrived at and the " Shenou-teanisms " resolved here could carry considerable practical-diacritic weight. We are, of course, in search of the *converging* of the various symptoms, the cumulative evidence. Despite all this, we shall still have to contend with numerous instances of untypical Shenoute, where one cannot improve upon Zoega's " *existimo* ", " *arbitror* ", " *nisi fallor* ", " *conjicio* " and the like. A nice methodological issue is that of the SUB-CORPUS OF QUOTATIONS, mainly biblical, interwoven in the text. There is again the technical difficulty of recognizing a quoted segment of the text where it is not signalled as such (by ⲨⲤⳲⳲ ⳤⲈ-, ⲚⲐⲈ ⲈⲦⲤⳲⳲ ⳤⲈ-, ⲀⲨϢ ⲞⲚ/ⲠⲀⲖⲒⲚ ⲞⲚ/ⳘⲠⲈⲒⳘⲀ ⳤⲈ-, and the like; an instance of unsignalled quotation is *Ch.* 115.23f. = *Mt.* 3:12). More importantly, these quotations (and, significantly, biblical *reminiscences*) give us a glimpse into an extraneous system of grammar, where, for example, ϢⲀⲦⲚⲀⲨ contrasts with Shenoute's own ϢⲀⲚⲦⲈⲞⲨ ϢⲰⲠⲈ (§2.5.0.2), ⲦⲀⲢⲈⲨⲤⲰⲦⳘ with Shenoute's paradigm of post-imperatival forms (§7.2.1.1.5), in application to which many of the statements made below are simply not valid. She-noute's own awareness of this contrast of norms is evident, since he puts it to rhetorical use, switching now and again to the Scripture diasystem, ringing diaphasic changes, achieving archaic, pathos-carrying, authoritative effects. As a rule, I have left quotations and reminiscences out of my account, nevertheless referring to them on occasion in contrastive terms; excerpt-quotations, as well as Shenoute's own conscious archaisms, will be duly noted.

Admittedly, in the exposition I have not always drawn uniformly on all sources: unpublished MSS have been called on mainly for scarcely documented phenomena. For some studies (notably Ch. 7, the conjunctive) I have used a core corpus (Leipoldt + Chassinat) with added peripheral evidence, aiming for a higher degree of homogeneity for some central issues.

0.1.2 SHENOUTE'S STYLE. A measure of Shenoute's literary standing (" the greatest of all writers in the Coptic language ", WORRELL 1945:22) is the frequency of comments on his style. A brief review of these not always favourable reactions is rewarding, since it illustrates the traditional approach to Coptic idiomatic syntax. ZOEGA (1805), though not the first to edit fragments of Shenoute's work — this distinction goes to Mingarelli — first noted the extremes which Shenoute's " *dicendi modus* " can attain, a very important piece of information indeed: on the one hand, he observes (588) " *sententiarum emphatica inversio... fervidae illae declarationes... epistolae illae parabolis et paradigmis refertae... scripta stylo plano atque fluido digesta* "; on the other hand (*ibid.*, 483) " *stylus pedestris et humilis... lectu facilis, stylus placidior... quam is quo uti solet* ". The first of the two, Shenoute's idiosyncratic, overwrought and often overstating mood is naturally the one most often pointed out; either admiringly: " the fury, eloquence and beauty of the language " (Hyvernat in the introduction to his manuscript catalogue of

from those of other homiletic writers, and especially of his successor, Besa, cannot be solved on a stylistic basis alone (see §0.1.2) but must wait for a comprehensive statement of Shenoute's linguistic usage, a Grammar, Phraseology and Lexicon of Shenoute. The attribution by stylistic impression alone has occasionally misled editors (notoriously Amélineau, even Crum in a few of his " Sh "s in the Dictionary, also in his catalogues). See on this issue Ladeuze, *Étude sur le cénobitisme pakhômien* (1898) 151f.; Kuhn, *Muséon* 66:225f. (1953), 71:376ff. (1958), and in the introduction to his edition of Besa (CSCO 157/copt.21, 1956) p.xiii f. The so-called " Pseudo-Shenoute " texts (ed. Kuhn, CSCO 206-7/copt.29-30, 1960 with an unedited parallel codex, *B.L.Or.* 12689) have a different standing: they seem to be somehow based on, and to contain, genuine Shenoute material (SHISHA-HALEVY 1975:472f., 477, 1976b:362f.). Regarding Leipoldt's No.76 and non-shenoutean fragments included in Amé-lineau's edition, see the Appendix.

[6] MALKIEL 1959.

1886-7 to the Woide-Clarendon Press collection, now in the Bodleian Library, Oxford); " L'auteur le plus original, le plus passionné, celui dont la langue est la plus riche et le vocabulaire le plus complet " (Amélineau, *Miss.* IV [1895] 497) or with more or less discerning criticism: " La phrase de Schenoudi n'est pas la phrase assez simple, assez analytique, des autres auteurs coptes; c'est une phrase compliquée, aussi synthétique qu'elle peut l'être, tourmentée, coupée d'incises et de propositions subordonnées " (Amélineau, *Œuvres de Schenoudi* I [1907] xiv)[7]. LEIPOLDT, the great editor of Shenoute, also comments somewhat adversely on his stylistic idiosyncrasies (1903:§§11,13: his characterization, albeit subjective and psychologistic, is at times quite apt): " Ihm fehlt die harmlose Naivetät, fehlt die schlichte Einfalt, fehlt die kindliche Ausdrucksweise... ". Leipoldt distinguishes between " depression " and " exultation " in Shenoute's mood, in his works he distinguishes between, on the one hand, the sermons, which exhibit a style " recht hölzern " and in which " fliessen Worte und Sätze ruhig dahin. Die einzelnen Teile werden breit und äusserlich von einander geschieden, die Gedanken oft und fast ungeschickt wiederholt. Selbst den Ermahnungen... fehlt es an Kraft und Wärme ", and, on the other, the epistles, in which more emotion is in evidence: " sprunghaft... überstürzen sich die Sätze ". WORRELL's comment is more restrained (1945:24): " His style is not polished, but it shows some rhetorical skill. He is original and difficult... he had a great command of the language and shaped it ". Obviously, none of the critics make an attempt to glimpse, through the personal style and rhetoric of our author, the true pageant of native, idiomatic (and often colloquial) Coptic: " style " has obliterated syntax, and the *point de repère* is yet again the norm of Scripture Coptic.

0.2 STATEMENT OF METHODOLOGICAL ORIENTATION

In this series of studies I shall view grammatical phenomena from a European-structuralist viewpoint. This is not the place and there is hardly the space to embark here on a detailed account of this school, since even the European brand of structuralist linguistics, far from being a monolithic school with an agreed, easily epitomizable code of procedure, is rather an ensemble of individualistic, frequently eclectic approaches, tenets and codifications[8]; what follows is a concise programmatic exposé of the most consequential principles of analytic policy to which I adhere in this work.

0.2.1.1 RELATIONSHIPS, SYNTAGMATIC AND PARADIGMATIC. OPPOSITION AND NEUTRALIZATION.
A language element can be described as having a value (role, function, meaning), as grammatically operative, only in terms of its relationship to other elements[9]: syntagmatic (linear, (co)textual) or paradigmatic (commutative, categorial) relationship. The former is interpretable in terms of dependence, rection (government), conditioning, (in)compatibility, sequence (arrangement, placement); the latter in terms of opposition and of relevance, and its negation, neutralization; of substitution and category.

---

[7] Observing nevertheless that Shenoute's style could at times be quite different: " Il avait ses moments d'accalmie, où sa phrase était limpide... les lions ne rugissent pas toujours, ils badinent quelquefois et jouent avec leurs lionceaux " (*ibid.*). Note Amélineau's characteristic eloquence. Without rating too highly his grammatical acumen, it is nevertheless amusing to note that Amélineau writes of Shenoute's sentences with subordinate clauses in which one is liable to go astray, unless one holds firmly to the rules of grammar, " règles encore peu connues que d'ailleurs l'auteur viole, et avec la plus magnifique désinvolture " (*ibid.*, and see too pp. xxix ff.).

[8] Some valuable retrospective surveys and guides for further reading: LEPSCHY 1972 (see p. 152f. for further state-of-the-art reports); MOHRMANN *et al.* 1961, esp. pp. 126ff., 196ff., 294ff.; articles by Koerner, Engler, Lepschy, Hymes and Fought in SEBEOK, ed. 1975:717-1176; see also BAZELL 1954, COSERIU 1969, and numerous works referred to below. I must first deny all intention to convey an impression of a nice-and-tidy code of procedure, and confess my awareness of the inevitable superficialities. The following paragraphs are neither a general linguistics manifesto nor a *profession de foi*, but jotted highlights of orientation for the grammatical studies to follow.

[9] In Saussure's words (GODEL 1954:63): " Il n'y a jamais rien qui puisse résider dans *un* terme ", cf. SAUSSURE 1949:150ff.; BENVENISTE 1963:16; SIERTSEMA 1965:94f., COSERIU 1969:58ff.; this is the meaning of " grammatical system ": there are no elements outside it.

The simplest oppositions [10] are *binary* (including *privative*, with two poles or terms related to each other as *marked : unmarked* [11]). Any one member of an opposition may be *zero* [12] or neutral (non-functional). Neutralization (*Aufhebung*, suppression of opposition) is a syntagmatic-and-paradigmatic event just as significant as opposition [13]: the governed or conditioned representative member in a case of neutralization cannot be said to have any meaning, since meaning depends on and presupposes opposition, the possibility of choice [14], the existence of a paradigm. (Incidentally, any change in the number of terms in a paradigm entails a reassignment of the meaning of the individual members.) Neutralization, like opposition, is only definable for a specific environment.

0.2.1.2 PATTERN AND CATEGORY. A category is expressed, realized and defined by a substitution-list or *paradigm* (of affixes, syntagms or constructions), which is its *signifiant* [15]. This paradigm is in turn valid (being resolvable) only in a given environment. Accordingly, the category is definable only by its localization, in terms of the sequence/substitution set of coordinates. The category is a constituent part of a *pattern*: the pattern is defined as *an ordered sequence of categories (paradigms)*; but since commutation is dependent on the extent of environment established as relevant [16], pattern delimitation is a component of decisive importance in the definition. Pattern boundaries, however, are relative (in the sense that they are gradable on a scale of rank of ever-decreasing extent, from text-entirety downwards [17]). Consequently, established classes or categories are correspondingly gradable on a scale of varying analytic delicacy [18].

0.2.1.3 PROFILE OF A GRAMMATICAL PHENOMENON; IDENTITY; MODELS. As stated above, the identification of a grammatical entity is effected by a positional/commutational localization: the point where the coordinates of compatibility and commutability meet in this identificational matrix is its analytic identity, its name [19]: this, no more, no less, is the analytic information we can give on it. We may add,

[10] Classified by TRUBETZKOY (1939:60ff.); see COSERIU 1969:120ff. Oppositions are formal *and* functional, in a formal system and a *système de valeur*, as the two faces of the *signifiant - signifié* linguistic coin. We accordingly adopt as the basic premise in analytic procedure that a *formal* difference must mean a *functional* one.

[11] TRUBETZKOY 1939:67, 77, 84; MARTINET 1965:180ff.; see below Ch.5, footnote 24.

[12] On the (by definition) structural concept of a "zero element" (significant absence) see SAUSSURE 1949:123f., 163f., MEIER 1961, with abundant literature.

[13] See classifications and discussion by TRUBETZKOY 1936, 1939:69ff., 206f.; HJELMSLEV 1939 (SIERTSEMA 1965:180ff.); COSERIU 1969:125, 132, 234ff.; ROBINS 1970:41ff.

[14] An example: the circumstantial conversion as an expansion of an indefinite nominal nucleus can only be said to be "adnominal" — no more; whereas each of the two main verbal expansions of a *definite* noun, viz. the relative and circumstantial, has its "meaning", respectively, attributive and adnexal modification.

[15] "Paradigm" — not in its arbitrarily restricted, traditional, schoolbook sense of "substitution-list in the minimal (morphologic, 'word') environment", but also in the sense of commutability in the larger-than-word extent, including paradigms of constructions. See SIERTSEMA 1965:175ff., 262ff., SEILER 1967:517f. (No.1).

[16] An example: the converters: є-circ., є-Sec. Tense, єтє- (relative), nє- (preterite) constitute a single category (paradigm) only in the extent of the minimal environment, namely the converted conjugation form (or predication in general). Their mutual commutability ceases to be true once we extend the pattern boundaries to include, say, the immediately preceding paradigm; this "morphological" category is still further fragmentated if the operative environment is extended even more.

[17] HALLIDAY 1961:251, 261. See §0.2.2.

[18] HALLIDAY 1961-260f.

[19] Cf. SAUSSURE 1949:150ff. This is the policy adopted here regarding the difficult theoretical dilemma of *identity* vs. *homonymy*, which will often arise in the course of the following descriptions. An item will be judged and "named" only by reference to the above criteria, to which one must add allo-forms in order to synthesize a "surname". For example: the plural definite article and the "nota relationis" are both represented in Coptic by a nasal phoneme; their distinct identities, however, are established on the basis of (a) their paradigms and syntax, (b) their allomorphs in a specific corpus (e.g. in Chassinat's edition of Shenoute: n-/m- for the *nota relationis*, n-/m-/n-/n-/nє- for the plural article). Another example: ϣαρє-/ϣα- (aorist affirmative base) *vs.* ϣα-/ϣαρο= (preposition).

or occasionally prefer, a synthetic statement: the various (conditioned) alloforms of our entity. This gives us a different facet of its identity, which, together with the analytic one, I consider the complete descriptive statement to be made concerning any grammatical element. It follows that we must not, indeed cannot, " import " any external pre-conceived notion into the grammar of a language as a ' category ". This *caveat* is immediately and eminently applicable to the part-of-speech assignment of a given element, to which we shall have the opportunity to return now and again [20].

I must here briefly refer to a meta-meta-linguistic perplexity, one that is usually ignored in general linguistic discussion, namely, the so-called " hocus-pocus " *vs.* " God's truth " nature of theoretical constructs [21]. While we pretend to depict in our descriptions a *modèle de récepteur* situation, it is often obvious that the presented models are really of our own creation. It might be claimed, and with very good reason, that any synthesizing model, departing from, assuming or preceding [22] the unstructured data is inevitably an artificial (and to a varying extent arbitrary) construct, superimposed on the data material. This may also apply in general to what we call " structure " and " system " [23]. Nonetheless, I consider these models (a) legitimate, valid and viable, provided they be based on sound observation; (b) desirable, in the sense of " constructive ", effectively encoding meta-linguistic information in a conventionally decodable manner [24]. Still, it cannot be claimed that they are exclusively or universally *true*.

0.2.2 LEVELS, HIERARCHIES, DIRECTIONS OF ANALYSIS. Among the meta-linguistic models or " fictions " referred to in the preceding paragraph are some which I consider fallacious and which I have tried to avoid in the present exposition. First and foremost among these is the *stratification* of analysis, the " levels ". Even without resorting to the special pleading warranted by the singular typological reasons [25] that make Coptic much less subject to the preliminary theoretical distinction between *word* and *sentence*, *morphology* and *syntax* than Indo-European or Semitic languages, the advisability as well as the validity and legitimacy of this particular model must be (and often has been) questioned [26]. The analysis must, I believe, be *continuous*, text-to-morpheme, class-and-member; the word would be but a stage in this downward analysis, an intermediate pattern-unit, defined (like other patterns) by inner constituency, sequence, prosodic characterization and boundary signalling, a syntagm [27] like others.

---

[20] Cf. BARRI 1975b:§6; BAUM 1976:139-143. Indeed, I accept without reservation Sapir's dictum (*Language* 125) that " No logical scheme of the parts of speech — their number, nature, or necessary confines — is of the slightest interest to the linguist. Each language has its own scheme. Everything depends on the formal demarcation it recognizes ". Written sixty years ago, one cannot, unfortunately, dismiss this warning today as no longer necessary. Similarly, one must sadly concede that Halliday's optimistic belief (*Studies in Linguistic Analysis*, 1957, p. 57) that " transference of grammatical categories is a dead horse no longer to be flogged " cannot have been uttered with Coptic in mind. See also §0.3 and Chapter 1, footnote 1.

[21] GARVIN 1954:74f.; HOUSEHOLDER 1952; BAUM 1976:139-143.

[22] Cf. Saporta, *Word* 12:12 (1956): " It is clear that linguistic patterns are highly patterned. What is not clear is whether this fact is best considered the result of a linguistic analysis or the basis for this analysis "; SCHUCHARDT (SPITZER 1928:411f.): " Nun gibt es Systeme, die schon fertig in den Dingen liegen und von uns nur entdeckt werden, und Systeme, die wir bilden, um sie in die Dinge hineinzulegen... Systeme dieser Art haben nur zeitweilige und bedingte Geltung "; also *ibid.* 299f.

[23] Consider HALLIDAY's definitions (1961:246f., 254ff.).

[24] Cf. HALL's " fictions " (1965).

[25] Cf. MISTELI's typologically oriented review of Stern's *Grammatik* (1982:448ff., 454 " no words, only groups — larger or smaller, closer or looser "); STERN xi f., STEINTHAL–MISTELI 1893:272f.; and see the discussion of the Coptic " word " below, §6.0.2.3, with further references.

[26] See BARRI 1977:13ff., 21ff., 24ff. for a critical research-historical survey of the question; on the problems involved in defining the word, see LYONS 1968:194-208; HALLIDAY 1961:261. Cf. De Groot " Wort und Wortstruktur ", *Neophilologus* 24/25: 221-233 (1939/40); De Boer, " Morphologie et syntaxe ", *CFS* 6:5-25 (1946/7); and the telling reponses in *Acts of the Sixth Congress of Linguists* (1949), discussion of Question III. For Coptic see already STERN 1880:XI.

[27] In the Saussurean sense (SAUSSURE 1949:170), cf. Frei, *Studia Gratulatoria Groot* (1962) 139: " combinaison de deux ou plusieurs unités également présentes qui se suivent ". This is also Baudouin de Courtenay's use of the term (*A Baudouin de Courtenay Anthology*, tr. and ed. E. Stankiewicz, 1972 p. 267).

Coptic morphology could be conceived of naïvely, as a study, synchronic or diachronic, of *purely formal* inner regularities of structure, with no functional correlates (e.g. for the nominal and infinitive " classes ") [28].

Another synthesizing hierarchy which I reject in synchronic description is that of primary *vs.* secondary functions [29]. This is, I believe, an arbitrary and distorting distinction: there is no hint in the actual, i.e. environment-defined, signalling function of elements, of any scale of precedence or importance. (One encounters terms like " primary " or " main " and " original " — both in the only meaningful, *diachronic* sense, and in a vague uncommitted sense — often confusedly understood as attributes of " use ", " function " and the like.) On the other hand, *rule ordering* or *analytic (descriptive) order* [30] is acceptable as a descriptive artifice, a necessary heuristic means of interrelating observables, not a dynamic theory of what actually takes place in the system [31]. Another hierarchy which I adopt implicitly is that of *analytic delicacy*, distinguishing between the resolution of primary and secondary classes [32].

0.2.3 NON-ATTESTATION. An inevitable embarrassment of a structural corpus-based grammar (perhaps more acute with a dead language, where no informant can extend our corpus at need) is having to puzzle out the *significance of non-attestation*. Even in a corpus as extensive as ours, the non-occurrence of some theoretically possible or expected element or construction must be weighed for possible structural significance, status of *case vide*, as against fortuitousness: we must see our way to distinguishing between systemic and accidental non-occurrence [33]. This perplexity is all the more acute here, since the present study is not an exhaustive inventory-catalogue of all paradigmatic or even syntagmatic possibilities, but an account of grammatical *structure*: the lists in this work should be seen as open-ended, due to the certainty of the corpus being eventually extended and the ever-present possibility of a descriptive oversight. In my opinion, the only theoretically acceptable way out of this predicament is the one, based on an examination of the distribution-structure, suggested by ROSÉN (1968). If a non-attestation of item (entity, phenomenon) x is dependent upon a specific environment and environmental properties, upon a specific pattern P_1, and it can be shown that a different pattern, P_2 in which x does occur, is in this respect in complementary (suppletive) distribution with P_1, we may consider the non-occurrence of x in P_1 a *fact of grammatical absence* [34] which we should not expect to find refuted (by a chance attestation) in the corpus under observation. If, however, x does not feature in any complementary environment, the non-attestation may be interpreted as mere non-occurrence, possibly to be rectified in the near future (unless yet another pattern, P_3, including x, is eventually found to be in an " allo "-relationship with P_1).

---

[28] Somewhat in the sense of MARTINET's use of the term (1967:§4.6 " l'étude des variantes de signifiant "), or Vergote's in his *Grammaire copte* (Ia, 1973, " morphologie synthématique ").

[29] See (for example) KURYŁOWICZ 1964; criticism by E. Koschmieder in *Die Welt der Slawen* 7:409-22 (1962).

[30] See BLOOMFIELD 1933:212f.; ROSÉN 1964:§46, 1970; BARRI 1977:21 (" the order of what the linguist does "). I have a similar view also of that other phenomena-relating metalinguistic construct, the *transformation*, except as a presentation device (cf. SCHUCHARDT [SPITZER 1928:296]: " Umkehrung ist zwar statisch vorhanden, aber nicht genetisch ").

[31] " *Structural* " as distinct from *linear* (sequential) order (BLOOMFIELD 1933:210; TESNIÈRE 1965:16f., 19ff.; ROSÉN 1970) has a different standing altogether, reflecting, in my opinion, linguistic reality and not a model of convenience. Another non-dynamic structuring device employed below is that of *Immediate-Constituents* (IC) analysis.

[32] HALLIDAY 1961:272f.

[33] For instance, the comparison of " adverb " paradigms in the various positions and functions is meaningless unless one can estimate their limits.

[34] Some examples: ⲛⲧⲉⲓⲍⲉ " thus " is *absent* as predicate in the Bipartite pattern, since it is predicated in the ⧺ Predicate – ⲡⲉ⧺ pattern (§1.2.1.2); *ⲙⲁⲣⲉⲕ-/ⲙⲡⲣⲧⲣⲉⲕ- are *absent*, since the imperative fills their slots; the ⧺*Second Tense (negative) → focal interrogative modifier⧺ is *absent* in the ⧺ Sec. Tense + interrogative focal modifier⧺ pattern, since a different construction, viz. ⧺ interrogative modifier → (negative) First Tense⧺ supplies the " missing " item.

0.2.4 THE SAUSSUREAN DUALITIES [35]. Corpus-based description makes unnecessary stand-taking on the *synchrony : diachrony* model, which is probably no less fictive and conveniently idealizing than others [36]. Structural description and the very concept of system are essentially static, just as they are primarily internal, i.e. non-comparative. The situation as regards the *langue : parole* dichotomy is somewhat more complicated. This distinction has often been criticized as inadequate, and additional stratification has been suggested. HJELMSLEV's conception fluctuates between three and four main strata of language, adding the "norm", an essentially social and system(*langue*)-oriented, abstract set of rules, and the "usage", a *parole*-oriented, also socially determined set of habits [37]. COSERIU [38] introduces the "norm" as an intermediate level, allowed for in the abstract system of the language and its individual adaptation (the *parole* is its concrete realization). The norm allows for individual variation, with the selection and fixation of variants. In the context of these two reconcilable views, what we are attempting to discern in the present study would be Shenoute's *usage* and the Coptic literary *norm* behind it. The textual realization is the *parole*, while the features of the innermost core or deepest layer, the Coptic-Sahidic *langue*, are abstractable from a series of *norm* reports. "Usage" approximates "idiolect" (in Bloch's definition, "an individual's set of linguistic habits"), and it is Shenoute's idiolect, or whatever layer of it is reflected in his written works, that we aim at portraying, with no reference to other idiolects, dialects or other subdivisions of the Coptic language, or to any "general" (i.e. not syncorporal) formulation or synthetic-panoramic conception of grammar.

0.2.5 MACRO-SYNTACTIC ANALYSIS

0.2.5.1 TEXTUAL STRUCTURE (SYNTAGMATICS). The realization of (a) the circular nature of pattern delimitation (*paradigm* ⌐ ⌐ *extent of resolution environment*), (b) the fact that continuous text-to-morpheme analysis is the only way to break this circularity, and (c) the fact that the "context-free" syntactic unit has as little meaning or relevance in the functioning of a language as the illusory isolated morphological one — all this must lead us to recognize the *text* as the prime syntactic unit, the prime pattern, the prime analyzable entity, subdivisible again and again [39]. Just as the "word", definable in ad-hoc junctural terms, exists (i.e. functions) only with reference to its environment (phrase and clause), so these too cannot claim any automatic, intrinsic prominence, or pre-analytic status of self-evident significance, but are referable to phrase/clause-including subtextual stretch units. The macro-syntactic view of grammatical phenomena has been adopted, on occasion, in traditional ("sentence") grammar, in offhand, opportunistic forays into the "context". The context has been constantly, more or less consciously, consulted, "employed" as an aid for determining function [40], but rarely formalized, included in the pattern, except in the consideration of traditional (stylistics- or rhetorics-oriented [41]) cases, like conditional complexes, *consecutio temporum*, etc. In the present work (esp. Chs. 2 and 7) I attempt a formal description of the grammatically relevant context or COTEXT, i.e. "cotext patterns" [42], "cotext-

---

[35] See LEPSCHY 1972:Ch.II, with further reading indicated.

[36] HALL 1965:337.

[37] This is an oversimplified account of Hjelmslev's complicated and mobile terminology (see SIERTSEMA 1965:140ff.).

[38] 1969:151f., 1971:53-72, 1975:39ff.

[39] In HALLIDAY's terminology (1961:251, with n. 30) this descending analysis is gradable on a scale of "*rank*".

[40] Cf. Polotsky's exemplary application of the context in the *Études* (POLOTSKY 1944).

[41] Several important syntactic phenomena, originally treated in a para-grammatical frame of reference, such as rhetorical "figures", will be of interest to us in the following pages; "Anredestil", "enumerative Redeweise", "polare Redeweise", "parataktischer (appositioneller) Nachtragsstil", "anacolouthon", "anaphora/cataphora", "ellipsis", "pairing", "parenthesis", "colon", "protasis - apodosis", and others.

[42] I am using "cotext" for the relevant textual (syntagmatic) environment, reserving "context" for both extra-linguistic, situational, background environment of sphere of validity and the not directly relevant textual one.

sensitive rules " (Lyons). An important feature of the textual linear system is the coherence or *cohesion* of its constituent parts; this will occupy us in several junctions. Another, closely related feature, constituting the basis for the discussion in Ch. 2, is the *thematic structure* of the text: the concatenation and development of ' theme + rheme ' patterns, involving the concepts of the information unit and its *focus*.

0.2.5.2 The second, PARADIGMATIC dimension of the textual system may be conveniently called the " paradigm of validity ", i.e. " the textual category for which a given grammatical-systemic statement is valid ". This is approximately the *texteme* in the textological structure or *texture* (cf. the paradigm in the syntagmatic sequence). It is clear, for instance, that the system recoverable in a narrative text (or narrative stretch) is quite different from that resolved, say, in a dialogue, where the grammatical inventory is much richer, perhaps maximal. One text (corpus component) may comprise several textemes or text classes, which should be distinguished and separated, in theory, in the pre-analytic stage. In reality, they are resolved in a circular process, on the strength of analysis results. The value (= function) of an element in one text-class is different, by structural definition, from its value elsewhere [43]. The definition of textual categories, text (sub)species or types, by reference to the grammatical system and structural distinctive features is one of the objectives of such text-based investigations as the present one.

0.2.5.2.1 THE RHETORICAL DIALOGUE is our case in point, the grammatically definable textual type most in evidence in Shenoute's writing. Without a rather involved delving into the particulars and theory of the dialogue [44] and an application of what we know of Shenoute's (and, in general, Byzantine) rhetorical theory and norms [45], it would be difficult to meet the challenge of a full and precise definition of this textual type. This would in any case require separate treatment, and must remain outside the scope of the present discussion. A few brief notes will perhaps give an idea of some of its features. (a) It is a one-way dialogue, an enhanced and distended allocution (with a captive and mute addressee). (b) " Rhetoricity " is a transcurrent (in a different sense, " suprasyntactic ") category, intersecting others; the " rhetorical dialogue " may include real dialogues, real and rhetorical narratives ("*paradeigmata*") [46]. (c) The first- and second-person referential system is pivotal, with several subsystems (e.g. WE [= I + you]: THEY, I : YOU [metaphorically THOU], WE : YOU, etc.). (d) Among grammatical peculiarities, we find constructions (incl. the so-called " figures "), word-order idiosyncrasies, " values " of constructions, e.g. the polemic function of the Cleft Sentence, characteristic particles and modifiers, and lexical preferences.

---

[43] Some striking Coptic cases in point: ЕЧNΑСШТМ (Second Future) is jussive in a preceptive cotext; NE- (pret. converter) expresses a *durative past* outside a narrative stretch, but signals (with ΠΕ) " *Relief*" (Weinrich) or tempo- or dimension-varying in a narrative cotext; ЕΑЧСШТМ (circ. perfect) is *continuative* in a narrative cotext; the conjunctive is a typical non-narrative form (partly corresponding to ΑЧ- (ΑΥШ) ΑЧ-, ΑЧ- ЕТРЕЧ- in narration). For the Second Tense, a cotext-bound, macrosyntactic category *par excellence*, see Ch. 2. Note that both NE- and the Second Tense are exponents of specific macrosyntactic status (§2.0.1.1), and can only be described adequately in a " context-sensitive grammar " (LYONS 1968:235ff.).

[44] Perhaps the most significant definitional feature of dialogue in this connection is its complexity: it is analyzable into two sub-structures of *allocution* and *response*, each with a distinct grammatical system of its own. Although not every dialogue is a " Wechselrede ", this may be taken as the ideal form.

[45] See MÜLLER 1956:54 (n. 3), 61ff.

[46] Some constituents of the rich paradigm inventory of the rhetorical dialogue: *rhetorical narrative* (*III* 38, 78); *real narrative* (*III* 208f., *IV* 198f.); *letters* (*III* 21,25); *invective address* (*Ch.* 19ff.); *report of conversation* (*Ch.* 50ff.); *praising address* (*Ch.* 84ff.); *dialogue within dialogue within dialogue* (*Ch.* 93ff., 97); *generic dialogue* (*III* 51), *dialogue within narrative* (*III* 38f.). Note that the system recoverable from the rhetorical narrative is much fuller than that of the non-rhetorical historical one, including such features as the Second Tense, conjunctive (§7.2.4.2), conditional constructions, etc.

0.2.5.3 REFERENCE. It would be out of place here to enlarge upon the current text-linguistic schools, trends, individual variations and controversies. Most theoreticians of this doctrine [47] underline its superior capabilities for dealing with problems of sub-textual grammar which the sentence-grammatical approach cannot satisfactorily solve. Some main concerns and preoccupations of text-linguistic study are: analysis of discourse structure [48], textual typology [49], textual system [50], thematic text structure (" Functional Sentence Perspective ", see §2.0.2.3) [51], and cohesion in the text [52].

0.3 THE MODIFIER: A PRIMARY OR HYPER-CATEGORY

...ⲀⲨⱲ ⲚϤⲀⲀⲚ ⲚⲘⲠⱲⲀ ⲚⲞⲨⲘⲀ ⲚⲘⲦⲞⲚ... (*IV* 176.3)

ⲈⱲϪⲈ ⲦⲈⲦⲚϤⲒ ϬⲈ ⲘⲘⲀⲨ ⲘⲠⲈϯϪⱲ ⲘⲘⲞϤ ⲈⲒϪⱲ ⲘⲘⲞϤ ⲀⲚ ⲌⲀⲢⲞⲒ ⲘⲀⲨⲀⲀⲦ (*IV* 96.12f.)

ⲀⲀⲔ ⲚⲈⲖⲀⲬⲒⲤⲦⲞⲚ ⲌⲘⲠⱲⲀϪⲈ ⲚⲦⲈⲔⲦⲀⲠⲢⲞ,

ⲚⲅⲀⲀⲔ ⲚⲀⲦⲚⲞⲈⲒ ⲌⲚⲦⲘⲎⲦⲈ ⲚⲚⲤⲀⲂⲈⲈⲨ (*IV* 41.9f.)

ⲞⲨⲢⱲⲘⲈ ⲈⲀⲠⲚⲞⲨⲦⲈ ϯ ⲚⲀϤ ⲚⲞⲨⲘⲚⲦⲈⲢⲞ ⲌⲒϪⲘⲠⲔⲀⲌ,

ⲚϤⲦⲘⲀⲀϤ ⲚⲘⲠⱲⲀ Ⲛϯ-ϬⲞⲘ ⲚⲀϤ ⲚⲢ-ⲠⲈⲦⲚⲀⲚⲞⲨϤ ⲚⲌⲎⲦⲤ...

ⲚⲦⲀϤⲞⲨⱲⲘ ⲚⲌⲎⲦⲤ ⲌⲚⲞⲨ; (*A 2* 364).

The present series of studies is concerned with the definition, resolution, compatibilities and commutations which constitute the taxonomic profile of the Coptic modifier. An impression of the range of its distribution can be obtained by studying the excerpts quoted above. This category, including all adnominal, adverbal [53], adnexal, and ad-pattern [54] satellites or expansions, would be considered, according to one's point of view, either *synthetic*, conveniently grouping together and condensing a number of paradigms in a continuous distributional structure [55]; or *analytic*, at a low level of delicacy [56]. This is a *primary* category, subdivisible, at a higher level of resolution (at which level the studies are actually conducted) into secondary classes, and these into yet more fragmented subclasses. Although I cannot see any real incongruity between the two conceptions, I prefer the first (" polyparadigmatic hyper-cat-

---

[47] Some general programmatic, introductory, state-of-the-art or bibliographical reports: DRESSLER 1973, 1978; DRESSLER–SCHMIDT 1973; HARTMANN 1971; 1975. See also the introductory chapters in WEINRICH 1977; GRIMES 1975.

[48] See, for instance, HARRIS 1952; DANEŠ 1970; GÜLICH–HEGER–RAIBLE 1974; WEINRICH 1977, etc.

[49] E. G. HAUSENBLAS 1964; GÜLICH–RAIBLE 1972; WERLICH 1975.

[50] See the excellent WEINRICH 1977; a solitary work for (Late) Egyptian, HINTZE 1950-2.

[51] See, for instance, FIRBAS 1966; HALLIDAY 1967; BENEŠ 1968; DANEŠ 1974.

[52] PALEK 1968, HALLIDAY–HASAN 1976.

[53] " Noun " and " verb " have never been explicitly defined for Coptic. Those acquainted with this issue in pre-Coptic Egyptian will agree this is a far from trivial matter. They are definable, like other parts of speech, only in terms of pattern: " noun " — the paradigm expanding determinator pronouns (§§5.1.1.0.1f.), expanding the pre-object allomorph of a verb lexeme, privileged to occupy the actor slot of a verbal predication pattern etc.; " verb " — a conjugation-form (defined by POLOTSKY 1960a:§1). Thus the verb lexeme (traditionally " infinitive ") is a nominal sub-class privileged to occupy the third position in the Tripartite pattern, not (with some exceptions) expanding ⲞⲨ-, i.e. in a different " determination " category from other noun sub-classes and finally alternating (true of some of the members of this sub-class) in regular proclitic pre-object allomorphs. This *cumulative* definition for Coptic corresponds to the " categorial " one, characterizing a part-of-speech by a cluster of morphological categories (case-gender-number, tense-mode-person) in use in languages of a different type. See SCHUCHARDT, SPITZER 1928:275.

[54] Note that " adnominal " and " adverbal " are telescoped ways of saying " modifying the noun/verb syntagm ". By " ad-pattern " I mean " modifying a *predicative* pattern ", usually used of a Nominal Sentence. " Adnexal " (" *adpredicative* " in SHISHA-HALEVY 1972) means " modifying by attaching or adjoining a (predicative) nexus "; see §7.1.3.

[55] The traditional and conventional conception of the part-of-speech proves on examination to be synthetic on two counts: first, as a *conglomerate* of categories rather than a single one; second, in mingling arbitrarily semasiological, syntactic and morphologic considerations of classification. See BRINKER 1972:63ff., and §0.2.1.3 above.

[56] See HALLIDAY 1961:272f.

egory ") for its " propaganda value ", as conveying more cogently the idea of the distributional conti-
nuity of the expansion — more specifically, the obliteration of the major traditional categorial differentiation of ADVERB *vs.* ADJECTIVE as a deep dichotomy (obviously the result of an imported and pre-
conceived " part of speech " metalinguistic model). This is especially striking for the *adverb*. The Coptic
" adverb " is by no means a specialized qualifier of verbs. Nor is the attributive satellite marked by N-
characterized in any way as adnominal (N-modifiers constitute a crucial intermediate sub-category of
postadjunctive modifiers which may profitably be considered the *point d'appui* for the primary category).
Under the heading of " MODIFIER ", all sub-categories, all paradigms, are to be judged in their own light,
and no other differentiation is necessary or meaningful. By (as it were) reshuffling and respacing them,
we arrive at a position where we can consider the grammatical facts free of pre-analytic compartmen-
talization.

0.3.1　The term MODIFIER has here an exclusively formal, tagmemic reference: " satellite ", " expansion ". The semasiological aspect of the category is extremely variegated and is not, probably cannot
be, an operational criterion for grammatical classification.

0.3.2　Four representative realizations or manifestations of this category are treated here: (a) the
modifier in unmarked, or position-marked, or morphematic cohesion with its nucleus (modificatum):
Chs. 1, 3, 4; (b) the modifier (adnominal/adpronominal) in anaphoric cohesion with its nucleus: the augens
(Ch. 6); (c) the conjunctive, a verbal *adnexal* modifier (N-marked, combining the interdependences of
nucleus-satellite and [logical] subject-predicate): Ch. 7; (d) the *focal* modifier (presented in a discussion
of focalization patterns in general): Ch. 2. For a fuller impression and more details of these four manifestations, it is suggested the reader consult the Table of Contents opening each chapter.

0.4 RETROSPECT: COPTIC GRAMMATICAL RESEARCH

In view of the aims of the present work, which are fundamentally reoriented in respect to the traditional approach to Coptic grammar, I keep the critical examination of Coptological grammatical tradition
to a minimum. It is of course impossible to treat studies of the pre-Polotsky era alongside a consideration
of Polotsky's momentous contributions [57]. Several research-historical or state-of-the-art appreciations [58]
have commented in more or less strong terms on the methodologically neglectful research history of
Coptic grammar — indeed, the sad fact that general linguistic method and interest have to a considerable
extent passed Coptic by is as true today as it was a hundred years ago, perhaps more true [59]. Without

---

[57] Most of the issues discussed in this work have not yet been treated *in extenso* by our Master. Only in one instance (the
Second Tenses, Ch. 2) have I presumed to question his findings, but even there our differences are traceable to a basic divergence in
methodological *Weltanschauung*. Prof. Polotsky's statements are by no means invalidated, and what I suggest is an alternative
(in my opinion advantageous) view of the facts, conceivable only after he had blazed a trail to understanding the system.

[58] POLOTSKY 1971:55f.; SCHENKEL 1972, esp. 169ff. (on structuralism. Incidentally, Coptic, the language which played so crucial
a role in Champollion's decipherment, is sadly underrepresented in this volume commemorating the 150th anniversary of this event);
CALLENDER 1973a:59f. on the rare structuralist approach; 61 ff., on Polotsky (Callender's implied reservation about Polotsky's
structural method is unwarranted, although it is true that he has never openly broken with traditional [non-structural] 19th-century
principles and models. As a matter of fact, Polotsky has never pledged himself to any one school of general linguistic method.)
JUNGE 1974a is mainly a meta-meta-linguistic discussion, a critique of Schenkel's and Callender's papers. FUNK 1978a; MINK
1978.

[59] POLOTSKY 1970:558. The severance of Coptic grammatical scholarship from general linguistics — a subject worthy of
special study — is as old as Stern's *Grammatik*, published at the very time (1880 - the publication year of H. Paul's *Prinzipien
der Sprachgeschichte*) that next door, so to speak, the Neogrammarian Doctrine emerged full-fledged from the controversies of
the eighteen-sixties and seventies. Today one observes, not without envy, the methodologically careful, even pampering description
of the minutest, most exotic " native dialect " (Pacific, Amerindian, Papuan...), and the smooth incorporation of living and dead
Near and Far Eastern languages among those constituting the object of current general linguistic research — while Coptic, a para-

dwelling on individual descriptive flaws — examples can be found all over the place — one can compile a list of " seven deadly sins ", the more flagrant lapses in method since Stern's *Grammatik*. These are all the more blameworthy in dead-language grammar, where methodology ought to be, if anything, more rigorous, since one has no " native speaker " to check and control one's findings by or to extend one's corpus at wish. They are as follows, in a *diminuendo* order of persistence (not necessarily of consequence): A view of phenomena which is: *not corpus-based*, i.e. unhomogenous; *unstructural*, i.e. atomistic and absolutistic [60]; *uncotextual* (self-restricted to an arbitrarily delimited extent of analysis); *neglectful of the interdependence of signifié and signifiant*, form and function (also the distinction of alternation and variation). This view has been overtly *ethnocentric* [61], in terminology as well as in many " docile " calques of extraneous categories, even in circumstances patently pointing to language-specific phenomena. (As a matter of fact, terminology often precedes and motivates the postulation of categories, as is inevitable when one proceeds unstructurally.) *Synchronic* treatment is often adulterated with *diachronic* reflections [62], the descriptive *listener's model* with *generative, speaker's model* formulations.

0.4.1 Perhaps it would not be out of place — if only as a curiosity — to close this section with five typological statements made of Coptic, mostly in the last century. Read today, they convey at worst the overpowering impression of utter detachment from the reality of the language; at best, they capture something — not always the same something, always subjective, always inadequate — of the flavour of Coptic. They have nothing particular to do with details of grammar, but with an accumulated contrastive impression in quest of the *mot juste* [63]. Note the consensus on the austerity, lack of sophistication and of complexity of the language [64] — an unmistakable sign that Shenoute has been left out of consideration:

MINGARELLI (1785:82): " ... verum haec lingua, ut libere dicam quod sentio, non modo simplex mihi videtur, sed etiam rudiuscula... insuavis, stridula, compositis vocabulis abundans, inops potius quam copiosa ".

PEYRON (1841:159, " monitum "): " Finem Grammaticae impono, quin de Syntaxi dicam. Praeterquam quod enim in lingua geometrica, cuiusmodi Copticam esse vidimus, par est Syntaxis, quae ordinem naturalem sequitur, neque inversionem verborum patitur ".

STEINTHAL–MISTELI (1893 [65]:107f.): " Formsprache... anreihend... nicht wortig... befriedigende Gestaltung des ganzen Satzes ... (268) ... nackte steife Einfachkeit. (272) ... Mumiengeist... (301) ... grammatische Armut und Nüchternheit ".

classical, almost " nostratic " language, a treasure-trove of grammatical notabilia, has yet to be discovered. The truth is, Coptic has been falling between all possible stools, especially those of " pagan " Egyptology and the study of Eastern Christianity (with the magnificent exception of the Erman–Sethe–Polotsky lineage). The current fashionable flurry of interest in Gnosticism, proceeding on the whole as if the grammatical description of pre-Nag Hammadi Coptic is a *fait accompli*, may prove to be yet another milestone in the luckless progress of Coptic linguistics.

[60] Stern, more than any of the pre-Polotsky grammarians, may claim some structuralist sympathy. Consider his predilection for a dichotomic presentation of binary (often privative) categories: *Relation* vs. *Annexion*; *conjugierter* vs. *conjugationsloser Satz*; *Dauerzeit* vs. *Ereigniszeit* (§§369, 494); *Tätigkeit* vs. *Zustand* (p. 172f.); *Umstand* vs. *Handlung* (§440); *mittelbare* vs. *unmittelbare Anknüpfung* (d. Objekts, §489), with some only negative terms, like *unabhängig* (§480), *präfixloser Satz, nicht nominales Subject* (§370), etc.

[61] This usually means an Indo-European and/or Semitic prejudicial " squint " (Jespersen's term) in description; see POLOTSKY 1959:457 (= *CP* 236). This attitude is more subtle in the typologist's essentially contrastive treatment: the prevailing spirit is rather that of STEINTHAL–MISTELI's " Wo fände sich desgleichen im Indogermanischen oder Semitischen? " (1893:50).

[62] Justly reprimanded by Vergote (*BiOr* 6:101f. [1949]) and FUNK 1978a:105; see now Schenke, *OLZ* 76:347f. (1981).

[63] I am leaving out here some diachronic-typological observations, like Hintze, *ZPh* 1:96ff. (1947) and the apt criticism by SCHENKEL 1966 a; briefly, MINK 1978:97f. in traditional Humboldtian terminology (analytic, synthetic, " wurzelflektierend ")

[64] Cf. for Egyptian DAUMAS (1952:34): " L'égyptien a eu parfois de la peine à reproduire la souplesse de la syntaxe grecque... "; he (and others) probably have in mind mainly *word-order* properties.

[65] The Coptic and Egyptian information is given esp. on pp. 267-301, but various reflections on Coptic may be found *passim*.

AMÉLINEAU (1895, *apud* Schmidt, *Pistis Sophia*, 1925, xxiii): " Cette langue ignore les longues phrases... c'est une langue éminemment analytique et non point synthétique... les phrases procèdent toujours par petits membres très clairs, presque indépendants les unes des autres... jamais, au grand jamais, nous ne rencontrons en copte ces périodes à incises compliquées à trois ou quatre membres différents, dont les éléments sont unis les uns aux autres d'une manière synthétique, si bien que l'intelligence de la phrase entière ne peut être obtenue qu'avec le dernier mot ".

Compare STERN's on the whole unexceptionable account of Coptic word-order (*Grammatik* §635): " Die Wortstellung... bewahrt die Regelmäßigkeit und Klarheit... Die längsten Perioden, und die Sprache liebt sie weit auszudehnen, zeigen immer den nämlichen einförmigen Bau, indem die paratactische Gedankenabwicklung nur durch die Participia und Relativa oder durch den Conjunctiv oder durch den Infinitiv unterbrochen wird. Die Klarheit, welche der Sprachgeist vom Gedanken fordert, führt seine genaue Zergliederung herbei, wenn er mehrfach und verwickelt ist. Von allen Redefiguren ist daher keine häufiger im koptischen Satzbau als die Prolepsis. Das Zusammendrängen vieler Begriffe in derselben Construction wird dadurch vermieden und der Rede eine gewisse Ruhe und Anschaulichkeit verliehen ". There can be no doubt of the preeminence of STERN as a grammarian of insight and penetration (see n. 60).

0.5 TECHNICAL NOTIFICATION

0.5.1 PATTERNS. The scheme of treatment for a given pattern consists in general of the following main stages and sections: (a) *general observations*, (b) *paradigm*, or *category constituency*, with token documentation, (c) *special observations* on selected individual members of the paradigm, (d) (for some patterns) *documentation*: representative examples followed by references " in bulk ".

0.5.2 EXAMPLES quoted are representative and selected, unless a given phenomenon is less than well attested, when most or all of the examples in my files are given. The number of examples varies according to the strength of documentation [66]. Additional references (not necessarily all) will follow, in a " *Zitatennest* " (following DENNISTON's maxim, " the reader should be allowed to bathe in examples "). Examples are translated only when they are in any way problematic, or if this is necessary or useful or has any bearing upon the argument.

0.5.3 SPECIAL SYMBOLS and typographical devices used:

' . . . . '	symbolizes	a non-autonomous pattern
# . . . . . . #		an autonomous pattern
+		syntagmatic compatibility (not necessarily sequence [contiguity])
→		syntagmatic compatibility *and* sequence (contiguity)
*		unattested (hypothetical) form
(*)		rare or unique form
~		fluctuation, variation
{ }		a morpheme, *with its paradigm* (unqualified substitutability; e.g. {ⲡⲉ}, {ⲡ-}).
‿		open juncture
] [		juncture boundary
‖		paradigm (substitution group)

The text is followed by an Appendix of Shenoute sources; Bibliographical Reference List; Indices (Index of Terms and Subjects; Index of Coptic Words, Phrases and Constructions; Index Locorum).

---

[66] Cf. Lagarde's " Zwei Beispiele sind etwas wenig, wenn man ' oft ' sagt " (*Aus dem deutschen Gelehrtenleben*, 1881, 26).

CHAPTER 1

A POLYPARADIGMATIC PATTERNING OF MODIFIERS IN UNMARKED, POSITION-MARKED OR MORPHEMATIC COHESION

1.0.1 PROBLEMS OF SYNTHESIS: PRECONCEIVED IDEAS OF THE " ADVERB " AS A PART OF SPEECH; THE COPTIC " ADVERB "; N-SATELLITES

1.0.1.1 With no other part of speech is it more pertinent to question its definition and demarcation than with the " adverb ": this part of speech refutes the claims for universal validity, conflicts with language-specific realities and is generally arbitrary to the point of being unworkable. This is so unanimously felt today that this statement is almost banal; yet " adverb ", even if now and then joined or replaced by more modern nomenclature, features as commonly as ever in the grammatical register. Trying to deal here with this almost embarassing theme as succintly and as pertinently to the task in hand as possible, I shall limit myself to a few observations of a general and historical nature.

1.0.1.2 The traditional and still conventional approach to defining parts of speech [1] mingles uncontrollably notional, morphematic and syntactic considerations. This alone would appear objectionable, even were one to accept the by itself questionable premise of a grammar " where everything is either this or that " [2], and even were one prepared to tolerate the ethnocentric and/or universalistic bias in tackling what are, first and last, language-specific issues. Such " pre-fabricated " pre-analytic entities — to be identified in (or, in reality, forcibly accommodated to) the structure of every individual language — must be supplanted by structurally conceived categories or category groupings and role relationships: " form-classes " defined by position and commutation.

1.0.1.3 Judged by the traditional lights and pronouncements, the adverb is seen to be a non-category, a negatively defined, " waste-basket " pigeonhole absorbing such elements as are not eligible for classification as other parts of speech, bordering on and merging into others (notably the conjunction [συνδεσμός] and " particles ") [3]. Within this amorphous aggregate, the sole consistently operative, definitional constituent is the adverb as *verb qualifying* or verb-adjunctal, *adverbal* (subsuming, with greater sophistication of classification, a subclass of " sentence modifiers " — see below, §1.1.2.2) [4]. This function, really a mixture of syntagmatic and reference-logical phenomena, has nothing natural or immutable about it, and, far from being self-evident, must be given careful consideration, the more so in cases like that of Coptic, where " verb " and " adverbal " need precise definition, where " adverbal " also applies to the status of a paradigm of verb forms [5]. All this apart, it must be stressed that (a) adverbal status, although central in forming the detached conception of the " adverb " part of speech, is by no means coextensive with its entire functional spectrum [6], (b) there looms in the background of this conception the metalinguistic proportion model [7]: *adverb(/adverbal)* ≈ *adjective(/adnominal)* — that is to say, the

---

[1] From the almost inexhaustible critical literature on this aspect of traditional grammar, I shall quote only DE SAUSSURE 1949:152f., TESNIÈRE 1965:51f., PAUL 1920:§244ff., MATTHEWS 1974:43ff. (" Our traditional parts of speech have not been handed to us on tablets of stone "). See also the Preliminary Chapter, note 20.

[2] Cf. HOCKETT 1967:936 (with Sapir's famous " all grammars leak ").

[3] On the Stoic Greek συνδεσμός, μεσότης and πανδέκτης see SCHMIDT 1839:37, 45f., ROBINS 1966:10ff.; see PINKSTER 1972: 35ff. for Latin grammatical theory. There are discussions of this approach in AHLMAN 1938:19f., KARCEVSKIJ 1936:107f., SECHE-HAYE 1950:65, THESLEFF 1955, e.g. p. 15 n. 1. It is hard to detect a qualitative difference between the descriptive treatment of " adverbs " in modern Coptic grammars and (say) that of TUKI 1778, who variously refers to adverbials as " *adverbium* ", " *particula* ", " *littera* " (N-, Є-), simply " *vox* " (ХЄКААС) АУШ is " *adverbium* " (203ff., see §1.3.10 below); so is ЄРЄ-; ЅАѲН is " *particula seu praepositio* ", NѲЄ " *particula seu adverbium* ". (I fully concur with Tuki's designation of N- as a " *littera coniunctiva* " [96ff.].) CALLENDER 1970:327ff. (App. IV) does ask some of the relevant questions — in fact, his is the only penetrating examination of this subject — but is, I believe, handicapped by his generative frame of reference. Instead of function and distribution, he is interested in derivation models and transformational (i.e. dynamic) relationships; my own approach is diametrically opposed to his.

[4] A further source of complications is that " adverbal " in " general " application includes modification of the substantive verb (— what about true Nominal Sentences?) and ῥῆμα was after all used also for " clause ", " phrase " or rather " utterance " (Plato, *Cratylus* 399b): cf. STEINTHAL 1890:137f.

[5] Clause Conjugation forms, the circumstantial conversion, conjunctional sentence-forms, various eventive forms (ЅМ̅ПТРЄЧ-, МN̅N̅САТРЄЧ-).

[6] Cf. SCHOEMANN 1862:160f.

[7] See for instance SECHEHAYE 1950:64f., REGULA 1951:75, KURYŁOWICZ 1964:19f. Among the classical grammarians, see

affinity of two distinct functions, related in a transformational or hierarchic model and by some corresponding formal (morphological) correlation — regular at least cardinally, and at least in the "inflecting" Indo-European and Semitic languages. On the other hand, a different point of view goes even further, subsuming "adverb" and "adjective" under a single cover-term [8], with various subdivisional properties; here the syntagmatic *satellital* essence of the two categories overrules morphological considerations. It is this latter approach which I adopt, as being of advantage in Coptic, where neither hierarchy nor transformation is (in my opinion) called for to locate "adverb"/"adjective" in a *système de valeur* [9], and where there is no clear-cut morphematic dichotomy between adnominals and adverbals, and hence no *a priori* call for a correlation theory, in brief, where no content can be given to the concepts "adverb" and "adjective" other than the syntagmatic + paradigmatic information that amounts to their respective distributional structures.

1.0.2 In Coptic, then, it is the "adjective-adverb" or MODIFIER which is analytically isolable as a prime category. The N-satellite marker, a typological show-piece and one of Coptic's most cogent messages for general linguistic experience [10], may be taken as the Coptic modifier (satellite, expansion) exponent *par excellence*. The multi-functional nature of N-constructions has been the subject of many discussions. The typological ones are often tainted by preoccupation with the corresponding Indo-European(-Semitic) structure ("Is N- a case morpheme? If so, which case?"), while the Coptological ones [11] show a predilection for (diachronic) speculation rather than (synchronic) description. In this work, I shall be concerned with N- in several different pattern-types: as adverbal, generally and specially, in the present chapter; as adverbal and focalized, in Chapter 2; as adverbal object-expansion, in Chapter 3; in adnominal construction, here and in Chapter 4, and so on. Thus, the only exposition feasible at this point is necessarily a generic and loose one.

The Coptic "adverb" is not usually a lexical (morphematic) entity but a syntagm. That is to say, lexical "adverbs", not grammatically analyzable and marked only by grammatical compatibilities [12], are the exception. The largest group by far among adverbally privileged elements consists of *prepositional phrases* [13], preposition-marked modifiers. Prominent among these are modifiers marked by N-/MMO⸗, which invite some fundamental questions about their nature, identity and function. The crux, the hub

---

Scholia Dion. Thrax (Hilgard) 233.25-7; Priscian *Inst.* (Hertz) XV 1 (" hoc enim perficit adverbium verbis additum, quod adiectiva nomina appellativis nominibus adiuncta "), II 16 (of the Stoics) " necnon etiam adverbia nominibus vel verbis connumerabant, et quasi adiectiva verborum ea nominabant "; see SCHOEMANN 1862: Ch. 10 (esp. pp. 136, 157ff.), PINKSTER 1972:37.

[8] Compare the *viśesaka* in Indian grammatical tradition (CARDONA 1973:85 n. 6), possibly also Dion. of Halicarnassus' ἐπίρρημα in the etymological (preterminological?) meaning. See SANDMANN 1939, esp. 91, LYONS 1966:216ff.

[9] I differ here with Polotsky's " transpositional " approach to the Egyptian-Coptic verb (e.g. POLOTSKY 1976 esp. §§1.1-3; see §2.0.0.1 below). Polotsky implicitly assumes the validity of a universal distinction of *adverb* vs. *adjective* vs. *substantive*, on which he bases a categorization of (in Coptic, converted) verb forms, even though neither " adjective " nor " adverb " have been defined for Coptic. On the other hand, taking " adverbial " and " adjectival " as coterminous with " adverbal " and " adnominal " is open to objections (see above).

[10] Ever a pet subject of the typologists, these constructions have been intelligently treated by STEINTHAL 1847, MISTELI 1882: 433ff., STEINTHAL-MISTELI 1893:281, SCHWARZE-STEINTHAL 1850:460.

[11] Some noteworthy if not always unexceptionable accounts: STERN §§183, 236, 333ff., 509, 513, 533f., KICKASOLA 1975:230, BÖHLIG 1977. Crum's struggle to put the morphs in lexicological order (*Dictionary* 215-6) is telling.

[12] Cf. (in a sense) KARCEVSKIJ's " *determinant à marque zéro* " (1936:107f.), although he also has here in mind the negative essence and the frequent non-rectional nature of adverbial links. Coptic modifiers are lexemic, not modulus categories (Whorf); " function-words " (Fries), not a morphosyntactic category as in many Indo-European languages.

[13] Nucleus-satellite IC-analysis of the prepositional phrase is, I believe, impossible in Coptic (*pace* NAGEL 1980:90) — although the preposition does presuppose the noun, and is therefore in a *determination* dependency with it. Unlike Indo-European prepositions, which are often modifiers further expanded, Coptic prepositional phrases are exocentric complexes, and are, judged by this criterion (see KURYŁOWICZ 1936:88) " a single word ". In dependency-grammatical terms, the preposition (including N-) " belongs " to the verb syntagm, not to the noun.

of this perplexity lies in the merging in Coptic of the following extra-Coptic (or " universal ") terms of relationship; on the one hand (syntagmatically) *adnominal/adverbal*; on the other hand (paradigmatically), *adverbial/direct-object* marking/*predicative-constituent* marking [14]. Different treatments place the burden of the problem at different nodes of this multiple furcation [15]. An all-important (though rarely mentioned) feature of the N-modifier is that, more than any other in the prepositional-phrase class, it is essentially *post-adjunctive*: indeed, it is the clearest manifestation in Coptic of the '*nucleus → satellite*' *Grundrichtung* or basic syntagmatic sequence [16]: except for certain fixed combinations (see §1.1.2.2), the major tagmemic polarity feature, viz. the opposition of ante- *vs.* post-location, is neutralized for N-. N-modification is the Coptic adjunct expansion *par excellence*, the quintessential satellite. I would therefore agree unreservedly with the old typologists' evaluation of N- as a *general relator*, satellite signall " *nota relationis* " [17], the reference of the relationship being resolved by the environment.

1.1   NON-PREDICATIVE MODIFIER STATUS

1.1.1   ADNOMINAL MODIFIER ROLE: ' NOUN SYNTAGM → MODIFIER '

(A) GENERAL OBSERVATIONS: (1) The presence here of such members of the adnominal paradigm(s) as are associated (by familiarity) with the *adverbal* status is often explained in transformationalist terms as the result of a " reduction of a relative construction " [18] or as an overall nominalization of a verbal nucleus and its expansion(s) [19]. I consider this aetiology unhelpful and unnecessary, as is also the underlying assumption that there is something derived, secondary or marginal in the adnominal occurrence of an " adverb " [20]: any " explanation " of this order must be held irrelevant and extrinsic to the structura, significance of this ocurrence.

---

[14] It must be stressed that these functional mergers are not exclusive to Coptic. For some basic illuminating statements, see BECKER 1841:597f. (" *prädikativer Genitiv* ", adnominal + predicative), also SCHOEMANN 1862:151f.; VON DER GABELENTZ 1869:383 (adverbal + object, adverbial + predicative); FROBEEN 1898:30ff., 38f. (adverbial + adnominal + predicative); cf. also SANDMANN 1946 on the French *parler haut*, *dire vrai* (adverbial + object + predicative).

[15] BÖHLIG 1977 sees the hub of the problem in the adnominal ("genitive") *vs.* adverbal (" object ") distinction; likewise SCHWARZE–STEINTHAL 1850:460f. MISTELI 1882 considers the " case " choice; KICKASOLA 1975:230ff. treats the subdivision within the adverbal expansion construction. Compare STEINTHAL 1847:49 " (N) *notiones alias in alias vergentes indicat* ". See now also LAYTON 1981:240ff.

[16] Significantly, we find in (Nitrian?) Bohairic a neat distinction of ⧺ ΚΑΛⲰⲤ - *vs.* - ⲚΚΑΛⲰⲤ ⧺, the former a non-adjunctal, non-satellital, adclausal premodifier, the latter an adverbal adjunctal satellite (cf. also ⧺ ⲠⲀⲒⲢⲎϮ- *vs.* -ⲘⲠⲀⲒⲢⲎϮ ⧺). Whether or not the fact that some Bohairic (also " Middle Egyptian " and Sahidic?) prepositions are preeminently post-adjunctal and need a modifier nucleus in premodifier status (⧺ⲚⲎⲢⲎⲒ ⲮⲈⲚ- *vs.* -ⲮⲈⲚ⧺) is germane here still has to be established.

[17] STEINTHAL 1847:45 " *merae relationis signum* ", 50 " N *relativum* ", 46 " *exponens indefinitae relationis cuiusdam* ", " N *cum linea mathematica, qua duo puncta conjungantur aut inter se referantur apte comparari posse mihi videtur* ". STEINTHAL–MISTELI 1893:281 " *allgemeiner grammatischer Weiser* ".

[18] So STEINITZ 1969:114ff., BRINKER 1972:138ff. This is in fact SCHENKEL's (1966) analysis of the ME *b3k jm* construction, which he considers an " *apokoinou* " one of a predicative adverb. Truly adnominal, according to him (57f.) are only adjective-expanding modifiers. Cf. RUDNITZKY 1956:130ff.

[19] STEINITZ 1969:118ff., BRINKER. *ibid.*, Obviously, some (notably rection-type) constructions could be advantageously analyzed in IC-terms as (*article*) + (*verb lexeme* + *modifier*): ⲞⲨⲔⲦⲞ ⲈⲠⲀⲌⲞⲨ (*A 2* 76), ⲠⲰⲚⲌ ϢⲀⲈⲚⲈⲌ (*IV* 32.8), ⲠⲌⲀⲢⲈⲌ ⲈⲠⲆⲒⲔⲀⲒⲞⲚ (*Ch.* 106.20f.) ⲠⲘⲞⲨ ⲌⲘⲠⲚⲞⲂⲈ (*Berl.* 1613 2 ⲦⲒⲐ), as could — most cogently of all — regular nominalizations: ⲦϬⲒⲚⲂⲰⲔ ⲈⲌⲞⲨⲚ (*K* 9298), ⲦϬⲒⲚⲈⲒ ⲘⲠⲞⲨⲀ ⲠⲞⲨⲀ ⲈⲌⲢⲀⲒ ⲈⲚϬⲒⲬ ⲘⲠⲚⲞⲨⲦⲈ (*Ch.* 94.31ff.), ⲦϬⲒⲚⲬⲒⲦⲀϬⲤⲈ ⲚⲤⲰϤ (*P* 130[5] 35 vo), ⲦⲘⲚⲦⲢⲈϤϮⲦⲰⲚ ⲈⲌⲞⲨⲚ ⲈⲚⲈⲚⲈⲢⲎⲨ (*P* 131[5] 19 ro) and so on. The distinction between adnominal and adverbal (" object ") N- is in these circumstances unfounded (see below).

[20] " *Extrinsèque* " (SECHEHAYE 1950:66ff.). Consider KARCEVSKIJ's cogent observation on the incidental nature of the adverb's relationship with the verb (1936:110f.).

(2) The uniformity of the adnominal modifier paradigm may be broken by several (partly overlapping) transformational or analytic expedients: distinguishing between (a) modifiers predicatable in the Bipartite Pattern (§1.2.1.1), differently predicatable and unpredicatable ones, (b) syntagms interpretable as (*article*) + (*verb lexeme + modifier*) [21] and those analyzable as (*article + noun*) + *modifier*, the former with a sub-group of (*article*) + (*nominalization exponent + (verb-lexeme + modifier*)): ΠΡЄЧΡ-ϨШΒ ЄΠϨΟΜΝΤ (*K* 934) ΤЄΚϬΙΝϹϨΑΙ ШΑ- (*III* 13.12f.) [22], (c) various dependency types, see §1.1.2.1: rectional *vs.* complementational modification (especially relevant with verb lexemes, but not excluded with noun-lexeme " valency ").

(3) The *augens*, a specific ad(pro)nominal modifier is discussed in detail in Chapter 6 [23].

(4) Among the important adnominally occurring *verbal* modifiers, we find the attributive *relative* conversion, the adnexal *circumstantial* [24] and *conjunctive* (§7.1.3 below, also §§7.3-4).

(B) CONSTITUENCY AND PARADIGMS (an open-ended listing) [25]:

		Ν-/ΜΜΟ=	see §1.3.1, spec. obs.
		ΝΤЄ-/ΝΤΑ=	spec. obs.
		ΝΤΟΟΤ=	*III* 180.1
		ΜΝ-	spec. obs.
		ϨΙ-	spec. obs.
		Є-/ЄΡΟ=	*Ch.* 135.37, *Wess. 9* 86b 24f., spec. obs.
Є	ϨΟΥΝ	Є-/ЄΡΟ=	*III* 87.15
Є	ϨΡΑΙ	Є-, ЄΧΝ-	*Ch.* 17.47ff., 94.31ff.
ШΑ	ϨΡΑΙ	Є-	*Ch.* 56-7
		ϨΝ-/ΝϨΗΤ=	*III* 168.5f., 195.26f.
	ϨΡΑΙ	ϨΝ-/ΝϨΗΤ=	*IV* 74.13
Є	ΒΟΛ	ϨΝ-/ΝϨΗΤ=	*III* 194.22
Є	ΒΟΛ	ϨΙΤΝ-	*IV* 29.26f.
		ϨΙΧΝ-	*Ch.* 117.34ff.
		ϨΑΤΝ-	*P* 130² 102 ΚΒ
		ϨΑϨΤΝ-	*III* 157.11f.
		ΝϹΑ-	*III* 42.4
		Ν-/ΝΑ=	*III* 206.16
		ЄΤΒЄ-	*III* 25.10
		ШΑ-, ШΑΤΝ-	*IV* 32.8, *III* 72.20
		ΠΑΡΑ-	*III* 141.27f.
		ΚΑΤΑ-	*IV* 106.15f.

[21] ϨΑΡЄϨ , after FREI 1966, with Π- the nucleus (§5.1.1).

     Π   Є-

[22] ЄϨΟΥΝ Є- modifying action-nouns: ΠΙϹΤΙϹ (*III* 87.15), ΑΓΑΠΗ (*Ch.* 88.53ff., *P*131⁴ 88 ΡΛΑ), ΜΟϹΤЄ (*III* 135.25f.), ΜΝΤϹΤΜΗΤ (*Ep.* 66), etc., is specifically adnominal, replacing a simple preposition (mostly Ν-) in the adverbial status. The actor here is usually expressed pronominally in a possessive article (ΠЄЧ-, ΠЄΚ- etc.), and the whole can be rendered " ...which I (you, we...) have for... ", following (*III* 172.18) ΠΟΥШШ ЄΤЄΟΥΝΤΑΝЧ ЄϨΟΥΝ Є- (also *III* 118-9).

[23] Borderline cases like ΝΑ=, ЄΡΟ=, ϨΑΡΙϨΑΡΟ= as well as kindred non-augential modifiers like ΝΟΥШΤ, ΜΜΑΤЄ are discussed in the present chapter or in chapter 6.

[24] A distinction neutralized (in favour of the circumstantial) after a non-Π-determinated nucleus (SHISHA-HALEVY 1972, esp. 75-128; 1976c:n. 3).

[25] Ordered by and large on principles of approximate relative frequency, which are of course subject to change as more or new attestations are taken into consideration. Many slots in the three paradigms may be zero-realized. Properly speaking, the first position in the 'nom. nucleus — modifier' syntagm is occupied by the determinator paradigm (§5.1.1.0.1), which is expanded by the noun lexeme; either may be further expanded by the augens (Ch. 6) and the modifier paradigms here displayed.

ε	ВОΛ	ОҮТЄ-	*P* 130² 5 ПЄ
		NNАϨPN-	*P* 130⁵ 100 КН
		ХЄ-	*Ch.* 158.52f., spec. obs.
		ХIN-	*Ch.* 76.8ff.

NϨОҮО (§1.3.1.3), TЄNОҮ (§1.3.4), NАМЄ, ϨNОҮМЄ (§1.3.5), ΑΛΗΘШC (§1.3.11.1.2), ϨОΛШC (§1.3.11.1.1), КАΛШC §1.3.11.1.3), ϨОМОIШC (§1.3.11.1.4), ϨАПΛШC (§1.3.11.1.7), МОNОN (§1.3.11.2.1.1) МАΛΛОN, МАΛIСТА (§1.3. 11.2.1.4), АҮШ (§1.3.10).

(C) Sᴘᴇᴄɪᴀʟ ᴏʙsᴇʀᴠᴀᴛɪᴏɴs: (1) N-/MМО⸗ [26], NTЄ-/NTА⸗: (a) It would seem that any account of these elements and their intricate functional structure must start with a statement of position regarding the identity or homonymy of adnominal N- (with ПЄЧ- a partly suppletive pronominalization [27]) and adverbal N-/MМО⸗. I believe this approach is methodologically unsound, and that the only alternative to speculation in this case lies in a structural definition (cf. §3.1.2.0.1) [28]. Adnominal N- occurs, as a *nota relationis*, in syntagms with a value which (say) an Indo-European-oriented observer could identify with that of his own attributive or possessive syntagms; still, the significance of this for the Coptic *innere Form* must not, to say the least, be overstated.

(b) N-modification of a nominal nucleus can occur with (usually before) other modifiers. The sequenc*I* of several modifiers may (here as with adverbal modification, §1.1.2.1) be subjected to IC-analysis: (*II*e 90.2) (ΛΑΑҮ NPШМЄ) ϨIВОΛ / (*ibid.* 217.23) (ϨАϨ NTАМЄIОN) NϨНТЧ / (*Ch.* 17.47ff.) [(ПINОϬ) NКPIМА] Є(ϨPАI ЄХШN) [29] and so on.

(c) N-, the adjunct-characteristic κατ' ἐξοχήν, is prenominal; instances like (*Ch.* 98.36ff.) ОҮМNTЄPО NШАЄ-NЄϨ or (*IV* 159.13 codd.) ПϨШВ NКАТАСАPϮ I take to be a case of N- governing a nominalized ("hy-postasized") modifier — or rather *governing a determinator*, expanded by a modifier: see §5.1.1. N- is no less a symptom indicative of the "nominalness" of a syntagm than are the determinators: indeed, N- and the determinators always occur conjointly, in a nuclear syntagm further expanded by a noun lexeme or modifier, see §1.1.1.1.

(d) I fear the present account cannot claim to give the last enlightening word on the (allomorphic?) distribution of N- *vs.* NTЄ-/NTА⸗. The grammar-books' threadbare and lacunary statement for Sahidic [30], to the effect that (a) NTЄ- expanding an indefinite noun, governs a definite one, and (b) NTЄ- expands an already expanded noun — although correct and workable in a general way for Shenoute [31], would

---

[26] See §1.0.1.2 above, Chs. 3 and 4. Qᴜᴇᴄᴋᴇ (1981:260) does not consider this N- prepositional; what matters synchronically is its satellite status.

[27] Note МПВ(О)ΛN- (*Ch.* 93.44ff.), pronominally МПЄЧВОΛ (*ibid.* 100.1), Shenoute follows here Akhmimic usage (*Dictionary* 33-4).

[28] I am of course aware of the diachronic roots and grounds for the distinction made between the "properly adnominal" N (< Eg. *n*) and "adverbal + predicative + prepositional" N (< Eg. *m*), and also that "in the midst of synchrony we are in diachrony". Nonetheless, I firmly believe in the feasibility of a synchronically-termed consistent description of the *status quo* resulting from the historical event of the merging of {*m*} and {*n*}.

[29] In Frei's dependence model (Fʀᴇɪ 1966):

[30] For example, Sᴛᴇʀɴ §292ff. (not completely separating the Sahidic and Bohairic systems), Tɪʟʟ §111ff. (including an example with a demonstrative-expanding nucleus — *Joh.* 12:34 — which I would rather analyze as ПЄI(ШНPЄ NTЄПPШМЄ).

[31] Consider (*IV* 26.2) ϨОТЄ NTЄПNОҮТЄ / (*III* 214.18) ОҮАГГЄΛОС Н ОҮП͞Н͞А NTЄПNОҮТЄ / (*Ch.* 101.35ff.) ϨЄNКЄАГАΘОN NTЄПКАϨ / (*A 2* 92) NЄТϨНП NTАҮ / (*A 2* 451, not Sh.) ТЄϨIН ЄТСОҮТШN NTЄТАPЄТН / (*P* 130² 48 СКΔ) ТPАСОҮ ММЄ NTЄПХОЄIС / (*IV* 195.14) ϨPЄ NIМ

conflict especially with instances of ' ∅- + N- (*def.*) ', e.g. (*A 1* 133) ⲍⲱⲥ ⲯⲏⲣⲉ ⲙⲡⲟⲩⲟⲉⲓⲛ / (*A 2* 453, not Sh.) ... ⲯⲱⲡⲉ ⲛⲣⲱⲙⲉ ⲙⲡⲛⲟⲩⲧⲉ/ⲛⲯⲏⲣⲉ ⲛⲧⲟⲣⲅⲏ, ' (*indef.*) + ⲛⲧⲉ- (*indef.*) ' e.g. (*A 2* 433, not Sh.) ⲍⲉⲛⲟⲓⲕⲟⲇⲟⲙⲏ ⲛⲧⲉⲍⲉⲛⲯⲏⲣⲉ ⲯⲏⲙ and ' (*def.*) + ⲛⲧⲉ- (*def.*) '. e.g. (*A 2* 420, not Sh.) ⲛⲉⲩⲥⲛⲗⲱⲕⲥ ⲛⲧⲉⲡⲛⲟⲃⲉ / (*ibid.* 452) ⲛⲯⲏⲣⲉ ⲛⲧⲉⲡⲡⲉⲧϫⲟⲥⲉ / (*P* 130² 55 ⲧⲓⲥ) ⲡⲟⲩⲱⲯ ⲛⲧⲉⲡⲉϥϩⲏⲧ ⲉⲑⲟⲟⲩ / (*P* 130⁵ 22 ⲫⲙⲑ) ⲛⲁⲡⲟⲥⲧⲟⲗⲟⲥ ⲛⲧⲉⲡϫⲟⲓⲥ / even (*P* 130² 62 ⲟⲉ) ⲛⲉⲩⲕⲁⲧⲁⲥ̧ⲁⲣⲝ ⲛⲧⲁⲩ. Pending the findings of a special study, I suggest that an original opposition of N- *vs.* ⲛⲧⲉ- (essential possession *vs.* incidental possession or appurtenance), usually neutralized in accordance with the above statements, is maintained· in isolated cases, perhaps with a limited inventory of noun lexemes in the nucleus [32] where N- is the marked exponent of essential possession, with ⲛⲧⲉ- either an unmarked or non-possessive relator. The whole issue is a component of the multi-faceted theme of determinator syntax (cf. §5.1.1). Observe, however, that like N-, ⲛⲧⲉ is not exclusively adnominal (ⲛⲉⲧⲉⲣⲉⲍⲉⲛⲕⲟⲟⲩⲉ ⲁⲍⲉ ⲛⲁⲩ ⲛⲧⲉⲧⲏⲩⲧⲛ *Ch.* 101.38ff.), although N- is a regular direct-object expansion mark (Ch. 3), while ⲛⲧⲉ- is a non-rectional modifier.

(e) See §6.0.1 for N- introducing a lexicalizing apposition following a pronominal nucleus: (*III* 96.21) ...ⲍⲁⲣⲟⲥ ⲛⲧⲡⲉ, (*Ch.* 102.9f.) ...ⲉⲣⲟϥ ⲛⲅⲉⲛⲟⲥ ⲛⲓⲙ, even (*A 2* 403) (ⲡⲓⲑⲉ) ⲙⲙⲱⲧⲛ ⲙⲡⲉⲥⲛⲁⲩ. This construction must be kept apart, if only for the reason that a non-determinator pronominal nucleus (predominant in the augential modification patterns, Chapter 6) does not feature in the nucleus paradigm of adnominal N-. (On the affinity between ' *noun → modification* ' and ' *pronoun → apposition* ', see §4.3.)

(2) ⲉ-: this is the only common, unmistakably *rectional* modifier in our paradigms. Instances like (*A 2* 396) ⲟⲩⲯⲁϫⲉ ⲉϫⲟⲟϥ or (*IV* 152.2) ⲟⲩⲍⲱⲃ ⲉⲁⲁϥ are a case apart: the modification here is dependent on the environment of the noun syntagm as well as on the formal nucleus. (On ⲉⲍⲟⲩⲛ ⲉ- see n. 22.)

(3) ⲍⲓ-, ⲙⲛ-: the distinction between the non-coordinating modifier ⲍⲓ- (e.g. in *Ch.* 208.43f. (ⲛ)ⲍⲟ ⲍⲓⲍⲟ) and the coordinating ⲍⲓ- (ⲧⲃⲃⲟ ⲍⲓⲙⲉ *III* 34.17) can be stated in terms of the distributional relationship of the latter, which coordinates zero-determinated nouns, with ⲙⲛ-, which serves to coordinate {ⲡ-}/{ⲟⲩ-}-determinated noun syntagms: ⲍⲉⲛⲟⲩⲱⲙ ⲙⲛⲍⲉⲛⲥⲱ (*P* 130² 37 ro), ⲟⲩⲍⲕⲟ ⲙⲛⲟⲩⲉⲓⲃⲉ (*ibid.*), ⲡⲛⲟⲩⲃ ⲙⲛⲡⲡⲁⲧ (*Ch.* 116.57f.), ⲛⲍⲟⲩ ⲙⲛⲛⲭⲁⲧϥⲉ (*P* 130² 59 ⲟ); with ∅- ⲛⲓⲙ (§§3.1.1.2.1(3), 5.1.1.0.1) we find ⲁⲩⲱ/-ⲍⲓ-/-ⲙⲛ- (*P* 131⁵ 28 ro) ϭⲱⲛⲧ ⲛⲓⲙ ⲍⲓⲟⲣⲅⲏ ⲛⲓⲙ ⲙⲛⲁⲯⲕⲁⲕ ⲛⲓⲙ ⲙⲛⲕⲁⲕⲓⲁ ⲛⲓⲙ, also *Ch.* 21.33ff., 48.54ff., etc. The pronominal state of ⲙⲛ- is found only in coordinative instances like (*III* 22.17) ⲛⲁⲛ ⲛⲙⲙⲉ or (*BM* 209 ⲗⲑ) ⲉⲣⲱⲧⲛ ⲛⲙⲙⲁⲛ, see §1.1.2.4.1.

(4) ⲍⲁ(ⲍ)ⲧⲛ- (a) Consider the following instructive example, in which the adnominal modifier is disjoined from the same prepositional phrase in predicative status and adnominal (relative) form: (*III* 157.11ff.) ⲡ̄ⲍⲗⲗⲟ ⲍⲁⲍⲧⲏⲛ... ⲑⲗⲗⲱ ⲍⲁⲍⲧⲛⲧⲏⲩⲧⲛ... ⲛⲍⲗⲗⲟⲓ ⲉⲧⲍⲁⲧⲛⲧⲏⲩⲧⲛ. This does not mean that the adnominal modifier is a " reduced " form of the relative construction, but only that their significations in the given context are sufficiently close. (b) Note the prevalence of *indefinite* nuclei (this is also true for ⲍⲣⲁⲓ ⲛⲍⲏⲧ⸗). Does this imply a prosodically conditioned adnominal placement of an *adverbal* (or adclausal) modifier — the indefinite nucleus, as it were — attracting the modifier to its vicinity? Compare ⲛⲓⲙ ⲉⲛⲉⲍ (§1.3.6 below).

(D) Documentation:

N-: exx. *passim* (esp. in §§1.3. and Ch. 4), and consider (*P* 130⁵ 16 ro) ⲍⲉⲛⲕⲉⲛⲟⲩⲧⲉ ⲙⲡⲃⲗⲡϫⲟⲉⲓⲥ / (*P* 130⁴ 140 vo) ⲟⲩⲁ ⲛⲑⲉ ⲛⲛⲓⲁⲧⲛⲟⲩⲧⲉ / (*III* 221.9) ⲡⲟⲩⲁ ⲡⲟⲩⲁ ⲛⲛⲉⲧⲉⲙⲡⲟⲩⲕⲧⲟⲟⲩ ⲉⲃⲟⲗ... / (*IV* 73.11) ⲗⲁⲁⲩ ⲙⲙⲁ

ⲍⲓⲥⲱ ⲛⲓⲙ ⲛⲧⲉⲡⲙⲟⲩ / (*BLOr.* 6807(2) f. 7) ⲟⲣⲅⲏ ⲛⲓⲙ ⲛⲧⲁϥ. A strikingly conflicting *locus* is (*P* 130⁵ 22 ⲫⲙⲑ) ⲛⲁⲡⲟⲥⲧⲟⲗⲟⲥ ⲛⲧⲉⲡϫⲟⲓⲥ *vs.* ⲙⲡⲣⲟⲫⲏⲧⲏⲥ ⲧⲏⲣⲟⲩ ⲙⲡⲉⲛϫⲟⲉⲓⲥ. *NB.* (*P* 130⁴ 127 ⲙⲃ) ⲡⲉⲍⲣⲟⲟⲩ ⲛⲍⲉⲛⲁⲅⲅⲉⲗⲟⲥ.

[32] This is, I think, the situation in Bohairic; here, however, we have wheels within wheels, since the determinators themselves are exponents — perhaps the primary ones — of this distinction. In Sahidic too, an instance like (*P* 130⁵ 21 ro) ⲛⲉⲩⲯⲏⲣⲉ ⲙⲛⲛⲉⲩⲯⲉⲉⲣⲉ ⲛⲧⲉⲧⲥⲁⲣⲝ proves that " possession " and " ⲛⲧⲉ-appurtenance " are compatible, hence distinct categories.

ⲘⲘⲞⲞⲨ / ⲠⲒⲤⲀ ⲘⲘⲞⲤ, ⲠⲈⲒⲤⲀ ⲘⲚⲠⲀⲒ ⲘⲘⲞⲤ (*A 1* 106, *IV* 95.17, *III* 204.8) / (*A 1* 276 = *Ch.* 117.19f.) ⲦⲈⲒⲌⲈ ⲘⲘⲞⲞⲨ ⲦⲈ " this is their way " / -Ⲣ-ⲦⲠⲈ ⲘⲘⲞⲞⲨ (*A 1* 150, 306).

Ⲉ-/ⲈⲢⲞⲤ: ⲨⲘⲘⲞ Ⲉ- (*A 2* 102, the rection of ⲨⲘⲘⲞ being Ⲉ-), ⲠⲀⲖⲖⲞⲦⲢⲒⲞⲤ ⲈⲢⲞⲤ (*A 2* 32) / (*A 1* 465) (ⲂⲰⲔ) ⲚⲌⲰⲠ ⲈⲢⲞⲞⲨ / (*III* 18.28) ⲀⲦⲚⲞⲂⲈ ⲈⲠⲈⲤⲈⲞⲞⲨ / (*IV* 5.5f.) ⲠⲚⲀⲨ ⲈⲠⲌⲞ. For adnominal ⲈⲦⲢⲈ- — ⲞⲨⲖⲞⲄⲞⲤ ⲈⲦⲢⲈ- (*III* 218.14), ⲦⲤⲒⲚⲨⲀⲖ... ⲈⲦⲢⲈ- (*IV* 67.24), ⲦⲈⲨⲚⲞⲨ ⲈⲦⲢⲈⲚ- (*Wess. 9* 155b 3ff.) — see §7.4.

ⲈⲌⲞⲨⲚ Ⲉ-: see footnote 22, to which add (*A 1* 16) ⲠⲈⲦⲚⲈⲞⲞⲨ ⲈⲌⲞⲨⲚ ⲈⲞⲨⲞⲚ ⲚⲒⲘ ⲀⲨⲰ ⲈⲌⲞⲨⲚ ⲈⲢⲞⲒ ⲌⲰ / (*A 2* 256) ⲞⲨⲘⲞⲨⲨⲦ ⲈⲌⲞⲨⲚ ⲈⲠⲔⲰⲦ.

ⲈⲌⲢⲀⲒ (ⲈⲬⲚ-): (*Wess. 9* 148a 1f.) ⲔⲈⲀⲚⲞⲘⲒⲀ ⲈⲌⲢⲀⲒ ⲈⲬⲰⲔ / (*III* 210.18) ⲠⲈⲤⲠⲰⲦ Ⲏ ⲠⲈⲤⲔⲰⲦⲈ ⲈⲌⲢⲀⲒ / (*Ch.* 17.47ff.) ⲠⲒⲚⲞⲦ ⲚⲔⲢⲒⲘⲀ ⲈⲌⲢⲀⲒ ⲈⲬⲰⲚ.

ⲌⲚ-/ⲚⲌⲎⲦⲤ: (*P* 130² 48 ⲤⲔⲆ) ⲌⲀⲌ ⲈⲘⲀⲦⲈ ⲌⲚⲚⲈⲦⲞⲨⲀⲀⲂ / (*P* 131⁵ 4 ⲅⲟ) ⲞⲨⲀ ⲚⲌⲎⲦⲦⲎⲨⲦⲚ / (*IV* 73.11) ⲖⲀⲀⲨ ⲚⲨⲰⲚⲈ ⲌⲘⲠⲈⲨⲤⲰⲘⲀ / (*P* 131⁷ 25 ⲅⲟ) ⲀⲨ ⲌⲚⲚⲈⲨⲘⲌⲀⲖ ⲚⲈⲦⲢ-ⲌⲰⲂ ⲔⲀⲖⲰⲤ / (*A 2* 120) ⲔⲈⲘⲈⲖⲞⲤ ⲌⲘⲠⲈⲔⲤⲰⲘⲀ / (*ibid.* 245) ⲞⲨⲦⲀⲖⲈ ⲌⲚⲦⲈⲨⲞⲨⲈⲢⲎⲦⲈ ⲤⲚⲦⲈ / (*K* 9291) ⲠⲚⲀⲨ ⲌⲘⲠⲌⲞ, ⲠⲚⲀⲨ ⲌⲘⲠⲌⲎⲦ / (*Ch.* 118.44f.) ⲞⲨⲘⲀ ⲚⲘⲦⲞⲚ ⲌⲚⲘⲠⲎⲨⲈ / (*IF* 67 apud *Dictionary* 147b) ⲌⲈⲚⲖⲀⲀⲨ ⲌⲚⲚⲦⲞⲠ / (*III* 217.23) ⲌⲀⲌ ⲚⲦⲀⲘⲈⲒⲞⲚ ⲚⲌⲎⲦⲈ / (*ibid.* 168.5ff.) ⲠⲘⲞⲨ ⲦⲎⲢⲈ ⲌⲘⲠⲚⲞⲂⲈ, ⲠⲰⲚⲌ ⲦⲎⲢⲈ ⲌⲚⲦⲆⲒⲔⲀⲒⲞⲤⲨⲚⲎ.

ⲌⲢⲀⲒ ⲌⲚ-/ⲚⲌⲎⲦⲤ: (*IV* 74.13) ⲞⲨⲀ ⲌⲢⲀⲒ ⲚⲌⲎⲦⲚ / (*P* 130² 63 ⲟⲌ) ⲌⲞⲈⲒⲚⲈ ⲌⲢⲀⲒ ⲚⲌⲎⲦⲚ... ⲞⲨⲞⲚ ⲌⲢⲀⲒ ⲚⲌⲎⲦⲦⲎⲨⲦⲚ, sim. *III* 152.5f.; sim. (ⲞⲨⲞⲚ ⲚⲒⲘ) *III* 126.1, (ⲢⲰⲘⲈ) *K* 927, *P* 131⁷ 45 ⲣⲟ, (ⲌⲀⲌ) *A 2* 301.

ⲈⲂⲞⲖ ⲌⲚ-: (*III* 194.22) ⲞⲨⲀⲄⲄⲈⲖⲞⲤ ⲈⲂⲞⲖ ⲌⲚⲦⲠⲈ / (*Ch.* 144.46ff.) ⲠⲈⲦⲤⲞⲨⲦⲰⲚ ⲈⲂⲞⲖ ⲌⲘⲠⲈⲦⲤⲞⲨⲦⲰⲚ, ⲠⲚⲞⲨⲦⲈ ⲈⲂⲞⲖ ⲌⲘⲠⲚⲞⲨⲦⲈ, ⲠⲨⲎⲢⲈ ⲈⲦⲞⲨⲀⲀⲂ ⲈⲂⲞⲖ ⲌⲘⲠⲈⲒⲰⲦ ⲈⲦⲤⲘⲀⲘⲀⲀⲦ.

ⲌⲒ-: (*Wess. 9* 132a 28f.) ⲞⲨⲨⲀⲬⲈ ⲌⲒⲂⲞⲖ / (*ibid.* 112b 27f.) ⲌⲈⲚⲔⲞⲞⲨⲈ ⲌⲒⲂⲞⲖ / (*III* 90.2) ⲖⲀⲀⲨ ⲚⲢⲰⲘⲈ ⲌⲒⲂⲞⲖ.

ⲈⲂⲞⲖ ⲌⲒⲦⲚ-: (*IV* 29.26f.) ⲌⲈⲚⲨⲎⲢⲈ ⲘⲚⲌⲈⲚⲨⲈⲈⲢⲈ ⲈⲂⲞⲖ ⲌⲒⲦⲘⲠⲚⲞⲨⲦⲈ / (*A 2* 304) ⲞⲨⲦⲰⲚⲦ ⲈⲂⲞⲖ ⲌⲒⲦⲘⲠⲚⲞⲨⲦⲈ / (*III* 158.7f.) ⲌⲈⲚⲚⲞⲦ ⲚⲔⲢⲒⲘⲀ ⲈⲂⲞⲖ ⲌⲒⲦⲘⲠⲚⲞⲨⲦⲈ.

ⲨⲀ-: (*III* 142.28f.) ⲘⲠⲨⲀ ⲚⲈⲒ ⲨⲀⲢⲞⲚ / (*BKU* 180² 11.21, *Wess. 9* 138c-d, *Ench.* 82a) ⲞⲨⲰⲚⲌ ⲨⲀⲈⲚⲈⲌ.

Ⲛ-/ⲚⲀⲤ: (*P* 131⁸ 84 ⲫⲟ) ⲞⲨⲔⲖⲎⲢⲞⲚⲞⲘⲒⲀ ⲚⲀⲤ / (*III* 126.5f.) ⲦⲈⲨⲘⲚⲦⲤⲀⲂⲈ ⲚⲀⲨ ⲘⲀⲨⲀⲀⲨ.

ⲌⲀⲦⲚ-: (*IV* 35.27f.) ⲖⲀⲀⲨ ⲌⲢⲀⲒ ⲚⲌⲎⲦⲚ Ⲏ ⲌⲀⲦⲚⲦⲎⲨⲦⲚ ⲚⲦⲰⲦⲚ / (*Wess. 9* 150a 14ff., d 22f., *IV* 28.22) ⲌⲞⲒⲚⲈ ⲌⲀⲦⲚⲦⲎⲨⲦⲚ / (*K* 9291) ⲠⲦⲰ ⲌⲀⲦⲚⲚⲈⲚⲈⲢⲎⲨ.

ⲚⲚⲀⲌⲢⲚ-: (*BM* 253 ⲚⲎ) ⲌⲈⲚⲨⲘⲘⲞ ⲚⲚⲀⲌⲢⲀⲨ / (*P* 130⁵ 100 ⲔⲎ) ⲨⲀⲨⲨⲰⲠⲈ ⲚⲀⲦⲨⲀⲨ ⲚⲚⲀⲌⲢⲘⲠⲚⲞⲨⲦⲈ.

ⲈⲂⲞⲖ ⲞⲨⲦⲈ-: (*P* 130² 5 ⲠⲈ) ⲠⲠⲞⲚⲎⲢⲞⲤ ⲈⲂⲞⲖ ⲞⲨⲦⲈⲞⲨⲞⲚ ⲚⲒⲘ.

ⲠⲀⲢⲀ-: (*IV* 206.12f.) ⲌⲈⲚⲢⲰⲘⲈ ⲘⲠⲞⲚⲎⲢⲞⲤ ⲀⲨⲰ ⲚⲢⲈⲨⲢ-ⲚⲞⲂⲈ ⲠⲀⲢⲀ ⲢⲰⲘⲈ ⲚⲒⲘ.

ⲔⲀⲦⲀ-: (*Wess. 9* 131a 9f.) ⲦⲈⲨⲠⲖⲀⲚⲎ ⲔⲀⲦⲀⲢⲞⲨ / (*IV* 69.15f.) ⲔⲈⲌⲰⲂ ⲔⲀⲦⲀⲦⲈⲒⲌⲈ / (*Ch.* 167.56ff., *IV* 31.4, 159.13, *III* 74.16) ⲌⲈⲚⲈⲒⲞⲦⲈ ⲔⲀⲦⲀⲠⲈⲒⲂⲒⲞⲤ / (*P* 130² 107 ⲅⲟ) ⲌⲈⲚⲈⲒⲞⲦⲈ ⲔⲀⲦⲀⲤⲀⲢⲬ.

ⲈⲦⲂⲈ-: (*P* 130⁴ 50 ⲤⲔ) ⲠⲰⲚⲌ ⲈⲦⲂⲈⲦⲆⲒⲔⲀⲒⲞⲤⲨⲚⲎ.

ⲬⲈ-: (*Wess. 9* 129b 30f.) ⲠⲒⲨⲀⲬⲈ ⲬⲈ-ⲌⲞⲘⲞⲞⲨⲤⲒⲞⲤ / (*A 2* 343) ⲠⲈⲒⲢⲀⲚ... ⲬⲈ-ⲌⲞⲨ / (*BM* 253 ⲚⲎ) ⲠⲈⲒⲤⲬⲎⲘⲀ ⲬⲈ- (" which means ") ⲘⲞⲚⲀⲬⲞⲤ / (*A 1* 155) ⲚⲈⲒⲞⲠⲈ ⲬⲈ-ⲤⲰⲌⲈ / (*III* 59.8) ⲞⲨⲘⲀ ⲬⲈ-ⲂⲈⲖⲀⲘⲰⲚ / (*P* 130⁴ 124 ⲖⲤ) ⲢⲀⲚ... ⲬⲈ-ⲞⲨⲎⲎⲂ ⲌⲒⲘⲞⲚⲀⲬⲞⲤ.

1.1.1.1 MODIFIERS IN NOUN SYNTAGMS. In the syntagm ' *determinator → modifier* ', the modifier expands the nuclear determinator pronoun. This is not a " hypostase " except by virtue of a pattern [33]. The inventory of modifiers is here shorter than in the post-lexeme paradigm (§1.1.1), and includes many Greek loan-modifiers and in general mostly fixed expressions, clichés and calques. The ensuing noun syntagm is often (for some modifiers, usually) the predicate of a bimembral Nominal Sentence.

(1) Nucleus: {ⲡ-}: (*IV* 53.4) ⲠⲌⲀⲐⲎ ⲘⲠⲞⲨⲞⲈⲒⲚ / (*A 1* 302) ⲠⲌⲞⲨⲚ ⲚⲌⲎⲦⲞⲨ / (*Teza* 684) ⲠⲨⲀ ⲈⲚⲈⲌ, appositive after ⲠⲚⲞⲨⲦⲈ (§4.3) / ⲠⲈⲂⲞⲖ ⲌⲚ-, Ⲛ(Ⲉ)ⲈⲂⲞⲖ ⲌⲚ- Ⲛ- (*Ench.* 89a, *P* 130² 109 ⲫⲟ, *III* 114.25, *IV* 126.29, *Ch.* 47.49f., *Wess. 9* 131a 13f., *K* 9294, *P* 130⁴ 122, 130⁵ 22, *A 1* 289, etc.) / (*Ch.* 97.35f.) ⲘⲠⲢⲞⲤⲞⲨⲞⲈⲒⲨ. No instance of the feminine determinator ⲧ- is known to me. The possessive determinators: (*III* 20-1) ⲚⲀⲬⲒⲚⲠⲔⲀⲒⲢⲞⲤ / ⲚⲈⲨⲔⲀⲦⲀⲤⲀⲢⲬ (*IV* 122.24 cod., *A 2* 526 etc.).

---

[33] ·In principle and from this point of view on a par with the ⧧ *modifier* + ⲡⲉ ⧧ pattern (§1.2.1.2).

(2) Nucleus: {ⲟⲩ-}: ⲟⲩⲕⲁⲧⲁⲣⲱⲧⲛ (*III* 116.17, 117.5f.) / ⲟⲩⲡⲁⲣⲁ(ⲧⲉⲩ-/ⲧⲉⲛ-/ⲧⲉⲕ)ⲫⲩⲥⲓⲥ (*Ch.* 21.26f., *IV* 112.24, *P* 130⁵ 24 ⲣⲡⲃ) / ⲟⲩϣⲁⲉⲛⲉϩ (*A 2* 236) / (*A 2* 418, not Sh.) ⲟⲩⲡⲣⲟⲥⲟⲩⲟⲉⲓϣ (*vs.* ⲟⲩϣⲁⲉⲛⲉϩ on line 12) / ϩⲉⲛⲕⲁⲧⲁⲥⲁⲣⲝ (*IV* 81.5, 112.7, *P* 130⁵ 111 ro) / (*III* 107.17ff.) ⲟⲩⲉⲃⲟⲗ ϩⲓⲧⲙⲡⲛⲟⲩⲧⲉ.

(3) Nucleus: Ø-, after the modifier marker ⲛ-: — ⲛϣⲁⲉⲛⲉϩ (*IV* 38.15, *A 2* 465) / (*IV* 159.13) — ⲛⲕⲁⲧⲁⲥⲁⲣⲝ, *v.l.* ⲕⲁⲧⲁⲥⲁⲣⲝ, §1.1.1 / (*III* 58.29) — ⲛⲕⲁⲧⲁⲉⲓⲱϩⲁⲛⲛⲏⲥ / (*A 2* 100, *IV* 162.5) ⲙⲡⲁⲣⲁⲡϣⲓ, parall. ⲡⲁⲣⲁⲡϣⲓ, line 6.

(4) A (unique?) case of real hypostase [34]: ϣⲁϩⲓⲣⲟⲩϩⲉ " until evening " (*IV* 84.10, 92.2, *v.l.* ϣⲁⲣⲟⲩϩⲉ), which however may be explained by metanalytic analogy with ϩⲓⲧⲟⲟⲩⲉ < ϩⲧⲟⲟⲩⲉ (the latter being etymologically primary). ⲉⲛⲉϩ (§1.3.6), historically a prepositional phrase, is unanalyzable in Coptic.

1.1.2.0.1 Predication-modifying role. The adverbal modifier. Valency. Postadjuncts vs. premodifiers. The adverbal [35] modifier is found to occur in either of two patterns, viz. # *verb syntagm* + *modifier* #, where it is postadjunctive, and # *modifier* + *verb syntagm* #, where it is either focal (one construction in a set of focalization patterns, see §§2.4-6) or *adclausal* (in the sense of " in relation to the whole pattern or clause as such "), *premodifying* [36]. In the latter case (§1.1.2.2) we cannot speak of an expansion or adjunction: I take the function of the modifier here rather as *presetting*, orientating in advance, prelocating the clause in a framework of local, temporal, modal relationships [37]; the modifier is preparatory, in a sense *given* and (like conditional or temporal protases) often *topical* (cf. §2.0.2.1). Thus, although the convenient term " premodifier " will be employed in the following discussion, it stands rather for " presetter ", " predeterminer " or the like. No small difficulty here lies in uncovering the syntactic structure of the pattern [38]. Two alternative analyses present themselves: (a) The whole # *modifier* + *clause* # complex precludes nucleus-satellite analysis, that is to say, cannot be binarily analyzed in terms of a centre-and-periphery hierarchy, yet can be stated as a " determination " dependence, the premodifier presupposing the clause and not *vice versa*. (This is not unlike the preposition-noun dependence.) (b) Not in line with the basic Coptic *nucleus* → *satellite* syntagmatic sequence (but in accordance with that of the " mediator " lexeme premodifier construction, §3.4), we analyze the complex as ' *expansion* → *nuclear clause* ' [39].

[34] Cf. Karcevskij 1936:109f.

[35] " Adverbal ": in adjunctal or at any rate non-nexal relationship with a conjugation form (here " verb syntagm " [VS]). It goes without saying that further subcategorization of the verb is still called for—or a precise compatibility determination of certain modifiers with certain conjugation forms.

[36] The generally accepted (if language-specifically elusive and complicated) distinction of *sentence-* vs. *component-*modifier has been extensively treated for various languages; cf. Kern's *Satz-* vs. *Prädikatsbestimmung*, Gabelentz 1869:380,383f., Sechehaye 1950:164f. (" compléments de phrase "), Greenbaum 1969, Mathesius 1975:140f., Allerton and Cruttenden in *Lingua* 34:1-30 (1974).

There is no discussion of this issue for Coptic (but cf. Funk 1978b:96ff., 101ff., esp. §4.1.2, on the " conjugation mediators ", which Funk considers to be sentence modifiers of a kind; see §3.4 below on the " lexeme premodifiers ").

[37] Cf. Weinrich 1977:226ff., 268f., etc. on the " obstinate signals " which premodify sentences and larger subtextual units, up to text extent.

[38] The correlations and interactions of placement (*e.g.* initial, post-verbal, final) function (adverbal, adclausal) and syntagmatic structure are too complex, and involve factors too multifarious (including considerations of prosody, prominence, even style) to be thus summarily dismissed. As in any other issue of word order, a unified theory must be evolved in this case. (Cf. Jacobson 1964 for a painstaking scanning study of English modifier placement.)

[39] Note too the functionally difficult, if formally sharp, difference between premodifiers preceding an uncharacterized clause-form (' ⲕⲁⲗⲱⲥ ⲁⲕϫⲟⲟⲥ ') and a *focal* (nexus-constituent) modifiers. With the latter, the initial position is a feature of the predicative pattern (' ⲕⲁⲗⲱⲥ ⲉⲩϫⲱ ⲙⲙⲟⲥ '). Often, the actual difference in function escapes one. (Formally too, there is the possibility of transition from one construction to the other, with ⲉ- and ϫⲉ- " devalued " to a post-modifier clause form; see below, esp. §1.3.11 passim, and §2.5.0.1.).

1.1.2.1 THE POSTADJUNCTIVE ADVERBAL MODIFIER

(A) GENERAL OBSERVATIONS: (1) NUCLEUS - EXPANSION. The verb syntagm is expanded by the modifier; more precisely, it is the verb lexeme that is expanded. Some modifiers may be further expanded in their turn (§1.1.2.4). The prepositional phrase, however, can be analyzed only as a *determination* dependence, the preposition being the *determinant* — presupposing the noun, which is the determinate.

(2) VALENCY STRUCTURING (see also §3.0.1.2). Status hierarchy is the foremost question raised in this construction, since we usually have more than one modifier expanding one verb syntagm. This is primarily a matter of IC-analysis, of analytic model, of definition in terms of sequence and commutation, and — most crucial — of finding criteria for distinguishing between *complementation* (which is optional, grammatically unrestricted, non-rectional, hence pertinent and meaningful) and *rection* (conditioned, i.e. non meaningful) of the verbal nucleus [40]. In this regard, Crum's *Dictionary* is notoriously unhelpful (we are lucky, though, to have such a varied and extensive — if unstructured — inventory of attested combinations). A study of verb valency (actantial properties or potential) in Coptic is an urgent grammatical and lexicological *desideratum*. A specimen structured display of combination possibilities follows:

(α_1, β_1): $\#$ VS $+$ *modifier* $\#$; in matrix terms, positions [41] $(\emptyset)$ and (1).

(α_1): (K 9294) ⲥⲥⲱⲃⲉ ⲛⲥⲱⲟⲩ

(β_1): (K 913) ⲯⲁⲩⲡⲱⲧ ⲉⲙⲁⲩ

(α_1): *rection*, " object " (see §3.0.1) or " case " [42]. The modifier here is a co-constituent of the verb lexeme (" V + "), and no other actant is addable: " bivalent verbs ". The modifier, being conditioned, is here a *mot vide*, devoid of own meaning, commutable only with $\emptyset$- [43], if that [44]. The rection case *par excellence* is that of the mediate direct object marked by ⲛ-/ⲙⲙⲟ⸗, discussed in detail below (Ch. 3). Some other bivalent lexemes: ⲥⲱⲧⲡ (ⲛ-), ⲥⲁⲣⲉⲥ (ⲉ-), ⲯⲱⲡⲉ (ⲛ-), various reflexive verbs (ⲙⲧⲟⲛ, ⲯⲟⲩⲯⲟⲩ).

(β_1): *complementation*. The modifier in position (1) is optional, freely commutable, hence meaningful, semasiologically contributive, distinctive and indeed defining.

(α_2, β_2): $\#$ VS $+$ *modifier*$_1$ $+$ *modifier*$_2$ $\#$; matrix: $(\emptyset)$-(1)-(2).

(α_2): (III 130.6) ...ⲉⲧⲭⲓ ⲙⲙⲟⲩ ⲛⲅⲟⲛⲥ / (IV 54.16) ⲉⲩⲉⲧⲥⲁⲃⲟⲟⲩ ⲉⲡⲥⲗⲗⲟ [45] / (III 204.5f.) ⲯⲁⲣⲉⲧⲥⲓⲟ ⲙⲡⲟⲉⲓⲕ ⲙⲛⲡⲙⲟⲟⲩ " satiate thee (2nd fem.) with... " / (IV 79.14) ⲍⲙⲡⲧⲣⲉⲩⲁⲓⲧⲉⲓ ⲙⲙⲟⲟⲩ ⲙⲙⲟⲩ — the identity of ⲙⲙⲟ⸗ is here structurally definable (§3.1.2.0.1) / (ibid. 82.28) ...ⲉⲍⲟⲃⲥⲕ ⲙⲙⲟⲟⲩ / (III 166.22) ⲡⲯⲓ ⲉⲧⲟⲩⲛⲁⲯⲓ ⲙⲙⲟⲩ

---

[40] On this famous issue, see TESNIÈRE 1965:127ff. (actants *vs.* circonstants; his two criteria are patently inadequate. The formal one, very ethnocentric, conflicts with our ⲛ-, while the semasiological one cannot be accepted on its own). See also FREI 1964:35f., HELBIG 1971:33ff., BRINKER 1972:130ff., 154ff. (" In diesem Bereich ist noch fast alles zu tun "). This distinction is all too often vague and elusive (witness the " essentiality " *vs.* " erasability " test). For further references, see §3.0.1.2 below. (In Coptic, cases like ⲭⲉⲣⲟ⸗ and ⲭⲉⲛⲁ⸗ — see Černý, *ZÄS* 97: 44-6 [1971] — are clearly instances of non-rectional expansion turned rectional.)

[41] " Position " in a structural, not sequential sense, and potentially realizable by zero.

[42] ROSÉN 1977:168ff.

[43] This, together with absence of complementation (non-pertinent absence), correspond to *Dictionary's* " Intr. ", CHERIX's " absolut ".

[44] Consider ⲛⲁⲩ ⲉ-/ⲉⲃⲟⲗ, where ⲉ- cannot be zeroed. (The *rectum* of ⲉ- can be zeroed, by replacement by ⲃⲟⲗ). As a matter of fact, zeroing takes place by definition in this pattern only, not in the complementation construction, where the absence of a modifier does not have a grammatical significance.

[45] " Let the elder be informed about them ". So too (A 2 310) ⲧⲥⲁⲃⲉ-ⲡⲉⲧⲛⲍⲟ ⲉⲍⲟⲟⲩⲧ. In (IV 198.20) ⲁⲩⲧⲥⲁⲃⲟⲓ ⲉⲣⲟⲩ " I was informed about him ", the role of slots (1) (" direct object ") and (2) is reversed; the essential point here is *the existence of two governed slots*, one of which is ⲉ- marked. (See also POLOTSKY 1933:418 n. 1 [not in *CP*], on ⲧⲁⲙⲟⲟⲩ ⲉ-).

ⲚⲌⲈⲚⲢⲰⲘⲈ / (*BM* 204 oz) ⲚⲈⲦϤⲘⲈⲈⲨⲈ ⲈⲢⲟⲟⲨ ⲈⲟⲨⲟϭⲠⲟⲨ / (*III* 106.29) ⲀϤⲦⲤⲦⲟ ⲀⲈ ⲈⲂⲟⲗ ⲚⲚⲰⲀϫⲈ ⲘⲘⲈ [46] / (*ibid.* 106.18f.) ⲈⲦⲢⲈⲨⲦⲤⲈϤ-ⲘⲟⲟⲨ ⲚⲤⲈⲦⲘⲘⲈϤ-ⲟⲈⲒⲔ.

($β_2$): (*III* 185.17f.) ⲌⲘⲠⲦⲢⲈⲠⲌⲗⲗⲟ ⲈⲒ ⲈⲂⲟⲗ ⲌⲒⲦⲈⲦⲎⲨⲦⲚ / (*Ch.* 162.18f.) ⲈⲨⲰⲰ ⲈⲂⲟⲗ ⲌⲒⲂⲟⲗ / (*ibid.* 23.54ff.) ⲚⲦⲟⲟⲨ ⲀⲚ ⲚⲈⲦⲈⲰⲀⲔⲈⲒ ⲚⲌⲎⲦⲟⲨ ⲌⲚⲌⲈⲚⲢⲀⲤⲟⲨ, structurally different ⲌⲚ-.

($α_2$): *Double rection*: two conditioned expansions of a *trivalent* verb lexeme. Consider also ϭⲚⲦϤ ⲈϤ-, ⲌⲀⲢⲈⲌ ⲈⲢⲟϤ ⲈϤ- [47].

($β_2$): *Double complementation.* We find here very frequent mixed ($α + β$) constructions [48]: ($α_1 + β_1$): (*III* 98.12) ⲈⲤⲠⲟⲦⲠⲈⲦ ⲘⲘⲟⲟⲨ ⲈⲌⲢⲀⲒ Ⲉ- / (*A* 2 234) ⲦⲈⲚⲠⲒⲤⲦⲒⲤ ⲈⲦϪⲎⲔ ⲈⲂⲟⲗ ⲈⲌⲟⲨⲚ ⲈⲢⲟϤ / (*K* 9294) ⲚⲦⲟⲤ ⲠⲈⲦ-ⲟⲨⲰⲀϫⲈ ⲈⲢⲟⲤ ϫⲈ- [46]. ($α_1 + β_2$): (*A* 2 361) ⲀϤⲌⲀⲢⲈⲌ ⲈⲢⲟⲤ ⲚⲀϤ ⲈⲨⲘⲚⲦϫⲠⲒⲟ / (*Ch.* 26.51ff.) ⲠⲈⲤⲟⲨⲰⲰ ⲈⲦⲤⲘⲈ ⲘⲘⲟⲟⲨ ⲚⲌⲎⲦϤ ⲌⲚⲟⲨⲘⲈ / (*III* 187.8) ⲈⲦⲈⲦⲚⲦⲚⲚⲟⲟⲨ ⲘⲘⲟⲟⲨ ⲚⲀⲚ ⲚⲌⲀⲌ ⲚⲤⲟⲠ / (*Leyd.* 301) ⲚⲚⲈⲢⲰⲘⲈ ⲤⲈⲔ-ⲦⲈϤ-ⲌⲟⲒⲦⲈ ⲈⲌⲢⲀⲒ ⲔⲀⲔⲰⲤ. ($α_2 + β_1$): (*III* 107.12) ⲈϤⲘⲟⲦⲚ ⲚⲤⲢ-ⲘⲗⲀⲌ ⲈⲂⲟⲗ ⲟⲨⲂⲈ- / (*IV* 2.3) ⲚⲈⲦⲈⲢⲈⲠϫⲟⲈⲒⲤ ϤⲒ-ⲢⲟⲟⲨⲰ ⲌⲀⲢⲟⲚ ⲚⲌⲎⲦⲟⲨ.

($α_3$) (uncommon): (*A* 2 397) …ⲈⲦⲢⲈϤⲔⲀⲀϤ ⲔⲀⲌⲎⲨ ⲘⲘⲟϤ / (*III* 112.10f.) ⲚⲈⲦⲈⲢⲈⲚⲈⲨⲌⲂⲎⲨⲈ ⲟⲨⲰⲚⲌ ⲘⲘⲟⲟⲨ ⲈⲂⲟⲗ ϫⲈ-ⲌⲈⲚⲔⲀⲔⲈ ⲚⲈ.

($β_3$): (*IV* 106.12) …ⲈⲔⲰⲦⲈ ⲈⲌⲟⲨⲚ ⲈⲂⲟⲗ ⲈⲠϫⲒⲚϪⲎ / (*A* 2 87) ⲚϤⲰⲟⲠ ⲢⲰ ⲀⲚ ⲚⲦⲈⲒⲌⲈ ⲌⲢⲀⲒ ⲚⲌⲎⲦⲈ ⲦⲈⲚⲟⲨ. ($α_1 + β_3$): (*III* 208.17f.) ⲚⲈⲦⲟ ⲚⲀϤ ⲦⲈⲚⲟⲨ ⲚⲎⲒ ⲪⲀⲚⲈⲢⲟⲚ / (*Ch.* 116.36ff.) ⲤⲈⲚⲀⲢ-ⲢⲘⲘⲀⲟ ⲌⲚⲌⲈⲚⲌⲂⲎⲨⲈ ⲠⲀⲄⲀⲐⲟⲚ] ⲌⲚⲟⲨⲢⲰⲘⲈ ⲚⲟⲨⲰⲦ ⲀⲨⲰ ⲌⲚⲟⲨⲔⲰⲦ ⲚⲟⲨⲰⲦ] ⲈⲨϫⲰⲢⲀ: IC-analysis adds in these complex cases a vital hierarchical resolution (see below).

($β_4$): (*IV* 175.10f.) ⲚⲀⲚⲟⲨ-ⲈⲒ ⲟⲚ ⲈⲌⲢⲀⲒ ⲌⲒϫⲰϤ ⲌⲚⲚⲔⲰⲦⲈ ⲚⲦⲈⲌⲒⲎ ⲈⲦⲂⲈ ⲚⲈⲦⲚⲀⲌⲈ ⲚⲀⲨ ⲌⲀⲢⲀⲦϤ.

($α_1 + β_4$): (*III* 116.25ff.) ⲀϤⲔⲦⲟ ⲚⲦⲈϤϭⲒϫ ⲌⲢⲀⲒ ⲚⲌⲎⲦ ⲌⲚⲟⲨⲘⲔⲀⲌ ⲚⲌⲎⲦ ⲈⲚⲀⲰⲰϤ ⲔⲀⲦⲀⲠⲀⲘⲠⲰⲀ ϫⲈ-ⲀⲒⲢ-ⲚⲟⲂⲈ ⲘⲠⲈϤⲘⲦⲟ ⲈⲂⲟⲗ.

(3) IC-ANALYTIC DECISIONS are essential in certain cases: (a) Denominal derived " compound verbs "[49]: ' Ⲡ-Ⲍⲗ ⲘⲘⲟϤ ' may be analyzed as bivalent (Ⲡ-Ⲍⲗ | ⲘⲘⲟϤ) or trivalent (Ⲡ- Ⲍⲗ ⲘⲘⲟ⸗). (b) Occasionally one hesitates between assigning two successive modifiers to a single or two separate slots: ⲈⲒ ⲈⲌⲢⲀⲒ Ⲉ- (expanded modifier, see §1.1.2.4) or ⲈⲒ ⲈⲌⲢⲀⲒ Ⲉ-. We do not have any means of resolving this dilemma, except that of semasiological evaluation (which would not help us out anyway in case (a), and is in- conclusive and arbitrary even in case (b)). (c) In instances of ($β_2$...), IC-analysis is often enlightening (see exx. above).

(4) The manifold TEXT-COHESIVE function of modifiers does not directly concern us here, as the seg- ment under examination is ' *VS + modifier* ' alone; nevertheless, the compatibility of both grammatical (i.e. conjugational) and lexical elements of the verb syntagm with their modifiers [50] must be investigated. This is hardly feasible in a study such as the present one, which aims at a syntactic schematization of the modifier system (see below, §§1.3). It must be undertaken as part of a monographic, systematic treat- ment of verbal syntax and semantics for individual conjugational environments and semasiological syntagmatics. Other *desiderata* are the investigation of modifier occurrence, collocations and of modifier

---

[46] With syntagmatic (sequential) and structural (analytic) orders conflicting. As a general rule (with some well-known exceptions, see POLOTSKY 1961) the further away a modifier is from the verb lexeme, the less grammatically involved it is with it; this does not apply, though, to positions (1)-(2) of the matrix.

[47] At least one possible description of the adnexal ' *noun+circumstantial* ' complex expanding a verb would involve distin- guishing between a bivalent lexeme (ϭⲒⲚⲈ/ⲌⲈ Ⲉ- + *direct object*) and its trivalent homonym ϭⲚⲦϤ/ⲌⲈ ⲈⲢⲟϤ ⲈϤ-, ⲚⲀⲨ ⲈⲢⲟϤ ⲈϤ-, ⲌⲀⲢⲈⲌ ⲈⲢⲟϤ ⲈϤ-, etc. I have found (SHISHA-HALEVY 1972:77-82) this homonymy also for ϫⲰ, Ⲧ, ⲦⲰⲰ, ϫⲠⲟ, ⲦⲀⲌⲟ and other verbs.

[48] A striking case of lexemes both rectionally and complementationally expandable is that of Ⲧ (and ϫⲒ): Ⲧ Ⲛ- | ⲈⲌⲟⲨⲚ/ⲈⲌⲢⲀⲒ/ⲟⲨⲂⲈ-/ⲘⲚⲚⲤⲀ-/Ⲉ-, ϫⲒ Ⲛ- | Ⲉ-/ⲈϫⲚ-... also ⲚⲒϤⲈ Ⲛ- | ⲈⲌⲟⲨⲚ/Ⲉ(ⲌⲢⲚ)-/ⲚⲤⲀ-...

[49] See §3.1.2.2.2 for a discussion and an extensive listing of these syntagms.

[50] Cf. WEINRICH 1977 *passim* (e.g. 71), SEILER 1968, KLUM 1961 (esp. 86 ff.), STEINITZ-SCHÄDLICH 1970, etc.

mobility in the utterance (this last is here selectively attempted). Specific pronoun-including modifiers are exponents of a cohesion scheme: the *augens*, discussed in Ch. 6: (*A 1* 122) ЕРЕСООУN ТШN Н ЕРЕЕІМЕ ТШN Н ЕІNАЕІМЕ ТШN АNОК. So (less regularly) are anaphoric elements included in the expansions: (*IV* 128.11f.) ПNОВЕ ЕNТАNМЕЕУЕ ЕШААТЧ ЕВОЛ ММОN ЕТВНННТЧ, ЕТВНННТЧ resuming П(NОВЕ), ШААТЧ resuming ПЕN(СОN) in the preceding cotext / (*P* 130⁴ 88 ro) N†СООУN ММОК АN ХЕ-NТК-NІМ / (*ibid.* 89 vo) МПРТРЕПЕКСШМА ҀЕ КNNЕ ХЕКАС NNЕҀТАКОК / (*III* 130.7f.) ПАІ ЕТММАУ АУШ NЕІКООУЕ ПNОУТЕ NАКРІNЕ ҀNТМНТЕ МПАІ МNNАІ ЕТММАУ. (In a future general study of Coptic text-grammar, and specifically text cohesion ["texture"], this issue of phoric expansions must take a foremost place [see §3.1.1.1.0.1, 5.1.1.1 and 6.0.2.2(8) for some special anaphoric features].) Otherwise, the modifier stands in unmarked (or morphematically marked) cohesion with its nucleus [51].

(5) Specifically ADVERBAL VERB-FORMS (though not, except for the conjunctive, Ch. 7, discussed here) must be considered members of the modifier paradigm: the conjunctive and other Clause Conjugation forms, the adverbal circumstantial forms [52], vested [53] (ҀШС-, ҀОТАN-, ХІN- etc. + Е-) and unvested (Е-), conditional forms and constructions, the coeventive (ҀМПТРЕҀ-), posteventive (МNNСАТРЕҀ-) and precursive (NТЕРЕҀ-) [54], the last being post-adjunctively in marked placement; various conjunctional constructions (including ХЕ-). Although certainly modifiers and syntactically akin to the mixed bag of items specified in the inventory below, they form a class apart in respect of word order, not being accommodated by the 'Ø-(1)-(2)...' matrix. They are mostly non-rectional (the circumstantial and conjunctive — Ch. 7 — are adnexal).

(B) CONSTITUENCY. The following is an open-ended inventory, a checklist rather than a true paradigmatic presentation. It is a paradigm in the sense that these modifiers do occur in adverbal postadjunctive status and in the compatibilities and order indicated. A few words are called for concerning the exhaustiveness and validity of claims made here. Since we deal here with lexemes (or rather elements in the no man's land common to grammar and lexicon), the lists and combination possibilities cannot be taken as closed (especially as the corpus may yet be extended, and "productivity" in a dead language must be a matter of inference rather than assumption). References are representative (I have no statistics on frequency. More references are given for the rarer items).

(1) *prepositions*

Е-(А-)/ЕРО॒	"to, for, concerning etc.", *III* 184.13, *Ch.* 127.24, *Mun.* 104.
ЕРАТ॒	"to (chez)", *Ch.* 155.46f. (*Dictionary* 303).
ЕРN-/ЕРШ॒, ЕРО॒	"to, on (the mouth of...)", *Ch.* 48.53f., *A 1* 241, *BM* 253 NҀ, *P* 131⁴ 154 ΛЕ; *P* 130⁴ 127 МВ; *Z* 246 РІΔ. Almost only with ТШМ, ОУШN (*Dict.* 289b).
ЕТN-/ЕТООТ॒	"to (hand of...)" *III* 214.1, *A 1* 113, *A 2* 26 (*Dict.* 427b).
ЕҀЕN-	"πρός", *Wess. 18* 143a 25ff. *Dict.* 685a (also in Besa; cf. (Е)ҀN-, spec. obs. 3).
ЕҀРN-/ЕҀРА॒	"towards (the face of...)", rare, usually with ЕҀОУN *A 1* 465 (*Dict.* 649).
ЕХN-/ЕХШ॒	"on, upon, over, against", *III* 40.8, *Ch.* 198.34f. (*Dict.* 757-8).
АХN-, ЕХN-/АХШ॒, ЕХШ॒	"without", *III* 42.5, *IV* 113.16, *A 2* 519 (*Dict.* 25-6).
ЕТВЕ-/ЕТВННТ॒	"about, because of..., for the sake of...", *Miss.* 279, *III* 108.19f.

---

[51] Compare the cohesive zeroing of the non-rectional modifier in a 'КШ ЕВОЛ → КШ' cotext pattern (see §3.1.1.1.0.1 for exx.); cf. STEINITZ 1969:15ff.

[52] SHISHA-HALEVY 1972, first chapter.

[53] *Ibid.*, Introduction, Chapter 3.

[54] *Ibid.* §§1.4.1-3.

MN-/NMMA⸗	" with, and- ", *III* 219.24, *Ch.* 136.5.
N-/MMO⸗	" in relation to, in, with, direct object etc. ", *III* 108.19f., *IV* 7.5 (spec. obs. 1).
N-/NA⸗	" to, for ", *III* 173.25, *Ch.* 131.23f.
(M)ПB(O)Λ-, NBΛΛA⸗	" outside of, beside " (exx. in *Dict.* 33-4).
NNA2PN-/NNA2PA⸗	" in the presence of..., before ", *Wess.* 9 119a 19f., *III* 54.19.
NCA-/NCⲰ⸗	" after, behind, beyond ", *Ch.* 127.45f., *III* 219.12.
MNNCA-/MNNCⲰ⸗	" after ", *P* 130⁴ 104 ⲣⲕⲅ, *Ch.* 134.37ff., *A 1* 13.
NTN-/NTOOT⸗	" with, in the hand of... ", *IF* 123 (apud *Dict.* 523b), *III* 145.1 (*Dict.* 427-8).
OYBE-/OYBH⸗	" against, opposite ", *III* 159.11, *Ch.* 120.42f., 197.23f.
(OYTE-)/OYTⲰ⸗	" between, among ", *Ch.* 146.33ff.
ⲰA-/ⲰAPO⸗	" (up) to, until, towards ", *IV* 33.18, *A 1* 16.
2A-/2APO⸗	" under, on behalf of, for ", *Wess.* 9 155b 5, *Mun.* 100.
2AEIAT⸗	" under the observation of ", *P* 130⁴ 59 ro.
(2APN-)/2APⲰ⸗	" under the mouth of..., before ", *Ch.* 157.55ff., *Rossi 2/3* 54, *A 2* 166 (*Dict.* 289-290).
2APAT⸗	" under foot of... ", *A 2* 299 (*Dict.* 303b).
2A(2)TN-/2A(2)TH⸗	" under (hand of...), with, among ", *III* 27.16, 150.14, 157 *passim*, *IV* 62 *passim* (*Dict.* 428b).
2I/2IⲰⲰ⸗	" on, in, at " *III* 213 *passim*, *Ch.* 174.3f.
2IPN-/2IPⲰ⸗	" at, upon (mouth/door of...) ", *III* 118.3, *Rossi 2/3* 51, *IF* 307 (apud *Dict.* 290a) (*Dict.* 290a).
2ITN-/(2ITOOT⸗)	" by, through ", *III* 24.22, 196.20 (*Dict.* 428-9).
2ITOYN-/2ITOYⲰ⸗	" beside, next ", *A 2* 52, *IV* 120.19 (*Dict.* 444b).
2IXN-/2IXⲰ⸗	" (up)on ", *Wess.* 9 141a 28, *Ch.* 18.26f. (*Dict.* 758-9).
(E)2HT⸗	" of " with Ⲣ-2OTE *IV* 156.19, *K* 9294, *Mun.* 177, *Ch.* 151.20, *Mich.* 158 14a.
2N-/N2HT⸗	" in, at, with, etc. ", *Ch.* 110.16, *IV* 7.1; " to " — sp. obs. 3 2N-.

(2) *prepositions (of Greek origin and/or with no presuffixal allomorph); modifiers*

ANTI-	§1.3.11.5
AYⲰ	§1.3.10
ENE2	§1.3.6
ETI	§1.3.11.6
EIC-	" for " (temporally), *III* 89.10, 218-9, *IV* 172.6, *P* 130⁵ 79 Λ: ...EIC2OYO ECE NPOMПE ＋ⲰⲰ 2NNEYAⲄⲄEΛION (*Dict.* 85b).
KAN	§1.3.11.6
XⲰPIC	§1.3.11.5
KATA(PO⸗)-	§1.3.11.5
MEXPI-	§1.3.11
NOYEⲰ-	" without ", *IV* 91.20 (*Dict.* 502a).
NAME	§1.3.5.1
ПAΛIN	§1.3.11.3
ПAPA(PO⸗)-	§1.3.11.5
ПPOC-	§1.3.11.5
TAXY	§1.3.11.4
TENOY	§1.3.4
TⲰN	" where/whence? ", see *Ch. 2*, esp. §2.2 (e.g. *A 1* 33).

ⲦⲰⲚⲞⲨ, etc.	§1.3.9
ⲰⲀⲦⲚ-	" except ", P 130[1] 133 ⲦⲔⲐ (Dict. 593).
ⲌⲞⲦⲀⲚ	§1.3.11.6
(Ⲍ)ⲞⲦⲒ ⲆⲈ ⲬⲈ-	A 2 338.
ⲌⲰⲤ	§1.3.11.5
ⲌⲞⲤⲞⲚ, ⲈⲚⲌⲞⲤⲞⲚ	§1.3.11.6
ⲬⲈ-	conjunctional, explicative, gerundial (" saying ") etc., III 81.24f., Wess. 9 126b 3ff., Ch. 116.18ff., 143.34f.
ⲬⲒⲚ-	" since ", III 218.9, IV 39.27f. (Dict. 772-3).
noun + noun	§1.3.3
(reiterated noun)	
Ø-noun	§1.3.2

(3) *expandable modifiers* (cf. §1.1.2.4)

ⲈⲂⲞⲖ	" out ", IV 98.4 (Dict. 34).
ⲈⲠⲀⲌⲞⲨ	" back ", A 1 24 (Dict. 284b).
ⲈⲠⲈⲤⲎⲦ	" down " Ryl. 70 ⲤⲚⲂ (Dict. 60a).
ⲈⲐⲎ	" to the front, forwards ", Mun. 91 (Dict. 641a).
ⲈⲌⲞⲨⲚ	" in(side) ", III 115.21 (Dict. 685-7).
ⲈⲌⲢⲀⲒ₁	" up ", A 2 113, 234 (ⲘⲞⲨⲌ " fill ") (Dict. 698-9, spec. obs. 2).
ⲈⲌⲢⲀⲒ₂	" down ", IV 59.3, A 1 404 (the setting sun) (Dict. 700, spec. obs. 2).

ⲈⲂⲞⲖ	Ⲉ-/ⲈⲢⲞ⸗	BKU 180 (ⲠⲰⲰⲚⲈ).
	ⲈⲬⲰ⸗	RE 10 161a 2.
	Ⲛ-/ⲘⲘⲞ⸗	III 118.29, Wess. 9 108a 16ff.
	ⲚⲦⲚ-	IF 123 (apud Dict. 523b).
	ⲞⲨⲦⲈ-/ⲞⲨⲦⲰ⸗	Ch. 145.39f., Mun. 103, P 130[2] 92 ⲠⲤ, 130[4] 120 ⲔⲌ, A 2 109.
	ⲌⲀ-	IV 101.16.
	ⲌⲀⲢⲰ⸗	Ch. 135.30f.
	ⲌⲎⲦ⸗	P 130[5] 37 vo (ϬⲰⲰⲦ) (prenom. ⲌⲎⲦϤ Ⲛ- 130[2] 44 ⲢⲒⲆ).
	(ⲌⲒ-)ⲌⲒⲰⲰ⸗	Wess. 9 171b 8.
	ⲌⲒⲦⲚ-/ⲌⲒⲦⲞⲞⲦ⸗	IV 204.13, Ch. 111.48f.
	ⲌⲒⲬⲚ-/ⲌⲒⲬⲰ⸗	A 1 452, A 2 336 (ⲦⲰⲞⲨⲚ), IV 49.16, Ch. 116.2f.
	ⲌⲚ-/ⲚⲌⲎⲦ⸗	III 162.10, IV 19.15.
	ⲘⲘⲀⲨ	IV 121.6.
	ⲦⲰⲚ	see §2.6.3
	ⲬⲈ-	IV 21.7, P 130[4] 100 vo.
(Ⲛ)ⲤⲀⲂⲞⲖ		IV 152.22
	ⲘⲘⲞ⸗	IV 74.23.
ⲰⲀⲂⲞⲖ		Z 246 ⲠⲂ.
ⲌⲒⲂⲞⲖ		A 2 26, Ch. 162.8f.

ⲈⲌⲞⲨⲚ	Ⲉ-/ⲈⲢⲞ⸗	IV 24.4f., 6.10ff.
	ⲈⲌⲢⲚ-/ⲈⲌⲢⲀ⸗	Ch. 13.45f., K 9345, IV 116.19f.
	Ⲛ-	IV 63.2.

	ⲟⲩⲧⲱ⸗	*Ch.* 90.5f.
	ϩⲛ-	*A 2* 304 (ⲥⲟⲟⲩϩ), *P* 130^{4} 103 ⲣⲕⲃ, *Mun.* 177 ("hit") (sp. obs. 3).
	ϣⲁ-	*Ch.* 23.25.
ⲛϩⲟⲩⲛ	ϩⲁ-	*P* 130^{1} 141 ⲧⲙⲑ ("hit").
		IV 98.6f.
	ϩⲛ-/ⲛϩⲏⲧ⸗	*III* 142.25f.
	ⲛ-	*IV* 98.6f.
ⲥⲁϩⲟⲩⲛ		*A 1* 381.
ϣⲁϩⲟⲩⲛ	ⲉ-	*A 2* 380, *IV* 41.24.
ϩⲓϩⲟⲩⲛ		*A 2* 26.
	ⲙⲙⲟ⸗	*IV* 155.3.

ⲉϩⲣⲁⲓ "up", "down" ("up + down"?)	ⲉ-/ⲓⲉⲣⲟ⸗	*IV* 24.13f., *Wess. 9* 154a 14f.
	ⲉⲧⲟⲟⲧ⸗	*IV* 20.22.
	ⲉϫⲛ-/ⲉϫⲱ⸗	*IV* 67.18, 200.6.
	ⲛⲙⲙⲁ⸗	*IV* 11.15f., *P* 131^{5} 58 ⲓⲍ (ϣⲱϣ).
	ϩⲁ-	*Z* 247 ⲣⲕⲍ, *P* 130^{5} 128 ⲧⲙⲑ (ⲥⲙⲙⲉ).
	ϩⲁϩⲧⲛ-	*III* 27.15f.
	ϩⲓ-	*IV* 98.2.
	ϩⲛ-	*Ryl.* 67 ⲧϥⲋ, *P* 130^{4} 93 ⲣⲙⲇ.
	ⲧⲱⲛ	*A 2* 513.
	ⲟⲩⲧⲱ⸗	*IF* 163 (apud *Dict.* 495a).
(ⲛ)ϩⲣⲁⲓ	ϩⲓ-	*P* 130^{4} 126 ⲗⲑ.
	ϩⲛ-/ⲛϩⲏⲧ⸗	*III* 156 *passim*, *IV* 204.16, *III* 193.18.
ⲥⲁⲛϩⲣⲉ		"above", *Ench.* 57b (*Dict.* 700).
ϩⲓϩⲣⲉ		"up", *A 1* 150 (*Dict.* 700a).
ϣⲁϩⲣⲁⲓ	ⲉ-	*III* 142.8.

ⲉⲑⲏ	ⲙⲙⲟ⸗	*IV* 95.16.
ⲛⲥⲁⲑⲏ		*IV* 113.1.
ϩⲁⲑⲏ		*IV* 48.10.
ϩⲓⲑⲏ		*IV* 40.13.
ϩⲓϩⲏ	ⲙⲙⲟ⸗	*IV* 95.20.

(C) Special observations: (1) ⲛ-/ⲙⲙⲟ⸗ (see §§1.0.1, 1.1.1, 1.3.1 and *passim*). I consider the question of material identity subordinate to that of structural (i.e. functional) identity, which is determined by the slot occupied in the valency matrix and by commutability. Occasional analytic perplexities may arise (gen. obs. 3): ⲣ-$\overset{0}{\text{ⲡ}}$ⲙⲉⲉⲩ$\overset{1}{\text{ⲉ}}$ ⲛ- or ⲣ-$\overset{0}{\text{ⲡ}}$$\overset{1}{\text{ⲙ}}$ⲉⲉⲩⲉ ⲛ- (adnominal ⲛ-; ⲣ-ⲡⲉϥⲙⲉⲉⲩⲉ corroborates the second alternative.)

(2) ⲉϩⲣⲁⲓ in a well-known syncretism; a phonological merger has caused two distinct Egyptian "prepositional adverbs" [55] ("up", *r-ḥry* and "down", *r-ẖry*) to merge in Sahidic Coptic into a single

[55] Edel 1959:18.

entity " up or down ", " inclininglу, slopingly ". This at least is the *communis opinio* [56]. It remains to be seen whether the " up/down " distinctive feature — the functional burden — is situated in the verbal nucleus (or perhaps in its context), or whether this opposition is neutralized, for any given combination of ' lexeme + ЄϨⲢⲀⲒ + preposition ', in favour of one or the other sense: ⲔⲰ ЄϨⲢⲀⲒ meaning " lay *down* ", ЄⲒ ЄϨⲢⲀⲒ Є- " descend " only, ⲀⲖЄ ЄϨⲢⲀⲒ (*III* 99.1, [ⲦⲀⲖⲞ] *IV* 156.3) " ascend, go up ", and so on: consider (*III* 107.1, 111.2, *Miss.* 283) ЄⲒ ЄϨⲢⲀⲒ Є- " fall down into ", (*A 2* 192) ЄⲒ ЄϨⲢⲀⲒ ϨⲚ- " sprout up from ", (*A 1* 97) -ⲦⲀⲀϤ ЄϨⲢⲀⲒ ЄⲚЄϤⲞⲨⲰϢ ⲘⲠⲞⲚⲎⲢⲞⲚ " deliver (down) to ", (*IV* 24.16) ϨⲰⲘ ЄϨⲢⲀⲒ ЄϪⲚ- " trample, tread down ", (*ibid.* 13f.) -ⲚⲞϪⲞⲨ ЄϨⲢⲀⲒ ЄⲠⲔⲰϨⲦ " down to ", (*Ch.* 60) (of the sun) ЄⲒ/ⲚⲎⲨ ЄϨⲢⲀⲒ " rise ", ⲂⲰⲔ/ⲚⲀ ЄϨⲢⲀⲒ " set ", and so on. It may well be that one of the two senses — ЄϨⲢⲀⲒ " down "? — is unmarked environmentally, while the other is so marked; this must be settled by corpus-based investigation. May cases of " doubt " (*Dictionary* 698b) really be cases of indifference? Consider (*III* 210.18) ⲠЄⲤⲔⲰⲦЄ ЄϨⲢⲀⲒ ϨⲀⲢⲒϨⲀⲢⲞⲤ, (*IV* 64.6) ⲘⲞⲔϨ ЄϨⲢⲀⲒ ЄϪⲚ-, (*ibid.* 55.20f.) ⲞⲨⲰⲦⲂ ЄϨⲢⲀⲒ Є- etc., where the direction is immaterial.

(3) (ЄϨⲞⲨⲚ) ϨⲚ- " into ", pron. ЄϨⲞⲨⲚ ЄϨⲢⲀ⸗ (*Dictionary* 684b, Polotsky 1939:113 = *CP* 377, Layton 1981:244f.): (*A 1* 202) ⲚⲤЄϯ ЄϨⲞⲨⲚ ϨⲘⲠЄⲚϨⲞ/ (*P* 131[1] 139 ⲦⲘⲤ) ϯ-ⲀⲀⲤ ЄϨⲞⲨⲚ ϨⲘⲠϨⲞ/ЄϨⲞⲨⲚ ЄϨⲢⲀⲨ; also ϤⲒ-ⲒⲀⲦⲔ ЄϨⲢⲀⲒ ϨⲚ- (*Z* 247 ⲢⲒⲂ), ⲂⲰⲔ ЄⲂⲞⲖ/ϨⲚ- (*P* 130[2] 24 ⲪⲚЄ; of viper's venom: " into body "), ϢⲀⲨϢⲒⲂЄ ⲘⲠⲆⲒⲔⲀⲒⲞⲚ ϨⲘⲠϪⲒⲚϬⲞⲚⲤ ⲀⲨⲰ ⲠⲦⲂⲂⲞ ϨⲘⲠϪⲰϨⲘ (*P* 130[4] 104 ⲢⲔⲄ). ⲂⲰⲔ ЄϨⲞⲨⲚ ⲚϨⲎⲦ⸗ (*P* 130[5] 16 vo) seems to indicate a complete merging of this compound preposition with ϨⲚ-/ⲚϨⲎⲦ⸗ " in " (Akhm. ⳉЄⲚ- vs. ⳉЄⲚ-). ЄϨⲚ- (e.g. in Besa ed. Kuhn 79 ⲚЄⲦⲚⲎⲨ ЄϨⲘⲠЄⲨϨⲎⲦ, also common in " Middle Egyptian " Coptic) is Є + the same.

1.1.2.2 Premodifiers. Adclausal (adpattern) modifiers

(A) General observations: (1) Above (§1.1.2.0.1) the point was made that the modifier preceding the predicative pattern [57] or opening the clause is not adjunctal, but presets or predetermines the circumstances or attitude in/under which the predication is to be understood as valid. It thus realizes an option for a specific staging or structuring of the information given in the clause, related to the option of topic-comment arrangement. Postadjunctive modification has a broader potential of paradigmatic/syntagmatic extent (embodying as it does the valency matrix, rection and complementation) than premodification. Particularly significant is the absence in the case of pre- or adclausal modification of the opposition between rection and complementation, so crucial in postadjunctive modification. Paradigmatically speaking, the premodifier (insofar as it is opposed to a corresponding postadjunctive homonym) realizes a *marked* option in a binary category of placement. Syntagmatically, it is different in that it is free of matricial structuring. There seems to be a restriction on the number of premodifiers to any single clause, these being much fewer than the number of possible postadjunctive modifiers, and usually not exceeding three or four premodifiers to a clause.

(2) Premodifiers relate to the content of the entire clause. The degree of their integration with it may vary, it is also related to their macro-syntactic standing [58]. It is difficult to estimate this degree (in all probability, on a gradient scale). Prosodically, premodifiers are more autonomous syntactically

[56] Černý 1976:291f.

[57] See §3.3 for the lexeme/stative modifiers.

[58] See §7.3.1 for #*modifier* + *conjunctive*# syntagms; §§1.3.11 *passim* for the *premodifier*-ϪЄ-clause integration type. It is interesting to note that the variant -ⲞⲤ of -ⲰⲤ Greek-origin modifiers is much more prevalent in postadjunctive position, which is apparently sufficiently characterizing, than in premodifier status. Note too the Nitrian Bohairic distinction of # ⲔⲀⲖⲰⲤ- *vs.* -ⲚⲔⲀⲖⲰⲤ#. For Ⲛ- with Greek-origin modifiers, see Crum 1926, I 251f. (n. 8), Kahle 1954:104.

than postadjuncts, since they usually constitute independent cola and may be disjoined by enclitics from the body of the clause [59].

(3) Criteria for identifying adclausal elements proposed for a modern language [60], such as their eligibility as foci of negation, of interrogation, of information, are only in part applicable to Coptic, a dead language. The focalizability test, for instance, shows that there is a subdivision of unfocalizable premodifiers, but most share a potential focal status with the postadjuncts (see §§2.4-6). Indeed, I find more essential the distinction between the non-focal — in relation to the rest of the clause, topical — preposed modifier on the one hand and the focalized one on the other.

(4) Here too, one must consider verb forms sharing in the modifier paradigm: the circumstantial (e.g. *Ch.* 110.26ff., *IV* 187.6ff.), coeventive (2ⲘⲠⲦⲢⲈϤ-, e.g. *III* 58.21f., *IV* 128.4ff.), posteventive (ⲘⲚⲚⲤⲀ-ⲦⲢⲈϤ-, e.g. *III* 133.24 ff.), precursive (ⲚⲦⲈⲢⲈϤ-, in unmarked placement; e.g. *III* 24.7f., *IV* 206.1ff.) [61], conditional forms and syntagms ((2ⲞⲦⲀⲚ/ⲔⲀⲚ) ⲈϤϢⲀⲚ-, ⲈϤϢⲰⲠⲈ, ⲈϤⲬⲈ-, ⲈⲚⲈ-). The augential modifiers (Chapter 6) are absent in this paradigm.

(B) CONSTITUENCY: Only the most common premodifiers are here presented (premodification being an open option, exhaustivity is precluded in this case, in which more and more members are added as one comes across them). Those premodifiers for which placement opposition is rare or absent are marked with an asterisk.

Ⲛ-	ⲚⲦⲈⲓ2Ⲉ §1.3.1.2, ⲚⲐⲈ Ⲛ- *III* 112.16, Ⲛ2ⲞⲨⲞ §1.3.1.3, ⲚϢⲞⲢⲠ *III* 55.15, ⲚⲞⲨⲞⲈⲓϢ ⲚⲓⲘ *IV* 99.16, ⲘⲠⲞⲞⲨ *Teza* 683.
ϢⲀ-	ϢⲀ2ⲢⲀⲓ Ⲉ- *A 1* 171.
2Ⲛ-	*III* 73.10ff., 2ⲚⲞⲨⲘⲈ (§1.3.5.2).
ⲈⲦⲂⲈ-	*Wess. 9* 141a 25ff., ⲈⲦⲂⲈ-ⲬⲈ- *A 2* 334.
ⲀⲬⲚ-	" without ", *A 2* 245f., *Wess. 18* 97b 9ff.
2ⲓⲦⲚ-	*III* 113.12.
*ⲈⲠ2ⲀⲈ	§1.3.7, ⲈⲠⲘⲀ Ⲛ- *Young* passim, Ⲉ2ⲢⲀⲓ Ⲉ- *III* 88.8, ⲈⲠⲬⲓⲚⲬⲎ §1.3.7.3.
ⲬⲓⲚ-	ⲬⲓⲚⲦⲈ2ⲞⲨⲈⲓⲦⲈ *P* 130⁴ 139 ro, ⲬⲓⲚⲈⲚⲈ2 §1.3.6.
2ⲢⲀⲓ 2Ⲛ-	*III* 73.9f., *IV* 99.16.
ⲈⲂⲞⲗ 2Ⲛ-	*P* 130⁴ 129 ⲘⲈ, *IV* 36.21.
ⲈⲓⲤ-	*Ch.* 173.56ff.
ⲘⲚⲚⲤⲀ-	*P* 130⁴ 111 ⲪⲚⲄ-Ⲇ.
ⲚⲚⲀ2ⲢⲚ-	*P* 130² 37 ro ⲚⲚⲀ2ⲢⲎⲦⲚ ϢϢⲈ...
ⲚⲀⲘⲈ	§1.3.5.1
ⲦⲈⲚⲞⲨ	§1.3.4
*ⲀⲨϢ	§1.3.10
Ø-noun	§1.3.2; esp. ⲤⲞⲠ in 2Ⲁ2 ⲚⲤⲞⲠ, ⲤⲞⲠ — ⲤⲞⲠ —, etc.

Greek-origin premodifiers (§§1.3.11 passim): ⲀⲚⲦⲓ- (esp. in ⲀⲚⲦⲓⲦⲢⲈϤ-, ⲀϤ-, a favourite Shenoutean figure, e.g. *A 2* 7-8, ⲬⲰⲢⲓⲤ-, ⲔⲀⲦⲀ-, 2ⲰⲤ-, *ⲘⲀⲗⲓⲤⲦⲀ, *ⲘⲀⲗⲗⲞⲚ, *ⲞⲨ ⲘⲞⲚⲞⲚ, *ⲠⲀⲗⲓⲚ ⲞⲚ, ⲈⲔⲘⲈⲢⲞⲨⲤ, *ⲔⲀⲚ, *ⲘⲞⲄⲓⲤ, ⲈⲦⲓ, *ⲠⲗⲎⲚ, ⲤⲬⲈⲆⲞⲚ, *ⲦⲀⲬⲀ.

---

[59] See Ch. 6, esp. §6.0.3. This is also borne out by punctuation (e.g. *Ch.* 53.13, 56.28, 163.12; 21.2, 36.22, 113.50; 115.38; 120.10; 141.21 etc.). Compare too SHISHA-HALEVY 1975:483 b.4, c.3,4.

[60] GREENBAUM 1969, esp. 24f., 119f., 230f.

[61] For extensive documentation and a discussion, see SHISHA-HALEVY 1972 §§1.1.1, 1.4.1.1.2, 1.4.1.2.2., 1.4.2.1.

(C) SPECIAL OBSERVATIONS: (1) 2N: ' 2N-OY + *infinitive* ', only in Shenoute's infrequent (Biblicizing) use of the so-called tautological infinitive, the syntagm used in certain languages to focalize (by topicalizing + focalizing) a verb lexeme: see GOLDENBERG 1971 (a penetrating and detailed, language-specific as well as typological-comparative study of these constructions). I consider the Coptic construction borrowed; for the authentic, stylistically neutral Coptic means of verb focalization (the autofocal Second Tense) see §2.1. Some exx. for the Shenoutean tautological infinitive: (*P* 130² 42 PH) MH 2NOYPAϢE NCENAPAϢE AN / (*P* 130⁴ 110 ΦNB) 2NOYXΠIO MAPNXΠIO NNENEPHY / (*A 2* 49) ...XEKAC 2ϢϢN 2N2APE2 NIM ENNA2APE2 EΠEN2HT / (*ibid.* 380) 2NOYEI KNHY. Also *III* 183.4, 188.6, *IV* 121.4f. (and cf. — post-adjunctively — *A 1* 274, *Wess. 9* 90b 1ff., 156c 7ff.). Outside certain stereotyped expressions, 2PAI 2N- seems to be the premodifier alternant of 2N-.

(2) Premodifiers of Greek origin are here statistically more weighty than in the post-adjunctive constituency — many are exclusively premodifiers, with no placement opposition. It would seem that Greek supplies here real conjuncts and disjuncts (in the terminology of GREENBAUM 1969), in which the Egyptian stock of Coptic is very meagre. (The similarity to the particle situation is striking, if indeed particles too are not to be taken as premodifiers.)

1.1.2.3 MODIFIERS IN A NOMINAL SENTENCE [62]

(A) GENERAL OBSERVATION: Since here too one encounters a placement distinction, the question must be asked whether the same functional differentiation in evidence with verbal predications is valid in nominal-predication patterns which have their own specific, relatively rigid prosodic structure (cf. §6.0.3.3; 6 note 36). This structure must be considered a possible factor motivating the placement of modifiers. Initially, we note here three placements:

(a) *post-predicate* (adjunctal, adlexemic?): 2ENATNOYTE ΦANEPON NE (*A 2* 485);

(b) *pattern-final* (adclausal?) [63]: OY ΠE +PHNH N2ENPϢME NNA2PMΠNOYTE (*III* 75.10);

(c) *prepattern* (adclausal?) — premodifier: NAME ΠEЧHI ΠE TEKKΛHCIA (*A 2* 332).

These possibilities, observable for example in the bimembral ⧧ *predicate*-{ΠE} ⧧ pattern [64], must yet be empirically evaluated by reference to syntactic and prosodic motivating factors (for instance, extensive adlexemic modification is usually pattern-final; contrast (*Wess. 9* 117a 10 ff.) OY EPON ΠE or (*Ench.* 87a) 2ENEBOΛ N2HTN AN NE with (*Leyd.* 347) 2ENEBOΛ NE 2MΠEЧCϢMA ETOYAAB. This leaves us, at least in theory, with the simplified binary opposition of post-predicate + pattern-final *vs.* prepattern. See also §6.0.3.4 for the polar placement conditioning of certain modifiers; some (NA⸗, NAME, augentia) occur only as colon-second, i.e. in post-predicate placement. In one pattern, post-predicate and pattern-final placements coalesce: (*IV* 102.16) ...EANON-2ENPM2E EBOΛ 2NTMNT2M2AΛ NΘYΛH / (*Leyd.* 348) ANON-OYCϢMA NOYϢT 2MΠEXC. More precisely, we note six different cases:

(1) ⧧ *predicate* + {ΠE} (*nominal subject*) ⧧ [64]:   " non-extensive " modification: (a), (b), (c)
                                                         " extensive " modification: (b), (c)

---

[62] CALLENDER (1970:98-110) discusses, with ample illustration, the subcategorization and semasiological compatibility of " adverbials " with Nominal-Sentence patterns. He does not enter placement issues (see also *ibid.* 134-143 and CALLENDER 1973b:196).

[63] The modifier following the pronominal subject or the apposite lexical (or demonstrative) one. I do not include here cases of the modification of a verb syntagm in position (a): (*IV* 21.16f.) OYϢNE EЧMHN EBOΛ ΠE.

[64] SETHE 1916:§§95-99, 107-9, cf. also 131-3; POLOTSKY 1962:426f. (= *CP* 431f.); CALLENDER 1970 Ch. III *passim*.

(2)   # *pronominal subject* → *nom. predicate* # [65]: (b), (c)

(3)   # *subject* + ΠЄ + *nom. predicate* # [66] (see spec. obs. below): (a) (pattern-second, here post-subject), (b), (c)

(4)   *Focal* modifiers, marked or unmarked as such in their construction: (*Wess. 9* 142d 22ff.) ZЄN-ΧΡЄICTIANOC ZNOY NЄ: these are left out of the present discussion (see §2.7.3.3).

(5)   Basically different is the nominal-focus Cleft Sentence, where a premodifier may precede the verbal *glose* (theme) constituent: (*III* 55.15f.) NTOOY NϢOΡΠ NЄNTAYMЄCTϢϤ.

(6)   A distinct *Wechselsatz* Nominal Sentence pattern ("balanced construction"), where the two (pro)-nominal terms — lexically identical or related — are symmetrically reversible and (as regards thematic structure) of equal rank, i.e. subject/predicate alternatingly. On this pattern, more syntactic and prosodic information is still needed (see Ch. 6, n. 37 below). Consider (*A 2 2*) NЄϤMЄΛOC NЄ NЄTN-MЄΛOC ЄKMЄΡOYC / (*Ch.* 59.31ff.) ΠϢI NTΠЄ ΠЄ ΠϢI MΠKAZ, cf. (*Miss.* 281) NΘЄ MΠЄTNKOTK ЄϤΠAZT ЄΧMΠЄϤZO ЄϤKΛΧ-ΠAT ЄϤΧϢ MMOC ΧЄ-ЄϤϢΛHΛ TЄ ΘЄ MΠЄTNKOTK...

(B) CONSTITUENCIES: the most common or notable modifiers are here included, all of category (1) above. An asterisk marks those modifiers for which placement opposition is neutralized or reduced.

Position (a):

*NA= [67]	(*A 1* 102) OYϢΙΠЄ NAI ΠЄ.
*MMO=	(*Ch.* 117.19f.) TЄIZЄ MMOOY TЄ; cf. the difficult common formula in the Bruce Codex 'ΠЄIΡAN MMOOY NЄ'.
*N-	(*A 2* 21-2) NTOϤ NCAϤ ΠЄ AYϢ NTOϤ MΠOOY ΠЄ AYϢ NTOϤ ON MMHNЄ ΠЄ; compare with *Ch.* 63-4, which finishes with NTOϤ ΠЄ NOYOЄIϢ NIM, i.e. pos. (b).
*ЄΡO=	(*Wess. 9* 117a 10f., 147d 28f.) OY ЄΡO= ΠЄ / (*A 2* 464) TANAΓKH ЄΡOI TЄ
* NNAZΡA=	(*III* 203.8) ZЄNBOTЄ NNAZΡЄ NЄ / (*P* 130⁴ 141 vo) OYΠONHΡON NNAZΡAϤ ΠЄ (sim. ZЄNΠONHΡON *A 2* 512).
NZOYO	(§1.3.1.3) (*III* 19.2) OYAΓAΘON NZOYO ΠЄ.
NAMЄ, AΛHΘϢC	(§§1.3.5.1, 1.3.11.1.2) (*RE 11* 16a 17) ZЄNЄBIHN NAMЄ NЄ / (*Wess. 9* 144c 4f.) NTOOY NAMЄ NЄ / (*A 2* 402) OYZOTЄ ΓAΡ AΛHΘϢC ΠЄ / (*Ryl. 67* TϤC) OYKAKO-ΔAIMϢN AΛHΘϢC ΠЄ ΠΡϢMЄ.
ΦANЄΡON	(*A 2* 485) ZЄNATNOYTЄ ΦANЄΡON NЄ.
KATA-	(*Ryl. 67* TϤC) OYΡϢMЄ MЄN KATAΘIKϢN MΠNOYTЄ ΠЄ ΠΡϢMЄ.
TЄNOY	(§1.3.4) (*IV* 20.10) OY TЄNOY TЄ TЄΧΡЄIA...

Position (b):

N- [68]	(*Ch.* 64.1ff.) NTOϤ ΠЄ NOYOЄIϢ NIM.
* N- "for"	(*IV* 92.22f.) ZЄNΠONHΡON NЄ NNЄTNAAMЄΛЄI.
ZN-	(*III* 222.8) ZЄNΡMMAO NЄ ZMΠNOYTЄ / (*P* 130⁴ 58 IΔ) ZЄNATNOBЄ ON NЄ AYϢ ZЄNΧΡHCTOC ΓAΡ NЄ ZNNЄYZBHYЄ THΡOY.
* ZIΧN-	(*III* 190.18) OYCOϬN ΠЄ ZIΧNTAΠЄ MΠΡϢMЄ NΔIKAIOC.

---

[65] POLOTSKY *ibid.*, CALLENDER 1970 Ch. III *passim*, (SETHE 1916:§§60-62, 64-66).

[66] POLOTSKY 1962:426f. (= *CP* 431f.), CALLENDER 1970 Chs. I, II *passim*, (SETHE 1916:§§135, 143-4).

[67] Cf. POLOTSKY 1961:313 (= *CP* 417).

[68] Here belongs NΘЄ in (*III* 118.5f.) OYΔIKAIOC ΠЄ NΘЄ NNЄNTAYNKOTK.

* NNAϨPN-   (*Ch.* 117.49ff.) ϨЄNOY ГAP NЄ NNAϨPN- / (*P* 130⁴ 139 гo) OY ϨШШϤ NЄ NЄIMNTA-
                     CЄBHC NNAϨPNTAГAПH...

ШA-   (*IV* 21.17) OYMKAϨ NϨHT ПЄ ШATCYNTЄΛЄIA.

KATA-   (*III* 22.12f. 16) ПOYЄIШT AN ПЄ KATATAϪIC, ПOYCON ПЄ KATACAPϪ / (*ibid.* 59.22f.)
                     OYOOϨЄ NЄCOOY TЄ KATAПШAϪЄ MПϪOЄIC (also *ibid. ibid.* 26f., 28f.).

*ЄTPЄ-   (*IV* 29.26) MПNAY AN ПЄ ПAI ЄTPЄ- (also *ibid.* 178.13f., 187.9f.; see §7.4).

*ЄПTHPϤ   (§1.3.7.2) (*III* 68.11) ϨЄNOY ϨШШϤ NЄ ЄПTHPϤ.

*ЄϨPAI ЄϪN-, *ЄBOΛ ϨN-   (*A 2* 32) ϨЄNϨAП NЄ NЄIШAϪЄ ЄϨPAI ЄϪШN / (*III* 89.6) ϨЄNϨOOY NЄ ЄBOΛ ϨN-
                     ϨЄNϨOOY.

*ϪЄ-   (*III* 107.23f.) ANON-NIM H ϨЄNOY NЄ NЄNШI ϪЄ-ЄϤNATPЄNIMHHШЄ COYШNN.

TЄNOY   (§1.3.4; see spec. obs.) (*A 1* 293) TAI TЄ ΘЄ TЄNOY AYШ ШAЄNЄϨ.

NAMЄ   (§1.3.5.1) (*III* 95.23f.) OYГAMOC ПЄ ПAI NAMЄ / (*A 1* 305) OYHI ГAP ПЄ NAMЄ
                     ϨITШBЄ ϨIШNЄ.

ФANЄPON   (*P* 130⁴ 125 ΛϨ) ϨЄNATNOYTЄ NЄ ФANЄPON.

Position (c):

*AYШ   (§1.3.10)

*ONTШC   (§1.3.11.1.6, e.g. *III* 40.9f.).

*ПANTШC   (§1.3.11.1.5, e.g. *Ch.* 59.31ff.).

*ϨOMШC   (§1.2.11.1.4, e.g. *Ch.* 80.15ff.).

*ϨOMOIШC   (§1.3.11.1.4, e.g. *A 2* 464).

*MAΛΛON, MAΛICTA   (§1.3.11.2.1.4, e.g. *A 2* 510-511).

*ЄTI   (§1.3.11.6, e.g. *III* 89.6).

ЄTBЄПAI   (*III* 74.14) ЄTBЄПAI ПKAIPOC ПЄ...

KATA-   (*Cat.* 42.21f.) KATAOYOIKONOMIA MЄN TЄϤMAAY TЄ, KATATMNTNOYTЄ ΔЄ ЄT-
                     ϪOCЄ TЄϤϨMϨAΛ TЄ.

*TЄNOY GЄ-   (§1.3.4, e.g. *III* 77.4).

NAMЄ, AΛHΘШC   (§§1.3.5.1, 1.3.11.2) (*A 2* 332) NAMЄ ПЄϤHI ПЄ TЄKKΛHCIA / (*ibid.* 371) ПЄK-
                     NOYTЄ NAMЄ ЄTЄOYNOYTЄ AN ПЄ " your god, who is not truly a god " / (*III*
                     114.12) AΛHΘШC OYAГAΘON ON ПЄ ПAI.

(C) SPECIAL OBSERVATIONS: (1) Appraising the data by reference to opposition/function/modifier, we arrive at the following statements:

Position (a) neutralizes *adnominal* and *adclausal* modification [69].

Position (b) is *adclausal*. Insofar as it is pertinent, it is relatively rare.

Position (c) is the placement of a *premodifier*.

(2) The " trimembral " pattern ⧣ *subject* + *copula* (ПЄ) + *nom. predicate* ⧣ is prosodically different from the bimembral ⧣ *predicate* + {ПЄ} + (*lex. subject*) ⧣: Ch. 6 footn. 37. The modifier-placement situation is quite different in this case, and in the post-subject position we find a paradigmatically and syntagmatically more extensive constituency: (*A 2* 76) ПШϤ NTЄΨYXH NϨЄNPШMЄ ЄYAPXЄI MNNЄTOY-APXЄI MMOOY ПЄ ϪOOC ϪЄ- / (*ibid.* 364) APA ПOYNOϬ NOYШHPЄ ЄBOΛ ϨNTMNTPMMAO ЄNTAПЄϤЄIШT TAAC NAϤ ПЄ OYϨOOY / (*IV* 51.6f.) ПNAY NTШOYN NTЄYШH ЄP-ϨШB ЄPOϤ ПЄ ПAKOOY. Rarely, one finds similarly

---

[69] On the functional yield of the placement of circumstantial forms adnominal to a predicate in the bimembral pattern (placement that may be prosodically conditioned or neutralized), see SHISHA-HALEVY 1972:100-105 (§2.1.2.3) and 1976a:34.

" loose " junctural conditions even in the bimembral pattern, in circumstances as yet obscure: (A 2 304) ⲋⲉⲛϢⲏⲣⲉ ϢⲎⲙ ⲀⲚ ⲈⲘⲠⲀⲦⲞⲨⲤⲞⲨⲚ-ⲦⲘⲈ ⲚⲈ ⲚⲈⲦⲚⲈⲒⲢⲈ ⲚⲚⲀⲒ ⲚⲀⲨ.   However, this may be an instance of the distinct " *Wechselsatz* " pattern, the junctural contour of which is similar to that of the trimembral Nominal Sentence, see (a) (6) above.

(3) The placement of ⲚⲚⲀⲊⲢⲚ- (also of ⲊⲒⲪⲚ-, and other prep. phrases?) may also be regulated by prosodic weight: presuffixally, these occur in pos. (a); prenominally — esp. before a further expanded noun — in pos. (b).   We need more exx. to establish this mechanism beyond doubt.

(4) ⲦⲈⲚⲞⲨ in position (b) (§1.3.4) may represent the *intercolary*, conditioned placement of this modifier/ particle (ⲦⲀⲒ-ⲦⲈ-ⲐⲈ " thus " being taken as a single colon).

1.1.2.4.1 Modifiers as nuclei: modifiers modified[70].   Prominent here are the three cardinal directional-motional modifier syntagms (Ⲉ)ⲂⲞⲖ, (Ⲉ)ⲊⲞⲨⲚ, (Ⲉ)ⲊⲢⲀⲒ, which are expansible by an impressive list of prepositions (see the inventory and spec. observations in §1.1.2.1), thereby constituting the intricate, subtle system of spatial-relational orientation so typical of Coptic.   These systematized complexes apart, I have noted the following modifiers expanding others:

ⲚⲊⲞⲨⲞ " rather, even (more) ": (III 222.4) ⲔⲀⲖⲰⲤ ⲚⲊⲞⲨⲞ / premodifying in (III 126.23f.) ⲊⲚⲚⲈⲒⲞⲨⲞⲈⲒϢ ⲦⲈⲚⲞⲨ, ⲚⲊⲞⲨⲞ ⲀⲈ ⲊⲚⲚⲈⲞⲨⲞⲈⲒϢ ⲚⲊⲀⲈ / (A 1 11) ⲚⲊⲞⲞⲨ ⲚⲒⲘ, ⲚⲊⲞⲨⲞ ⲀⲈ ⲊⲚⲚⲤⲀⲂⲂⲀⲦⲞⲚ / (ibid. 39) ⲈⲂⲞⲖ ⲊⲒⲦⲞⲞⲦⲈ... ⲚⲊⲞⲨⲞ ⲀⲈ ⲈⲂⲞⲖ ⲊⲒⲦⲞⲞⲦⲚ.

ⲘⲘⲀⲦⲈ " only ": (IV 24.6f.) ⲊⲘⲠⲈⲨⲖⲀⲤ ⲘⲘⲀⲦⲈ ⲀⲨϢ ⲊⲘⲠⲈⲨⲊⲎⲦ ⲀⲚ.

ⲈⲘⲀⲦⲈ " very ": (P 130⁴ 139 ro) ⲔⲀⲖⲰⲤ ⲈⲘⲀⲦⲈ.

ⲘⲀⲖⲖⲞⲚ, ⲘⲀⲖⲒⲤⲦⲀ " especially ": (III 77.19) ⲊⲘⲠⲈⲊⲞⲞⲨ... ⲘⲀⲖⲖⲞⲚ ⲀⲈ ⲊⲚⲦⲈⲨϢⲎ / (IV 78.7f.) ⲚⲊⲀⲊ ⲚⲤⲞⲠ ⲘⲀⲖⲒⲤⲦⲀ ⲘⲠⲚⲀⲨ ⲈⲦⲚⲚⲀϢⲰⲚⲈ.

ⲊⲀⲠⲖⲰⲤ " simply ": (A 1 204, IV 196.3, Ch. 162.4f. etc.).

Add also the following cases, in my opinion of modification rather than rection: ⲬⲰⲢⲒⲤ (+ *circumstantial*) (IV 108.8), ⲔⲀⲚ (+ *conditional/circumstantial*) (*passim*, e.g. III 19.28, 22.9, 40.16, 19ff.), ⲈⲦⲒ (+ *circumstantial*) (III 210.23, IV 191.12). ⲊⲞⲘⲞⲒⲰⲤ (§1.3.11.1.4) and ⲞⲨ ⲘⲞⲚⲞⲚ (§1.3.11.2.1) are likely candidates for the modifier-premodifier role.

1.1.2.4.2 Modifiers coordinated/disjoined.   Coordination and disjunction in Coptic, even for the simpler, more obvious word classes, are far from clear and matter-of-fact constructions.   The most acute issue here is the exact status of ⲀⲨϢ (§1.3.10) and Ⲏ and their relation to -∅- and other elements like ⲞⲨⲀⲈ and ⲈⲒⲦⲈ. ⲀⲨϢ (ⲞⲚ) and Ⲏ (ⲚⲦⲞϤ) are used to coordinate/disjoin modifiers: (III 181.4) ⲊⲘⲠⲈⲞⲨⲞⲈⲒϢ ⲦⲈⲚⲞⲨ ⲀⲨϢ ⲞⲚ ⲊⲘⲠⲈⲞⲨⲞⲈⲒϢ ⲚⲊⲀⲈ / (P 130² 59 o) ⲈⲘⲞⲨ ⲀⲨϢ ⲈⲰⲚⲊ / (Ch. 32.19ff.) ⲈⲂⲞⲖ ⲊⲚⲦⲠⲈ ⲀⲨϢ ⲈⲂⲞⲖ ⲊⲚⲦⲈ-ⲤⲦⲢⲀⲦⲒⲀ... / (IF 88 apud *Dictionary* 236b) ⲈⲂⲞⲖ ⲘⲘⲞⲞⲨ Ⲏ ⲊⲒⲪϢⲞⲨ / (III 130.3f.) ⲊⲚⲞⲨⲘⲚⲦⲦⲨⲢⲀⲚⲚⲞⲤ Ⲏ ⲚⲦⲞϤ ⲊⲚⲞⲨⲘⲚⲦⲀⲒⲔⲀⲒⲞⲤ / (P 130² 63 oz) ⲊⲀⲊⲦⲎⲚ Ⲏ ⲊⲀⲊⲦⲚⲦⲎⲨⲦⲚ.   So are ⲞⲨⲀⲈ and ⲈⲒⲦⲈ -ⲈⲒⲦⲈ: (A 2 519) ⲈⲬϢⲒ (" without me ") ⲞⲨⲀⲈ ⲊⲀⲢⲞⲔ ⲘⲀⲨⲀⲀⲔ / (III 116.16f.) ⲈⲒⲦⲈ ⲊⲘⲠⲈⲚⲤϢⲞⲨⲊ ⲈⲊⲞⲨⲚ ⲈⲒⲦⲈ ⲊⲚⲚⲈⲠⲒⲤⲦⲞⲖⲎ / (P 130²

---

[70] Although in a general sense — with reference to the semantics of the interrelationship between ⲈⲂⲞⲖ ⲊⲚ- and ⲊⲚ-, ⲈⲊⲞⲨⲚ Ⲉ- and Ⲉ- (etc.) — the nuclear modifier may be taken as " precising " or even " reinforcing " the preposition (so *Dictionary*, passim; cf. Stern §516, p. 340) — this being a case of the " semasiological nucleus " (see §4.2), the preposition does not coincide with the grammatical nucleus, the modifier.   I have no doubt that the modifier here *is* nuclear, in a syntactic sense.   Some prepositions (e.g. ⲞⲨⲦⲈ-, ⲈⲊⲢⲚ-) are rare in Shenoute and are analytically " renewed ", replaced by expanded modifiers (ⲈⲂⲞⲖ ⲞⲨⲦⲈ-, ⲈⲊⲞⲨⲚ ⲈⲊⲢⲚ-).   In certain references, too, prepositions are replaced by 'modifier+preposition' syntagms: ⲊⲚ- " from " (see n. 96) by ⲈⲂⲞⲖ ⲊⲚ-, ⲊⲒ- " from " by ⲈⲂⲞⲖ ⲊⲒ-, Ⲉ- " against " by ⲈⲊⲞⲨⲚ Ⲉ-, ⲊⲚ- " into " by ⲈⲊⲞⲨⲚ ⲊⲚ-, ⲈⲬⲚ- " on-to " by ⲈⲊⲢⲀⲒ ⲈⲬⲚ- and so on.   Needless to say, this system deserves a thorough structural monographic treatment, isolating semasiological ranges as well as grammatical distribution.   For the theoretical background, cf. Karcevskij 1936:110, Tesnière 1965:127ff., Jacobson 1964:36, Pinkster 1972:108ff.

62 ⲟⲉ) ⲉⲓⲧⲉ ⲍⲛⲧⲉⲍⲣⲉ ⲉⲓⲧⲉ ⲍⲛⲟⲃⲥⲱ ⲉⲓⲧⲉ ⲍⲙⲡⲉⲩⲱⲛⲉ. Modifier coordination by means of ⲙⲛ- is extremely rare in Shenoutean Sahidic: (*IV* 120.12f.) ⲉⲍⲟⲩⲛ ⲍⲛⲛⲉⲛⲥⲩⲛⲁⲅⲱⲅⲏ... ⲙⲛ-ⲍⲣⲁⲓ ⲍⲙⲡⲧⲟⲡⲟⲥ ⲙⲡⲉⲛⲉⲓⲱⲧ is a special case, with ⲡⲙⲁ appositive to the modifiers. *Iteration* of the same modifier may be interpreted as an expressive case of zero-marked coordination, favoured by Shenoutean style: ⲍⲟⲗⲱⲥ ⲍⲟⲗⲱⲥ (*III* 138.23, *IV* 75.25), ⲉⲙⲁⲧⲉ ⲉⲙⲁⲧⲉ (*A 2* 87, 301), ⲙⲙⲏⲛⲉ ⲙⲙⲏⲛⲉ (often ⲁⲩⲱ ⲙⲙⲏⲛⲉ ⲙⲙⲏⲛⲉ, *III* 77.19f., *IV* 66.15, 69.1f., 205.18, *A 1* 285, *Ench.* 85a): this is an "insistence" emphasizing procedure [71], used only with a small subgroup of modifiers. Another idiomatic and typical construction employs the copulative (ⲙⲛ-) ⲛⲙⲙⲁ=, mainly to add another pronominal *rectum* to a usually '*prep.* + *pronoun*' prepositional phrase [72]: (*Ch.* 27.24) ⲍⲁⲣⲱⲕ ⲛⲙⲙⲁⲩ / (*III* 184.21f., *BM* 209 ⲗⲑ) ⲉⲣⲟⲓ ⲛⲙⲙⲏⲧⲛ / (*ibid.* 211.11) ⲙⲙⲟⲟⲩ ⲛⲙⲙⲁϥ / (*Leyd.* 302) ⲟⲩⲧⲱⲧⲛ ⲛⲙⲙⲁⲩ / (*Wess. 9* 112a 4f.) ⲉⲧⲃⲏⲏⲧ ⲛⲙⲙⲉ / (*Ch.* 147.14f.) ⲉⲛϫⲟⲉⲓⲥ ⲛⲙⲙⲁⲥ, but also with an additional *nominal rectum* to a '*prep.* + *pronoun*' phrase: (*III* 191.31) ⲛⲙⲙⲁⲩ ⲙⲛⲡⲛⲟⲩⲧⲉ (ⲙⲛ- in two different identities) / (*Wess. 18* 97b 9ff.) ⲁϫⲛⲧⲕ ⲙⲛⲡⲉⲕⲡⲛⲁ / (*Wess. 9* 146a 1 ff., 10ff.) ⲡⲉⲟⲟⲩ ⲛⲁⲕ ⲙⲛⲡⲉⲕⲱⲏⲣⲉ.

1.2 THE PREDICATIVE MODIFIER

In the following paragraphs, we consider a set of patterns in which the modifier is not adjunctal, but is in a *nexal* relationship with a pronoun/noun-syntagm constituent. These patterns do not all form a paradigm [73]: the two major ones are selected by the predicated modifier, that is to say, are in complementary distribution, constituting together one "arch-pattern" of modifier predication.

1.2.1.1 THE BIPARTITE PATTERN: NOUN SYNTAGM/PREFIXED PERS. PRONOUN → MODIFIER [74]

(A) GENERAL OBSERVATION: In this pattern we must distinguish two sub-patterns:

(1) *subject* (*theme*): {ⲡ-} determinator pronoun (+ noun lexeme)/prefixed pers. pronoun/demonstrative pronoun; *predicate* (*rheme*): modifier (of the inventory, below), and

(2) *subject* (*theme*): {ⲟⲩ-} or Ø-determinator pronoun (+ noun lexeme)/indefinite pronoun/indeterminable; *predicate* (discontinuous): (affirm.) ⲟⲩⲛ — modifier, (neg.) ⲙⲛ — modifier [75]. Basic and converted forms of the pattern are considered.

(B) CONSTITUENCY:

ⲛ-   ⲙⲡⲟⲟⲩ (*A 1* 379), ⲛⲧⲡⲉ (*A 1* 245), ⲛⲍⲣⲁⲓ ⲍⲛ- (*III* 201.18), ⲛⲍⲣⲁⲓ ⲛⲍⲏⲧ= (*A 1* 119), ⲛⲍⲟⲩⲛ (*III* 24.19f.), ⲙⲡⲃⲟⲗ (*Ench.* 88b), ⲙⲡⲉϥⲙⲧⲟ ⲉⲃⲟⲗ (*III* 27.10), ⲙⲡⲉⲓⲙⲁ (*Ch* 162.44), ⲙⲡⲉⲙⲍⲓⲧ etc. (*IV* 120.15f.), ⲛⲧⲙⲏⲧⲉ (*Ch.* 197.39f.), ⲙⲡⲉ(ⲕ)ⲕⲱⲧⲉ (*Ch.* 30.12f.), ⲛⲑⲉ (*A 1* 246) etc. (open-ended list).

---

[71] Cf. HOFFMANN 1936:104ff.

[72] STERN:559. Compare (*Ch.* 63.6) ⲛⲟⲩⲛ ⲛⲙⲙⲁϥ "ours and his".

[73] Cf. CALLENDER 1973b and 1970, Ch. VI. Certain members of his "paradigm" are not considered in the present discussion, namely, the *verbal* predicated ⲟ (ⲛ-), ⲱⲡⲉ (ⲛ-), ⲱⲟⲟⲡ (ⲛ-). In addition to their being verbal, their selection is differently motivated than the lexically suppletive or complementary members of the set considered here: Callender's "mixed paradigm" is one of a single type — the *basic unmarked predication* of a modifier (see however in §1.2.1.3.1 below).

[74] POLOTSKY 1960a:§§5-6, 8-9, 12, 19-15; NAGEL 1980:83. See now QUECKE, *Or* 52:298ff. (1983).

[75] POLOTSKY 1960a:§§19ff., 35; NAGEL 1980:77ff. I treat both subpatterns conjointly and do not attribute primacy to either. In superscriptions like (*III* 26.25, *IV* 22.1) ⲍⲉⲛⲕⲟⲩⲓ ⲛⲱⲁϫⲉ ⲛⲛⲁⲍⲣⲛ- we do not have a Bipartite construction at all (the modifier belongs to the '*noun* + *modifier*' predicate group, while the heralded text itself — a ⲡⲉ-substitute — is the subject). On the other hand, ‖ ⲉⲓⲥ + *noun syntagm* + *modifier* ‖ is a deictic presentative alternant (affirmative only) of both Bipartite subpatterns: (*IV* 91.11) ⲉⲓⲥ-ⲧⲉⲕⲕⲗⲏⲥⲓⲁ ⲅⲁⲣ ⲙⲡϫⲟⲉⲓⲥ ⲍⲙⲡⲕⲁⲍ ⲧⲏⲣϥ / (*ibid.* 161.2f.) ⲉⲓⲥ-ⲥⲁⲉⲓⲛ ⲍⲙⲙⲁ ⲛⲓⲙ ⲍⲙⲡⲕⲁⲍ ⲧⲏⲣϥ (see NAGEL 1980:80ff.).

ΝΤΟΟΤ⸗	(*III* 211.4).
ΜΜΟ⸗	(*Ch.* 148.37f., 42f., *IV* 96.24; see spec. obs.).
ΜΜΑΥ	" there " (*Ch.* 11.9f.).
Ν-/ΝΑ⸗	ΠΕΟΟΥ ΝΑ⸗ (*IV* 197.7, *RE 10* 160b 20 etc.), ΟΥΟΕΙ ΝΑ⸗ (*Wess. 9* 129a 1, 8f.) (see spec. obs.).
(ΜΝ-)/ΝΜΜΑ⸗	(*III* 101.6f., *IV* 160.13, *Ch.* 53.13, 193.53f.).
ΕΡΟ⸗	(*Ch.* 98.51f., 102.19, *Rossi 2/3* 58, *IV* 43.28, *P* 130² 32 ΛΒ: ΝΧΕΙΡΟΓΡΑΦΟΝ ΕΤΕΡΟЧ, (see spec. obs.).
Ε2ΡΑΙ ΕΧΝ-/ΕΧⲰ⸗	very common: ΠΕΥΚΡΙΜΑ Ε2ΡΑΙ ΕΧⲰΙ (*Miss.* 280), ΠΕΣΝΟЧ ΝΝΕΙΡⲰΜΕ Ε2ΡΑΙ ΕΧΜΠΑΙ (*A 1* 98), ΠΕΥⲤⲰϢ Ε2ΡΑΙ ΕΧⲰΟΥ Ч2ΙΧⲰΟΥ ΓΑΡ (*P* 130² 113 ΡΗ); also *P* 130⁵ 69 vo, 131⁵ 80 ro (adaptation of *Act.* 18:6?).
ΕΧΝ-	(*A 2* 304, 346; see spec. obs.).
2Α-/2ΑΡΟ⸗	(*IV* 74.12, *Ch.* 15.33f., *P* 131⁵ 20 ΡΠZ).
2ΑΡΑΤ⸗	(*III* 38.10).
2ΑΡⲰ⸗	(*Ch.* 119.1, *P* 131⁶ 81 vo).
2Α(2)ΤΝ-/2Α(2)ΤΗ⸗	(*III* 157 passim, *Ch.* 106.9f., *Cat.* 42.39).
2Ι-/2ΙⲰⲰ⸗	(*IV* 74.7f., *Wess. 9* 138a 29f., *III* 156.13), 2Ι2ΟΥΝ, 2ΙΒΟΛ (*III* 31.19, 52.20, *A 1* 15), 2ΙΟΥΝΑΜ, 2Ι2ΒΟΥΡ (*III* 14.5f.).
2ΙΧΝ-/2ΙΧⲰ⸗	(*Ch.* 46.35ff., *A 1* 13, *K* 924) .
2Ν-/Ν2ΗΤ⸗	(*IV* 86.2, *III* 14.4, *Ch.* 90.42ff., *P* 130⁴ 49 ro).
(ΟΥΤΕ-)/ΟΥΤⲰ⸗	(*Miss.* 234).
ΟΥΒΕ-/ΟΥΒΗ⸗	(*Ch.* 70.12, *Mun.* 102).
(ΝΑ2ΡΝ-)/ΝΑ2ΡΑ⸗	(*Ch.* 108.49f.).
ⲤΑ-ΠΕⲤΗΤ	(*Cairo* 8007, *Berl. Sitz.* 430).
ΜΝΝⲤΑ-	(*BM* 253 ΝZ).
ΝⲤⲰ⸗	(*IV* 24.8).
2ΡΑΙ 2Ν-	(*A 2* 175), 2ΡΑΙ 2ΙΧΝ-/2ΙΧⲰ⸗ (*A 1* 99, *III* 189.15), 2ΡΑΙ ΟΥΤΕ-/ΟΥΤⲰ⸗ (*Ch.* 156.12f., 163 apud *Dictionary* 495a), 2ΡΑΙ ΕΧΝ- (*P* 130¹ 37 ΡΝZ, *A 1* 799), 2ΡΑΙ Ν- (*P* 130¹ 126 ΡΚⲤ), cf. Ν2ΡΑΙ 2Ν-/Ν2ΗΤ⸗ (*A 1* 191 etc.).

(C) SPECIAL OBSERVATIONS: (1) ΜΜΟ⸗ is used to predicate so-called "*inalienable*" possession (Lévy-Bruhl's term, see ISAČENKO 1954:141ff.), and is selected by a special sub-paradigm of noun lexemes: (Ε)ΚΙΒΕ (*Ch.* 148.37ff.), ΤΝ2 (*IV* 96.24, *P* 130² 39 ΡΑ), ΑΠΕ (*A 1* 251), ⲤΑ " beauty " (*K* 9320), 6ΙΧ, ΟΥΕΡΗΤΕ (*Ch.* 87.9f. 27ff.), ΠΑΤ (*III* 143.28), ΒΑΛ (*P* 131⁵ 80 ro) and of course 6ΟΜ (*IV* 51.14f.), and possibly many more. This is a field which must be further investigated also in other contexts, notably that of the combinatorics of ' determinator + noun + possessive expansion (Ν-/ΝΤΕ-) ' [76]. We may here have a gradient parameter on a scale of syntactic features converging on a given lexeme (a striking case — valency being another — of "lexemic syntax").

(2) Predicative Ν-/ΝΑ⸗ features in a historically interesting, if synchronically problematic pattern [77]. ΟΥΟΕΙ (Ν-) occurs in most conversions (ΕΤΕΟΥΟΕΙ Ν- *Rossi 2/3* 37, *P* 130⁴ 139 vo; ΝΕΟΥΟΕΙ Ν- *IV* 94.24, *Wess. 9* 142d 9; ΕΟΥΟΕΙ Ν- [circ.] *IV* 4.12f.), yet cannot properly speaking be taken as an (indeterminable)

---

[76] Cf. HAVERS 1931:§92; STEINTHAL–MISTELI 1893:292, 299. In Coptic, a "*be*-language" as regards predication of possession, the opposition ΟΥΝ (ΝΤΑ⸗ - : ΜΜΟ⸗) is one of unmarked *vs.* inalienable possession. On inalienable possession see also ROSÉN, *Lingua* 8:264-293 (1959).

[77] GARDINER 1957:§114.1, SATZINGER 1976:198f.

noun, but rather as part of a composite predicate. ПЄΟΟΥ Ν- is neither convertible nor negativable (moreover, the П- determination is here not really pertinent).

(3) ЄΡΟ=: predicative only in the sense " to one's debit, one's duty/responsibility " (cf. *Dictionary* 51), prenominally ЄΡΟϤ Ν-, not Є-.

(4) ЄϪΝ-: in three instances where the absence of ΟΥΝ- with an indefinite noun may be due to special modulation of the utterance (idiomatic exclamation, rhetorical question)[78]: (*A 2* 304) ΜΗ ΟΥϬѠΝΤ ⲀΝ ЄΒΟⲖ ϨΙΤΜΠΝΟΥΤЄ ЄϨΡⲀΙ ЄϪΝΟΥΟΝ ΝΙΜ... / (*ibid.* 346) ΜΟЄΙϨЄ ЄϪΝΜΟЄΙϨЄ, but cf. (*Cat.* 43.29) ϨЄΝ[ΜΟЄΙϨЄ ЄϪΝΜΟЄΙϨЄ] ΝЄ / (*A 1* 188) ΟΥⲖΥΠΗ ЄϪΝΟΥⲖΥΠΗ, ΟΥΘⲖΙΨΙϹ ЄϪΝΟΥΘⲖΙΨΙϹ...

1.2.1.2 # MODIFIER → ПЄ

(A) GENERAL OBSERVATIONS: (1) The modifier predicated by this pattern — known as a " Nominal Sentence ", after the word class more " typically " constituting its predicate — is not unknown, but has never really been treated separately and in detail[79]. This predicate position is in fact only one of the positions in which the modifier vies with the noun syntagm: another is in the satellital slot following the determinators (§1.1.1.1)[80]. In fact, the Nominal Sentence predicates a *determinator pronoun* followed by its lexeme[81]. In our pattern, however, the modifier is invariably non-determinated.

(2) The modifier predicate precedes the pronominal subject ПЄ. The pattern may be negated, and is (rarely) converted, only in the relative conversion.

(3) *Suppletivity*: A modifier in this pattern does not occur as predicative in the Bipartite (§1.2.1.1). That is to say, it is complementary with the Bipartite, and no opposition obtains between the two predicative patterns (two " allo-syntagms " of a single " syntagmeme " predicating a modifier). See §0.2.3.

(4) It may not be going too far to suggest that in the ever accumulating instances of '*present/perfect circumstantial* + ПЄ' (see QUECKE 1977b:302, BROWNE 1978a:7 = 53, 1979b:200, to whose exx. add *Judith* 14:14, and many [Nitrian] Bohairic examples, e.g. in Hyvernat's 1886 *Actes des Martyrs*), the circumstantial is predicated in the very pattern examined here. It is a predication especially on a higher level of analysis — the macrosyntactic level — signalling a " backgrounding " of the evolving action. 'ΝЄϤϹѠΤΜ ПЄ' might accordingly be taken to contain (beside the actor and verb lexeme) *two* distinct relational signals: ΝЄ- for the narrative framework characterization, -ПЄ for the macrosyntactic backgrounding (cf. CALLENDER's " situational " subject, 1970:205ff.; also ПЄ as *apodosis marker*, with fut. [*III* 158.7f., *P* 130[1] 135 ΤⲀΓ]; POLOTSKY 1939:110 = *CP* 374).

(B) CONSTITUENCY:

Ν- ΝΤЄΙϨЄ *IV* 84.14, see spec. obs.
ΝΘЄ *III* 75.16f., see spec. obs.; ΝΘЄ ΜΠЄΝΤⲀϤЄΙΡЄ ΤЄ ΘЄ ΜΠЄΤЄΜΠϤЄΙΡЄ (*IV* 159.11f.).

[78] See NAGEL 1970:80.

[79] See among STERN's exx. on pp. 300 (*Marc.* 13:33), 302 (*I Cor.* 9:18), 305 (*Ps.* 8:1); TILL §248; CALLENDER 1970:37ff.114f. SETHE 1916:§109 treats our construction together with # (det. + adv.) ПЄ #, apparently considering it a case of " article omitted ".

[80] Yet another is the "*glose*" — or verbal topic — constituent in the focus-initial focalization constructions (§§2.4-6 below). Indeed, I believe that the sharp noun : " adverb " dichotomy which forms the matrix of Polotsky's conception of Egyptian grammatical structure, is considerably blurred in Coptic (cf. also SHISHA-HALEVY 1978).

[81] The not infrequent instances of # *bare noun* (or *zero-determinated noun*?) -ПЄ # merit a special discussion (this is nowhere treated as a distinct case, and is not included in the constituency lists in CALLENDER 1970). We may have here a pattern with apparently limited predicate and subject constituencies, possibly also special environmental properties. Some Shenoutean exx.: (*Ch.* 183.23) ..ЄΡⲀϢЄ ПЄ ΝⲀΥ / (*A 2* 34, 114) ...ЄΜΟΙϨЄ ПЄ ΝⲀΥ... / (*A 1* 210) ϢΙΠЄ ПЄ ϪΟΟΥ / (*A 2* 395) Η ΟΡΓΗ ⲀΝ ПЄ ϪΟΟϹ / (*Or.* 159.34ff.) ...ЄϹΙϢЄ ПЄ ΘЄ... ЄΒΟΤЄ ПЄ ΘЄ...

ΠΑΡΑ-	ΠΑΡΑΚΕΚΟΥΙ ΠΕ + *conjunctive* (*A 2* 390, §7.3.1), ΠΑΡΑΠΕΥΟΥϢϢ ΓΑΡ ΠΕ Ε- (*RE 10* 161a 16f.), ΠΑΡΑΤΡΕΥ- ΠΕ (*A 2* 75).
ΚΑΤΑ-	ΚΑΤΑΠΕΥΕΙΝΕ ΠΕ ΠΕΙΝΕ ΝΝΕΖΒΗΥΕ (*Wess. 9* 110a 14ff., *IV* 65.12f., neg.)
ϢΑ- [82]	ϢΑΠΕΙΜΑ ΤΕ ΤΕΤΝΜΝΤ-ΖΗΤ ΝΟΥϢΤ ΝΜΜΑΝ (*P* 130¹ 135 ΤΛΓ-Δ), *Ch.* 59-60, 60.7ff. (adaptation of *Mark* 13:27).
ⲬΙΝ-	*Ch.* 59.55ff., 60.4ff. (adapt. of *Mark* 13:27).
ΕΠⲬΙΝⲬΗ	ΕΠⲬΙΝⲬΗ ΝΑΥ ΤΕ ΤΕΥΖΥΠΟΜΟΠΗ (*IV* 46.18, see §1.3.7.3.1; also, in a quotation, *III* 45.17f.).
ΖΑΘΗ	ΕΝΕΖΑΘΗ ΓΑΡ ΠΕ ΕΜΠΑΤΕΠΟΥΟΕΙΝ ΑΥϢ ΠϢΝΖ ΕΙ ΕΠΚΟΣΜΟΣ (*A 2* 247).
ΖΙΤΟΥϢ⸗	ΠΕΤΖΜΠΠΙΡΕ Η ΠΟΥϢΝΖ ΕΒΟΛ ΜΠΟΥΟΕΙΝ... ΖΙΤΟΥϢΥ ΜΠΣΟΒΤ ΔΕ ΕΤΖΙΒΟΛ ΠΕ (*III* 52.18ff.).
ΕΒΟΛ ΖΝ-	ΠΕΥⲬΠΟ ΔΕ ΕΒΟΛ [ΠΕ] ΖΜΠΙϢΤ... (*Wess. 9* 147b 10ff.).
ΤϢΝ	ΕΒΟΛ ΤϢΝ ΠΕ ΝΙΖΒΗΥΕ ΕΤⳠΟΟΜΕ (*A 2* 333, *A 1* 8, *Ench.* 93a; cf. §2.6.3.2).

(C) Special observations: (1) ΝΤΕΙΖΕ is by far the most common modifier in this construction. We find the following varieties of this pattern:

(a) ΝΤΕΙΖΕ(ΟΝ) {ΠΕ} + *noun syntagm* (*III* 103.4, *IV* 80.21, *III* 74.17f. codd., *Ch.* 75.44ff., 194.9ff., 24ff., 65.6f., 156.56ff., *A 2* 537, *A 2* 337, *Wess. 9* 86a 28ff. etc.).

(b) ΝΤΕΙΖΕ ΟΝ ΤΕ Ν + *noun syntagm* (sgl./plur.) (*IV* 163.25, 164.2, 111.4, *Ch.* 193.25f., *Wess. 9* 86b 1ff.).

(b') ΝΤΕΙΖΕ ΟΝ ΤΕ + *noun syntagm* (plur.) (*IV* 106.2).

(b'') ΝΤΕΙΖΕ ΟΝ ΤΕ + *clause*: ΝΤΕΙΖΕ ΟΝ ΤΕ ΝΑϢ ΝⲌΕ ΠΕΤΕΟΥΝΤΑΥ ΜΜΑΥ ΜΠΣΟΟΥΝ... ΕΝΥΝΑΝΑΥ ΑΝ ΕΠΑΓΓΕΛΟΣ ΑΥϢ ΝΥΣΟΥϢΝΥ... ΝΤΕΙΖΕ ΟΝ ΤΕ ΝΙΜ ΠΕΤΝΑΟΥϢϢ... (*P* 130² 47-8 ΣΚΓ-Δ).

(c) ΝΤΕΙΖΕ ⲌϢϢ⸗ Ν + *noun syntagm* (*III* 48.24f.).

This pattern (like other ΘΕ-constructions: ΝΘΕ Ν-, ΤΑΙ ΤΕ ΘΕ Ν-, ΤΑΙ ΤΕ ΤΕ(Υ)ⲌΕ...) is expandable by a subnexal constituent: *noun + adnexal circumstantial* (Shisha-Halevy 1972:82ff. and see footnote 99 below): (*III* 48.24f.) ΝΤΕΙΖΕ ⲌϢΟΥ ΝΝⲌΕΛΛΗΝ ΜΝⲌΑΙΡΕΤΙΚΟΣ ΝΙΜ ΕΥΜΕΕΥΕ ΝΝΑⲌΡΑΥ ⲬΕ- / (*A 1* 267) ΝΤΕΙΖΕ ΟΝ ΠΕ ΠΕΥⲌΜⲌΑΛ ΕΛΙΣΣΑΙΟΣ ΕΑΥΤΟΥΝΕΣ-ΝΕΤΜΟΟΥΤ, also *IV* 163-4, *Ch.* 193.25-39. Here the subnexal unit forms part of the overall nexus in the pattern. Pattern (2) may be regarded as anacoluthic. ΟΝ is clearly an essential (if not indispensable) component of this pattern in its different forms.

(2) In (*III* 47.19) ΝΕΥΜΕΡΙΣ ΝΕ ΝΘΕ ΕΤΣΗΖ ⲬΕ- we have properly speaking a different pattern, the copular ⧻ *subject - copula - predicate* ⧻ Nominal Sentence predicating the modifier ΝΘΕ.

1.2.1.3 Miscellaneous patterns

1.2.1.3.1 The stative of ΕΙΡΕ, Ο, supplies a convenient *outil grammatical* for predicating the important group of Ν-modifiers in a durative framework [83], which relates paradigmatically to the Nominal Sentence as an incidental *vs.* inherent predication: ΠΡϢΜΕ ΕΤΟ ΝΑΥ ΝΑΠΕ (*A 1* 251). Whereas the " copular " (i.e. incomplete-predication) -Ο is empty of verbal-lexical content, other statives, forming a paradigm with this -Ο (Ν-) and expandable by Ν- as well as by other modifiers, supply various *Aktionsart* characterizations of the basic nexus: -ϢΟΟΠ, -ΟΥΗⲌ, -ΚΗ, ⲌΜΟΟΣ... (consider *III* 98.19, 134.12f., *IV* 44.25, 50.23, *Ch.* 57.45ff., 59.46ff., 50.43ff., *Ench.* 93a, etc.) [84]. Ν-modifiers can occur, of course, as predicative (" *adnexal* ") complements of many other verbs (of which only ΕΙΡΕ — and ϢϢΠΕ? — are in regular trans-

---

[82] See Wiesmann 1927:67 and Jernstedt 1929:128, on *III* 97.14f. (quoting *Prov.* 6:26).
[83] Callender 1970:248-279 (cf. our Chapter 3, note 4).
[84] Callender 1970:279ff., 1973b.

formative relationship with their statives): ⲀⲨϤⲒⲦⲞⲨ ⲚⲀⲒⲬⲘⲀⲖⲰⲦⲞⲤ (*A 2* 252), ϤⲚⲀⲦⲰⲞⲨⲚ ⲚⲤⲰⲘⲀ ⲘⲠⲚⲈⲨⲘⲀⲦⲒⲔⲞⲚ (*ibid.* 401), ⲀⲔⲀⲀⲔ ⲚⲂⲞⲦⲈ (*Wess. 9* 118a 24ff.) [85].

1.2.1.3.2 The prenominal allomorph of ⲈⲒⲢⲈ is used to predicate certain prepositions *in the Tripartite Conjugation* [86]: Ⲣ-ⲈⲢⲞ⸗ (*IV* 12.21, perf., *A 1* 162, conj., *Wess. 18* 127a 30, conj., ⲀⲢⲞ⸗); Ⲣ-ⲄⲒⲬⲰ⸗ (*Wess. 9* 171b 25f., perf.); Ⲣ-ⲠⲀⲢⲀ- (*IV* 3.20, *P* 130[4] 105 ⲢⲔⲈ: ⲖⲀⲀⲨ ⲈⲀϤⲢ-ⲠⲀⲢⲀⲦⲈϤⲪⲨⲤⲒⲤ); Ⲣ-ⲄⲒⲦⲠⲈ (*A 2* 192, fut. III, *ibid.* 441, not Sh., conj.).

1.2.1.3.3 A marginal yet I believe well established pattern predicates a modifier with a *zeroed subject (theme)* [87]: ⲈⲦⲂⲈ-, in *irrealis* protases: (*A 2* 113-4) ⲈⲚⲈⲈⲦⲂⲎⲎⲦⲞⲨ (i.e. ⲚⲈⲠⲖⲎⲄⲎ) ⲠⲀⲢⲀⲔⲈϢⲎⲘ ⲠⲈ ⲚⲦⲈⲠⲈⲦⲢ-ⲠⲀⲌⲢⲈ ⲈⲢⲞⲚ ⲤⲖⲀⲀⲦⲈ ⲘⲚⲌⲈⲚϢⲰⲚⲈ / (*A 2* 398) ⲌⲀⲘⲞⲒ ⲞⲚ ⲈⲚⲈⲈⲦⲂⲈⲞⲨⲘⲚⲦⲀⲦⲤⲞⲞⲨⲚ Ⲏ ⲞⲨⲘⲚⲦϢⲎⲢⲈ ϢⲎⲘ (i.e. it was done). Negatively (" were it not for... "), with ⲚⲤⲀⲂⲎⲖ: (*A 2* 514) (" people say secretly about me) ⲬⲈ-ⲚⲤⲀⲂⲎⲖ ⲈⲦⲂⲎⲎⲦϤ ⲀⲨⲰ ⲬⲈⲚⲈⲚⲞ ⲘⲠⲈⲚⲬⲞⲈⲒⲤ, ⲚⲈⲚⲚⲀϤ5Ⲱ ⲀⲚ ⲠⲈ / (*P* 131[5] 56 ro) ⲔⲀⲒ ⲄⲀⲢ ⲀⲖⲎⲐⲰⲤ ⲚⲤⲀⲂⲎⲖ ⲈⲦⲂⲈⲚⲤⲞⲠⲤ ⲘⲘⲒⲬⲀⲎⲖ ⲈⲦⲞ ⲚⲤⲞⲂⲦ ⲈⲢⲞⲚ ⲚⲈⲢⲈⲚⲆⲀⲒⲘⲰⲚ... ⲚⲀⲦⲀⲔⲞ ⲚⲦⲠⲞⲖⲒⲤ ⲦⲎⲢⲤ, but also with ⲈⲚⲈⲈⲦⲂⲈ... ⲀⲚ: (*A 1* 158) ⲈⲚⲈⲈⲦⲂⲈⲠⲈⲒⲌⲰⲂ ⲀⲚ ⲚⲈⲞⲨⲚϢ5ⲞⲘ ⲈⲦⲢⲈⲌⲈⲚⲔⲞⲞⲨⲈ ⲦⲀⲘⲒⲞⲞⲨ, compare (*IV* 156.26) ⲈⲚⲈⲈⲦⲂⲈⲦⲀⲄⲀⲠⲎ ⲀⲚ ⲚⲒⲤ̄ ⲚⲈⲒⲬⲰ ⲚⲚⲀⲒ...

ⲌⲚ-	also in an unfulfillable protasis: (*IV* 94.23) ⲈⲚⲈⲌⲚⲞⲨⲘⲚⲦⲌⲀⲌ ⲚϢⲀⲬⲈ, ⲚⲈⲨⲚⲀϢ5Ⲙ-5ⲞⲘ ⲀⲚ ⲚⲀⲠⲀⲦⲀ ⲘⲠⲈⲦⲢⲞⲈⲒⲤ...
ⲚⲚⲀⲌⲢⲚ-:	(*III* 107.6) ⲀⲖⲎⲐⲰⲤ ⲚⲚⲀⲌⲢⲀⲒ ⲌⲰⲤ ⲈϢⲬⲈ-ⲚⲞⲨⲎⲌ ⲚⲤⲀⲞⲨⲤⲀ / (*Ch.* 135.50ff.) ⲚⲚⲀⲌⲢⲀⲔ ⲘⲈⲚ ⲌⲰⲤ ⲈϢⲬⲈ-ϤⲘⲞⲔⲌ, ⲀⲖⲖⲀ ⲚⲚⲀⲌⲢⲚⲚⲈⲦⲚⲞⲈⲒ ⲀⲚ / (*IV* 159.11f.) ⲚⲚⲀⲌⲢⲚⲚⲢⲰⲘⲈ ⲄⲀⲢ ⲌⲰⲤ ⲈϢⲬⲈ-ⲚⲐⲈ ⲘⲠⲈⲚⲦⲀϤⲈⲒⲢⲈ ⲦⲈ ⲐⲈ ⲘⲠⲈⲦⲈⲘⲠⲈϤⲈⲒⲢⲈ — in this case ⲌⲰⲤ (ⲈϢⲬⲈ-) may be the theme.
ⲚⲦⲈⲒⲌⲈ:	see §1.2.1.2, spec. obs. (1), sub-pattern (c).
ⲔⲀⲖⲰⲤ:	(*III* 222.4) ⲔⲀⲖⲰⲤ ⲚⲌⲞⲨⲞ ⲈⲚϢⲀⲚⲤⲀⲌⲰⲚ ⲈⲂⲞⲖ ⲚⲚⲈⲚⲚⲞⲂⲈ — here the conditional may well be the theme / (*IV* 109.8) ⲔⲀⲖⲰⲤ ⲞⲚ " it is well " / (*P* 130[2] 105 ⲦⲘⲄ) ⲈϢⲬⲈ-ⲔⲀⲖⲰⲤ ⲚⲠⲤⲞⲞⲨⲚ, ⲔⲀⲖⲰⲤ ⲚⲌⲞⲨⲞ ⲚⲦ5ⲒⲚϢⲀⲬⲈ... ⲔⲀⲖⲰⲤ ⲚⲦⲘⲚⲦⲤⲀⲂⲈ... ⲔⲀⲖⲰⲤ ⲚⲦⲘⲚⲦⲢⲘⲚⲌⲎⲦ.
ⲔⲀⲔⲰⲤ:	(*IV* 80.2f.) ⲔⲀⲔⲰⲤ ⲚⲌⲈⲚⲖⲀⲞⲤ ⲈⲨⲤⲰⲔ ⲘⲘⲞⲞⲨ ⲚⲬⲚⲀⲌ [88].

1.2.2 THE MODIFIER FOCALIZED: ⧺ SECOND TENSE → MODIFIER ⧺ AND OTHER PATTERNS. See Chapter 2.

1.2.3 THE MODIFIER IN A PREDICATION-PRESUPPOSING ZEUGMATIC PATTERN: 'PRONOUN/NOUN SYNTAGM → MODIFIER'

(A) GENERAL OBSERVATIONS: (1) This is a well-attested, typical Shenoutean construction which I believe has not had the attention it deserves: a syntagm of *noun/independent pronoun + modifier* is included in a larger syntagmatic complex, in which it expands a nuclear unit comprising some or most of the following components: *subject (pro)noun, object (pro)noun, verb lexeme, adjunctal* or *predicative modifier*, and in one of several cohesion possibilities with the constituents of this unit — often in antithetic configuration:

---

[85] {ⲞⲨ-} is not excluded from the predicative post-Ⲛ-position (ⲠⲖⲀⲤⲤⲈ ⲘⲘⲞϤ ⲚⲞⲨⲢⲰⲘⲈ, Ⲣ-ⲔⲀⲌ ⲚⲞⲨⲢⲰⲘⲈ *Cat.* 42.16f., 43.6, ϢⲰⲠⲈ ⲚⲌⲈⲚⲢⲰⲘⲈ ⲚⲦⲈⲠⲚⲞⲨⲦⲈ *Ench.* 93a, and so on) while {Ⲛ} is. This is another syntagmatic factor subdividing the determinator category into Ø-, {ⲞⲨ-} *vs.* {Ⲛ-} (another is the alternation of the two Bipartite subpatterns, see §1.2.1.1).

[86] POLOTSKY 1959:459 (+ n. 3) (= *CP* 237.), cf. STERN p. 315.

[87] Cf. §§7.1.3, 7.3... for ⧺ (*modifier* - Ø) + *adnexal conjunctive* ⧺, a pattern much more common than the minimal ⧺ *mod.* - Ø ⧺ one (for which cf. TESNIÈRE 1965: 186ff.). For Egyptian ⧺ *mod.* – Ø ⧺ cf. JUNGE 1978:§7.1.2.

[88] Perhaps also (exclamatory, *III* 146.20) ⲠⲖⲎⲚ ⲠⲬⲞⲈⲒⲤ ⲌⲘⲠⲈⲔ5ⲰⲚⲦ ⲀⲚ (cf. *Ps.* 6:2, 37:2).

(*Ch.* 102.19ff.) ЄΡЄΠΒΑΛ ΜΜΑΥ ЄΤΒЄΝΑΥ ΑΥШ ΠΜΑΑΧЄ ЄΤΒЄСШΤΜ / (*Ch.* 46.12ff.) ΤЄΤΝΤШΡΠ ΜΜΟΟΥ, ΖΟΙΝЄ ΝΧΙΝΧΗ ΖЄΝΚΟΟΥЄ ΖΑΖЄΝΚΟΥΙ ΝΤΙΜΗ / (*Ch.* 28.18ff.) ΝЄΝΤΑΥΧШΚ ЄΒΟΛ ЄΝΝЄΥЄΠΙΘΥΜΙΑ (sic) ΝΜΜΑΚ ΑΥШ ΝΤΟΚ ΝΜΜΑΥ / (*III* 211.10f.) ЄЧЄΙΡЄ ΜΜΟΟΥ (i.e. ΜΜΝΤΑСЄΒΗС) ΝΖΗΤΟΥ ΑΥШ ΝΤΟΟΥ ЄΒΟΛ ΖΙΤΟΟΤЧ.

(2) I consider this "zeugmatic" pattern [89] a representation of the nuclear pattern structure, projected into the textual sequence — a representation with a higher degree of cohesion with the nuclear unit than would be effected by its simple repetition. This is an *outline* construction, a suspended or (to borrow from architectural terminology) a *corbel* or *cantilever* "overhanging" construction. In preference to this somewhat over-graphic descriptive nomenclature, one may adopt the negative or detractive *incompleteness* and *omission*, with the rhetoric-stylistic "*elleipsis*"[90] or the generative "gapping". "*Apokoinou*", another traditional term, is more descriptive than the others but also insufficiently specific.

(3) As regards the informational or thematic-functional structure of this construction, I think one can validly regard the '*noun syntagm + modifier*' complex as relatively predicative (rhematic), with its subject (theme) — a cohesive-anaphoric one — zeroed within it. Alternatively, the modifier alone can be considered predicative, and the noun *prominently topical* (§2.0.2.1) there being a nexal relationship between the two.

(B) CONSTITUENCY (open-ended list):

N-   (*Ch.* 47.1ff.) ШΑΤЄΤΝШΑΤΟΥ, ΖΟΙΝЄ ΝΟΥΖΝΟ ΝСΟΥΟ... ΖЄΝΚΟΟΥЄ ΝΟΥΧΟΥΤΗ ΜΜΑΑΧЄ, ΖЄΝΚΟΟΥЄ ΝΟΥΡΤΑΒ / (*ibid.* 168.3ff.) ΝΤЄΙΖЄ ΟΝ ΠЄ ΟΥСΟΝ ΝΟΥСΟΝ ΑΥШ ΟΥСШΝЄ ΝΟΥСШΝЄ / (*A 2* 153) ΝΑШЄΝШΗΡЄ ЄΤΚШ ΝСШΟΥ ΝΝЄΥЄΙΟΤЄ ΑΥШ ΝЄΙΟΤЄ ΝΝЄΥШΗΡЄ ΑΥШ ΝΖΟΟΥΤ ΝΝЄΥΖΙΟΜЄ ΑΥШ ΝЄΖΙΟΜЄ ΝΝЄΥΖΑΙ.

Є-   (*A 2* 60) СЄЄΡΟΥ ЄΛΑΥ, ΠЄЧΜΑΝΝΚΟΤΚ ЄΤΒΒΟЧ, ΠΝΑ ЄΛΑЧ... ΠΖΑΠ ЄΤΑΛЧ ЄΧΝΧΙ-ΖΟ, ΝΝΗСΤЄΙΑ ЄΖΑΡЄΖ ЄΡΟΟΥ / (*Ch.* 54.19ff.) ΤΟΥЄΡΗΤЄ ЄСШΟΟΠ ΖΜΠСШΜΑ ЄΤΒЄΜΟΟШЄ, ΝϬΙΧ ЄΠЄΥΖШΒ, ΝΤЄΙΖЄ ΟΝ ΠΜΟΝΑΧΟС ЄΤΡЄЧСϬΡΑΖΤ.

ЄΖΟΥΝ Є-   (*P* 131[4] 88 ΡΛΔ) ЄЧΝΑΟΥШΝΖ ΟΝ ΝΤЄЧΑΓΑΠΗ ЄΖΟΥΝ ЄΡΟΝ, ΑΥШ ΑΝΟΝ ΖШШΝ ЄΖΟΥΝ ЄΝЄΝЄΡΗΥ.

ЄΧΠ-   (? *A 1* 188, 9× — in line 6 a lacuna where the nodal verb would have been) ΟΥΛΥΠΗ ЄΧΝΟΥΛΥΠΗ, ΟΥΘΛΙΨΙС ЄΧΝΟΥΘΛΙΨΙС, ΟΥΑΝΑΓΚΗ ЄΧΝΟΥΑΝΑΓΚΗ...

ΖΝ-/ΝΖΗΤ⸗   (*IV* 60.19f.) (ЄΥΝΑΒШΚ ЄΥΡШΜΤ), СΝΑΥ ΖΝΝЄΤΡ-САΒΒΑΤΟΝ, ΑΥШ ΟΥΑ ΖΝΝЄΤЧΙ ΜΠΡΟΟΥШ... / (*Ch.* 118.26ff.) ΑЧΚΑ-ΤЄЧϬΙΧ ΖΙΧШΝ ΑΥШ ΤЄЧϬΟΜ ΝΖΗΤΝ.

ΖΑ-   (*Ch.* 89.33ff.) ΝЄΙΝΑϯ ΠЄ ΝΝΑΜΝΤШΡΠΜΜΙСЄ ΖΑΤΑΜΝΤШΑЧΤЄ... ΠΚΑΡΠΟС ΝΖΗΤ ΖΑΠΝΟΒЄ ΝΤΑΨΥΧΗ.

(ΜΝ-)/ΝΜΜΑ⸗   (*A 2* 20) СЄΠШΡШ ΜΠЄΥΠΡΗΥ ΖΑΡΟЧ ΝΜΜΑΥ (i.e. the Devil and his followers) ΑΥШ ΝΤΟЧ ΝΜΜΑΥ.

ΝΝΑΖΡΝ-   (*III* 221.4ff.) ΝΤЄΙΖЄ ΟΝ ΟΥΖЄΘΝΟС ΝΑСЄΒΗС ΝΝΑΖΡΜΠΖЄΘΝΟС ΝЄΥСЄΒΗС, ΑΥШ ΟΥΑΡΧШΝ ΝΝΑΖΡΝΟΥΑΡΧШΝ, ΟΥΡΜΜΑΟ ΝΝΑΖΡΝΟΥΡΜΜΑΟ... ШΑΖΡΑΙ ЄΟΥΛΗСΤΗС ΜΠЄЧΜЄΤΑΝΟΙ ΝΝΑΖΡΜΠЄΝΤΑЧΜЄΤΑΝΟΙ.

ΚΑΤΑ-   (*III* 220.20)... ΠΟΥΑ ΠΟΥΑ ΚΑΤΑΤЄЧΤΑΞΙС / (*ibid.* 110.8f., *P* 131[4] 90 ΡΛΗ) ΠΟΥΑ ΠΟΥΑ ΚΑΤΑΤЄЧΜΙΝЄ...

ЄΒΟΛ ΖΙΤΟΟΤ⸗   (*III* 211.10, quoted above).

ЄΤΒЄ-   (*Ch.* 102.19ff., quoted above; 24ff.) ЄΡЄΤΜΝΤΡΜΜΑΟ ШΟΟΠ ЄΤΒЄΝΑ, ΑΥШ ΤЄΖΟΥСΙΑ ЄΤΒЄΡΖΑΠ / (*A 2* 473-4) ΜΝΛΑΑΥ ΝΖΑΜШЄ ЄΜΝΤЧ-ΒΑШΟΥΡ ЄΤΒЄШШШΤ Η ΠΛЄΝΤΗΝ ЄΤΒЄΟΥЄΙСЄ.

ΧЄ-   (*Wess. 9* 149b) ΝШΗΡЄ ШΗΜ ЄΥСШΒЄ ΧЄ-Ι͞С, ΝЄΤΧΙΟΟΡ ΝΟΥΜΟΟΥ ΧЄ-Ι͞С, ΝЄΤΠΗΤ ΖΑΠΖΟ ΝΝΒΑΡ-

---

[89] See STERN:306f., TILL 1954:387 n. 8 (for Egyptian, cf. Gilula, *JNES* 35:27 [1976]).
[90] Cf. GERBER 1885:457-476.

ⲂⲀⲢⲞⲤ ⲬⲈ-ⲓ̅ⲥ̅, and so on (7×): the basic unit (a 23ff.) is *Sec. Present* + ⲬⲈ-ⲓ̅ⲥ̅ / (*III* 39. 19ff.) ⲦⲀⲒ ⲦⲈ ⲐⲈ ⲞⲨⲀ ⲬⲈ-, ⲔⲈⲞⲨⲀ ⲈⲦⲂⲈ-, ⲔⲈⲞⲨⲀ ⲈⲦⲂⲈ-.

1.3 SYNTHETIC INFORMATION: A SELECTIVE EXAMINATION OF INDIVIDUAL MEMBERS OF THE CATEGORY AND THEIR PROPERTIES

The following is a generally catalogic study of the *marking* of certain modifiers for modifier status and their distribution, with consideration of their functioning inside various *nucleus + modifier* constructions.

Coptic modifiers are either analyzable, i.e. syntagmatic (§§1.3.1-3, 1.3.5, 1.3.7-8) or unanalyzable — morphematic or lexemic (§1.3.4-6, 1.3.9-10). The nature of the modifiers of Greek origin (§1.3.11) is not clear. Even those with a recognizable original morphological factor (-ⲰⲤ, -ⲞⲚ) cannot be taken as fully analyzable in Coptic, where there is nothing to prove, for instance, that -ⲰⲤ is a suffixed morpheme (it is evidently not productive, i.e. in a motivation relationship, even in the Greek-origin sub-system of Coptic). Nevertheless, modifiers of this type do have a mark, a recurring formal characteristic — albeit with a degree of uniqueness [91] — and are thus more " grammaticalized " than, say, ⲦⲀⲬⲨ or the native ⲦⲀⲒ and ⲦⲰⲚⲞⲨ.

1.3.1 Ⲛ-MARKED MODIFIERS. The distribution and external syntagmatics of this, the most characteristic of " adverbial " markers, are treated elsewhere. Here I wish to dwell on some specific, well-defined Ⲛ-syntagms. Ⲛ- precedes noun syntagms (including the infinitives) in various environmentally determined adnominal and adverbal functions. There is, however, a mixed bag of recurring Ⲛ-phrases that are more or less fixed as complements of *modality* (time/space/manner) for the nuclear verb. This is Ⲛ- as a " relational " preposition [92], occurring in regular, lexicalized, predictable collocations, which correspond to modal (often de-adjectival) " adverbs " in inflecting languages.

(a) *Localization in space* [93]: ⲘⲠⲂ(Ⲟ)Ⲗ Ⲛ- " outside " (*III* 71.16, *P* 130⁴ 99 vo), ⲘⲠⲔⲰⲦⲈ " around " (*Ch.* 33.17f.), ⲚⲞⲨⲘⲀ (*IV* 91.14), ⲚⲎⲒ ⲈⲎⲒ ⲀⲨⲰ ⲘⲠⲈⲒⲘⲀ ⲈⲠⲀⲒ " from [93] house to house and from this place to that " (*IV* 92.20).

(b) *Localization in time*: expressions of occasion, event and duration: ⲘⲠⲒⲞⲨⲞⲈⲒϢ (*IV* 185.12), ⲚⲞⲨⲞ-ⲈⲒϢ ⲚⲒⲘ (*IV* 1.12), ⲚⲞⲨⲞⲈⲒϢ " once (upon a time) " (*IV* 185.1), ⲚⲞⲨⲌⲞⲞⲨ (*IV* 54.19), Ⲛ2ⲘⲈ Ⲛ2ⲞⲞⲨ (*Ch.* 105.52), ⲘⲠⲤⲞⲠ (*IV* 67.23), ⲚⲔⲈⲤⲞⲠ (*IV* 83.20), Ⲛ4ⲦⲞⲞⲨ ⲚⲤⲞⲠ (*IV* 74.6), ⲚⲞⲨⲤⲞⲠ (*IV* 67.10), ⲘⲠⲈⲒⲤⲞⲠ Ⲏ ⲚⲚⲈⲚ-ⲔⲈ2ⲞⲞⲨ (*A 2* 82), ⲘⲠⲚⲀⲨ (*IV* 67.25), ⲚⲚⲀⲨ ⲚⲒⲘ (*IV* 175.8f.), ⲚⲀⲢⲬⲀⲒⲞⲤ " of old " (*III* 19.14, see §4.2.2.1), ⲚⲤⲀ4 " yesterday " (*A 1* 50), ⲘⲘⲎⲚⲈ " daily ", see below, ⲚϢⲞⲢⲠ " at first " (*IV* 73.12), ⲘⲠⲞⲞⲨ " today " (*III* 95.22f.) ⲘⲠⲞⲞⲨ Ⲏ Ⲛ12ⲞⲞⲨ (*III* 114.11), ⲚⲦⲈⲨⲚⲞⲨ " at once " (*III* 99.11), ⲚⲞⲨⲚⲞⲨ ⲈⲂⲞⲖ 2ⲚⲞⲨⲚⲞⲨ " at any given hour " (*III* 87.8), ⲚⲞⲨⲔⲞⲨⲒ ⲚⲀⲠⲢⲎⲦⲈ " for a short instance " (*IV* 67.19), ⲚϢⲀⲈⲚⲈ2 " for ever " (*IV* 6.12, see §1.1.1.1), ⲚⲦⲢⲞⲘⲠⲈ " this year " (*P* 130⁴ 140 ro) and many more.

---

[91] Compare the status of some semi-analyzable imported derivational suffixes in English: *-tain, -sist, -ceive*... Morphematic " uniqueness " (and analyzability or " transparency ") seems to be a gradient property. Almost all research remains to be done with regard to the Shenoutean *Graecitas Coptica*. We have no way of measuring the difference in grammatical transparency between such variants as ⲔⲀⲖⲰⲤ and ⲔⲀⲖⲞⲤ; of some relevance here may be the Bohairic alternation of ⧻ ⲔⲀⲖⲰⲤ - and - ⲚⲔⲀⲖⲰⲤ⧻ (but also ⧻ⲠⲀⲒⲢⲎ+ - and - ⲘⲠⲀⲒⲢⲎ+⧻).

[92] ⲘⲘⲞ꞊ enters this issue only as a resumptive representative of Ⲛ-: (*A 2* 489) ⲚⲐⲈ ⲚⲦⲀⲨⲤⲞⲚⲦⲈ ⲘⲘⲞⲤ / (*ibid.* 397) ⲚⲐⲈ ⲈⲦⲈⲢⲈⲚⲢⲈ4ⲈⲠⲒⲐⲨⲘⲈⲒ ⲈⲠⲀⲅⲀⲐⲞⲤ ⲚⲀⲚⲀⲨ ⲈⲢⲞⲚ ⲘⲘⲞⲤ / (*ibid.* 65) ⲠⲤⲞ6Ⲛ ⲀⲨⲰ ⲠⲚⲈ2 ⲈϢⲀⲢⲈⲦⲀ2ⲤⲈ ⲘⲘⲞⲞⲨ.

[93] Cf. (on the fluctuation Boh. Ⲛ- ~ 6ⲈⲚ-) PIEHL 1902, ANDERSSON 1904:11ff.; see ⲘⲘⲀⲨ (and n. 96 below) on the syncretism of locative (" in ") and ablative (" from ") semantics in ⲦⲰⲚ etc.

(c) *Determination of manner/degree*: N2O-2I2O " face to face " (*III* 153.12, *Ch.* 208.43f., *P* 130² 48 PKⲀ), NOYKOYI (*A 1* 150), NKEKOYI (*III* 99.12), N2OYO " rather ", " even (more) ", see below; NBPPE " anew " (*A 2* 314), NTEI2E " thus ", see below; NAꙎ N2E " how? " (*Wess. 9* 148a 18ff.), NⲐE N-/ET- " in the manner of / that " (*III* 51.19, 104.26), NXNA2 " violently " (*A 1* 44), NNOYX " falsely " (*P* 130² 39 vo); with infinitives [94]: NOYꙎ2M " again " (*A 1* 74), N2ꙎⲠ " in hiding " (*A 1* 465), NXIOYE " by stealth " (*A 2* 495), etc.

1.3.1.1 Certain N-syntagms deserve more leisurely attention. First, the cases of " unique " or " near-unique " morphemes, in which the isolation of N- (in its allomorph M-) leaves us with a non-recurring, or almost non-recurring — hence, morphologically undefinable — morph as the residue of the syntagm [95].

(a) The deictic " pro-modifier " MMAY is a case in point. -MAY does recur in EMAY " thither " (*IV* 62.3), but nowhere else. MMAY is a pro-modifier (a more grammaticalized, anaphoric modifier, representing 2N-/N- prepositional phrases) meaning " there " (often predicative, *III* 211.9, *Ch.* 116.13) or " thence " (*III* 99.2, *IV* 121.6f. [96]).

(b) Another instance is the excluding, focusing adjunct MMATE " only ", which is again in paradigm with E-MATE as a sole companion, on which paradigm its analyzability is to be based. Both are post-adjunctive only, and neither is ever predicative. EMATE " very " [97] is far removed semasiologically: usually adverbal (NAꙎE-ⲠTꙎ2 EMATE: *A 2* 29, *A 1* 247 written MMATE, *III* 13.22, *IV* 70.5, etc.), it is often adnominal: (*A 2* 296) 2ENKOYI EMATE / (*ibid.* 499) ⲀIKAIOC EMATE / (*ibid.* 317) N2A2 NCOⲠ EMATE, sim. *III* 21.20, 169.13 / (*Ch.* 146.15f.) OYNO6 EMATE NBꙎ NEⲖOOⲖE, etc. EMATE is occasionally reiterated (§1.1.2.4.2). MMATE, which has a special affinity with the augens MAYAA⸗ (§6.1.4.1) is preeminently adnominal, and occurs most typically, stylistically speaking, in (or in conjunction with) a clause including a local (" *Satzglied* ") negation: " not only..., but (also)... " (*e.g. III* 173.12f., 184.17f.; see in more detail, and with more exx., §2.9.1.2.2, also §6.2) — also in syntagm with EIMHTI " but for ", which precedes ' (*pro*)noun MMATE ' (*IV* 62.20) or, less usually [98], governs E-: EIMHTI EMATE E- (*IV* 91.12). MMATE may modify another modifier: (*IV* 24.6f.) 2MⲠEYⲖAC MMATE / (*III* 50.4ff.) 2NOYⲠⲖHⲅH NXNOY4 NBPBP MMATE. I know of no clear instance of adverbal MMATE.

(c) MMHNE " daily " is another instance of the " unique morpheme ". Exclusively postadjunctive, it occurs *adverbally* (*III* 145.23, *IV* 69.23, *Ch.* 201.44ff.), *adclausally* (*A 2* 21-2 NTO4 ON MMHHNE ⲠE) and (rarely) *adnominally* (ⲠNAY NOYꙎM MMHNE *IV* 153.22).

---

[94] N + *infinitive* occurs *rectionally* after certain verbs: APXEI (*III* 44.12), 6M-6OM (*III* 109.19), COOYN (*III* 105.18), EI (*Ch.* 201. 45ff.).

[95] Cf. BLOOMFIELD's famous " *cranberry* " (1935:160f.), on which see also R. Harris, *Synonymy and Linguistic Analysis* Oxford: Blackwell, 1973, p. 66ff.

[96] The syncretism of " locative " and " ab/delative " is evident with many other modifiers (notably TꙎN " whence ", *Wess. 9* 127 b 8ff., 14ff., 128 a 1ff.) and prepositions, esp. 2I- (2IXꙎ4 *Ming.* 89b, and 2IBOⲖ *III* 150.5), 2N-, 2A- (resolved in EBOⲖ 2N-, EBOⲖ 2A-) — see the entries in *Dictionary*. Incidentally, this may add an improvement to my interpretation of the Shenoutean TꙎ ETꙎ — *WZKM* 69:33-9 (1977) — to be understood as " whence — whither? ". This suggestion, communicated to me by W.-P. Funk, is corroborated by an unpublished example (*P* 130⁴ 105 PKE) TꙎ ETꙎ TENOY XINNXE-ME EXI-6OⲖ, XINMⲠⲀIKAION EXIN6ONC, XINⲠTBBO EXꙎ2M, where XIN- E- would agree well with a " whence - whither " frame of reference.

[97] Rare instances of MMATE used for EMATE, " very " (the reverse does not occur, to my knowledge): *A 1* 53, 247, 244.

[98] Usually ' EIMHTI E-(*pro*)noun MAYAA⸗ ' (*III* 90.3, 124.6, 136.20 etc.), or with no modification (*III* 45-6, *IV* 91.17f.); ' EIMHTI + noun ': (*III* 52.10f., *IV* 62.5, etc.). In Shenoute, the paradigm following EIMHTI includes: (E)-(*pro*)noun MMATE/MAYAA⸗, ETPE4CꙎTM, XE-*perfect/present/Nominal Sentence, conjunctive* and *modifiers* (*III* 138.11f., incl. the circumstantial, *IV* 60.25f., 61.2). See §7.3.1.1.

1.3.1.2 ⲚⲦⲈⲒⲌⲈ " thus " occurs: (a) *Postadjunctively, adverbally*: (*III* 222.12) ⲘⲀⲢⲚⲘⲞⲔⲘⲈⲔ ⲈⲢⲞⲚ ⲚⲦⲈⲒⲌⲈ, typically expanding the verbs ⲬⲰ and ⲈⲒⲢⲈ (*III* 18.3, 28.3, 37.7, 49.16, etc.); *adnominally*: (*A 1* 65) ⲚⲈⲒⲌⲂⲎⲨⲈ ⲚⲦⲈⲒⲌⲈ.

(b) *Initially*, as an *adclausal premodifier*, in a verb clause: (*III* 141.20) ⲚⲦⲈⲒⲌⲈ ⲀⲨϢⲰⲠⲈ ⲌⲘⲠⲘⲀ ⲈⲦⲘⲘⲀⲨ ⲚⲐⲈ ⲘⲠⲞⲨⲌⲞⲢ / (*ibid*. 148.4f.) ⲚⲦⲈⲒⲌⲈ ⲚⲈϤⲬⲰ ⲚⲚⲈϤϢⲀⲬⲈ ⲚⲚⲈⲦⲘⲠϢⲀ ⲚⲤⲰⲦⲘ ⲈⲢⲞⲞⲨ.

(c) *Initially*, in the constructions: (1) # ⲚⲦⲈⲒⲌⲈ (ⲌⲰⲰ⸗) ⲞⲚ (Ⲛ-) *noun syntagm* (+ *circumstantial*) #: (*III* 48.24f.) ⲚⲦⲈⲒⲌⲈ ⲌⲰⲞⲨ ⲚⲚⲌⲈⲖⲖⲎⲚ... ⲈⲨⲘⲈⲈⲨⲈ ⲚⲚⲀⲌⲢⲀⲨ ⲬⲈ-ⲈⲨϢⲞⲞⲠ ⲌⲘⲠⲞⲨⲞⲈⲒⲚ / (*IV* 104.7f.) ⲚⲦⲈⲒⲌⲈ ⲞⲚ ⲦⲘⲀⲀⲨ ⲚⲦⲤⲨⲚⲀⲄⲰⲄⲎ ⲈⲤⲚⲀⲈⲒⲢⲈ ⲌⲰⲰⲤ ⲞⲚ ⲚⲦⲈⲒⲌⲈ — the circumstantial here is adnominal and adnexal [99].
(2) # ⲚⲦⲈⲒⲌⲈ ⲞⲚ + [*noun syntagm* + *modifier*] # : (*III* 221.4f., 11f.) ⲚⲦⲈⲒⲌⲈ ⲞⲚ ⲞⲨⲌⲈⲐⲚⲞⲤ ⲚⲀⲤⲈⲂⲎⲤ ⲚⲚⲀⲌ-ⲢⲘⲠⲌⲈⲐⲚⲞⲤ ⲚⲈⲨⲤⲈⲂⲎⲤ, ⲚⲦⲈⲒⲌⲈ ⲞⲚ ⲞⲨⲤⲞⲚ ⲈϤⲬⲀⲌⲘ ⲚⲚⲀⲌⲢⲚⲞⲨⲤⲞⲚ ⲈϤⲞⲨⲀⲀⲂ. The modifier appears to be predicative here within its information unit — the bracketed constituent being articulated as *topic* + *comment* (or *theme* + *rheme*); ⲚⲦⲈⲒⲌⲈ itself is topical in relation to the whole: *topic* + (*topic* + *comment*).
(3) # ⲚⲦⲈⲒⲌⲈ (ⲞⲚ) + [*noun syntagm* + *clause*] #: (*III* 98.11ff.) ⲚⲦⲈⲒⲌⲈ ⲞⲚ ⲦⲈⲤⲌⲒⲘⲈ ⲈⲦϢϢⲰⲦ ⲚⲚⲈⲤⲤⲀⲢⲌ ⲘⲘⲒⲚ ⲘⲘⲞⲤ ⲞⲨ ⲠⲈⲦⲤⲚⲀⲬⲞⲞϤ / (*ibid*. 109-110) ⲚⲦⲈⲒⲌⲈ ⲄⲀⲢ ⲚⲞⲨⲞⲈⲒϢ ⲚⲒⲘ ⲚⲈⲦⲤⲰⲦⲘ ⲔⲀⲔⲰⲤ ϢⲀϤⲌⲰⲠ ⲈⲢⲞⲞⲨ — the noun is extraposed and later resumed.
(4a) ⲚⲦⲈⲒⲌⲈ (ⲞⲚ) ⲠⲈ (ⲚⲦⲈⲒⲌⲈ predicative: §1.2.1.2): (*IV* 84.14) ⲚⲦⲈⲒⲌⲈ ⲞⲚ ⲠⲈ ⲞⲨⲢⲰⲘⲈ Ⲏ ⲞⲨⲤⲌⲒⲘⲈ ⲈⲨϢⲀⲚⲢ-ⲀⲦϬⲞⲘ ⲌⲚⲞⲨϢⲰⲚⲈ.

(4b) ⲚⲦⲈⲒⲌⲈ focalized by a verbal topicalization-form (see Ch. 2, esp. §2.4): (*III* 76.8) ⲚⲦⲈⲒⲌⲈ ⲄⲀⲢ ⲈⲚⲦⲀⲨ-ⲬⲞⲞⲤ...

1.3.1.3 ⲚⲌⲞⲨⲞ occurs: (a) *Postadjunctively, adverbally* (" rather ", " greatly ", " [even] more ", " on the contrary "): (*IV* 5.8) ϤⲤⲞⲦⲠ ⲚⲌⲞⲨⲞ / (*ibid*. 18.12) ⲤⲈⲚⲀⲦⲀⲘⲞⲚ ⲀⲨⲰ ⲦⲚⲚⲀⲈⲒⲘⲈ ⲚⲌⲞⲨⲞ / (*Ch*. 23.19ff.) Ⲏ ⲈⲔϤⲒ-ⲢⲞⲞⲨϢ ⲌⲀⲠⲢⲰⲘⲈ ⲌⲚⲞⲨ... ⲈⲔⲞⲨⲈϢ-ⲘⲞⲞⲨⲦϤ ⲚⲦⲞϤ ⲚⲌⲞⲨⲞ / (*III* 38.24) †ⲚⲀⲘⲒϢⲈ ⲞⲨⲂⲎⲔ ⲚⲌⲞⲨⲞ / (*A 2* 341) (they asked whether) ⲚⲀⲚⲞⲨ-ⲠⲈⲒⲌⲰⲂ, (I answered:) ϤⲌⲞⲞⲨ ⲚⲌⲞⲨⲞ, also *III* 115.17f., 146.16, 163.22, *IV* 18.12, 82.10f., *Ch*. 85.13ff. In a typical figure, ⲚⲌⲞⲨⲞ combines the sense of " rather, on the contrary " with a Second-Tense *autofocal* construction (see §2.1.7), e.g. (*III* 212.8f.) ⲠⲈⲦⲬⲰ ⲘⲘⲞⲤ ⲬⲈ-ⲀⲒⲤⲞⲨⲚ-Ⲓ̄Ⲥ̄... ⲈⲚⲈⲒⲢⲈ ⲚⲚⲀⲒ ⲚⲦⲀⲚⲢ-ⲀⲦⲤⲞⲞⲨⲚ ⲘⲘⲞϤ ⲚⲌⲞⲨⲞ / (*Ch*. 171.2f.) (ⲌⲢⲀⲒ ⲄⲀⲢ ⲌⲘⲠⲔⲀⲒⲢⲞⲤ ⲈⲦⲞⲨⲘⲈⲈⲨⲈ ⲈⲠⲀⲒ... ⲬⲈ-ⲞⲨⲀⲦⲚⲀ ⲠⲈ...) ⲈϤⲞ ⲚⲚⲀⲎⲦ ⲚⲌⲞⲨⲞ.

(b) *Adclausally*, in a Nominal-Sentence pattern (§1.1.2.3, " on the contrary "): (*III* 113.20) ⲞⲨⲖⲀⲤ ⲈϤⲬⲀⲌⲘ ⲚⲌⲞⲨⲞ ⲠⲈ ⲠⲖⲀⲤ ⲚⲚⲀⲤⲈⲂⲎⲤ / (*ibid*. 115.28) ⲈϢⲬⲈ-ⲞⲨⲦⲀⲖⲀⲒⲠⲰⲢⲞⲤ (sic) ⲀⲖⲎⲐⲞⲤ (sic) ⲠⲈ... ⲞⲨⲘⲀⲔⲀ-ⲢⲒⲞⲤ ⲞⲚ ⲀⲖⲎⲐⲰⲤ ⲚⲌⲞⲨⲞ ⲠⲈ... / (*IV* 3.4) ⲠⲈⲦⲈⲢⲈⲚⲢⲰⲘⲈ ⲘⲈⲈⲨⲈ ⲈⲢⲞϤ ⲬⲈ-ⲞⲨⲤⲞⲨⲞ ⲠⲈ ⲈⲞⲨⲦⲰⲌ ⲌⲰϤ ⲚⲌⲞⲨⲞ ⲠⲈ, also *III* 19.2, *IV* 60.23, 108.27 etc.

(c) *Adnominally* (" too much ", " even, especially, in particular "): (*III* 221.18) ⲔⲈⲌⲰⲂ ⲚⲌⲞⲨⲞ / (*IV* 77.2) ⲚⲈⲨⲘⲚⲦⲘⲀⲒⲦⲞ ⲚⲌⲞⲨⲞ / (*IV* 9.20f.) ⲠⲔⲈⲒⲞⲨⲆⲀⲤ ⲚⲌⲞⲨⲞ / (*Ch*. 30.45ff.) ⲚⲦⲞⲔ ⲌⲰⲰⲔ ⲚⲌⲞⲨⲞ. It is, in this status, usually a *premodifier*, semasiologically close to ⲘⲀⲖⲖⲞⲚ, ⲘⲀⲖⲒⲤⲦⲀ (§1.3.11.2.1.4), in the sense of " especially ", " so much more " — a focusing adjunct: usually ' ⲚⲌⲞⲨⲞ ⲆⲈ + *noun* ' (prosodically a colon by itself): *III* 37.17f., 106.12f., 108.19f., 112.13, *IV* 23.7, *Ch*. 74.18f., etc.

(d) ⲚⲌⲞⲨⲞ expanding or premodifying another modifier [100]: (*III* 222.4) ⲔⲀⲖⲰⲤ ⲚⲌⲞⲨⲞ / (*III* 181.19f.) ...ⲈⲦⲢⲈⲨ†-ϬⲞⲘ ⲚⲦⲞϤ ⲚⲌⲞⲨⲞ / (*Ch*. 18.28f.) ⲚⲦⲈⲒⲌⲈ ϬⲈ ⲚⲌⲞⲨⲞ (*A 1* 11) ⲚⲌⲞⲞⲨ ⲚⲒⲘ, ⲚⲌⲞⲨⲞ ⲆⲈ ⲌⲚⲚⲤⲀⲂⲂⲀⲦⲞⲚ.

---

[99] Cf. SHISHA-HALEVY 1972:75ff., 81ff.: consider ⲚⲐⲈ/ⲦⲀⲒ ⲦⲈ ⲐⲈ Ⲛ-[*noun* + *circ*.] (*IV* 82.1f.) ⲚⲐⲈ ⲚⲚⲔⲈⲀⲢⲄⲞⲤ ⲚⲢⲰⲘⲈ ⲈⲨϢⲀⲀⲦ ⲚⲤⲂⲰ / (*Wess*. 9 91b 6ff.) ⲦⲀⲒ ⲦⲈ ⲐⲈ ⲚⲚⲒⲀⲦⲤⲂⲰ ⲈⲦⲘⲘⲀⲨ ⲈⲨⲬⲰⲔ ⲈⲂⲞⲖ ⲚⲦⲈⲠⲒⲐⲨⲘⲒⲀ ⲚⲦⲈⲨⲮⲨⲬⲎ / (*A 1* 162-3) ⲦⲀⲒ ⲦⲈ ⲦⲈⲚⲌⲈ ⲠⲢⲀⲚ ⲀⲨⲰ ⲠⲈⲤⲬⲎⲘⲀ ⲈⲚⲚⲀⲔⲀⲀⲨ ⲚⲦⲚⲘⲞⲞϢⲈ / (*A 2* 138) ⲦⲀⲒ ⲦⲈ ⲐⲈ ⲚⲚⲀⲢⲬⲎⲄⲞⲤ ⲚⲚⲌⲈⲐⲚⲞⲤ ⲈⲦⲞ ⲚⲀⲦⲚⲀⲌⲦⲈ ⲬⲒⲚⲚϢⲞⲢⲠ ⲈⲀⲨⲤⲰⲠ ⲈⲌⲞⲨⲚ ⲌⲘⲠⲦⲞⲠⲞⲤ ⲚⲔⲀⲔⲈ. Note in the last example the opposition between the two adnominal expansion forms: ⲈⲦ- *attributive*, and Ⲉ- *adnexal*.
[100] ⲚⲌⲞⲨⲞ itself is expanded, in the sense of " more than... ", by Ⲉ + *noun* (incl. *infinitive*: III 77.2, *A 1* 56, *III* 131.10).

Note here especially ⲚⲌⲞⲨⲞ + *circumstantial*, in the sense of "especially when": (*Wess. 9* 138c 19f.) ...ⲈⲚϬⲒⲚⲈ ⲘⲠⲨⲒⲚⲈ ⲚⲚⲈⲦⲨⲰⲚⲈ ⲚⲌⲞⲨⲞ ⲆⲈ ⲈⲚϤⲒ ⲘⲠⲢⲞⲞⲨⲨ ⲚⲚⲈⲦⲈⲘⲘⲚⲦⲞⲨ-ⲢⲰⲘⲈ ⲘⲘⲀⲨ.

(e) Initially, ⲚⲌⲞⲨⲞ is rare: (*III* 147.14) ⲚⲈⲒⲨⲞϪⲚⲈ ⲚⲀⲒ ⲘⲀⲨⲀⲀⲦ ϪⲈⲚⲚⲀⲨⲰⲠⲈ ⲞⲚ ⲚⲤⲔⲀⲚⲆⲀⲖⲞⲚ... ⲚⲌⲞⲨⲞ ⲆⲈ ⲚⲈⲒⲞⲨⲰⲨ ⲀⲚ ⲠⲈ ⲈⲖⲨⲠⲈⲒ ⲚⲚⲈⲤⲚⲎⲨ ⲦⲎⲢⲞⲨ ⲘⲠⲒⲤⲦⲞⲤ.

1.3.2 Zero-marked noun syntagms in modifier status[101] are restricted to certain temporal or spatial localizing expressions and the modal pronominal ⲖⲀⲀⲨ "at all", "anyhow". Related to this lack of marking is the syntagmatic zero — the absence of resumption of initial nouns: contrast (*IV* 58. 19f.) ⲠⲈⲌⲘⲈ ⲚⲌⲞⲞⲨ ⲚⲚⲈⲢⲰⲘⲈ ⲈⲨⲔⲀⲞⲈⲒⲔ ⲚⲦⲞⲞⲦϤ ⲈⲠⲦⲎⲢϤ, with (*ibid.* 54.29) ⲠⲈⲌⲘⲈ ⲚⲌⲞⲞⲨ ⲦⲎⲢϤ ⲚⲚⲈⲨⲈⲨⲠⲒⲤⲈ ⲚⲌⲎⲦϤ ⲈⲠⲦⲎⲢϤ. This cohesional distinction is indicative, since it determines the noun as *modifying* the subsequent clause, not serving as its topic (§6.0.1).

(1) ⲈⲚⲈⲌ: see §1.3.6.

(2) ⲦⲈⲢⲞⲘⲠⲈ, ⲦⲢⲢⲞⲘⲠⲈ "yearly", "— a year"[102], distributive. *Postadjunctive, adnominal* (to ⲤⲞⲠ only): ⲚⲞⲨⲤⲞⲠ ⲦⲈⲢⲞⲘⲠⲈ (*P* 131⁵ 13 ro), ⲚϤⲦⲞⲞⲨ ⲚⲤⲞⲠ ⲦⲢⲢⲞⲘⲠⲈ (*IV* 74.6f.), also *ibid.* 58.1, 91.8.

(3) ⲤⲞⲠ: initially, as *adclausal premodifier*: ⲌⲀⲌ ⲚⲤⲞⲠ "often" (*III* 146.28, 147.9,18, etc.) — contrast with the postadjunctive — ⲚⲌⲀⲌ ⲚⲤⲞⲠ (*III* 107.14, 139.11). *Postadjunctive*: ⲞⲨⲤⲞⲠ (*A 2* 397), ⲨⲞⲘⲦ ⲚⲤⲞⲠ (*Ch.* 106.52ff.). The disjunctive ⲤⲞⲠ — ⲤⲞⲠ, ⲞⲨ/ⲌⲈⲚⲤⲞⲠ — ⲞⲨ/ⲌⲈⲚⲤⲞⲠ "now... now... ", "at times... at times... " (*III* 19.20ff., 70 *passim*, 77-8, 110.9f. etc.) is usually a premodifier.

(4) ⲨⲞⲢⲠ ⲘⲈⲚ- "first of all", "at first" is initial and adclausal: *III* 164.5, *IV* 128.6, *Ch.* 204.19f., *P* 130² 54 ⲠⲄ, 130⁵ 39 vo.

(5) ⲌⲞⲞⲨ in ⲠⲈⲌⲘⲈ ⲚⲌⲞⲞⲨ (*IV* 58.19).

(6) ⲢⲞⲨⲌⲈ, ⲌⲦⲞⲞⲨⲈ "at evening", "at dawn" (*IV* 65.26). This is a peculiar case, in which the only synchronic indication of nominal status is the occurrence of these words after prepositions, notably ⲌⲒ-, ⲨⲀ-, Ⲉ-, ϪⲒⲚ-, Ⲛ- (*IV* 60.14, 61.1, 92.13f., *Ch.* 51.22, 145.26f., *P* 130¹ 139 ⲦⲘⲈ: ⲚⲢⲞⲨⲌⲈ ⲀⲨⲰ ⲌⲦⲞⲞⲨⲈ). ⲢⲞⲨⲌⲈ ⲠⲈ (*IV* 60.21) is inconclusive, in view of the # modifier - ⲠⲈ# pattern (§1.2.1.2). There is however some basis for considering ⲌⲒ- in ⲌⲒⲦⲞⲞⲨⲈ (and even in ⲌⲒⲢⲞⲨⲌⲈ, *IV* 92.2 cod. C ⲨⲀⲌⲒⲢⲞⲨⲌⲈ *v.l.* ⲨⲀⲢⲞⲨⲌⲈ) metanalytically fused with the lexeme and somehow connected with the (radical) Ⲍ in ⲌⲦⲞⲞⲨⲈ[103] — I know of no attestation for * ⲌⲒ-ⲌⲦⲞⲞⲨⲈ (see *Dictionary* 728a; consider also *Miss.* 282, *IV* 104.4f. ⲌⲒⲢⲞⲨⲌⲈ ⲀⲨⲰ ⲌⲒⲦⲞⲞⲨⲈ). Consequently, these expressions may not properly belong here, but are — at least to some extent — modifiers by lexical right, like ⲦⲀⲬⲨ or ⲦⲰⲚⲞⲨ. (ⲌⲒⲢⲞⲨⲌⲈ also occurs as an *adnominal* modifier: *P* 131⁵ 133 ro ⲦⲤⲨⲚⲀϮⲤ ⲌⲒⲢⲞⲨⲌⲈ.)

(7) ⲖⲀⲀⲨ "at all", "anyhow", "in anything" is *postadjunctive only*: (*III* 137.23) ...ⲈⲘⲠⲒϪⲒⲦⲞⲨ ⲚϬⲞⲚⲤ ⲖⲀⲀⲨ / (*IV* 18.18f.) ⲚⲤⲀⲄⲀⲚⲀⲔⲦⲈⲒ ⲖⲀⲀⲨ ⲀⲚ ⲈⲠⲆⲒⲔⲀⲒⲞⲤ / (*Thompson* D ⲚⲐ) ⲘⲠϤⲀⲌⲈⲢⲀⲦϤ ⲖⲀⲀⲨ ⲞⲨⲂⲈ- (v.l. *A 2* 246 ⲚⲖⲀⲀⲨ).

---

[101] Cf. Schenkel 1966:58 ("absolute substantives" — they are in fact neither absolute nor "asyntactic", but lack an overt marking of the "adverbial" syntactic function). Junge 1978:73-84, esp. 76, 81ff, arrives, through equating "prepositional phrase" (*qua* "adverb") with "noun" (in "adverbial status" yet *qua* "noun") at the far-reaching and to me unacceptable — since procedurally exceptionable — identification (in Middle Egyptian) of nominal and "adverbial" nexus, at least in "deep structure". This error is due, I believe, to misapplication (and misjudgement of the significance) of commutability. To judge by the occasional *variae lectiones*, the characteristic zeroed in Coptic is in all probability the Ⲛ- + ⲌⲚ- syncretism (see footnote 93).

[102] von Lemm 1972b:377f., Daumas 1952:119f. (*Dictionary* 297a).

[103] Černý 1976:302f. suggests for ⲌⲦⲞⲞⲨⲈ a hybrid etymology: *ḥd−t3* + *dw3w*: Crum gives in *Dictionary* 727b-728a ⲌⲒⲦⲞⲞⲨⲈ and ⲌⲒⲦⲀⲀⲨⲈ as specifically Shenoutean and Akhmimoid (A, A²) forms, but does not consider the possibility that these are syntagms, analyzable to a degree.

(8) ⲡⲃⲟⲗ " out(side) ", *postadjunctive*: (*III* 103.18f.) ⲁⲩⲛⲟⲭⲟⲩ ⲉⲃⲟⲗ ⲡⲃⲟⲗ / (*IV* 110.9f.) ⲍⲱⲃ ⲛⲓⲙ ⲉⲧⲟⲩⲛⲁⲁⲁⲩ... ⲉⲩⲛⲁⲁⲁⲩ ⲡⲃⲟⲗ ⲙⲡⲉⲩⲍⲱⲃ ⲛ6ⲓⲭ ⲛ̄ⲩⲁⲩⲁⲁϥ... (v.l. ⲙⲡⲃⲟⲗ), also *IV* 33.27, 113.24f., *A 1* 70. *Adnominally*: (*IV* 112.17f.) ⲍⲱⲃ ⲛⲓⲙ ⲡⲃⲟⲗ ⲙⲡⲕⲁⲧⲁⲇⲁⲝⲓⲥ (sic).

1.3.3 ITERATION-MARKED NOUN SYNTAGMS IN MODIFIER STATUS

1.3.3.1 The syntagm ' *∅-noun lexeme → ∅-noun lexeme* ' is a member of the *postadjunctive* modifier paradigm and occupies a slot in the valency matrix with no further marking: (a) as a *distributive-distensive-particularizing* complement in the second (or following) post-verbal slot: (*Ch.* 183.52f.) ⲁⲩ-ⲩⲁⲁⲧⲟⲩ ⲙⲉⲗⲟⲥ ⲙⲉⲗⲟⲥ sim. *III* 106.2 / (*IV* 19.19f.) ⲥⲉⲛⲁⲡⲟⲧⲡⲧ ⲉⲡⲕⲁⲍ ⲧⲁ6 ⲧⲁ6 / (*ibid.* 199.2) ...ⲉϥⲕⲱ ⲙⲙⲟⲟⲩ ⲉⲍⲣⲁⲓ 6ⲟⲡⲉ 6ⲟⲡⲉ / (*P* 130[5] 19 ⲣⲇ) ⲛⲉϥⲭⲱⲗⲕ ⲟⲩⲟⲛⲍ ⲉⲃⲟⲗ ⲍⲓⲱⲩϥ ⲏ ⲛⲍⲏⲧϥ· ⲙⲁ· ⲙⲁ· / (*A 1* 77) ⲩⲁⲛⲧⲟⲩⲧⲁⲁϥ ⲕⲟⲩⲓ ⲕⲟⲩⲓ ⲛⲧⲟⲟⲧⲟⲩ [104] / (*ibid.* 108) ⲩⲁⲣⲉⲟⲥ2ⲟⲩ ⲡⲟ6ⲉ ⲡⲟ6ⲉ ⲏ ⲗⲁⲕⲙ ⲗⲁⲕⲙ, or (b) as a *rectional* expansion [105] — an " object ", in the first post-verbal position (see §3.0.1): (*HT H* 1 ro) ⲛⲉⲛⲉⲓⲟⲧⲉ ⲛⲧⲁⲩⲭⲱⲗⲉ ⲥⲙⲁ2 ⲥⲙⲁ2 ...ⲕⲁⲛ ⲙⲁⲣⲛ̄ⲕⲱⲧϥ ⲇⲉ ⲍⲱⲱⲛ ⲭⲁⲗⲉ ⲭⲁⲗⲉ, parall. (ⲭⲁⲗⲉ ⲭⲁⲗⲉ ⲍⲱⲱⲛ) *P* 131[4] 161 vo — expansion focalized by Second Perfect / (*ibid.* 2 vo) ⲛⲉⲛⲉⲓⲟⲧⲉ ⲉⲩⲥⲟⲟⲩ2 ⲉ2ⲟⲩⲛ ⲧⲃⲁ ⲧⲃⲁ ⲛⲥⲁⲧⲉⲉⲣⲉ — note the *open juncture* of the *verb + iteration-marked rectional modifier* syntagm / (*III* 29.28) ⲉⲓⲕⲱⲧϥ ⲭⲁⲗⲉ ⲭⲁⲗⲉ — the iteration-marked object-expansion focalized by the Second Present / (*A 2* 26) ⲛⲍⲉⲗⲗⲏⲛ... ⲛⲧⲁⲛⲥⲱⲃ2 ⲙⲡⲉⲩⲉⲓⲱⲧ ⲡⲇⲓⲁⲃⲟⲗⲟⲥ ⲣ-ⲟⲩⲗⲡⲉ ⲟⲩⲗⲡⲉ ⲍⲓⲱⲟⲩ / (*A 1* 108) ⲛⲉⲧⲛⲁⲣ-ⲁⲥ ⲏ ⲡⲗⲁ6ⲉ ⲡⲗⲁ6ⲉ. The iteration of cardinal numbers [106] — ⲟⲩⲁ ⲟⲩⲁ, ⲥⲛⲁⲩ ⲥⲛⲁⲩ, ⲥⲛⲧⲉ ⲥⲛⲧⲉ... — occurs either in complement or rection status: (*A 1* 12, in part parall. *BM* 992 vo) ⲛⲉⲧⲉⲩⲁⲣⲉⲡⲭⲟⲉⲓⲥ ⲓ̅ⲥ̅ ⲭⲟⲟⲩⲥⲟⲩ ⲥⲛⲁⲩ ⲥⲛⲁⲩ / (*IV* 60.28) ⲉⲧⲙⲕⲁ-ⲩⲉⲉⲣⲉ ⲩⲏⲙ ⲉⲃⲱⲕ ⲥⲛⲧⲉ ⲥⲛⲧⲉ / (*P* 130[5] 64 ⲣⲟⲥ) ⲥ2ⲁⲓ (the heart's secrets) ⲟⲩⲁ ⲟⲩⲁ / (*IV* 84.8) ⲛⲛⲉⲩⲁⲛⲁⲅⲕⲁⲍⲉ ⲙⲙⲟⲟⲩ ⲉⲛⲏⲥⲧⲉⲩⲉ ⲥⲛⲁⲩ ⲥⲛⲁⲩ / (*ibid.* 103.6f.) ⲉⲩⲉⲓⲣⲉ ⲥⲛⲁⲩ ⲥⲛⲁⲩ ⲏ ⲩⲟⲙⲛⲧ ⲩⲟⲙⲛⲧ.

1.3.3.2 ' *∅-noun → ∅-noun* ' is bracketed and marked by ⲛ- as the *predicative complement* of forms of ⲉⲓⲣⲉ: (*Miss.* 279f., parall. *P* 130[5] 69 ro) ⲧⲍⲱⲛⲏ ⲉⲧⲟ ⲙⲡⲗⲁ6ⲉ ⲡⲗⲁ6ⲉ / (*A 1* 240) ⲁⲩⲁⲁⲩ ⲛⲩⲁⲩ ⲩⲁⲩ / (*III* 110.17) -ⲣ-ⲟⲩⲉⲓ ⲛⲥⲓⲩϥ ⲥⲓⲩϥ / (*IF* 85, apud *Dictionary* 378a) -ⲁⲁϥ ⲙⲡⲗⲁ6ⲉ ⲡⲗⲁ6ⲉ ⲏ ⲥⲓⲩⲃ ⲥⲓⲩⲃ (*IV* 172.10, *Mun.* 160, *P* 130[2] 99 ⲣ̅ⲭ̅ⲉ, *IF* 188 apud *Dictionary* 422b) ...ⲉϥⲟ ⲛ6ⲱⲧ2 6ⲱⲧ2.

1.3.3.3 *Adnominally*, we find ' *∅-noun → ∅-noun* ' (with restricted constituency) in -ⲙⲙⲓⲛⲉ ⲙⲓⲛⲉ (2ⲓⲁⲩⲁⲛ ⲁⲩⲁⲛ) (*Ch.* 183.43f., *Wess.* 9 127b 8f., *A 2* 116, *P* 130[4] 91 ⲣ̅ⲙ̅) with the sense of " each and every... ".

1.3.3.4 In this sense (" each and every... ", complexive/comprehensive universal plurality [107]) the iterated ' *determinator + noun* ' syntagm occurs in various syntactic statuses even with a definite determinator: (*A 1* 395) -2ⲱⲙ ⲉ2ⲣⲁⲓ ⲉⲭⲛⲑⲁⲓⲣⲉⲥⲓⲥ ⲑⲁⲓⲣⲉⲥⲓⲥ / (*ibid.* 155) -2ⲙⲡⲕⲁⲓⲣⲟⲥ ⲡⲕⲁⲓⲣⲟⲥ / (*III* 126.16) 6ⲓⲛⲉ... ⲙⲡ2ⲱⲃ ⲡ2ⲱⲃ / (*ibid.* 204.6f) ⲩⲁⲣⲉⲧⲥⲓⲟ ⲟⲛ ⲙⲡⲛⲟⲃⲉ ⲡⲛⲟⲃⲉ / (*A 2* 21) ⲛ4ⲣ-ⲡⲣⲱⲙⲉ ⲡⲣⲱⲙⲉ ⲁⲩⲱ ⲡⲥⲟⲛ ⲡⲥⲟⲛ ⲁⲩⲱ ⲧⲉⲥ2ⲓⲙⲉ ⲧⲉⲥ2ⲓⲙⲉ... / (*III* 110.8f.) ⲡⲟⲩⲁ ⲡⲟⲩⲁ ⲕⲁⲧⲁⲧⲉϥⲙⲓⲛⲉ / (*IV* 73.19f.) ⲡⲣⲱⲙⲉ ⲡⲣⲱⲙⲉ ⲉⲧ2ⲙⲡⲏⲓ... ⲁⲩⲱ ⲧⲟⲩⲉⲓ ⲧⲟⲩⲉⲓ... ⲉⲩⲉ2ⲱⲛ ⲉⲧⲟⲟⲧⲟⲩ...

1.3.3.4.1 The iterated lexeme is rarely found expanding (and bracketed by) a single determinator, meaning " assorted... " (plural only): (*A 1* 108) 2ⲉⲛ2ⲟⲉⲓⲧⲉ ⲏ 2ⲉⲛ2ⲃⲟⲟⲥ ⲏ 2ⲉⲛⲥⲗⲡⲉ ⲥⲗⲡⲉ / (*A 2* 26) 2ⲉⲛⲟⲩⲁ

---

[104] Also ⲩⲏⲙ ⲩⲏⲙ (*A 1* 101) ⲁϥⲱⲭⲛ ⲩⲏⲙ ⲩⲏⲙ, cf. ⲟⲩⲩⲏⲙ ⲟⲩⲩⲏⲙ (*A 1* 150), coordinated with ⲕⲁⲧⲁ2ⲟⲟⲩ 2ⲟⲟⲩ.

[105] Cf. (for Turkish and Modern Armenian) GODEL 1945:10f.: *acı acı gülüyordu* (" adverbe "), *yumurta çiğ çiğ yemek* (" prédicat indirect du sujet ou de l'objet ").

[106] GODEL 1945:11f., HOFMANN 1936:20ff.

[107] DAUMAS 1952:27f. (cf. STERN §273).

OYA " τινες, *aliqui* " / (*Ch.* 156.48f.) NIOYNOY OYNOY " those various hours " / (*A 1* 108) ΠΛϬΕ ΠΛϬΕ ΝΤΟΟΥ ΝΕ " a collection of assorted rags " (ΝΤΟΟΥ is the augens, §6.1.3).

1.3.4 ΤΕΝΟΥ (once ΝΤΕΝΟΥ, *A 1* 262, collated) occurs in several formal/functional manifestations, ranging from the fully temporal " now " through the " nynegocentric " [108] *hic-et-nunc*, through various contextual values of actuality to particle-like interclausal relator role accompanied by prosodic symptoms.

1.3.4.1 ΤΕΝΟΥ *adverbal, postadjunctive*, often clause-final: " now ", frequently in collocation with other time-indications: (*A 2* 53) ΕΡΕΙΟΥΔΑC ϢΟΟΠ ΤϢΝ ΤΕΝΟΥ / (*ibid.* 159) CϢΤΜ ϨϢϢϤ ΕΤΜΝΤϢΒΗΡ ΝΝΑ ΜΠΗΥΕ ΤΕΝΟΥ / (*III* 203.15f.) ΕΝΕΡΕΠΝΟΥΤΕ ΝΑϢΑΧΕ ΝΜΜΕ ϨΙΧΜΠΚΑϨ ΤΕΝΟΥ / (*ibid.* 219.4) (ΠΕΙϢΑΧΕ) ΑΙΕΙΜΕ ΕΡΟϤ ΤΕΝΟΥ ϨΝΤΕΙΡΟΜΠΕ ΤΑΙ — note the tense / (*IV* 1.23f.) ΕΝϢΑΝΡ-ΒΟΛ ΕΠΡϢΚϨ ΝΝΕΤΜΜΑΥ ϨΜΠΙΜΑ ΤΕΝΟΥ / (*ibid.* 98.25f.) +COOYN ΧΕ-ΕΙΡ-ΟΥ ΧΙΝΝϢΟΡΠ ΑΥϢ ΟΝ ΤΕΝΟΥ / (*P* 130² 40 ΡΑ) ΟΥΟΝ ΝΙΜ ΕΤΕΜΠΟΥΜΕΤΑΝΟΙ... ϨΜΠΕΙΜΑ ΤΕΝΟΥ — again, note the compatibility of the perfect with ΤΕΝΟΥ; also in (*P* 130⁴ 126 Μ) ΝΕΝΤΑΝ- ϢΡΠΧΟΟΥ ΤΕΝΟΥ " even now ". Additional exx.: *III* 182.19, 188.17f., 206.22, 208.17, 131.5f., 150.7, *IV* 6.17f., 1.24, *Ch.* 82.12ff., etc. etc.

1.3.4.1.1 Postadjunctively, we often find ΤΕΝΟΥ in idiomatic collocation (coordinated or disjoined) with other temporal modifiers: (*A 1* 287) ϨΜΠΕΟΥΟΕΙϢ ΕΤΜΜΑΥ Η ΝΤΟϤ ΤΕΝΟΥ / (*IV* 36.2, 98.26, *A 2* 107 etc.) ΧΙΝΝϢΟΡΠ ΑΥϢ ΟΝ ΤΕΝΟΥ / (*IV* 197.9) ΤΕΝΟΥ ΑΥϢ ΝΟΥΟΕΙϢ ΝΙΜ / (*ibid.* 206.22) ΤΕΝΟΥ Η ΝΤΟϤ ΜΠΕΟΥΟΕΙϢ ΕΤΜΜΑΥ — note the inverse order on line 28 / (*A 1* 293) ΤΕΝΟΥ ΑΥϢ ϢΑΕΝΕϨ / (*III* 194.19f.) ΕΙΤΕ ϨΙΧΜΠΚΑϨ ΤΕΝΟΥ ΕΙΤΕ ϨΜΠΕϨΟΟΥ ΜΠϨΑΠ / (*P* 130⁴ 118 ΚΓ) ΝΑΡΧΑΙΟC ΑΥϢ ΟΝ ΤΕΝΟΥ.

1.3.4.2 ΤΕΝΟΥ *colon-enclitic* [109] (— ΤΕΝΟΥ —, -ϬΕ/ΟΝ ΤΕΝΟΥ —): " now then ", " in our time and place ", " in the case under discussion, in this instance ", " at this point in the argument ", " following/in view of what has been said ". Here the shift from clause-segment modification through adclausal reference to *contextual interclausal linkage* [110] is most evident: ΤΕΝΟΥ approaches here the role of a *superordinating particle*, with a corresponding difference in prosodic status, inferable from the placement: (*A 1* 57) ΜΗ ΝΤϢΤΝ ΤΕΝΟΥ ΝΕΤΜΕ ΝΝΕΤϨΙΤΟΥϢΝ / (*A 2* 65) ΝϴΕ ΤΕΝΟΥ ΕΤΕΡΕΤΠΑΡϴΕΝΟC ϨΝΟΥΜΕ... ϢΛΗΛ (vs. the bride in Song of Songs) / (*ibid.* 298) ΝΑϢ ΝϨΕ ΤΕΝΟΥ ΚΑΤΑΝΙϢΑΧΕ ΝCΕΝΑΝΟΙ ΑΝ / (*A 1* 335) ΕΤΒΕΟΥ ΤΕΝΟΥ ΠΕΥ- ϢΜϢΕ CϨ²ΟΥΟΡΤ ΑΝ / (*ibid.* 297) ΝϴΕ ϨϢϢΝ ΟΝ ΤΕΝΟΥ ΕΤΝΡ-ΝΟΒΕ / (*III* 144.26) ΟΥΚΟΥΝ ΝΑΙ ΤΕΝΟΥ ΕΤΜΜΑΥ ΝΕΤΝΑΧΟΟC ΧΕ- / (*Ch.* 171.30ff.) ΟΥ ϬΕ ΤΕΝΟΥ ΠΕ- / (*IV* 183.7) ΕΝΜΕΕΥΕ ΕΟΥ ϬΕ ΤΕΝΟΥ. Striking here is the frequent occurrence after ΝϴΕ-/ΚΑΤΑϴΕ- (also *A 2* 191, *Ench.* 85a, 87b, 92-3, *III* 18.27f., *Wess.* 9 148c 9f. etc.) and, in intercolary placement (§6.0.3), after ΤΑΙ ΤΕ ϴΕ [111] (*III* 142.16, 167.13,21); also after the antecedent in a relative construction [112] (*III* 205.22f. ΠΕΙΒΙΟC ΤΕΝΟΥ ΕΤΕΝϨΗΤϤ, also *IV* 121.26 / *III* 206.7 ΠΙΤϢϢ ΤΕΝΟΥ ΕΝΤΑϤΝΤΕ ΕϨΟΥΝ ΕΡΟϤ / *IV* 111.14 ΤΑΙ ΤΕΝΟΥ ΕΤϢΟΟΠ ΜΠΜΑ ΜΠΡΟ), after the predicate in a Nominal Sentence [113] (*A 2* 306 ΟΥ ΕΡΟΙ ΤΕΝΟΥ ΠΕ- / *IV* 20.10 ΟΥ ΤΕΝΟΥ ΤΕ ΤΕΧΡΕΙΑ / *III* 170.9 ΠΕΤΕϢϢΕ ΟΝ ΤΕΝΟΥ ΠΕ), and following the focus in focalization patterns (" Cleft Sentences ", see Ch. 2): (*A 2* 451, not Sh.) ΠΑΙ ΤΕΝΟΥ ΠΕΤϤΟΥϢΝϨ ΜΜΟϤ ΕΒΟΛ / (*Wess.* 9 121b 16ff.) ΝΑϢ ϬΕ ΝϨΕ ΤΕΝΟΥ ΕΤΕΤΝΚϢΛΑΥΕ. In all these cases it is the prosodic contour of the clause that motivates the placement of ΤΕΝΟΥ, and a full temporal value is not rarely found here.

---

[108] *Vs.* " allocentric ": Klum 1961:86ff., 223ff.
[109] See §6.0.3.
[110] See Klum 1961:248 n. 1 and 248ff.; Greenbaum 1969:55f. (" *transitional* " vs. temporal conjuncts).
[111] Cf. Polotsky 1961:§12.
[112] Polotsky 1961:§§12, 20.
[113] Polotsky 1961:§§8 (p. 308 = *CP* 412), 18.

1.3.4.3 ⲦⲈⲚⲞⲨ *initial*, an *adclausal premodifier*: ⲦⲈⲚⲞⲨ ⲆⲈ —, ⲀⲖⲖⲀ ⲦⲈⲚⲞⲨ — is temporal, often opposed to another foregoing temporal modifier: *Ch.* 31.27ff. (*vs.* Ⲛ(ⲞⲨ)ⲞⲨⲞⲈⲒⱲ), sim. *IV* 185.2f., 13f., *Ch.* 143.13ff. (*vs.* ⲌⲀⲐⲎ ⲘⲠⲞⲞⲨ, so too in 150.37ff., *A 2* 86, *P* 130² 104 vo), *Ch.* 204.19ff. (*vs.* ⱲⲞⲢⲠ ⲘⲈⲚ-), *IV* 105.9 (*vs.* ⲌⲀⲐⲎ ⲘⲠⲀⲦⲚ-). ⲦⲈⲚⲞⲨ ⳠⲈ- is relatively rare: " now then ", " at this stage of the argument ": *III* 77.4 ⲦⲈⲚⲞⲨ ⳠⲈ ⲞⲨ ⲦⲈ ⲦⲘⲚⲦⲀⲤⲈⲂⲎⲤ, also *A 2* 159, 248. Note ⲈⲦⲒ ⲞⲚ ⲦⲈⲚⲞⲨ (*Ch.* 91.20f.) a calque of ἔτι καὶ νῦν?

1.3.4.4 ⲦⲈⲚⲞⲨ *adnominal* to situational nouns: Ⲡ(Ⲉ)ⲒⲘⲀ (*Ch.* 57.45ff., *A 2* 240, 314, 461, 462, *IV* 1.24), Ⲡ(Ⲉ)ⲒⲤⲎⲨ, ⲚⲒⲌⲞⲞⲨ (*A 1* 463, *A 2* 87, *III* 145-6, *P* 130¹ 126 ⲢⲘⲀ, 130⁴ 49 ro), ⲠⲈⲒ-/ⲚⲈⲒⲞⲨⲞⲈⲒⱲ (*III* 106.8f., 126.17,23, 180.19f.,24f., *A 2* 427), ⲠⲈⳞⱲⲚⲌ (*Rossi* 2/3 16), ⲦⲈⲚⲪⲨⲤⲒⲤ (*IV* 113.2).

1.3.4.5 ⲦⲈⲚⲞⲨ is occasionally found in noun-syntagm status (cf. §1.1.1.1) — in origin, of course, it goes back to ⲦⲈ-determinated ⲞⲨⲚⲞⲨ, when it was a case of the " zero-marked noun as modifier " (§1.3.2): ⲐⲒⲚⲦⲈⲚⲞⲨ (*P* 130⁴ 50 ⲤⲔ), ⱲⲀⲌⲞⲨⲚ ⲈⲦⲈⲚⲞⲨ (*P* 130⁵ 105 ⲪⲠⲌ).

1.3.5.1.1 ⲚⲀⲘⲈ " truly ", " really " (cf. ⲀⲖⲎⲐⲰⲤ, §1.3.11.1.2), occurs *postadjunctively, adverbally*: (*A 2* 501) ⲬⲈ-ⲚⲚⲈⳞⲠⱲⲤ ⲚⲀⲘⲈ ⲈⲂⲞⲖ ⲌⲘⲠⲚⲞⲨⲦⲈ / (*A 1* 171) ⲀⲨⲤⲰⲞⲨⲌ ⲄⲀⲢ ⲚⲀⲘⲈ ⲈⳬⲘⲠⳢⲞⲈⲒⲤ / (*A 1* 213) ⲚⲈⲦⲞⲨⲞⲚⲌ ⲈⲂⲞⲖ ⲚⲀⲘⲈ ⲬⲈ-ⲌⲈⲚⲘⲀⲢⲦⲨⲢⲞⲤ ⲚⲈ / (*IV* 159.8) ⲈⲦⲢⲈⳞⲌⲀⲤⲦⳞ ⲚⲀⲘⲈ ⲈⲦⲂⲈⲠⲚⲞⲨⲦⲈ / (*Ch.* 68.6ff.) ⲀⲚⲞⲚ ⲦⲚⲤⲞⲞⲨⲚ ⲀⲚ ⲈⲖⲀⲀⲨ — ⲦⲚⲤⲞⲞⲨⲚ ⲀⲚ ⲚⲀⲘⲈ / (*Ench.* 80a and often in " Vita Monachorum " passages) — ⲈⲦⳲⱲⲚⲈ ⲚⲀⲘⲈ. More exx.: *III* 165.20, 170.21, *IV* 57.17f., 156.24, *Ch.* 62.11ff., etc.

1.3.5.1.2 As *adclausal/adverbal*, ⲚⲀⲘⲈ may occupy the colon-second position (or share it); this may be due to the prosodic contour of the construction: (*A 2* 371) ⲠⲈⲔⲚⲞⲨⲦⲈ ⲚⲀⲘⲈ ⲈⲦⲈⲞⲨⲚⲞⲨⲦⲈ ⲀⲚ ⲠⲈ / (*RE 11* 16a 17) ⲌⲈⲚⲈⲂⲒⲎⲚ ⲚⲀⲘⲈ ⲚⲈ ⲚⲈⲦⲘⲘⲀⲨ cf. *RE 10* 162b 16 ⲌⲈⲚⲈⲂⲒⲎⲚ ⲀⲖⲎⲐⲞⲤ (sic) ⲚⲈ and §1.1.2.3 / (*IV* 32.2f.) ⲚⲀⲒ ⲚⲀⲘⲈ ⲚⲦⲀⲨⱲⲰⲠⲈ (Sec. Perfect) ⲚⲤⲒⲞⲨⲢ ⲈⲦⲂⲈⲦⲘⲚⲦⲈⲢⲞ ⲘⲠⲚⲞⲨⲦⲈ / (*III* 173.26) ⲌⲀⲘⲞⲒ ⲞⲚ ⲚⲀⲘⲈ ⲈⲚⲈⲨⲚⲀ+ⲖⲞⲄⲞⲤ ⲌⲀⲢⲞⲞⲨ / (*Wess.* 9 156c 7 ff.) ⲬⲈⲔⲀⲤ ⲚⲀⲘⲈ ⲈⳞⲈⲤⲘⲞⲨ ⲈⲢⱲⲦⲚ ⲌⲚⲤⲘⲞⲨ ⲚⲒⲘ. More exx.: *Ench.* 82a, *Wess.* 9 144c 4f., *Ch.* 142.49f., 155.33ff., *Or.* 157.3, 165.42f., *A 2* 27, etc.

1.3.5.1.3 ⲚⲀⲘⲈ *initial*, a *premodifier*: (*A 1* 72) ⲚⲀⲘⲈ +ⲘⲈⲈⲨⲈ ⲬⲈ-. Here I include cases of ⲀⲨⱲ ⲚⲀⲘⲈ —: (*A 2* 332) ⲀⲨⱲ ⲞⲚ ⲚⲀⲘⲈ ⲠⲈⳞⲎⲒ ⲠⲈ ⲦⲈⲔⲔⲖⲎⲤⲒⲀ / (*III* 71.17f.) ⲀⲨⱲ ⲚⲀⲘⲈ ⲌⲚⲀⲀⲨ ⲚⲒⲘ ⲘⲠⲞⲨⱲⱲⲦ... / (ibid. 191.22) ⲦⲈⲚⲀⲨ ⲈⲢⲞⲞⲨ ⲀⲨⱲ ⲚⲀⲘⲈ ⲦⲈⲤⲞⲞⲨⲚ ⲀⲚ ⲘⲘⲞⲞⲨ / (*Ch.* 77.23ff.) ⲀⲨⱲ ⲚⲀⲘⲈ ⲚⲈⲚⲚⲀⲈⲒⲘⲈⲠⲈ — or ⲀⲖⲖⲀ ⲚⲀⲘⲈ —: (*III* 217.2f.) ⲀⲖⲖⲀ ⲚⲀⲘⲈ ⳞⲚⲀⲢⲌⲞⲨⲈⱲⱲⲠⲈ ⲚⲦⲞⳞ ⲈⳞⲞⲨⲀⲀⲂ... / (*III* 131.15f. Cod. B, parall. *A 2* 196) ⲀⲖⲖⲀ ⲚⲀⲘⲈ ⲠⲈ ⲚⲈⳞⲞⲨⱲⱲ ⲠⲈ ⲈⲦⲢⲈⲨⲔⲰ ⲚⲀⲨ ⲈⲂⲞⲖ, see §6.0.3.3 for the " foreshadowed " ⲠⲈ; also ⲀⲢⲎⲨ ⲚⲀⲘⲈ- (*III* 140.30f.), ⲔⲀⲒⲄⲀⲢ ⲚⲀⲘⲈ- (*III* 146.23), ⲚⲀⲘⲈ before a conditional complex (*III* 70.17f.) [114].

1.3.5.1.4 ⲚⲀⲘⲈ *postadjunctive, adnominal* — very common, occurring with most determinators: " true ", " real ", " veritable ", " genuine ": ⲠⲒⲤⲦⲞⲤ ⲚⲀⲘⲈ (*III* 15.16, 137.14, *IV* 21.5, *A 1* 14, etc. etc.) / (*A 2* 96) ⲞⲨⱲⲚⲈ ⲚⲀⲘⲈ / (ibid. 55, *Ch.* 34.53ff.) ⲚⲢⲘⲚⲚⲞⲨⲦⲈ ⲚⲀⲘⲈ / (*III* 223.16) ⲚⲈⲨⲤⲈⲂⲎⲤ ⲚⲀⲘⲈ / (*A 2* 402, 407, etc.) ⲚⲈⳬⲢⲈⲒⲤⲦⲒⲀⲚⲞⲤ ⲚⲀⲘⲈ / (*A 2* 60) ⲠⲀⲰⲢⲞⲚ ⲚⲀⲘⲈ / (*IV* 80.23) ⲌⲈⲚⲈⲒⲞⲦⲈ ⲚⲀⲘⲈ / (*Ch.* 168.44ff.) ⲞⲨⲘⲚⲦⳬⲀⳢⲈ ⲈⲠⲚⲞⲨⲦⲈ ⲚⲀⲘⲈ — ⲚⲀⲘⲈ expands here the whole ' *noun + modifier* ' group / (*IV* 129.11) ⲠⲈⲚⲈⲒⱲⲦ ⲀⲨⱲ ⲦⲈⲚⲘⲀⲀⲨ ⲚⲀⲘⲈ / (*Ch.* 140.20) ⲚⲞⳞ ⲚⲀⲘⲈ / (*III* 39.26) ⲚⲤⲰⲦⲠ ⲚⲀⲘⲈ ⲘⲠⲚⲞⲨⲦⲈ — note the position

---

[114] Consider (*Or.* 159-160) ⲀⲨⱲ ⲈⲞⲨⲈⲒ ⲚⲀⲘⲈ ⲦⲈ " she really is one " (i.e. an adulteress), varying with ⲀⲨⱲ ⲚⲀⲘⲈ ⲈⲞⲨⲈⲒ ⲦⲈ. Both are clear cases of the modifier ⲀⲨⱲ, translatable here as " and what is more ", " and moreover " (§1.3.10).

of ΝΑΜΕ / (*Ch.* 93.19ff.) ΝΕϥϢΒΕΕΡ ΝΑΜΕ ᴢΜΠΕⲬⲤ — note placement. Examples of ' *noun* - ΝΑΜΕ - *relative* ' are often ambiguous, but occasionally adnominal beyond doubt, with the relative adding further characterization: (*Ch.* 9.30f.) ΤϹΗϥΕ ΝΑΜΕ ΕΤ6ΟⲬ6Ⲝ / (*ibid.* 191.28ff.) ΠΡΕϥΡ-ΝΟΒΕ ΝΑΜΕ ΕΤΡΟΟΥΤ, ΠΑϹΕΒΗϹ ΝΑΜΕ ΝΤΑΥΕΙΑ-ΤΟΟΤΟΥ ΝϹⲰϥ (contrast with the ambiguous *Or.* 160.34ff. ΝΑΘΗΤ ΝΑΜΕ ΕΤΡ-6ΡⲰᴢ ΜΠΟΕΙΚ). Very occasionally, the second-position placement in the group is motivated, ΝΑΜΕ modifying the whole complex: (*IV* 115.15) ΝΑΙ ΝΑΜΕ ΝΤΕΙΜΙΝΕ. Note ΑᴢΕ ΝΑΜΕ " yes, indeed ": (*A 2* 106) ᴢⲰϹ ΑᴢΕ ΝΑΜΕ ΑΡΗΥ ΝΤΟϥ " yes, indeed, perhaps even... " / (*ibid.* 308) ΚΑΝ ΑᴢΕ ΝΑΜΕ ΕΥϢΑΝ-.

1.3.5.2 ᴢΝΟΥΜΕ is rather less common [115]:

1.3.5.2.1 *Postadjunctive, adverbal*: (*Ryl.* 67 ΤϥΘ) ΟΥΝΡⲰΜΕ ΕΡΕΤΕΚΜΕ ΝᴢΗΤΟΥ ᴢΝΟΥΜΕ / (*A 2* 109) ΝΕΤΡΟΕΙϹ ΕΡⲰΤΝ ᴢΝΟΥΜΕ / (*IV* 3.26) ϹΕ+-ΕΟΟΥ ΝΑΥ ᴢΝΟΥΜΕ / (*Ch.* 26.50ff.) ΠΕϹΟΥⲰϢ ΕΤϹΜΕ ΜΜΟΟΥ ΝᴢΗΤϥ ᴢΝΟΥΜΕ / (*III* 108.13f.) ΕΝΕΝΤΑΝΡ-ΠΕΚΟΥⲰϢ ᴢΝΟΥΜΕ / (*III* 28.6) ΕΥΡΑΝΑϥ ΜΠΝΟΥΤΕ ᴢΝΟΥΜΕ. Additional exx.: *Ch.* 21.6ff., 112.21ff., *III* 185.12f., *IV* 108.12f., *A 2* 416, 472, etc. More unusually, we find the expression postadjunctively modifying a Nominal Sentence: (*III* 171.9f.) ᴢΕΝΠΙϹΤΟϹ ΑΝ ΝΕ ΟΥΤΕ ᴢΕΝΡΕϥ+- ϹΒⲰ ΑΝ ΝΕ ᴢΝΟΥΜΕ. In (*A 1* 250) ΑΥⲬⲰΚ ΕΒΟΛ ᴢΝΟΥΜΕ ΑⲬΝΤϢΑΜ we may have ᴢΝΟΥΜΕ modifying a modifier: " truly without ", and its placement secondary (conditioned).

1.3.5.2.2 Initially, as a premodifier, ᴢΝΟΥΜΕ is extremely rare, if to be found at all. The one possible instance I have noted (*III* 120.24f., 27ff.) is a nice case of the focalized modifier, preceding a complex topic made up of its own *topic* (theme) + *comment* (rheme) — see Ch. 2: ΝΕΤⲬⲰ ΜΜΟϹ ⲬΕ-ΝΤΑΥⲬΟΟΥ ΤΗΡΟΥ ΕΡΟΝ, ΕΒΟΛ ⲬΕ-ᴢΝΟΥΜΕ ΝΤΑΥⲬΟΟΥ ΕΤΒΕΝΕΤΜΜΑΥ.

1.3.5.2.3 The lower incidence of ᴢΝΟΥΜΕ compared with ΝΑΜΕ is especially striking in the adnominal status, in which relatively few examples have come to light (almost all from *Ch.*): (*Ch.* 53.54f., 70.38f.) ⲬΡΕΙϹΤΙΑΝΟϹ (ΝΙΜ) ᴢΝΟΥΜΕ / (*ibid.* 25.27f.) ΠΑΠΕⲬⲤ ᴢΝΟΥΜΕ / (*ibid.* 79.40f.) ΝϢΗΡΕ ΜΠΝΟΥΤΕ ᴢΝΟΥΜΕ / (*Wess. 9* 147c 1 ff.) ΝϹΟΦΟϹ ΑΥⲰ ΜΠΙϹΤΟϹ ᴢΝΟΥΜΕ — all in commendatory collocations.

1.3.6 ΕΝΕᴢ " ever " is synchronically [116] unanalyzable, sharing the syntactic privileges of a noun:

1.3.6.1 *Adverbally-postadjunctively* (compatible with the perfect and future, less usually aorist — " the two faces of eternity ") it rarely occurs marked by Ν-: (*A 1* 295) ΜΗ Α6ΕΛΑΑΥ ΜΠΡΟΦΗΤΗϹ ΤⲰΟΥΝ ΝΕΝΕᴢ ᴢΜΠῙΗ̄Λ̄, but usually without any marking for modifier status (§1.3.2.): (*Ch.* 32.36ff.) ΜΠΚΑ- ᴢΕΡΑΤΚ ᴢΜΜΕ ΕΝΕᴢ, ΜΠΕΤΑΙΟ ΟΝ ϢⲰΠΕ ΝΑΚ ΕΝΕᴢ / (*Gol. Jelanskaja* 1b) ΜΗ ϢΑΡΕΠΝΟΥΤΕ ϢⲰΠΕ ΜΝΠΟΝΗΡΟϹ Ν- ΡⲰΜΕ ΕΝΕᴢ Η ΟΥΝ6ΟΜ ΕΝΕᴢ ΝΟΥΡⲰΜΕ ΝΟΥϢΤ ΜΠΟΝΗΡΟϹ ΕⲬΙ-ΟΥΝΟ6 ΜΜΗΝϢΕ Ν6ΟΝϹ / (*P* 130⁵ 17 Ρᴢ) ΜΗ ΚΝΑϢ- ⲬΟΟϹ ΡⲰ ΕΝΕᴢ ⲬΕ- / (*P* 130² 24 ΦΝΑ-Ε) ΑΡΕⲬΕΡΕ-ᴢΗΒϹ ΔΕ ΟΝ ΕΝΕᴢ... ΑΡΕΤϹΑΒΕ-ΡⲰΜΕ ΔΕ ΟΝ ΕΝΕᴢ ΕΠ2Οϥ... / (*P* 130⁴ 105 ΡΚΕ) ΝΤΑΠΡΗ ΜΝΠΟΟᴢ 6Ⲱ ΝΑϢ Ν2ΟΟΥ ΕΝΕᴢ ΝΟΥΕϢΝΕΙ Ε2ΡΑΙ / (*Wess. 9* 120b 3ff.) ΜΠΕΠϹΑΤΑΝΑϹ ΒⲰΚ Ε2ΟΥΝ ΕΡⲰΜΕ ΕΝΕᴢ / (*III* 153.10f.) ΜΠΚΝΑΥ ΕΡΟϥ ΕΝΕᴢ / (*IV* 17.11f.) ΝϹΕΝΑⲬΙ-ϢΙΠΕ ΑΝ ΕΝΕᴢ. As in other languages (notably old and modern Indo-European ones), ΕΝΕᴢ, which frequently features in interrogative sentences predicating ΝΙΜ " who? ", fluctuates here between the post-verbal and post-pronominal (or adpronominal: ΝΙΜ ΕΝΕᴢ " whoever? ") placements. From (*A 2* 518) ΝΤΑΝΙΜ ΕΙΜΕ ΕΝΕᴢ ΝΝΕΙΡΟΜΠΕ ΤΗΡΟΥ... ⲬΕ- / (*ibid.* 153) ΝΤΑΝΙΜ ΝΡⲰΜΕ Ρ-ΔΙΚΑΙΟϹ ΕΝΕᴢ, through (*A 2* 463) ΝΤΑΝϹⲰΤΜ ᴢΙΤΝΝΙΜ ΕΝΕᴢ ⲬΕ- / (*A 1* 77) ΝΤΑΙⲬΟΟϹ ΕΝΙΜ ΕΝΕᴢ ⲬΕ-, to (*A 2* 151) ΝΤΑΝΙΜ ΕΝΕᴢ... Ϲ2ΑΙ / (*A 2* 18) ΝΤΑΝΙΜ ΝϢϹ ΕΝΕᴢ ΚΑΝΕϹΟΟΥ 2ΜΠΟ2Ε / (*RE 10* 162a 5) ΝΙΜ ΕΝΕᴢ ΠΕΝΤΑϥΕΙΡΕ ΝΑΚ ΝϢΟΡΠ... / (*Young* ΙΓ) ΝΙΜ 6Ε 2ⲰϢϥ ΕΝΕᴢ ΠΕΤΝΑΥΤΡΠ-ΛΑΑΥ...

---

[115] Postadjunctive, adverbal ᴢΝΟΥΜΝΤΜΕ is a near-synonym (*III* 158.28, *Ench.* 80b).
[116] See ČERNÝ 1976:36.

1.3.6.2 *Initially*, we find only ϫⲓⲛⲉⲛⲉ2, premodifying the *negative perfect* (*A 2* 241, 341, *III* 216) [117].

1.3.7 ⲉⲡ-*marked modifiers* are mostly analyzable as ⲉ + *def. article* + *noun*, yet with a remarkably high degree of semasiological fusion:

1.3.7.1 ⲉⲡ2ⲁⲉ " finally ", initial (premodifier) only, usually ⲉⲡ2ⲁⲉ ⲇⲉ — (contextually marked): (*III* 103.20) ...ⲉⲡ2ⲁⲉ ⲇⲉ ⲁⲩⲙⲟⲟⲩⲧⲟⲩ / (*A 1* 260) (on children's playful constructions) ...ⲉⲡ2ⲁⲉ ⲇⲉ ⱳⲁⲩⲧⲁⲕⲟⲟⲩ ⲧⲏⲣⲟⲩ / (*IV* 8.12) ⲉⲡ2ⲁⲉ ⲇⲉ ⲁⲩ2ⲓⲧⲟⲟⲧⲟⲩ ⲉⲡⲣⲣⲟ ⲙⲡⲧⲏⲣ4. Also *A 2* 166, *P* 131⁴ 151 ⲙ.

1.3.7.2 ⲉⲡⲧⲏⲣ4 is the native equivalent (showing also formal similarity) of 2ⲟⲗⲱⲥ (§1.3.11.1.1):

1.3.7.2.1 Postadjunctively, *adverbally* (ⲉⲡⲧⲏⲣ4 is only postadjunctive): " at all ", " in any way ": (*IV* 70.23) ⲛⲛⲉⲩⲕⲁⲁⲩ ⲉⲡⲧⲏⲣ4 ⲉⲧⲣⲉⲩⲉⲓⲣⲉ 2ⲓⲛⲁⲓ 2ⲣⲁⲓ ⲛ2ⲏⲧⲛ / (*ibid.* 72.15) ⲛⲛⲉⲣⱳⲙⲉ 2ⲣⲁⲓ ⲛ2ⲏⲧⲛ ⱳⱳ 2ⲓⱳⲟⲩ ⲉⲡⲧⲏⲣ4 / (*Ch.* 187-8) ⲛⲉⲅⲣⲁⲫⲏ ⲛⲁ+-2ⲏⲩ ⲙⲙⲟⲛ ⲁⲛ ⲉⲡⲧⲏⲣ4 / (*III* 132.3f.) ...ⲉⲧⲙⲧⲣⲉⲩⲃⲱⲕ ⲉ2ⲟⲩⲛ ⲉⲣⲟ4 ⲉⲡⲧⲏⲣ4 (scil. ⲉⲡⲕⲁ2 ⲉⲛⲧⲁ4ⲉⲣⲏⲧ ⲙⲙⲟ4 ⲛⲁⲩ) / (*P* 130⁵ 36 vo) ⲡⲕⲁⲕⲉ ⲁ4ⲁⲛⲁⲭⲱⲣⲉⲓ ⲛⲁ4 ⲉⲃⲟⲗ ⲉⲡⲧⲏⲣ4. In two instances, we may have ⲡⲧⲏⲣ4 for ⲉⲡⲧⲏⲣ4 (zeroing ⲉ-?: *A 2* 310, 311, uncollated).

1.3.7.2.2 *Adnominally*: " What(so)ever ", expanding only ⲗⲁⲁⲩ, usually 6ⲉⲗⲁⲁⲩ — note the placement: (*A 2* 313-314) 6ⲉⲗⲁⲁⲩ ⲛ2ⲛⲟ ⲉⲡⲧⲏⲣ4 ⲛⲧⲉⲛⲥⲱⲙⲁ... 6ⲉⲗⲁⲁⲩ ⲛⲣⱳⲙⲉ ⲉⲡⲧⲏⲣ4 ⲛⲭⲣⲉⲓⲥⲧⲓⲁⲛⲟⲥ / (*ibid.* 258-9) ⲗⲁⲁⲩ ⲙⲙⲉⲗⲟⲥ ⲉⲡⲧⲏⲣ4 / (*IV* 59.13) 6ⲉ ⲗⲁⲁⲩ ⲛⲣⲁⲛ ⲛⲧⲉⲓ2ⲉ ⲉⲡⲧⲏⲣ4 / (*P* 130¹ 15 ro) ⲗⲁⲁⲩ ⲛⲣⱳⲙⲉ 2ⲟⲗⲱⲥ... ⲗⲁⲁⲩ ⲛⲛⲕⲁ ⲉⲡⲧⲡⲣ4... ⲗⲁⲁⲩ ⲛ2ⲟⲟⲩ ⲉⲡⲧⲏⲣ4. Also *III* 90.1, *IV* 58.14f., 112.1f., *A 2* 316.

1.3.7.3.1 ⲉⲡϫⲓⲛϫⲏ " in vain, uselessly, with no effect, for no reason, without provocation " [118]. Postadjunctive, *adverbal*: (*III* 124.12) ...ⲁⲩⲱ ⲁⲛⲟⲕ ⲛⲧⲁⱳⱳⲡⲉ ⲉⲓⲙⲟⲥⲧⲉ ⲙⲡⲉⲧ2ⲓⲧⲟⲩⱳⲓ ⲉⲡϫⲓⲛϫⲏ (sim. *ibid.* 131.4, 139.15,27) / (*ibid.* 123.8) ⲛⲁⱳ 6ⲉ ⲛ2ⲉ ⲉⲓⲛⲁϫⲓ-ⲛⲁⲓ ⲉⲧⲙⲙⲁⲩ ⲛ6ⲟⲛⲥ ⲏ ⲛⲧⲁ0ⲙⲕⲟⲟⲩ ⲉⲡϫⲓⲛϫⲏ / (*Ch.* 96.5ff.) ...ⲉⲥⲟⲣⲙⲉⲥ ⲉⲡϫⲓⲛϫⲏ / (*P* 131⁶ 30 ⲣⲙⲉ) ⲛ2ⲓⲥⲉ ⲉⲧⲩⱳⲟⲟⲡ ⲉⲡϫⲓⲛϫⲏ... ⲡⲉⲧⲧⲁⲓⲟ ⲙⲙⲟ4 ⲁⲛ ⲉⲡϫⲓⲛϫⲏ. Also *III* 30.22f., 123.8, *IV* 81.11f., 94.15f., 106.12, 116.22f., *P* 131⁵ 19 ro, 130¹ 139 ⲧⲙⲥ (+-ⲧⱳⲛ ⲉⲡϫⲓⲛϫⲏ " without provocation "). ⲉⲡϫⲓⲛϫⲏ is often focalized by a Second Tense: (*A 1* 446) ⲉⲣⲉⲡⲟⲩ2ⲓⲥⲉ ⲙⲛⲡⱳⲟⲩ ⱳⲟⲟⲡ ⲉⲡϫⲓⲛϫⲏ / (*A 2* 415) ⲛⲧⲁⲓⱳⲡ-2ⲓⲥⲉ ⲉⲡϫⲓⲛϫⲏ ⲁⲩⲱ ⲛⲧⲁⲓⲕⲁ-2ⲧⲏⲓ ⲉⲡϫⲓⲛϫⲏ ⲁⲩⲱ ⲛⲧⲁⲓ4ⲓ ⲉ2ⲣⲁⲓ 2ⲁⲧⲉⲓⲁⱳⲏ ⲙⲙⲟⲕ2ⲥ ⲉⲡϫⲓⲛϫⲏ / (*Berl.* 1613 1 ⲕ0) ⲉⲣⲉⲡⲉⲡⲣⲟⲫⲏⲧⲏⲥ ⱳⲁϫⲉ ⲉⲡϫⲓⲛϫⲏ. *Adnominally*, ⲉⲡϫⲓⲛϫⲏ is less usual: (*IV* 94.15f.) 2ⲉⲛ2ⲓⲥⲉ ⲉⲡϫⲓⲛϫⲏ / (*A 1* 298) 2ⲉⲛⲁⲛⲁⱳ ⲉⲡϫⲓⲛϫⲏ. *Premodifier*: ⲉⲡϫⲓⲛϫⲏ (ⲁⲛ) ⲁ4- *A 2* 131, *Ch.* 139. 19f., *III* 55.14f. For predicative ⲉⲡϫⲓⲛϫⲏ see §1.2.1.2.

1.3.7.3.2 ⲛϫⲓⲛϫⲏ " without remuneration, gratis ", (rarely) " for no reason " is mostly opposed to ⲉⲡϫⲓⲛϫⲏ: (*Ch.* 92.25ff.) ⲛⲉⲧⲉⲣⲉⲛⲣⱳⲙⲉ ⲣ-2ⲱⲃ ⲛⲁⲩ ⲛϫⲓⲛϫⲏ, sim. (ⲣ-2ⲱⲃ) *Berl.* 1611 5 ⲗⲥ, *P* 130³ 113 vo / (*P* 131⁷ 25 ro) 4ⲁ2ⲉⲣⲁⲧ4 ⲛ6ⲓⲡⲥⲁⲉⲓⲛ 2ⲓⲣⲙⲡⲣⲟ ⲉ4ⱳⲓⲛⲉ ⲛⲥⲁ+ⲛⲁ2ⲣⲉ ⲛϫⲓⲛϫⲏ / (*IV* 160.17f.) ⲛϫⲓⲛϫⲏ *vs.* 2ⲁ-ⲡⲉⲩⲃⲉⲕⲉ / (*III* 83.7f.) ⲛϫⲓⲛϫⲏ opposed to 2ⲁ2ⲉⲛⲕⲟⲩⲓ ⲛⲧⲓⲙⲏ. Rarely, ⲛϫⲓⲛϫⲏ (neutral? consider *Ch.* 106.62ff.) seems synonymous with ⲉⲡϫⲓⲛϫⲏ (*A 1* 276) ⲛⲣⲉ46ⲛ-ⲁⲣⲉⲓⲕⲉ ⲉⲡⲛⲟⲩⲧⲉ ⲛϫⲓⲛϫⲏ. Both are apparently disjoined in (*Ench.* 89b) ⲛ0ⲉ ⲉⲛ[ⲧⲁⲛⲁⲁⲥ] ⲛϫⲓⲛϫⲏ [ⲁⲛⲟⲛ] 2ⱳⱳⲛ ⲏ [ⲉⲡϫⲓⲛ]ϫⲏ.

1.3.7.4 ⲉⲡⲉ2ⲟⲩⲟ " too much, in excess ", postadjunctive: (*P* 130⁴ 131 vo) ⲉⲣⱳⲁⲛⲡⲉⲧ2ⲉⲣ-ⲉⲣⱳⲧⲉ ⲉ4-ⲛⲉⲕⲓⲃⲉ ⲉⲡⲉ2ⲟⲩⲟ... / (*III* 133.20) 4ⲙⲟⲥⲧⲉ ⲙⲙⲟⲛ ⲉⲡⲉ2ⲟⲩⲟ / (*IV* 155.8) ⲛ4ⱳⲓⲛⲉ ⲁⲛ ⲉⲡⲉ2ⲟⲩⲟ / (*Wess. 9* 140c

---

[117] ⱳⲁⲉⲛⲉ2 occurs adnominally (§1.1.1), in this status, also marked by ⲛ- (§1.1.1.1).
[118] Cf. Gk. εἰκή; CHERIX 1979:100, *Dictionary* 747b (Crum does not indicate a difference between ⲉⲡϫⲓⲛϫⲏ and ⲛϫⲓⲛϫⲏ, except for the preponderance of δωρεάν as the equivalent of the latter). For the predicative ⲉⲡϫⲓⲛϫⲏ (ⲡⲉ) see §1.2.1.2.

9ff.) ...ⲠⲀⲎⲚ ⲬⲈⲔⲀⲤ ⲚⲚⲈⲚⲔⲀⲢⲰⲚ ⲈⲠⲈⲌⲞⲨⲞ. Adnominally, we find (*III* 200.22f.) ⲘⲘⲀⲒⲚⲞⲂⲈ ⲈⲠⲈⲌⲞⲨⲞ and perhaps (130⁵ 40 ⲘⲄ) ⲌⲈⲚⲬⲢⲒⲤⲦⲒⲀⲚⲞⲤ ⲌⲰⲞⲨ ⲚⲈ ⲈⲠⲈⲌⲞⲨⲞ — unless the last example is adclausal.

1.3.7.5 For ⲈⲠⲘⲀ, see §7.4.

1.3.7.6 ⲈⲠ + *infinitive*: ⲈⲠⲰⲚⲌ (*III* 218.5ff.), ⲈⲠⲞⲨⲰⲚⲌ ⲈⲂⲞⲀ (*Ch.* 114.53f.) ⲈⲠⲈⲰⲈⲠ-(sic)ⲌⲈⲚⲯⲨⲬⲎ ⲈⲢⲞⲴ (*Wess. 9* 117a 24ff.). Whether or not this is a free procedure — an open-ended (productive) paradigm — remains to be established by more evidence [119].

1.3.8 ⲌⲒⲞⲨⲤⲞⲠ " (all) together " reveals a remarkable distribution:

1.3.8.1 *Final*, modifying a coordination: ' X ⲀⲨⲰ/ⲘⲚ-Y ⲌⲒⲞⲨⲤⲞⲠ ': (*IV* 108.5f.) ⲚⲦⲞⲞⲨ ⲌⲰⲞⲨ ⲈⲨⲘⲘⲀⲨ ⲘⲚ ⲚⲈⲨⲈⲢⲎⲨ ⲌⲒⲞⲨⲤⲞⲠ / (*III* 13.13) (ⲦⲈⲔϬⲒⲚⲤⲌⲀⲒ) ⲰⲀⲠⲀⲈⲂⲒⲎⲚ ⲀⲨⲰ ⲚⲈⲚⲈⲂⲒⲎⲚ ⲌⲒⲞⲨⲤⲞⲠ / (*ibid.* 63.9f.) ⲌⲈⲚⲦⲰⲌ ⲈⲚⲀⲰⲰⲞⲨ ⲈⲘⲀⲦⲈ ⲘⲚ ⲌⲈⲚⲢⲞⲞⲨⲈ ⲌⲒⲞⲨⲤⲞⲠ ⲘⲚⲌⲈⲚⲔⲈⲚⲦⲎϬ ⲈⲨⲞⲰ / (*P* 131⁴ 157 vo) ⲌⲈⲚⲰⲀⲬⲈ ⲈⲢⲈⲚⲈⲦⲬⲰ ⲘⲘⲞⲞⲨ ⲘⲚⲚⲈⲦⲠⲒⲤⲦⲈⲨⲈ ⲚⲀⲨ ⲚⲀⲌⲈ ⲈⲌⲢⲀⲒ ⲈⲌⲈⲚⲌⲒⲈⲒⲦ ⲚⲔⲀⲔⲈ ⲌⲒⲞⲨⲤⲞⲠ.

1.3.8.2 *Ad(pro)nominal* (in fact *augential* — see Ch. 6, esp. §6.1), modifying a (usually plural) pronoun, often with (and following) ⲦⲎⲢ≠: (*P* 131⁴ 87 ⲢⲀⲀ) ⲀⲨⲰⲰ ⲈⲂⲞⲀ ⲌⲒⲞⲨⲤⲞⲠ / (*IV* 191.7f.) ⲈⲨⲰⲞⲞⲠ ⲦⲎⲢⲞⲨ ⲌⲒⲞⲨⲤⲞⲠ ⲌⲚⲦⲘⲚⲦⲈⲢⲞ ⲘⲠⲈⲬ̅Ⲥ̅ / (*A 2* 299) ⲈⲢⲈⲤⲞⲞⲨⲌ ⲈⲌⲞⲨⲚ ⲌⲒⲞⲨⲤⲞⲠ (addressed to the congregation), adverbal? Cf. (ⲤⲰⲞⲨⲌ ⲈⲌⲞⲨⲚ) *IV* 158.16, *A 2* 298 / (*A 2* 292) ...ⲈⲦⲢⲈⲠⲚⲞⲨⲦⲈ ⲬⲞⲞⲤ ⲚⲀⲨ ⲌⲒⲞⲨⲤⲞⲠ / (*IV* 89.2f.) ...ⲚⲤⲈⲦ ⲘⲘⲞⲞⲨ ⲚⲀⲨ ⲌⲒⲞⲨⲤⲞⲠ / (*P* 131⁶ 23 [ⲞⲐ]) ⲀⲚⲞⲚ ⲦⲎⲢⲚ ⲌⲒⲞⲨⲤⲞⲠ ⲘⲀⲢⲈⲚⲤⲈⲠⲤ-ⲠⲚⲞⲨⲦⲈ / (*P* 130⁵ 37 vo) ⲞⲨⲞⲚ ⲚⲒⲘ ⲌⲒⲞⲨⲤⲞⲠ ⲚⲦⲀⲨⲦⲀⲚⲌⲞⲨⲦⲞⲨ. Also *IV* 67.8, *A 1* 68, *P* 131⁴ 86 ⲢⲀ.

1.3.9 ⲦⲰⲚⲈ, (rarely) ⲦⲰⲚⲞⲨ "very (much)", "greatly" is always postadjunctively adverbal, and expands only the present tense: (*A 1* 58) ⲦⲚⲰⲀⲀⲦ ⲦⲰⲚⲈ ⲚⲦⲀⲔⲞⲴ, ⲦⲈⲀⲨⲠⲈⲒ ⲦⲰⲚⲈ / (*ibid.* 68) ⲦⲈⲦⲘⲀⲒⲎⲨ ⲦⲰⲚⲈ / (*A 2* 319) ⲦⲢ-ⲰⲠⲎⲢⲈ ⲘⲘⲰⲦⲚ ⲦⲰⲚⲈ / (*III* 25.6) ⲦⲚ ⲰⲠ-ⲌⲘⲞⲦ ⲦⲰⲚⲈ / (*ibid.* 117.17) ⲦⲈⲦⲚⲘⲞⲔⲘⲈⲔ ⲘⲘⲰⲦⲚ ⲦⲰⲚⲞⲨ / (*IV* 193.9) ⲀⲔⲦ-ⲈⲞⲞⲨ ⲘⲠⲚⲞⲨⲦⲈ ⲦⲰⲚⲈ ⲌⲘⲠⲈⲔⲤⲰⲘⲀ.

1.3.10 ⲀⲨⲰ " also ", " too ", " moreover ", " and indeed ", " furthermore " (cf. *adeo*) — a focusing additive conjunct. This I believe is its true nature, even as a coordinator, which is misrepresented when we take it "simply" as a coordinative conjunction [120]. The modifier status of ⲀⲨⲰ is made conspicuous by the grammatical asymetry of its flanking constructions (especially — a typical figure — *basic tense* + ⲀⲨⲰ + *circumstantial*, mostly Nom. Sentence and perfect) [121]: this is a significant normal phenomenon rather than a violation of coordination restrictions — indeed, this is not conjunctional coordination in its usual accepted sense [122]: (*A 1* 171) ⲦⲚⲀⲀⲢⲬⲈⲒ ϬⲈ ⲚⲬⲈ-ⲠⲈⲦⲰⲞⲞⲠ ⲀⲨⲰ ⲈⲚⲦⲞⲴ ⲞⲚ ⲠⲈⲦⲰⲞⲞⲠ / (*Ch.* 79.51ff.) ⲚⲀⲰ ⲚⲌⲈ ⲠⲈⲨⲞⲨⲰⲰ ⲀⲚ ⲠⲈ ⲠⲞⲨⲰⲰ ⲚⲚⲀⲀⲒⲘⲰⲚ, ⲀⲨⲰ ⲈⲠⲞⲨⲰⲰ ⲚⲚⲀⲀⲒⲘⲰⲚ ⲠⲈ ⲠⲈⲨⲞⲨⲰⲰ / (*IV* 24.2f.) ⲀⲨⲢ-ⲠⲀⲒⲀⲂⲞⲀⲞⲤ ⲚⲂⲀⲀⲈ, ⲀⲨⲰ ⲈⲞⲨⲂⲀⲀⲈ ⲢⲰ ⲠⲈ / (*ibid.* 75.20ff.) ...ⲦⲠⲞⲢⲚⲒⲀ ⲘⲚⲠⲬⲒⲞⲨⲈ ⲘⲚⲠϬⲞⲀ ⲘⲚⲌⲰⲂ ⲚⲒⲘ ⲈⲴⲌⲞⲞⲨ... ⲀⲨⲰ ⲈⲚⲀⲒ ⲚⲈⲦⲴⲚⲀⲈⲒ ⲈⲌⲞⲨⲚ ⲈⲦⲂⲎⲎⲦⲞⲨ ⲚϬⲒⲠⲬⲀⲬⲈ (*III* 125.7f.) ⲌⲈⲚⲂⲀⲀⲈ ⲚⲈ ⲈⲨⲤⲞⲢⲘ... ⲀⲨⲰ ⲈⲌⲈⲚⲦⲞϬⲈ

---

[119] Cf. the grammaticalized Bohairic ⲈⲠⲬⲒⲚ(ⲦⲈ)- (Stern §§470-2, Mallon–Malinine §§271, 273). In Sahidic, we may have a calque of the Greek εἰς/πρός + *infinitive* (Blass–Debrunner §402.2.5).

[120] Shisha-Halevy 1972:183f., 1975:474, 1976a:33; cf. Layton 1979:174(II).

[121] Cf. §7.1.2.2 for the conjunctive as another " pseudo-coordinative " verb form. Cf. in Bohairic *Acta Martyrum* (CSCO) II 205.12, 268.2, and compare the Late Egyptian ḥr (esp. ḥr jw-, with no circumstantial preceding: see Wente, *Late Ramesside Letters*, 1967, 58 n. *b*; *Chronique d'Égypte* 44:272f.; Satzinger 1976:231f.). Compare Jacobsson 1977:49f., for English *and*.

[122] See Dik 1972:25ff.; Greenbaum 1969:52ff.; Pinkster 1972:111ff., 116ff. Note that ⲀⲨⲰ does enter Tesnière's broad "*jonctif*" category (Baum 1976:89ff.). Other instructive constructions are ⲀⲨⲰ ⲘⲚ- (*Wess. 9* 174d 7f., 175a 23; *Dictionary* 170 — cf. the Boh. ⲀⲀⲀ ⲚⲈⲘ), pre-apodotic ⲀⲨⲰ: #ⲚⲦⲈⲢⲈⲴ-, ⲀⲨⲰ — # (*III* 110.19f.) — see Layton 1979:173. For comparable Greek " adverbial " functions see Goodwyn §859f., Kühner-Gerth II 253ff., Mayser 2/1 343f., 2/3 143ff., Blass–Debrunner §422.2.

ΝΕ ΕΜΠΕΠΝΟΥΤΕ ΤΟϬΟΥ / (*RE 10* 162a 13ff.) ...ΑΚΤΟΟΒΟΥ ΝΑΥ ΤΗΡΟΥ ΑΥШ ΕΑΚΤΡΕΥΚΛΗΡΟΝΟΜΕΙ ΜΠШΝ2 ШΑΕΝΕ2 / (*P* 130¹ 137 ΤΛΗ) ΝΕΝϹΝΗΥ 2ШΟΥ ΝΕ ΑΥШ ΕΠΕΝΕΙШΤ ΤΗΡΝ ΠΕ ΠΝΟΥΤΕ / (*Berl.* 1613 6 vo) ΝΚΟΥΙ ΕΤΝΕΙΡΕ ΜΜΟΟΥ ЧШΠ ΜΜΟΟΥ ΕΡΟЧ 2ΝΤΕЧΜΝΤΧΡΗϹΤΟϹ ΑΥШ Ε2ΕΝΚΟΥΙ ΝΕΝΤΑΝΑΑΥ ΕΤΒΕΤΜΝΤϬШΒ ΜΠΕΝϹШΜΑ. / (*A 2* 177) ΑЧΕΙ ΕΒΟΛ 2ΝΤΕΝΤΑЧΠΛΑϹϹΕ ΜΜΟϹ 2ΝΘΗ ΑΥШ ΕΑЧϯ-ΚΕ2ΟΥΕΤΑΙΟ ΝΤΠΑΡΘΕΝΟϹ ΕΤΟΥΑΑΒ ΜΑΡΙΑ / (*ibid.* 265) ΚΛШΜϹ ΑΥШ ΕΑΚϯ ΝΤΕΚϬΟΜ ΤΗΡϹ Ε2ΡΑΙ ΕΠΠΕΘΟΟΥ / (*B.L.Or.* 3581 *A* 131ϹΝΒ-Γ) ΑΤΕΤΝΚΛΗΡΟΝΟΜΕΙ ΜΜΟЧ 2ΜΠΤΒΒΟ... ΑΥШ ΝΤΟЧ 2ШШЧ ΕΑЧΚΛΗΡΟΝΟΜΕΙ ΜΜШΤΝ... Also *A 2* 26, 299, *Or.* 159-160 (note 114). This is a characteristic (and diagnostically useful) construction. Even more distinctive is ΑΥШ ΕΜΟΓΙϹ " and hardly, and barely " [123]. Compare the remarkably similar role of ΠΑΛΙΝ and ΜΑΛΙϹΤΑ before the circumstantial (see below).

1.3.11 The question of GREEK LOAN-MODIFIERS is naturally tied up with that of the status of non-Egyptian words in Coptic generally, and, more specifically, with the nature and degree of their assimilation into the Coptic grammatical system — one aspect of the typological issue of the Greek-induced element on Coptic grammar. This difficult subject is outside the scope of the present study [124]. My view, however, is that we are here up against a gradient, not dichotomic (" loan-words " *vs.* " foreign words ") phenomenon of assimilation. The assimilation scale can be established in terms of productivity, of integration in the Coptic semasiological system, and (sometimes) in terms of phonological structure and properties — all three criteria presupposing in-depth monographic investigation, in addition to the procedure in vogue, viz. the collection of Greek-origin items.

1.3.11.1 -ШϹ-*characterized modifiers* are but partly analyzable (see above, §1.3.0.1) and their listing is apparently limited (or at best half-open-ended, meaning that more and more members may turn up, yet without a substantiatable claim to free productivity in Coptic). Although this phonemic configuration is certainly indicative (or rather co-indicative) of modifier status, their transparency and analyzability are not absolute. The most common instances are discussed in the following paragraphs:

1.3.11.1.1 2ΟΛШϹ (2ΟΛΟϹ, 2ШΛШϹ) " at all ", " wholly " (similar in function and distribution to ΕΠΤΗΡЧ, §1.3.7.2) occurs

(a) *Adverbally, postadjunctively* — note the significant variation in spelling (exclusive to this position!): Usually we find here a negatived or negative-implication verb (" at all "): (*A 2* 548) ΜΠΟΥΡ-ΝΟΒΕ 2ШΛШϹ / (*IV* 69.19f.) ΝΝΕΥϯ-2ΝΑΑΥ ΝΑΥ 2ΟΛШϹ ΝΤΕΙ2Ε / (*ibid.* 99.20f.) ΝΤΝШΙΠΕ ΑΝ 2ΟΛШϹ / (*ibid.* 93.6) ΝϹΕΜΟΚ2 ΑΝ 2ΟΛШϹ ΕΝΟΕΙ ΜΜΟΟΥ / (*P* 130⁴ 156 Τ2Ε) Νϯ-2ΟΤΕ ΑΝ 2ΟΛШϹ / (*A 1* 105-6) ΝΕΙШΝΕ ΕϯΟΥΑШΟΥ ΑΝ... ΕΤΡΕΥШΠΕ 2ΟΛШϹ 2ΜΠΑϹШΜΑ / (*III* 43.5f.). (It is blasphemy to say:) ΟΥΝΡШΜΕ ΜΟΥ 2ΟΛШϹ ΕϪΜΠΕΝ-ΤΑЧΠΛΑϹϹΕ ΜΜΟΟΥ. More exx.: *III* 38.16, 135.25ff., *IV* 62.25f., 94.1, 124.9, 200.2,25, *Ch.* 44.35ff., *A 1* 47, 97, etc. Less frequently, we see 2ΟΛШϹ modifying an affirmative verb, with the meaning " completely, wholly, totally, altogether ": (*A 1* 251) ϹΕϹΗ2 2ΟΛШϹ ΡШ (-ΡШ 2ΟΛШϹ in *P* 130¹ 138 ΤΜ, 131⁴ 89 ΡΛϹ) / (*IV* 124.7f.) ΝΕΤΝΑΝΚΟΤΚ ΕΥ2ΗΝ Ε2ΟΥΝ 2ΟΛШϹ. In this position, 2ΟΛШϹ (in contradistinction to ΕΠΤΗΡЧ) may be intensified by reiteration: §1.1.2.4.3.

(b) 2ΟΛШϹ (2ΟΛΟϹ) ΡШ- " actually ", " on the whole ", is a (relatively rare) *premodifier*: (*K* 928) 2ΟΛШϹ ΡШ ΝΑШΕΝΡШΜΕ ΕΤΟ ΝΑЧ ΝΑΠΕ / (*P* 131⁴ 142 Κ) 2ΟΛΟϹ ΡШ ΕШϪΕ-ΚШΑΑΤ ΝΚΕ2ШΒ ΑЧΟΥΑ2Ч ΕΡΟЧ / (*III* 36.15) 2ΟΛШϹ ΡШ ΝЧΝΑШΤΑΛϬΕ-ΠШЧ ΑΝ — also *A 1* 47.

---

[123] SHISHA-HALEVY 1976a:33, §1.3.11.6 below and §7.3.1.

[124] See WEISS 1968, and (for statement of the problem, with suggestions towards its solution and relevant literature) MINK 1978:95ff. See now also VERGOTE in YOUNG (ed.) 1981:339ff.; ANBA GREGORIUS 1981 is the most recent study in a series unfortunately wanting in theoretical considerations: p. 205ff. on " adverbs ".

(c) *Adnominally*, ⲋⲟⲗⲱⲥ, ⲋⲟⲗⲟⲥ modifies postadjunctively the indefinites ⲗⲁⲁⲩ, ⲣⲱⲙⲉ, ⲕⲉⲟⲩⲁ in the sense of "what(so)ever": (*A 1* 14) ⲋⲉⲗⲁⲁⲩ ⲛⲋⲛⲁⲩ ⲋⲟⲗⲱⲥ, sim. *IV* 87.19f., *III* 92.9, *K* 921 / ⲋⲉⲗⲁⲁⲩ ⲛⲣⲱⲙⲉ ⲋⲟⲗⲱⲥ (*IV* 44.24, 45.4, 87.8f., 206.18, 81.5, etc.) / (*P* 130¹ 15 ro) ⲗⲁⲁⲩ ⲛⲣⲱⲙⲉ ⲋⲟⲗⲱⲥ... ⲗⲁⲁⲩ ⲛⲛⲕⲁ ⲉⲡⲧⲏⲣϥ / (*IV* 107.29) ⲧⲉϥⲥⲱⲛⲉ ⲏ ⲧⲉϥⲙⲁⲁⲩ ⲏ ⲕⲉⲟⲩⲉⲓ ⲋⲟⲗⲱⲥ.

1.3.11.1.2 ⲁⲗⲏⲑⲱⲥ "truly" (cf. ⲛⲁⲙⲉ, ⲋⲛⲟⲩⲙⲉ, §1.3.5) occurs

(a) *Postadjunctively, adverbally* ("truly", "really"): (*A 2* 464), parenthetically, ⲕⲁⲛ ⲉⲩⲭⲉ-ϯⲙⲉⲋ ⲅⲉ ⲛⲱⲓⲡⲉ ⲧⲉⲛⲟⲩ ⲉⲧⲃⲉⲧⲁⲁⲙⲉⲗⲉⲓⲁ-ϯⲙⲉⲋ ⲅⲁⲣ ⲁⲗⲏⲑⲱⲥ-... / (*A 2* 174, *Ryl.* 67 ⲧϥⲟ) ⲁⲛⲱⲱⲡⲉ ⲁⲗⲏⲑⲱⲥ ⲛⲑⲉ ⲛⲛⲓⲁⲕⲁⲑⲁⲣⲧⲟⲥ, also *IV* 25.8.

(b) In a Nominal Sentence (§1.1.2.3) it is adnominal/adclausal (status neutralized), with a variation ⲁⲗⲏⲑⲱⲥ/ⲁⲗⲏⲑⲟⲟⲥ: (*A 2* 402) ⲟⲩⲋⲟⲧⲉ ⲅⲁⲣ ⲁⲗⲏⲑⲱⲥ ⲡⲉ ⲛⲁⲩ... / (*RE 10* 162b 16) ⲋⲉⲛⲉⲃⲓⲏⲛ ⲁⲗⲏⲑⲟⲟⲥ ⲛⲉ / (*III* 115.26ff.) ⲟⲩⲧⲁⲗⲁⲓⲡⲱⲣⲟⲥ ⲁⲗⲏⲑⲟⲟⲥ ⲡⲉ... ⲟⲩⲙⲁⲕⲁⲣⲓⲟⲥ ⲟⲛ ⲁⲗⲏⲑⲱⲥ ⲛⲋⲟⲩⲟ ⲡⲉ... Also *Ch.* 195.3ff., *A 2* 395, *Cat.* 43.28.

(c) *Initially* — always -ⲱⲥ — the premodifier ⲁⲗⲏⲑⲱⲥ means "indeed", "really": (*A 2* 191) ⲁⲗⲏⲑⲱⲥ ⲕⲟ ⲙⲙⲛⲧⲣⲉ ⲉⲣⲟⲕ ⲙⲁⲩⲁⲁⲕ / (*ibid.* 473) ⲕⲁⲓ ⲅⲁⲣ ⲁⲗⲏⲑⲱⲥ ⲟⲩⲋⲟⲧⲉ ⲡⲉ ⲭⲟⲟⲥ / (*IV* 25.2f.) ⲁⲗⲏⲑⲱⲥ ⲟⲩⲱⲓⲡⲉ ⲁⲩⲱ ⲟⲩⲭⲡⲓⲟ ⲛⲋⲟⲩⲟ ⲡⲉ / (*III* 107.6) ⲁⲗⲏⲑⲱⲥ ⲛⲛⲁⲋⲣⲁⲓ ⲋⲱⲥ ⲉⲩⲭⲉ-, see §1.2.1.3.3 / (*P* 130⁵ 71 ⲥⲋⲁ) ⲁⲗⲏⲑⲱⲥ ⲥⲉⲛⲁⲭⲛⲟⲩⲛ ⲋⲁⲋⲱⲃ ⲛⲓⲙ ⲉⲑⲟⲟⲩ. Also *III* 114.21, 161.29f., 212.17. *Wess.* 9 145b 29ff. ⲙⲁⲗⲗⲟⲛ ⲇⲉ ⲁⲗⲏⲑⲱⲥ ⲭⲉ- (*Ch.* 129.21ff.) with the *varia lectio* ⲙⲁⲗⲗⲟⲛ ⲇⲉ ⲁⲗⲏⲑⲱⲥ (*III* 35.2) could also be interpreted as ⲁⲗⲏⲑⲱⲥ expanding ⲙⲁⲗⲗⲟⲛ (§1.3.11.2.5).

(d) *Adnominally*, ⲁⲗⲏⲑⲱⲥ/ⲁⲗⲏⲑⲟⲟⲥ is rather rare compared with ⲛⲁⲙⲉ: (*A 2* 18) ⲡⲥⲟϭ ⲁⲗⲏⲑⲱⲥ / (*RE 10* 164a 4) ⲋⲉⲛⲋⲱⲃⲉ ⲁⲗⲏⲑⲟⲟⲥ / (*Cat.* 42.29) ⲡⲉⲱⲃⲏⲣ ⲋⲱⲱϥ ⲁⲗⲏⲑⲱⲥ ⲛⲛⲉⲡⲣⲟⲫⲏⲧⲏⲥ.

1.3.11.1.3 ⲕⲁⲗⲱⲥ "well", "rightly", "beneficially"[125] and ⲕⲁⲕⲱⲥ "badly", "harmfully, with evil intent", "ill" occur

(a) *Postadjunctively* — very often clause-finally, thus probably adclausal rather than adverbal: (*III* 80.17) ϯⲟ ⲋⲱⲱⲧ ⲛⲋⲙⲋⲁⲗ ⲛⲁⲩ ⲕⲁⲗⲱⲥ, sim. *ibid.* 111.23f. / (*ibid.* 220.23) ⲛⲉⲛⲧⲁⲩⲭⲱⲕ ⲉⲃⲟⲗ ⲛⲧⲉⲩⲇⲓⲁⲕⲟⲛⲓⲁ ⲕⲁⲗⲱⲥ, sim. (ⲭⲱⲕ ⲉⲃⲟⲗ ⲕⲁⲗⲱⲥ) *IV* 4.5 / (*P* 130⁴ 139 ro) ⲉⲁⲩⲕⲱⲧϥ ⲅⲉ ⲕⲁⲗⲱⲥ ⲉⲙⲁⲧⲉ / (*IV* 157.2f.) ⲛⲟⲓ ⲛⲛⲉⲅⲣⲁⲫⲏ ⲕⲁⲗⲱⲥ / (*A 2* 498) ⲡⲉⲛⲧⲁⲡⲡⲉⲧⲟⲩⲁⲁⲃ ⲭⲟⲟϥ ⲕⲁⲗⲱⲥ, ⲁⲛⲟⲩϥ ⲕⲁⲕⲱⲥ / (*ibid.* 333) ϥⲥⲱⲧⲙ ⲕⲁⲕⲱⲥ ⲛϭⲓⲡⲙⲁⲁⲭⲉ ⲁⲩⲱ ϥⲛⲁⲩ ⲕⲁⲕⲱⲥ ⲛϭⲓⲡⲃⲁⲗ / (*IV* 95.10) ⲛⲛⲉⲣⲱⲙⲉ ⲥⲉⲕ-ⲧⲉϥⲋⲟⲓⲧⲉ ⲉⲋⲣⲁⲓ ⲕⲁⲕⲱⲥ, with many more exx., e.g. *III* 93.2, 110.1, 119.10f., 153.8, 217.13f., *IV* 73.22, 118.27, 162.21, *A 1* 302 etc.

(b) Less usually, ⲕⲁⲗⲱⲥ occurs *initially* as a *premodifier* (with the perfect): (*III* 222.3) ⲕⲁⲗⲱⲥ ⲁⲡⲉⲩⲁⲅⲅⲉⲗⲓⲟⲛ ⲧⲥⲁⲃⲟⲛ / (*IV* 8.4) ⲕⲁⲗⲱⲥ ⲁϥⲭⲟⲟⲥ / (*Ch.* 104.37f.) ⲕⲁⲗⲱⲥ ⲁⲕⲭⲉ-ⲡⲁⲓ / (*P* 130² 109 ro) ⲕⲁⲗⲱⲥ ⲟⲩⲛ ⲁⲧⲉⲅⲣⲁⲫⲏ ⲱⲁⲭⲉ — more often, both ⲕⲁⲗⲱⲥ and ⲕⲁⲕⲱⲥ tend to predicative status[126]: either focalized by a Second Tense/circumstantial topicalization form (§2.6.1): (*A 2* 338) ⲉⲧⲃⲉ-ⲡⲁⲓ ⲕⲁⲗⲱⲥ ⲉⲩⲭⲱ ⲙⲙⲟⲥ / (*P* 130⁴ 122 ⲗⲃ) ⲕⲁⲗⲱⲥ ⲁⲩⲱ ⲇⲓⲕⲁⲓⲱⲥ ⲉⲩⲱⲱ... in the # *modifier* -∅ # predication pattern (§1.3.1 3.3) or before a conditional topicalization form: (*III* 222.4f.) ⲕⲁⲗⲱⲥ ⲛⲋⲟⲩⲟ ⲉⲛⲱⲁⲛⲥⲁⲋⲱⲛ ⲉⲃⲟⲗ ⲛⲛⲉⲛⲛⲟⲃⲉ.

(c) *Adnominally*, we find ⲕⲁⲗⲱⲥ modifying only a verb-nominalization: (*A 2* 547) ⲧⲉⲩϭⲓⲛⲉⲓ ⲱⲁⲣⲟⲟⲩ ⲕⲁⲗⲱⲥ ⲋⲓⲧⲛⲛⲁⲅⲅⲉⲗⲟⲥ.

---

[125] See Abel 1876-7:549ff. for a conceptual study of καλῶς (cf. Blass–Debrunner §102.3).
[126] Cf. Paul 1920:§200.

1.3.11.1.4 ϨΟΜⲰⲤ " nevertheless ", " at all events ", " however that may be, for all that, even so "
(*licet, quoadminus*)[127] and ϨΟΜΟΙⲰⲤ (often spelled ϨΟΜ(Λ)ΙΟ/ⲰⲤ) " likewise, similarly ", are to an extent
functionally conflated in our corpus, with ϨΟΜΟΙⲰⲤ encroaching on the semasiological range of ϨΟΜⲰⲤ [128].

(a) Questionably, *postadjunctively-adverbally*: ϨΟΜΟΙⲰⲤ only (not ϨΟΜⲰⲤ): (*III* 99.14) Λ[ⲎⲘ]ΟⲨⲦⲈ
ⲈⲢ[ΟΟⲨ] ϨΟΜΟΙⲰⲤ / (*A 2* 262) ⲈⲨⲚⲀⲈΙⲢⲈ ⲚⲀⲎ ϨΟΜΛΙΟⲤ ⲔⲀⲦⲀⲠⲈⲎⲘⲠⲨⲀ / (*ibid.* 378-9) ...ⲈⲦⲢⲈⲠⲀⲠΙⲤⲦΟⲤ Ⲣ-ⲢⲘⲘⲀΟ
ⲀⲨⲰ ⲠⲠΙⲤⲦΟⲤ ϨΟΜΟΙⲰⲤ, Ⲏ ⲬⲈⲠⲈⲨⲤⲈⲂⲎⲤ Ⲣ-ⲄⲢⲰⲤ ⲀⲨⲰ ⲠⲀⲤⲈⲂⲎⲤ ΟⲚ ϨΟΜΟΙⲰⲤ — in all cases I would prefer an *ad-
(pro)nominal* interpretation (" to him too ", " the believer likewise "...) — compare the adnominal premodifier [129] in (*III* 220.21) ⲚⲨΟⲢⲠ ⲘⲈⲚ ⲚⲈⲠΙⲤⲔΟⲠΟⲤ, ϨΟΜΟΙⲰⲤ ⲘⲠⲢⲈⲤⲂⲨⲦⲈⲢΟⲤ.

(b) *Initially* we find both as additive or concessive conjuncts: ϨΟΜⲰⲤ " nevertheless ": (*A 1* 382)
ϨΟΜⲰⲤ ⲤⲈΟ ⲚⲀⲦⲚⲀϨⲦⲈ ⲈⲢΟⲎ ⲚϬΙⲚϨⲈⲖⲖⲎⲚ / (*III* 13.9) ϨΟΜⲰⲤ Ⲛ+ϬⲚ-ⲈΙⲚⲀⲬΟΟⲤ ⲀⲚ ⲬⲈΟⲨ / (*Ch.* 125.10ff.) ϨΟΜⲰⲤ
ⲈΙⲚⲀⲨⲈⲦ-ⲠⲨⲀⲬⲈ ⲈⲂΟⲖ / (*ibid.* 128.33ff.) (even though I do not wish to say it) ϨΟΜⲰⲤ ⲈⲦⲂⲈⲦⲨⲪⲈⲖⲈΙⲀ ⲚⲚⲈⲦ-
ⲤⲰⲦⲘ +ⲚⲀⲬΟΟⲎ, sim. *ibid.* 57.51 ff., 80.15ff.. ϨΟΜΟΙⲰⲤ " nevertheless ": (*IV* 195.8f.) (Even if there are
people who are pained to hear that " the Kingdom of God is not eating and drinking ") ϨⲰΜΛΙΟⲤ ⲠⲚΟⲨⲦⲈ
ⲠⲚⲦⲀⲎⲤⲘⲚ- (sic) ⲠΟⲨⲰⲘ ⲘⲚⲠⲤⲰ ⲀⲖⲖⲀ ⲈⲨⲘⲚⲦⲀⲦⲤⲈΙ ⲀⲚ,... / (*A 2* 464) ⲔⲀⲚ ⲈⲨⲬⲈ-+ⲘⲈϨ ϬⲈ ⲚⲨΙⲠⲈ... ϨΟΜΙⲰⲤ
ⲦⲀⲚⲀⲄⲔⲎ ⲈⲢΟΙ ⲦⲈ ⲈⲦⲢⲀⲬΟΟⲤ. ϨΟΜΟΙⲰⲤ " likewise ": (*III* 66.12f.) ϨΟΜΙⲰⲤ ⲆⲈ ΟⲚ ⲦⲆΙⲀΘⲎⲔⲎ ⲚⲂⲢⲢⲈ ⲈⲤ+
ⲀⲚ ΟⲨⲂⲈ ⲚⲈΙⲨⲀⲬⲈ (*v.l.* ϨΟΜΛΙΟⲤ); also *ibid.* 31.23f., 67.2. In titles, superscriptions (with date or theme
of the homily; not part of the corpus): *III* 102.9, *IV* 11.1f. (ϨΟΜΛΙΟⲤ/ΟΜΟΙⲰⲤ).

1.3.11.1.5 ⲠⲀⲚⲦⲰⲤ (ⲠⲀⲚⲦΟⲤ a common spelling), " no doubt ", " necessarily ", " without fail ",
" eventually ", " as a matter of course ", " naturally ", " assuredly ", " possibly ", " perhaps ".

(a) *Clause-finally*, as *adclausal* postadjunctive modifier, usually with an *apodotic future* tense (the
protases being ⲈⲎⲨⲀⲚ-, ⲈⲨⲬⲈ- or the protasis-equivalent ⲠⲈⲦ(ⲚⲀ)-, ⲠⲈⲚⲦⲀ-): (*A 2* 535) ⲈⲢⲨⲀⲚⲠⲈⲦϨⲢ-
ⲈⲢⲨⲦⲈ ⲈⲎ-ⲚⲈⲔΙⲂⲈ ⲈⲠⲈϨΟⲨΟ, ⲠⲈⲤⲚΟⲎ ⲚⲀⲈΙ ⲈⲂΟⲖ ⲠⲀⲚⲦⲰⲤ / (*ibid.* 360) ⲈⲨⲬⲈ-ⲠⲢⲰⲘⲈ ΟⲨⲨⲨ ⲀⲚ ⲈⲔⲀⲀⲨ ⲚⲤⲰⲎ
ⲈϨⲚⲀⲎ, ⲎⲚⲀⲔⲀⲀⲨ ⲠⲀⲚⲦⲰⲤ ⲈϨⲚⲀⲎ ⲀⲚ / (*ibid.* 165) ⲈⲨⲬⲈ-ⲠΟⲨⲰϨⲈ ⲚⲀⲚⲈⲬ-ⲦⲀⲂⲰ ⲀⲚ ⲈⲠⲘΟΟⲨ ⲈⲦⲂⲈⲚⲦⲂⲦ ⲈⲦϨΟΟⲨ,
ⲎⲚⲀ+ΟⲤⲈ ⲠⲀⲚⲦΟⲤ ⲚⲚⲈⲦⲚⲀⲚΟⲨΟⲨ / (*ibid.* 249-250) ⲠⲈⲦⲚⲀⲘⲈⲢⲈ-ⲠⲬΟⲈΙⲤ ⲀⲚ... ⲎⲚⲀⲈΙ ⲠⲀⲚⲦⲰⲤ ⲈⲦΟΟⲦⲎ ⲘⲠⲈⲬⲠΙΟ
ⲘⲚⲠⲚΟϬⲚⲈϨ / (*III* 213.19) ⲚⲈⲦⲖⲨⲠⲈΙ ⲄⲀⲢ ⲔⲀⲦⲀⲠⲚΟⲨⲦⲈ, ⲠⲚΟⲨⲦⲈ ⲚⲀϤΙ-ⲦⲈⲨⲖⲨⲠⲎ ⲠⲀⲚⲦⲰⲤ / (*ibid.* 214.10f.)
ⲚⲈⲦⲈΙⲢⲈ ⲚⲚⲀΙ, ⲤⲈⲚⲀⲘΟⲨⲦⲈ ⲈⲢΟΟⲨ ϨⲰΟⲨ ⲠⲀⲚⲦⲰⲤ ⲬⲈ ⲚⲄⲈⲚⲈⲀ ⲚⲦⲆΙⲔⲀΙΟⲤⲨⲚⲎ / (*Ch.* 182.15ff.) ⲦⲈⲦⲈⲚⲤΟⲨⲰⲚϨ
ⲚⲀⲎ ⲈⲂΟⲖ ⲀⲚ, ⲤⲈⲚⲀⲦⲀⲀⲤ ⲚⲀⲨ ⲠⲀⲚⲦⲰⲤ. More exx.: *III* 24.14, *IV* 3.17f., *Ch.* 134.48ff., 161.28ff., *A 2* 14,
165 etc. Rarely, adclausal ⲠⲀⲚⲦⲰⲤ is found outside this configuration (" no doubt "): (*IV* 6.23f.) ϨⲀⲠⲤ
ⲠⲀⲚⲦⲰⲤ ⲈⲦⲢⲈⲨⲬΙ-ϬΟⲖ / (*A 2* 455) (explication of " ⲈⲎⲬⲎⲔ ⲈⲂΟⲖ ") ⲠⲈⲦⲬⲎⲔ ⲈⲂΟⲖ ⲠⲀⲚⲦⲰⲤ ⲠⲈ ⲠⲀΙ ⲈⲦⲈⲢⲈ-
ⲠⲨⲀⲬⲈ ⲚⲦⲈⲪⲨⲤΙⲤ ⲚⲀⲬⲰⲔ ⲈⲂΟⲖ ⲈϨⲢⲀΙ ⲈⲬⲰⲎ.

(b) *Initially*, ⲠⲀⲚⲦⲰⲤ occurs before the present (or present-equivalent) tense, less usually before the
perfect, with the sense " no doubt ", " as is well known ", but also with nuances of " possibly ", even
" perhaps "[130]: (*Ch.* 55.1ff.) ⲠⲀⲚⲦⲰⲤ ⲠⲈⲔϨⲦΟ ϬⲘ-ϬΟⲘ ⲠⲀⲢⲀϨⲀϨ / (*ibid.* 59.31ff.) ⲠⲀⲚⲦⲰⲤ ⲠⲨΙ ⲚⲦⲠⲈ ⲠⲈ ⲠⲨΙ
ⲘⲠⲔⲀϨ / (*III* 196.16) ⲠⲀⲚⲦⲰⲤ ⲢⲰ ⲘⲠⲈⲚⲚΟⲈΙ ⲘⲠⲨⲀⲬⲈ — also *IV* 2.6, *Ch.* 56.29ff., 120. 21ff., *A 2* 454.

(c) The imported (unanalyzable?) ΟⲨ ⲠⲀⲚⲦⲰⲤ [131] " not indeed ", " certainly not ", in a rhetorical
question: (*IV* 2.20ff.) ⲈⲦⲂⲈ ΟⲨ... ΟⲨ ⲠⲀⲚⲦⲰⲤ ⲈⲦⲂⲈ... / (*ibid.* 10.4ff.) ϨΙⲦⲚΟⲨ ⲈⲨⲬⲰ ⲘⲘΟⲤ ⲬⲈ-... ΟⲨ ⲠⲀⲚⲦⲰⲤ
ϨΟⲈΙⲚⲈ ⲬⲈ-... ϨⲈⲚⲔΟΟⲨⲈ ⲬⲈ-...

---

[127] BLASS–DEBRUNNER §450.2.
[128] As early as classical Greek: cf. KÜHNER-GERTH II 280, 4; SCHWYZER II 554, 582f.
[129] See MAYSER 2/2:184, 170 on the placement of adnominal ὁμοίως.
[130] Cf. Lee, *Mus* 83:137f. (1970).
[131] BLASS–DEBRUNNER §433.2.

1.3.11.1.6 ⲟⲛⲧⲱⲥ, ⲟⲛⲧⲟⲥ " indeed ", " in fact, actually ", " truly " occurs only in initial position, and often (typically) introduces an apodotic present or future after ⲉϢⲭⲉ-/ⲉϤϢⲁⲛ- protases, as a kind of superordinator (" then indeed... "): (*III* 37.2, parall. *Ch.* 132-3) ⲉϢⲭⲉ-ⲧⲛⲉⲡⲓⲑⲩⲙⲉⲓ ⲉⲧⲃⲃⲟ, ⲟⲛⲧⲱⲥ ϤⲟⲩⲱϢ ⲛⲍⲟⲩⲟ ⲉⲧⲃⲃⲟⲛ / (*III* 25.24f.) ⲉϢⲭⲉ-ⲧⲉⲧⲛⲥⲟⲟⲩⲛ ⲙⲡⲛⲟⲩⲧⲉ ⲏ ⲧⲉⲧⲛⲏⲡ ⲉⲓⲥ̅ ⲟⲛⲧⲱⲥ ⲧⲉⲧⲛⲙⲡϢⲁ ⲙⲡⲥⲁⲍⲟⲩ... / (*Ch.* 26.40ff.) ⲉⲓϢⲁⲛⲭⲟⲟⲥ ⲭⲉ-ⲛⲧⲁⲩⲥⲛⲧ-ⲧⲉⲃⲇⲉⲗⲗⲏ ⲭⲉ-ⲉⲩⲛⲁⲧⲛⲧⲱⲛⲅ ⲉⲣⲟⲥ ⲟⲛⲧⲱⲥ ⲕⲟⲩⲱⲧⲃ ⲙⲙⲟⲥ ⲉⲃⲟⲗ ⲁⲩⲱ ⲕⲣ-ⲍⲟⲩⲟ ⲉⲣⲟⲥ / (*ibid.* 100.52ff.) ⲛⲧⲱⲧⲛ ⲇⲉ ⲉⲧⲉⲧⲛϢⲁⲛⲧⲙⲣ-ⲍⲱⲃ ⲍⲛⲛⲁⲓ ⲧⲏⲣⲟⲩ ⲉⲧⲣ-ⲍⲟⲩⲟ ⲛⲏⲧⲛ, ⲟⲛⲧⲱⲥ ⲧⲉⲧⲛⲁⲣ-ⲍⲧⲏⲧⲛ, ⲟⲛⲧⲱⲥ ⲧⲉⲧⲛⲁⲗⲩⲡⲉⲓ / (*ibid.* 79.19ff.) ⲉϢⲭⲉⲡⲁⲥⲉⲃⲏⲥ ⲡⲉⲧϮ-Ϭⲟⲙ ⲙⲡⲇⲁⲓⲙⲱⲛ ⲉⲍⲣⲁⲓ ⲉⲭϢϤ, ⲟⲛⲧⲱⲥ ⲟⲩⲙⲁⲕⲁⲣⲓⲟⲥ ⲡⲉ ⲡⲉⲩⲥⲉⲃⲏⲥ. Also *III* 40.9f. (with the apod. preceding the protasis), 67.22, 22.20ff., *IV* 21.14, *Ch.* 116. 53ff. (before the whole cond. complex). Elsewhere, too, ⲟⲛⲧⲱⲥ occurs mostly before the present tense or Nominal Sentence: (*III* 75.16) ⲟⲛⲧⲱⲥ ⲟⲩⲁⲑⲏⲧ ⲍⲱⲱϤ ⲁⲩⲱ ⲟⲩϢⲁϤⲧⲉ ⲡⲉ / (215.2f.) ⲟⲛⲧⲱⲥ ⲛϮⲧⲁⲉⲓⲏⲩ ⲣⲱ ⲁⲛ ⲛⲛⲁⲍⲣⲁⲓ, also *III* 13.5, 114.27 (fut.), 212.9f., *Ch.* 169.22ff. It is unusual with the perfect: (*IV* 7.11f.) ⲡⲉⲭⲁⲩ ⲭⲉ-... ⲟⲛⲧⲱⲥ ⲁⲩⲟⲩⲱⲛⲍ ⲉⲃⲟⲗ ⲛⲧⲉⲩⲙⲛⲧⲁⲧⲛⲟⲩⲧⲉ ⲉⲥϢⲏϢ ⲙⲛⲧⲟⲣⲅⲏ...

1.3.11.1.7 VARIA: (a) (ⲍⲁⲡⲁⲍ) ⲍⲁⲡⲗⲱⲥ [132], usually adnominally to ⲣⲱⲙⲉ ⲛⲓⲙ, ⲟⲩⲟⲛ ⲛⲓⲙ, ⲍⲱⲃ ⲛⲓⲙ, (but also adclausally), typically recapitulating and summing up (as an " attitudinal conjunct ") the idea or category underlying a preceding detailed list or account: (*A 2* 416) (following a list of useless items) ...ⲁⲩⲱ ⲍⲁⲡⲁⲍ ⲍⲁⲡⲗⲱⲥ ⲍⲱⲃ ⲛⲓⲙ ⲉⲙⲛⲛⲟⲩϤⲣⲉ ⲍⲓⲱϢϤ / (*IV* 54.6ff.) (following a list of toilsome tasks) ⲍⲁⲡⲁⲍ ⲍⲁⲡⲗⲱⲥ ⲍⲱⲃ ⲛⲓⲙ ⲉⲧⲟⲩⲛⲁⲍⲓⲥⲉ ⲛⲍⲏⲧⲟⲩ ⲡⲁⲣⲁⲧⲉⲩϬⲟⲙ / (*A 1* 16) (following a description of a dog's physical actions) ⲍⲁⲡⲗⲱⲥ ⲙⲉⲗⲟⲥ ⲛⲓⲙ ⲛⲧⲁϤ Ϣⲁⲕⲛⲁⲩ ⲉⲣⲟϤ ⲍⲛⲟⲩⲛⲟϬ ⲛⲁⲡⲉⲓⲗⲏ, also *A 2* 260, *P 131*[6] 13 vo. With the meaning " simply ": (*A 2* 228) ⲡⲥⲁⲉⲓⲛ ⲉϢⲁϤⲃⲱⲕ ⲁⲛ ⲉⲣⲁⲧϤ ⲛⲟⲩⲟⲛ ⲛⲓⲙ ⲍⲁⲡⲗⲱⲥ ⲉⲣ-ⲡⲁⲍⲣⲉ ⲉⲣⲟⲟⲩ (hardly even to wealthy patients) — note ⲛⲧⲉⲓⲍⲉ ⲍⲁⲡⲗⲱⲥ " simply thus " (§1.1.2.4, *IV* 196.3, *Ch.* 162.5, *A 1* 204).

(b) ⲇⲓⲕⲁⲓⲱⲥ, ⲇⲓⲕⲁⲓⲟⲥ, before the First Perfect: (*IV* 9.22f.) ⲇⲓⲕⲁⲓⲱⲥ ⲁϤⲡⲱⲧ ⲉⲃⲟⲗ ⲙⲙⲟⲟⲩ ⲛϬⲓⲡⲉⲥⲙⲟⲩ / (*P 130*[4] 54 Ϥⲁ) ⲇⲓⲕⲁⲓⲱⲥ ⲁⲡⲉⲑⲣⲟⲛⲟⲥ ⲛⲉⲟⲟⲩ ⲙⲉⲥⲧⲱⲟⲩ, also *III* 109.13. Focalized by the Second Present/ circumstantial (§2.6.1): (*III* 47.3f.) ⲇⲓⲕⲁⲓⲱⲥ ⲉⲩⲙⲟⲥⲧⲉ ⲛⲛⲁϤ ⲉⲧⲟⲩⲱⲍ ⲉⲭⲛⲍⲛⲁⲁⲩ ⲛⲓⲙ ⲛⲁⲕⲁⲑⲁⲣⲧⲟⲛ / (*P 130*[4] 122 ⲁⲃ) ⲕⲁⲗⲱⲥ ⲁⲩⲱ ⲇⲓⲕⲁⲓⲱⲥ ⲉⲩ-. Postadjunctive (rare): (*Ryl.* 69 ⲛⲅ) Ϥⲛⲁⲭⲟⲟⲥ ⲛⲁⲩ ⲇⲓⲕⲁⲓⲱⲥ ⲭⲉ-...

(c) ⲡⲛⲉⲩⲙⲁⲧⲓⲕⲱⲥ (terminological), postadjunctive: (*Ch.* 208.25ff., Sh. ?). ... ⲉϤϢⲙϢⲉ ⲛⲁϤ ⲡⲛⲉⲩⲙⲁⲧⲓⲕⲱⲥ.

(d) ⲧⲉϢⲥ " so long ", postadjunctive (*A 2* 254).

(e) ⲍⲱⲥⲁⲩⲧⲱⲥ " just so ", premodifier (*A 1* 258).

1.3.11.2 -ⲟⲛ-CHARACTERIZED MODIFIERS may — at least as one possibility — be interpreted as *position-marked nouns* [133].

1.3.11.2.1.1 The attitudinal ⲙⲟⲛⲟⲛ " but, yet ", " only ", " however ", " besides ", " at all events " occurs initially, adclausally: (*IV* 110.19) ⲙⲟⲛⲟⲛ ⲛⲛⲉⲣⲱⲙⲉ ⲍⲣⲁⲓ ⲛⲍⲏⲧⲉⲛ (sic) ⲛⲟⲩⲟⲉⲓϢ ⲛⲓⲙ ⲭⲟⲟⲥ... / (*ibid.* 173.4) ⲙⲟⲛⲟⲛ ⲛⲛⲉⲣⲱⲙⲉ ⲟⲩⲱⲙ-ⲍⲛⲟ ⲛⲧⲉⲓⲍⲉ..., also *III* 18.18f., *IV* 53.15f., 56.11f., 60.23f., 66.12, *P 131*[7] 45 vo — all in a typical construction with a *negative jussive* form; in text- or paragraph-beginning: (*III* 86.16) ⲙⲟⲛⲟⲛ Ϯⲧⲁⲩⲟ ⲛⲟⲩⲟⲛ ⲛⲓⲙ ⲉⲧⲟⲩⲏⲍ ⲍⲉⲙⲡⲉⲓϮⲙⲉ (sic) ...ⲭⲉ-... / (*ibid.* 182.1) ⲙⲟⲛⲟⲛ ⲡⲉⲥⲡⲉⲣⲙⲁ ⲛⲛⲉⲛⲉⲓⲟⲧⲉ ⲛⲁϢⲱⲡⲉ Ϣⲁⲉⲛⲉⲍ ⲛⲉⲛⲉⲍ..., also *IV* 114.16 / (*IV* 109.9f.) ⲙⲟⲛⲟⲛ ⲛⲧⲟⲟⲩ ⲉⲧⲛⲁϮ-ⲗⲟⲅⲟⲥ ⲍⲁⲍⲱⲃ ⲛⲓⲙ " only they " / (*A 2* 380-1) ⲙⲟⲛⲟⲛ ⲟⲩⲛϬⲟⲙ ⲙⲙⲟⲛ ⲉⲍⲱⲧⲡ ⲉⲡⲛⲟⲩⲧⲉ ⲉⲛⲍⲟⲥⲟⲛ ⲉⲙⲛⲁⲅⲅⲉⲗⲟⲥ... ⲛⲁϢϬⲙ-Ϭⲟⲙ ⲉⲡⲟⲣⲭⲛ ⲉⲧⲁⲅⲁⲡⲏ ⲙⲡⲛⲟⲩⲧⲉ " only so long as... ". Premodifying a noun-equivalent: (*IV* 4.9f.) ⲙⲟⲛⲟⲛ ⲛⲉⲧⲛⲁⲉⲓⲣⲉ ⲛⲛⲉⲍⲃⲏⲩⲉ ⲙⲡⲣⲁⲛ ⲥⲉⲛⲁϢⲱⲡⲉ ⲙⲙⲁⲕⲁⲣⲓⲟⲥ ⲙⲙⲁⲩ, or a modifier: (*IV* 54.23f.) ⲉⲩⲛⲁⲟⲩⲟⲙϤ ⲛⲁⲩ..., ⲙⲟⲛⲟⲛ ⲉⲩⲥⲡⲟⲩⲇⲁⲍⲉ ⲁⲛ, so too (changing Leipoldt's division and punctuation) *ibid.* 162.21.

---

[132] PREISIGKE 1.155 (+ suppl. 27).

[133] It will be remembered here that the ex-adjectival morphs -ⲟⲥ/-ⲟⲛ have an allomorphic distribution in modifier status in Coptic: see §4.

1.3.11.2.1.2 ΟΥ ΜΟΝΟΝ... ΑΛΛΑ..., "not only... but (also/even)...", the well-known Greek configuration [134], occurs in Shenoute in an interesting array of constructions. Generally speaking, ΟΥ ΜΟΝΟΝ is followed (as in the Greek original) by a noun or noun-equivalent (ΠΑΙ, ΠΕΤ-, also ΧΕ- with noun/modifier), but after ΑΛΛΑ the framework terms are looser, and quite a few possibilities present themselves:

(1) ' ΟΥ ΜΟΝΟΝ (ΧΕ-) [135] *noun*, ΑΛΛΑ- *noun*' may be the stereotype: (*III* 47.24f.) ΤΑΜΙΟ ΓΑΡ ΝΙΜ, ΟΥ ΜΟΝΟΝ ΧΕ-ΝΡΩΜΕ, ΑΛΛΑ ΝΚΕΤΒΝΟΟΥΕ ΜΝΝΕΘΗΡΙΟΝ..., *ibid.* 68.18f. (ΟΥ ΜΟΝΟΝ ΧΕ-ΝΕΝΤΑΥ-, ΑΛΛΑ ΩΑ2ΡΑΙ ΟΝ Ε-), *IV* 159.13f.

(2) ΟΥ ΜΟΝΟΝ ΧΕ-, ΑΛΛΑ... (ΟΝ) gives the impression of being actually superimposed on various textual segments: ΟΥ ΜΟΝΟΝ ΧΕ- [*protasis*], ΑΛΛΑ [*protasis + apodosis*] (*III* 16.19ff.), [*extraposition*] ΟΥ ΜΟΝΟΝ ΧΕ-, ΑΛΛΑ... ΟΝ (*IV* 15.10ff.), ΟΥ ΜΟΝΟΝ ΧΕ- [*premodifier + verb syntagm*], ΑΛΛΑ- *verb syntagm* (*III* 36.3ff. *IV* 156.12ff.), ΟΥ ΜΟΝΟΝ ΧΕ- [*adnominal circumstantial*], ΑΛΛΑ- [*adnominal circumstantial*] (*III* 76.11f.), ΟΥ ΜΟΝΟΝ ΧΕ- [*infinitive*], ΑΛΛΑ- [*conjunctive*] (*IV* 4.10ff.). Simpler cases: ΟΥ ΜΟΝΟΝ ΧΕ-ΜΕΥ-, ΑΛΛΑ ΩΑΥ-ΟΝ (*III* 31.8f.), ΟΥ ΜΟΝΟΝ ΧΕ-ΑΥ-, ΑΛΛΑ ΑΥ- (*III* 29.10ff.), ΟΥ ΜΟΝΟΝ ΧΕ-ΝΤΝ- ΑΝ, ΑΛΛΑ (Ε)ΝΡΠΚΕ- (*III* 108.8f.), ΟΥ ΜΟΝΟΝ ΧΕ-ΩΑΥ-, ΑΛΛΑ (ΟΝ) ΣΕΝΑ- (*III* 48.9), and so on (more exx.: *III* 90-1, 93.24f., 104.1ff., *IV* 21.2ff., 30.19ff., 95.19ff., *Ch.* 93.35ff., etc.).

(3) Mixed construction: ΟΥ ΜΟΝΟΝ ΔΕ ΠΑΙ ΧΕ-ΑΙΧΝΟΥΤΝ, ΑΛΛΑ ΑΙΡ-ΑΝΑΩ ΟΝ (*III* 139.10f.), ΟΥ ΜΟΝΟΝ ΧΕ-Α2Α2 ΧΙ-ΣΜΟΥ... ΑΛΛΑ ΝΕΤΝΑ ΟΝ ΕΡΑΤΥ ΜΠΝΟΥΤΕ (*IV* 22.18ff.), ΟΥ ΜΟΝΟΝ ΧΕ-2ΑΠΕΥΒΕΚΕ, ΑΛΛΑ ΟΥΔΕ [136] ΟΝ ΝΧΙΝΧΗ (*IV* 160.17f.).

(4) ΟΥ ΜΟΝΟΝ + *verb syntagm*, without ΧΕ-, is rare: (*III* 114-5) +ΝΑΧΟΟΣ ΧΕ-ΟΥ ΜΟΝΟΝ ΝΑΩΕ-ΝΕΤΡ2ΩΒ... ΑΛΛΑ ΝΑΩΩΟΥ ΟΝ ΝΟΙ-ΝΑΡΓΟΣ.

(5) "Solitary" ΟΥ ΜΟΝΟΝ: (*III* 40-1) ΟΥ ΜΟΝΟΝ ΧΕ-+Ο ΝΧΑΧΕ ΕΡΟΟΥ / (*ibid.* 115.2f.) ΟΥ ΜΟΝΟΝ ΧΕΝΣΕΕΙΡΕ ΑΝ ΝΝΑΤΕΧΡΙΑ ΜΠΣΩΜΑ ΟΥΔΕ ΝΑΤΕΨΥΧΗ.

1.3.11.2.2 ΦΑΝΕΡΟΝ "manifestly" is postadjunctive: adnominal (verb nominalization): (*Ench.* 78b) ΝΡΕΥΡ-ΝΟΒΕ ΦΑΝΕΡΟΝ; adnominal/adclausal: (*A 2* 485, *P* 130⁴ 125 ΛΖ) 2ΕΝΑΤΝΟΥΤΕ ΦΑΝΕΡΟΝ ΝΕ / (*III* 208.17f.) ΝΕΤΟ ΝΑΥ ΤΕΝΟΥ ΝΗΕΙ ΦΑΝΕΡΟΝ. Expanding a modifier: (*A 1* 204) 2ΝΝΕΥΤΟΠΟΣ ΦΑΝΕΡΟΝ.

1.3.11.2.3 ΣΧΕΔΟΝ "almost", premodifying ΝΘΕ "almost like": (*Ch.* 119.47ff.) ΕΥΤΑΚΗΥ ΕΥΒΗΛ ΕΒΟΛ ΣΧΕΔΟΝ ΝΘΕ ΝΝΙ2ΑΛΟΥΣ / (*P* 130⁴ 105 ΡΚϚ) ΚΑΝ ΕΥΩΑΝΣΒΟΚ ...ΣΧΕΔΩΝ (sic) ΝΘΕ ΜΠΟΥΟΕΙΝ ΜΠΟΟ2, ΙⲤ ΝΑΜΑ2ΟΥ ΝΑΥ ΟΝ (i.e. the benefactor's property).

1.3.11.2.4 (?) ΛΟΙΠΟΝ "well then", "thus", "consequently", *initial* (attitudinal, dis/conjunct) premodifier: (*P* 131⁵ 43 Ρ, not Sh.?) ΛΟΙΠΟΝ ΜΝΛΑΑΥ ΝΗΥ Ε2ΟΥΝ ΩΑΡΟΝ / (*ibid.* 63 vo) ΛΟΙΠΟΝ ΩΑΥΚΟΛΑ-ΖΕ..., also 131⁶ 42 ro (Sh.?), 131⁷ 25 ro — no instance in texts of certain Shenoutean authorship.

1.3.11.2.5 ΜΑΛΛΟΝ, ΜΑΛΙΣΤΑ

1.3.11.2.5.1 ΜΑΛΛΟΝ (ΔΕ) "rather", "even more, so much more", "especially", attitudinal dis-/conjunct. (a) ΜΑΛΛΟΝ ΔΕ [137] + *predication* (*III* 24.21f., 68.9f.); (b) ΜΑΛΛΟΝ ΔΕ + *modifier*: (*Ch.* 93.46ff.) ...ΜΑΛΛΟΝ ΔΕ 2ΝΝΕΨΑΛΜΟΣ / (*III* 77.19) 2ΜΠΕ2ΟΟΥ, ΜΑΛΛΟΝ ΔΕ 2ΝΤΕΥΩΗ / (*A 2* 510-511) ΜΑΛΛΟΝ

---

[134] See KÜHNER–GERTH II 257, MAYSER 2/3:118; cf. DAUMAS 1952:128f.

[135] ΧΕ- before a noun, predication form or modifier, appears to be part of the ' ΟΥ ΜΟΝΟΝ ΧΕ- ΑΛΛΑ- ' framework rather than sharing in the paradigm after ΟΥ ΜΟΝΟΝ.

[136] KÜHNER-GERTH II 257.

[137] MAYSER 2/3:127.

ⲆⲈ ⲈⲌⲈⲚⲠⲞⲚⲎⲢⲞⲤ ⲚⲈ ⲚⲈⲦⲈⲒⲢⲈ ⲘⲘⲞⲞⲨ " especially since ", also *P* 131⁴ 92 ⲢⲘⲂ;   (c) ⲘⲀⲖⲖⲞⲚ ⲆⲈ + *noun* (-*equivalent*) " in particular " (*III* 222.9f., *P* 130⁴ 122 ⲖⲂ); ⲘⲀⲖⲖⲞⲚ ⲆⲈ ⲬⲈ- [*neg. protasis* + *apodosis*] " especially since ": (*IV* 19.19) ⲘⲀⲖⲖⲞⲚ ⲆⲈ ⲬⲈ-ⲈⲚⲈⲞⲨⲢⲘⲢⲀⲨ ⲀⲚ ⲠⲈ... ⲚⲈⲤⲚⲀⲌⲰ ⲀⲚ ⲠⲈ / (*ibid.* 99.21f.) ⲘⲀⲖⲖⲞⲚ ⲆⲈ ⲬⲈ-ⲈⲔⲨⲀⲚⲦⲘⲦ ⲚⲀⲨ... ⲈⲔⲚⲀⲢ-ⲂⲞⲖ ⲀⲚ. In ⲘⲀⲖⲖⲞⲚ ⲆⲈ ⲀⲖⲎⲐⲰⲤ ⲬⲈ- (*III* 35.2, ⲬⲈ-less variant in *Ch.* 129.21ff.), ⲬⲈ- may alternatively be understood as the formal marking of the inter-dependence of the clause and the premodifier ⲀⲖⲎⲐⲰⲤ, the conjunct ⲘⲀⲖⲖⲞⲚ or both: cf. ⲘⲀⲖⲒⲤⲦⲀ ⲬⲈ- (below).   (d) ⲠⲞⲤⲰ/ⲠⲞⲤⲞ ⲘⲀⲖⲖⲞⲚ " how much more...? " is a rhetorical question, *in apodosi* after ⲈⲨⲬⲈ-, usually with a Second Tense/circumstantial topicalization form (§2.6.1; ⲠⲞⲤⲰ was originally — and is synchronically [138]? — focal): *III* 97.24f., *Ch.* 74.54ff., 119.30ff., *A 2* 396 (+ First Future). Occasionally, ⲠⲞⲤⲰ ⲘⲀⲖⲖⲞⲚ occurs in the predication-presupposing pattern (§1.2.3): (*III* 42.3f.) ⲈⲨⲬⲈ-ⲚⲤⲞⲂⲨ ⲀⲚ ⲈⲞⲨⲀ ⲚⲚⲬⲀⲬ, ⲠⲞⲤⲞ ⲘⲀⲖⲖⲞⲚ ⲚⲢⲰⲘⲈ / (*Ch.* 59.17ff.) ⲈⲨⲬⲈ-ⲚⲈⲌⲂⲎⲨⲈ ⲄⲈ ⲚⲚⲢⲰⲘⲈ ⲨⲞⲞⲠ ⲚⲦⲈⲒⲌⲈ, ⲠⲞⲤⲰ ⲘⲀⲖⲖⲞⲚ ⲠⲚⲞⲨⲦⲈ...; also *III* 29.23.

1.3.11.2.5.2   ⲘⲀⲖⲒⲤⲦⲀ (often similar in meaning to ⲘⲀⲖⲖⲞⲚ) " certainly " [139], " not to mention, let alone ", " so much more ", " even ", " most of all, above all ", " on the contrary " [140], " especially since, considering that... ", " what's more ".

(a) ⲘⲀⲖⲒⲤⲦⲀ + *predication form*: (*III* 94.3f.) ⲘⲀⲖⲒⲤⲦⲀ ⲦⲚⲀⲬⲞⲞⲤ ⲬⲈ- " certainly " / (*P* 130⁵ 39 ro) Ⲏ ⲘⲀⲖⲒⲤⲦⲀ ⲆⲈ ⲀⲠⲘⲞⲨ ⲄⲰⲢⲄ ⲈⲢⲞⲤ / (*III* 22.16) ⲘⲀⲖⲒⲤⲦⲀ ⲠⲞⲨⲤⲞⲚ ⲠⲈ ⲔⲀⲦⲀⲤⲀⲢⳜ " even " / (*III* 96.2) ⲘⲀⲖⲒⲤⲦⲀ ⲚⲈⲦⲠⲞⲢⲚⲈⲨⲈ... ⲚⲀⲒ ⲚⲀⲘⲈ ⲚⲈ ⲚⲨⲞⲨⲬⲈⲦ-ⲠⲈⲨⲢ-ⲠⲘⲈⲈⲨⲈ ⲈⲂⲞⲖ " on the contrary " / (*IV* 178.12) ⲘⲀⲖⲒⲤⲦⲀ ⲠⲞⲨⲞⲈⲒⲨ ⲠⲈ ⲀⲨⲰ ⲦⲈⲨⲚⲞⲨ ⲚⲦⲰⲞⲨⲚ ⲌⲀⲠⲌⲒⲚⲎⲂ " so much more ", etc.: more exx.: *III* 110.16, 183.24f., 203.2f., *IV* 86.1f., 153.10, *Ch.* 100.8ff., etc.

(b) ⲘⲀⲖⲒⲤⲦⲀ + *modifier* (" even ", " especially "): (*IV* 78.8) ...ⲚⲌⲀⲌ ⲚⲤⲞⲠ, ⲘⲀⲖⲒⲤⲦⲀ ⲘⲠⲚⲀⲨ ⲈⲦⲚⲚⲀⲨⲰⲚⲈ / (*ibid.* 155.22) ...ⲘⲀⲖⲒⲤⲦⲀ ⲌⲚⲚⲦⲞ ⲚⲚⲈⲦⲌⲒⲦⲞⲨⲰⲞⲨ. Very frequently with a circumstantial (" especially since ", " considering that .. ", " actually "): (*III* 87.10) ⲘⲀⲖⲒⲤⲦⲀ ⲈⲚⲚⲀ ⲈⲘⲀⲨ / (*RE 10* 161a 31ff.) ⲈⲚⲈⲞⲨⲘⲈⲢⲞⲤ ⲚⲞⲨⲰⲦ... ⲠⲈⲚⲦⲀⲔⲦⲀⲘⲒⲞⲨ, ⲚⲦⲔ-ⲞⲨⲘⲞⲒⲌⲈ, ⲘⲀⲖⲒⲤⲦⲀ ⲈⲀⲔⲦⲀⲘⲒⲈ-ⲠⲦⲎⲢⲤ " how much more, considering that... " / (*Wess. 18* 128b 1ff.) ...ⲘⲀⲖⲒⲤⲦⲀ ⲈⲢⲈⲦⲈⲄⲢⲀⲪⲎ Ⲣ-ⲘⲚⲦⲢⲈ ⲘⲚⲚⲈⲤⲨⲀⲬⲈ / (*Ch.* 53.7ff.) ...ⲘⲀⲖⲒⲤⲦⲀ ⲈⲠ-ⲬⲞⲈⲒⲤ ⲠⲈⲦⲬⲰ ⲘⲘⲞⲤ / (*BMCat.* 80, No. 195) ⲘⲀⲖⲒⲤⲦⲀ ⲈⲚⲦⲔ-ⲞⲨⲞⲨ ⲌⲰⲨⲤ ⲚⲚⲀⲌⲢⲘⲠⲄⲰⲚⲦ ⲚⲦⲞⲢⲄⲎ...; also *III* 96.12f., 124.5f., 142.23, 200.18f., *IV* 33.5f., 100.8f.

(c) ⲘⲀⲖⲒⲤⲦⲀ + *noun* (" even ", " especially ", " not to mention, let alone ", " namely "): *IV* 1.8f., 4.8, 30.16, 110.3f., 112.2, *III* 82.8f., 91.7f., 106.11f., 112.1 — " especially "; *III* 36.16, 43.7f., *IV* 161.19f., 172.8f. — " certainly not "; *III* 74.16, 213.3f. — " even "; *IV* 100.18, *Ch.* 26.8ff., *P* 130⁴ 139 ro — " not to mention "; *Ch.* 67.21ff., 71.39f., 78.51ff. — " namely ".

(d) Most striking of all, ⲘⲀⲖⲒⲤⲦⲀ ⲬⲈ-: (1) a distinctive, well-attested construction of consecutive " prospective " subordination, ⲘⲀⲖⲒⲤⲦⲀ ⲆⲈ ⲬⲈ- + *Future III* or ⲘⲀⲖⲒⲤⲦⲀ ⲬⲈ- + *Second Future*: *III* 150.25f. (" especially so as to... "); 159.29f. (" certainly [not] so as to... "), also *IV* 115.13, 52.18; *III* 166.28f., 17.19f. (" let alone that... "); *III* 181.17f. (" so much more/certainly that... ").

(2) ⲘⲀⲖⲒⲤⲦⲀ (ⲆⲈ) ⲬⲈ- + *conditional complex*, " especially since ": (*III* 51.2f.) ⲘⲀⲖⲒⲤⲦⲀ ⲬⲈ-ⲈⲦⲈⲦⲚⲨⲀⲚⲦⲘ-ⲤⲀⲌⲰⲦⲚ ⲈⲂⲞⲖ... ⲚⲀⲨ ⲚⲌⲈ ⲈⲦⲈⲦⲚⲀⲢ-ⲂⲞⲖ... / (*IV* 42.1ff.) ⲘⲀⲖⲒⲤⲦⲀ ⲆⲈ ⲬⲈ ⲈⲚⲈⲚⲦⲀⲨⲞⲂⲨⲞⲨ Ⲏ ⲈⲨⲨⲀⲚⲞⲂⲨⲞⲨ... ⲚⲈⲢⲈⲦⲈⲒⲘⲒⲚⲈ ⲚⲢⲰⲘⲈ ⲚⲀⲨⲘⲤ. Compare *Ch.* 65.22ff. (ⲘⲀⲖⲒⲤⲦⲀ ⲈⲨⲬⲈ-... + *apodosis*, without ⲬⲈ-).

(3) " Especially since ": (*III* 86.20) ⲘⲀⲖⲒⲤⲦⲀ ⲬⲈ-ⲠⲔⲀⲒⲢⲞⲤ ⲌⲞⲤⲈ, perhaps also *ibid.* 103.13, unless here ⲬⲈ- is conditioned by a preceding verb. The nature of the dependence between ⲘⲀⲖⲒⲤⲦⲀ and the ⲬⲈ-clause is far from clear. ⲬⲈ- may be pertinent, (co-)characterizing (α) a consecutive construction premodified

---

[138] Although the sequence introduced by ⲠⲞⲤⲰ ⲘⲀⲖⲖⲞⲚ is focal in relation to the topicalizing ⲈⲨⲬⲈ-protasis, I believe ⲠⲞⲤⲰ ⲘⲀⲖⲖⲞⲚ itself is focal in the apodosis.

[139] See GREENBAUM 1969:132ff. on the English *certainly*.

[140] Cf. MAYSER 2/1-53 (" adversativ-korrektiv ").

by ⲘⲀⲖⲒⲤⲦⲀ (cf. ⲈⲂⲞⲖ ⲦⲰⲚ ⲬⲈ-ⲈⲨⲚⲀ-, §2.6.3.2) or (β) causality. On the other hand, ⲬⲈ- may be an exponent of an explicit syntactic connection between the premodifier and its sequence [141], characteristic in Coptic of pre-elements of Greek extraction. A third alternative, that ⲬⲈ- is in these cases a mark of the predicative status of the premodifier [142], cannot be entirely dismissed, even though the usual cotextual tests for topic/focus isolation cannot be applied here.

1.3.11.3 ⲠⲀⲖⲒⲚ (ⲆⲈ) ⲞⲚ " (and/but) again ", " but then ", " alternatively " — additive/replacive/item-presenting conjunct [143]: a premodifier, introducing (often in a series of predications, quotations or in reporting) an additional predication: (*III* 54.19) ⲠⲀⲖⲒⲚ ⲞⲚ ⲠⲈⲬⲀⲨ / (*ibid.* 58-9) ⲞⲨⲰⲰⲤ ⲦⲈ... ⲠⲀⲖⲒⲚ ⲞⲚ ⲞⲨⲞⲞⲌⲈ ⲚⲈⲤⲞⲞⲨ ⲦⲈ... ⲞⲨⲢⲈⲨⲬⲒ-ⲤⲂⲰ ⲦⲈ ...ⲠⲀⲖⲒⲚ ⲞⲚ ⲞⲨⲢⲈⲨⲦ-ⲤⲂⲰ ⲦⲈ / (*Ch.* 24.27f.) ⲤⲈⲚⲀⲈⲒⲘⲈ ⲈⲢⲞⲔ... ⲠⲀⲖⲒⲚ ⲞⲚ ⲤⲈⲦⲀⲌⲞ ⲘⲘⲞⲔ... / (*III* 110.18) ⲠⲀⲖⲒⲚ ⲞⲚ ϢⲀⲨⲦ-ⲔⲈⲞⲨⲈⲒ ⲈⲦⲞⲞⲦⲨ. ⲠⲀⲖⲒⲚ ⲞⲚ ⲬⲈ- is common in quotation series (*A 2* 340, *IV* 33.3f. etc.); ⲠⲀⲖⲒⲚ ⲞⲚ may add a whole premodified complex: (*III* 71.14f.) ⲠⲀⲖⲒⲚ ⲞⲚ ⲌⲚⲚⲈⲒⲢⲞⲘⲠⲈ ⲚⲞⲨⲰⲦ ϢⲈ ⲚⲀⲒⲬⲘⲀⲖⲰⲦⲞⲤ ⲈⲀⲚⲤⲞⲞⲦⲞⲨ / (*IV* 45.22) ⲠⲀⲖⲒⲚ ⲞⲚ ⲘⲚⲚⲤⲀⲚⲈⲒⲌⲂⲎⲨⲈ ⲦⲎⲢⲞⲨ ⲚⲤⲈⲒⲚ-ⲌⲈⲚⲢⲰⲘⲈ... Additional exx.: *III* 110.11f., 59.22, 90.7ff., 127.20f., *IV* 1.17f., 127.4, 168.9, *Ch.* 68.15f., *A 1* 261-2, *P* 131⁴ 157 vo, etc. ⲠⲀⲖⲒⲚ (ⲞⲚ) + *circumstantial* — " moreover " — is used much in the same way as ⲀⲨⲰ premodifying a circumstantial form (§1.3.10): (*III* 212.22) (" the roads are different from one another ") ...ⲠⲀⲖⲒⲚ ⲞⲚ ⲈⲞⲨⲌⲒⲎ ⲚⲞⲨⲰⲦ ⲦⲈ ⲈⲚⲀϢⲈ-ⲚⲔⲞⲦⲤ Ⲏ ⲘⲘⲞⲈⲒⲦ ⲘⲠⲈⲤⲤⲰⲢⲘ / (*A 1* 75) (" The sins he says you have been forgiven ") ⲠⲀⲖⲒⲚ ⲈⲀⲠⲔⲀⲔⲈ ⲈⲒ ⲈⲂⲞⲖ ⲈⲨⲞⲨⲎⲌ ⲚⲤⲀⲠⲞⲨⲞⲈⲒⲚ... ⲠⲀⲖⲒⲚ ⲈⲀⲢⲈⲠϢⲌⲦ ⲘⲠⲤⲒϢⲈ ⲈⲬⲘⲠⲈ-ⲌⲖⲞⲦ...

1.3.11.4 ⲦⲀⲬⲨ, ⲦⲀⲬⲎ " quickly ". Here (differently from the -ⲞⲚ-group) there is no morphologically related " masculine " or " animate " counterpart [144]. This is a fairly common modifier, invariably *postadjunctive* but for rare cases of secondary (prosodically motivated) intercolary placement [145]: (*III* 40.6) ⲚⲈⲦⲠⲒⲤⲦⲈⲨⲈ ⲦⲀⲬⲨ ⲚϢⲀⲬⲈ ⲚⲒⲘ / (*Ch.* 114.62f.) ⲀⲨⲰ ⲚⲤⲈⲞⲨⲞⲘⲞⲨ ⲦⲀⲬⲨ / (*ibid.* 132.31f.) ⲀⲨⲦⲂⲂⲞ ⲦⲀⲬⲨ / (*A 2* 5) ⲀⲖⲰⲦⲚ ⲘⲘⲀⲨ ⲦⲀⲬⲨ / (*ibid.* 121) ⲔⲞⲨⲰϢ ⲈⲈϢⲘ-ⲞⲨⲔⲰⲌⲦ ⲦⲀⲬⲨ / (*P* 130⁴ 123 ⲖⲄ) ⲤⲈⲚⲀⲦⲰⲞⲨⲚ ⲦⲀⲬⲎ / (130⁴ 127 ⲘⲂ) ⲈⲚⲈⲘⲠⲈⲚⲈⲦⲨⲒ-ⲢⲞⲞⲨϢ ⲞⲨⲘⲈⲨ ⲦⲀⲬⲎ / (*Wess.* 9 140a 13ff.) ⲈⲨⲔⲰⲦⲈ ⲚⲤⲀⲦⲔⲒⲂⲈ ⲦⲀⲬⲨ. Also *III* 35.4ff., 87.12f,. 198.10f., *IV* 85.4, 155.7f., *Ch.* 130.23f., *A 2* 47, 390, *Miss.* 279, *K* 9040, etc. Aberrant conditioned placement: (*A 2* 53-4) ⲦⲀⲒ ⲦⲈ ⲐⲈ ⲦⲀⲬⲨ ⲚⲦⲀⲨⲞⲨϢⲦⲂ ⲈⲂⲞⲖ.

1.3.11.5 Prepositions of greek origin

(a) ⲔⲀⲦⲀ " according to... ", " by " (distributive), and ⲠⲀⲢⲀ " beside " [146], " in comparison with ", " beyond " are certainly more common in all-Greek, more or less terminological, phrases or clichés: ⲠⲀⲢⲀⲦⲈⲚⲪⲨⲤⲒⲤ (*III* 224.19, *IV* 112.24f., *P* 130⁴ 104 ⲢⲔⲆ, *A 2* 459), ⲠⲀⲢⲀⲪⲨⲤⲒⲤ (compound noun?) (*III* 77.24,

---

[141] Cf. Tobler 1886:51ff., Tesnière 1965:188ff.

[142] Cf. Rosén 1979:461ff.

[143] Greenbaum 1969:47ff., 59f. Compare the famous humorous application of adjunct-conjunct homonymy in Mark Twain's " Buck Fanshaw's Funeral " — " he's dead again ".

[144] §4.2.2.1.

[145] The diachronic question (here acute, but arising in each individual instance of non-native Coptic word) of why a given Greek lexeme was chosen to replace an Egyptian one (or, to put it the other way round, why this or that Egyptian element was destined to be replaced) is not pointless, even if almost hopelessly difficult to answer. (It but paraphrases H. Schuchardt's basic dictum that the history of linguistic forms is written — and must be studied — in terms of *individual case histories*, and not of wholesale change). Of course, one cannot approach problems of this order without a satisfactory structural-synchronic account of Egyptian and Coptic lexical systems.

[146] See von Lemm 1972a:239f., Nagel 1973a:113ff., Anba Gregorius 1981:211ff., 217ff. I have found no instance of ⲔⲀⲦⲀ in the sense " against " or " as for " (Godron, *BIFAO* 63:135-7 [1965]).

208.20, 216.4f.), ⲕⲁⲧⲁⲧⲉⲩⲫⲩⲥⲓⲥ (*III* 219.20, *IV* 113.2), ⲕⲁⲧⲁⲥⲁⲣⲝ (*III* 22.16, *IV* 31.1, etc.), ⲕⲁⲧⲁⲧⲁⲝⲓⲥ (*III* 22.13, 220.20), ⲕⲁⲧⲁⲡⲉⲓⲃⲓⲟⲥ (*III* 74.16, *IV* 59.16f.), ⲕⲁⲧⲁⲕⲁⲓⲣⲟⲥ (*IV* 21.18, *P* 130⁴ 118 ⲕⲅ, *Ch.* 66.41f., *A 2* 379), ⲕⲁⲧⲁⲥⲁⲃⲃⲁⲧⲟⲛ (*IV* 54.14, *Ch.* 51.23, *A 1* 14, *P* 130⁵ 28 vo), ⲕⲁⲧⲁⲟⲓⲕⲟⲛⲟⲙⲓⲁ (*III* 219.6, *RE 10* 162b 23), ⲕⲁⲧⲁⲡⲕⲟⲥⲙⲟⲥ (*III* 214.6f.), ⲕⲁⲧⲁⲛⲉⲅⲣⲁⲫⲏ (*III* 160.28, *IV* 34.22f.), etc. Both occur freely in collocation with Egyptian nouns (also in recurring clichés — yet not zero-determinated?) — statistically (by number of occurrences) predominantly so; ⲕⲁⲧⲁ is by far the better attested (with almost 400 occurrences in Leipoldt, vs. less than 40 for ⲡⲁⲣⲁ; ⲕⲁⲧⲁⲑⲉ and distributive instances are numerically perhaps more important): ⲕⲁⲧⲁⲡⲉⲩⲙⲡϣⲁ (*IV* 2.9) ⲕⲁⲧⲁⲡⲟⲩⲉⲥⲥⲁⲥⲛⲉ (*ibid.* 12.18f.), ⲕⲁⲧⲁⲡⲉⲥⲟⲩⲱϣ (*ibid.* 11.8), ⲡⲁⲣⲁⲧⲉⲛⲅⲟⲙ (*III* 134.19), ⲡⲁⲣⲁⲧⲉⲛⲙⲡϣⲁ (*P* 130⁵ 65 vo), ⲡⲁⲣⲁⲣⲱⲙⲉ ⲛⲓⲙ (*III* 143.1), etc. Of all Greek-origin prepositions, only ⲕⲁⲧⲁ and ⲡⲁⲣⲁ have pre-pronominal allomorphs (ⲕⲁⲧⲁⲣⲟ⸗ ⲡⲁⲣⲁⲣⲟ⸗: *III* 116.17, 117.5f., 11, *RE 10* 162b 8, *P* 130⁵ 37 vo).

(b) ⲁⲛⲧⲓ " instead of " occurs typically before ⲧⲣⲉϥⲥⲱⲧⲙ (less usually before the non-causative infinitive) in a common, indeed distinctively Shenoutean figure " instead of (doing this or that), we (etc.) did/do... ": *III* 51.10f., 115.5ff., *IV* 82.10f.,24f., 107.18, *A 2* 53, 54, 48, 466, *Wess. 9* 94a 3ff., 118b 11ff., 127b 26ff., etc. (see §1.1.2.2). With infinitives: *IV* 92.11f., *Wess. 9* 117a 20f. With non-verbal nouns: *III* 213.14, 214.14.

(c) ϩⲱⲥ " as ", " as if " [147] occurs as a *premodifier*, " vesting " [148] a circumstantial form, with or without ⲉϣⲭⲉ- (*Ch.* 207.18f., *Leyd.* 366, *Wess. 9* 143a 17ff., *IV* 92.6, etc.), rarely with an unconverted predication (Nominal Sentence, Cleft Sentence: *Ch.* 30.36f., *Wess. 9* 87b 21ff.). ϩⲱⲥ ⲉϣⲭⲉ preceding the autofocal Second Tense (§2.1.5): *III* 96.25, etc. Prepositionally, ϩⲱⲥ is well attested with native and Greek nouns: ϩⲱⲥⲛⲟⲩⲧⲉ (*III* 88.24), ϩⲱⲥϣⲙⲙⲟ (*ibid.* 135.5) ϩⲱⲥⲧⲩⲣⲁⲛⲛⲟⲥ (*ibid.* 40.14), ϩⲱⲥⲥⲁⲣⲕⲓⲕⲟⲥ (*ibid.* 63.8), etc.

(d) ⲭⲱⲣⲓⲥ " without ", " but for " precedes ⲧⲣⲉϥⲥⲱⲧⲙ (*Wess. 9* 108b 21f.), the non-causative infinitive (*III* 25.4f.) and noun lexemes, usually in recurring expressions, such as ϣⲱⲛⲉ and ⲁⲛⲁⲅⲕⲏ (*IV* 51.4, 98.7f., *P* 130⁵ 69 vo); with other nouns: *P* 130⁵ 15 vo (ⲡⲛⲟⲙⲟⲥ), *ibid.* 23 ⲣⲟⲏ (ⲛⲉϥⲕⲉⲡⲟⲛⲏⲣⲟⲛ), *III* 70.2,11 (ⲛⲟⲩⲟⲟⲧⲉ, ⲛⲉⲩⲕⲉⲧⲃⲛⲟⲟⲩⲉ), *IV* 95.23 (ⲙⲛⲧⲁⲧⲥⲟⲟⲩⲛ), 125.3 (ⲛⲁⲓ), 157.24 (ⲟⲩⲣⲱⲙⲉ ⲏ ⲟⲩⲥϩⲓⲙⲉ), etc. ⲭⲱⲣⲓⲥ is expandable by another modifier — a circumstantial: (*IV* 108.8) ⲭⲱⲣⲓⲥ ⲉⲩⲙⲙⲁⲩ.

(e) ⲡⲣⲟⲥ [149], relatively rare, seems to occur in fixed expressions: ⲡⲣⲟⲥⲟⲩⲟⲉⲓϣ, ⲡⲣⲟⲥⲟⲩⲕⲟⲩⲓ " for a (short) while " (*III* 35.4f., 131.17, *RE 11* 15b 2, 16a 7f., *RE 10* 164a 25f., *P* 130² 7), ⲡⲣⲟⲥⲧⲉⲩⲛⲟⲩ " for a while " (*A 2* 105, *P* 130⁴ 114 ϭⲉ, 130⁵ 93 vo), ⲡⲣⲟⲥϩⲉⲛⲕⲟⲩⲓ ⲛϩⲟⲟⲩ (*P* 130⁴ 38 vo, opp. ϣⲁⲉⲛⲉϩ), ⲡⲣⲟⲥⲑⲉ (*P* 131⁸ 84 ro).

1.3.11.6 Greek loan-modifiers: miscellaneous

(1) ϩⲱⲥⲧⲉ " consequently ", " and so ", expanded by the conjunctive (§ 7.3.1.1), with ⲉⲧⲣⲉϥ- (*ibid.*), premodifying the circumstantial (*IV* 87.4), Nom. Sentence (*ibid.* 183.2).

(2) ⲕⲁⲛ " at least " [150], " even ". Before the jussive or imperative (*III* 66.6f., *IV* 37.22, *Ch.* 82.7f., 87.46f., 116.30f., *A 1* 256, *A 2* 369-370, *P* 131⁷ 71 ro (ⲉϣϫⲉⲛⲅⲛⲁⲣ-ⲡⲁⲣⲑⲉⲛⲟⲥ ⲁⲛ... ⲕⲁⲛ ⲙⲡⲣⲡⲟⲣⲛⲉⲩⲉ) etc.); before ⲟⲩⲛ (*Ch.* 157.55f.), the present (*ibid.* 31.5ff.) and perfect (*ibid.* 138.5ff.); adnominally (" even ", *III* 222.15); ⲕⲁⲛ... ⲕⲁⲛ... is a disjunctive framework (" either... or... ", " be it..., or be it... "), usually for circumstantial forms (*III* 222.8f., *IV* 11.9, 109.20f., 111.8f., 154.12, etc.). As a concessive premodifier [151], with the conditional, ⲉϣϫⲉ or (rarely) ⲉϣⲱⲡⲉ, also with the circumstantial (" even if ", " even

---

[147] Stern §§607, 617, 622; Jelanskaja 1966:197ff.; Shisha-Halevy 1972:175f. Cf. Haardt, *WZKM* 57:78 (1961).
[148] Shisha-Halevy 1972:168 and §0.3.2.
[149] Anba Gregorius 1981:221f.
[150] Blass–Debrunner §374b (with Tabachowitz 41).
[151] Stern §628, Jelanskaja 1966:159f., Shisha-Halevy 1972:171ff.

though ": *III* 19.28f., 28.11, 22.9f., 40.16,19ff., 91.18, *IV* 3.27f., 114.8, *Ch.* 139.12ff., *Wess. 9* 140b 19ff., 179a 22, *Ep.* 56, etc.); less usually, precedes a basic tense in this role (*III* 93.20f., 23).

(3) (ⲉⲛ)ⲍⲞⲤⲞⲚ, ⲈⲪⲞⲤⲞⲚ [152], " so long (as...) ", " insofar (as...) ", " as soon (as...) ", usually with the circumstantial (ⲈⲚⲌⲞⲤⲞⲚ is the more common): circ. present (*III* 27.27, *Ch.* 70.9, *Wess. 9* 152a 20ff., etc.), circ. perfect (*III* 31.23f., *RE 11* 17b 42f.), circ. Nominal Sentence (*IV* 74.15, 75.1,12); rarely, with a Basic Tense (perfect or present, *IV* 20.2, 104.21, *Ch.* 112.16ff.). ⲈⲪⲞⲤⲞⲚ is rare: (*RE 11* 16a 27f.) ⲈⲪⲞⲤⲞⲚ ⲄⲀⲢ (ⲉ)ⲚⲦⲎⲄ ⲈⲌⲞⲨⲚ ⲈⲠⲚⲞⲨⲦⲈ ⲀⲨⲰ (ⲉ)ⲚⲌⲈⲖⲠⲒⲌⲈ ⲈⲢⲞⳓ, ⳓⲚⲀⲞⲨⳡⳡⳓ ⲘⲠⲬⲀⳓⲈ ⲌⲀⲚⲈⲚⲞⲨⲈⲢⲎⲦⲈ. ⲌⲞⲤⲞⲚ occurs (only in *Ch.*?) with Basic Tenses ("insofar as "): *Ch.* 16.43ff., 125.19ff.; note the disjunctive ⲌⲞⲤⲞⲚ... ⲌⲞⲤⲞⲚ... (" a little... a little... ", *IV* 162.2f.).

(4) ⲌⲞⲦⲀⲚ [153], with the circumstantial future (rare: " whenever ", *Ch.* 72.41ff., in parallel to ⲠⲈⲦⲚⲀ-, *ibid.* 73.34ff.), usually with the conditional, in the same sense (*III* 63.22, *IV* 63.6, 10.22f. — *v.l.* conditional without ⲌⲞⲦⲀⲚ — *Ch.* 68.3, etc.).

(5) ⲘⲞⲄⲒⲤ [154], " hardly ", also a rhetorical negation: see §7.3.1 — with the conjunctive, focalized by the Second Perfect (*III* 24.23), also converted with its clause as ⲈⲘⲞⲄⲒⲤ, in this case often premodified by ⲀⲨⲰ (§1.3.10; see references in §7.3.1).

(6) ⲀⲖⲖⲀ " but, however ", *passim*; opening apodosis " nonetheless " (*A 2* 333); before modifiers (*IV* 56.6, *Wess. 9* 173c 19ff.), with conjunctive.

(7) ⲈⲒⲘⲎⲦⲒ " otherwise ", see §7.3.1.1.

(8) ⲦⲀⲬⲀ (ⲬⲈ-) [155] " possibly ", " by chance ", " perhaps ", " apparently ", with conjunctive (*A 2* 369), Second Tenses — present (*A 2* 434, not Sh.), future (*ibid.* 440, not Sh.), Basic Tense (*ibid.* 434, not Sh., *P* 131⁷ 39 ro ⲦⲀⲬⲀ ⲞⲨⲚⲌⲞⲒⲚⲈ ⲌⲘⲠⲦⲢⲈⲨⲤⲰⲦⲘ ⲈⲢⲞⲒ ⲤⲈⲚⲀⲬⲞⲞⲤ ⲬⲈ...). Also for (rhetorical) interrogation? [156]

(9) ⲠⲞⲖⲖⲀⲔⲒⲤ " often " (*A 2* 415, not Sh., before a conditional complex).

(10) ⲈⲨⲦⲀⳠⲒⲀ (εὐταξία, " in good order "): (*A 2* 257) ⲆⲞⲔⲒⲘⲀⲌⲈ ⲘⲠⲌⲰⲂ ⲈⲨⲦⲀⳠⲒⲀ " precisely " [157].

(11) ⲈⲔⲘⲈⲢⲞⲨⲤ (*A 2* 2) ⲚⲈⳓⲘⲈⲖⲞⲤ ⲚⲈ ⲚⲈⲦⲚⲘⲈⲖⲞⲤ ⲈⲔⲘⲈⲢⲞⲨⲤ " in part "/" alternatingly " [158].

(12) ⲦⲞⲦⲈ " then " (*P* 130⁵ 83 ⲢⲒⲀ) ⲀⲘⲞⲨ ⲚⳡⲞⲢⲠ ⲈⲂⲞⲖ ⲌⲚⲚⲈⲔⲀⲔⲀⲐⲀⲢⲤⲒⲀ ⲦⲞⲦⲈ ⲚⲄⲬⲞⲞⲤ ⲬⲈ-ⲠⲀⲤⲰⲦⲎⲢ.

(13) ⲈⲦⲒ " still ": ⲈⲦⲒ ⲞⲚ ⲦⲈⲚⲞⲨ (cf. ἔτι καὶ νῦν *Ch.* 91.20f.); premodifying: a Nominal Sentence (*III* 89.6f.), a circumstantial form (" when still... ", *III* 210.23, *IV* 191.12), ⲞⲨⲚ (*P* 130⁵ 66 ⲞⲄ) Ⲉⳝ ⲞⲨⲚⲌⲀⲌ ⲆⲒⲤⲦⲀⳌⲈ; adnominal (*Young* ⲅ).

(14) ⲞⲨⲔⲈⲦⲒ " not any more ", with a negative clause: (*Ch.* 80.31ff.) ⲀⲨⲰ ⲞⲨⲔⲈⲦⲒ ⲚⳓⲚⲀⳡⳓⲘ-ⳓⲞⲘ ⲀⲚ ⳓⲈ ⲈⲢⲞⳓ (for this ⳓⲈ cf. §6.0.3.2).

(15) ⲠⲖⲎⲚ " yet ", " however " — paragraph opener, subtextual initial-boundary marker (*III* 117.20, 183.22, 84.8, 200.4f., *IV* 64.25, etc. [159]).

---

[152] Stern §622, Jelanskaja 1966:197ff., Shisha–Halevy 1972:174ff.

[153] Stern §622, Jelanskaja 1966:197ff., Shisha–Halevy 1972:173f.

[154] Cf. Crönert 1903:98 n. 2; Preisigke 2.113 (+ suppl. 183); Mayser 1/3 120, 2/2 184 (ⲘⲞⲄⲒⲤ is usually predicative: §§7.1.3, 7.3.1 — cf. Brugmann IF 27:262f. [1910]). For (ⲀⲨⲰ) ⲈⲘⲞⲄⲒⲤ see Shisha–Halevy 1976a:33 (cf. Browne 1979b:202, on *Luc.* 23:53).

[155] Blass–Debrunner §360.2, Anh. §456.3, Drescher 1969:96f.

[156] Jannaris §1749. See also Lee, *Mus* 83:137-8 (1970).

[157] Lampe 577, Liddell-Scott 734. Cf. εὐτάκτως (Mayser 1/3 124, 2/2 177, 183, Preisigke 1.623). Compare ⲠⲀⲢⲢⲎⲤⲒⲀ Drescher 1970:149ff.).

[158] Here reminiscent of *I Cor.* 12:27. Cf. Mayser 2/2 38, 390; Preisigke 1.75.

[159] In (*III* 17.27) ⲠⲖⲎⲚ ⲬⲈ-ⲀⲔⲬⲞⲞⲤ ⲬⲈ- appears to be explicative: "but since you have said...", with a second clause (18.3) ⲈⲀⲒⲬⲞⲞⲤ ⲚⲀⲔ ⲬⲈ- "and I said to you..." and the main clause (18.6f.) ⲘⲚⲚⲤⲀⲠⲈⲒⳡⲀⲬⲈ ⲘⲚⲚⲔⲞⲞⲨⲈ ⲦⲎⲢⲞⲨ ⲚⲦⲀⲒⲬⲞⲞⲨ ⲚⲀⲔ ⲀⲒⲦⲀⲘⲞⲔ ⲬⲈ...

Chapter 2

THE ADVERBAL MODIFIER FOCALIZED: THE SECOND TENSE
IN MICRO-/MACROSYNTACTIC AND CATEGORIAL PERSPECTIVE

2.0.0.1 RESEARCH-HISTORICAL: POLOTSKY'S TREATMENT OF THE SECOND TENSE

In retrospect, there is no denying that the story of the redemption of the Second Tense, the Sleeping Beauty among Coptic grammatical categories, is, in more than one way, the story of modern Coptic linguistics. The unveiling of the nature of this category initiated a renaissance of grammatical scholarship, which is thus precisely datable to 1944, the publication year of POLOTSKY's momentous *Études de syntaxe copte*, where it is treated on pp. 24-97 (with earlier tentative statements in POLOTSKY 1934:60, 63f. = *CP* 368f. and 1937 for Coptic, and 1940 for Late Egyptian and Coptic. Subsequent restatements of the pan-Egyptian category may be found in POLOTSKY 1960a:§§11ff., 30ff., 1965:§§16ff., 22ff., 1970:566f., 1973: 136ff., 1976:§§2.3-7, 3.9). A brief resumé: according to Polotsky, the Second-Tense conjugation form is to be conceived of as a *verbal nominalization*, with the privilege of actor (nominal grammatical subject) status in the Bipartite (# *nom. actor* + " *adverbial* " *predicate* #) pattern. The " adverb " (our modifier) following the Second Tense is thus its predicate; the ensuing construction is typologically (formally and functionally) comparable to " Cleft Sentence " patterns in other languages (§2.0.2.2.4 below), where a nominalized verb construction (" that... ", " que... ") serves as logical subject (" *glose* ", topic) for a non-verbal (" adverbial ") logical predicate (" *vedette* ", focus: see below for my terminology). In

Polotsky's more recent transformational formulation (1976), the nominalization of the verb by means of the Second-Tense converter is correlated to its demotion to subject status and the promotion of an " adverbial " adjunct to predicate status.

In setting out from, and taking issue with, Polotsky's conception and systematization (which, if the truth be told, have not yet been properly digested and applied by the Copto-Egyptological community at large, even today [1]), despite its truly awe-inspiring elegance and simplicity, shaping order out of chaos, and its law-like standing [2], I wish once more to state my conviction that his statements are not invalidated by the following observations; they are as cogent as ever — in their own procedural frame of reference. What I offer here is an alternative assignment of the facts, motivated by a different set of methodological principles. One may recall here VON DER GABELENTZ's typically Neogrammarian proviso (1875:159): " Es dürfte hier... streng zu scheiden sein zwischen dem Gesetze und den Einschränkungen " (in our case, *extensions*, rather) " welche dieses durch den Sprachgebrauch erlitten hat ". I mean to portray in this chapter Shenoute's *Sprachgebrauch*, no more, no less, and let the rule look after itself. My alternative to the Master's neat scheme [3] is less elegant, amorphous, and non-modular though not unstructured, but perhaps less reproachable for what I regard as a methodological flaw insofar as strictly synchronic description is concerned: the postulation of an " orthodox " or normal-and-original functional core [4] with a periphery of secondary, extended sub-functions [5], with no integration of all roles in the framework of a unified (even if complex and fragmentated) functional theory, or its paradigmatic association with other relatable forms or patterns. I can hardly conceive of any synchronic meaning for " extension " or " divergence ". Within the terms of reference of his own orientation, Polotsky's description is of course impeccable. If you reject it, you are faced with the realization that the syntax of the Second Tenses is so complex as to rule out any simple one-rule statement to define its workings.

My reservations concerning Polotsky's view of the Second Tenses may be condensed into the following comments:

(a) I confess myself agnostic about the alleged *substantival* nature of the form. This claim (in Pootsky's argumentation for Coptic [6]) is unmistakably traceable to the model (Bipartite or Bipartite-like), to which the form is assigned, and not to argument from independent or cross-evidence from other, intersecting patterns [7] which would pin down the form as nominal (cf. the corresponding Middle Egyptian *mrr.f* form, which features in subject/predicate status in Nominal Sentence patterns, governed by pre-

[1] See HORN's apt remarks (1980:64 n. 6).

[2] See for instance HORN 1980:63f.

[3] A neatness more warranted in Old and Middle Egyptian (though rare exx. such as *Coffin Texts* III 202 *n jśst jr.f tm.k swr wsšt* " But why wilt thou not drink urine? " still remain unintegrated in the main theory unless the topic here is " adverbial ").

[4] Possibly representing this core as the norm derives less from a conviction of a synchronic state than from a subtle, perhaps not conscious historical bias induced by the successive juxtaposition of all phases of Egyptian in the second Étude (which is as much a study of a diachronic category as a series of synchronic accounts). Obviously, a possible statistical preponderance of this core pattern (a preponderance never really established) is irrelevant as a synchronic argument. (Incidentally, the " Middle Egyptian " [" Oxyrhynchite "] dialect of Coptic which is generally not innovative, goes even much further than Sahidic in favouring these so-called " extensions ".)

[5] POLOTSKY 1944:51-3 (= *CP* 155-7), 1960a:§32 Obs. " Such ' exceptions ', which are relatively not at all numerous, can be brought under a limited number of heads and understood as extensions of the basic function... Inasmuch as they deviate from the structure of the ' Second Tenses ' they are secondary (' emplois abusifs '), but it is not in the least suggested that they should ' be dismissed as improper uses '. They can be ' dismissed ' only in the sense that they do not invalidate the definition of the basic function ". Is there not more than a suggestion of circularity in this definition?

[6] POLOTSKY 1944:66ff. (= *CP* 170ff.), 1960a:§11 and 32 Obs.

[7] The " actual Coptic usage " which is argued as amply demonstrating this nominal nature (POLOTSKY 1960a:408 = *CP* 254) is not specified, unless this refers again to the Bipartite pattern (subject) assignment of the form; see (b) below. Negation by means of N- AN, adduced as proof, is hardly conclusive, as this is the general negator of non-verbal nexus, adjunct and component, rather than an index of the nominal character of a term.

positions, object-expansion of transitive verbs, and so on [8]). This statement (of the nom. nature of the form) is therefore circular. It is also (at least in implication, but explicitly in 1976) dependent on a transformational approach to syntactic analysis, and also on some "diachronic inertia" or extrapolation from established historical facts. This question acquires a special edge when the *circumstantial* (modifier-paradigm) topicalization form (§2.5) is considered, and when the whole question is approached from the "signalling", i.e. listener's, angle: of what function is the Second-Tense converter an exponent? What does it signal, in the unfolding of the discourse? More on this subject in §2.8.3.

(b) The association of the Second Tense with the Bipartite pattern [9], while historically well-founded, s synchronically "leaky" and aprioristic. At issue here are the very rudiments of the definition of at pattern: the substitution and prosodic features do not match in the Second-Tense and Bipartite patterns (for the latter, see §1.2.1.1); the nominal status of the Second Tense — a *sine qua non* for the Bipartite assignment — is actually *dependent* on this assignment; finally, the *Second-Tense modifier* construction is only one in a set of at least five major patterns featuring this and related forms. There is hardly any synchronic justification for considering this particular one *primary*, even if all the indications suggest it is *original*, historically speaking.

(c) Clauses, like other grammatical unities, should be classified in terms of inner structure *and* in terms of their function in the larger units of which they are part. This, the macrosyntactic aspect (in my view a key factor in the description of our form) has been under-treated in Polotsky's analysis, which does point out the value of contextual configurations favouring the occurrence of the Second Tense, but nowhere formalizes the context (or rather the COTEXT, i.e. the syntactically and not merely situationally relevant segment of the text) as part of an ultra-clausal pattern, which may not only lead to greater predictability of a Second-Tense "event" but is inevitable and indispensable at some stage of a descending analysis and in the treatment of the question as one of *category exponence* and *signalling*.

2.0.1 MORPHOSYNTAX

2.0.1.1 ON CONVERSION IN GENERAL. I retain here this term of dynamic implication (POLOTSKY 1960a:§10; later understood as exponence of "transpositions"), which I use to mean the mark or signal of a specific definable syntactic standing, not a transformationally conceived *shifting* of status, either within or outside a preconceived set of part-of-speech compartments [10]. I can see no reason for tagging the converters as "syntactic" or "non-syntactic" [11]. The circumstantial and relative converters have internal (micro-)syntactic function, marking a conjugation-form as adjunctal/adnexal modifier, with part

---

[8] See POLOTSKY 1944:82f. (= *CP* 186f.), 1964:276f., 1976:§§2.1, 2.3-7; FRANDSEN 1975. The affinity of the "emphatic" with the relative forms, so cogently put by Polotsky, is problematic in the case of some allomorphs of the Coptic converter, and for others, out of the question.

[9] POLOTSKY 1944:66f. (= *CP* 170f.), 1960a:§§11, 30. In his forthcoming work, Polotsky comments for the first time on the differences (in prosody and constituency) between the Bipartite and the Second-Tense constructions, yet retains the old affiliation as a kind of sub-pattern of the Bipartite (this is indeed inevitable in the "transpositional" verbal system, where the Second Tense constitutes the substantival term).

[10] POLOTSKY 1976. For the theoretical background of word-class shifting, cf. Vachek, *Dictionnaire de linguistique de l'École de Prague* (1960) 23f. ("conversion"), Dokulil, *TCLP* 3:215-239 (1968), BAUM 1976:34f., 110ff. ("translation", "transference").

[11] Cf. the distinctions made by POLOTSKY 1960a:§§10-11 (the Sec. Tense kept apart from all other converters). Although he does not here specify or define how "conversion" is to be understood, his current transposition theory of the converters as exponents of *adverbial* (circumstantial), *adjectival* (relative) and *substantival* (Sec. Tense) transformation of the verb could be referred to. However, this would leave the *preterite* converter a case apart, outside this system.

neutralization: after a non-ⲡ-determinated nucleus, the circumstantial represents the opposition terms, as it does after a verbal nucleus. Elsewhere an opposition obtains: the circumstantial expressing *adnexal*, the relative *attributive* modification [12]. The Second Tense and preterite converters, on the other hand, have a higher-level or macro-syntactic signalling function. The preterite converter [13] marks a transition, " gear shift ", change of tempo (into " slow motion "), perspective (" low relief ", in WEINRICH's term) or dimension (into " setting ") in the narrative structure. The Second Tense highlights and delimits a stage — and thus resolves the structure — in the thematic or informational development of the dialogic or expository discourse [14]. Neither are satellites, but prime filaments in the texture of discourse — the " imperfect " in the narrative, eventual — the Second Tense in the thematic non-eventual texture. Both realize a *staging* option (see below) exercised by the speaker/narrator.

2.0.1.1.1 MORPHOLOGY. The Second Tense converter is an exponent of a category different from and intersecting that of tense [15]. Its incompatibility with Clause Conjugation forms is as much correlatable with their extra-temporal standing as with their non-autonomous syntaxic one (indeed both aspects must be but different faces of the same coin). Its incompatibility with Nominal Sentence patterns (which however do have their own topicalization forms, §2.5) may also be due to the special para-temporal type of predication but may also have historical roots.

The following allomorphs of the converter are found in Shenoute [16]:

(a) (1) ⲉ-, prenominally ⲉⲣⲉ-, before the Bipartite conjugation forms, in focalization patterns (1) to (6). Note the following: ⲉⲣⲁ- Second Future, sec. person sgl. fem. [17] (*A 1* 50, 445, *A 2* 8, 11, etc.); the Akhmimoid ⲉ- prenominally, rare [18] (*Wess. 9* 146c 6ff. ⲉⲡⲓϣⲁϫⲉ ϫⲉ-ⲍⲟⲙⲟⲟⲩⲥⲓⲟⲥ ⲥⲏⲍ ⲧⲱⲛ, *v.l.* ⲉⲣⲉ- 129b 30ff.).

(2) ⲉ-ⲟⲩⲛ-/ⲙⲛ- [19], patterns (1) and (6): *Ch.* 186.41ff., *A 2* 45, *A 1* 415. Note (α) ⲉⲙⲛ- as a "that"-form? *K* 9316 ⲙⲛⲛⲥⲁⲧⲣⲉⲩⲥⲟⲩⲛ-ⲡⲥⲟⲟⲩⲛ ⲧⲏⲣϥ ⲁⲩⲱ ⲉⲙⲛⲕⲉⲛⲟⲩⲧⲉ ⲛⲥⲁⲓⲧ; (β) ⲟⲩⲛ-/ⲙⲛ — the existence predication, not the indefinite-actor allo-form for the Bipartite syntagmeme; the Sec. Tense form in this case is without ⲟⲩⲛ-/ⲙⲛ- [20].

(3) ⲉ-ⲟⲩⲛⲧⲁ⸗/ⲙⲛⲧⲁ⸗ [19], patts. (1)-(3): *III* 71.23 (cod. C), 85.14, *Cat.* 43.16, *BMCat.* 94 (213 ⲗⲏ), *P* 131[6] 19 ⲙⲅ.

---

[12] SHISHA–HALEVY 1972:§2.1.1, 1976c:134 n. 3; see §§7.1.3, 7.3, 7.4 below.

[13] An adequate functional account of preterite conversion — for once without reference to the Greek imperfect — is long overdue. For the mysterious ⲡⲉ with this, otherwise converted or basic forms, see §1.2.1.2, gen. obs. 4.

[14] In fact, WEINRICH's " *relief* " (1977:91ff., etc.) would, in a somewhat different sense, apply to both roles; this is " subordination " or " inclusion " (*pace* FUNK 1981:196) on a higher, macrosyntactic, level of analysis.

[15] The question of whether or not this is a " mood "-type category (ČERNÝ–GROLL Ch. 26, §10.6: " polemic mood ") is one of terminological taste rather than of essential policy. Our category is tense-intersecting, functionally definable by intra- and inter-clausal relationships as an option of " staging ". (Incidentally, the " mood "-definition would have to apply to the [equally polemic] Cleft Sentence with nominal *vedette*, which however is not treated as a 'mood' by Prof. Groll.)

[16] NB. This inventory gives an overall picture of the distribution of the allomorphs; the actual constituency, drastically curtailed in many patterns, will be added under the relevant headings. Moreover, *circumstantial* (§2.5) and Basic tense themes (§2.6.2) in the distributional picture, should, properly speaking, be included in the morphological muster.

[17] POLOTSKY 1960a:§59.

[18] SHISHA–HALEVY 1976b:360f.

[19] POLOTSKY 1944:49f. (= *CP* 153f.), 1957a:232f. (= *CP* 232f.), 1960a:§§33ff.

[20] POLOTSKY 1960a:§§21, 35.

(4) ε + " adjective-verbs " [21], patts. (1) and (2): ⲉⲛⲁⲁ(ⲁ)⸗ (*Ch.* 135.44f., *Wess. 9* 130b 23f. = 147a 2ff.), ⲉⲛⲁⲓⲁⲧ⸗ (*A 2* 51, *Cl. Pr.* 33 1), ⲉⲛⲁⲛⲟⲩ⸗ (*Leid.* 302 = *IV* 96.3).

(5) ⲉϣϣⲉ, patt. (2): ⲉϣϣⲉ... ⲛⲟⲩⲏⲣ (*A 2* 464).

(6) ⲉⲟⲩⲟⲓ (ⲁⲛ) ⲛ-, circumstantial? patt. (6): ⲛⲁϣ ⲛ2ⲉ ⲉⲟⲩⲟⲓ ⲁⲛ... (*A 2* 155).

(7) ⲉ2ⲛⲁ⸗ (?) [22] *III* 161.30: patt. (2) or (6).

(b) ⲉϣⲁϥ- [23], pattern (2): *IV* 18.2; pattern (1): *A 2* 479 ⲡⲏⲣⲡ ⲉϣⲁϥⲧⲣⲉⲛⲃⲁⲗ ⲛⲛⲉⲧϣⲥⲕ 2ⲛ2ⲉⲛⲏⲣⲡ ... ⲉⲣ- ⲉⲗⲏⲁⲕⲏⲙⲉ.

(c) ⲛⲧ-(ⲁϥ-) fluctuates with ⲉⲛⲧ(ⲁϥ-) (§2.0.1.1.2); patts. (1) to (4) [24].

I have found no evidence in Shenoute for this converter before Tripartite negative bases or ⲛ-ⲁⲛ negatived patterns. Indeed, a drastic reductive change seems to have taken place here, compared with the system depicted in the *Études* and " Coptic Conjugation System ": negative conjugation forms are either unmarked as themes or (much more rarely) so marked by the circumstantial (in focus-initial patterns, see §§2.5-6 below) [25].

In the Second Present (converted Bipartite) we find as predicate, beside the durative infinitive, also the *stative* and the *predicative modifier*: (*Ch.* 76.46f.) ⲉϥⲥⲏ2 ⲅⲁⲣ ⲛⲧⲉⲓ2ⲉ ⲭⲉ- (*A 2* 114) ⲉⲥϣⲟⲟⲡ ⲧⲱⲛ / (*Ch.* 102. 19f.) ⲉⲣⲉⲡⲃⲁⲗ ⲙⲙⲁⲩ ⲉⲧⲃⲉⲛⲁⲩ / (*P* 130⁵ 119 ⲅⲟ) ⲉⲣⲉ 2ⲙⲡⲁ2ⲏⲧ 2ⲱⲥ ⲙⲁⲁⲩ ⲛⲟⲩⲙⲏⲛϣⲉ ⲛϣⲏⲣⲉ / (*Ch.* 159.33f.) ⲉϥ2ⲛⲧⲉⲩⲙⲏⲧⲉ ⲛⲟⲩⲏⲣ.

2.0.1.1.2 Second-power conversion. Polotsky (1957a:232 = *CP* 232, 1960a:§§11 Obs., 18) points out the compatibility of the circumstantial and Second Perfect converters [26], in a second-power conversion ⲉⲛⲧⲁϥ- (analyzable, in IC terms, as ε[ⲛⲧ(ⲁϥ-...)] (pattern 2). This has a practical implication in a corpus where ⲉⲛⲧ- (rel. perf.) is neatly opposed to ⲛⲧ- (Sec. Perf.). This is not the case in our corpus, where ⲉⲛ- and ⲛ- (and generally ε + nasal/syllabic nasal) fluctuate. The situation seems even more hopeless for the circumstantial converter before the ε-allomorph of the Sec. Tense (see below for a solitary instance of ⲉⲉⲣⲉ-). Here, zero is clearly the norm. Nevertheless, in cases where an " asyndetic parataxis " is improbable (that is, outside the narrative perfect [27], or in " list-/catalogic style " [28] and other suitable contextual configurations), absence of coordination or disjunction may imply a (zeroed) circumstantial converter. Some especially striking, recurring or typical instances follow:

[21] Polotsky 1944:51 (= *CP* 155), 1960a:§37.

[22] Cf. Polotsky 1957a:231f. (= *CP* 232).

[23] See Quecke 1979:440, Polotsky 1944:95f. (= *CP* 199f.).

[24] In *Chassinat*, ⲛⲧⲁϥ- seems to be the norm (with rare exceptions) for both converters, Sec. Tense and relative, except for line-final ⲛ- which is often written ⲉⲛ- (e.g. 42.34, 67.53, 84.12, 102.14 *vs.* 55, etc.). Elsewhere in *Ch.* ⲉⲛⲧⲁϥ- may be construed as circumstantial + Sec. perfect (e.g. in 150.24ff. ⲛ0ⲉ ⲙⲡⲁⲓ ⲉ(ⲛⲧⲁϥⲡⲱ2 ⲛⲛⲉϥ20ⲉⲓⲧⲉ ⲉⲧⲃⲉ-); not however in 158.1ff., where ⲉⲛⲧ- (rel.) and ⲛⲧ- (Sec.) are neatly opposed.

[25] Polotsky 1960a:§18.

[26] See too Funk 1981:184f. (circ. of Sec. Fut. in " Middle Egyptian "). The relative and Second Tense converters appear to be incompatible (cf. Funk, *TU* 119, 1976, p. 58 n. 2, but see Polotsky 1960:405 n. 3 = *CP* 251). Examples which could be taken as *preterite conversion* of the Second Present (cf. in Boh. ⲛⲉⲁϥⲑⲱⲛ *I Cor.* 12:17,19): *A 1* 241 (collated, Borg. 189 ⲣ2ⲏ) ⲉⲛⲉ·ⲉⲣⲉⲡⲛⲟⲩⲧⲉ ⲉⲛⲉⲣⲅⲉⲓ ⲁⲛ ⲙⲡⲁⲓⲕⲁⲓⲟⲛ 2ⲛⲛⲉⲧⲉⲛⲟⲩϥ ⲛⲉ ⲛⲟⲩⲟⲉⲓϣ ⲛⲓⲙ, ⲛⲉⲣⲉⲡⲭⲓ ⲛ6ⲟⲛⲥ ⲛⲁⲣ-ⲡⲕⲟⲥⲙⲟⲥ ⲛⲕⲁⲕⲉ ⲡⲉ (not to be confused with the *interrogative* ⲉⲛⲉ before the Sec. Present: *Ch.* 95.25ff., *P* 130⁵ 66 ⲟⲣ, *BMCat.* 79, 194 f. 4).

[27] E.g. *Ch.* 84-5, 132.28ff., *III* 47.11, *IV* 198.1ff.; see Layton 1979:184ff., and compare Havers " *veni-vidi-vici*-style " (1931:153).

[28] E.g. *Ch.* 32.36ff., 57.40ff., 66 *passim*, *III* 191.21f., *IV* 22.5ff. etc.; cf. the so-called " rhetorical asyndeton " and Havers' " enumerative Redeweise " (1931:114, 154).

(1) ε/∅-εϥ- [29]: the unique εερε-: (*IV* 107.5f.) ⲀϨⲢⲞϤ ϨⲞⲞⲨⲦ ⲘⲚⲤϨⲒⲘⲈ, ⲈⲈⲢⲈϨⲒⲘⲈ Ⲟ ⲚⲞⲨ ⲘⲚϨⲞⲞⲨⲦ ϨⲢⲀⲒ ⲚϨⲎⲦⲚ "What has a man to do with a woman, while in what capacity is a woman to be with a man among us?"; *circ.* + *negatived Sec. Present*: (*IV* 38.22ff.) Ⲏ ⲈⲢⲈⲦⲘⲚⲦⲈⲢⲞ ⲚⲘⲠⲎⲨⲈ ⲤⲂⲦⲰⲦ ⲚⲚϨⲞⲞⲨⲦ ⲘⲀⲨⲀⲀⲨ, ⲈⲚⲈⲤⲤⲂⲦⲰⲦ ⲀⲚ ⲚⲚⲈϨⲒⲞⲘⲈ... "... it being for the women that it is not ready...".

(2) the recurring and formulaic ⲈⲒϪⲰ ⲘⲠⲀⲒ ϪⲈ- "by which I mean to say...", a Shenoutean expression, marking and introducing the "hermeneia" after an allegory: (*Ch.* 102.19ff.) ⲔⲀⲒ ⲄⲀⲢ ⲈⲢⲈⲠⲂⲀⲖ ⲘⲘⲀⲨ ⲈⲦⲂⲈⲤⲰⲦⲘ ⲈⲒϪⲰ ⲘⲠⲀⲒ ϪⲈ ⲈⲢⲈⲦⲘⲚⲦⲢⲘⲘⲀⲞ ϢⲞⲞⲠ ⲈⲦⲂⲈⲚⲀ ⲀⲨⲰ ⲦⲈϮⲞⲨⲤⲒⲀ ⲈⲦⲂⲈⲢ-ϨⲀⲠ / (*P* 130⁴ 103 ⲢⲔⲂ) ⲈϢϪⲈ-ⲠϬⲈⲢⲰⲂ ϨⲚⲚⲈⲚϬⲒϪ ⲀⲨⲰ ⲦⲤⲎϬⲈ ⲈⲦⲂⲈⲞⲨ ⲠⲘⲞⲨⲒ ⲘⲠⲠⲞⲨϢⲚϢ ⲦⲰⲢⲠ ⲘⲠⲈⲤⲞⲞⲨ... ⲈⲒϪⲰ ⲘⲠⲀⲒ ϪⲈ-ⲈϢϪⲈ-ⲀⲚⲞⲚ-ϨⲈⲚⲤⲀⲂⲈⲈⲨ ⲀⲨⲰ ⲀⲚⲤⲞⲨⲚ-ⲚϨⲀⲠ ⲘⲠⲚⲞⲨⲦⲈ... ⲈⲦⲂⲈⲞⲨ ⲦⲚⲠⲀⲢⲀⲂⲀ ⲘⲠϨⲀⲠ ⲀⲨⲰ ⲦⲚϪⲒ ⲚϬⲞⲚⲤ. Also *P* 131⁴ 155 ⲖⲎ, 156 ⲖⲐ, 130² ⲢⲞⲎ, 70 ⲢⲠⲆ, 74 ⲢϤⲂ, *K* 9316, etc., etc.

(3) ε/∅ ⲚⲦⲀ-: (*Ch.* 146.52ff.) ⲘⲎ ⲚⲦⲀⲠⲈⲭ̅ⲥ̅ ⲈⲒ ⲀⲚ ⲈⲂⲞⲖ ϨⲘⲠⲒⲎ̅Ⲗ̅ ⲔⲀⲦⲀⲤⲀⲢⲝ- ⲚⲦⲀⲦⲈⲔⲔⲖⲎⲤⲒⲀ ⲈⲒ ⲈⲂⲞⲖ ⲚϨⲎⲦϤ / (*Ming.* 318) ⲦⲘⲎⲤⲈ ⲆⲈ ⲘⲠⲚ- (say, know or sim.) ϪⲈ-ⲈⲤⲤⲨⲚϨⲒⲤⲦⲀ ⲘⲘⲞⲤ ϨⲚⲀϢ ⲚⲄⲀⲘⲞⲤ ⲚⲦⲀⲨϪⲒⲞⲨϢ ⲘⲘⲞⲤ ⲚⲀϢ ⲚϨⲈ / (*A* 2 312) ⲀϢ ⲚⲖⲀⲞⲤ Ⲏ ⲀϢ ⲚⲤⲨⲚⲀⲄⲰⲄⲎ ⲈⲚⲦⲀⲠⲚⲞⲨⲦⲈ ϮⲤⲂⲰ ⲚⲀⲨ ϨⲚⲞⲨϢⲢϪ ⲚⲦⲈⲚϨⲈ (see §2.5.1.2) / (*P* 131⁴ 87 ⲢⲀⲂ) ⲠⲀⲚⲦⲰⲤ ⲞⲚ ⲈⲚ̅ⲦⲀⲨϪⲒⲦϤ ⲈⲂⲞⲖ ⲈⲦⲀⲔⲞϤ ϨⲚⲞⲨⲘⲚⲦⲀⲄⲢⲒⲞⲤ... ⲚⲀϢ ⲚⲦⲞϤ ⲚϨⲈ ⲈⲨⲚⲀϮ-ⲤⲞ ⲈⲦⲀⲔⲞ ⲚⲦⲈⲨⲮⲨⲬⲎ — a clear instance, with the circumstantial focalization-pattern preceding a main-clause interrogative one. Note that the syllabicity of the Ⲛ in ⲚⲦⲀ- is maintained after the converter. / (*Ch.* 41.42ff.) ⲚⲀⲠⲈⲭ̅ⲥ̅ ⲚⲈ ⲚⲦⲀϤⲦⲀⲀⲨ ⲚⲀⲨ ⲈⲨⲀⲠⲞⲖⲀⲨⲤⲒⲤ / (*III* 95.20ff.) ⲠⲢⲘⲘⲀⲞ ⲘⲘⲈ ⲚⲦⲀϤⲢ-ϨⲎⲔⲈ ⲈⲦⲂⲎⲎⲦⲚ ⲈⲠϪⲞⲈⲒⲤ ⲚⲚⲔⲀ ⲚⲒⲘ ⲠⲈ ⲚⲦⲀϤⲢϨⲘϨⲀⲖ ⲈⲦⲂⲈⲠⲢⲰⲘⲈ "the true rich one, who became poor for our sake, being the Lord of all things, it being for man's sake that he became a slave..."; *III* 71.18f. quoted below in §2.1.7.2.

(4) Two special cases where the postulation of the zero-variant of the circ. converter is called for by the syntactic structure: adnexal complementation to ⲦⲀⲒ ⲦⲈ ⲐⲈ/ⲚⲐⲈ ⲘⲠ-, ⲚⲦⲈⲒϨⲈ ⲞⲚ ⲠⲈ [30], or in the ⲠⲀⲒ ⲉ- appositive relative clause with a focalized modifier (ⲠⲀⲒ ⲈⲦ- for unfocal predication) [31]: (*Ch.* 64-5) ⲚⲐⲈ ⲄⲀⲢ ⲚⲚϢⲞⲢⲠ ⲚⲢⲰⲘⲈ ϨⲘⲠⲠⲀⲢⲀⲆⲈⲒⲤⲞⲤ ⲚⲦⲀϤϮ-ϪⲢⲞⲠ ⲚⲀⲨ ⲚϬⲒⲠϪⲀϪⲈ ϨⲚϨⲈⲚϢⲞϪⲚⲈ ⲚⲔⲢⲞϤ ⲀϪⲚϨⲢⲞⲞⲨ ⲈϤϢϢ ⲈⲂⲞⲖ "... while it is crying out voicelessly that the Enemy made them stumble by iniquitous counsels" / (*Ch.* 194.24ff.) ⲚⲦⲈⲒϨⲈ ⲞⲚ ⲠⲈ ⲠⲠⲀⲦⲢⲒⲀⲢⲭⲎⲤ ⲀⲂⲢⲀϨⲀⲘ ⲈⲚⲦⲀϤϪⲒ ⲚⲚⲒⲚⲞϬ ⲚⲤⲘⲞⲨ ⲈⲂⲞⲖ ϨⲒⲦⲘⲠⲚⲞⲨⲦⲈ ⲈⲦⲂⲈⲦⲈϤ-ⲘⲚⲦⲘⲀⲒϢⲘⲘⲞ "... it being because of his love of strangers that he received these great blessings" / (*III* 142.16ff.) ⲦⲀⲒ ⲞⲚ ⲦⲈ ⲐⲈ ⲦⲈⲚⲞⲨ ⲘⲠⲀⲒ ⲘⲚϨⲈⲚⲔⲞⲞⲨⲈ ⲈⲚⲦⲀⲨⲤⲰϢ ⲚⲚⲈⲚⲈⲒⲞⲦⲈ ⲈⲚⲦⲀⲨⲚⲔⲞⲦⲔ ⲘⲠⲈⲞⲨⲞⲈⲒϢ ⲈⲚⲈⲨϢⲞⲞⲠ ⲚⲘⲘⲀⲨ "... it being at the time when they (the Fathers) were still with them that they disdained them" / (*III* 31.22f.) ⲚⲀⲒ ⲈⲢⲈⲠⲈⲨⲦⲀⲖϬⲞ ϢⲞⲞⲠ ⲈⲂⲞⲖ ϨⲒⲦⲘⲠⲚⲞⲨⲦⲈ ⲘⲀⲨⲀⲀϤ "Those whose healing is *from God alone*" / (*III* 224.21f.) ⲚⲈⲒϢⲀϪⲈ ⲚⲀⲒ ϨⲒⲦⲞⲞⲦⲞⲨ ⲈⲢⲈⲠⲈⲚⲂⲒⲞⲤ ⲚⲀⲀⲚⲀⲒ. Also *III* 206.10ff., *Ch.* 84.29ff., 130 37ff. One must bear in mind that our hesitation in several of the exx. above between the 'circumstantial + adjunct' and 'circumstantial + (Sec. Tense + modifier nexus)' stems from the inability to predict with any confidence the occurrence of a Sec.-Tense construction — to place the boundary-line between the formal *mise en relief* and the *construction plane*. This selection may however be taken as fairly representative of those cotextual constellations where a regular Sec.-Tense "event" might be expected.

Incidentally, no certain example of the Sec. Tense of ⲚⲈ- is attested in Shenoute (POLOTSKY 1960a: §18[f.]); a possible instance is *III* 203.15f. (" Had you kept all your good deeds,) ϮⲘⲈⲈⲨⲈ ϪⲈ-ⲈⲚⲈⲢⲈⲠⲚⲞⲨⲦⲈ ⲚⲀϢⲀϪⲈ ⲚⲘⲘⲈ ⲦⲈⲚⲞⲨ ⲚⲐⲈ ⲚⲦⲀϤϢⲀϪⲈ ⲚⲀⲢⲭⲀⲒⲞⲤ ⲘⲚϨⲀϨ...

---

[29] A probable case is *Ch.*89.12ff. ⲘⲀⲢⲈϤⲤⲰⲦⲘ ⲈⲠⲈⲠⲢⲞⲪⲎⲦⲎⲤ ⲈϤϪⲰ ⲚⲚⲀⲒ ⲈⲦⲂⲎⲎⲦϤ ⲀⲚ ⲀⲖⲖⲀ ⲈⲦⲂⲎⲎⲦⲚ (of the same type — circ. + neg. nexus — are *IV* 64.1ff., 65.11ff.). This interpretation is not however the only one possible: the negation may well be of an *adjunct to a circumstantial verb*, not of the nexus between a Second Tense and a modifier. The absence of any punctuation between ⲈϤϪⲰ ⲚⲚⲀⲒ and ⲈⲦⲂⲎⲎⲦϤ in the *Ch.* example may be of significance.

[30] SHISHA-HALEVY 1972:§2.1.1.2; see our §1.2.1.2.

[31] *ibid.* §2.1.3.2.2.

2.0.1.2 On a question of identity and homonymy: sec. tense vs. circumstantial, sec. tense vs. relative. On a strictly Sahidic-internal and synchronic basis [32], there is, on the one hand, no a priori distributional reason to reject the morphological identity of Second Perf. (Є)ΝΤΑ- with the rel. perfect or of Second Aorist ЄϢΑ- with the relative *or* circumstantial aorist, or of Second Tense Є- in all other cases, with the circumstantial converter [33], all featuring here in a set of patterns with remarkable functional affinity (and to this extent too belonging together). On the other hand, if we apply a strict structural-analytic definition of identity, every single pattern occurrence of the morph, i.e. its syntagmatic/paradigmatic localization, must be considered its " name ", leaving us with a fragmentation of at least *five* possible entities, some homonymous [34]. Let us take a closer look at the distributional structure of Є- and (Є)ΝΤ- (again as if we are innocent of all historic and extra-Sahidic knowledge, and not taking (Є)ΝΤ-, ЄΤЄ- matter-of-factly as allomorphs of Є-). We must bear in mind that this structure is (a) somewhat distorted, since it is incomplete without the suprasegmental distinctive feature of each pattern, and (b) arbitrary to a degree, since the definition of the critical extent is variable (§§0.2.1.2, 0.2.5.1). Moreover, not all environments considered are commensurate.

	Є-	ЄΑ-	ЄΜЄ-	ЄϢΑ-	(Є)ΝΤ-
adnominal (adnexal:attributive)	+	+	+	+	+
adverbal	+	+	+	(—) [35]	—
initial, non-thematic	+	+	—	—	—
initial, thematic (patts. 2-3)	+	—	(?)	+	+
final, non-thematic	+	+	+	+	+
final, thematic (patts. 4-6)	+	+	(?)	+	+
autofocal (patt. 1)	+	—	(?)	+	+
final, focal	+	+	—	—	—
initial, focal	+	+	—	—	—

One notes the maximal distribution of Є- [36], and the similar distribution of (Є)ΝΤΑ- and ЄϢΑ-, ЄΜЄ- (for the latter, the evidence is inconclusive), but most instructive are the patterns in which all are opposed as one paradigm, namely, (4) to (6); we cannot therefore interrelate them as allomorphs of the same archimorpheme. Moreover, the circumstantial and Second Tense converters are compatible (§2.0.1.1.2) and

---

[32] Diachronic information, at least from pre-Demotic Egyptian, points to the identity of the " emphatic " forms and relative forms (POLOTSKY 1976: esp. §§2.1, 2.3), with the absence of gender-number concord — i.e. a tagmemic feature — the sole distinctive feature of the former: *mrr.f* and *sḏm.n.(tw).f, j.jr.f sḏm* are relative forms, with further bifurcation purely functional, i.e. their formal *Merkmal* as " emphatic " or " relative " is their very construction, not a mere *correlation with* this construction. The inference from dialects in which the two are distinct (e.g. FUNK 1981:194, from " Middle Egyptian ") is, I believe, unwarranted: the merger in Sahidic, a diachronic event, has synchronic systemic consequences: it is these we must report on.

[33] So already EDGERTON (1935:261ff.): " (separating the forms) seems to lack empirical reality ".

[34] Consider exx. of the type (*A 2* 463-4) ⲌⲰⲂ ⲚⲒⲘ ⲚⲦⲀϤⲀⲀⲨ, ⲚⲦⲀϤⲀⲀⲨ ⲦⲎⲢⲞⲨ ⲈⲦⲂⲈⲠⲈⲚⲞⲨⲬⲀⲒ, neatly showing the pattern way to defining identity.

[35] No certain examples of adverbal circumstantial for ϢⲀϤ- are known to me (candidates are *Wess.* 9 91b 1, 140a 12, 145b 20). For ⲈⲘⲈϤ- we do have some unambiguous exx. (*III* 94.20, *IV* 38.4f., *Mun.* 107). The circ. present appears to supply the circumstantial for the affirmative aorist (consider *Ch.* 130.46f., *III* 94.19, *IV* 15.24 etc.). (A possible " Middle Egyptian " example is *Mt.* 11:19: ⲌⲀϤⲒ ⲚⲘ̄ⲠϢⲎⲢⲈ ⲘⲠⲢⲰⲘⲈ ⲈϢⲀϤⲞⲨⲞⲘ ⲈϢⲀϤⲤⲰ).

[36] Historically speaking this is hardly surprising, as this is a merger of the functional ranges of both *jw-* and *j.jr-*.

thus prove their categorial disparity (unlike the relative and Second Tense converters). The negation test — N(ЄЧ-) ΛN for the Sec. Tense, Є(NЧ- ΛN) for the circumstantial — used by POLOTSKY (1960:§28 Obs.) to establish their distinctness, does not seem to me conclusive, since it might be argued that it is this arrangement (or, from a different angle, juncture) *differentia specifica* which characterizes the ЄЧ-form as a thematic pre-focal component of a nexus — N.B.: no NЄЧ- ΛN in patts. (1), (3), (4)-(6); thematic ЄNЧ- ΛN in (5) —, *vs.* non-thematic (rhematic or a nexus in itself, adnexal); the negation arrangement here assumes the functional burden. To sum up my view on this subject [37]: On the analytic plane, I accept the homonymy of the Sec. Tense and circumstantial, Sec. Tense and relative, perhaps even with a greater fragmentation: Є-, NT- are signals of different purport in different environments. On a more synthetic plane of description, I would prefer to regard the circumstantial as a component in a pattern set, the Sec. Tense a component in another, due consideration being given to their paradigmatic and syntagmatic encounters. This policy is adopted in the present discussion.

An altogether different matter is the *practical* question of distinguishing the circ./relative from the Second-Tense converters. Since we are not here concerned with " forms " but with patterns, this is rarely of consequence. Consider, for instance, the final-consecutive ХЄ-/ХЄKΛΛC ЄЧNΛ-. Is the converter circumstantial or Second Tense? Did the question have any meaning for the Coptic decoder of this syntagm?

2.0.2 THE THEORETICAL BACKGROUND. Even a superficial attempt at an IC and functional analysis of Second Tense constructions brings home two points: (a) The components are not of necessity reflected in the clause structure, but must be referred both to information in the preceding stretches of the text (" cotext ") and to this cotext as *syntactically* relevant to and in cohesion with the Second-Tense construction. The resolvable units, "predication", "subject", "predicate", "predicative component" etc., constitute a whole structure which, quite apart from (and beyond) the pattern-specific syntactic realization and articulations, is meaningful in an ultra-clausal "logical" or rather *informational* system of reference [38]. (b) We realize there are, even in this sense of structure, predicates and predicates, subjects and subjects; we feel the difference between a " non-emphatic " or paradigmatically unmarked subject/predicate and an " emphatic " one (to use provisionally one of a host of semi-opaque and cryptic synonyms for " strengthening "). This is a real opposition with formal correlates, a paradigm of grades or types of predication, of *thematicity* and of *focality* — see below.

2.0.2.0.1 THEORETICAL-TERMINOLOGICAL SYSTEMS: TOPIC - COMMENT - FOCUS / GIVEN - NEW; COTEXT-SENSITIVE GRAMMAR. Without pretending to span within these limits the considerable questions involved, I shall give below a brief review of some important theoretical systems. (a) A preliminary step, very important for our purpose, is to recognize the *optional, subjective* nature of the informational

---

[37] On the theory of this difficult issue, see HARRIS 1951, esp. §§13.31, 13.41, 15.2-3; HOUSEHOLDER 1971:196ff., 220f. (on the limitations of the complementary-distribution test).

[38] POLOTSKY 1944 (e.g. 30f. = *CP* 134f., 57ff. = *CP* 161ff.), 1962:414ff. (= *CP* 419ff.). Polotsky was the first to replace (for Coptic) " grammatical subject " by *actor* (1960a:§3) and thus restore " subject " — and " predicate " — to their original " logical " frame of reference, brilliantly demonstrating the analytic advantage of this essential reinstatement: in Coptic, " grammatical predicate " — a contradiction in terms — has no analytic meaning. An early statement (the earliest in modern linguistics?) on the distinction of logical and grammatical structures, may be found in BECKER 1836:15ff., and later 1841:579ff. (In what is in fact the early edition of [1836], namely the *Deutsche Grammatik* of 1829, the " grammatical predicate " still reigns supreme. See HASELBACH 1966:198ff., 209f.) Next we find the " psychological " subject/predicate in VON DER GABELENTZ 1869:378; WEIL 1879 (see pp. 14f., 20f.); TOBLER 1886:5ff., 88ff., and on in the typologistic-psychologistic trend of 19th-century " *Sprachwissenschaft* ", parallel and antagonistic to the Neogrammarian mainstream. (The fact that the " psychological " terms are preeminent in PAUL 1920 shows how over-simplifying it is to regard him as the " spokesman of ths Neogrammarians " in all respects.)

organization of the discourse [39], like numerous other phenomena of grammar (some cases of word-order regulation, selection of " particles " and other inter-clausal relators, some tenses, etc.). This is not the grammaticality of dependence and conditioning. This realization is vital, lest we look in vain for a single simple " responsible factor " for the occurrence of a Second Tense, and lest we lose sight of our main task, which is to clarify the *signifié* of the Second-Tense *signifiant* or mark; it is not to attempt to account for its presence. (b) Within clause boundaries, we have a ' *theme + rheme* ' structure. THEME — in HAL-LIDAY's definition (1967:212) [40] a " point of departure [41], what is being talked about, what I am talking about now "; RHEME — " what is being said about the theme ". This is the *thematic* structure, grammatical in the sense that it is " purely syntactic " (*ibid*. 199f., 211f.), i.e. on clause level, intra-clausal. (c) Halliday rightly stresses the presence of another independent yet related structure: the *informational* one, in the *information block* or *unit*, which may, or may not, coincide with clause extent. The weak point — " bridge ", overlap or liaison factor between the two structures where it is all too easy to slip from one to another and confuse them, is the identity or disparity of the " given " (" what you were/I was talking about ", in Halliday's definition) with the theme. They *can* be identical, but this is not always the case. " Givenness " is a cotextual factor [42]: the " given " segment — the (co)text-bound one [43] — I would here name TOPIC. It is the cotextual component or representative in the clause, ideally coinciding with the theme but often distinct from it, with the theme in cohesion with it in one way or another — always in a different structure and to a different extent (the subtextual segment of the information unit, which may even include the paragraph and larger textual subdivisions). Halliday's " theme proper " (1967:200) is my " theme " and " topic " combined. The theme is Janus-faced, with relations of one grammatical kind inside its clause, and of a different kind backwards with its cotext. The Second Tense can be treated properly only in terms of reference of a cotext-sensitive grammar, since it involves the speaker's option of " staging " the information. It is a cotext-form *par excellence*, in evaluating which the degree of cotext boundness is crucial; it must be examined both in terms of ' theme - rheme ' and ' topic - focus ' structures. (d) In parallel with the rheme, predicated (" installed ") on the theme inside the clause, the topic — in

---

[39] HALLIDAY 1967:220: " [The concept of theme] is based on the notion of choice — it represents an option on the part of the speaker "; GRIMES 1975:323ff.: " ...choice of one of a number of possible ways of ' staging ' the information ".

[40] Also 1967:464. I generally adopt and apply here Halliday's main ideas and terminology. For a good summary of his own scheme, see HALLIDAY 1967:241ff., 1972:162ff.; also JONES 1977:81ff. However, I use the term " topic " and extend the application of " information unit " up to and beyond the paragraph.

[41] This linear-axis conception of the theme can be traced from WEIL's " point du départ, notion initiale " (1879:20f.), corresponding to VON DER GABELENTZ's " psychological subject " (1869:378: " das, woran, worüber ich den Angeredeten denken lassen will " — while the psych. predicate is " das, was er sich darüber denken soll ", that is, the predicate in a subject-dependent definition; see too *idem* 1901:365ff., 369f.). Similarly, BLÜMEL's *A(usgangspunkt)* → *Z(iel)* (1914); BALLY's (1950: e.g. §32) and GOSSEN (1951) *thème* → *propos*, MÜLLER-HAUSER (1943) *thème* → *énoncé* Theme → rheme is used by AMMANN (1920), and, following him, LÖPFE 1940), yet he occasionally mixes or approximates the logical and grammatical structures, e.g. on p. 22, talking of word-order — " vom Thema zur Aussage, vom Handelnden zur Handlung "; see HASELBACH 1966:211 — a *rapprochement* of unfortunate and far-reaching consequences, traceable to the belief in " the natural ' vocation ' [of certain word-classes] to symbolize subject and predicate " (SANDMANN 1954:101). Compare here the equally formalistic classical ῥῆμα (ROBINS 1966:7ff.: Aristotle's ῥῆμα, " set of words functioning in their capacity as the second component of a two-part sentence "; for the Stoic definition see SCHMIDT 1839:61). In the Prague School we find an evolution: from Mathesius' two-faced definition of the theme, covering both our " theme " and " topic " — " that which is known or at least obvious in the given context, and from which the speaker proceeds " (*apud* FIRBAS 1964) to DANEŠ and FIRBAS' improved version, separating utterance-level (theme → rheme) from text-level (given → new): DANEŠ 1974, JONES 1977:60ff.

[42] The " original sin " of many a terminological stumble in this context is carelessness in distinguishing between " known " (" assumed as known "), " accepted ", " given ", anaphora nucleus and " basis of the *énoncé* ". See CHAFE 1976, ALLERTON 1978.

[43] SGALL 1974:28: " [Elements the speaker reminds of as elements] known from the context, from the situation or from general conditions of the given utterance "; this is too comprehensive, and again mixes clause- and cotext-levels.

its information unit — prepares us for the FOCUS, the hub and kernel of this structure. (HALLIDAY 1967: 200ff., 207, defines it in prosodic terms which are not much help for Coptic, although they do not conflict with what we know of the tonicity of focal segments.) The focus is *new* in relation to the topic — a matter of relative, not absolute value [44]; it is usually coincident with the rheme. The focus is the message nucleus.

The Second-Tense form may, in correlation with and as a component of certain cotextual patternings (§2.0.2.4), be the *theme* (often ≠ topic) [45], focalizing its rheme (patts. 2-3). It may be self-focalizing, with topic and focus, theme and rheme, all in one (pattern 1). It may be a *topic* (= theme), following its focus (rheme) (patts. 4-6).

2.0.2.1 TOPICALIZATION, THEMATIZATION: MEANS AND PARADIGM [46].
In the first place, one notes measures applied to the *nominal* theme: its " isolation " by various means, especially its extrapositive detachment from the main structure — so-called *segmentation* [47], with or without additional marking [48], with or without resumption. The *verbal* thematic component may be nominalized and treated as a nominal theme; it may be de-finitized, with its lexemic and grammatical constituents separated [49]. However, the theme may also be unmarked in any way except by its slot in the clause (compare the actor noun/pronoun in the Coptic conjugation form [50]). It may then receive an additional, " over- " characterization, usually by prosodic and/or placement-shift (such as segmentation) highlighting, thus realizing what amounts to a *distinct member in a binary paradigm of thematicity*, the PROMINENT THEME [51], which ought to be explicitly related to the unmarked member and not impressionistically subsumed under " emphasis " or " *Hervorhebung* ".

2.0.2.2.1 FOCALIZATION AND FOCALITY: MEANS, PARADIGM, VALUES.
Focalization — the marking as focus [52] — and thematization are two faces of the same coin, since theme or topic-marking constructions achieve by the same token the effect of focus-marking. Still, there are patterns in which only the focus is marked (e.g. prosodically or by a particle) and others where both focus and theme/topic are marked (notably the Cleft Sentence, §2.0.2.2.4). Here too we must distinguish between a focus indicated by virtue of basic syntactic properties — an unmarked member in the focality paradigm (ⲘⲘⲀⲨ in ⳝⲘⲘⲀⲨ),

---

[44] Consider the distinction between " structurally new ", i.e. " anaphorically new " (also " inherently new " in the case of closed systems, such as prepositional sets) and non-anaphoric, situational " newness " (HALLIDAY 1967:204ff.). See too DANEŠ 1974:109ff. This corresponds to the " *Hauptbegriff* " (not subject-dependent) definition of logical predicate (from BECKER 1836: 18ff. onwards).

[45] See §2.7.2 for specific ⧺ *topic* → (theme + rheme/focus)⧺ schemes.

[46] For some general (also typological) material, see HALLIDAY 1967:211f.; JONES 1977:91ff., 174ff.; DAHL 1974:18; GRIMES 1975:343f.

[47] MÜLLER-HAUSER 1943:152ff., GOSSEN 1951:164ff., following BALLY (1950:§§79-99).

[48] Such as pre-Demotic *jr-* (cf. MÜLLER-HAUSER 1943:226ff.). On the affinity of topicalization and protasis cf. JUNGE 1978: 66ff.

[49] Cf. EBELING 1905:113-128 (" Dispiacere non mi dispiacete "); GOLDENBERG 1971; also the use of English " do " outside the interrogative/negative allomorphic role (" do go ", " he did say so " — functionally very close to our pattern (1), ' ⲈⲔⲖⲞⲂⲈ '). In the case of the Greek " Second Tenses " (ROSÉN 1957, esp. pp. 135f., 150f.), the whole εἰμί + *participle* syntagm is, in its external relationships, thematic; internally, however, it constitutes a nexus.

[50] Cf. " procédés de position ", MÜLLER-HAUSER 1943:92ff.

[51] HALLIDAY 1967:213f., 216; DAHL 1974:18 (" emphatic topic "); JONES 1977:169ff. (see also 3ff., 6ff.). Compare REGULA's " mise en relief thématique " (1966). In a somewhat different, currently used sense of " prominent ", Coptic is a *topic-prominent* language, a language that marks its topics rather than its " subjects " or directly marking the focus. CALLENDER's "focusing" (1970:186ff.) seems to include the prominent topic.

[52] Not to be confused with focus or rheme *isolation* (e.g. by the " question test "). See JONES 1977:68f., 76f., 87f. The two issues are of course related, since it is with the marking of a focus (or the focalization value of a mark) that we are concerned.

and one in the framework of a marked topicalization " truss " or a special focalization pattern (ЄЧMMAY), the marked member [53]. The Second-Tense converter is either a prominent-thematization (often also top-icalization) signal *or* (pattern 1) a mark of self-focality. The pattern-initial focus (§§2.4-6) appears to be yet another member of this paradigm, half-way between the unmarked and high-focality extremes.

2.0.2.2.2 Although focality is an *absolute* grammatical category, it has relative functional values, resolved by the macrosyntactic structure: (a) *Polemicity* determined and varied by the cotext (it is, for instance, different in text-initial position, different in the response-substructure of dialogue, yet again in reference to a contrast); (b) a high " Communicative Dynamism " level (see definition of *CD* in §2. 0.2.3), i.e. a high degree of contribution to the development of the informational progression (high " ac-releration "); (c) the " emphasis " value. This is an elusive, vague notion, evading grammatical frames of reference, subjectively envisaged on a variety of levels, from synonymity with " focality " to being celegated to extra-grammatical territories [54]. I adopt a broad definition, close to Weinrich's " *Relief* ": any divergence or variance from the textual environment level, with appropriate sub-categorization. We may, for instance, have an emphasis of contrast [55], of specification (vs. characterization) [56], distinctive or isolating emphasis (cf. POLOTSKY 1944:33f. = *CP* 137f.).

2.0.2.2.3 Focality may be (language-specifically) non-pertinent — conditioned or inherent (in these cases, not subject to cotextual macrosyntactic analysis, and not in opposition to a non-focal occurrence outside the scheme of values referred to above). This is the important case of the *interrogative* modifiers and pronouns, cogently applied by POLOTSKY in his study of the Second Tense [57]. This is of consequence, not only for the informational patterning of these cases, but also for the very placement of the foci (see §2.8.1 below).

2.0.2.2.4 THE CLEFT SENTENCE AND THE SECOND TENSE. Probably the most familiar set of focalization patterns, well known in a certain European *Sprachbund* and (thanks to Polotsky) in Egyptian-Coptic, is the so-called CLEFT SENTENCE (" *phrase coupée* ") [58]. In general terms, these are patterns

---

[53] See HALLIDAY's definition (1967:207f.: " The unmarked focus does not imply any preceding information ").

[54] Cf. THESLEFF 1955:12ff. (semantic-psychologistic, with sub-categorization into " emphasis ", " intensification ", " ampli-fication ", " strengthening "); WEIL 1879:9 (types: rhetorical, logical, affective, grammatical; an instance of " rhetorical emphasis ", and a logical freak, is the case of *two simultaneous foci* in a single information unit: see §2.7.1.3.1. below, and cf. LÖPFE 1940:24); MOORHOUSE 1959:73ff.; HALLIDAY 1967:203f., 207; DRESSLER 1968:77ff.

[55] Cf. CHAFE 1976:33ff., and (for the stylistic aspect) FEHLING 1969:36-47, 271-9, 295-307.

[56] Cf. the attempt at structuring emphasis in LÖPFE 1940:27f.

[57] 1944:29ff. (= *CP* 133ff.), 87 (= *CP* 191); CALLENDER 1971 (esp. p. 21. Callender discusses the relations between topicali-zation, Cleft-Sentence focalization and the inherently focal interrogatives, in a generative framework). We still need an investigation of *non-interrogative* modifiers of inherent focality (like MOΓIC -, §1.3.11.6, or KAΛШC -, §1.3.11.1.3; cf. §2.5.0.1). See PAUL 1920:§200; KARCEVSKI 1936:109. Strikingly comparable are the Irish " adverbs " which occur usually or exclusively in Cleft Sentence patterns: *amhlaidh* " thus ", *minic* " often ", *ar éigean* " hardly ", Welsh *braidd* (*y*-), cf. our MOΓIC in foc. patt. (4).

[58] For Cleft Sentence analysis and terminology, see POLOTSKY 1937:2f. (= *CP* 100f.), 1944:57ff. (= *CP* 161ff.), 1962a: 413 n. 1 (= *CP* 418), 1976:§2.5; CALLENDER 1970:Ch. IV, 1971. For the French construction, see DAMOURETTE-PICHON §§1554-66 (coining " *vedette* " and " *glose* " for the focus and theme-topic); MÜLLER-HAUSER 1943:205-215. For some early discus-sion, see BECKER 1841:542, 600; TOBLER 1886:121, 196 n. 2 f. For English, see JESPERSEN 1937:83-9, 1954:147ff. For Latin, LÖFSTEDT 1966. For some general or typologic-comparative studies, see BECKMAN 1934:29ff.; DRESSLER 1973:54, 57ff.; GRIMES 1975:341f.; COYAUD 1979:119. The Celtic Cleft Sentence constructions are most interesting. To the best of my knowledge, they have not yet been structurally studied. See H. Lewis, *Celtica* 3:295f. (1956), for the so-called " mixed sentence " in Welsh; H. Wagner, *Das Verbum in den Sprachen der britischen Inseln* (Tübingen 1959) 81f., 173f.; H. Lewis' famous " The Sentence in Welsh " (*Proc. Brit. Academy* 1942); MACCANA 1973; most of Pokorny's rather superficial *substratum* articles, and many dialect-specific sketches (e.g. by Fink, Bergström, O'Nolan, Strachan, Dottin).

focalizing a (pro)noun or modifier by means of a nominalizing (less frequently, " adverbializing ", see §2.5) thematization of the verb. The focus and its theme are in a nexal relationship, realized in Indo-European by the verb " be " as copula, with an additional arrangement (word-order) focalization procedure, *viz.* preposing the focus to the theme, with (in most cases) the entailed syntactic feature of a formal cataphoric pronominal subject, to which the theme is appositive: " *It is... who/which/that...* ", " *C'est... qui/que...* ". Polotsky's identification of the Egyptian and Coptic Second-Tense verb form with the *glose* (Cleft Sentence theme) presents the following difficulties: (a) Formally the comparability is imperfect, since there is no " clefting " [59] in Egyptian and Coptic — the order of the terms which Polotsky has in mind is *theme → rheme* or *topic → focus*, and (b) the nominalness of the theme is not incontestably established. I suggest that it would be preferable to regard the Second Tense as a form which plays a role in several patterns, some of which — our patts. (4-6) — are formally closer to the particular Indo-European Cleft Sentence than others. The Second-Tense converter, an exponent of thematicity or focality — in short, a signal of specific *Functional Sentence Perspective / Communicative Dynamism* (§2.0.2.3) properties — should not, I believe, be confined in a descriptive Procrustean bed. Like other focalization patterns, the Cleft Sentence is still in need of more precise statements of value. It is (for instance) cataphoric, i.e. non-polemic, " presentative ", in certain textual slots (e.g. in text-initial position, at the opening to a parable or " *paradeigma* ", in the answer to a question, and in a description) [60]. Needless to say, subsuming all these as allo-patterns under one heading *a priori* is largely unwarranted, since we lack those suprasegmental features which would distinguish them formally. Also, the paradigmatic standing of the Cleft Sentence, i.e. its relation to unmarked-focality members of its paradigm, varies considerably from one language to another. (On a selective [impresssionistic] scale ranging from advanced devaluation [Welsh], through ever higher pertinacy roles in Irish, French, British literary English, to full focality status in other Germanic languages, I would grade Coptic somewhere between Irish and French, rather in the proximity of the latter.)

2.0.2.3 THE ORGANIZATION OF INFORMATION. This organization, static and dynamic, is what one has to look out for when attempting to formalize the relations of the thematic/topical component with its environment. We must apply some gradient notion like COMMUNICATIVE DYNAMISM ("CD"), in FIR-BAS' definition [61]: " The extent to which the element contributes towards the development of the communication ", higher cotextual interdependence meaning a lower grading of CD; always considering, however, that there is always some noticeable development and some factor of cotextual boundness (absolute idling [*Leerlauf*] is as much a myth as is absolute cotextual independence), and that constructing a scale of CD is difficult because of the continuous spectrum-like nature of such a scale, with countless subjectively postulated intergradations between the extremes of very low and very high grading. The arbitrariness and subjective quality of the following schematization are therefore to be expected. The following points must be borne in mind: (a) Attention must focus on the skeleton — the extremes and major intermediate points of reference — in this gradation, rather than the minor ones, which are not always formally correlatable. (Note that CD is essentially a *junctural* — cohesional — concept, hence by nature a continuum; see §6.0.2.) (b) We cannot *predict* the degree or contour of CD. This is decided, i.e. made clear, only after the pattern in question, with all its constituent signals, is completed. (c) Often one must distinguish between the CD-grading of the Second-Tense *form* and that of its *construction*, in which case we have rather a CD-*contour* in the given extent. (d) The CD gradation cuts across other formal typo-

---

[59] In transformational jargon, " clefting " is synonymous with " focalization ".
[60] Cf. ROTHENBERG 1971, MACCANA 1973 (esp. 104ff.); see SHISHA-HALEVY 1975:477.
[61] *Apud* DANEŠ 1974:19; see FIRBAS 1964, BENEŠ 1968, JONES 1977:64ff.

logies of the focus (interrogative/non-interrogative, word-class, rhetorical/non-rhetorical). (e) The two scales below, I and II, must be superimposed symmetrically onto each other. The higher and lower CD in these scales (like topicalizaffion and focalization) are but the two faces of one and the same coin (we are after all concerned here with *links*, i.e. formal indications of cohesion, various grammatical and se-mantic anaphoric signals referring back to *prius dicta* or *prius nota*, and with *delimitations*, i.e. indications of the absence or negation of a link; see §6.0.2). (f) Note the high incidence of grades 3-4 on both scales·

SCALE I:	(LOWER CD) ⟶ (HIGHER CD)
grade ∅	ΝΕΤΧΟϹΕ ΕΥΧΟϹΕ ΕΤΒΕΝΕΥΠΡΑΞΙϹ ΝΑΓΑΘΟΝ (*A 1* 163).
grade 1-2 (a)	ΕΡΕΠΟΥΟΕΙΝ ΜΠΟΟϨ ΜΝΝϹΙΟΥ ΝϨΗΤϹ (i.e. in the night; not even the nexus is new) (*A 2* 248).
grade 1-2 (b)	ΕΤΒΕΠΑΙ ΝΤΑΠΕΙΝΟϬ ΝϹΑϨΟΥ ΕΙ ΕϨΡΑΙ ΕΧΜΠΕΙϨΓΕΜΩΝ (*III* 26.8ff.; only the nexus is new; all terms are anaphoric).
grade 2	ΕΡΕΠΑΙ ΝΑϢΩΠΕ ΝΑΝ (*Ch.* 88.2f.; ΠΑΙ focal).
grade 3	ΝΤΑΙΧΕ-ΠΑΙ ΕΙϹΟΟΥΝ ΧΕ- (*A 2* 73).
grade 3-4 (a)	ΝΤΑΥΕΙ ΤΩΝ (*III* 87.12f., context implied).
grade 3-4 (b)	ϨΙΤΝΟΥ ΕΑϨΑϨ Ρ-ϢΜΜΟ ΕΡΩΤΝ, ΜΗ ϨΙΤΝ- ΑΝ (*A 1* 89, *prius notum* rhetorically assumed).
grade 3-4 (c)	ΕΝΝΑϢΧΟΟΥ ΤΗΡΟΥ ΑΝ (*A 2* 238-9), ΕΥΧΙ-ϬΟΛ (*IV* 51.17).
grade 4-5	ΝΤΑΝϹΩΤΜ ϨΙΤΝΝΙΜ ΕΝΕϨ ΧΕ- (*A 2* 463).

SCALE II:	(LOWER CD) ⟵ HIGHER CD)
grade ∅	"ΕϤϨΚΛΕΙΤ" (*Ch.* 81.7; *lemmatic* role).
grade 1	"ΕΝϢΩΝΕ" (*A 1* 56), "ΕΙΜΟϹΤΕ ΜΜΟΟΥ" (*III* 123.1f.): §2.1.4. ΕΥΝΑΕΙ (*IV* 61.29, jussive), ΕΥΡ-ΝΟΒΕ (*IV* 80.2) — all patt. (1).
grade 1-2	ΕΙΝΑΟΥΕΜ-ΟΥ (*Ch.* 105.17f.).
grade 2	ΕΙΟ ΜΜΑΤΟΙ, ΕΙΟ ΝϨΗΓΕΜΩΝ (*A 1* 43), ΕΙΟ ΝΑϢ ΝϨΕ (*A 1* 104).
grade 2-3 (a)	ϨΜΠΕϨΟΟΥ ΕΤΟΥϢΑΧΕ ΕΡΟϤ ΧΕϤΟ ΝΝΑΗΤ, ΝΤΑϤΡ-ΘΕ ΝΤΟϤ ΝΟΥΑΤΝΑ (*III* 76.19f.).
grade 2-3 (b)	ΕΝΑΙΑΤϤ ΑΝ... ΧΕ-..., ΑΛΛΑ ΕΝΑΙΑΤϤ... ΕϤϢΑΝ (*Cl. Pr.* 33, 1; the whole configuration has high CD, inequally divided between the constituents).
grade 3-4	ΝΤΑϤϹΜΝΤ-ΜΠΗΥΕ ΝΑϢ ΝϨΕ (*Ming.* 288), ΕΤΒΕΟΥ ΕΚΟ ΝΚΡΟϤ (*A 2* 146).
grade 3	ΕΡΕΙΟΥΔΑϹ ϢΟΟΠ ΤΩΝ ΤΕΝΟΥ (*A 2* 53), ΕΤΒΕΟΥ... ΕΙΝΑΟΥΑϨΤ ΝϹΑ-, ΕΤΒΕΟΥ Ν†ΝΑΟΥΑϨΤ ΑΝ ΝϹΑ- (*Ch.* 72.1ff.).
grade 4-5	ϨΙΤΝΟΥ ΕΑϨΑϨ Ρ-ϢΜΜΟ ΕΡΩΤΝ, ΜΗ ϨΙΤΝΝΝΟΜΟϹ ΑΝ (*A 1* 89).
grade 5	ΕΡΕΠΒΑΛ ΜΜΑΥ ΕΤΒΕΝΑΥ (*Ch.* 102.19ff.; all terms and nexal relationship - *prius nota*)

2.0.2.4 THE SYNTAGMATICS OF NEXUS: A NOTE (see §2.8). In considering the ⧣ theme + rheme ⧣ limited unit we set out (as did Polotsky) from a pattern arranged ' theme → rheme '. The association of the theme with the initial position is often pointed out and considered a basic or normal placement [62],

---

[62] Cf. BECKER 1841:§122 (586ff.; see HASELBACH 1966:210); VON DER GABELENTZ 1869:379f.; WEIL 1879:20f.; HALLIDAY in DANEŠ (ed.) 1974:52.

this order reflecting the logical " *marche des idées* " [63], as well as the macrosyntactic " thematic progression " [64], the progression from *given* to *new* [65], low to high CD, the rhetorical φυσικὴ τάξις. (Indeed, thematic/rhematic role is a matter of position rather than of pattern slot.) However, this ideal arrangement is in opposition [66] to certain *focus-initial* patterns which, while mostly understated [67] in pan-Coptic or diachronic exposition, are nevertheless fully constitutional, even decisive features of the synchronic picture: they realize yet another type, constitute yet another member in the paradigm of focality.

Although *nucleus - satellite* dependence analysis does not necessarily suit or match the *theme - rheme* analysis (BARRI 1978), the latter can be mapped onto the former, the two being compatible (witness the adnexal modification of the circumstantial and conjunctive; see §7.1.3).

2.0.2.5 THE SECOND TENSE: AN INTEGRATED VIEW OF INFORMATION STRUCTURING AND FUNCTION. With the reminder that any syntaxization we may carry out must be incomplete without suprasegmental data, we arrive at the following correlational picture (note in particular the characteristics of pattern (1), accounting for its being our point of departure in the present description, at variance with Polotsky's):

(a)

pattern	function	Sec.-Tense/circumstantial	clause
(1)	autofocal	theme + rheme, ≠ topic; formal topic, focalization signal	= information unit
(2)-(3)	heterofocal	topic-constituent or topic-resumptive; theme: given information	less than information unit
(4)-(6)	heterofocal	theme = topic: given information	less than information unit

(b)

pattern	nexus structure [68]	inform. structure contour	inform. unit
(1)	irrelevant	no information resumption	Sec. Tense form
(2)-(3)	Sec. Tense → focus	direct inform. resumption [69]	Sec. Tense + focus
(4)-(6)	focus → Sec. Tense	indirect inform. resumption	Sec. Tense + focus

pattern	clause CD contour (inform. development)	converted-form CD grading
(1)	high ungraduated rise	very high
(2)-(3)	moderate graduated rise	very low
(4)-(6)	high ungraduated rise + dip	moderately high

---

[63] WEIL 1879:12f.

[64] FIRBAS 1966, 1967; DANEŠ 1970.

[65] HALLIDAY 1967:205, 211.

[66] " Tension " is Firbas' expression (JONES 1977:65ff.). In Coptic there is quite possibly some " tension " between the Egyptian topic-initial patterns and the typically Coptic, " Indo-European " fronting of the focus.

[67] Mentioned by POLOTSKY 1944:48ff. (= *CP* 152ff.); cf. STERN §521.

[68] Only for pertinent, i.e. not inherent, focality; only for pertinent, i.e. unconditioned, order (§2.6.3.1.2).

[69] Often clarified as " given information " *after* the focus, i.e. the focus resolves the informational structure.

2.1-3   THEME/TOPIC-INITIAL PATTERNS

2.1 THE AUTOFOCAL SECOND TENSE CONSTRUCTION: SECOND-TENSE CONJUGATION FORM — FOCALIZATION PATTERN (1)

2.1.1 # ⲉϥ + modifier #. Differing with Polotsky, I begin my exposition with the autonomous Second Tense, a self-contained unit, thus simpler in the macro-syntactic view (even if historically problematic): the self-focalizing " ⲉϥⲥⲱⲧⲙ " (etc., see next paragraphs) and " ⲉϥⲙⲙⲁⲩ ", with which we shall deal here[70]: a high-CD, low-cotext-boundness information unit: ⲉⲩⲣⲁϣⲉ " what they are doing is rejoicing ", " they are doing nothing but rejoicing " (cf. Anglo-Irish " It's rejoicing they are"); ⲉϥ2ⲛⲁⲙⲛⲧⲉ " he is in Hell, and nowhere else ". The verb lexeme or modifier is focal, but in a different or higher degree of focality than in the basic conjugation-form[71]. This applies where the opposition obtains, and not in the case of ⲉϥⲧⲱⲛ (+ nom. actor): ⲉⲥⲧⲱⲛ ⲧⲙⲛⲧⲙⲁⲓ2ⲟⲙⲛⲧ, ⲉⲥⲧⲱⲛ ⲧⲁⲛⲟⲙⲓⲁ... ⲉⲩⲧⲱⲛ ⲇⲉ ⲛⲥⲁⲣⳅ... (A 2 336-7), ⲉⲣⲉⲛⲉⲛⲕⲉⲉⲥ ⲧⲱⲛ (A 1 212), sim. A 2 393, Ch. 166.28f., III 67.17ff. etc. In this focus of inherent focality we have an instance of neutralization of focality grading (§2.0.2.2.3). The modifiers of *pertinent* focality occurring here (needless to say, in the Sec. Present only; an open-ended focus paradigm, yet incomparably more restricted than and not overlapping the §1.2.1.1 inventory): 2ⲛ-/ⲛ2ⲏⲧ⸗, 2ⲓ-, ⲛⲧⲟⲟⲧ⸗, ⲛⲥⲱ⸗ (not in the Bipartite pred. list); the anaphoric ⲙⲙⲁⲩ; the expanded modifier 2ⲣⲁⲓ (2ⲛ-). The internal nexus is usually affirmative, sometimes negatived by (ⲛ) — ⲁⲛ (§2.9.1.1): " Where is Judas now? " — ⲉϥ2ⲛⲁⲙⲛⲧⲉ (A 2 53) / ⲡⲟⲩⲁ ⲙⲉⲛ (of the animals) ⲉϥⲛⲛ2ⲁⲗⲁⲧⲉ ⲉⲧ2ⲛⲙⲙⲟⲟⲩ, ⲁⲩⲱ ⲡⲕⲉⲟⲩⲁ ⲉϥ2ⲛⲛⲭⲁⲧϥⲉ ⲉⲧ2ⲓⲭⲙⲡⲕⲁ2 (Wess. 9 91a 26ff., parall. Sh. quoted in BLOr. 8811 ⲥⲙ) / ⲉⲥⲛⲥⲱⲛ ⲉⲣ-ⲛⲟⲃⲉ ⲁⲩⲱ ⲉⲧⲙⲉⲓⲣⲉ (Ch. 65.13f.) / ⲡⲙⲁ ⲇⲉ ⲟⲛ ⲉⲧⲉⲣⲉⲡⲉⲡⲛⲁ ⲙⲡⲭⲟⲉⲓⲥ ⲛ2ⲏⲧϥ, ⲉⲥⲙⲙⲁⲩ ⲛ6ⲓⲧⲙⲛⲧⲣⲙ2ⲉ (P 130⁵ 50 ⲥⲕ, cf. Ch. 138.27ff.) / ⲉⲣⲉⲡⲣⲱⲙⲉ ⲛⲧⲟⲟⲧⲥ, ⲉⲥ2ⲛⲧⲟⲟⲧϥ ⲁⲛ ⲙⲡⲣⲱⲙⲉ (IV 12.14) / ⲉⲣⲉⲛⲛⲟⲃⲉ 2ⲛⲛⲁⲭ2ⲉ ⲁⲛ, ⲁⲗⲗⲁ 2ⲛⲛⲉⲛ2ⲏⲧ (A 2 340); sim. A 2 248, Ch. 93.55ff., etc.

We encounter an analogous construction with *verb* lexemes[72], in durative *and non-durative* conjugation patterns. In the following paragraphs, I shall present certain cotext-functional categories typifying this verbal marked focus and more or less stereotyped, i.e. predictable.

2.1.2 TOPICAL (" RHETORICAL ") QUESTIONS[73].   Second Future, rarely Sec. Aorist, ⲉⲩⲛ(ⲧⲁ⸗). (Ch. 70.49ff.) ⲙⲏ ⲉϥⲛⲁϥⲓ-ⲟⲩ6ⲉⲣⲱⲃ ⲉ2ⲣⲁⲓ ⲉⲣⲟⲓ ⲏ ⲉϥⲛⲁⲁⲁⲧ ⲛ2ⲏⲕⲉ, ⲙⲏ ϥⲛⲁϣⲉⲓⲛⲉ ⲛⲟⲩⲥⲁ2ⲟⲩ ⲉⲭⲱⲓ, ⲙⲏ ϥⲛⲁϣϯ ⲛⲁⲓ ⲛⲟⲩⲙⲛⲧⲣⲙⲙⲁⲟ ⲏ ⲉϥⲛⲁⲙⲉ2-ⲡⲁⲏⲓ ⲛⲁⲅⲁⲑⲟⲛ ⲏ ⲉϥⲛⲁⲧⲁⲗ6ⲟⲓ 2ⲛⲛⲁϣⲱⲛⲉ (the two Basic Future[74] variants predicate -ϣ-) / (BMCat. 94, No. 213 ⲗⲏ) ⲙⲏ ⲉⲩⲛⲧⲁⲛ-ϣⲁⲭⲉ ⲙⲙⲁⲩ ⲉⲭⲱ / (A 1 108 coll.) ⲙⲏ ⲉϣⲁⲣⲉⲡⲁ2ⲟⲩ ⲁⲛ (i.e. the rags) ⲏ ϣⲁⲣⲉⲟⲥ2ⲟⲩ / (Ch. 186.41ff.) ⲁⲣⲁ ⲉⲟⲩⲛ2ⲉⲛⲧⲛ2 ⲙⲡⲛⲟⲩⲧⲉ ⲡⲡⲁⲛⲧⲟⲕⲣⲁⲧⲱⲣ / (Miss. 279)

---

[70] POLOTSKY 1960a:§30.

[71] Cf. POLOTSKY 1944:52f.(=CP 156f.).

[72] THESLEFF's (1955:14f.) " We do not think of degrees of walking " is simply not true (cf. DRESSLER 1968). It is not, however, with " degrees (of a verbal concept) " that we are concerned, but with the phenomenon, common in Indo-European as well as outside it, of a verb-form privileged to occur in marked focalization patterns. (Curiously, the " imperfective " or enhanced *Aktionsart* postulated for the " emphatic " form in the pre-Polotskyan grammar of Middle Egyptian comes here to mind.)

[73] POLOTSKY 1944:31ff. (= CP 135ff.). Cf. ROSÉN 1957:149(f.) for this role of the Greek ' εἰμί + participle ' " Second Tenses ".

[74] I have no exx. of Basic Tenses *on their own* as rhetorical questions. ⲭⲉ-ⲁⲣⲁ + Future I (Ch. 84.17ff.) is not a question, but an instance of the sceptical or half-hopeful nuance of ἄρα (esp. clear in εἰ, ἐὰν ἄρα see DENNISTON 37f.; BLASS–DEBRUNNER §375; KÜHNER–GERTH II 324ff.). In Coptic, ⲭⲉ- indicates that ⲁⲣⲁ here is not a second-position particle, but a clause-initial one (for the merging of ἄρα and ἄρα see, i.a. JANNARIS §1748c; KÜHNER–GERTH II 318 Anm.; DENNISTON 44.Our ⲭⲉ-ⲁⲣⲁ- may simply be: ὅτι ἄρα- (DENNISTON 38f.).

H ЄϢАУNЄ2ПЄ АN ЄПЄТNАМОУ / (*A 1* 70) МН АРТА2ОС РϢ ЄСПАРАВА... H ЄІТМАІО ММОС ХЄ-АСХϢ N2ЄNϢАХЄ NСϢ... H N†ϢП АN NNЄNТАСХООУ NСϢ... ХЄ-2ЄNNОВЄ NЄ (note that here, as elsewhere often — §§2.6.3, 2.7.3 — a Second Bipartite variates with a Basic Tripartite or negative Bipartite). Other exx.: *III* 90.15, 91.13f., *Ch.* 43.48ff., 195.47ff., *Wess. 9* 138a, *A 1* 125 etc. This case may be conceived of in two ways (beyond the general contextual circumstance of " emphatic-discourse " manner). On the one hand, as a *topicalization* form on a high level of textual analysis[75]: the question is — in macro-syntactic analysis — the topic of the answer, here zeroed[76]. The rhetorical question — stylistically an argumentational flourish or gambit — is grammatically an independent, self-contained dialogue unit, with the zeroing of the response component signalled by the form of the question-allocution. On the other hand, these questions have an affinity with *declarative* forms or syntagms (the rhetorical ἐκφώνησις vs. ἐρώτησις; cf. " Did he run! "[77]). One is given the impression that rhetoricity is a kind of *suprasyntactic* category, with overt syntactic signalling.

2.1.3 JUSSIVE/PRECATIVE/PRECEPTIVE/PROMISSIVE ЄЧNАСϢТМ. Affirmative, rarely negatived; 3rd person, 1st person, rarely 2nd person.

(*III* 210.13) ЄЧNАЄІ / (*Ch.* 192.24ff.) ТОРГН ЄNТАЧТϢМNТ ЄРОС АУϢ АСТϢМТ ЄРОЧ, АУϢ ОN ЄСNАТϢМТ ЄРОЧ (" ... and let it! ") / (*III* 20.17f.) ЄРЄПNОУТЄ... NАТАКО NТАѰУХН (apodotic imprecation, opp. to NNЄI- negative pledge, ЄІЄ- hopeful solicitation or self-promise) / (*III* 218.5ff.) ЄКЄМА2ОУ NРϢМЄ ЄПϢN2, ЄКЄ- МА2ОУ NЛАОС ЄПϢN2... ЄКNА2АРЄ2 ЄРООУ ЄВОЛ 2NϢТОРТР NІМ, ЄКNАР2ОУЄ-МА2ОУ NРϢМЄ ЄПϢN2; / (*III* 19.6, promise) ЄУNАР-ВОЛ ЄТОРГН / (*IV* 72-3, hortative) ЄNАСМN-(sic)ПЄУВЄКЄ NММАУ, H ЄNА† (sic) NАУ NТА- СОУ... H NNАNАУ (sic) ХЄ-ЄNNА†-ОУ NАУ NϢВЄІϢ / (*A 2* 505-6, neg. hortative) ЄNNАΘАІВЄ АN N2ЄNАТ- 6ОМ H 6ОТПОУ ЄВОЛ / (*IV* 61.27f., neg. jussive) ЄУNАХІТОУ ЄРООУ АN. Additional exx.: *IV* 103 *passim* (ЄУNА-, negative NNЄ-); 61-2; *Ch.* 187.2f.; *A 2* 144; preceptive, *IV* 53.24, 54.3, 63.19, 71.2, 81 *passim*, etc.

This Akhmimoid isogloss[78] is intriguing both from the syntactic point of view (does it have a " that "- clause role? cf. the OE-ME prospective *sdm.f* in this function[79]) and that of its formal and functional relations with the conjunctional future syntagms ХЄ-/ХЄКАС ЄЧNА-, which are still in need of thorough investigation. The co-existence of the ЄЧNА- jussive with the classical Sahidic МАРЄЧ-[80] is noteworthy: the latter is marked as rhetorical, with the former preceptive and unmarked (МПРТРЄ- is common to both terms)[81].

2.1.4 " QUOTATION-FORM ", GLOSSING AND LEMMATIC ROLES[82]

2.1.4.1 The Second Tense used in quoting or attributing a subjective[83] claim, thought or statement that is thereby more or less strongly *discredited* (" ... so they say " would approximately convey this meaning); Second Present (very rarely, Sec. Perfect); all persons; affirmative only?

---

[75] JONES 1977:179ff. (" high/mid-level themes, to define or open a subject area ", 184).

[76] VON DER GABELENTZ 1975:136f., 156.

[77] Cf. TOBLER 1899:18ff., EBELING 1905:137-142 (" Che hai paura? ", esp. 140), VON DER GABELENTZ 1901:183. Note also the unmistakable functional affinity with the English tag-construction: " He ran, didn't he? ".

[78] SHISHA-HALEVY 1976b:363.

[79] Cf. POLOTSKY 1964:271f. (= *CP* 56f.), 1976:§2.7 (for ME, cf. JUNGE 1978:§8.4.2).

[80] POLOTSKY 1950:80ff. (= *CP* 215ff.); cf. QUECKE 1979:443f.

[81] See §7.2.1.1.2. In the " Vita Monachorum " passages we also come upon the special jussive ЄТМТРЄЧ-, very common in the non-Shenoutean Leipoldt's No. 76 (*IV* 129-153, see note in the Appendix) but also found in *IV* 171.17; jussive ЄТРЄЧ- *IV* 71.14, neg. ЄТМ- 66.12 (see Ch. 7, note 63).

[82] Cf. ROSÉN 1957:149 (the Greek " Second Tense " in this function).

[83] Cf. POLOTSKY 1944:39ff. (= *CP* 143ff.): here at least STERN (§§601, 372) is vindicated.

(*A 1* 56) ⲚⲈⲦⲬⲰ ⲘⲘⲞⲤ ⲌⲢⲀⲒ ⲚⲌⲎⲦⲈ ⲬⲈ-ⲈⲚⲨⲰⲚⲈ, ⲤⲈⲞⲨⲰⲘ... (sim. ⲈⲨⲨⲰⲚⲈ *IV* 85.26, 154.26) / (*K* 9028 ro) ⲈⲨⲘⲈⲈⲨⲈ ⲬⲈ-ⲈⲨⲞⲚⲌ, ⲈⲨⲘⲞⲞⲨⲦ; ⲀⲨⲰ ⲈⲨⲘⲈⲈⲨⲈ ⲬⲈ-ⲈⲨⲌⲎⲚ ⲈⲌⲞⲨⲚ ⲈⲠⲚⲞⲨⲦⲈ, ⲈⲨⲞⲨⲎⲨ ⲈⲂⲞⲖ ⲘⲘⲞϤ / (*III* 92.21) ⲈⲨⲬⲰ ⲘⲘⲞⲤ ⲬⲈ-ⲈⲨⲨⲖⲎⲖ ⲈⲘⲈⲨⲢ-ⲌⲰⲂ [84] / (*RE 10* 159 b 30ff.) ⲘⲠⲈϤⲂⲰⲔ ⲈⲬⲘⲠⲀⲌⲎⲦ ⲈⲚⲈⲌ ⲬⲈ-ⲈⲒϯ-ⲤⲂⲰ Ⲏ ⲬⲈ-ⲈⲒ-ⲬⲠⲒⲞ... / (*P* 130⁵ 70 ⲠⲌ) ⲚⲈⲦⲬⲰ ⲘⲘⲞⲤ ⲬⲈ (Ⲉ)ⲚⲤⲞⲞⲨⲚ ⲘⲘⲞϤ (sim. *Ch.* 179.41ff.) / (*III* 123.2, 150.29) (" saying ") ⲬⲈ-ⲈⲒⲬⲒ ⲘⲘⲞⲞⲨ ⲚⳠⲞⲚⲤ, ⲬⲈ-ⲈⲒⲘⲞⲤⲦⲈ ⲘⲘⲞⲞⲨ (sim. 139.17, 124.17f., 143.21, 133.20, 123.1f.) [85] / (*III* 117.27f.) ⲀⲒⲬⲞⲞⲤ ⲀⲚⲞⲔ ⲌⲘⲠⲀⲨⲀⲒ ⲚⲦⲀⲘⲚⲦⲀⲐⲎⲦ ⲬⲈ-ⲚⲦⲀϤⲚⲀⲨ ⲚⳠⲒⲠⲬⲞⲈⲒⲤ ⲬⲈ-... / (*IV* 200.20) ⲀⲚⲈⲦⲘⲠⲈϤⲔⲰⲦⲈ ⲘⲈⲈⲨⲈ ⲬⲈ-ⲚⲦⲀϤⲠⲰⲨⲤ. Additional exx.: *III* 124.18, 141.24, *IV* 102.20f., *Ryl. Cat.* 32 (No. 68 Ⲥⳤ). Rare instances of undiscredited (yet equally subjective) quotation: (*A 1* 248, of a wine) ⲨⲀⲨⲬⲞⲞⲤ ⲈⲢⲞϤ ⲬⲈ-ⲈϤⲬⲀⲬⲰ / (*A 1* 258) ⲞⲨⲚⲌⲈⲚⲔⲞⲞⲨⲈ ⲆⲈ ⲞⲚ ⲈⲨⲀⲨⲞⲨⲰⲘ ⲘⲠⲈⲦⲌⲒⲂⲞⲖ ⲘⲘⲞⲞⲨ (i.e. of the fruits) ⲬⲈϤⳌⲞⲖⳠ (i.e. ⲬⲈ- ⲈϤ-?) ⲀⲨⲰ ⲈϤⲔⲒⲰⲞⲨ ⲀⲨⲰ ⲈⲚⲀⲚⲞⲨϤ.

2.1.4.2 LEMMATIC ⲈϤⲤⲰⲦⲘ: rare (cf. §2.7.2.4). (*Ch.* 81.6f.) ⲔⲀⲒⲦⲞⲒⳌⲈ ⲀⲨⲬⲞⲞⲤ ⲬⲈ ⲈϤⲌⲔⲀⲈⲒⲦ (Esau; this may however be the circumstantial of *Gen.* 25:29) / (*IV* 181.11) ⲞⲨ ⲆⲈ ⲠⲈ " ⲈⲨⲞⲨⲎⲌ ⲚⲤⲰⲞⲨ " (the source text, 181.10f., has ⲚⲈⲦⲈⲢⲈⲚⲞⲨⲞⲨ ⲞⲨⲎⲌ ⲚⲤⲰⲞⲨ. The answer here reveals a different, somewhat surprising possibility [86]: " ⲞⲨⲎⲌ ⲚⲤⲰⲞⲨ " ⲠⲈ ⲬⲈ-).

2.1.5 ⲈⲂⲞⲖ ⲀⲚ ⲬⲈ- (" not because "), ⲌⲰⲤ ⲈⲨⲬⲈ- (" as if ") + Second Tense. These are two co-textual constellations apparently calling (as an option) for a higher focality of the included verb:

(a) ⲈⲂⲞⲖ ⲀⲚ ⲬⲈ-/ⲈⲂⲞⲖ ⲬⲈ- (less common) + Second Present/Perfect; affirmative only; usually in strongly antithetic environment (focus of contrast) [87]; the Sec. Tense in the first or both terms of the antithesis, occasionally varying with a Basic Tense. (*A 2* 299-300) ⲈⲂⲞⲖ ⲀⲚ ⲬⲈ-ⲚⲦⲀⲠⲀⲒ ⲖⲒⲂⲈ ⲀϤⳌⲈ ⲈⲌⲢⲀⲒ ⲈϤⲢⲒⲘⲈ / (*A 1* 44) ⲈⲂⲞⲖ ⲀⲚ ⲬⲈ-ⲚⲦⲀϤⲢ-ⲠⲈⲐⲞⲞⲨ ⲚⲌⲞⲨⲞ ⲈⲢⲞⲚ ⲀⲠⲚⲞⲨⲦⲈ ⳠⲰⲚⲦ ⲈⲢⲞϤ ⲀϤⲘⲞⲞⲨⲦϤ... ⲀⲖⲖⲀ ⲈⲂⲞⲖ ⲬⲈ-ⲚⲦⲀ ⲚⲈⲌⲞⲞⲨ ⲘⲠⲈϤⲰⲚⲌ ⲬⲰⲔ ⲈⲂⲞⲖ / (*K* 9315) (" the arrogant man cannot accept the moral principle ") ⲈⲂⲞⲖ ⲀⲚ ⲬⲈ-ⲈϤⲬⲞⲤⲈ ⲈⲠⲖⲞⳠⲞⲤ ⲚⲚⲈⳠⲢⲀⲪⲎ / (*A 1* 131-2) (" he violated his oath ") ⲈⲂⲞⲖ ⲀⲚ ⲬⲈ-ⲈϤⲢ-ⲌⲞⲦⲈ Ⲏ ⲈϤⲨⲒⲠⲈ, ⲀⲖⲖⲀ ⲈⲂⲞⲖ ⲚⲦⲞϤ ⲬⲈ-ⲀⲠⲞⲨⲰⲨ ⲚⲚⲢⲰⲘⲈ ⲚⲦϤ ⲈⲌⲢⲀⲒ ⲈⲨⲤⲀⲌⲞⲨ / (*P* 130¹ 139 ⲦⲘⲈ)... ⲈⲂⲞⲖ ⲀⲚ ⲬⲈ-ⲈⲦⲈⲦⲚⲨⲀⲀⲦ ⲚⲦⲈⲦⲚⲚⲎⲤⲦⲈⲒⲀ ⲘⲚⲦⲈⲦⲚⲘⲈⲖⲎⲦⲎ, ⲀⲖⲖⲀ ⲈⲂⲞⲖ ⲚⲦⲞϤ ⲬⲈ-ⲚⲦⲈⲦⲚϪⲎⲔ ⲀⲚ ⲈⲂⲞⲖ ⲌⲚⲦⲘⲈⲌ-ⲈⲒⲀⲦⲦⲎⲨⲦⲚ. Also *A 1* 53, *III* 66.2f., 116.18f., *Wess. 9* 86b 30ff.

(b) (ⲌⲰⲤ) ⲈⲨⲬⲈ + Second Perfect. Affirmative only; perhaps in complementary distribution with ⲌⲰⲤ ⲈⲨⲬⲈ + circumstantial for the Bipartite [88] (cf. the Second Perfect allomorph after the irrealis ⲈⲚⲈ-): (*A 2* 33) (ⲌⲀⲌ ⲈⲀⲨⲦⲀⲔⲞ ⲌⲚⲞⲨⲤⲨⲚⲈ) ⲌⲰⲤ ⲈⲨⲬⲈ-ⲚⲦⲀⲞⲨⲌⲀⲦⲎⲨ ⲨⲈϤ-ⲠⲈⲨⲞⲨⲰⲨ ⲈⲂⲞⲖ / (*III* 208.5) ⲀⲒⲚⲀⲨ ⲀⲚⲞⲔ ⲈⲞⲨⲀ ⲈⲨⲬⲈ-ⲚⲦⲀϤⲦⲀⲌⲈ-ⲞⲨⲌⲞϤ Ⲏ ⲞⲨⲆⲢⲀⲔⲰⲚ [89] / (*III* 215.23f.) ⲌⲰⲤ ⲈⲨⲬⲈ-ⲚⲦⲀⲠⲎⲒ ⲦⲎⲢϤ ⲌⲘⲞⲞⲤ Ⲏ ⲔⲒⲘ ⲚⲌⲀⲌ ⲚⲤⲞⲠ / (*A 2* 362) ⲌⲰⲤ ⲈⲨⲬⲈ-ⲚⲦⲀⲨⲦⲰⲘ ⲚⲚⲂⲀⲖ ⲚⲦⲈⲒⲘⲒⲚⲈ ⲚⲢⲰⲘⲈ — ⲚⲦⲀⲨⲦⲞⲘⲞⲨ ⳠⲀⲢ ⲀⲖⲎⲐⲰⲤ, cf. *III* 96.25, parall. *Or.* 161.37ff.; see next paragraph.

---

[84] In (*III* 45.5) (" raise their hands ") ⲬⲈ-ⲈⲨⲨⲖⲎⲖ we may have a circumstantial after ⲬⲈ- "as if..." (sim. to ⲌⲰⲤ ⲈⲨⲬⲈ- + circ., SHISHA–HALEVY 1972:§3.2.4.5).

[85] When the person indicated is different from the speaker, we may have here instances of indirect-speech shifting (*III* 91.15f. ⲬⲈ-ⲈϤⲤⲈⲨⲌ-ⲘⲎⲎⲨⲈ, 133.20 ⲬⲈ-ⲈϤⲘⲞⲤⲦⲈ ⲘⲘⲞⲚ) or, much more frequently, unshifted person (*III* 124.17f. ⲬⲈ-ⲈⲔⲬⲒ ⲘⲘⲞⲚ ⲚⳠⲞⲚⲤ) or, also very common, quoted reference in terms of " real person " (*III* 123.2 ⲬⲈ-ⲈⲒⲬⲒ ⲘⲘⲞⲞⲨ ⲚⳠⲞⲚⲤ). These phenomena, which belong in the sphere of " *Erlebte Rede* " (" *style indirecte libre* ") and the formalities of inclusion and cohesion, need yet to be thoroughly investigated.

[86] Cf. *RE 10* 159a 13ff. (parall. BM 253 ⲚⲎ) ⲈⲦⲂⲈⲞⲨ ⲀⲒⲬⲞⲞⲤ ⲬⲈ-ⲦⲰⲰⲘⲈ (referring to the preceding ⲚⲈⲦⲦⲞⲞⲘⲈ ⲈⲢⲞϤ ⲀⲨⲰ ⲈϤⲦⲞⲞⲘⲈ ⲈⲢⲞⲞⲨ) / (*A 2* 492) (ⲀⲨⲤⲞⲔⲔ ⲚⲀⲨ ⲈⲠⲀⲌⲞⲨ) ⲤⲞⲔⲔ ⲈⲠⲀⲌⲞⲨ ⲠⲈ... / (*A 2* 245) (ⲀϤⲦⲚⲚⲞⲞⲨϤ) ⲦⲚⲚⲞⲞⲨϤ ⲦⲰⲚ. See §2.7.2.4.

[87] Cf. POLOTSKY 1944:39 (= *CP* 143), 53 f. (= *CP* 156f.).

[88] SHISHA–HALEVY 1972:§§3.2.4.3-4. Consider ⲌⲰⲤ ⲈⲨⲬⲈ + circ. future (*Ch.* 22.34ff.), rarely, + circ. perfect (*IV* 92.6), + neg. circ. pres. (*IV* 115.25). Note the zero alternant before a Nominal Sentence (*Ch.* 30.36f., *Wess. 9* 87b 21f., *IV* 182.7f. etc). I admit the evidence for the circumstantial (as against Sec. Present) allomorph is not strong; however, the evidence for (ⲚⲐⲈ) ⲌⲰⲤ - with ⲈⲀϤ- and circ. Nominal Sentence (*ibid.* §§3.2.4.1.2) is corroborating.

[89] Cf. SHISHA–HALEVY 1972:§3.2.4.4 for the syntax of " reporting a vision ".

2.1.6 The rare PARENTHETIC SECOND TENSE occurs in interruptions of a narrative stretch, by which the narrator intercalates (or often "postcalates") his opinion or personal attitude ("narrator's aside"), but also meets the need to clarify or justify a particular choice of words. Note the unmistakable role which particles play here [90]. We find the Sec. Perfect, affirmative and negatived: (*Or.* 161.37ff., parall. *III* 96.25) ⲍⲱⲥ ⲉⲯⲭⲉ-ⲛⲧⲁⲩⲡⲱⲥ ⲛⲍⲏⲧ — ⲛⲧⲁⲩⲡⲱⲥ ⲅⲁⲣ (sim. *A 2* 369, quoted in the prec. paragraph) / (*A 2* 246) ...ⲉⲁⲛⲛⲁⲩ ⲉⲟⲩⲟⲛ — ⲛⲧⲁⲛⲥⲱⲧⲙ ⲁⲛ — ⲉⲁⲯⲕⲁ-ⲛⲉⲯⲯⲏⲣⲉ ⲉⲃⲟⲗ ⲍⲙⲡⲙⲟⲟⲩ.

2.1.7 Less schematizable, but still to some extent predictable, are miscellaneous circumstances in which the autofocal Second Tense occurs:

2.1.7.1 In *disjunctive configurations* (ⲥⲟⲡ — ⲥⲟⲡ —, ⲍⲟⲉⲓⲛⲉ — ⲍⲟⲉⲓⲛⲉ —, etc.), varying with Basic Tenses; affirmative only; Second Aorist, Second Present.

(*A 1* 249, coll.) ⲛⲣⲱⲙⲉ ⲛⲉ: ⲥⲟⲡ ⲙⲉⲛ ⲉⲯⲁⲩⲭⲓ-ⲙⲉ, ⲥⲟⲡ ⲇⲉ ⲟⲛ ⲉⲯⲁⲩⲭⲓ-ⲭⲟⲗ; ⲥⲟⲡ ⲯⲁⲩⲥⲱⲧⲙ, ⲥⲟⲡ ⲇⲉ ⲯⲁⲩ-ⲣ-ⲁⲧⲥⲱⲧⲙ; ⲍⲉⲛⲍⲟⲟⲩ ⲯⲁⲩⲧⲃⲃⲟⲟⲩ, ⲍⲉⲛⲍⲟⲟⲩ ⲇⲉ ⲟⲛ ⲉⲯⲁⲩⲭⲁⲍⲙⲟⲩ; ⲍⲉⲛⲥⲏⲩ ⲉⲯⲁⲩⲣ-ⲍⲧⲏⲩ ⲉⲭⲛ ⲛⲉⲩⲛⲟⲃⲉ, ⲍⲉⲛⲥⲏⲩ ⲇⲉ ⲟⲛ ⲉⲯⲁⲩⲕⲧⲟⲟⲩ ⲉⲍⲣⲁⲓ ⲉⲣⲟⲟⲩ; ⲍⲉⲛⲟⲩⲟⲉⲓⲯ ⲉⲯⲁⲩⲣⲓⲙⲉ ⲭⲉ-ⲁⲩⲗⲁⲁⲩ, ⲍⲉⲛⲕⲉⲟⲩⲟⲉⲓⲯ ⲉⲯⲁⲩⲣⲁⲯⲉ... ⲍⲉⲛⲉⲃⲟⲧ ⲏ ⲍⲉⲛⲣⲟⲙⲡⲉ ⲉⲯⲁⲩⲣ-ⲛⲁⲅⲁⲑⲟⲛ, ⲍⲉⲛⲣⲟⲙⲡⲉ ⲉⲯⲁⲩⲣ-ⲙⲛⲧⲁⲥⲉⲃⲏⲥ ⲛⲓⲙ / (*III* 42.19f.) (ⲧⲁⲓ ⲧⲉ ⲑⲉ ⲉⲧⲉⲣⲉⲡⲛⲟⲩⲧⲉ ⲟⲓ-ⲕⲟⲛⲟⲙⲉⲓ ⲙⲡⲣⲱⲙⲉ ⲕⲁⲧⲁⲡⲉⲧⲉⲍⲛⲁⲯ), ⲍⲟⲉⲓⲛⲉ ⲙⲉⲛ ⲉⲯⲁⲩⲕⲁⲁⲩ ⲛⲥⲉⲱⲥⲕ ⲍⲙⲡⲓⲙⲁ, ⲍⲉⲛⲕⲟⲟⲩⲉ ⲉⲯⲁⲩⲯⲓⲧⲟⲩ ⲉⲃⲟⲗ ⲧⲁⲭⲏ. Also *III* 110.9ff., *IV* 8.11f., perhaps *Berl. Sitz.* ⲍⲟⲓⲛⲉ ⲅⲁⲣ ⲉⲩⲭⲱ ⲙⲙⲟⲥ ⲭⲉ-... ⲍⲉⲛⲕⲟⲟⲩⲉ ⲇⲉ ⲭⲉ-... ⲍⲉⲛⲕⲟⲟⲩⲉ ⲇⲉ ⲭⲉ-... ⲍⲟⲓⲛⲉ ⲇⲉ ⲉⲩⲭⲱ ⲙⲙⲟⲥ ⲭⲉ-... ⲙⲙⲁⲛⲓⲭⲁⲓⲟⲥ ⲇⲉ ⲉⲩⲭⲱ ⲙⲙⲟⲥ ⲭⲉ-..., unless here the ⲭⲉ-clauses are focalized; *Ench.* 78a.

2.1.7.2 In the second or both terms of antithetic configurations [91]; affirmative, negative; Second Present, Aorist, Perfect.

(*Ch.* 207.19ff., Sh.? adaptation of the famous *Mark* 5:39) ⲙⲡⲉⲡⲇⲓⲕⲁⲓⲟⲥ ⲅⲁⲣ ⲙⲟⲩ ⲁⲗⲗⲁ ⲉⲯⲛⲕⲟⲧⲕ / (*III* 71.18f., possibly a case of circumstantial + Sec. Perfect) ⲍⲛⲁⲁⲩ ⲛⲓⲙ ⲉⲙⲡⲟⲩⲯⲯⲱⲧ... ⲁⲗⲗⲁ ⲉⲛⲧⲁⲩⲟⲩⲱⲍ ⲉⲣⲟⲟⲩ ⲛⲍⲟⲩⲟ / (*III* 33.9f.) ⲙⲡⲉⲯⲟⲩⲱⲍ ⲉⲧⲟⲟⲧⲯ ⲉⲯⲁⲭⲉ... ⲁⲗⲗⲁ ⲛⲧⲁⲯⲣⲡⲕⲉⲣ-ⲍⲧⲏⲯ ⲉⲭⲛⲛⲉⲯⲛⲟⲃⲉ / (*III* 108.9) ⲟⲩ ⲙⲟⲛⲟⲛ ⲭⲉ-ⲛⲧⲛⲭⲉ-ⲗⲁⲁⲩ ⲛⲁⲩ ⲁⲛ, ⲁⲗⲗⲁ (ⲉ)ⲛⲣⲡⲕⲉⲡⲁⲣⲁⲕⲁⲗⲉⲓ; for ⲟⲩ ⲙⲟⲛⲟⲛ see §1.3.11.2.1.1; for -ⲣⲡⲕⲉ-, §3.3.1 (a similar example: *Ch.* 157.20ff.) / (*III* 212.7ff.) ⲡⲉⲧⲭⲱ ⲙⲙⲟⲥ ⲭⲉ-ⲁⲓⲥⲟⲩⲛ-ⲓ̄ⲥ̄, ⲉⲛⲉⲓⲣⲉ ⲛⲛⲁⲓ ⲛⲧⲁⲛ-ⲣ-ⲁⲧⲥⲟⲟⲩⲛ ⲙⲙⲟⲯ ⲛⲍⲟⲩⲟ / (*IV* 157.21ff.) (Instead of plucking the plant) ⲛⲧⲁⲩⲧⲱ6ⲉ ⲙⲙⲟⲯ ⲛⲧⲟⲯ. Similar exx.: *III* 40.11ff., 76.19ff. (parall. *Ch.* 171.7ff.), *A 2* 241.

2.1.7.3 VARIA. (a) The Second Tense *in apodosi* (cf. SHISHA-HALEVY 1973): (*K* 926) ⲉⲓⲯⲁⲛⲕⲣⲓⲛⲉ ⲙⲙⲟⲕ... ⲉⲓⲣ-ⲛⲟⲃⲉ, ⲉⲕⲯⲁⲛⲕⲣⲓⲛⲉ ⲙⲙⲟ ...ⲉⲕⲣ-ⲛⲟⲃⲉ; (*Wess. 9* 110a 11f.) ⲉⲓⲯⲁⲛⲭⲟⲟⲥ ⲛⲉ ⲉⲓⲣ-ⲛⲟⲃⲉ / (*IV* 79-80) ⲡⲉⲧⲛⲁⲣⲁⲛⲁⲯ ⲉⲣⲟⲓ ⲏ ⲛⲯⲥⲱⲕ ⲙⲙⲟⲓ ⲛⲭⲛⲁⲍ... ⲉⲩⲣ-ⲛⲟⲃⲉ. These examples may, however, all be cases of focalized *object* (§2.3.1; cf. " ⲉⲕⲭⲓ-6ⲟⲗ ", and (c) below).

(b) " Dramatic " Second Present (" Koinzidenzfall ") [92]: (*III* 29.27f.) ⲁⲛⲟⲕ ⲍⲱⲯⲧ ⲟⲛ ⲉⲓⲕⲱⲧⲯ-ⲭⲁⲗⲉ ⲭⲁⲗⲉ ⲁⲩⲱ ⲉⲓⲛⲟⲩⲭ ⲉⲧⲧⲱⲙⲉ, perhaps (*IV* 64.26f.) ⲡⲁⲓ ⲇⲉ ⲉⲓⲭⲱ ⲙⲙⲟⲯ ⲭⲉ-.

---

[90] Cf. SHISHA-HALEVY 1976a:37 n. 18. Basic (durative) tense (opistho-)parentheses: ...ⲛⲯⲡⲱ2 ⲇⲉ ⲟⲛ—ⲯⲡⲏ2 ⲣⲱ (*III* 113.13f.) ⲧ6ⲁⲉⲓⲟⲓ 6ⲉ 2ⲓⲟⲩⲥⲟⲡ... ⲉⲃⲟⲗ ⲭⲉ-ⲧ6ⲁⲓⲏⲩ ⲣⲱ 2ⲛⲛⲁ2ⲃⲏⲩⲉ (*A 1* 70) / " ⲛⲉⲛⲛⲁ2ⲱ ⲁⲛ ⲡⲉ " — ⲙⲡⲟⲩ ⲣⲱ (*IV* 96-7: Leipoldt: "*locus corruptus*") / ⲡⲛⲟⲩⲧⲉ ⲡⲭⲟⲉⲓⲥ ⲡⲉⲭ̄ⲥ̄ ⲓ̄ⲥ̄ ⲛⲁⲯⲁⲁⲧⲛ ⲉⲃⲟⲗ ⲙⲙⲟⲯ — ⲏ ⲥⲉⲯⲁⲁⲧ ⲣⲱ (*A 2* 24. Cf. *A 1* 135 ⲯⲛⲁⲥⲓ ⲅⲁⲣ ⲏ ⲁⲯⲥⲓ ⲣⲱ / (*A 1* 132) ...ⲭⲉ-ⲉⲩⲉⲙⲟⲩ ⲏ ⲣⲱ ⲁⲩⲙⲟⲩ / (*A 1* 150) ⲁ ⲡⲁⲓ ⲁⲥⲁⲓ ⲏ ⲯⲛⲁⲁⲥⲁⲓ ⲣⲱ — instances of the *figura Sinuthiana*) / ⲡⲉⲓⲏⲓ ⲉⲯⲉⲯⲱⲡⲉ ⲉⲡⲩⲯⲯ ⲏ ⲛⲭⲁⲉⲓⲉ — ⲥⲉⲟ ⲣⲱ ⲛⲭⲁⲉⲓⲉ (*A 2* 8) / ⲕⲁⲛ ⲉⲯⲭⲉ-ⲧⲙⲉ2 6ⲉ ⲛⲯⲓⲡⲉ ⲧⲉⲛⲟⲩ... — ⲧⲙⲉ2 ⲅⲁⲣ ⲁⲗⲏⲑⲱⲥ — 2ⲟⲙⲓⲯⲥ (sic)... (*A 2* 464).

[91] POLOTSKY 1944:39f. (= *CP* 156f.).

[92] This may be related to the " synchronous present ", " Koinzidenzfall " or, as it is usually known today, " performative discourse " role of the Second Present, which I find well attested outside Shenoute (esp. in documentary or epistolary formulae): " hereby... ", an act meant to be considered as carried out at the very time of — and *by* — being announced. Consider the formulary ⲉⲓⲥⲧⲟⲓⲭⲉⲓ (" I concur with "), ⲉⲓⲍⲟⲙⲟⲗⲟⲅⲉⲓ (" I admit, agree "), ⲉⲓⲟ ⲙⲙⲛⲧⲣⲉ (" I testify "), ⲉⲓⲱⲣⲕ (" I swear "), ⲉⲓⲕⲓⲛⲁⲩ-ⲛⲉⲩⲉ (" I vouch for "), ⲉⲓⲯⲡ-ⲧⲱⲣⲉ (" I promise "), as well as the less formulary or non-formulary ⲉⲓⲧ (ⲉⲃⲟⲗ) (" I sell ", Till, *Rechts-*

(c) Occasional instances of Second Perfect predicating P- (cf. (a) above; is the object of P-, or the whole 'P + object' syntagm focalized?): (*IV* 67.2f.) ⲤⲈⲞⲨⲞⲚ⳾ ⲈⲂⲞⲖ... ϪⲈ-ⲚⲦⲀⲨⲢ-ⲀⲦϬⲞⲘ / (*IV* 199.7f.) Ⲁ⳾ⲚⲢⱲⲘⲈ (sic) ⲈⲒ ⱲⲀⲢⲞⲒ... ⲈⲦⲂⲈⲚⲈⲨⲦⲂⲚⲞⲞⲨⲈ, ϪⲈ-ⲘⲈⱲⲀⲔ ⲈⲚⲦⲀⲨⲢ-⳾ⲒⲔ ⲈⲢⲞⲞⲨ.

2.2 THE HETEROFOCAL SECOND-TENSE CONSTRUCTION: ⧣ SEC. TENSE CONJ.-FORM → MODIFIER ⧣ — FOCALIZATION PATTERN (2)

In Polotsky's analysis, this is the original, core model: a master structure, which he identifies with, or approximates to, the Bipartite pattern, and from which he deduces the nominal (substantival) nature of the Second Tense, its " transposed " status and the transformative shift of the modifier, from adjunctal to predicative status. The 'theme → rheme' arrangement of the nexus terms is here the " classic " one which (when pertinent, i.e. not conditioned by internal — focus — or external factors) is integrated in a *thematic progression*, or gradual, concatenated evolvement of the communication [93].

2.2.1 The FOCUS CONSTITUENCY is here the largest of all focal paradigms, and is impressively close to that of the adverbal adjunctal modifier (§1.1.2.1). Both lists being open-ended, it is difficult to estimate to what degree they overlap.

Ⲉ- (*Ch.* 16.47ff.), ⲈⲚϪⲒⲚϪⲎ (§1.3.7.3), ⲈⲦⲢⲈ- (*Ch.* 129.2ff.), Ⲉ + inf. (*III* 191.26f.).

ⲈⲂⲞⲖ ⳾Ⲛ-	(*Ch.* 34.18ff.)/⳾ⲒⲦⲚ- (*Ch.* 9.5ff.) / ⲦⱲⲚ (*A 1* 281, §2.6.3.2)
ⲈⳲⲞⲨⲚ Ⲉ-	(*Ch.* 20.31f.).
ⲈϪⲚ-	(*Ch.* 152.30ff.).
ⲈⲦⲂⲈ-	(*III* 122.24f.), ⲈⲦⲂⲈϪⲈ- (*III* 100.16f.).
ⲔⲀⲦⲀ-	(*IV* 16.2f.).
Ⲛ-/ⲘⲘⲞ⸗	(dir. obj., *IV* 51.16f.; introd. predicative, *III* 67.12; " in, at, by ", *Wess. 9* 87a 11ff.).
Ⲛ-/ⲚⲀ⸗	(*III* 165.16ff.).
ⲘⲚ-	(*III* 98.3,7,10).
ⲚⲚⲀ⳾ⲢⲚ-	(*III* 134.15).
ⲚⲤⲀ-	(*Ch.* 55.8ff.).
ⲠⲢⲞⲤ-	(*P* 130² 80 ro).
ⲞⲨⲂⲈ-	(*III* 65.14).
ⱲⲀ-	(*Ch.* 28.38f.).
⳾Ⲁ-	(*Ch.* 17.24ff.).
⳾Ⲁ⳾ⲦⲚ-	(*Miss.* 283).
⳾Ⲓ-	(*Ch.* 25.14ff.).
⳾ⲒⲦⲚ-	(*III* 28.25f.).
⳾ⲒϪⲚ-	(*III* 80.25f.).
⳾Ⲛ-	(*Ch.* 14.32ff.).
⳾ⲰⲤ-	(*Ch.* 97.21ff.).
ϪⲈ-	(var. roles; *III* 137.23ff., *Ch.* 62.1f., *Wess. 9* 149a-b).
ϪⲈⲔⲀⲤ	(*III* 120-7ff.).
ϪⲒⲚ-	(*Ch.* 65.15ff.).

Clause Conjugations (Ⲉ⳽ⱲⲀⲚ-, ⱲⲀⲚⲦⲈ-, ⲚⲦⲈⲢⲈ- (?) *A 2* 51, 87; *not* conjunctive)

---

urk. 27.12; Crum, *Coptic Ostraca* 139.4), ⲈⲒⲘⲒⲤⲐⲞⲨ (" I lease ", Krall, *Rainer* 127.9), ⲈⲒⲠⲀⲢⲀⲔⲀⲖⲈⲒ (" I beg, appeal ", Till, *Ostraca* 243), ⲈⲒⱲⲒⲚⲈ (" I greet ", Stefanski-Lichtheim, *Ostraca* 158), ⲈⲒⲤⲘⲞⲨ ⲈⲢⱲⲦⲚ (" I bless you ", Crum, *Coptic Ostraca* 282), ⲈⲒⲘⲞⲨ (" I am dying ", *ibid*. 267). For this functional category in general and comparative view, see KOSCHMIEDER 1965:26-34, 46f.; R. HARRIS 1972; GRIMES 1975:71ff.; WEINRICH 1977:57.

[93] See §2.0.2.3-4. Compare the macro-syntactically marked role of the ⧣SUBJECT-*copula*-PREDICATE⧣ Nominal Sentence pattern (SHISHA-HALEVY 1976a:48f.).

Circumstantial (III 66.5f.).
Iteration-marked noun syntagms (§1.3.3).

The THEME/TOPIC CONSTITUENCY: ∈-/∈PE- converted Bipartite, aorist (affirmative), adjective-verbs, OYNTA⸗, ϢϢE, (∈)NT-converted perfect. The NEXUS is here affirmative or negated: §2.9.1.2.

2.2.2 GENERAL OBSERVATIONS. (1) For relatively few — even if, in absolute numbers, common — members of the above list, notably ∈TBE-, (∈BOΛ) ϨITN-, (ϨPAI, ∈BOΛ) ϨN-, ϨI-, ∈ϪN-, N- (NTEIϨE, NAϢ N-), there is an opposition or a compexly conditioned alternation with the focus-initial patterns: see §§2.4-6 below, esp. 2.6.4; those patterns have their own focus constituency paradigms, which feature some foci here absent (notably -ϢC-modifiers).

(2) For various *focalization figures* employing this pattern (the COMPLEX FOCUS: ∈YNAϪITK ∈PATϤ NNIM *Wess. 9* 117a 5f.; DOUBLE FOCALIZATION: NTANIM TCABOϤ ∈NIM *Wess. 9* 110a 9f.; the MULTIPLE DISJOINED FOCUS: NTAYKAAY ϨAϨTNNIM H ϨNAϢ NHI *Miss.* 283) see §2.7.1; for details concerning the syntagmatics of this pattern, for the coordination/disjunction of several themes, and for the isolation of the focus among several modifiers, see §2.8.4.

(3) For BASIC TENSE themes with several of these foci (notably TϢN, NOYHP, NAϢ N-) see §2.7.3.

(4) For the focusing modifiers MMATE, MAYAA⸗ and other augentia, co-marking the focus, see §§1.3.1.1, 2.9.1.2 *passim* and §6.2.1. ∈IϪϢ MMOϤ AN ϨAPOI MAYAAT (*IV* 96.13) / ∈ϤϢOOΠ ϨMΠEYΛAC MMATE AYϢ ϨM-ΠEYϨHT AN (*IV* 24.6f.).

SPECIAL OBSERVATIONS. (1) For N-/MMO⸗ and the problems involved, see §§1.0.1, 1.1.2.1, etc. It is evident that not all of its functional spectrum shares the same focalization properties: while NAϢ NϨE " how? " features in both focus- and topic-initial patterns, N- as object-expansion always follows its theme, as do most of the more " lexical " syntagms of N- (for NϨOYO and NTEIϨE focalized, see *III* 131.10, *Wess. 9* 174d 29ff., *III* 76.8ff., *IV* 195.4).

(2) ∈-: in MΠOYTAAC NAN ∈TPENCOYN-TEϨIH... AΛΛA NTAYTAAC NAN ∈COYN- (*III* 191.25ff.) we have a remarkable instance of the focus being heralded by a cataphoric element in the theme (§5.2.2.1), indicating yet again the compatibility of the ' nucleus - satellite ' and the ' theme - rheme ' dependences (the latter is " mapped on " the former).

(3) TϢN " where? ", focalizable also in pattern (1), with an immediate explication of the actor-pronoun by a noun syntagm, §6.0.1; ∈CϢOOΠ TϢN TEϨIH ∈TMMAY (*A 2* 114) / ∈PEIOYΛAC ϢOOΠ TϢN TENOY (*A 2* 53) / ∈CNAϨE ∈POϤ TϢN (*A 2* 336; sim. with ϨE or ϬINE, *A 1* 62, 306, *III* 72.9f. etc.). " Whence? " (see Ch. 1, footnote 96): ∈PECOOYN TϢN ϪE- (*A 1* 67; sim., with ∈IME or COOYN, *A 1* 72, 122, *Wess. 9* 143d 1ff. etc.) / NTAΠEINEϨ THPϤ ∈I TϢN ∈ϨPAI ∈- (*III* 72.24f., sim. *ibid.* 17f., 87.12) / ∈PENCϢNT NAϢϢΠE TϢN H ∈BOΛ ϨITNNIM (*A 2* 412). For TϢN following a Basic Tense, see §2.7.3.2.3.

(4) The CIRCUMSTANTIAL focus features in some typical focalization figures, such as the " *Wechsel-satz* "-like # ∈Ϥ— ∈Ϥ— # construction and the " No sooner... than... " combination: see (with further reff.) §2.7.1.1. Some non-rhetorical examples: NAI ΔE ∈IϪϢ MMOOY ∈IOY∈Ϣ-TNOOϤPE (sic) ∈NENP∈ϤϪI-ϨAΠ (*P 130*⁵ 40 MΓ) / NAI ∈P∈∈IP∈ MMOOY TENOY ∈P∈COOYN (*III* 206.13) / ∈T∈TNAKPINE MMOI ∈IϨATNTHYTN AN (*III* 25.17f.) / NTAΠϪOEIC KAAϤ AN ∈ϤϬM-ϬOM ∈ΠPϢME, AΛΛA ∈P∈ΠPϢME ϬM-ϬOM ∈POϤ (*Ch.* 16-17): these last examples call our attention to the fact that the circumstantial, even when not focal, is an *adnexal* modification form, i.e. it adjoins a nexus or predicative dependence to a verb or noun (§7.1.3). In the focalized circumstantial we have a " promoted " or marked degree of adnexation. Some figure-type instances of this kind may belong rather to the focus-initial pattern (6): ∈YMOCTE MMϢTN AN ∈YϪϢ NHTN NNAI (*Wess. 9* 158a 30ff.) / ∈ITOΛMA ∈IϪϢ NNAI (*Mun.* 96).

(5) ⲉⲁϥ- occurs theme-like in a few instances[94], always in *contrastive context*: ⲁⲥϯ-ⲟⲩⲱ ⲛⲟⲩ; ⲛⲟⲩⲧⲏⲏⲃⲉ ⲁⲛ ⲏ ⲛⲧⲟϥ ⲕⲉⲙⲉⲗⲟⲥ, ⲁⲗⲗⲁ ⲉⲁⲥϯ-ⲟⲩⲱ ⲛⲛⲕⲁⲣⲡⲟⲥ ⲛⲧⲇⲓⲕⲁⲓⲟⲥⲩⲛⲏ (*Ch.* 183.2ff.) "... but it is the fruits of righteousness it sprouted" / ⲉⲣⲉⲧⲡⲉ ⲏ ⲡⲉⲥⲧⲉⲣⲉⲱⲙⲁ ⲕⲏ ⲁⲛ ⲉϩⲣⲁⲓ ⲉϫⲛϩⲉⲛⲙⲁ ⲛⲧⲉⲡⲕⲁϩ ⲛⲑⲉ ⲛⲧⲙⲉⲗⲱⲧ ⲉⲧⲕⲏ ⲉϫⲙⲡⲏⲓ, ⲁⲗⲗⲁ ⲉⲁϥⲟϥⲧϥ ϩⲛⲧⲉϥϭⲟⲙ (*Ch.* 59.46ff.) "... but it is with His power that He fastened it". As appears from two other examples (*Ch.* 171.10ff. = *III* 76.20ff. and *III* 163.19ff.), these are perhaps better interpreted as cases of the non-thematic circumstantial premodified by the constrastive conjunct rather than focalization patterns.

2.2.3 Some assorted examples. *Affirmative nexus*: (*P* 130[5] 79 ⲁ, not Sh.?) ⲛⲧⲁⲡⲉⲓϣⲁϫⲉ ϭⲱⲗⲡ ⲉⲣⲟⲓ ⲁⲓⲉⲓⲙⲉ ⲉⲣⲟϥ ⲧⲉⲛⲟⲩ ϩⲛⲧⲉⲓⲣⲟⲙⲡⲉ ⲧⲁⲓ / (*ibid.* 61 ⲗⲉ) ⲉⲣϣⲁⲛⲡⲉϩⲙⲟⲩ ⲇⲉ ⲃⲁⲁⲃⲉ ⲉⲩⲛⲁⲙⲟⲗϩϥ ⲛⲟⲩ / (*A 1* 104) ⲛⲧⲟⲕ ⲅⲁⲣ ⲉⲧⲥⲟⲟⲩⲛ ϫⲉ-ⲉⲓⲟ ⲛⲁϣ ⲛϩⲉ ("... how I am (physically)"; sim.[95] *A 2* 516 "... how they stand", *Or.* 154.39f.) / (*Ch.* 54.19ff.) ⲧⲟⲩⲉⲣⲏⲧⲉ ⲉⲥϣⲟⲟⲡ ϩⲙⲡⲥⲱⲙⲁ ⲉⲧⲃⲉⲙⲟⲟϣⲉ / (*Wess. 9* 86a 16ff.) ⲛⲧⲁⲡⲉⲓⲧⲁⲕⲟ ⲛϯⲁⲉⲓⲏⲥ ⲉⲓ ⲉϩⲣⲁⲓ ⲉϫⲙⲡⲉⲓⲙⲏⲏϣⲉ ⲛⲑⲉ ⲙⲡϣⲱϩ ⲛⲟⲩⲕⲁⲧⲁⲕⲗⲩⲥⲙⲟⲥ ⲙⲡⲟⲩⲟⲉⲓϣ ϫⲉ-ⲟⲩⲙⲟⲛⲟⲛ ϫⲉ-ⲙⲡⲉⲟⲩⲁ ⲛⲟⲩϭⲥ ⲛⲟⲩⲁ, ⲁⲗⲗⲁ ϫⲉ-ⲛⲉⲩⲣⲡⲕⲉⲣⲁϣⲉ ϩⲛⲧⲙⲛⲧⲁⲥⲉⲃⲏⲥ / (*III* 45.22ff.) ⲉⲧⲉⲧⲛϣⲱⲣⲡ ⲙⲙⲱⲧⲛ ⲛⲛⲓⲙ; ⲉⲧⲉⲧⲛϣⲙϣⲉ ⲛⲛⲓⲙ; ⲉⲧⲉⲧⲛⲁϯ-ϩⲏⲩ ⲛⲟⲩ ⲉⲧⲉⲧⲛϯ-ⲛϣⲟⲧ ⲛⲛⲉⲧⲛϩⲏⲧ; / (*A 1* 80) ⲉⲓⲛⲁϣϥⲓ ⲛⲛⲁⲃⲁⲗ ⲉⲣⲟⲕ ⲛⲁϣ ⲛϩⲉ / (*Ch.* 55.24ff.) ⲁⲛⲁⲩ ⲉⲡϩⲟⲩⲉⲡⲣⲟⲫⲏⲧⲏⲥ ⲓⲱϩⲁⲛⲛⲏⲥ ϫⲉ-ⲉϥϣⲁϫⲉ ⲛⲁϣ ⲛϩⲉ. For the last two exx. see §2.6.3.

Negated nexus (§2.9.1.2): (*III* 21.10) ⲛⲧⲁⲓⲥⲟⲩⲱⲛⲉ ⲅⲁⲣ ⲁⲛ ⲛⲃⲣⲣⲉ / (*A 2* 403) ⲛⲉϥⲛⲁϣⲁϫⲉ ⲅⲁⲣ ⲁⲛ ϩⲁⲣⲟϥ ⲙⲁⲩⲁⲁϥ, ⲁⲗⲗⲁ ⲉϥⲛⲁϫⲉ-ⲡⲉⲧϥⲛⲁⲥⲟⲧⲙⲉϥ / (*IV* 51.16f.) ⲛⲛⲉⲩⲥⲱⲃⲉ ⲁⲛ ⲛϩⲉⲛⲕⲟⲟⲩⲉ, ⲁⲗⲗⲁ ⲉⲩⲥⲱⲃⲉ ⲙⲙⲟⲟⲩ ⲙⲁⲩⲁⲁⲩ / (*III* 74.4ff.) ⲙⲟⲛⲟⲛ ⲉϣⲁⲩⲕⲱⲧ ⲁⲛ ⲙⲡⲏⲓ ⲙⲡϫⲟⲉⲓⲥ ⲡⲛⲟⲩⲧⲉ ϫⲉ-ⲉⲛⲛⲁⲙⲟϣⲧϥ ϫⲉⲛⲉϥⲥⲟⲩⲧⲱⲛ ⲁⲩⲱ ϫⲉⲛⲉⲛⲉⲥⲱϥ, ⲁⲗⲗⲁ ϫⲉ-ⲉⲛⲉⲙⲟϣⲧⲛ ⲁⲛⲟⲛ ⲛϩⲏⲧϥ ϫⲉ-ⲉⲛⲟ ⲛⲁϣ ⲛϩⲉ / (*A 2* 51) ⲉⲛⲁⲓⲁⲧⲛ ⲁⲛ ϫⲉ-ⲟⲩⲛ-ⲟⲩⲣⲁⲛ ϩⲓϫⲱⲛ, ⲁⲗⲗⲁ ⲉⲛⲁⲓⲁⲧⲛ ⲉⲣϣⲁⲛⲡⲥⲱⲧⲏⲣ ⲓ̅ⲥ̅ ⲛⲁϩⲙⲉⲛ.

2.3 THE HETEROFOCAL SECOND-TENSE CONSTRUCTION: # SECOND-TENSE CONJUGATION-FORM + PRONOUN/NOUN SYNTAGM # — FOCALIZATION PATTERN (3)

Here we witness the focalization of the actants: (pro)nominal actor as well as the object-expansion. According to Polotsky[96], this is again a secondary use, even in synchronic view. In broader structuradelineation, our pattern will have to be confronted with the Cleft Sentence with (pro)nominal *vedette* (POLOTSKY 1962a), and arrive at a statement of opposition and neutralization[97], of macro-syntactic circumstances favouring the one construction or the other. The concurrence of the two patterns is especially striking with the *interrogative*, i.e. inherently focal, members of the focus paradigm. Here I believe we are dealing with a stylistically variant construction, rather than a functionally opposed one. Note the unmistakably colloquial flavour of idiomatic expressions like ⲉⲕϫⲉ-ⲟⲩ "What do you say?", ⲉⲕⲣ-ⲟⲩ "How are you doing?". Here, however, I shall simply present the classified evidence for the Second-Tense pattern in Shenoute.

2.3.1 FOCALIZED OBJECT-EXPANSION. The FOCUS constituency: *interrogative pronouns* (inherently focal): ⲟⲩ "what?", ⲛⲓⲙ "who?", ⲁϣ (ⲛ-) "what...? which...?", ⲟⲩⲏⲣ "how much?". *Non-interrogative*: noun syntagms - determinators (ⲡ- ⲟⲩ- Ø-, §5.1.1.0.1) expanded by noun lexemes; ⲡ- ex-

[94] Cf. POLOTSKY 1944:48f. (= *CP* 152f.). See below, §2.5, for ⲉⲁϥ- as post-focal theme-topic.

[95] POLOTSKY 1940:245 (= *CP* 37).

[96] See POLOTSKY 1944:31 (= *CP* 135), 51f. (= *CP* 155f.). This is, in a way, tantamount to describing as "secondary" the use of the English "that..." as *glose*-form in Cleft Sentences with a (pro)nominal *vedette* ("It was my father that gave me the tie as a present"), cf. POLOTSKY 1944:§21. This is worth considering diachronically, but is synchronically unhelpful. See ROSÉN's (1957) non-hierarchic presentation (esp. p. 141ff.) of the foci for the Greek "Second Tenses".

[97] Cf. POLOTSKY 1944:§§20, 22; see §2.7.1.2 below for Cleft Sentence + Sec. Tense configurations.

panded by a relative form (indeterminable substantivized relative [98]); the possessive pronoun ΠΑ- expanded by a noun syntagm; indefinite pronouns: ΟΥ "something", ΟΥΗΡ "so much"; perhaps also personal pronoun + augens (*A 2* 238, quoted below). Noteworthy is the focalization of ΧΕ-ΟΥ "(saying) what?", where ΧΕ- forms part of the valency of ΧⲰ "say", and is cataphorically represented in the verbal nucleus (the theme; again, nexal dependence is mapped on a 'nucleus - satellite' phrase). The THEME constituency: Second Present and Future, Second Perfect (noticeably less common), ΕΜΝΤΑ⸗, Second Aorist. The NEXUS is affirmative only for interrogative foci, otherwise both affirmative and negated (by ΑΝ), §2.9.1.3.

DOCUMENTATION: *affirmative nexus*: (*A 2* 509) ΕΙΝΑΧΕ-ΟΥΗΡ ΤΕΝΟΥ; / (*A 2* 512) ΕΙΝΑΤϬΑΙΕ-ΑⲨ ΜΜΕΛΟC ΝΤΑΚΑ-ΑⲨ, Η ΕΙΝΑΡ-ΑⲨ ΜΜΕΛΟC ΝΤΑΛΛΑΙΠⲰΡΟC ΝΤΑΜΑΚΑΡΙΖΕ ΝΑⲨ / (*A 2* 17) ΕΚΡ-ΟΥ ΝΤΟΚ Ν2ΗΤΟΥ; (sim. ΕⲨ(ΝΑ)ΡΟΥ "What does/will do...?", "How is...?", *A 1* 201 / *P* 130² 75 ΓΟ ΕΥΡ-ΟΥ ΝΘΥΔΡΙΑ ΧΙΝΜΠΕΙΝΑΥ ΝΤΑCΟΥⲰϬΠ / *A 2* 86, 481, 341, *Ch.* 117.6f., 166.48f., *III* 49.19, *IV* 98.25f., etc.).
ΕΙΧΕ-ΟΥ (*A 2* 366, *P* 130⁴ 99 vo etc.) but more usually Ε(Ч)ΧⲰ ΜΜΟC ΧΕ-ΟΥ (*A 2* 58, *Ch.* 143.36ff.), also Sec. Future, Perfect (*A 2* 56, 397, 387, *IV* 186.13 answered by ΠΕΧΑЧ ΧΕ-, pointing to suppletion between ΧⲰ and ΠΕΧΑ⸗).
ΧΕ-ΟΥ expands other verbs in the Second Tense, without cataphoric reference: ΟΥⲰⲰΒ (*Ch.* 132.26ff., Sec. Perf.); Ρ-2ΟΤΕ (*III* 105.29f., Sec. Pres.); +-2ΑΠ (*P* 131⁴ 86 ΡΛ); (*P* 131⁶ 19 ΜΓ) ΕΜΝΤΑΝ-ΟΥ ΜΜΑΥ; ΕΜΝ-ΤΑΝ-ΡΟΕΙC ΜΜΑΥ / (*Ch.* 28.46f.) ΕЧΝΑΤΑ2Ε-ΝΙΜ / (*Wess. 9* 171c 2 ff.) ΝΤΑΙΧΕ-ΠΕ+CΟΟΥΝ ΜΜΟЧ / (*A 2* 509) ΕΚΟΥⲰΜ-ΝΟΒΕ ΑΥⲰ ΟΥ2ΡΕ ΑΝ / (*Wess. 9* 171d 1ff.) ΝΕΤⲨΟΟΠ ΓΑΡ ΜΝΠΔΙΑΒΟΛΟC ΕⲨΑΥCΟΥΝ-ΝΑΠΔΙΑΒΟΛΟC ΧΙ-ϬΟΛ (ΕЧΧΙ-ϬΟΛ) is focal only (*III* 187.18f., *IV* 51.17, 64.26f., *Ch.* 185.34f., etc. — it can of course be circumstantial, i.e. non-initial: *Ch.* 185.45f., 187.51) / (*Mun.* 102) ΕⲨΧΕ-ΜΠΟΥΚΑ-ΠΝΟΥΤΕ ΝΑΥ ΕΙΕ ΕΥ-ΝΑΚΑ-ΡⲰΜΕ;

Negated nexus (rare): (*A 2* 238-9) ΕΝΝΑⲨΧΟΟΥ ΤΗΡΟΥ ΑΝ / (*Wess. 9* 171c 6f.) ΟΝΤⲰC ΕΙΧΙ-ϬΟΛ ΑΝ / (*Ch.* 96.9f.) ΝΤΑΙΧΕ-ΟΥⲨΑΧΕ ΑΝ Ν2ΟΥΟ ("I have not said a single superfluous thing") / (*IV* 94.3ff.) ΕⲨΑΥ-ⲨⲰⲰϬΕ-ΠⲰΝΕ ΑΝ Η ΝCΕΠΟΛ2Ч ΝϬΙΝΕΤΝΑΧⲰΡΠ ΕΡΟЧ, ΑΛΛΑ ΕⲨΑΥⲨⲰⲰϬΕ ΝΤΟΟΥ ΕΒΟΛ 2ΙΤΟΟΤЧ ("It is not the stone which is wounded or cut by those who stumble against it; it is rather they who are wounded by it" — the first part of the translation is not literal).

2.3.2 FOCALIZED ACTOR EXPRESSION is much less usual. FOCUS constituency: interrogative pronouns: ΝΙΜ, ΑⲨ, ΟΥΗΡ (*Thompson* E vo); non-interrogative foci are rare and mostly found in ambiguous examples: personal pronoun + augens; ΠΑΙ; the expanded determinators Π-, ΟΥ. THEME constituency (in order of frequency): Second Perfect (the only form with interrogative foci), Second Future, Present. NEXUS: affirmative only.

DOCUMENTATION: (*A 2* 18) ΝΤΑΝΙΜ ΝⲨⲰC ΕΝΕ2 ΚΑ-ΝΕCΟΟΥ 2ΜΠΟ2Ε ΑΥⲰ ΤⲨΑΙΡΕ 2ΜΠΤΡΕЧΜΟΥ... (sim. ΝΤΑΝΙΜ ΕΝΕ2...[99]: *A 2* 151, 153, 518, *Berl.* 1613 ΤΙΘ) / (*P* 131⁵ 4 vo) ΕΡΕΝΙΜ ΝΑΝΑ ΝΑΝ / (*Ch.* 203.51f.) ΝΤΑΑⲨ ΝΕΚΚΛΗCΙΑ Ρ-2ⲰΒ / (*Ch.* 24.53f.) ΤΔΟΚΙΜΗ ΓΑΡ ΕΡΕΟΥ2ΕΛΠΙC ΕΝΑΝΟΥC ΟΥΗ2 ΝCⲰC ΝΝΑ2ΡΝ- (or is ΝCⲰC/ΝΝΑ2ΡΝ- focalized?) / (*A 2* 299-230) (ΕΒΟΛ ΑΝ ΧΕ-ΝΤΑΠΑΙ ΛΙΒΕ ΑЧ2Ε Ε2ΡΑΙ ΕЧΡΙΜΕ) ΝΤΑΡΕΠⲨⲰC Ν2ΗΤ ΝΤΟ ΕΡΕΡΙΜΕ Ε2ΡΑΙ ΕΧⲰЧ "... it is *you* rather who have cried yourself into a stupor"; similarly *IV* 94.3ff. (ΕⲨΑΥⲨⲰⲰϬΕ-ΠⲰΝΕ ΑΝ)... ΑΛΛΑ ΕⲨΑΥⲨⲰⲰϬΕ ΝΤΟΟΥ ΕΒΟΛ 2ΙΤΟΟΤЧ "... it is they rather who are wounded by it".

---

[98] See §3.1.1.2.1.
[99] See §1.3.6 for the syntax of ΕΝΕ2.

2.4-6 Focus-initial patterns

2.4 Heterofocal second-tense construction: # modifier → sec.-tense conjugation-form # — focalization pattern (4)

2.4.0.1 In the following paragraphs, we consider a set of patterns (which are reminiscent of Western-type Cleft Sentences, §2.0.2.2.4) in which the focus precedes the topicalization form, and the focalization is (co-)signalled by a tagmemic feature of arrangement — the initial placement of the focus [100]. I shall consider the following complexities involved: (a) Pattern selection — patts. (2) vs. (4-5) —, rule-ordered, determined by the macro-syntactic relationships of the patterns. (b) The distinct focality type or grade of the initial focus, wherever an opposition obtains between it and the post-theme focus. (c) In the focus-initial patterns, the determination of the topic form by morphosyntactic factors: Tripartite/Bipartite, affirmative/negative topic and nexus. (Among topic forms here we must consider the morphologically unmarked Basic Tenses [§2.6.2].) (d) Idiosyncratic properties of focus classes or individual foci (inter-rogative/non-interrogative; ⲚⲀ Ϣ ⲚⲌⲈ, ⲈⲦⲂⲈⲞⲨ, ⲈⲂⲞⲖ ⲦⲰⲚ). (e) The existence of a pattern for which the topic form — ⲈϤ(ⲚⲀ)-, ⲈϢⲀϤ- — cannot be disambiguized: a syncretism neutralization of Second Tense and circumstantial: pattern (6). In §2.6.4. below, I shall attempt to sketch the structural picture emerging from the data of §§2.4.1-2.6.3.

2.4.1 Focalization pattern (4). Focus constituency. Of the interrogative foci so typical of patts. (5) and (6), none is here focalized. We find here only the peculiar ⲈⲂⲞⲖ ⲦⲰⲚ, dealt with in detail in §2.6.3. Non-interrogative modifiers (in order of frequency): ⲈⲦⲂⲈ- (esp. ⲈⲦⲂⲈⲠⲀⲒ, ⲈⲦⲂⲎⲎⲦ⸗); (ⳌⲢⲀⲒ/ⲈⲂⲞⲖ) 2Ⲛ- (often in the distinctive ⳌⲘⲠⲀⲒ —); (ⲈⲂⲞⲖ) 2ⲒⲦⲚ-; ⲚⲦⲈⲒ2Ⲉ; ⲈⳘⲚ-; ⲘⲚⲚⲤⲰⲤ; ⲘⲞⲅⲒⲤ [101]; ⲚⲦⲈⲢⲈ-, 2ⲞⲤⲞⲚ. Topic constituency: only ⲚⲦⲀϤⲤⲰⲦⲘ. Nexus: affirmative; negated (by — ⲀⲚ after the focus: §2.9.2.1).

Documentation: *affirmative*: (*III* 26.8) ⲈⲦⲂⲈⲠⲀⲒ ⲚⲦⲀⲠⲈⲒⲚⲞⳆ ⲚⲤⲀⳌⲞⲨ ⲈⲒ Ⲉ2ⲢⲀⲒ ⲈⳘⲘ- / (*Leyd.* 410) ⲈⳘⲘⲠⲀⲒ ⲈⲚⲦⲀϤⲈⲒ Ⲉ2ⲢⲀⲒ ⲈⲠⲒϢϢⲚⲈ / (*Wess.* 9 131a 2ff.) ⲈⲂⲞⲖ ⲦⲰⲚ ⲚⲦⲀ2ⲰⲢⲒⲅⲈⲚⲎⲤ ⲤⲰⲞⲨ2 Ⲉ2ⲞⲨⲚ... / (*P* 131⁵ 67 vo) 2ⲘⲠⲀⲒ ⲞⲚ ⲚⲦⲀϤⳘⲞⲞⲤ ⳘⲈ... ⲚⲦⲀⲠⳘⲞⲈⲒⲤ ⳘⲞⲞⲤ ⲞⲚ ⲈⲦⲂⲈⲠⲀⲒ ⳘⲈ-. Note the chiastic arrangement, re-curring in this pattern combined with pattern (2); also *Wess.* 9 144b-c, 153b-c, etc. / (*Cat.* 42.22) ⲚⲦⲈⲒ2Ⲉ ⲅⲀⲢ ⲈⲚⲦⲀⲚⲈⲒⲞⲨⲀ̄Ⲓ (sic) ⲖⲒⲂⲈ / (*Wess.* 9 152c 17ff.) 2ⲒⲦⲘⲠⲀⲒ ⲞⲚ ⲚⲦⲀⲨⳘⲞⲞⲤ ⲚⳆⲒⲚⲈⲄⲢⲀⲪⲎ ⳘⲈ- / (*P* 131⁴ 88 ⲢⲀⲅ) 2ⲢⲀⲒ 2Ⲛ ⲦⲘⲚⲦⳘⲀⳘⲈ... ⲚⲦⲀⲤⲢ-2ⲞⲨⲞ ⲚⳆⲒⲦⲀⲄⲀⲠⲎ / (*III* 210.21f.) ⲘⲚⲚⲤⲰⲤ ⲚⲦⲀⲚⲀⲒ ⲦⲎⲢⲞⲨ ⲤⲰⲞⲨ2 ⲈⲢⲞⲤ "Only afterwards did all those (*scil.* demons) gather against it (*scil.* the misguided soul)"; *v.l.* Basic Perfect / (*A 2* 430, not Sh.) ⲚⲦⲈⲢⲈϤⲦⲤⲒⲞϤ ⳘⲘⲞϤ (i.e. of the honey) ⲚⲦⲀⲠⲈϤⲤⲦⲞⲘⲀⳆⲞⲤ ⲀⲚⲀⲦⲢⲈⲠⲈ / (*IV* 162.2f.) 2ⲞⲤⲞⲚ ⲀⲠⲀⲒ ⲦⲦⲰϤ Ⲉ2ⲞⲨⲚ ⲚⲦⲀⲠⲀⲒ ⲈⲚⲦϢϤ (sic) ⲈⲂⲞⲖ (i.e. ⲦⲈϤⲚⲀ2ⲂⲈ; the sense here is "as soon as..."; see §7.2.3.2).

Negated nexus (affirmative topic only) [102]: (*A 1* 113) ⲈⲦⲂⲈⲘⲠⲈ̄ⲐⲞⲞⲨ ⲀⲚ ⲘⲀⲨⲀⲀⲨ 2ⲢⲀⲒ Ⲛ2ⲎⲦⲈ ⲚⲦⲀⲠⲀⲒ-ϢⲰⲠⲈ / (*Wess.* 9 144c 24ff.) ⲈⲦⲂⲈⲠⲈⲐⲂⲂⲒⲞ ⲀⲚ ⲘⲀⲨⲀⲀϤ ⲚⲦⲀϤⳘⲞⲞⲤ ⳘⲈ... Additional exx.: *III* 24.23 (focus: ⲘⲞⲅⲒⲤ), 76.8 (ⲚⲦⲈⲒ2Ⲉ), *Ch.* 136.41ff. (2ⲢⲀⲒ 2Ⲛ), *A 2* 499 (2ⲚⲞⲨⲤⲞⲞⲨⲦⲚ), *P* 130² 68 ⲢⲠ (ⲈⲦⲂⲈ-), 71 ⲢⲠⲤ (ⲈⲂⲞⲖ 2ⲒⲦⲞⲞⲦ⸗).

2.5 The circumstantial topicalization: # modifier/(pro)noun → circumstantial con-jugation-form # — focalization pattern (5)

---

[100] Mentioned in passing by Polotsky 1944:44 (= *CP* 148), and (with reference to negation) in 1960a:§32. If one is to judge by these statements, Polotsky recognizes solely a # focus + Sec. Tense # pattern. See also Stern §521.

[101] See §§1.3.11.6, 7.3.1.

[102] Cf. Polotsky 1960a:§32.

2.5.0.1 As may be gathered from the topic and focus constituency lists, this pattern (not mentioned as such in the *Études* [103]) transcends or cuts across a double modular, historically founded dichotomy of Polotsky's: between the "substantival" (thematic) and "adverbial" (adjunctal) verb-forms [104], and between the two complementary Cleft Sentence patterns — one with initial (pro)nominal vedette (focus) and ΠΕΤ- *glose* (theme/topic), and the other with initial Second-Tense theme and subsequent modifier focus [105]. This pattern could be considered separately as a lower-grade member in the focality paradigm, with its topic verging on a marked NON-INITIAL VERB-FORM. This is perhaps due to the devaluating effect of the inherently focal, hence (in terms of focality grading) not pertinent, interrogative pronouns or modifiers. (This is somewhat corroborated by the high incidence of ΝΖΑΖ ΝϹΟΠ "often", ΕΤΒΕΠΑΙ "therefore", ΚΑΛϢϹ "well" [106] and other, not characteristically focal premodifiers [107].)

2.5.0.2 Two constructions may belong here, which however stand apart: 'ϢΑΝΤΕΟΥ ϢϢΠΕ', rarely ϢΑΤΝΑΥ "until when...?", followed by a circumstantial present or circumstantial negative perfect [108], and 'ΕΙϹ + temporal expression + ΕϤ-/ΧΙΝΤΑ-'. (*A 2* 105) ϢΑΝΤΕΟΥ ϢϢΠΕ ΕΥΕΙΡΕ ΝΝΕΙΒΟΤΕ ΖΝΜΜΑ ΕΤΟΥΑΑΒ / (*III* 36.24f. = *Ch.* 132.26ff.) ϢΑΝΤΕΟΥ ϬΕ ϢϢΠΕ ΑΝΟΝ ΜΠΕΝΠϢΖ ΝΝΕΝΖΗΤ / (*P* 131⁴ 144 ΡⱫΗ) ϢΑΝΤΕΟΥ ϬΕ ϢϢΠΕ ΕΝϮ ΝΟΥΖΟΟΥ ΝϹΑΟΥΖΟΟΥ ΜΠΕΝΚΤΟΝ ΕΠΝΟΥΤΕ / (*P* 131⁵ 47 ro) ϢΑΝΤΕΟΥ ϢϢΠΕ ΕΝΜΗΝ ΕΒΟΛ ΖΝΝΕΝΜΝΤΝΑϢΤΖΗΤ / (*K* 9068) ϢΑΤΝΑΥ ΕΜΠϤΤΑΝΖΕΤ-ΠΝΟΥΤΕ / (*Ryl. Cat.* 34, No. 70 ϹΜΒ) ΕΙϹΑΟΥΗΡ ΝΟΥΟΕΙϢ ΧΙΝΤΑΠΑΙ ΤΑΖΟϤ / (*A 1* 71) ΕΙϹΖΟΥΟ ΕΕΒΟΤ ϹΝΑΥ ΕΝΟΥϢϢ ΕΤΡΕΤΝΡ-ΟΥΖΗΤ ΝΟΥϢΤ. Although it is probable that these are true focalization patterns with the circumstantial, a thematic topicalization constituent, one cannot help feeling that the circumstantial is (also?) in a complementation or contentualization relationship with the focus. These constructions must be further investigated, with the syntax of time expressions in general.

2.5.1 FOCUS constituency: interrogatives: ΑϢ, ΟΥΗΡ; ΝΑϢ ΝΖΕ, ΖΙΤΝΟΥ; non-interrogative: numbers; ΖΑΖ Ν-; ΖΕΝ-; (Ν)ΖΑΖ ΝϹΟΠ, ΖΕΝϹΟΠ, ΖΕΝΜΗΗϢΕ ΝϹΟΠ [109]; -ϢϹ-modifiers; ΕΤΒΕ-; ΖΝ-; ΕΙΜΗΤΙ Ε- [110];

---

[103] Cf. however 1944:48f. (= *CP* 152f.). See SHISHA–HALEVY 1972:§2.2.1.2, 1975:475f., 1976a:36f., 1976b:137, 1978. For the Cleft Sentence with *pronominal vedette* and circumstantial *glose*, cf. BROWNE 1978b, 1979b:202.

[104] Cf. POLOTSKY's most explicit and elaborate exposition of this thesis in 1976, also 1965 (esp. 99 47-50); an early sketch is 1944:91ff. (= *CP* 195ff.).

[105] See POLOTSKY 1944:57ff. (*CP* 161ff.). Striking analogies to the (partial) overlapping of the Cleft-Sentence patterns are to be found in the ongoing blurring of the functional boundaries of the *that/wh-/∅-glose* markers in the English Cleft Sentence, *a-/y-* in Modern Welsh (in Gaelic, *a-* is the sole *glose*-marker). For some comparative notes on the circumstantial *glose*-form, see POLOTSKY 1944:59 (= *CP* 163) n. 2, SHISHA–HALEVY 1978:64ff. In a different approach, our circumstantial *glose* may be conceived of as a zero conversion or *conversion base* (cf. SHISHA–HALEVY 1972:§§2.1.3.1, 2.2.1.3, 2.3.1.2), thus perhaps analogous to the zero-marked *glose* in English: "It's on Wednesday the show opens". A third alternative would be the interpretation of the circumstantial as a *participle* form (cf. the Greek "Second Tenses", ROSÉN 1957, and SHISHA–HALEVY 1976c). A construction which recalls Gardiner's "missing link", namely a ΠΕΤ-*glose* after an "adverbial" *vedette* (Gardiner, *JEA* 33:97f. [1947]) actually occurs in *Ryl.* 368 (*Cat.* 172).

[106] Cf. its native counterpart 'ΟΥΑΓΑΘΟΝ ΠΕ + inf.', in which ΟΥΑΓΑΘΟΝ is microsyntactically predicative, yet macrosyntactically thematic (see §7.1.3).

[107] Compare the devaluated status of the Welsh (Old to Modern) so-called "abnormal order" (as distinct from the "mixed order" or "mixed sentence", a true functionally operative Cleft Sentence): if any element other than the verb opens the clause, it is followed by a "phantom" relative: *Ef a welei carw* "He saw a stag", *At y cwn y doeth ef* "He went to [look at] the dogs", *Y march a gymerth* "He accepted the horse" (from the MW *Pedeir Keink Y Mabinogi*). Is our circumstantial also but a marked non-initial verb form?

[108] See (with reff.) SHISHA–HALEVY 1976b:361ff.; add some exx. quoted here, and the unpubl. non-Shenoutean yet Shenoute-emulating *BL Or.* 8811 ⱫΗ, with Basic (neg.) Future.

[109] Zero-marked noun syntagm in modifier status, §1.3.2.

[110] Cf. §§1.3.11.6, 7.3.1.1.

ⲭⲓⲛⲉⲛⲉⲍ; circumstantial present. Topic constituency: (*affirmative topic*) ⲉⲁϥ-, ⲉⲟⲩⲛ-, (*negatived topic*, ⲉ(ⲛ)ϥ(ⲛⲁ)- ⲁⲛ; ⲉⲙⲡϥ-, ⲉⲙⲡⲁⲧϥ-, ⲉⲟⲩⲟⲓ ⲁⲛ, ⲉ + Nom. Sentence + ⲁⲛ. Nexus: affirmative, negated (§2.9.2.3).

2.5.2 Observations. (1) ⲉⲁϥ-; Polotsky 1944:48f. (= *CP* 152f.)[111] offers two alternative explanations: it is either a true circumstantial topicalization or a Sahidic relic corresponding to Fayumic ⲁⲁϥ- (see *ibid*. 71 = *CP* 175; 94f. = *CP* 198f.). (Compare now the " Middle Egyptian " Second Perfect ⲉⲍⲁϥ-, which may still arguably be circumstantial in form.) With reference to synchronic and internal structure, I believe a circumstantial interpretation is inevitable. For ⲉⲁϥ- as a possible *prefocal* theme form, see §2.2, spec. obs. (5).

(2) ⲉⲙⲡϥ-; replacing ⲉⲧⲉⲙⲡϥ- (Polotsky 1944:88f. = *CP* 192f., 1960a:§18), yet compare the Demotic *i.ir-bn.pn.f sdm* (Polotsky 1944:88 = *CP* 192, Johnson 1976:186f.). (3) ⲉⲛϥ — ⲁⲛ replaces ⲉⲧⲉⲛϥ — ⲁⲛ, still uniquely attested (Polotsky 1944:89 = *CP* 193). Incidentally, in all cases of a negatived topic, the arrangement factor is neutralized — the focus is always initial.

2.5.3 Documentation[112]. *Affirmative nexus* — affirmative or neg. topic; mostly interrogative focus: (*Ryl. Cat.* 34 No. 70 ⲥⲙⲉ) ⲟⲩⲏⲣ ⲛⲧⲩⲡⲟⲥ ⲙⲡⲟⲛⲏⲣⲟⲛ ⲉⲁⲩⲭⲟⲕⲟⲩ ⲉⲃⲟⲗ / (*A 1* 312) ⲁⲩ ⲛⲗⲁⲟⲥ ⲏ ⲁⲩ ⲛⲥⲩⲛⲁⲅⲱⲅⲏ ⲉⲛⲧⲁⲡⲛⲟⲩⲧⲉ ϯⲥⲃⲱ ⲛⲁⲩ ⲍⲛⲟⲩⲱⲣⲭ ⲛⲧⲉⲛⲍⲉ (This may be an instance of circumstantial + Sec. Perfect, §2.0.1.1.2, i.e. a topic comprising a whole included Cleft Sentence: " What people or what congregation did God *like us, firmly* teach ? ") / (*Wess. 9* 147c 22f.) ⲛⲁⲩ ⲛⲍⲉ ⲉⲟⲩⲛⲗⲗⲁⲩ ϣⲟⲟⲡ ⲍⲁⲧⲉϥⲍⲏ / (*A 1* 305) ⲛⲁⲩ ⲛⲍⲉ ⲉⲩⲛⲟⲅ ⲁⲛ ⲡⲉ ⲡⲣⲱⲙⲉ / (*Miss.* 278) ⲛⲁⲩ ⲛⲍⲉ ⲉⲟⲩⲛⲟⲃⲉ ⲛⲁⲛ ⲁⲛ ⲡⲉ / (*A 2* 155) ⲛⲁⲩ ⲛⲍⲉ ⲧⲉⲛⲟⲩ ⲉⲟⲩⲟⲓ ⲁⲛ ⲛⲛⲉⲧⲥⲱⲕ ⲛⲛⲉⲩⲉⲣⲏⲩ ⲉⲍⲣⲁⲓ ⲉⲛⲓⲍⲓⲉⲓⲧ ⲉⲧⲙⲙⲁⲩ ⲛⲕⲁⲕⲉ ⲍⲓⲅⲟⲥⲙ / (*P 130²* 47 ⲥⲕⲅ) ⲛⲁⲩ ⲛⲍⲉ ⲡⲉⲧⲉⲟⲩⲛⲧⲁϥ ⲙⲙⲁⲩ ⲙⲡⲥⲟⲟⲩⲛ ⲛⲛⲉⲅⲣⲁⲫⲏ· ⲉⲛϥⲛⲁⲛⲁⲩ ⲁⲛ ⲉⲡⲁⲅⲅⲉⲗⲟⲥ… / (*Rossi 2/3* 76) ⲛⲁⲩ ⲛⲍⲉ ⲡⲭⲟⲉⲓⲥ ⲛⲁⲛⲟⲩⲅⲥ ⲁⲛ… ⲉⲍⲣⲁⲓ ⲉⲭⲱ, ⲏ ⲉⲛϥⲛⲁⲣⲁϣⲉ ⲁⲛ ⲉⲭⲛⲛⲉⲛⲧⲁⲩⲉⲓⲣⲉ ⲙⲡⲡⲉⲧⲛⲁⲛⲟⲩϥ / (*P 131⁶* 117 vo) ⲛⲁⲩ ⲛⲍⲉ ⲉⲛϥⲛⲁⲣⲟⲉⲓⲥ ⲁⲛ ⲛⲍⲟⲩⲟ / (*Wess. 9* 86b 21ff.) ⲍⲓⲧⲛⲟⲩ ⲡⲉⲛⲧⲁϥⲣ-ⲛⲁⲓ ⲧⲏⲣⲟⲩ ⲛⲁϥ ⲛⲍⲙⲍⲁⲗ… ⲉⲁϥⲣ-ⲉⲃⲏⲛ ⲍⲓⲱϣϥ ⲛⲅⲓⲡⲇⲁⲓⲙⲟⲛⲓⲟⲛ ⲉⲧⲙⲙⲁⲩ / (*A 2* 301) ⲍⲉⲛⲙⲏⲛϣⲉ ⲛⲥⲟⲡ ⲉⲙⲁⲧⲉ ⲉⲙⲁⲧⲉ ⲉⲁⲍⲁⲍ ⲛⲧⲉⲓⲙⲓⲛⲉ ⲛⲣⲱⲙⲉ ϯ ⲟⲩⲃⲉⲧⲙⲉ, ⲁⲩⲱ ⲉⲁⲍⲁⲍ ⲣ-ϣⲙⲙⲟ ⲉⲧⲥⲩⲛⲁⲅⲱⲅⲏ / (*A 2* 7) ⲟⲩ ⲅⲁⲣ ⲛϣⲁⲭⲉ… ⲉⲙⲡⲟⲩⲣⲍⲟⲩⲉⲭⲟⲟⲩ ⲛⲛⲉⲧⲟⲩⲏⲍ ⲍⲛⲛⲉⲓⲧⲟⲡⲟⲥ / (*A 1* 111) ⲍⲁⲍ ⲛⲥⲟⲡ ⲉⲁⲡⲭⲟⲉⲓⲥ ⲡⲛⲟⲩⲧⲉ… ⲟⲩϣϣ (sim. *III* 145.25, 146.8, 147.9, 148.11ff.[113]) / (*A 2* 90) ⲍⲁⲍ ⲛϣⲁⲭⲉ ⲛⲧⲉⲓⲍⲉ ⲉⲁⲓⲭⲟⲟⲩ ⲍⲙⲡⲁⲙⲕⲁⲍ ⲛⲍⲏⲧ… (sim. *Cat.* 42.25) / (*III* 206.4ff.) ⲍⲉⲛⲙⲛⲧⲣⲙⲛⲍⲏⲧ ⲍⲉⲛⲥⲟⲟⲩⲛ ⲍⲉⲛⲕⲟⲥⲙⲏⲥⲓⲥ ⲍⲉⲛⲉⲛⲧⲟⲗⲏ ⲉⲩⲟⲩⲁⲃ (sic) ⲍⲉⲛⲙⲛⲧⲡⲁⲣⲑⲉⲛⲟⲥ ⲍⲉⲛⲕⲉⲍⲃⲏⲩⲉ ⲙⲙⲟⲓⲍⲉ ⲉⲁⲥⲟⲩⲱⲛⲟⲩ ⲧⲏⲣⲟⲩ (sim. *A 1* 113 ⲍⲉⲛⲍⲃⲏⲩⲉ ⲍⲉⲛⲧϣϣ ⲉⲗⲗⲁⲩ…) / (*III* 69.18f.) ⲧⲁⲓⲟⲩ ⲙⲛⲥⲛⲁⲩ ⲉⲁⲩⲭⲡⲟⲟⲩ ⲁⲩⲱ ⲉⲁⲛⲭⲟ ⲉⲃⲟⲗ ⲉⲛⲉⲛⲧⲁⲩⲙⲓⲥⲉ ⲛⲧⲉⲩⲭⲣⲓⲁ / (*A 2* 318-19, coll.) ⲉⲧⲃⲉⲛⲉⲛⲭⲱϣⲙ ⲙⲛⲛⲉⲛⲥϣϣϥ… ⲡⲭⲟⲉⲓⲥ ⲁⲩⲱ ⲡⲁⲅⲅⲉⲗⲟⲥ ⲉⲙⲡⲁⲧϥⲃⲱⲗ ⲉⲃⲟⲗ ⲛⲙⲙⲁⲛ (*v.l.* ⲙⲡⲁⲧϥ-) / (*Wess. 18* 140b 8ff.) ⲍⲛⲛⲁⲓ ⲟⲛ ⲧⲏⲣⲟⲩ ⲉⲙⲡⲉⲩⲍⲏⲧ ⲅⲛ-ⲁⲣⲓⲕⲉ ⲉⲣⲟⲟⲩ ⲁⲛ / (*Or.* 160.3ff.) ⲉϣϫⲉ-ⲉⲧⲃⲏⲏⲧⲕ ϣ ⲡⲙⲁⲓⲍⲗⲇⲟⲛⲏ ⲉϥⲍⲟⲟⲩ ⲉⲁⲡⲣⲱⲙⲉ ⲛⲉⲭ-ⲧⲉϥⲥⲍⲓⲙⲉ ⲉⲃⲟⲗ / (*BMCat.* 92, No. 211 2 ro) ⲇⲓⲕⲁⲓⲱⲥ ⲉⲁϥⲣ-ϣⲙⲙⲟ ⲉⲣⲟ / (*III* 56.17f.) ⲙⲉϣⲁⲕ ⲅⲁⲣ ⲉϥⲇⲟⲕⲓⲙⲁⲍⲉ ⲛⲧⲉⲥⲁⲅⲁⲡⲏ ⲉⲁϥⲍⲟⲡϥ ⲉⲣⲟⲥ ⲡⲣⲟⲥⲟⲩⲕⲟⲩⲓ.

Negated nexus - affirmative topic: (*Leyd.* 390) ⲙⲏ ⲉⲧⲃⲉⲛⲉⲓⲍⲃⲏⲩⲉ ⲁⲛ ⲛⲧⲉⲓⲙⲓⲛⲉ ⲉⲁⲡϣⲁⲭⲉ ⲉⲧⲥⲏⲍ ⲭⲟⲟⲥ ⲛⲁⲛ ⲭⲉ- / (*Wess. 9* 106a 7ff.) ⲙⲏ ⲉⲧⲃⲉⲧⲙⲛⲧⲥⲧⲙⲏⲧ ⲁⲛ ⲉⲁⲛⲁⲓ ⲉⲧⲙⲙⲁⲩ ⲭⲱⲕ ⲉⲃⲟⲗ ⲛⲍⲱⲃ ⲛⲓⲙ ⲉⲛⲁⲛⲟⲩϥ… (cf. the parall. *P 130²* 71 ⲣⲡⲉ, quoted §2.6.2).

[111] Earlier discussions: Stern §423 (*Ming.* 119 = *III* 50.1, transl. as a Cleft Sentence with conditional *glose*); Steindorff 1904:§328 (" main clause "); Levy 1909:§254 (" main clause "); Spiegelberg 1909:156f.; Edgerton 1935:260; Till §334 (" Sec. Tense ", following Polotsky).

[112] Some non-Shenoutean exx. for the circumstantial topic (see Polotsky 1944:48f. = *CP* 152f.): Besa *ed.* Kuhn 32.16 (ⲛⲁⲩ ⲛⲍⲉ), *BLOr.* 8811 ⲥⲗ (ⲉⲧⲃⲉ-, *bis*), *Sap.* 16:1 (ⲉⲧⲃⲉⲡⲁⲓ) durative negative, ⲉⲛϥ(ⲛⲁ)-ⲁⲛ: *Rom.* 8:32 (Morgan; ⲛⲁⲩ ⲛⲍⲉ), *II Cor.* 3:8 (ⲛⲁⲩ ⲛⲍⲉ), *Heb.* 2:11 (ⲉⲧⲃⲉⲡⲁⲓ), *Col.* 2:5 (ⲍⲛ-), *Eccles.* 8:16 (ⲍⲛ-).

[113] Note the specially high incidence of this pattern in Leipoldt's No. 40 (*III* 116-151, esp. 141ff.), with its numerous paragraphs introduced by ⲉⲧⲃⲉⲡⲁⲓ.

Additional exx.: *III* 207.21f. (ΝΑϢ ΝϨΕ ΕΝϤΝΑ -ΑΝ), 216.10 (ϪΙΝΕΝΕϨ ΕΜΠΟΥ-), *A 2* 78, *A 1* 108, 463, *A 2* 13, 337 (all ΝΑϢ ΝϨΕ Ε + neg. Bip.); *A 2* 91, *III* 71.19f. Cod. C — all ΝΑϢ ΝϨΕ + circ. Nom. Sentence); *A 1* 89 (ϨΙΤΝΟΥ ΕΑ-), *III* 125.9ff. (ΕΤΒΕ- ΕΑΥϪΟΟϹ, v.l. ΑϤ-, 1.12), so too *IV* 29.3ff.; etc.

2.6 The heterofocal second-tense/circumstantial construction: # modifier/(pro)noun → ε + conjugation-form # — focalization pattern (6)

Here we must be content with pointing out the topicalization characteristic, which is a syncretism neutralization of the circumstantial and Second-Tense converters. We cannot resolve this Ε-, internally at least, although for some individual foci (esp. those with a low grading of focality, §2.5.0.1) one is tempted to identify the morph as circumstantial. In terms of segmental signalling, however, there is no escaping the fact that this is a case of neutralization [114].

2.6.1 Focus constituency. Interrogatives: ΟΥΗΡ; ΝΑϢ ΝϨΕ, ΕΤΒΕΟΥ, ϨΙΤΝΟΥ, ΕϪΝΟΥ, ΕΤωΝ; ΠΟϹω ΜΑΛΛΟΝ, ϢΑΝΤΕΟΥ ϢωΠΕ, ϢΑΤΝΑΥ (§2.5.0.2); non-interrogative: determinators (ΟΥ-, ϨΕΝ-); numbers; ΕΤΒΕ-, (ϨΡΑΙ, ΕΒΟΛ) ϨΝ-, Ν(ΤΕΙϨΕ), (ΕΒΟΛ) ϨΙΤΝ-, ϨωϹ-; ΜΜΑΥ, -ωϹ-marked modifiers; ΜΟΓΙϹ, ΕΙϹ + time expression; circumstantial, conditional. Topic constituency: ΕϤ(ΝΑ)-, ΕϢΑϤ-, Ε- + adjective-verbs. Nexus: affirmative, negated (both focus and nexus negativing: §2.9.2.3) [115].

Documentation. *Affirmative nexus*: (*Ch.* 188.40ff.) ΟΥΗΡ ΝΡωΜΕ ΝΔΙΑΒΟΛΟϹ ΕΥΟΥΟΟΛΕ ϨΝΝΑΓΑΘΟΝ ΜΠΚΑϨ / (*A 2* 300) ΟΥϨΟΟΥ ΜΝΟΥϢΗ ϹΝΤΕ ΕΡΕΠΑΙ ϢΟϪΝΕ ΝΑΥ / (*III* 207.8ff.) ϨΕΝΠΡΟΦΗΤΗϹ ϨΕΝΕΥΑΓΓΕΛΙΟΝ ϨΕΝΑΠΟϹΤΟΛΟϹ ϨΕΝΓΡΑΦΗ ΕΝΑϢωΟΥ ϨΕΝΚΑΘΗΓΕϹΙϹ ΝΤΕΝΕΤΟΥΑΑΒ ϨΕΝϢΑϪΕ ΜΝϨΕΝϹΒΟΟΥΕ... ΕΡΕΕΙΡΕ ΜΜΟΟΥ ΑΥω ΕΡΕϹωΤΜ ΝϹωΟΥ (circumstantial? cf. 206.4ff. The low-focality focus and marked non-initial verb are here in evidence) / (*III* 69.13f.) ϹΑϢϤ ΝϹΑΕΙΝ ΕΥϯ-ΠΑϨΡΕ / (*A 1* 96) ΟΥΜΝΤϪΑϪΕ ΜΝΟΥΕΙΡΗΝΗ ΕΥϢΟΟΠ ϨΝΤΕΙϬΙΝΚω ΕΒΟΛ / (*Ch.* 72.1ff.) ΕΤΒΕΟΥ ΕΙΝΑΟΥΑϨΤ ΝϹΑΟΥΔΑΙΜωΝ; ΕΤΒΕΟΥ ΝϯΝΑΟΥΑϨΤ ΑΝ ΝϹΑΠΕΧϹ; / (*P* 130[5] 55 ϤΖ) ΝΑϢ ΝϨΕ ΕΙΝΑϪω ΜΠΕΤΕΝϯϹΟΟΥΝ ΜΜΟϤ ΑΝ / (*A 1* 233) ΕΤωΝ ΕϢΑΥΝΟϪϤ, one term of a chiastic figure, see §2.6.3.1.2 (4) / (*Or.* 163.19ff.) ΠΟϹω ΜΑΛΛΟΝ ΕϤΝΑϯϹΟ... (sim. *Ch.* 74.54ff., 119.30ff., *III* 97.24 etc.) / (*Ch.* 135.44f.) ϨΙΤΝΟΥ ΕΝΑΑΑΥ ΕΝΕΥΕΡΗΥ / (*IV* 14.10f.) ΕΤΒΗΗΤϹ ΟΝ ΕϢΑϤΚΤΟϤ ΕΒΟΛ ϨΜΠΕϤϬωΝΤ / (*Mun.* 96) ΕΙΤΟΛΜΑ ΕΙϪω ΝΝΑΙ "It is daringly I am saying this" / (*A 2* 476) ΜΟΓΙϹ ΓΑΡ ΕΝΝΑΑΙϹΘΑΝΕ.

Negative nexus - affirmative topic, negatived focus or nexus: (*Ch.* 38.35ff.) ΕΡϢΑΝΤΒΑϢΟΡ ΑϢΚΑΚ ΕΒΟΛ ΑΝ... ΕΡΕΠΜΟΥΙ ΤΡΡΕ "It is not when the fox cries out that the lion is afraid" (the all-important ΑΝ is omitted in the parallel *III* 79.4ff.) / (*A 2* 519) ΕΤΒΗΗΤ ΑΝ ΕΚΝΑϨΥΠΟΤΑϹϹΕ ΝΑΙ, ΟΥΔΕ ΕΤΒΗΗΤΚ ΑΝ ΕΙΝΑϯ-ΠΜΑ ΝΑΚ ΕΡ-ϨωΒ ΝΙΜ... / (*IV* 117.23) ΝΝΕΝϯϢΙΠΕ ΝΗΤΝ ΑΝ ΕΝϪω ΝΗΤΝ ΝΝΑΙ "It is not shaming you that we tell you this" / (*A 1* 114) ΜΗ ϨωϹΑΘΗΤ ΑΝ ΕΡΕΠΑΙ ΤΑΜΟ ΜΜΟ.

More exx.: *III* 199.23f. (ΟΥΗΡ Ν- ΕΡΕ-), 72.2f. (ΕΒΟΛ ΤωΝ Η ϨΙΤΝΟΥ ΕΡΕ-), *A 2* 333 (ϨΝ- ΕϤ-), *III* 70.7 (ϤΤΟ Ν- ΕΥ-), *P* 130[4] 122 ΛΒ (ΚΑΛωϹ ΑΥω ΔΙΚΑΙωϹ ΕΥ-), *Rossi 2/3* 86, *A 2* 413, 338, *III* 46-7 *passim*,

[114] Not that extra-Sahidic evidence is of great help. On the one hand, Akhmimic instances point to a Second Tense ('ΑϤ-ΝΑϹωΤΜΕ'): *Ex.* 7:1 (ΝΕϨ ΝϨΕ), *Clem.* (Schmidt) 46.5 (ΕΤΒΕΟ), *Prov.* 7:20 (ϨΙΤΝ-), 11:31 (ΜΟΓΙϹ), *Gespr. Jesu* 9.11f. (ΜΝΝϹΕΚΕ-ΟΥΗΡ ΝΡΟΜΠΕ). Compare now the clear "Middle Egypt." evidence for the Sec. Tense (e.g. *Mt.* 12:26, 29, 34), also Fayumic-ME *Joh.* 13:28 (ΕΤΒΕΟΥ ΑϨΑϤ-) and (late) Bohairic exx. of ΝΑϢ ΝΡΗϯ ΑϤΝΑ- etc. (*Mon. of Macarius* 31.7 ϧΕΝΑϢ ΝϨΟ ΑΙΝΑ-). Polotsky 1934:64 (= *CP* 369), 1960a:§37b interprets ϨΙΤΝΟΥ ΕΝΑΑΑΥ (*Ch.* 135.44f.) as Second Tense (also 1960a:§32, *Ch.* 38.35ff.; 1944:39, 44 = *CP* 143, 148). On the other hand, one finds in Akhmimic ample evidence for Ε- as a post-focal topic characteristic (cf. Till 1928:§218j). This is common in *Gespräche Jesu* (ΠωϹ-ΕΚ- 10.2, ΕΤΒΕΟ-ΕΚ- 32.1, ΝΕϨ ΝϨΕ ΕΥΝΑ- 25.8, ΚΑΛωϹ Ε- 30.10f., 38.10). Compare in *Clemens* Ε- for the *initial* topic (our patt. 2), when occurring after an extraposition, i.e. prominent topicalization of the actor/object: 7.1, 19.1, 20.5, 20.8. At any rate, the Sahidic situation must be judged internally.

[115] For ΕΤΒΕΟΥ, ΝΑϢ ΝϨΕ, ΕΒΟΛ ΤωΝ see discussion and more evidence in §2.6.3-4. For ΝΤΕΙϨΕ see §1.3.1.2; for -ωϹ-modifiers, §1.3.11.1.

IV 109.8f. (all ⲕⲁⲗⲱⲥ/ⲇⲓⲕⲁⲓⲱⲥ ⲉϥ-); *III* 114.13, *IV* 33.22 (ⲍⲛⲛⲁⲓ, ⲍⲙⲡⲁⲓ ⲉⲩ-, ⲉⲩⲁ-), *A 2* 342 (ⲍⲣⲁⲓ ⲛⲍⲏⲧ⸗/ ⲉⲃⲟⲗ ⲍⲓⲧⲟⲟⲧ⸗ ⲉϣⲁⲣⲉ-), *IV* 161.12 (ⲙⲙⲁⲩ), *A 1* 107 (ⲉⲝⲛⲟⲩ ⲉϥⲛⲁ-), *A 2* 147 (ⲍⲓⲧⲛⲟⲩ ⲉⲣⲉ- ⲛⲁ-).

2.6.2 AN UNMARKED MEMBER OF THE FOCALIZATION PARADIGM: ⧣ MODIFIER → BASIC TENSE ⧣. This is, of course, the case only when the context warrants the distinction from the *non-focal premodifier* (see §1.1.2.2). With the proviso that suprasegmental features, unknown to us, probably constitute the most prominent feature of this pattern, one may say that here the topic is (segmentally) marked only by position — this being morphologically a zero-member of the post-focal topicalization paradigm. FOCUS constituency: the listing cannot be even attempted here (for certain foci — ⲉⲧⲃⲉⲟⲩ, ⲛⲁϣ ⲛⲍⲉ, ⲉⲃⲟⲗ ⲧⲱⲛ — the complementary relationship of this pattern with the others will be treated at length in §2.6.3-4[116]). We find here interrogative and non-interrogative prepositional phrases (notably ⲉⲧⲃⲉ-, (ⲉⲃⲟⲗ) ⲍⲓⲧⲛ-, ⲉⲡⲭⲓⲛⲭⲏ). TOPIC constituency: most frequently ⲁϥ-/ⲙⲡϥ-, ϣⲁϥ-, ⲛϥ(ⲛⲁ)- ⲁⲛ. The NEXUS is affirmative or negated (nexus or focus negativing, §2.9.2.4).

DOCUMENTATION (speciminal). *Affirmative nexus*: (*A 2* 305) ⲛⲁϣ ⲛⲍⲉ ⲡⲛⲟⲩⲧⲉ ⲛⲁϯ-ⲥⲟ ⲉⲡⲁⲓ / (*A 2* 334) ⲉⲃⲟⲗ ⲧⲱⲛ ⲧⲉⲛⲟⲩ ⲛⲉⲧϯ-ⲍⲧⲏⲩ ⲉⲡⲉⲥⲍⲁⲓ ⲙⲙⲁⲧⲉ... ⲁⲩⲙⲉⲉⲩⲉ ⲉⲡⲉⲓⲍⲱⲃ / (*P* 130⁵ 70 ⲡⲏ) ⲉⲧⲃⲉⲟⲩ ⲧⲉⲧⲛⲭⲓ ⲉⲃⲟⲗ ⲍⲙⲡⲙⲩⲥⲧⲏⲣⲓⲟⲛ ⲉⲧⲟⲩⲁⲁⲃ / (*III* 199.27f.) ⲉⲧⲃⲉⲟⲩ ⲙⲡⲟⲩⲁⲙⲁⲍⲧⲉ ⲙⲙⲟ ⲉⲧⲙⲉⲓⲣⲉ ⲛⲛⲉⲓⲃⲟⲧⲉ ⲧⲏⲣⲟⲩ.

Negated nexus: (*P* 130² 71 ⲣⲡⲉ) ⲙⲏ ⲉⲧⲃⲉⲧⲙⲛⲧⲥⲙⲛⲧ (sic, for -ⲥⲧⲙⲏⲧ) ⲁⲛ ⲁⲛⲁⲓ ⲭⲱⲕ ⲉⲃⲟⲗ ⲛⲍⲱⲃ ⲛⲓⲙ ⲉⲛⲁⲛⲟⲩϥ, ⲏ ⲉⲧⲃⲉⲧⲙⲛⲧⲁⲧⲥⲱⲧⲙ ⲁⲛ ⲛⲧⲟϥ ⲁⲛⲉⲓⲕⲟⲟⲩⲉ ⲭⲱⲕ ⲉⲃⲟⲗ ⲙⲡⲉⲓⲙⲏⲏϣⲉ ⲙⲡⲉⲑⲟⲟⲩ (cf. the parall. *Wess.* 9 106a 7ff. with ⲉⲁ- topics) / (*A 1* 353) ⲉⲡⲭⲓⲛⲭⲏ ⲅⲁⲣ ⲁⲛ ⲁⲡⲭⲟⲉⲓⲥ ⲙⲉⲥⲧⲉ-ⲛⲓⲟⲩⲇⲁⲓ (sim. 88, 366, 354, *Ch.* 139.19f., *III* 55.14f., 56.13) / (*A 1* 125) ⲉⲧⲃⲉⲟⲩⲍⲣⲉ ⲁⲛ ⲛⲧⲟϥ ⲛⲥⲁⲣⲕⲓⲕⲟⲛ ⲛⲭⲓⲟⲩⲉ ⲍⲓⲕⲣⲟϥ ⲁⲛⲉⲓⲣⲱⲙⲉ ϯ ⲙⲡⲁⲓ ⲉⲧⲟⲟⲧϥ ⲙⲡⲛⲟⲩⲧⲉ / (*IV* 156.26f.) ⲉⲛⲉⲉⲧⲃⲉⲧⲁⲅⲁⲡⲏ ⲁⲛ ⲛ̄ⲧ̄ⲥ̄ ⲛⲉⲓⲭⲱ ⲛⲛⲁⲓ, ⲛⲉⲟⲩ ⲡⲉ ⲡⲁⲣⲟⲟⲩϣ.

A focalization pattern as unfulfilled-condition protasis, with the topic resuming the irrealis function already signalled for the whole clause: (*P* 131⁴ 158 ro) ⲉⲧⲃⲉⲡⲁⲓ ⲍⲣⲁⲓ ⲍⲛⲧⲅⲟⲙ ⲁⲛ ⲙⲡⲉⲧϣⲁⲭⲉ ⲁⲗⲗⲁ ⲍⲣⲁⲓ ⲍⲛⲧⲉⲭⲁⲣⲓⲥ ⲙⲡⲉⲧⲭⲱ ⲙⲙⲟⲥ ⲭⲉ... ⲧⲅⲟⲙ... ⲙⲡⲉⲧⲛⲡ̄ⲛ̄ⲁ̄ ⲛⲁϣⲱⲡⲉ ⲉⲥϣⲟⲩⲉⲓⲧ.

2.6.3 A SELECTIVE EXAMINATION OF FOCI:

Aiming for a complex, full-dimensional paradigmatic picture of the patterns introduced in §§2.4-6, I shall now present the evidence from a different angle: *topic alternation for a constant given focus*. For this purpose, two foci are chosen, no doubt statistically the best represented of their kind: ⲉⲧⲃⲉⲟⲩ " why? " and ⲛⲁϣ ⲛⲍⲉ " how? "[117]. Since they feature also in the topic-initial pattern (2), this too must be integrated in the picture and related to the focus-initial patterns. A third, rather peculiar interrogative focus examined here for its topic paradigm is ⲉⲃⲟⲗ ⲧⲱⲛ " whence? ", " on what grounds? ".

2.6.3.1.1 ⲉⲧⲃⲉⲟⲩ, ⲛⲁϣ ⲛⲍⲉ in *focus-initial* patterns. This is indubitably the usual placement. The TOPIC is (a) a BASIC TENSE, for (1) *affirmative/negative* NON-DURATIVE (TRIPARTITE) CONJUGATION (ⲁϥ-/ ⲙⲡϥ-, ϣⲁϥ-, ϣϣⲉ), also NOMINAL SENTENCES, (2) *negatived* BIPARTITE CONJUGATION, (3) (SPECIALLY CONDITIONED) *affirmative* BIPARTITE CONJUGATION. TOPIC (b) is morphologically marked: (1) ⲉ- (*circumst./ Second*): ⲉϥ(ⲛⲁ)-, ⲉϣⲁϥ-, ⲉ- + adj.-verb; (2) *circumstantial* (affirm./neg.): ⲉ(ⲛ)ϥ(ⲛⲁ)- ⲁⲛ, ⲉⲟⲩⲛ-,ⲉ- + Nom. Sentence, ⲉⲁϥ- (for ⲍⲓⲧⲛⲟⲩ, n. 117). Note that (3) Sec. Tense ⲛⲧⲁϥ-, patt. (4), is not attested.

Assorted representative examples: a (1) *III* 199.27f., *Ch.* 76.40f., *Wess.* 9 118a 23f., *A 1* 68, *A 2* 458 (ⲛⲁϣ ⲛⲍⲉ ϣⲁⲣⲉ-), *A 2* 69 (ⲛⲁϣ ⲛⲍⲉ + neg. Nom. Sent.), *A 2* 19-20 (ⲉⲧⲃⲉⲟⲩ ϣϣⲉ neg.) etc.; a (2) *III* 102

---

[116] For several instances of this pattern in configuration with others, esp. (5)-(6), see 9.2.7.3.

[117] ⲍⲓⲧⲛⲟⲩ , incomparably less well attested, still gives in miniature the same distributional picture: a (1) *RE 11'*16a 15f., *A 1* 2, *A 2* 114; b (1) *Ch.* 135.44f., *III* 72.2f., *IV* 10.4, 23.2, *A 1* 175; b (2) *Wess. 9* 86b 21ff., *A 1* 89 (ⲍⲓⲧⲛⲟⲩ ⲉⲁ-).

passim, *IV* 99.24f., 42.16f., *Ch.* 64.2ff. etc.; a (3) instances are mostly classifiable as follows (some fall into more than one category):

A. Quotations or reminiscences of Scripture texts [118]: *RE 11* 18b 25f., *Wess. 9* 148b 2f., *Ench.* 66a, *Wess. 9* 171d 7f., *Cl. Pr.* 44 ⲕⲏ-ⲑ, *A 2* 342 (an adaptation of *Mt.* 15:18f. and *Marc.* 7:21); ⲛⲁϣ ⲛϩⲉ ⲛⲧⲱⲧⲛ ⲧⲉⲧⲛⲁⲣ-ⲃⲟⲗ... *BMCat.* 83 (No. 199 ⲧⲍⲁ), cf. *III* 51.3f., 65.12, *Ch.* 169.7ff.; *Mt.* 23:23, *Heb.* 2:3; also (non-scriptural) arguments attributed to persons other than Shenoute: *Ryl.* 69 ⲛⲅ, *A 2* 430 (not Sh.).

B. Instances of striking rhetoricity and pathos: "proforma" or pseudo-topicalization; sometimes, with the flavour of Bible text. Note in particular *series of multiple questions*: (*A 2* 388-9) ⲉⲧⲃⲉⲟⲩ ⲕⲟ ⲛϩⲙϩⲁⲗ... ⲉⲧⲃⲉⲟⲩ ⲕϩⲩⲡⲟⲧⲁⲥⲥⲉ... ⲁⲩⲱ ⲕⲥⲟⲡⲥ... ⲉⲧⲃⲉⲟⲩ ⲕⲥⲙⲟⲩ ⲉⲛⲥⲱⲛⲧ ⲛⲧⲡⲉ, ⲕϭⲱϣⲧ ⲇⲉ ⲟⲛ ⲉⲃⲟⲗ / (*A 2* 351-2) ⲉⲧⲃⲉⲟⲩ ⲛⲧⲟⲟⲩⲛ ⲡⲣⲱⲙⲉ ⲣ-ⲑⲩⲥⲓⲁ ⲁⲩⲱ ϥⲛⲁ; ⲉⲧⲃⲉⲟⲩ ⲇⲉ ⲟⲛ ϥϣⲗⲏⲗ ⲁⲩⲱ ϥⲛⲏⲥⲧⲉⲩⲉ; ⲉⲧⲃⲉⲟⲩ ϥⲁⲥⲕⲉⲓ... ⲁⲩⲱ ϥⲣ-ⲇⲓⲕⲁⲓⲟⲥⲩⲛⲏ; ⲉⲧⲃⲉⲟⲩ ⲉϥⲛⲁⲣ-ⲡⲓⲥⲧⲟⲥ... ⲁⲩⲱ ⲉⲧⲃⲉⲟⲩ ⲉⲛϣⲡ-ϩⲓⲥⲉ... ⲏ ⲉⲧⲃⲉⲟⲩ ⲇⲉ ⲉⲣⲉⲡⲣⲱⲙⲉ ⲛⲁϫⲓⲧϥ ⲛϭⲟⲛⲥ ... ⲏ ⲉⲧⲃⲉⲟⲩ ϥⲟⲩⲱϣⲙⲉ ⲙⲙⲟϥ / (*Or.* 156.7ff.) ⲉⲧⲃⲉⲟⲩ ⲕϩⲱⲥ ⲛⲧϣⲱⲧⲉ ⲙⲡⲉⲧϩⲓⲧⲟⲩⲱϥ ⲏ ⲕϣⲟⲣϣⲣ ⲙⲙⲟⲥ / (*A 2* 146) ⲉⲧⲃⲉⲟⲩ ⲉⲕⲟ ⲛⲕⲣⲟϥ ⲁⲩⲱ ⲕϫⲓⲟⲩⲉ ⲁⲩⲱ ⲕϣⲱⲗ ⲏ ⲉⲕⲕⲱ ⲛϩⲧⲏⲕ...

C. ⲉⲧⲃⲉⲟⲩ with Basic Bipartite in apodosi (similarly rhetorical topicalization?): (*A 1* 265) ⲉⲛⲉϥⲛⲁϯ-ϩⲏⲩ ⲁⲛ ⲉⲣⲟⲟⲩ, ⲛⲁϣ ⲛϩⲉ ϥⲛⲁϫⲟⲟⲥ ϫⲉ- / (*A 1* 239) (ⲉⲛⲉⲙⲡⲉ...) ⲛⲁϣ ⲛϩⲉ ⲕⲛⲁⲉⲣ-ⲛⲟⲉⲓⲕ ⲉⲧϩⲓⲙⲉ ⲙⲡⲉⲧϩⲓⲧⲟⲩⲱⲕ / (*P* 130[4] 103 ⲣⲕⲃ) ⲉϣϫⲉ-ⲡϭⲉⲣⲱⲃ ϩⲛⲛⲉⲛϭⲓϫ ⲁⲩⲱ ⲧⲥⲏϥⲉ, ⲉⲧⲃⲉⲟⲩ ⲡⲙⲟⲩⲓ ⲙⲛⲡⲟⲩⲱⲛϣ ⲧⲱⲣⲡ ⲙⲡⲉⲥⲟⲟⲩ... ⲉϣϫⲉ-ⲁⲛⲟⲛ-ϩⲉⲛⲥⲁⲃⲉⲉⲩ... ⲉⲧⲃⲉⲟⲩ ⲧⲛⲡⲁⲣⲁⲃⲁ ⲙⲡϩⲁⲡ / (*BLOr.* 3581A 71, No. 202 ⲣⲡⲇ) (ⲉϣϫⲉ...) ⲛⲁϣ ⲛϩⲉ ⲡⲥⲱⲙⲁ ⲏ ⲡⲣⲱⲙⲉ ⲧⲏⲣϥ ⲛⲁⲥⲙⲓⲛⲉ ⲏ ϥⲛⲁⲣⲁⲛⲁϥ ⲙⲡⲉⲛⲧⲁϥⲧⲁⲙⲓⲟϥ.

D. Several instances of ⲟⲩⲛ-/ⲙⲛ- before the durative (almost in complementary distribution with ⲉⲣⲉ-): (*A 2* 483) ⲛⲁϣ ⲛϩⲉ ⲟⲩⲛⲣⲱⲙⲉ ⲁⲩⲱ ⲟⲩⲛⲥϩⲓⲙⲉ ⲛⲁϣⲱⲡⲉ ϩⲛⲟⲩⲧⲃⲃⲟ, also *Ench.* 80a, *Or.* 157.39ff.

Topic b (1) *Wess 9* 144c 15ff., *Ch.* 28.13f.,34f., *III* 31.13f., *IV* 49.25f., *Or.* 156.21ff., 166.14ff.; b (2) *Wess. 9* 147c 22f. (ⲛⲁϣ ⲛϩⲉ ⲉⲟⲩⲛ + pres.), *III* 207.21f. (ⲛⲁϣ ⲛϩⲉ ⲉⲛϥ — ⲁⲛ), *Miss.* 278 (ⲛⲁϣ ⲛϩⲉ + ⲉ-Nom. Sent.), *Rossi 2*/3 76 (ⲛⲁϣ ⲛϩⲉ ⲡϫⲟⲉⲓⲥ ⲛⲁⲛⲟⲩϭⲥ ⲁⲛ... ⲏ ⲉⲛϥⲛⲁⲣⲁϣⲉ ⲁⲛ...), *III* 71.19f., *A 2* 78.

2.6.3.1.2 ⲉⲧⲃⲉⲟⲩ, ⲛⲁϣ ⲛϩⲉ in topic-initial pattern (2). This construction, statistically weaker than the preceding ones in *Leipoldt* and *Chassinat* [119] (approx. 33% for ⲛⲁϣ ⲛϩⲉ, less than 10% for ⲉⲧⲃⲉⲟⲩ) is *marked*, i.e. can be shown to be subject to statements of special conditions. In the great majority of cases — *condition 1* — it is included as marked by ϫⲉ-, a characterization of macro-syntactic status [120]

[118] Compare §7.2.1.1.5.1 for a similar convergence of rhetoricity/quotedness; §2.6.3.1.2 for rhetoricity/apodoticity/quotedness.

[119] Not counting the basically different instances of - ⲟ ⲛⲁϣ ⲛϩⲉ ("how is...?") where the '*topic* → *focus*' arrangement is obligatory, i.e. unopposed to a focus-initial construction. Moreover, the focality grading is here different: ⲛ- marks the *predicative complement* (*adnexal modifier*) of the "copular" (i.e. incomplete-predication) - ⲟ -. This, I believe, is the most important distinction between the two phrases 'ⲛⲁϣ ⲛϩⲉ'. Some Shenoutean exx. for -ⲟ ⲛⲁϣ ⲛϩⲉ: *III* 74.7, 103.13, *IV* 6.17, 37.20f., 98.12, 155.2f., *Mun.* 110, *Or.* 154.39f. etc.

[120] Cf. Polotsky 1934:63f. (= *CP* 368f.), Layton 1979:187f. I believe that his statement, to the effect that in indirect questions we have a Second Tense with ⲉⲧⲃⲉⲟⲩ, skips an all-important descriptive step, namely the conditioning of arrangement. Also, "postverbal whenever a Second Tense is used" (188) is simply an inversion of terms: a Second Tense is used in the topic-initial patterns. We must here observe the following *descriptive order*: (1) arrangement ruling, (2) topic-form selection ruling. A similar inversion of these terms occurs in Wilson's statement (1970:78 n. 3): "Questions with Future III which place the main stress of the sentence on the adverbial extension usually avoid putting the interrogative at the head of the sentence". I see both arrangements as constituting distinct focalization patterns: see §2.6.4. Historically speaking, this conditioning may be described as a preservation, in an "island" of special macrosyntactic circumstances, of the original '*topic* → *focus*' arrangement, the "renewed", inverted focus-initial pattern being restricted to the complementary circumstances. Synchronically, this is of course the Shenoutean situation: it is (as a random check of Wilmet's references for ⲉⲧⲃⲉⲟⲩ and ⲛⲁϣ ⲛϩⲉ quickly shows) quite different from that prevailing in the New Testament.

(ⲭⲉ-included focus-initial ⲉⲧⲃⲉⲟⲩ/ⲛⲁⲩ ⲛ2ⲉ are rare: about 3% of all initial attestations for ⲛⲁⲩ ⲛ2ⲉ, 13% for ⲉⲧⲃⲉⲟⲩ). Here belong probably also cases of pre-inclusion — see (4) below; circumstantial conversion of the whole focalization pattern, see §2.0.1.1.2, and adverbal expanding focalization pattern (the -ⲅⲛ-Sec.-Tense constr. type, §2.8.3). *Condition 2* is another, probably related macro-syntactic characterization: THEMATIC PROGRESSION §§2.0.2.4, 2.7.2), with resuming and linking topicalization of a verb occurring previously. *Condition 3* concerns yet another macro-syntactic relationship: ⲉⲧⲃⲉⲟⲩ/ⲛⲁⲩ ⲛ2ⲉ *in apodosi*, esp. of ⲉⲩⲭⲉ- (which is after all more of a topicalization marker than a true conditional), also of ⲉⲙⲙⲟⲛ " otherwise ".[121] *Condition 4*: certain RHETORICAL configurations: rhetorical questions, chiasm, " proforma " topicalization, pre-inclusion (§2.7.1.4.2), and multiple focalization (ⲛⲁⲩ ⲛ2ⲉ corresponding to other post-topic interr. foci). *Condition 5*: Scripture QUOTATIONS or REMINISCENCES or emulation of Scriptural (archaic, authoritative) style. Note however that for topic categories a (1) (neg.), a (2), b (2) (neg.) — that is, for the negative topic (the *nexus* is here invariably affirmative) — the arrangement is not pertinent. A negative topic does not occur as Second Tense, but only as Basic or circumstantial, and then only post-focally.

DOCUMENTATION: (1) ⲭⲉ-*inclusion*: *A 1* 71 (after ⲭⲱ), *A 2* 251 (ⲉⲓⲱⲣⲙ ⲉⲃⲟⲗ), *A 2* 257 (ⲇⲟⲕⲓⲙⲁ2ⲉ), 516 (ⲉⲓⲙⲉ), 541 (ⲛⲁⲩ), *P* 130² 70 ⲣⲡⲅ (ϯ-2ⲧⲏⲕ) ⲭⲉ-ⲉⲩⲁⲩⲧⲁⲕⲟ ⲛⲁⲩ ⲛ2ⲉ / 130⁵ 90 ro (ⲛⲁⲩ) ⲭⲉ-ⲉⲩⲱⲁⲭⲉ ⲛⲁⲩ ⲛ2ⲉ ⲙⲛⲛⲉⲛⲧⲁⲩⲉⲓ ⲉⲭⲓ-ⲃⲁⲡⲧⲓⲥⲙⲁ / *Ch.* 55.24ff. (ⲁⲛⲁⲩ), *IV* 156.19f. (ⲡⲣⲟⲥⲉⲭⲉ), 188.10f. (ⲱⲓⲛⲉ), 12f. (ⲥⲟⲟⲩⲛ), etc. etc.; this construction is very common.

(2) *Thematic progression*: (*Ch.* 199.23ff.) ⲡⲗⲏⲛ ⲛⲓⲙ ⲛⲉⲧⲛⲁⲣ-2ⲧⲏⲩ ⲁⲛ ⲛⲥⲁⲡⲇⲓⲕⲁⲓⲟⲥ; ⲉⲩⲛⲁⲣ-2ⲧⲏⲩ ⲇⲉ ⲛⲁⲩ ⲛ2ⲉ / (*BMCat.* 81, No. 197) ⲡⲣⲱⲙⲉ ⲅⲁⲣ ⲉⲧϯ ⲉⲙⲛⲥⲉ ⲙⲡⲉⲧⲩⲁⲁⲧ ⲉⲩⲛⲁϯ ⲁⲛ ⲙⲡⲉⲧⲩⲁⲁⲧ ⲉⲧⲃⲉⲟⲩ / (*Ch.* 73.4ff.) ' ⲁⲡⲥⲁⲧⲁⲛⲁⲥ ⲃⲱⲕ ⲉ2ⲟⲩⲛ ⲉⲣⲟⲩ ' ⲛⲧⲁⲩⲃⲱⲕ 2ⲱⲱⲩ ⲉⲧⲃⲉⲟⲩ — *lemmatizing* topicalization, §2.7.2.

(3) *In apodosi*: (*A 2* 19) (If they spare one, many will do so and transgress the law; if so,) ⲛⲧⲁⲩⲙⲟⲟⲩⲧ ⲁⲛ ⲙⲡⲉⲓⲕⲉⲟⲩⲁ ⲉⲧⲃⲉⲟⲩ / (*A 2* 194) ... ⲙⲙⲟⲛ ⲉⲩⲛⲁⲃⲱⲕ ⲉⲃⲟⲗ 2ⲓⲧⲟⲟⲧⲟⲩ ⲛⲁⲩ ⲛ2ⲉ / (*A 1* 69) (ⲙⲡⲉⲡⲉⲥⲩⲁⲭⲉ ⲣ-ⲩⲁⲩ ⲛⲉ, ⲏ ⲙⲡⲉⲡⲱ ⲣ-ⲩⲁⲩ ⲛⲁⲥ ⲛⲧⲟ) ⲛⲧⲉⲓ2ⲉ ⲟⲛ ⲉⲣⲉⲡⲟⲩⲱⲁⲭⲉ ⲛⲁⲣ-ⲩⲁⲩ ⲛⲁⲛ ⲛⲁⲩ ⲛ2ⲉ (ⲉ)ⲙⲡⲉⲛⲩⲁⲭⲉ ⲣ-ⲩⲁⲩ ⲛⲉ ⲁⲛ.

(4) *Rhetorical configurations*: (*A 2* 385) ⲏ ⲉⲕⲛⲁⲩⲟⲩⲩⲟⲩ ⲙⲙⲟⲕ ⲛⲁⲩ ⲛ2ⲉ ⲡⲁⲛⲟⲙⲟⲥ ⲛⲓⲟⲩⲇⲁⲓ / (*A 1* 158) ⲛⲁⲩ ⲛ2ⲉ ⲉⲓⲛⲁⲉⲓⲙⲉ ⲉⲛⲉⲩⲩⲓ ⲏ ⲉⲓⲛⲁϯ-ⲩⲓ ⲉⲣⲟⲟⲩ ⲛⲁⲩ ⲛ2ⲉ — a chiastic *disiunctio Sinuthiana* figure / (*P* 131⁴ 87 ⲣⲗⲁ-ⲃ) ⲛⲧⲁⲩ6ⲟⲡⲩ ⲇⲉ ⲛⲁⲩ ⲛ2ⲉ... ⲁⲣⲁ 2ⲛⲟⲩⲙⲛⲧⲭⲁⲭⲉ... / (*A 2* 530) ⲉⲥⲛⲁⲟⲩⲱ2 ⲛⲁⲩ ⲛ2ⲉ 2ⲙⲡⲏⲓ... ⲁⲩⲱ ⲁⲩ ⲧⲉ ⲑⲉ ⲉϯⲛⲁ2ⲙⲟⲟⲥ ⲉⲧⲉⲧⲣⲁⲡⲉ2ⲁ ⲙⲙⲟⲥ / (*III* 15.21) ⲉⲧⲉⲧⲛⲁⲭⲟⲟⲥ ⲛⲁⲩ ⲛ2ⲉ ⲭⲉ... — idiom? sim. *A 1* 61 / (*P* 130⁴ 84 ⲛ) ⲛⲧⲁⲩⲱⲛ ⲇⲉ ⲛⲁⲩ ⲛ2ⲉ· ⲛϯⲥⲟⲟⲩⲛ ⲁⲛ, ⲁⲩⲱ ⲛⲧⲁⲩⲡⲁⲣⲁⲅⲉ ⲛⲁⲩ ⲛ2ⲉ· ⲙⲡⲓⲉⲓⲙⲉ — pre-inclusion focalization figure / (*A 1* 71) ⲉⲛⲛⲁⲩⲁ2ⲉⲣⲁⲧⲛ ⲧⲱⲛ ⲏ ⲉⲛⲛⲁⲩⲩⲓ-ⲡⲣⲟⲟⲩⲩ ⲙⲡⲉⲓ2ⲱⲃ ⲛⲟⲩⲱⲧ ⲙⲛⲛⲉⲛⲉⲣⲏⲩ ⲛⲁⲩ ⲛ2ⲉ ⲁⲛⲟⲛ ⲁⲩⲱ ⲛⲧⲟ / (*III* 207.14ff.) ⲉⲣⲉⲛⲁ6ⲱⲧ ⲛⲁⲩ ⲛ2ⲉ ⲉ2ⲟⲩⲛ ⲉ2ⲣⲁⲩ ⲙⲡⲭⲟⲉⲓⲥ... ⲉⲣⲉⲛⲁⲩⲩⲓ-ⲡⲟⲩ2ⲟ ⲉ2ⲣⲁⲓ ⲧⲱⲛ... ⲉⲣⲉⲛⲁ6ⲱⲧ ⲛⲁⲩ ⲛ2ⲉ ⲉ2ⲟⲩⲛ ⲉ2ⲣⲁⲩ ⲙⲡⲉⲛⲩⲟⲣⲡ ⲛⲉⲓⲱⲧ / (*A 1* 62-3) ⲉⲣⲉⲛⲁ2ⲉ ⲉⲡⲩⲁⲭⲉ ⲉⲧⲥⲏ2 ⲧⲱⲛ... ⲏ ⲉⲩⲛⲁⲧⲱⲙⲉ ⲉⲣⲟ ⲛⲁⲩ ⲛ2ⲉ. In (*Ming.* 318) ⲧⲙⲏⲥⲉ ⲇⲉ ⲙⲡⲛ- [...] ⲭⲉ-ⲉⲥⲥⲩⲛ2ⲓⲥⲧⲁ ⲉⲃⲟⲗ 2ⲛⲁⲩ ⲛⲅⲁⲙⲟⲥ (ⲉ)ⲛⲧⲁⲩ-ⲭⲓ-ⲟⲩⲱ ⲙⲙⲟⲥ ⲛⲁⲩ ⲛ2ⲉ " Of the interest we do not (know) in what wedlock it is begotten, having been conceived in what way " we witness a case of the circumstantial conversion of a pattern (2) focalization construction (§2.0.1.1.2) — here too the non-initial placement of ⲛⲁⲩ ⲛ2ⲉ is evidently conditioned; cf. category (1) above.

(5) (*A 1* 80) ⲉⲓⲛⲁⲩⲩⲓ-ⲛⲁⲃⲁⲗ ⲉⲣⲟⲕ ⲛⲁⲩ ⲛ2ⲉ 2ⲙⲡⲁⲩⲗⲏⲗ ⲕⲟⲩⲓ ⲙⲙⲛⲧ2ⲏⲕⲉ.

---

[121] Cf. SHISHA–HALEVY 1972:§4.1.4.1 (on ⲉⲙⲙⲟⲛ as circumstantial conversion of ⲙⲙⲟⲛ " no, not "). Cf. now the clearly circumstantial ⲉⲙⲁⲛ " otherwise " in " Middle Egyptian " Coptic (*Mt.* 6:1, 9:17; Schenke).

2.6.3.2 The idiosyncratic ЄВОΛ ΤШΝ "whence?", "on what ground?", "how come?" enters the following constructions, with the topic paradigm following it including several members absent in other post-focal environments:

(a) *(initial)*		ΑϤ-	*A 2* 111, 140, 334... (unmarked topic)
		ЄϤΝΑ-	*P* 131⁵ 42 ro, *RE 10* 162b 25f., *A 2* 54
		ЄϤ-	*A 1* 64, *III* 72.2f.
ЄВОΛ ΤШΝ		ЄОΥΝ-	*A 2* 412
		ΝΤΑϤ-	*Wess. 9* 131a 2ff. [122]
	ХЄ-ΑϤ-		*P* 130⁴ 120 KH
	ХЄ-ОΥΝ-		*A 1* 67
	ХЄ-ЄϤЄ-		*Ryl.* 69 ẓ, *A 2* 62.
	ХЄ-ЄϤΝΑ-		*A 2* 9, *III* 87.7, 26.18ff., etc.
(ΝЄВОΛ ΤШΝ)	ΠЄ ХЄ-ЄϤΝΑ-		*A 2* 8 (coll.) [123]
	ЄΤΡЄ-		*III* 19.20f. [123]

(b) *(non-initial)*   ХЄ + Sec. Tense + ЄВОΛ ΤШΝ *A 1* 281, *Cl. Pr.* 38, 1 [124], *IV* 64.23.

Some representative examples: (*A 2* 140) ЄВОΛ ΤШΝ ΑΤЄΤΝΤΑΚΟ ΝΘЄ ΝΟΥϢЄ ЄϤΟΥΟϢϤ / (*A 2* 54) ЄВОΛ ΤШΝ ЄΡЄΝΙẒΒΗΟΥЄ ΝΚΑΚЄ ẒΙ6ОСΜ ... ΝΑ6ΛΟΜΛΜ ЄẒΟΥΝ ЄΡΟΝ / (*P* 130⁵ 48 vo) ЄВОΛ ΤШΝ ХЄ-ЄΡЄΠΑΙ ΝΑϤΙ ΝΤЄΙẒЄ ΤΗΡС / (*A 2* 412) ЄΜΝΚШẒΤ ΔЄ ϢООΠ ЄВОΛ ΤШΝ ЄОΥΝΟΥОЄΙΝ Η ϢΑẒ ΝΚШẒΤ ΝΑϢШΠЄ / (*A 1* 64) ЄΤВЄОΥ Η ЄВОΛ ΤШΝ ЄΙХШ ΝΝΑΙ ΝЄ / (*Wess. 9* 131a 2ff.) ЄВОΛ ΤШΝ ΝΤΑẒШΡΙ6ЄΝΗС СШОΥẒ ЄẒОΥΝ... / (*P* 130⁴ 120 KH) ЄВОΛ ΤШΝ ХЄ-ЄΡϢΑΝΤЄΨΥΧΗ Ρ-ΝΟВЄ ΑΥΤΑΑС ЄΠСШΜΑ / (*A 2* 9) ЄВОΛ ΤШΝ ХЄ-ЄΡЄОΥϢΗΡЄ ΝΑΛΥΠЄΙ ΜΠЄϤЄΙШΤ / (*A 2* 8 coll.) ΝЄВОΛ ΤШΝ ΠЄ ХЄ-ЄΥΝΑΡ-ΝЄẒΒΗΥЄ ΝΝΔΑΙΜШΝ / (*A 2* 62) ЄВОΛ ΤШΝ ХЄ-ЄΡЄΤСΑВЄ-ΠΔΙΑΒΟΛОС ЄΠОΥẒΗΤ.

2.6.4 Focus-INITIAL PATTERNS: STRUCTURAL ASSIGNMENT AND EVALUATION. The following chart and tables are based on the data presented in §§2.4–2.6.3. They are fairly complex yet not entirely satisfactory in accounting for functional intricacies. To understand correctly the relationships of pattern form and topic constituency, one must resort to proper *descriptive ordering*.

(a) DESCRIPTIVE-ORDER ("multiple-choice") FLOW CHART (⟶ : conditioning or entailement; "no opposition". ⟵⟶ : opposition; choice or selection).

---

[122] ЄВОΛ ΤШΝ proves the exception to the non-interrogative constituency of the focus in pattern (4).

[123] ХЄ- and ЄΤΡЄ- may be understood either as true "that"-form topicalizations, albeit with a distinct *prospective* colouring (not unlike the "prospective emphatic" in Old and Middle Egyptian, POLOTSKY 1969:473ff., 1976:§2.7; cf. the analogous Greek use of ἵνα (νά), JANNARIS §§1774b, 1911, pp. 566, 577). Compare the Akhmimic (*Gespr. Jesu* 32.11f.) ΝЄẒ 6Є ΝẒЄ ΑΤЄΠΟΥЄ ΠΟΥЄ ΝẒΗΤΝЄ ΡΠΙẒΑΜΤ... In ΝЄВОΛ ΤШΝ ΠЄ ХЄ-, ХЄ- is appositive to the pronominal subject in the ╫ modifier + ΠЄ╫ predication pattern (§1.2.1.2).

[124] Rarely, we find ЄВОΛ ΤШΝ following the Basic "*imperfectum futuri*" (*in apodosi*), §2.7.3.

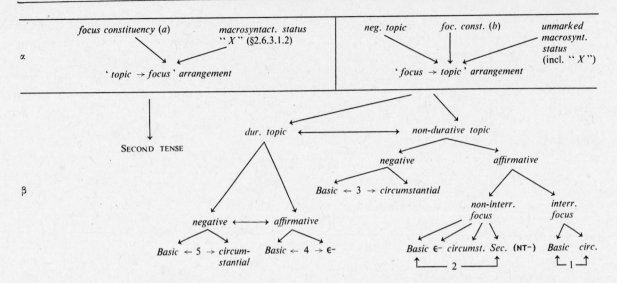

That is to say, we obtain five environments with five paradigms which must be expounded, at least *prima facie*. Closer inspection shows we can eliminate the very rare opposition (1), practically also (3).

(b) Neutralizations/oppositions in given environments/circumstances

topic form	*Basic Tense*	*Second Tense*	*circumstantial*	ɛ- (Sec. + circ.)
Basic Tense		non-interr.	non- dur. affirm. interr. (1)	affirm. dur. (4)
		perf. affirm. (2)	non-interr. affirm. (2)	non-dur. affirm. non-interr. ஶⲁϥ- (2)
			negative (3) (5)	
Second Tense	perfect affirm. non-interr. (2)		non-dur. affirm. non-interr. (2)	
circumstantial	non-dur. affirm. interr. (1)	non-dur. affirm. non-interr. (2)		
	non-interr. affirm. (2)			
	dur., non-dur. negative (3) (5)			
ɛ- (circumst. + Sec.)	non-dur. affirm. non-interr. ஶⲁϥ- (2)			
	dur. affirm. (4)			

(c) SIGNIFICANT DISTINCTIONS (FOCUS-INITIAL PATTERNS):

	affirm.: *neg.* TOPIC	*interr.*: *non-interr.* FOCUS	*affirm.*: *neg.* NEXUS
non-durative topic	+	+	—
durative topic	+	—	—

(d) INTERPRETATION. We note the existence of two separate, independent but successive conditioning sets at play: (α) PATTERN (arrangement) CONDITIONING, (β) TOPIC-FORM CONDITIONING. The " outputs " (a provisional one, of arrangement; a final one, of topic form) give us five paradigms or opposition environments. (1) The circumstantial member is extremely rare as compared with the bulk (dozens of occurrences) of the Basic Tense. (2) ⲀⳞ- has a full three-member paradigm, ⳜⲀⳞ-, a two-member one. (Note that focus constituency may also be operative.) Basic Tenses are opposed to converted ones as unmarked:marked topics (for the Nom. Sentence the circumstantial is the only way of marking). ⲈⲀⳞ- may be opposed to ⲚⲦⲀⳞ- as low-focality (or non-initial verb) marking *vs.* high-focality marking topicalization. Alternatively, the circumstantial belongs perhaps to a more colloquial system. (3) Here again circumstantial instances are very rare, and cannot be viewed as on a functional par with the Basic Tense. (4) Stylistic characterization? (5) See (2). Note that for the interrogative focus, topic-marking is redundant (focality being inherent).

2.7 STYLISTIC SYNTAX: COTEXT PATTERNS, " FIGURES ". In internal, non-contrastive view, " style " and " syntax " cannot be kept apart. The idiosyncratic realization of the grammatical potential of the *langue*, i.e. the idiolectal grammatical norm, is nothing but the writer's/speaker's style. This is no less true of macro-syntax: favoured or distinctive sub-textual stretches and configurations are nonetheless part and parcel of the functional system of grammar. In the following pages I review some of the familiar and recurring Shenoutean figures — those germane to the subject under discussion. Beyond the significance of their formal definition and their diagnostic value for identifying the Shenoutean text [125], they have some importance in an as yet non-existent frame of reference, that of COPTIC STYLISTICS.

2.7.1 RHETORICAL FOCALIZATION FIGURES

2.7.1.1 THE SECOND-TENSE THEME/TOPIC AND THE CIRCUMSTANTIAL FOCUS — patts. (2), (5), (6). Note in particular (a) the " *Wechselsatz* " or correlative " balanced " construction effect [126], where we have two ⲈⳞ-forms juxtaposed, and pattern (i.e. topic/focus) assignment is impossible and immaterial — the *topic - focus* structure is reversible: (*A 1* 68) ⲘⲎ ⲈⲘⲘⲈ ⲘⲘⲞ ⲈⲘⲘⲞⲤⲦⲈ ⲚⲦⲀⲠⲞⲗⲗⲈ, ⲈⲘⲘⲈ ⲘⲘⲞⲤ ⲈⲘⲘⲞⲤⲦⲈ ⲘⲘⲞ ⲚⲦⲞ, Ⲏ ⲈⲘⲘⲈ ⲚⲞⲨⲈⲒ ⲘⲘⲱⲦⲚ ⲐⲎⲢⲦⲚ... ⲈⲘⲘⲞⲤⲦⲈ ⲚⲞⲨⲈⲒ, Ⲏ ⲈⲘⲘⲞⲤⲦⲈ ⲚⲦⲞⳞ ⲚⲞⲨⲀ ⲊⲀⲐⲚ ⲈⲘⲘⲈ ⲚⲞⲨⲀ. Also, instances of the type (*Mun.* 96) ⲈⲒⲦⲞⲗⲘⲀ ⲈⲒⳜⲱ ⲚⲚⲀⲒ and (*Wess. 9* 158a 30ff.) ⲈⲨⲘⲞⲤⲦⲈ ⲘⲘⲱⲦⲚ ⲀⲚ ⲈⲨⳜⲱ ⲚⲎⲦⲚ ⲚⲚⲀⲒ / (*P* 130² 121 vo) ⲘⲠⲢⲘⲈⲈⲨⲈ ⳄⲈ-ⲈⲒⲘⲞⲤⲦⲈ ⲘⲘⲱⲦⲚ ⲈⲒⳜⲱ ⲚⲎⲦⲚ ⲚⲚⲀⲒ, ⲀⲗⲗⲀ ⲈⲒⲘⲈ ⲘⲘⲱⲦⲚ ⲊⲱⲤⲤⲞⲚ

---

[125] For some equally distinctive syntactic phenomena, see §§0.1.2, 2.7 *passim* and the index.

[126] Cf. POLOTSKY 1964:281f. (= *CP* 66f.), 1969:471f.; JUNGE 1978:115ff.; VERNUS 1981 (esp. 74ff.).

(*III* 122.20) ⲚⲀⲒ ⲆⲈ ⲈⲒⲭⲰ ⲘⲘⲞⲞⲨ ⲈⲈⲒⲦⲀⲘⲞ ⲘⲘⲰⲦⲚ / (*RE 11* 16a 39ff.) ⲈⲢⲈⲠⲖⲞⲄⲞⳝ ⲚⲞ6ⲚⲈ6 ⲀⲚ ⲈⳡⲭⲰ ⲘⲠⲀⲒ ⲞⲨⲆⲈ (Ⲉ)ⲚⲢⲀⲮⲈ ⲀⲚ... ⲀⲖⲖⲀ (Ⲉ)ⲚⲖⲨⲠⲈⲒ ⲚⲦⲞⳡ ⲚⲌⲞⲨⲞ.

(b) Instances of the " No sooner... than... " sense of the complex [127]: (*Ch.* 202-3) ⲈⲮⲀⳡⲮⲰⲠⲈ ⲈⳡⲦ ⲚⲦⲞⲞⲦⳡ ⲚⲞⲨⲞⲚ ⲚⲒⲘ ⲌⲚⲦⲈⲨⲬⲢⲈⲒⲀ ⲈⳡⲀⳝⲰⲞⲨ " (... Walking heavily in his eagerness;) and no sooner does he get the opportunity to aid somebody in need than he (walks) more lightly ".

2.7.1.2 TWO COMPLEMENTARY FOCALIZATION PATTERNS, COORDINATED/DISJOINED: Second-Tense construction, patt. (2) + Cleft Sentence with nominal/pronominal focus [128]. This is very common; the rhetorical effect of this juxtaposition of the focus-initial and theme/topic-initial patterns is of course *chiastic*. Often, these are *Disiunctio Sinuthiana* cases: (*A 2* 409) ⲈⲨⲈⲒⲢⲈ ⲘⲘⲞⲨ ⲚⲚⲒⲘ Ⲏ ⲚⲒⲘ ⲠⲈⲦⲚⲀⲮⲰⲠ ⲈⲢⲞⳡ ⲚⲚⲈⲨ-ⲠⲈⲦⲚⲀⲚⲞⲨⳡ / (*A 1* 52) ⲈⲒⲚⲀⲢ-ⲞⲨ Ⲏ ⲞⲨ ⲠⲈⲦⲚⲀⲀⲀⳡ / (*A 2* 378) "ⲈⲒⲕⲰ ⲚⲌⲦⲎⲒ ⲈⲠⲰⲚⲈ" — "ⲠⲢⲎ ⲠⲈⲦⲘⲞⲨⲢ ⲘⲘⲞⲒ" / (*Ench.* 67a) ⲚⲦⲀⳡⲮⲒⲂⲈ ⲌⲚⲞⲨ; ⲚⲦⲞⲕ ⲠⲈⲚⲦⲀⲕⳝⲒⲂⲈ / (*ibid.* 74b) ⲈⲦⲈⲦⲚⲎⲠ ⲈⲠⲰⲚⲌ — ⲠⲘⲞⲨ ⲠⲈⲦⲚⲀⲦⲰⲘⲦ ⲈⲢⲰⲦⲚ ⲌⲚⲞⲨⲮⳝⲚⲈ / (*RE 10* 163a 15f.) ⲚⲦⲀⲠⲕⲞⳝⲘⲞⳝ ⲦⲎⲢⳡ ⲮⲰⲠⲈ ⲈⲂⲞⲖ ⲌⲒⲦⲞⲞⲦⲕ, ⲀⲖⲖⲀ ⲠⲈⲕⳝⲦⲀⲨⲢⲞⳝ ⲠⲈⲚⲦⲀⳡⲕⲒⲘ ⲈⲠⲕⲀⲌ ⲦⲎⲢⳡ / (*III* 192.4) ⲈⳡⲮⲀⳝⲈ ⲈⲚⲒⲘ Ⲏ ⲚⲒⲘ ⲠⲈⲚⲦⲀⳡⳝⲞⲞⳝ...

2.7.1.3.1 DOUBLE SIMULTANEOUS (INTERROGATIVE) FOCALIZATION: (*Cat.* 42.27f.) ⲚⲒⲘ ⲠⲈⲦⳝⲰ ⲘⲘⲞⳝ ⲚⲚⲒⲘ [129] / (*Wess.* 9 110a 9f.) ⲚⲦⲀⲚⲒⲘ ⲦⳝⲀⲂⲞⳡ ⲈⲚⲒⲘ / (*A 2* 63) ⲚⲒⲘ ⲠⲈⲚⲦⲀⳡⲢ-ⲮⲞⲢⲠ ⲈⲚⲒⲘ / (*ibid.* 518-9) ⲚⲦⲀⲚⲒⲘ ⲈⲒⲘⲈ... ⳝⲈ-ⲚⲒⲘ ⲠⲈⲦⲚⲀⳡⲒ ⲌⲀⲚⲒⲘ ⲘⲘⲞⲚ Ⲏ ⳝⲈ-ⲚⲒⲘ ⲠⲈⲚⲦⲀⳡ⳼-ⲌⲎⲨ ⲈⲦⲈⲚⲒⲘ / (*RE 10* 160a 37) ⲚⲒⲘ ⲠⲈⲚⲦⲀⳡⲘⲈⲨⲦ-ⲚⲒⲘ. Compare (*Ch.* 128.43ff.) ⲀⲞⲨⲎⲢ ⲚⲈⲠⲒⳝⲕⲞⲠⲞⳝ Ⲣ-ⲞⲨⲎⲢ ⲚⲌⲞⲞⲨ ⲘⲚⲞⲨⲎⲢ ⲚⲞⲨⲮⲎ ⲘⲠⲒⲘⲀ.

2.7.1.3.2 Compare the extremely common COMPLEX (expanded, disjoined) FOCUS: (*A 1* 64) ⲈⲦⲂⲈⲞⲨ Ⲏ ⲈⲂⲞⲖ ⲦⲰⲚ ⲈⲒⳝⲰ ⲚⲚⲀⲒ ⲚⲈ / (*A 2* 8-9) ⲚⲀⳝ ⲄⲀⲢ ⲚⲌⲈ Ⲏ ⲈⲦⲂⲈⲞⲨ ⲈⲢⲈⲓⲦ ⲚⲀⲢ-ⲞⲨⲎⲒ Ⲏ ⲞⲨⲦⲞⲠⲞⳝ ⲚⲮⲘⲘⲞ ⲈⲢⲞⳡ / (*ibid.* 312) ⲈⲦⲂⲈⲞⲨ Ⲏ ⲈⳝⲚⲞⲨ ⲚⲌⲰⲂ (sim. 223-4, *III* 214.5) / (*Miss.* 283) ⲌⲀⲌⲦⲚⲚⲒⲘ Ⲏ ⲌⲚⲀⲮ ⲚⲎⲒ / (*Wess.* 9 151c 24ff.) ⲈⳝⲚⲞⲨ Ⲏ ⲈⳝⲚⲚⲒⲘ / (*A 1* 109) ⲈⲦⲂⲈⲚⲒⲘ Ⲏ ⲌⲀⲦⲚⲚⲒⲘ / (236) ⲈⲦⲂⲈⲞⲨ Ⲏ ⲌⲒⲦⲚⲞⲨ / (412) ⲦⲰⲚ Ⲏ ⲈⲂⲞⲖ ⲌⲒⲦⲚⲚⲒⲘ (sim. *P 131*[6] 14 vo) / (*III* 72.2f.) ⲈⲂⲞⲖ ⲦⲰⲚ Ⲏ ⲌⲒⲦⲚⲞⲨ (mostly striking instances of the *figura Sinuthiana*).

2.7.1.3.3 COMPLEX THEME (see §2.8.4), very common: (*A 2* 45) ⲚⲀⳝ ⲚⲌⲈ ⲈⳡⲚⲀⲢ-ⲮⲀⲨ... Ⲏ ⲈⲞⲨⲚⲞⲨⲢⲀⲚ ⲈⳡⲦⲘⲀⲒⲎⲨ ⲚⲀ⳼-ⲌⲎⲨ ⲘⲘⲞⳡ / (*ibid.* 525) ⲈⲚⲚⲀⲂⲰⲕ Ⲏ ⲚⲦⲀⲚⲂⲰⲕ... ⲈⲦⲂⲈ ⲠⲀⲒ ⲈⲦⲘⲘⲀⲨ / (*Leyd.* 410) ⲈⳝⲘⲠⲀⲒ ⲈⲚⲦⲀⳡⲈⲒ ⲈⲌⲢⲀⲒ ⲈⲠⲒⲮⲚⲈ Ⲏ ⲈⲚⲦⲀⲨⲚ-ⲚⲈⲒⲮⲰⲚⲈ ⲈⲌⲢⲀⲒ ⲈⳝⲰⳡ. Chiastically, (*Ch.* 119.445ff.) ⲈⲢⲈⲠⲈⳡⲌⲎⲦ ⲞⲨⲞⲮⳡ ⲚⲞⲨⲎⲢ ⲀⲨⲰ ⲈⳡⲦⲀⲕⲎⲨ (" discontinuous theme "); sim. *Ch.* 128.20ff.; compare also the conjunctive subcategorizing the theme (*Ch.* 7; e.g. *Ch.* 85.26ff., 89.18ff.).

2.7.1.4.1 The INDIRECT or " DISGUISED " FOCUS, with the interrogative included in an expansion of the Second-Tense verb (note again the compatibility of the *nucleus - satellite* and *theme - rheme* relationships). (*A 2* 413) ⲚⲦⲀⳡⳡⲰⲂⲦⳡ ⲘⲠⲈⲘⲦⲞ ⲈⲂⲞⲖ ⲚⲚⲒⲘ / (*IV* 105.5) ⲚⲦⲀⲨⲈⲒ ⲈⲌⲞⲨⲚ ⲮⲀⲢⲞⲚ ⲚⳝⲒⲞⲨⲈ ⲈⲚⲒⲘ / (*Wess.* 9 117a 5f.) ⲈⲨⲚⲀⳝⲒⲦⲕ ⲈⲢⲀⲦⳡ ⲚⲚⲒⲘ. Note the Basic Tense in (*Wess.* 9 133b 10ff.) ⲀⳡⳝⲈ ⲈⲌⲢⲀⲒ ⲈⲞⲨⲠⲈⲖⲀⲄⲞⳝ ⲚⲀⳝ Ⲛ6ⲞⲦ ⲘⲘⲚⲦⲀⳝⲈⲂⲎⳝ / (*P 130*[2] 103 ro) ⲈⳡⲚⲎⲨ ⲈⲢ-ⲞⲨ (sim. *IV* 94.13; *A 2* 513 ⲈⲒⲚⲀⲈⲒ ⲈⲌⲞⲨⲚ ⲚⲈ ⲈⲢ-ⲞⲨ).

2.7.1.4.2 The PREINCLUDED FOCALIZATION CONSTRUCTION is a very distinctive figure. There is

---

[127] Cf. POLOTSKY 1957b:114f. (= *CP* 48f.), 1964:277 (= *CP* 62) n. 1; DE CENIVAL 1972:43f.; VERNUS 1981:78ff.; BLASS 1960:5f. (with bibl., 6 n. 1): " Zwei Geschehen folgen einander so rasch, daß sie gleichzeitig werden: das ist schon eine Hyperbel. Wie können wir sie verstärken, wie noch mehr übertreiben? " See also PAUL 1920:§210; JESPERSEN *MEG* V §21.2.10, and numerous discussions for individual languages. Note ⲈⲮⲀⲨ- ⲈⲢⲮⲀⲚ- in the same sense, *IV* 20.12f. (" No sooner does the sun rise than the lamp is removed ").

[128] Cf. POLOTSKY 1944:62ff. (= *CP* 166ff.).

[129] Cf. Plato *Republ.* 332 c-d: ἡ τίσιν οὖν τί ἀποδιδοῦσα ὀφειλόμενον καὶ προσῆκον τέχνη.

here no formal marking of the dependence, beside the arrangement, which is inverse to the normal nucleus-satellite one in Coptic. (*P* 130² 74 ⲢⲨⲆ, parall. *Wess. 9* 108b 23ff.) ⲞⲨ ⲠⲈⲦⲈⲨⲚⲀⲀⲀⲨ (sic)· ⲢⲰⲘⲈ ⲚⲒⲘ ⲤⲞⲞⲨⲚ / (*IV* 64.15ff.) ⲈⲬⲞⲞⲤ ⲬⲈ-ⲚⲀⲨ ⲚⲌⲈ Ⲏ ⲚⲒⲘ ⲠⲈⲚⲦⲀⲨⲰⲬⲚⲈ... ⲈⲘⲘⲚⲢⲰⲘⲈ ⲤⲞⲞⲨⲚ / (*A 2* 223-4) ⲈⲨⲰⲞⲠ ⲈⲬⲚⲞⲨ Ⲏ ⲈⲦⲂⲈⲞⲨ ⲈⲨⲬⲈ-ⲘⲠⲈⲈⲒⲘⲈ Ⲛ†ⲚⲀⲬⲞⲞⲤ ⲀⲚ / (*P* 131⁴ 156Ⲙ) ⲈⲨⲰⲞⲠ ⲦⲰⲚ ⲦⲈⲚⲞⲨ ⲘⲀⲢⲞⲨⲦⲀⲘⲞⲚ / (*K* 9317) ⲞⲨ ⲠⲈⲦⲚⲀⲬⲞⲞⲨ Ⲛ†ⲤⲞⲞⲨⲚ ⲀⲚ Ⲏ ⲞⲨ ⲠⲈⲦⲚⲀⲦⲀⲨⲞⲨ Ⲛ†ⲈⲒⲘⲈ ⲀⲚ / *P* 130⁴ 84 Ⲛ is quoted above (§2.6.3.1.2). Compare the related constructions: (*Wess. 9* 148b 16ff.) ⲈⲬⲞⲞⲤ ⲆⲈ ⲬⲈ-ⲚⲀⲨ ⲚⲌⲈ ⲘⲚⲀⲀⲀⲨ ⲤⲞⲞⲨⲚ / (*Leyd.* 365) ⲈⲨⲬⲈ-ⲚⲀⲚⲞⲨⲨ Ⲏ ⲨⲌⲞⲞⲨ, ⲚⲒⲘ ⲚⲌⲎⲦⲦⲎⲨⲦⲚ ⲠⲈⲦⲤⲞⲞⲨⲚ ⲀⲚ / (*III* 210.7f.) ⲈⲒⲦⲈ ⲈⲨⲬⲈ-...Ⲏ ⲈⲨⲬⲈ-... ⲘⲠⲒⲈⲨϬⲘ-ϬⲞⲘ ⲈⲚⲞⲈⲒ / (*ibid.* 24.10f.) ⲠⲈⲦⲈⲢⲈⲠϨⲎⲦ ϬⲈ ⲘⲠⲞⲨⲀ ⲠⲞⲨⲀ ⲚⲀⲨⲞⲠⲨ ⲀⲨⲰ ⲠⲈⲨⲀⲀⲤ Ⲏ ⲠⲈⲦⲨⲚⲀⲨⲬⲞⲞⲨ ⲚⲦⲰⲦⲚ ⲈⲦⲤⲞⲞⲨⲚ / (*P* 130⁵ 125 vo, parall. *Cat.* 42.14f.) ⲈⲬⲞⲞⲤ ⲞⲚ ⲬⲈ-ⲚⲦⲀⲨⲰⲠⲈ ⲚⲢⲰⲘⲈ ⲚⲀⲨ ⲚⲌⲈ... ⲚⲦⲔ-ⲚⲒⲘ Ⲱ ⲠⲢⲈⲨⲦⲰϨ. The governing verbs are ⲤⲞⲞⲨⲚ, ⲈⲒⲘⲈ, ⲦⲀⲘⲞ, ⲚⲞⲈⲒ, ⲬⲰ; *no resumption is included in the construction* [130].

2.7.2 RHETORICAL TOPICALIZATION FIGURES (a selection)

2.7.2.1 # VERB^X → (VERB^X + FOCUS) #. The focalization pattern is coherent by repeating, as theme, a foregoing (usually rhematic) verb [131], often with a macro-syntactic topicalization marker.

2.7.2.1.1 Topicalization marked by ⲈⲨⲬⲈ-: (*Ch.* 191.46ff.) ⲈⲨⲬⲈ-ⲀⲨⲔⲀ-ⲢⲰⲘⲈ ⲚⲀⲨ ⲚⲦⲀⲨⲔⲀ-ⲌⲈⲚ-ⲤⲠⲀⲦⲀⲀⲀⲤ ⲀⲨⲰ ϨⲈⲚϨⲞⲨⲈⲬⲀⲬⲈ... / (*IV* 24.6f.) ⲈⲨⲬⲈ-ⲨⲨⲞⲞⲠ ⲞⲚ, ⲈⲨⲨⲞⲞⲠ ϨⲘⲠⲈⲨⲀⲀⲤ ⲘⲘⲀⲦⲈ ⲀⲨⲰ ϨⲘⲠⲈⲨϨⲎⲦ ⲀⲚ / (*III* 32.10f.) ⲈⲨⲬⲈ-ⲀⲨⲨⲒⲚⲈ ⲞⲚ ⲚⲤⲀⲞⲨⲨⲀϪⲈ, ⲈⲨⲀⲨⲨⲒⲚⲈ ϨⲚⲞⲨⲘⲚⲦⲌⲀⲔ / (*III* 85.13f.) ⲈⲨⲬⲈ-ⲞⲨⲚⲦⲨ-ⲞⲨϬⲞⲘ ⲄⲀⲢ ⲞⲚ, ⲈⲞⲨⲚⲦⲀⲨⲤ ϨⲚⲚⲈⲦⲔⲀ-ⲘⲀ ⲚⲀⲨ ⲚϨⲎⲦⲞⲨ. Especially typical of Shenoute is the pattern # ⲈⲨⲬⲈ- VERB^X → ⲈⲦⲂⲈⲞⲨ/ⲀϨⲢⲞ⸗/ⲚⲀⲨ ⲚⲌⲈ + VERB^X) #, often with more than one element repeated [132]: (*Ch.* 64.19ff.) ⲈⲨⲬⲈ-ϨⲚⲦϬⲞⲘ ⲘⲠⲨⲎⲢⲈ ⲚⲦⲀⲚⲞⲘⲒⲀ ⲈⲨⲦⲢⲈⲚⲢⲰⲘⲈ ⲈⲒⲢⲈ ⲚⲘⲠⲀⲢⲀⲪⲨⲤⲒⲤ, ⲈⲦⲂⲈⲞⲨ ⲚⲦⲞⲨ ϨⲚⲦϬⲞⲘ ⲘⲠⲈⲬⲤ̄... ⲚⲦⲚⲈⲒⲢⲈ ⲀⲚ... ⲚⲚⲀⲦⲈⲚⲪⲨⲤⲒⲤ — sim. *ibid.* 79.1ff. / (*A 2* 371) ⲈⲨⲬⲈ-ⲘⲚϬⲞⲘ ⲘⲘⲞⲔ ⲈⲈⲒⲢⲈ ⲚⲚⲈⲦⲢⲀⲚⲀⲨ ⲘⲠⲚⲞⲨⲦⲈ, ⲚⲀⲨ ⲚⲦⲞⲨ ⲚⲌⲈ ⲞⲨⲚϬⲞⲘ ⲘⲘⲞⲔ ⲈⲢ-ⲠⲞⲨⲰⲨ ⲦⲎⲢⲨ ⲘⲠⲈⲨϨⲎⲦ ⲘⲠⲞⲚⲎⲢⲞⲚ.

2.7.2.1.2 Topicalization marked by ⲈⲨⲨⲀⲚ-: (*Ch.* 104.5ff.) ⲈⲢⲨⲀⲚⲠⲘⲞⲚⲀⲬⲞⲤ ⲚⲎⲤⲦⲈⲨⲈ ⲘⲎ ⲈⲨⲚⲎ-ⲤⲦⲈⲨⲈ ⲚⲀⲔ Ⲏ ⲈⲔⲨⲀⲚⲈⲒⲢⲈ ⲘⲠϨⲀⲠ ⲘⲎ ⲚⲦⲀⲔⲀⲀⲨ ⲚⲀⲨ / (*Wess. 9* 110b 18ff.) ⲈⲢⲈⲨⲀⲚϬⲚ-ⲀⲢⲒⲔⲈ ⲈⲢⲈϬⲒⲚⲈ ⲈⲠⲈⲦⲀ ϨⲈⲢⲀⲦⲨ ϨⲚⲦⲞⲨⲘⲎⲦⲈ — compare (*Wess. 9* 111-2) ⲈⲨⲨⲀⲚ†-ⲘⲀⲈⲒⲚ ⲞⲚ ⲈⲠⲀϨⲞⲨ ⲈⲒⲘⲈ ϨⲰⲰⲨ ⲬⲈ-ⲈⲦⲂⲈⲚⲒⲘ Ⲏ ⲈⲦ-ⲂⲈⲞⲨ and (*IV* 11.9f.) ⲔⲀⲚ ϨⲈⲚⲀⲤ ⲈⲔⲦⲞⲤ ⲈⲠⲈⲤⲔⲰϨ Ⲏ ϨⲈⲚⲀⲤ ⲀⲚ ⲈⲀⲤⲔⲦⲞⲤ ϬⲈ ⲈⲂⲞⲀ ⲀⲚ ⲬⲈ-ⲀⲤⲤⲈⲒ ⲀⲀⲀⲀ..., actually a use of ⲈⲀⲨ- as both adverbal and topicalizing; also (*K* 933) ⲚⲤⲈⲚⲀⲢ-ⲨⲎⲢⲈ ⲀⲚ ⲈⲚⲈϨ ⲚⲞⲨⲈⲒⲰⲦ ⲞⲨⲦⲈ ⲤⲞⲚ ⲚⲞⲨⲤⲞⲚ, ⲈⲀⲨⲈⲒⲢⲈ ⲞⲚ, ⲚⲦⲀⲨⲈⲒⲢⲈ ⲈⲠϪⲒⲚϪⲎ.

2.7.2.1.2.1 ⲈⲒⲨⲀⲚⲬⲞⲞⲤ " If I say, when I say " is a striking topicalizing expression (cf. ⲈⲬⲞⲞⲤ " as to saying... ", exx. in §2.7.1.4.2 and n. 130): (*Cl. Pr.* 22 ⲦϪⲈ) ⲈⲒⲨⲀⲚⲬⲞⲞⲤ ⲬⲈ-†ϨⲞⲨⲨ, ⲈⲒϨⲞⲨⲨ ⲚⲀⲒ ⲘⲀⲨⲀⲀⲦ / (*A 2* 333) ⲈⲒⲨⲀⲚⲬⲞⲞⲤ ⲬⲈ-ⲠⲈⲒϨⲰⲂ ⲠⲀⲚϨⲀⲒⲢⲈⲦⲒⲔⲞⲤ ⲠⲈ... ⲈⲂⲞⲀ ⲦⲰⲚ ⲚⲈ ⲚⲒϨⲂⲎⲨⲈ ⲈⲦϬⲞⲞⲘⲈ ⲀⲨⲰ ⲚⲤⲰⲂⲈ / (*A 1* 281) ⲈⲨⲨⲀⲚⲬⲞⲞⲤ ⲄⲀⲢ ⲬⲈ-ⲈⲢⲈⲠⲆⲒⲀⲂⲞⲀⲞⲤ ⲘⲈⲈⲨⲈ ⲈⲨⲠⲞⲚⲎⲢⲞⲚ ⲚϨⲞⲨⲞ ⲈⲚⲢⲰⲘⲈ... ⲚⲦⲞⲨ ⲢⲰ ⲠⲈⲦⲤⲨⲘⲂⲞⲨⲀⲈⲨⲈ ⲚⲀⲨ / (*BLOr.* 3581A f. 160, No. 253 ⲚⲌ) ⲈⲒⲨⲀⲚⲬⲞⲞⲤ ⲬⲈ-ⲀⲦⲈⲄⲢⲀⲪⲎ †-ⲨⲒ ⲈⲠⲦⲂⲂⲞ ⲘⲠⲤⲰⲘⲀ ... ⲈⲚⲚⲀⲨⲬⲞⲞⲤ ⲞⲚ ⲬⲈ-ⲞⲨ ⲈⲦⲂⲈⲠⲬⲒⲚϬⲞⲚⲤ. Also *A 1* 410, *A 2* 295, 482.

---

[130] Compare the resumptions in the following case: (*P* 130⁵ 66 ⲞⲢ) ϨⲞⲦⲈⲒ ⲘⲈⲚ ⲄⲀⲢ ⲦⲚⲚⲀⲨ ⲈⲢⲞⲞⲨ (i.e. desire and anger) -ⲈⲦⲚϨ ⲰⲨⲬⲎ ⲠⲀⲒ ⲞⲨⲞⲚ ⲚⲒⲘ ϨⲞⲘⲞⲀⲞⲄⲈⲒ ⲘⲘⲞⲨ / (*A 2* 443, not Sh.) ϨⲞⲦⲈⲒ ⲆⲈ ⲠⲈϨⲞⲨⲞ ⲘⲠⲈⲚⲰⲚϨ... ⲈⲨⲀⲨⲔⲀⲦⲞⲢⲐⲞⲨ ⲘⲘⲞⲨ ϨⲒⲦⲚⲦⲈⲒⲠⲀⲢⲀⲦⲎ-ⲢⲎⲤⲒⲤ ⲚⲦⲈⲒⲘⲒⲚⲈ ⲞⲨⲞⲚ ⲚⲒⲘ ⲤⲞⲞⲨⲚ ⲘⲠⲀⲒ. Consider also the resuming and non-resuming constructions of ⲈⲬⲞⲞⲤ " as to saying ", a distinctive topicalization figure (§2.7.2.1.2.1): (*Ch.* 61.25ff.) ⲈⲬⲞⲞⲤ ⲆⲈ ⲬⲈ-ⲈⲨⲔⲰⲦⲈ ⲘⲘⲞⲨ ⲚⲀⲨ ⲚⲌⲈ... ⲞⲨⲀⲦϬⲞⲘ ⲠⲈ ⲈⲈⲒⲘⲈ ⲈⲠⲀⲒ / (*A 2* 392) ⲈⲬⲞⲞⲤ ⲬⲈ-ⲘⲠⲞⲨⲬⲒ-ⲂⲀⲠⲦⲒⲤⲘⲀ ⲚⲒⲘ ⲠⲈⲦⲞ ⲘⲘⲚⲦⲢⲈ ⲬⲈ-ⲀⲨⲬⲒ / (*Cat.* 42.14f.) ⲈⲬⲞⲞⲤ ⲆⲈ ⲬⲈ-ⲚⲦⲀⲨⲰⲠⲈ ⲚⲢⲰⲘⲈ ⲚⲀⲨ ⲚⲌⲈ... ⲚⲦⲔ-ⲚⲒⲘ ⲚⲦⲞⲔ Ⲱ ⲠⲢⲈⲨⲦⲰϨ / (*P* 130⁴ 115 ⲒⲌ) ⲈⲬⲞⲞⲤ ⲆⲈ ⲬⲈ-ⲚⲀⲨⲨⲞⲨ ⲚϬⲒⲘⲘⲀ ⲚⲘⲦⲞⲚ ⲈⲦϨⲚⲦⲘⲚⲦⲈⲢⲞ ⲚⲘⲠⲎⲨⲈ ⲠϨⲰⲂ ⲞⲨⲞⲚϨ ⲈⲂⲞⲀ ⲬⲈ-.

[131] Cf. POLOTSKY 1944:26ff. (= *CP* 130ff.).

[132] See MÜLLER 1956:62f.; cf. §3.1.1.1.0.1. for the anaphoric objects.

2.7.2.1.3 Relative topicalization. The antecedent is a pronominal or indefinite antecedent: (*IV* 4.2f.) ΝΕΤΧΟСΕ ΕΥΧΟСΕ ΕΤΒΕΝΕΥΠΡΑΞΙС ΝΑΓΑΘΟΝ / (*III* 115.8f.) ΜΗ ΖΝΑΥ ΝΙΜ ΕΤΕΡΕΠΝΑΗΤ + ΜΜΟΟΥ ΕΥ+ ΜΜΟΟΥ ΑΝ ΖΑΤΕΥΨΥΧΗ ΜΝ ΠΕΥСШΜΑ / (*A 2* 463-4) ΖШΒ ΝΙΜ ΝΤΑΥΑΑΥ ΝΤΑΥΑΑΥ ΤΗΡΟΥ ΕΤΒΕΠΕΝΟΥΧΑΙ.

2.7.2.1.4 Lᴇᴍᴍᴀᴛɪᴢɪɴɢ ᴛᴏᴘɪᴄᴀʟɪᴢᴀᴛɪᴏɴ — topicalization of a quotation or segment of a quotation [133]; very typical of Shenoute [134]. Note the following formal types: (a) Second-Tense marking of the full quote or its verbal part. (b) No formal marking of the verbal lemma, which is nevertheless a theme in our pattern (2). This is the most interesting construction, and argues for a level of cohesion (or grade of junctural delimitation [§6.0.2.]) between the lemmatic topic and its focus different — lower — from that between the usual theme/topic and its focus in patt. (2). (c) " Extraction " of a verbal segment or lexemic component in the quote and its incorporation — *in unaltered form* [135] — in a focalization pattern. (d) Extraction of a non-verbal segment of the quote and its incorporation in a focalization pattern. (e) No further explicit topicalization, but an annexation of an interrogative focus (with a zero topic ?) to the quote.

(a) (*A 2* 422, not Sh.) ΑΝΕΙΜΕ ΧΕ-ΝΑШ ΝΖΕ ΕΡΕ "ΝΒΑΛ ΜΠСΟΦΟС ШΟΟΠ ΖΝ ΤΕΥΑΠΕ " (*Eccl.* 2:14) / (*Ch.* 73.5ff.) " ΑΠСΑΤΑΝΑС ΒШΚ ΕΖΟΥΝ ΕΡΟΥ " — ΝΤΑΥΒШΚ ΖШШΥ ΕΤΒΕ ΟΥ; (*Joh.* 13:27) / (*Cat.* 42.12) " ΑΥ-ΤΝΝΟΟΥΥ " — ΝΤΑΥΤΝΝΟΟΥΥ ΤШΝ; (*Gal.* 4:4 paraphrased) / (*P* 131⁶ 19 ᴍᴦ) " ΕΤΕΤΝΜΙШΕ ΑΥШ ΤΕΤΝΡΠΟΛΕΜΟС ΜΝΤΗΤΝ ΜΜΑΥ " — ΕΜΝΤΑΝ-ΟΥ ΜΜΑΥ; ΕΜΝΤΑΝ-ΡΟΕΙС ΜΜΑΥ (*Jac.* 4:2).

(b) (*IV* 18.2) " ΥΝΑΧШΡ ΝΤΕΥСΝΥΕ " — ΥΝΑΧΟΡС ΕΡ-ΟΥ; ΕΥШШΤ ΝΖΕΝΤΒΝΟΟΥΕ ΧΝ-ΕΚШΝС ΝΖΕΝΡШΜΕ (*Ps.* 7:12) / (*A 2* 339) " ΥΝΑШШΠ ΜΠΕΝΝΟΥΤΕ " — ΥΝΑШШΠ ΕΟΥ; ΥΝΑШШΠ ΕΠΧΙ-ΚΒΑ (*Zach.* 9:7) / *A 2* 11) " ΝСΝΑΚΙΜ ΑΝ " — ΝСΝΑΚΙΜ ΑΝ ΖΝΟΥ; ΝСΝΑΚΙΜ ΑΝ ΖΝΤΜΝΤΝΟΥΤΕ ΕΥΜΝΤΑΤΝΟΥΤΕ, ΝСΝΑΚΙΜ ΑΝ ΖΝΝΑΤΕΦΥСΙС ΕΡ-ΝΑΜΠΑΡΑΦΥСΙС (*Ps.* 45:5) / (*III* 75.13f., parall. *Ch.* 169.11ff.) " ΜΜΝΡΑШΕ ШΟΟΠ ΝΝΑСΕΒΗС " — ΜΜΝΡΑШΕ ШΟΟΠ ΝΑΥ ΤШΝ, ΖΜΠΑΙШΝ ϬΕ ΕΤΝΗΥ ΧΝ-ΜΜΟΝ ΠΑΙ (*Is.* 48:22, 57:21) / (*Ch.* 183.1ff.) " ΑΙΡ-ΖΟΤΕ ΑΤΑСΑΡΞ +ΟΥШ " — ΑС+ΟΥШ ΝΟΥ; ΝΟΥΤΗΗΒΕ ΑΝ Η ΝΤΟΥ ΚΕΜΕΛΟС, ΑΛΛΑ ΕΑС+ΟΥШ ΝΝΚΑΡΠΟС ΝΤΔΙΚΑΙΟСΥΝΗ (*Ps.* 27:7) / (*Mun.* 142) " ΝΑΙ ΝΑΧΙШΚΑΚ ΕΒΟΛ ΖΝΟΥСΜΗ " — СΕΝΑΧΙШΚΑΚ ΕΒΟΛ ΤШΝ Η ΝΑШ ΝΖΟΟΥ; (? *Is.* 24:14).

(c) (*Ch.* 196.10ff.) " ΑΥΤСΙΟ ΝΟΥΨΥΧΗ ΕСΖΚΑΕΙΤ " — ΕСΖΚΑΕΙΤ ΜΠΝΑ ΕΛΑΥ ΑΥШ Π+ (*Ps.* 106:9) / (*III* 54.13) " ΕСΟ ΝΘΕ ΝΟΥΚΗΠΟС ΕΥΟΡΧ " — ΕΥΟΡΧ ΖΝΤΠΙСΤΙС ΜΝΤΕΝΤΟΛΗ ΜΝΤΕСΒШ ΜΠШΝΖ (*Cant.* 4:12) / (*A 2* 245) " ΑΥΤΝΝΟΟΥΥ " — ΤΝΝΟΟΥΥ ΤШΝ ΝСΑΤΡΕΥΤΝΝΟΟΥΥ ΕΒΟΛ ΖΙΤΟΟΤΥ ΑΥШ ΖΑΖΤΗΥ (*Gal.* 4:4) / (*Wess.* 9 98b 11ff.) " ΕΜΝΑΓΑΠΗ ΝΖΗΤ " — ΠΕΧΑΥ — " ΑΝΓ-ΟΥΛΑΑΥ " — ΕΜΝΑΓΑΠΗ ΝΖΗΤΥ ΕΝΙΜ ΝСΑΠΕΤΖΙΤΟΥШΥ; (*I Cor.* 13:2) / (*III* 45.17ff.) " ΕΠΧΙΝΧΗ ΝΗΤΝ ΠΕ ШΡΠ-ΤΗΥΤΝ " — ШΡΠ-ΤΗΥΤΝ ΕΡ-ΟΥ; ШΡΠ-ΤΗΥΤΝ ΕΟΥШШΤ Η ΕΟΥШΤΝ (*Ps.* 126:2) / (*III* 192.14f.-193.11) " ΜΝΤΧΑΧΕ ΖΙΑШΑΖΟΜ ΖΙΝΟϬΝΕϬ " — ...ΑШΑΖΟΜ ΖШШΥ ΕΝΙΜ Η Ρ-ΧΑΧΕ ΕΝΙΜ; (source ? Note that Ρ-ΧΑΧΕ represents the [non-verbal] expansion of ΜΝΤ-) / (*A 2* 330-1) " ΕΡΕ+-ΖΟΤΕ ΝΘΕ ΝΝϬΟΜ ΕΤΑΖΕΡΑΤΟΥ " — ΕΤΑΖΕΡΑΤΟΥ ΤШΝ Η ΕΝΙΜ; ΕΤΑΖΕΡΑΤΟΥ ΕΠΧΟΕΙС... (*Cant.* 6:4,10).

(d) (*A 2* 365) " ΠΕΥΕΟΟΥ ΝΑΒШΚ ΑΝ ΕΠΕСΗΤ ΝΜΜΑΥ " — ΕΠΕСΗΤ ΤШΝ ΝСΑΑΜΝΤΕ; (*Ps.* 48:17).

(e) (*Teza* 684) " ΑСШШΠΕ ΜΝΝСΑΝΙШΑΧΕ " — ΜΝΝСΑΑШ ΝШΑΧΕ; ΜΝΝСΑΤΡΕΥСΜΝ-ΤΟΟΤΥ ΜΝΑΒΙΜΕΛΕΧ (*Gen.* 22:1) / (*A 2* 386) " ΕΥΝΑΟΥШШΤ ΝΑΥ " — ΝΑШ ΜΜΙΝΕ ΝСΑΤΡΕΥΕΙΜΕ ΧΕ-ΠΕΤΕΟΥΝΤΑΥ-ΠШΗΡΕ ΟΥΝΤΑΥ-ΠΕΙШΤ; (*Joh.* 4:23) / (*A 1* 113) " +ΝΑΧΙ-ΖΑΠ ΝΜΜΗΤΝ ΑΥШ +ΝΑΧΙ-ΖΑΠ ΜΝΝШΗΡΕ ΝΝΕΤΝШΗΡΕ " — ΕΤΒΕΟΥ ΖШШΥ; (*Jer.* 2:9; sim. (?) *A 2* 57, *A 1* 299) / (*Ch.* 181.53ff.) " ΟΥΨΥΧΗ ΕСΟΥШΝΖ ΝΑΚ ΕΒΟΛ ΜΠΡΤΑΑС ΝΝΕΘΗΡΙΟΝ " — ΝΑШ ΝΘΗΡΙΟΝ; (*Ps.* 73:19).

---

[133] The Trimembral Nominal Sentence supplies another lemmatizing construction, *viz.* # "—" ΠΕ ΧΕ- # (after a quotation or allegory), e.g. *Ch.* 122.18ff.,28ff., 142.11ff., *A 2* 465-6, 491, *IV* 181.10ff.

[134] Thus, I believe, proving the Shenouteanity of *BLOr.* 6954 (12) vo [...]ΕΙΝ ΑΝ ΖΙΑШ ΝΖΙΗ; ΖΙΤΕΖΙΗ ΜΠΡΡΟ ΧΝ-ΖΙΤΕΖΙΗ ΜΠΧΑΙΕ (B. Layton's copy), probably our type (b).

[135] Cf. *BLOr.* 3581A 160 (No. 253 ΝΗ, parall. *RE 10* 159a 13ff.) (ΝΕΤΤΟΟΜΕ ΕΡΟΥ ...ΑΥШ ΕΥΤΟΟΜΕ ΕΡΟΟΥ) ΕΤΒΕΟΥ ΔΕ ΑΙΧΟΟС ΧΕ-"ΤШШΜΕ"; but *IV* 181.11ff. (ΟΥ ΔΕ ΠΕ ΧΕ-" ΕΥΟΥΗΖ ΝСШΟΥ ";) " ΟΥΗΖ ΝСШΟΥ " ΠΕ ΧΕ-; see n. 86.

2.7.3 Basic and second tenses: compatibility, opposition and neutralization

2.7.3.1 Compatibility. Coordination/disjunction; often, the Basic Tense (usually the first term) is negatived and/or non-durative (see also some of the exx. in §§2.1.2, 2.4-6). (*III* 191.25ff.) ⲘⲠⲞⲨⲦⲀⲀⲤ ⲚⲀⲚ ⲈⲦⲢⲈⲚ-, ⲀⲖⲖⲀ ⲚⲦⲀⲨⲦⲀⲀⲤ ⲚⲀⲚ Ⲉ- / (*III* 38.16f.) Ⲛ†Ⲣ-ⲌⲞⲦⲈ ⲀⲚ ⲌⲞⲖⲰⲤ ⲞⲨⲆⲈ ⲈⲒⲩⲦⲢⲦⲰⲢ ⲀⲚ (*v.l.* Ⲛ†ⲩⲦⲢⲦⲰⲢ ⲀⲚ) / (*A 2* 86) ⲤⲈⲚⲀⲬⲞⲞⲤ Ⲏ ⲈⲨⲬⲰ ⲘⲘⲞⲤ ⲬⲈ- / (*Wess. 9* 165c 27ff., parall. *III* 140.8) ⲌⲚⲞⲨⲚⲞⲌ ⲘⲘⲞⲤⲦⲈ ⲈⲔ-ⲚⲀⲠⲞⲢⲔⲚ Ⲏ ⲀⲔⲠⲞⲢⲔⲚ ⲈⲂⲞⲖ ⲌⲚⲦⲤⲨⲚⲀⲅⲰⲅⲎ.

2.7.3.2 Paradigms and alternation

2.7.3.2.1 The Basic Tense as a member in the post-focal topic paradigm (usually negatived and/or non-durative): §§2.6.2, 2.6.4.

2.7.3.2.2 The Basic Tense as a macro-syntactically conditioned alternant of the Ⲉ-topic: §2.6.3.1.1.

2.7.3.2.3 The Basic Tense (usually in ⲬⲈ-inclusion) as an unmarked prefocal theme (interrogative foci) [136].

(a) The focus ⲦⲰⲚ, the theme "ⲀⲨⲤⲰⲦⲘ": (*Wess. 9* 127b 8ff.) ⲀⲠⲒⲚⲦⲎⲊ ⲘⲘⲒⲚⲈ ⲘⲒⲚⲈ ⲈⲒ ⲦⲰⲚ... Ⲁ†ⲯⲰⲢⲀ ⲐⲎⲢⲤ ⲈⲒ ⲦⲰⲚ...; also 128a 1ff., *Ch.* 166.24ff., *BMCat.* 80 (No. 195), *A 2* 33; one instance of the Basic Present: (*Wess. 9* 117a 23ff., coll.) Ⲏ ⲠⲈⲨⲢⲀⲩⲈ ⲦⲰⲚ.

(b) The focus ⲚⲞⲨⲎⲢ, theme: *present*: (*P* 130² 45 ⲤⲒⲐ) ⲱ ⲤⲈⲞⲨⲞⲚⲌ ⲈⲂⲞⲖ ⲚⲞⲨⲎⲢ ⲬⲈ- / (*P* 130² 65 ⲢⲞ) ⲦⲚⲞⲨⲞⲚⲌ ⲈⲂⲞⲖ ⲚⲞⲨⲎⲢ ⲬⲈ- / (*IV* 35.18) (ⲬⲈ-)ⲦⲚⲦⲊⲀⲒⲎⲨ ⲚⲞⲨⲎⲢ; theme: *Basic Perfect*: (*III* 183.3) (ⲬⲈ-)ⲀⲨⲢ-Ⲁ-ⲚⲀⲩ ⲚⲞⲨⲎⲢ; theme: *adjective-verbs*: (*A 1* 374) ⲚⲈⲤⲰⲨ ⲚⲞⲨⲎⲢ, ⲚⲈⲊⲰⲨ ⲚⲞⲨⲎⲢ / (*A 1* 227) ⲚⲀⲚⲞⲨⲨ ⲀⲨⲰ ⲊⲤⲞⲖⲊ ⲚⲞⲨⲎⲢ. Additional exx.: *IV* 117.3f., 47.7f., *Ch.* 62.33ff., *Berl.* 1613 1 Ⲗ, *Ryl.* 69 ⲚⲄ, *Rossi* 2/3 26.

(c) The focus: ⲚⲀⲩ ⲚⲌⲈ, the theme: 'ⲀⲨⲤⲰⲦⲘ' (*P* 130² 36 vo) (†ⲌⲐⲎⲦⲚ ⲬⲈ-)ⲀⲨⲌⲰⲚ ⲚⲀⲩ ⲚⲌⲈ... ⲬⲈ.

2.7.3.2.4 The Basic Tense is very rare (perhaps significantly so) as a *varia lectio* for a marked theme/topic form: *III* 38.17, patt. (1); 210.21, patt. (4); *IV* 14.10, patt. (6); consider also (*BKU* 180² 8ff.) ⲈⲊ-ⲚⲀⲨⲤⲌ ⲚⲞⲨⲰⲚⲌ ⲩⲀⲈⲚⲈⲌ *vs.* (21) ⲊⲚⲀⲨⲤⲌ ⲚⲞⲨⲰⲚⲌ ⲩⲀⲈⲚⲈⲌ.

2.7.3.3 Other neutralizations

2.7.3.3.1 "Indifference", i.e. unmarkedness (or rare markedness) for the category of focality: (a) ⲚⲈ-converted forms (usually with ⲦⲰⲚ) [137]: (*Wess. 9* 148a 16ff.) ⲚⲈⲊⲦⲰⲚ ⲠⲈ...: ⲚⲈⲊⲌⲘⲞⲞⲤ ⲆⲈ ⲠⲈ ⲚⲀⲩ ⲚⲌⲈ; often the "future imperfect": (*RE 10* 162b 23f.) ⲚⲈⲨⲚⲀⲩⲱⲠⲈ ⲦⲰⲚ / (*Cl. Pr.* 22 ⲦⲈⲄ) ⲚⲈⲨⲚⲀⲦⲀⲔⲈ-ⲞⲨⲎⲢ ⲘⲯⲨⲬⲎ, also *RE 10* 164b 3f., *RE 11* 16b 16f., *P* 130² 87 vo.

(b) Inconvertible conjugation-forms: *Future III* + ⲚⲞⲨⲎⲢ (*III* 181.17f., 150.26), + ⲚⲚⲒⲘ (*III* 111.20), *conjunctive* (*A 2* 512) ⲈⲒⲚⲀⲦⲊⲀⲒⲈ-Ⲁⲩ ⲘⲘⲈⲖⲞⲤ ⲚⲦⲀⲔⲀ-Ⲁⲩ Ⲏ ⲈⲒⲚⲀⲢ-Ⲁⲩ ⲘⲘⲈⲖⲞⲤ ⲚⲦⲀⲖⲖⲀⲒⲠⲰⲢⲞⲤ ⲚⲦⲀⲘⲀⲔⲀⲢⲒⲌⲈ ⲚⲀⲩ; compare the *infinitive* expanded by interrogative modifiers (+ ⲈⲞⲨ, ⲈⲚⲒⲘ, *III* 45.18, 193.11).

(c) Nominal Sentence: + ⲚⲞⲨⲎⲢ (*Ch.* 104.47ff.), + ⲌⲚⲞⲨ (*A 2* 26), + ⲚⲀⲩ ⲚⲌⲈ (*A 2* 69, 154, 334, 403),

---

[136] Cf. Polotsky 1940:245 (= *CP* 37). Note that both ⲦⲰⲚ and ⲞⲨⲎⲢ are also indefinites — the homonymy is in fact resolved syntactically. ⲞⲨⲎⲢ in ⲞⲨⲚⲞⲨⲎⲢ ⲚⲂⲀⲤⲀⲚⲞⲤ ⲞⲨⲚⲞⲨⲎⲢ ⲚⲔⲞⲖⲀⲤⲦⲎⲢⲒⲞⲚ ⲊⲈⲈⲦ ⲈⲠⲢⲰⲘⲈ... (*P* 130⁵ 71 ⲤⲈⲄ, also *A 2* 331, *Wess. 9* 143d 12ff.) is a member of a paradigm including also the Second Tense (§2.3.2) and the Cleft Sentence with (pro)nominal *vedette*.

[137] Compare however Polotsky 1960b:25 (= *CP* 396) note 1. Has this something to do with the Akhmimic Second Perfect (ⲚⲀⲊ-)?

Cleft Sentence (nom. *vedette*) following ⲉⲧⲃⲉⲟⲩ (*Wess. 9* 105a-b). Note that while the Nom. Sentence is convertible *postfocally* (§§2.5.1, 2.6.3.1.1), the Cleft Sentence with (pro)nominal *vedette* is not.

2.7.3.3.2 After ⲭⲉ- and ⲉⲓⲉ-, the opposition of Basic *vs.* Second Tense is sporadically neutralized; consider *III* 21.14, 34.16, 91.10f., 167.6f., *Wess. 9* 117b 31ff., etc.

2.8   SECOND-TENSE CONSTRUCTIONS: NOTES ON PROSODY AND SYNTAGMATICS

2.8.1 PROSODY. All we know of the prosodic characteristics of focalization patterns is that the juncture between theme/topic and focus is open (§6.0.2). One notes the placement of ⲁⲛ, different from and more interesting than in the Bipartite (§2.9); that is about all, in patterns for which the suprasegmentals are of crucial diacritic significance [138]. There cannot be any doubt of the fundamentally different prosodic structure of topic-initial and focus-initial pattern groups, and of the existence of a gradation of differences between the individual patterns [139]. Consider the following instructive cases, indicative of the intricate network of prosodic states superimposed on the segmental skeletal pattern. We note that the focalization pattern usually consists of more than one colon (§6.0.3); also, the instances of strikingly extensive interposition between the theme-topic and focus components: (*III* 72.21) ⲉⲣⲉⲟⲩⲁ ⲛⲁϣϫⲟⲟⲥ / ⲟⲛ / ⲭⲉⲟⲩ " What more can one say? " / (*A 2* 431) ⲛⲧⲁⲓϣⲱⲡⲉ ⲅⲁⲣ ⲁⲛ / ⲡⲉϫⲁϥ / ⲙⲡⲟⲛⲏⲣⲟⲥ ⲛⲕⲉⲟⲩⲁ ⲁⲗⲗⲁ ⲛⲁⲓ ⲙⲙⲓⲛ ⲙⲙⲟⲓ / (*Wess. 9* 174d 29ff.) ⲛⲉⲛⲥⲟⲧⲡ ⲅⲁⲣ ⲁⲛ᾿ / ⲡⲉϫⲁⲩ / ⲛ2ⲟⲩⲟ ⲉⲡⲉⲛⲉⲓⲟⲧⲉ / (*IV* 183.7) ⲉⲛⲙⲉⲉⲩⲉ ⲉⲟⲩ/ϭⲉ ⲧⲉⲛⲟⲩ — a single colon / (*IV* 16.18f.) ⲉϣⲁⲩϫⲉⲣ-ⲥⲏϥⲉ ⲛⲓⲙ / ⲛⲧⲟϥ / ⲉⲃⲟⲗ 2ⲓⲧⲟⲟⲧⲥ / (*III* 209.13ff., codd. A, C) ⲉⲣⲉⲛⲛⲟⲃⲉ ⲅⲁⲣ ⲛⲛ2ⲉⲗⲗⲏⲛ ⲙⲛⲛⲁⲛⲉⲧⲟⲩⲱϣⲧ ⲧⲏⲣⲟⲩ ⲛⲛ2ⲉⲓⲕⲱⲛ ⲛⲛⲇⲁⲓⲙⲟⲛⲓⲟⲛ ⲉⲩⲟⲩⲟⲛ2 ⲉⲡⲛⲟⲩⲧⲉ ⲙⲁⲩⲁⲁϥ ⲁⲛ (A: ... ⲁⲛ ⲉⲡⲛⲟⲩⲧⲉ ⲙⲁⲩⲁⲁϥ) ⲁⲗⲗⲁ ⲉⲛⲕⲉⲣⲱⲙⲉ ⲟⲛ / (*A 2* 541) ⲉⲣⲉⲡⲉⲓⲛⲉ ⲙⲡⲉⲩⲕⲁⲡⲛⲟⲥ ⲁⲩⲱ ⲡⲉϥⲣⲱⲕ2 ⲉϥϣⲱⲃⲉ ⲉⲛⲉⲩⲉⲣⲏⲩ 2ⲛⲟⲩ / (*III* 102.12f., 19f.) ⲛⲁϣ ⲛ2ⲉ / ⲛⲧⲟⲕ / ⲛⲥⲉⲛⲁ ⲭⲓ-ϭⲟⲗ ⲉⲣⲟⲕ ⲁⲛ / (*BLOr* 3581A 71, No. 202 ⲣⲡⲇ) ⲛⲁϣ / ⲛⲧⲟϥ / ⲛ2ⲉ ⲡⲥⲱⲙⲁ ⲏ ⲡⲣⲱⲙⲉ ⲧⲏⲣϥ ⲛⲁⲥⲙⲓⲛⲉ... ⲛⲁϣ ⲛ2ⲉ / ⲛⲧⲟⲕ / ⲉⲕⲛⲁⲣϣⲁⲩ; see §§6.1.3.1-4.

2.8.2 NEXUS ARRANGEMENT; LOCATION OF THE THEME-TOPIC ‖ FOCUS SEAM: FOCUS ISOLATION. The question of identifying the focus on the basis of our segmental data arises in the common predicament of a topic-initial pattern (2) [140], where a non-interrogative focus is included in a group of modifiers of which any — or, conjointly, some — could be focal. The crux here is obviously the IC-analysis of the utterance into theme and rheme groups, with theoretical a well as practical implications [141]: the organization of the utterance in a relatively simple hierarchic structure [142], with the first section the verbal theme-topic, and the second the rheme-focus. Here again we are faced with the decisions of verbal valency — the distinction between rectional (componential) and complementational modification [143]. This, however, supplies us with a post-analytic *model* rather than a heuristic tool. I would like to point out here, in bold simplification, some facts regarding the arrangement of the pattern and placement of the focus. Generally

---

[138] Punctuation data are here of some value, though not immediately applicable or readily interpretable in prosodic terms. Several instances of a point or comma marking the Bipartition of focus-initial patterns have been quoted above (also *Wess. 9* 165c 27ff.); cf. (for LE) Wente, *JNES* 28:6 n. 37 (1969).

[139] A noteworthy distinction in the Subakhmimic John between two syllabifications of "in what way, how": ⲛⲉϣ ⲛ̄2ⲉ vs. ⲛⲉϣ ⲛ̄2ⲉ, corresponds to the distinction of *topic-initial* vs. *focus-initial* respectively, and may be indicative of prosodic differentiation: (ⲛ̄ⲉϣ) 6:25, 9:15.26; (ⲛⲉϣ) 3:4.9.12, 4:9, 5:44.47, 6:42.52, 8:33, 9:10.16.19.21, 12:34, 14:9.

[140] In patts. (1), (3) the placement of the focus is unambiguous; as it is in patt. (2) cases like ⲟ ⲛⲁϣ ⲛ2ⲉ (also the " disguised " focus, §2.7.1.4.1). In focus-initial patterns the focal constituent is by definition initial, and seems to be incompatible with non-focal premodifiers (§1.1.2.2); this point must however be further investigated.

[141] Cf. the general arguments in BARRI 1978 (esp. p. 256ff.).

[142] Cf. JUNGE 1972:33f., 1978:22, 32ff.

[143] JUNGE 1972:36ff.; see §1.1.2.0.1 above and §3.0.1 below.

speaking, two main groups are to be distinguished, with FINAL and NON-FINAL FOCUS. In cases of an in-
herent-focality (interrogative) focus, the placement (established by complex considerations) is immaterial,
non-pertinent. For the non-interrogative focus, however, the precise placement has an essential functional
value. The following illustration is representative of the main types; see §2.8.1 for the separation of theme
and focus and §2.8.4 for the discontinuous theme.

(a) FINAL FOCUS, the " ideal " arrangement (§2.0.2.4). The focus is interrogative or non-interrogative.
Adverbal modifications — rectional and complementational — follow the verb: (*A 2* 54) ⲏ ⲛⲧⲁⲛⲉⲓ ⲁⲛ
ⲉⲃⲟⲗ ⳛⲙⲡⲏⲓ ⲛⲧⲉⲛⲙⲛⲧⲕⲟⲥⲙⲓⲕⲟⲛ ⲉⲧⲃⲉⲧⲙⲣ-ⲛⲟⲃⲉ / (*A 2* 540) ⲉⲩⳛⲟⲃⲉ ⲧⲉⲛⲟⲩ ⲉⲣⲟ⳩ ⳛⲛⲟⲩ / (*A 2* 336) ⲉⲥⲛⲁⳋⲉ ⲉⲣⲟ⳩
ⲧⲱⲛ / (*A 1* 71) ⲉⲓⲙⲏⲣ ⲛⲙⲙⲁⲥ ⳛⲛⲟⲩ / (*Ryl.* 67 ⲩⲉ) ⲉⲩⲛⲁⳛⲱⲡⲉ ⲛⲁⲕ ⲙⲙⲉⲣⲓⲧ ⲛⲟⲩⲏⲣ / (*Ch.* 54.19ff.) ⲧⲟⲩⲉⲣⲏⲧⲉ
ⲉⲥⳛⲟⲟⲡ ⳛⲙⲡⲥⲱⲙⲁ ⲉⲧⲃⲉⲙⲟⲟⳛⲉ / (*ibid.* 183.57ff.) ⲉⲛⲛⲁⲡⲁⲣⲁⲇⲓⲇⲟⲩ ⲙⲙⲟⲛ ⲁⲛⲟⲛ' ⲧⲉⲛⲟⲩ ⲉⳋⲣⲁⲓ ⲉⲡⲕⲱⳋⲧ ⲛⲧⲅⲉ-
ⳋⲉⲛⲛⲁ ⲉⲧⲃⲉⳋⲉⲛⲛⲟⲃⲉ / (*III* 154.11) ⲉⲩⲛⲁⳍⲟⲧ⳩ ⲉⲃⲟⲗ ⳛⲙⲡⲉⳍⲗⲁⲟⲥ ⲛⲟⲩⲏⲣ / (*A 1* 100-1) ⲉⳛⳉⲉ-ⲛⲧⲁⲡⲁⲓ ⲥⲱⲕ
ⲉⳋⲣⲁⲓ ⲉⳋⳛ⳩ ⲛⲟⲩⳛⲓⲡⲉ ⲙⲡⲉⲙⲧⲟ ⲉⲃⲟⲗ ⲛⲛⲣⲱⲙⲉ ⳛⲙⲡⲧⲣⲉⳍⲡⲁⲣⲁⲃⲁ ⲙⲡⲉⲓⲁⲛⲁⳛ ⳉⲉ ⲉⲣⲉⲛⲉⲓⲣⲱⲙⲉ ⲛⲁⲣ-ⲃⲟⲗ ⲉⲡⳛⲓⲡⲉ
ⲧⲏⲣ⳩... Some more striking exx.: *III* 100.16f., 107.11ff., 122.24f., *Ch.* 23,15ff., *Wess. 9* 86a 16ff.

(b) NON-FINAL FOCUS. (1) Focus *interrogative*, adjuncts final: (*A 2* 464) (ⲉ)ⳛⳛⲉ ⲉⲡⲣⲱⲙⲉ ⲛⲟⲩⲏⲣ
ⲉⲩⲗⲏⲗ ⲛⳋⲁⳋ ⲛⲥⲟⲡ / (*A 1* 69) ⲉⲣⲉⲙⲟⲕⳋ ⲛⲟⲩ ⲛⲙⲙⲁⲥ / (*III* 98.3f.) ⲉⲩⲛⲁⲧ-ⳋⲁⲡ ⲉⲛⲓⲙ ⲉⲧⲃⲏⲏⲧⲟⲩ / (*Wess. 9* 128a
29ff.) ⲛⲧⲁⲩⲙⲉⲉⲩⲉ ⲇⲉ ⲧⲱⲛ ⲉⲧⲕⲉⲗⲁⲥⲉⲃⲉⲓⲁ / (*IV* 35.16f.) ⲉⲩⲛⲁⲛⲟⳍⲛⲉⳍ ⲛⲟⲩⲏⲣ ⲛⲛⲉⳍⲣⲙⲛⲏⲓ ⳋⲛⲟⲩⲕⲱⲙⳛ ⲙⲛⲟⲩⲥⲱⳛ⳩
/ (*III* 98.14) ⲏ ⲉⲩⲛⲁⲧ-ⳋⲁⲡ ⳋⲛⲟⲩ ⲉⲛⲉⲧⲙⲟⲩ ⳋⲣⲁⲓ ⳋⲛⲛⲉⲓⲃⲟⲧⲉ / (*P* 130[4] 105 ⲣⲕⲉ) ⲛⲧⲁⲡⲣⲏ ⲙⲛⲡⲟⲟⳋ ⳍⲱ ⲛⲁⳛ ⲛⳋⲟⲟⲩ
ⲉⲛⲉⳋ ⲛⲟⲩⲉⳛⲛⲉⲓ ⲉⳋⲣⲁⲓ. Consider also *III* 223.19, *IV* 154.20f., 189.7f.
(2) Focus *interrogative*, back extraposition final [144], adjuncts following the focus: (*A 2* 396) ⲉⳍⲛⲁⲧⲃⲃⲟ
ⲧⲏⲣ⳩ ⲛⲟⲩⲏⲣ ⲉⲃⲟⲗ ⳋⲛⲛⲟⲃⲉ ⲛⲓⲙ ⲛⳍⲓ-ⲡⲉⲧⲟⲩⲃⲁⲡⲧⲓⳋⲉ ⲙⲙⲟ⳩ / (*III* 170.19f.) ⲉⲩⲛⲁⲣ-ⲕⲁⲕⲉ ⲛⲟⲩⲏⲣ ⲛⳍⲓⳋⲉⲛⲣⲱⲙⲉ
ⲛⲁⲧⲥⲱⲧⲙ / (*ibid.* 169.23f.) ⲉⲩⲛⲁⲡⲱⲧ ⲛⲟⲩⲏⲣ 'ⲛⳍⲓⳋⲉⲛⲣⲱⲙⲉ ⲉⲩⲣ-ⳋⲟⲧⲉ ⳋⲏⲧ⳩ ⲙⲡⲛⲟⲩⲧⲉ / (*A 2* 114) ⲉⲥⳛⲟⲟⲡ ⲧⲱⲛ
ⲧⲉⳋⲓⲏ ⲉⲧⲙⲙⲁⲩ.

(c) Focus *non-interrogative*, back extraposition final/non-final (regulated by its extent, i.e. rhythmic
factors? [145]): (*III* 116.6f.) ⲛⲧⲁ⳩ⲧ ⲙⲙⲟⲟⲩ ⲛⲁⲕ ⲛⳍⲓⲓ̅ⲥ̅ ⲡⲉⲭ̅ⲥ̅ ⲡⲛⲟⲩⲧⲉ ⲁⲩⲱ ⲡⳛⲏⲣⲉ ⲙⲡⲛⲟⲩⲧⲉ / (*III* 117.28f.)
ⲛⲧⲁ⳩ⲛⲁⲩ ⲛⳍⲓⲡⳉⲟⲉⲓⲥ ⳉⲉ- / (*ibid.* 120.9) ⲉⲩⳉⲱ ⲇⲉ ⲛⲛⲁⲓ ⲛⳍⲓⲛⲉⲧⲙⲙⲁⲩ ⲉⲩⲧⲁⲙⲟ ⲙⲙⲟⲛ ⳉⲉ-.

2.8.3 THE SECOND TENSE AS A " THAT "-FORM. Above (§2.0.0.1) the point was made that nothing
in the synchronic set of relations of the Second Tense points unambiguously to its substantival nature.
Let us reconsider this issue, reviewing several constructions that may be taken as hinting at substantival
syntactic roles, probably integrated in a previous system but at any rate not perceptively so in the synchronic one. I have in mind

(a) The Second Tense (or at least an ⲉ-form) in patt. (2)-(3) focalization constructions *as object-
expansion of* ⳍⲓⲛⲉ *in a negated conjugation form*: (*A 1* 118) ⲛ⳩ⲛⲁⳍⲛ-ⲉ⳩ⲛⲁⳍⲓ-ⲛⲉ⳩ⲃⲁⲗ ⲁⲛ ⲉⳋⲣⲁⲓ ⲉⲡⲛⲟⲩⲧⲉ
ⲛⲁⳛ ⲛⳋⲉ / (*A 2* 520) ⲙⲛⲑⲉ ⲉⲧ⳩ⲛⲁⳍⲛ-ⲉ⳩ⲛⲁⲣ-ⲟⲩ ⲁⲛ (ⲁⲛ probably negatives the rel. future — "it is hardly
possible that he will not find what to do... "; I have however not collated the text); also *III* 13.9 (= *A 1*
221), *Ch.* 33.14f., 73.19ff. etc. [146]. Compare an instance of ⲉⲙⲛ-coordinated to a noun in object status:
(*K* 9316) ⲙⲛⲛⲥⲁⲧⲣⲉⲩⲥⲟⲩⲛ-ⲡⲥⲟⲟⲩⲛ ⲧⲏⲣ⳩ ⲁⲩⲱ ⲉⲙⲛⲕⲉⲛⲟⲩⲧⲉ ⲛⲥⲁ ⲓ̅ⲥ̅.

(b) An instance of a Second Present, non- or auto-focal, patt. (1), predicated by ⲡⲉ: (*A 1* 113 coll.)
ⲛⲧⲉⲥⲟⲟⲩⲛ ⲁⲛ ⳉⲉ-ⲉⲣⲉⲛⲕⲟⲧⲕ ⲡⲉ " You do not know that it means that you are asleep " [147].

---

[144] See §6.0.1. ⲛⳍⲓ- apparently tends to the final position when it introduces a prosodically more weighty noun syntagm.
[145] Cf. (for rhythmic considerations) §3.1.3.3.2.
[146] SHISHA–HALEVY 1976b:363 n. 33, with reff. (to the Shenoutean instances add those quoted here). Note that this may
well be a case of a (non-nominal) *interrogative clause* in direct-object status. Consider *Is.* 1:3 (Ciasca; quoted by Shenoute, in *Wess. 9*
153c 2f. parall. 178a 25ff.) ⲡⲁⲗⲟⲥ ⲙⲡⲉ⳩ⳍⲛ-ⲁⲛⲅ-ⲛⲓⲙ, *Man. Psalm-Book* 156.9 ⲙⲡⲟⲩⳍⲛ-ⲉⲩ ⲡⲉ ⲡⲛⲟⲩⲧⲉ.
[147] See STERN 1880:217 (two exx. of ⲛⲧⲁ- ⲡⲉ). Cf. CALLENDER 1970:205ff., and see §1.2.1.2, gen. obs. (4). For Egyptian, see POLOTSKY 1976:§2.6.4.

(c) The " conjunctional " use in Sahidic of the Sec. Perfect in the unfulfilled protasis after ⲉⲛⲉ- (e.g. *Ch.* 29.56ff.). Compare the Sec. Tense after (ⲍⲱⲥ) ⲉⲩϫⲉ- §2.1.4-5. I believe these unpredictable, isolated or fixed cases are inconclusive, and cannot be the basis for a synchronic "that"-form interpretation of the Second Tense (see nn. 146-7).

2.8.4 The complex theme/topic is made up of two or more (often discontinuous) coordinated or disjoined components, individually or conjointly marked for thematicity, in varying grades of mutual cohesion [148]. In ascending order of union and subcategorization:

(a) ' Sec.-Tense conjugation form + ⲁⲩⲱ/ⲏ + Sec.-Tense conjugation form ': (*A 2* 45) ⲛⲁϣ ⲛⲍⲉ ⲉⲩⲛⲁⲣ-ϣⲁⲩ... ⲏ ⲉⲟⲩⲛⲟⲩⲣⲁⲛ ⲉⲩⲧⲙⲁⲓⲏⲩ ⲛⲁⲧ-ⲍⲏⲩ ⲙⲙⲟⲩ / (*A 2* 372) ⲛⲁϣ ⲛⲍⲉ ⲉⲩⲛⲁ- ⲏ ⲉⲩⲛⲁ- / (*III* 73.8f.) ⲉⲣⲉⲡⲉⲧϭⲓ-ⲣⲟⲟⲩϣ ⲙⲟⲕⲙⲉⲕ ⲙⲙⲟⲩ ⲛⲧⲉⲓⲍⲉ ⲁⲩⲱ ⲉⲩⲗⲟⲅⲓⲍⲉ ⲙⲙⲟⲩ ϫⲉ- / (*Ch.* 119.45ff.) ⲉⲣⲉⲡⲉⲩⲍⲏⲧ ⲟⲩⲟϣϣ ⲛⲟⲩⲏⲣ ⲁⲩⲱ ⲉⲩⲧⲁⲕⲏⲩ sim. *ibid.* 128.20ff.; also *III* 119.2f., 134.16f., *IV* 63.24f., 107.1f., *Leyd.* 410, etc.

(b) ' Sec.-Tense Conjugation form (+ ⲁⲩⲱ/ⲏ) + " epithematic " circumstantial conjugation form' (rare) [149]: (*Ming.* 288) ⲛⲧⲁϥⲥⲙⲛⲧ-ⲙⲡⲏⲩⲉ ⲛⲁϣ ⲛⲍⲉ ⲁⲩⲱ ⲉⲁϥⲣ-ⲍⲓⲧⲡⲉ ⲙⲙⲟⲟⲩ ⲧⲏⲣⲟⲩ / (*III* 120.7f.) ⲙⲏ ⲛⲧⲁϥⲃⲱⲕ ⲉⲍⲣⲁⲓ ⲉⲧⲡⲉ... ⲉⲁϥⲉⲓⲛⲉ ⲉⲡⲉⲥⲏⲧ ⲛⲛⲉϥⲉⲛⲧⲟⲗⲏ (contrast with *III* 140.17 ⲙⲏ ⲛⲧⲁⲩⲃⲱⲕ... ⲁⲩⲉⲓⲛⲉ).

(c1) ' Sec. Perfect/Aorist + ⲁⲩⲱ/ⲏ + Basic Perfect/Aorist ' [150]: (*III* 218.1) ⲍⲱⲥ ⲉⲩϫⲉ-ⲛⲧⲁⲡⲏⲓ ⲧⲏⲣϥ ⲕⲓⲙ... ⲏ ⲁϥⲍⲙⲟⲟⲥ / (*ibid.* 219.3f.) ⲛⲧⲁⲡⲉⲓϣⲁϫⲉ ϭⲱⲗⲡ ⲉⲣⲟⲓ ⲁⲓⲉⲓⲙⲉ ⲉⲣⲟϥ ⲧⲉⲛⲟⲩ ⲍⲛⲧⲉⲓⲣⲟⲙⲡⲉ ⲧⲁⲓ / (*A 1* 108) ⲙⲏ ⲉϣⲁⲣⲉⲡⲁⲍⲟⲩ ⲁⲛ ⲏ ϣⲁⲣⲉⲟⲥⲍⲟⲩ. Also *III* 28.25f., 140.17, *IV* 157.22f.

(c2) ' Sec. Future/Aorist + ⲁⲩⲱ/ⲏ + conjunctive ': (*IV* 76.20f.) ⲛⲁϣ ⲛⲍⲉ ⲉⲣⲉⲛⲣⲱⲙⲉ ⲛⲥⲁⲃⲉ ⲛⲁⲧⲁϫⲣⲟ ⲍⲛⲧⲉⲩⲍⲩⲡⲟⲙⲟⲛⲏ ⲁⲩⲱ ⲛⲥⲉϫⲱⲕ ⲉⲃⲟⲗ ⲛⲍⲱⲃ ⲛⲓⲙ ⲉⲛⲁⲛⲟⲩⲩ / (*III* 40.11f.) ⲉϣⲁϥⲙⲉⲣⲓⲧϥ ⲛⲧⲟϥ ⲛⲍⲟⲩⲟ ⲁⲩⲱ ⲛϥⲣⲁϣⲉ ⲉϫⲱϥ; also *IV* 94.3 ff. Chiastically, in (*Ch.* 85.26ff.) ⲉⲣⲉⲡϫⲟⲉⲓⲥ... ⲛⲁⲥⲙⲟⲩ ⲉⲣⲟϥ ⲛⲟⲩⲏⲣ ⲁⲩⲱ ⲛϥⲧ-ⲉⲟⲟⲩ ⲛⲁϥ cf. 89.18ff.). In (*IV* 14.4f.) ⲉⲩⲛⲁⲧ-ⲍⲁⲡ ⲇⲉ ⲛⲧⲟϥ... ⲉⲃⲟⲗ ⲍⲓⲧⲛⲧⲁⲓ (ⲁⲩⲱ) ⲛⲥⲉⲕⲣⲓⲛⲉ ⲛⲟⲩⲟⲛ ⲛⲓⲙ ⲉⲃⲟⲗ ⲍⲓⲧⲟⲟⲧⲥ the focus is repeated and the conjunctive not markedly thematic.

2.9 Negation patterns: negatived focalization patterns, negated nexus, negatived adjuncts and pattern components

2.9.0.1 The gist of Polotsky's discussion of the negation of Second-Tense constructions [151] is the distinction between the negation of the theme-focus nexus (" main " or " primary " nexus, in Polotsky's current terminology) and the componential negativing of the theme (constituting in itself a " sub-" or " secondary " nexus). I would comment: (a) This distinction is tailored and indeed appropriate for the topic-initial construction, Bipartite-like focalization pattern (2). We have yet to specify the negation syntagmatics for the autofocal and focus-initial patterns. Polotsky treats the negation of these, esp. of pattern (4), briefly in the " Coptic Conjugation System " (1960a:§32), stating that (ⲛ)- ⲁⲛ is used, while the Second-Tense topic remains affirmative. One observes, however, that a negative topic is quite usual in focus-initial patterns. We must remember that these patterns replace in our corpus the theme/topic-

---

[148] Cf. (for *relative* conversion) Shisha-Halevy 1972:§2.1.3.1, 1976a:51.

[149] Cf. Shisha-Halevy 1972:137.

[150] Note the significant absence of this high-cohesion grade in the Bipartite conjugation.

[151] Mainly 1944:87ff. (= *CP* 191ff.), 1960a:§31f.; Kickasola 1975, esp. 103-137. The distinction of nexal vs. special negation is of course Jespersen's, in the fifth chapter of his classic " Negation in English and Other Languages " (1917; 1962:42ff.).

initial patterns for *negatived themes*, which as a matter of fact do not occur here. This renders the opposition of nexal *vs.* thematic negation meaningless: it does not obtain within the " classic " theme/topic initial construction. (Consider *A 2* 19 ΝΤΑΥΜΟΟΥΤ ΑΝ ΜΠΕΙΚΕΟΥΑ ΕΤΒΕΟΥ for the classical 'ΕΤΕΜΠΟΥ-'.) (b) It is legitimate to ask whether the two cases of nexal and thematic negation are not just two particular cases in a series of *possible incidence* of the negator, of different localizations of which one is nexal, another thematic. Two other particular localizations to be examined in the present context are the negativing of *an adjunct (modifier)* [152] and of the *focus*, both with an affirmative nexus. As a general rule one may say that for theme/topic-initial pattern (2) the nexal negation is located between the theme and the focus; otherwise (as a rule, with rare, prosodically motivated deviations) the ΑΝ-negation follows the segment it relates to [153]. (c) We should try to relate the affirmative form of each pattern to its negative one (whether or not the latter is regarded as a transform), and the *placement* of the negator to its *incidence* and functional role, in contributive relation to the focality of the pattern [154]. Below, I shall enumerate and selectively illustrate the negation patterns corresponding to focalization patterns (1) to (6) [155].

2.9.1 Theme/topic-initial patterns

2.9.1.1 PATTERN (1): THE AUTOFOCAL SECOND TENSE. *Present with focal modifier*: (*A 2* 462) ΤΜΝΤΕΡΟ ΝΜΠΗΥΕ ΕⲤ2ΜΠΕΙΜΑ ΑΝ Η ΠΑΙ / (*ibid.* 340) ΕΡΕΝΟΒΕ 2ΝΝΝΑΧ2Ε ΑΝ ΑΛΛΑ 2ΝΝΕΝ2ΗΤ; *rhetorical question*: (*Miss.* 279) Η ΕϢΑΥΝΕ2ΠΕ ΑΝ ΕΠΕΤΝΑΜΟΥ / (*A 1* 108) [156] ΜΗ ΕϢΑΡΕΠΑ2ΟΥ ΑΝ Η ϢΑΡΟΥΟⲤ2ΟΥ ΠΟϬΕ ΠΟϬΕ; *modal*: ΕϤΝΑ-: (*A 2* 505-6) ΕΝΝΑΘΛΙΒΕ ΑΝ Ν2ΕΝΑΤϬΟΜ... " Let us not distress " (also *IV* 61.27f., jussive; 154.14, hortative).

NEGATOR: ΑΝ. PLACEMENT: after the pattern or single expansion of the verb.

2.9.1.2 PATTERN (2): ⧧ THEME/TOPIC → MODIFIER ⧧

2.9.1.2.1 NEXAL NEGATION. (*Ryl. Cat.* 32, No. 68 ⲤϪΒ) ΝΕΥϢΟΒΕ ΑΝ Ε2ΕΝϢΗΡΕ ϢΗΜ / (*A 1* 183) ΜΗ ΝΕΝϢϢ ΑΝ ΝΝΙΓΡΑΦΗ ΝΟΥϢΤ / (*A 2* 403) ΝΕϤΝΑϢΑΧΕ ΓΑΡ ΑΝ 2ΑΡΟϤ ΜΑΥΑΑϤ ΑΛΛΑ ΕϤΝΑΧΕ-ΠΕΝΤΑϤⲤΟΤΜΕϤ / (*III* 131.10) ΝΝΕΙⲤΟΤΠ ΑΝ Ν2ΟΥΟ ΕΠΑΙ ΝΤΑϤΧΟΟⲤ... (also *IV* 51.16, *Wess.* 9 140b 3ff.) / (*III* 21.9f., ΝΤΑΙⲤΟΥϢΝΕ ΓΑΡ ΑΝ ΝΒΡΡΕ / (*ibid.* 17.1ff.) ΝΤΑϤΧΟΟⲤ ΑΝ ΧΕ-... ΑΛΛΑ ΝΤΑϤΧΟΟⲤ ΧΕ-... (sim. *IV* 111.20f.) 46.28f. etc.). Note also cases with the focusing modifier ΜΜΑΤΕ co-marking the focus: (*A 2* 52) ΝΤΑΥⲤ2ΑΙ-ΝΕΙϢΑΧΕ ΑΝ ΜΜΑΤΕ ΕΤΒΕ- / (*III* 50.4ff.) ΝΤΑΠΝΟΥΤΕ ϢΑΑΡ ΕΡΟϤ ΑΝ 2ΝΟΥΠΛΗΓΗ ΝΧΝΟΥϤ ΝΒΡΒΡ ΜΜΑΤΕ

---

[152] Cf. (for Egyptian) GUNN 1924:187f.; Satzinger, *Die negativen Konstruktionen im Alt- und Mittelägyptischen* (Berlin 1968), §46; Gilula, *JEA* 56:208ff. (1970), *JAOS* 92:560-5 (1972). On Coptic componential negation, see STERN §386 (" Wortnegation "), KICKASOLA 1975:219ff., 292ff.

[153] Cf. PRÄTORIUS 1881:757f.

[154] See SEILER 1952:79ff., 85f. He points out the tendency of the negator to be attached to the predicate, which is in a tug-of-war for the negation with the verb (see also MOORHOUSE 1959:4f.; JESPERSEN 1962:56ff.). In our case of focalization patterns, this tension is between the nexal and special (local) negation. The negation (acc. to Seiler) co- or over-characterizes the focus, contributing (macrosyntactically) to its focality. The negation delimits two statements, evoking the contrary one; cf. (p. 80) " Die Negation führt eine Affirmation nicht bloß zum Nullpunkt, sondern darüber hinaus in die entgegengesetzte oder gegenüberliegende Position... Die Negation konstatiert nicht bloß... das Nichtvorhandensein des Sachverhaltes A, sondern sie weist zugleich ausdrücklich auf diesen Sachverhalt A hin ". On the affinity of negation and " emphasis ", see also MOORHOUSE 1959:73ff. The affirmative focalized nexus (cf. " he *did* go ", " you *are* stupid ") is expressed in Coptic by means of the autofocal Second Tense.

[155] I cannot unfortunately report arriving at any definite statement regarding the distribution of ΑΝ *vs.* Ν- ΑΝ (cf. SHISHA-HALEVY 1976b:363f.). Pattern-specific information will be given below.

[156] The case of ΜΗ - ΑΝ is perhaps special (see PRÄTORIUS 1881:757f., SHISHA-HALEVY 1976a:43).

/ (*IV* 184.5f.) ⲚⲦⲀⲡⲉⲡⲣⲟⲫⲏⲦⲏⲤ ⲬⲟⲟⲤ ⲀⲚ ⲘⲘⲀⲦⲉ ⲉⲦⲉⲚⲦⲀⲤⲬⲡⲉ-ⲌⲀⲌ Ⲭⲉ-… / (*A 2* 390) ⲉⲣⲉⲚⲉⲨⲀⲅⲅⲉⲗⲓⲟⲚ ✝ ⲀⲚ ⲟⲨⲂⲉⲚⲉⲨⲉⲣⲏⲨ / (*Wess. 9* 138b 18ff.) ⲉⲩⲡⲀⲓⲇⲉⲨⲉ ⲘⲘⲟⲚ ⲀⲚ ⲌⲘⲡⲉⲩϬⲱⲚⲦ ⲀⲗⲗⲀ ⲌⲘⲡⲉⲩⲟⲨⲱϢ. Additional exx. for -ⲀⲚ-negation: *III* 21.1, 66.12f., *Ch.* 136.52ff., 65.15ff., *A 2* 150, 473, etc.

NEGATOR: — ⲀⲚ (all conj. forms), Ⲛ — ⲀⲚ (Bip., aor.), ⲚⲚ — ⲀⲚ (Bip.). THEME: affirmative[157]. PLACEMENT: (a) ⲀⲚ follows the theme/topic or its closest (usually rectional) expansion; (b) (with a nominal actor in the Tripartite Pattern) optionally after the actor expression.

2.9.1.2.2.1 FOCAL NEGATION (a). (*A 2* 312) ⲉⲨⲂⲀⲤⲀⲚⲓⲌⲉ ⲘⲘⲟⲟⲨ ⲉⲡϬⲓⲚϬⲏ ⲀⲚ ⲀⲗⲗⲀ ⲉⲣⲉⲚⲉⲦⲟⲨⲏⲌ ⲦⲏⲣⲟⲨ ⲌⲣⲀⲓ ⲚⲌⲏⲦⲚ ⲤⲟⲟⲨⲚ Ⲭⲉ-ⲉⲦⲂⲉⲟⲨ ⲏ ⲉⲬⲚⲟⲨ ⲚⲌⲱⲂ / (*III* 35.20) ⲚⲀⲓ ⲇⲉ ⲉⲓⲬⲱ ⲘⲘⲟⲟⲨ ⲉⲓⲦⲀⲓⲟ ⲀⲚ ⲘⲘⲟⲓ ⲘⲀⲨⲀⲀⲦ / (*Ch.* 89.12ff.) ⲘⲀⲣⲉⲩⲤⲱⲦⲘ ⲉⲡⲉⲡⲣⲟⲫⲏⲦⲏⲤ ⲉⲩⲬⲱ ⲚⲚⲀⲓ ⲉⲦⲂⲏⲏⲦⲩ ⲀⲚ (circ. of Sec. Present? other instances: *IV* 64.1f., 65.11ff.) / (*A 2* 87) ⲉⲚⲦⲀⲚⲉⲚⲦⲀⲨⲌⲉ ⲉⲌⲣⲀⲓ ⲉⲣⲟⲩ (i.e. the mud) ⲤⲗⲨⲦⲉ ⲚⲌⲏⲦⲩ ⲚⲐⲉ ⲚⲌⲉⲚⲡⲓⲣ ϢⲀⲚⲦⲉⲩⲡⲱϢ ⲀⲚ ϢⲀⲡⲉⲨⲙⲉⲣⲟⲤ ⲏ ϢⲀⲚⲦⲟⲨⲤⲱⲡ ⲀⲚ ϢⲀⲚⲉⲨⲙⲉⲣⲟⲤ ⲀⲗⲗⲀ ϢⲀⲚⲦⲟⲩⲟⲨⲱⲚⲌ ⲉⲂⲟⲗ ⲉⲨⲗⲟⲟⲙⲉ ⲀⲨⲱ ⲉⲨⲗⲀⲗⲱ ⲚⲌⲏⲦⲩ / (*III* 131.14f.) ⲚⲦⲀⲩⲬⲉ-ⲡⲀⲓ ⲚϬⲓⲡⲣⲱⲙⲉ ⲘⲡⲚⲟⲨⲦⲉ ⲌⲚⲟⲨⲙⲕⲀⲌ ⲚⲌⲏⲦ ⲀⲚ ⲘⲘⲀⲦⲉ / (*IV* 56.23ff.) ⲉⲚⲦⲀⲚⲉⲚⲉⲓⲟⲦⲉ ⲤⲨⲅⲬⲱⲣⲉⲓ ⲚⲀⲚ… ⲉⲦⲂⲉⲦⲙⲚⲦϬⲱⲂ ⲘⲘⲀⲦⲉ ⲀⲚ.

NEGATOR: — ⲀⲚ. THEME: affirmative. NEXUS: affirmative. PLACEMENT: immediately following the focus (or, if this is complex, after its first colon)[158]. Observe that ⲀⲚ in all probability co-marks the focus as such. This is the functional value of the adfocal placement. The opposition *nexal* vs. *focal* negation, existing only for this focalization pattern, is not easily reflected in English translation (cf. the subtle distinction, expressable in terms of Immediate Constituents, between " I am not feeling that well " and " I am feeling not that well " — a difference even more difficult to reproduce for the high-focality focalization pattern). Nevertheless, the distinction is unmistakenly there in Coptic syntagmatics. Both the affirmative nexus and the enhanced negative focus must play their part on the *plan du contenu*.

2.9.1.2.2.2 FOCAL NEGATION (b). *Second focus negated* or: (*affirmative* + *negative*) modifier focalized: (*IV* 24.6f.) ⲉⲩϢⲟⲟⲡ ⲌⲘⲡⲉⲨⲗⲀⲤ ⲘⲘⲀⲦⲉ ⲀⲨⲱ ⲌⲘⲡⲉⲩⲌⲏⲦ ⲀⲚ (*A 1* 380) ⲉⲩϢⲱϢⲦ ⲘⲘⲟⲟⲨ ⲚⲚⲇⲀⲓⲙⲟⲚⲓⲟⲚ, ⲘⲡⲚⲟⲨⲦⲉ ⲀⲚ / (*Ch.* 91.1ff.) ⲚⲀⲓ ⲘⲚⲚⲓⲕⲟⲟⲨⲉ ⲉⲩⲬⲱ ⲘⲘⲟⲟⲨ ⲉⲦⲂⲏⲏⲦⲚ ⲀⲨⲱ ⲉⲦⲂⲏⲏⲦⲟⲨ ⲀⲚ. Also *III* 29.7f., 34.11f., *RE 11* 16a 33ff., etc.

2.9.1.2.3 MODIFIER NEGATION[159]. (a) Expanding a Basic Tense (affirmative or negated): (*A 2* 464) ⲒⲤ ⲇⲉ Ⲍⲱⲱⲩ Ⲁⲩⲱⲡ̄ⲌⲓⲤⲉ ⲌⲚⲦⲤⲀⲣⲌ ⲉⲦⲂⲏⲏⲦⲩ ⲀⲚ ⲀⲗⲗⲀ ⲉⲦⲂⲏⲏⲦⲚ / (*A 1* 151) (ⲀⲨⲚⲀⲨ) ⲀⲨⲚⲀⲨ ⲉⲣⲟⲩ ⲀⲚ ⲚⲦⲉⲓⲌⲉ ⲌⲀⲡⲗⲱⲤ ⲀⲗⲗⲀ ⲀⲨϬⲓⲚⲡⲉ ⲘⲡⲟⲨϢⲱⲤ ⲘⲚⲡϬⲓⲤⲉ ⲘⲡⲉϥϢⲀⲌ / (*III* 200-1) ⲘⲡⲟⲨⲤⲣϥⲉ ⲉⲂⲟⲗ ⲌⲘⲡⲣⲟⲟⲩϢ ⲀⲚ ⲘⲡⲌⲱⲂ ⲚⲚⲉⲩϬⲓⲬ… ⲀⲗⲗⲀ ⲉⲂⲟⲗ ⲌⲘⲡⲣⲟⲟⲩϢ ⲘⲡϬⲓⲟⲨⲉ ⲘⲚⲡⲬⲱ̄ⲙ / (*IV* 116.12f.) ⲀⲚⲟⲚ ⲌⲱⲱⲚ ⲦⲚⲙⲟⲕⲌ ⲚⲌⲏⲦ ⲉⲦⲂⲏⲏⲦⲟⲨ ⲉⲦⲂⲉⲬⲉ-ⲘⲡⲟⲨⲣ-ⲌⲘⲌⲀⲗ ⲚⲀⲚ ⲀⲚ ⲕⲀⲦⲀⲡⲉⲚⲦⲟⲚ ⲚⲤⲀⲣⲕⲓⲕⲟⲚ ("not because") / (*III* 18.18ff.) ⲘⲟⲚⲟⲚ ⲚⲚⲉⲩⲣ-ⲙⲚⲦⲣⲉ ⲘⲡⲣⲀⲚ ⲘⲡⲬⲟⲉⲓⲤ ⲘⲚⲡⲉⲩⲬⲤ̄… ⲬⲉⲚⲚⲉⲟⲨⲚⲟⲂⲉ Ϣⲡ ⲀⲚ ⲉⲚⲉⲦⲚⲀⲉⲓⲣⲉ… ⲀⲗⲗⲀ Ⲭⲉ-ⲚⲚⲉⲕⲦⲱⲗⲙ ⲚⲦⲉⲕⲀⲅⲀⲡⲏ (" … not in order that… but in order that… "). Also *III* 20.2f., *Ch.* 85.8ff., *III* 116.16ff. (ⲀⲓⲬⲟⲟⲤ… ⲚⲉⲂⲟⲗ ⲀⲚ Ⲭⲉ-[160]), etc.

---

[157] KICKASOLA 1975:173; the example *Rom.* 14:6, quoted by POLOTSKY 1944:89 (= *CP* 193) for the neg. durative theme, is still unique, to the best of my knowledge.

[158] Cf. KICKASOLA 1975:103ff., 289f.; he obviously does not consider this an essential distinction.

[159] KICKASOLA 1975:219ff., 294ff. Note here (a) instances where Shenoutean ⲀⲚ corresponds to non-Akhmimicized Sahidic ⲟⲚ: *III* 16.7, *IV* 213.9 (*not* *IV* 116.13, as I erroneously suggested in 1976b:356); (b) a striking case of componential negation of a *bound morpheme*, non-adjunctal (*P* 130² 110 vo) ⲡⲉⲬⲀⲨ, ⲡⲉⲬⲀⲚ ⲀⲚ, cf. (130⁵ 97 ro) ⲡⲉⲬⲉ-ⲡⲚⲟⲨⲦⲉ, ⲣⲱⲙⲉ ⲀⲚ.

[160] Occasionally, ⲉⲂⲟⲗ ⲀⲚ Ⲭⲉ- seems to be in an ancolouthic, loosely connected or janus-faced construction: *III* 19.4f., 66.2, 185-6; cf. ⲉⲦⲂⲉⲟⲨ, Ⲙⲏ ⲉⲂⲟⲗ ⲀⲚ Ⲭⲉ- (*Ch.* 69.27ff., 73.8ff.) and Ⲙⲏ ⲉⲦⲂⲉ- ⲀⲚ (*Wess. 9* 105a 2ff.).

(b) Expanding a converted or inconvertible tense or extraconjugational (non-tense) verb form; all are *unmarked for thematicity*: (*A 2* 119) ⲛⲉⲩⲥⲱⲱϥ ⲛⲧⲁϥⲛⲧⲟⲩ ⲉⲃⲟⲗ ⲛⲍⲏⲧⲟⲩ ⲛⲟⲩⲥⲟⲡ ⲁⲛ ⲏ ⲥⲛⲁⲩ ⲁⲗⲗⲁ ⲛⲍⲁⲍ ⲛⲥⲟⲡ / (*III* 185.24ff.) ⲧⲁⲓ ⲧⲉ ⲑⲉ ⲛⲧⲁⲓⲍⲣⲟⲩ ⲍⲙⲡⲁϭⲱⲛⲧ ⲍⲛⲧⲉⲩϣⲏ ⲧⲏⲣⲥ ⲉⲧⲙⲙⲁⲩ ⲙⲙⲁⲧⲉ ⲁⲛ ⲙⲛⲡⲉⲍⲟⲟⲩ... ⲁⲗⲗⲁ ⲛⲍⲁⲍ ⲛⲥⲟⲡ ⲁⲓⲭⲉⲣⲟ... ⲍⲛⲟⲩϭⲱⲛⲧ / (*A 2* 400) ⲡⲉⲓⲥⲱⲙⲁ ⲡⲁⲓ ⲉⲧⲛⲁⲧⲱⲟⲩⲛ ⲍⲛⲧⲁⲛⲁⲥⲧⲁⲥⲓⲥ ⲍⲙⲡⲧⲣⲉϥϯ-ⲟⲩⲱ ⲁⲛ ⲛⲕⲉⲥⲱⲙⲁ ⲁⲗⲗⲁ ⲉⲧⲣⲉϥϯ-ⲟⲩⲱ ⲙⲙⲟϥ ⲙⲙⲓⲛ ⲙⲙⲟϥ / (*III* 19.16ff.) ⲛⲧⲟϥ ⲟⲛ ⲡⲉⲛⲧⲁϥⲍⲱⲛ ⲙⲛⲛⲥⲁⲧⲣⲉⲩⲥⲟⲩⲱⲛϥ ⲭⲉ-ⲛⲛⲉⲕϣⲡⲕ ⲁⲛ ⲙⲡⲣⲁⲛ ⲙⲡⲛⲟⲩⲧⲉ ⲙⲁⲩⲁⲁϥ ⲁⲗⲗⲁ ⲕⲉⲗⲁⲁⲩ ⲛⲁⲛⲁϣ " It is also He who commanded..., not only that... but also... " / (*III* 169.12f.) ⲙⲛⲛⲥⲁⲧⲣⲉⲕϯ-ⲥⲃⲱ ⲛⲁⲩ ⲛⲟⲩⲥⲟⲡ ⲁⲛ ⲟⲩⲧⲉ ⲥⲛⲁⲩ ⲁⲛ ⲟⲩⲧⲉ ϣⲟⲙⲧ ⲁⲛ ⲁⲗⲗⲁ ⲛⲍⲁⲍ ⲛⲥⲟⲡ / (*A 2* 414) ⲟⲩⲛⲍⲁⲍ ⲉⲩⲃⲱⲗ ⲛⲛⲉⲅⲣⲁⲫⲏ ⲍⲛⲟⲩⲥⲟⲟⲩⲧⲛ ⲁⲛ / (*ibid.* 465) ...ⲛⲥⲉⲧⲙⲣ-ⲃⲟⲗ ⲉⲡⲕⲱⲍⲧ ⲉⲧⲃⲉ ⲭⲉ-ⲙⲡⲟⲩⲣ-ⲡⲡⲉⲧⲛⲁⲛⲟⲩϥ ⲁⲛ ⲙⲙⲁⲧⲉ ⲏ ⲭⲉ-ⲙⲡⲟⲩϣⲡ-ⲍⲓⲥⲉ ⲉⲧⲃⲉⲡⲭⲟⲉⲓⲥ ⲁⲗⲗⲁ ⲙⲡⲟⲩⲕⲁⲧⲟⲟⲧⲟⲩ ⲉⲃⲟⲗ ⲍⲙⲡⲣⲱⲙⲉ. NB. The *simultaneous double placement* (the "foreshadowed enclitic", §6.0.3.3): (*A 2* 475) (ⲧⲁⲟⲓⲍⲉ) ⲧⲁⲓ ⲛⲧⲁⲛⲉⲧⲟⲩⲁⲁⲃ ⲭⲟⲟⲥ ⲁⲛ ⲉⲧⲃⲛⲏⲧⲟⲩ ⲁⲛ ⲁⲗⲗⲁ ⲉⲧⲃⲏⲏⲧⲛ ⲭⲉ-. Additional exx.: *Mun.* 96, *III* 111-2, 173. 11ff. (ϣⲁⲛⲧⲟⲩ- ⲁⲛ), 184.16ff. (ⲛⲑⲉ... ⲁⲛ), *IV* 47.8ff. (ⲍⲙⲡⲧⲣⲉ- ⲉⲧⲃⲉ- ⲙⲙⲁⲧⲉ ⲁⲛ) 57.17ff. (ⲉⲛϣⲁⲛ- ⲉⲧⲣⲉⲛ- ⲁⲛ ⲟⲩⲇⲉ ⲉⲧⲣⲉⲛ- ⲁⲛ), *Ch.* 177.13ff. (ⲡⲉⲧ- ⲉⲧⲃⲉ- ⲙⲙⲁⲧⲉ ⲁⲛ ⲁⲗⲗⲁ ⲉⲧⲃⲉ-) etc.

NEGATOR: (ⲛ?)- ⲁⲛ. PLACEMENT: following the modifier; rarely preceding it (intercolary, §6.0.3), or double.

(c) *modifier* (+ ⲁⲩⲱ) + *neg. modifier* expanding a verb form (affirm. or negatived): (*P* 130² 33 ⲗⲅ) ⲁϥⲣ-ⲛⲟⲃⲉ ⲉⲣⲟϥ ⲉⲡⲛⲟⲩⲧⲉ ⲁⲛ / (*III* 212.3f.) ϥⲁⲙⲁⲍⲧⲉ ⲙⲙⲟⲟⲩ ⲉⲧⲣⲉⲩϯ ⲉⲡⲁⲍⲟⲩ ⲉⲑⲏ ⲁⲛ / (*ibid.* 116.23f.) ⲁϥⲭⲓⲧ ⲉⲍⲟⲩⲛ ⲉⲩⲕⲁⲕⲉ... ⲁⲩⲱ ⲛⲉⲍⲟⲩⲛ ⲁⲛ ⲉⲩⲟⲩⲟⲉⲓⲛ / (*Mun.* 98, parall. *III* 169.14f.) ...ⲁⲩⲱ ⲛⲥⲉⲧⲙⲣ-ⲍⲛⲁⲩ ⲉⲥⲱⲧⲙ ⲕⲁ-ⲧⲁⲡⲟⲩⲱϣ ⲙⲡⲛⲟⲩⲧⲉ ⲁⲩⲱ ⲛⲕⲁⲧⲁⲡⲟⲩⲱϣ ⲁⲛ ⲙⲡⲟⲩⲁ ⲡⲟⲩⲁ ⲙⲙⲟⲟⲩ / (*A 1* 72) ⲉⲛⲉⲛⲧⲁⲥⲣ-ⲛⲟⲃⲉ ⲉⲡⲛⲟⲩⲧⲉ ⲉⲣⲟ ⲁⲛ, ⲛⲉⲣⲁⲥⲟⲡⲥ ⲉⲭⲱⲥ / (*Ch.* 153.36f.) ⲛⲉⲧⲥⲟⲟⲩⲍ... ⲍⲙⲡⲥⲱⲙⲁ ⲁⲩⲱ ⲍⲙⲡⲍⲏⲧ ⲁⲛ / (*III* 168.26) ⲛⲁⲛⲟⲩ-ϯ-ⲍⲏⲩ ⲛⲟⲩⲥⲃⲱ ⲛⲟⲩⲍⲁⲧ ⲁⲛ. Additional exx.: *III* 108.4f., *IV* 100.17f., 153.24f. etc.

NEGATOR: (ⲛ)- ⲁⲛ. PLACEMENT: following the second modifier or (ⲛ- ⲁⲛ) enclosing it. I consider the modifier in these cases (a-c) to be on the borderline of adjunct and focus, probably a gradient (non dichotomic) distinction: the two relationships are not mutually exclusive (§2.7.1.4.1). Here again, the negator seems to contribute towards enhancing — and co-marking — the focality of the modifier(s); consider the not uncommon case of ' ⲉϥⲥⲱⲧⲙ ' + neg. modifier, where we are at a loss to decide between the circumstantial and (circ. +) Second Present, e.g. *IV* 64.7ff., 65.11ff.

2.9.1.3 PATTERN (3): NON-MODIFIER FOCALIZATION (*object* only, §2.3.1). (*Ch.* 96.9f.) ⲛⲧⲁⲓⲭⲉ-ⲟⲩϣⲁⲭⲉ ⲁⲛ ⲛⲍⲟⲩⲟ / (*Wess. 9* 171c 7) ⲉⲓⲭⲓ-ϭⲟⲗ ⲁⲛ / (*IV* 94.3) ⲉϣⲁⲩϣⲱϭⲉ-ⲡⲱⲛⲉ ⲁⲛ / (*A 2* 509) ⲉⲕⲟⲩⲱⲙ-ⲛⲟⲃⲉ ⲁⲩⲱ ⲟⲩⲍⲣⲉ ⲁⲛ.

NEGATOR: ⲁⲛ. PLACEMENT: following the object. THEME: affirmative. No opposition between focal and nexal negation.

2.9.2 FOCUS-INITIAL PATTERNS

2.9.2.1 PATTERN (4): # *focus* → *Second Perfect* #. (*A 1* 81) ⲙⲏ ⲉⲧⲃⲉⲛⲁⲛⲟⲃⲉ ⲁⲛ ⲛⲧⲁⲕⲙⲁⲥⲧⲓⲅⲟⲩ ⲙⲙⲟⲓ / (*Wess. 9* 144c 24ff.) ⲉⲧⲃⲉⲡⲉⲑⲃⲃⲓⲟ ⲁⲛ ⲙⲁⲩⲁⲁϥ ⲛⲧⲁϥⲭⲟⲟⲥ ⲭⲉ- / (*A 1* 113) ⲉⲧⲃⲉⲙⲡⲉⲑⲟⲟⲩ ⲁⲛ ⲙⲁⲩⲁⲁⲩ... ⲛⲧⲁⲡⲁⲓ ϣⲱⲡⲉ.

NEGATOR: - ⲁⲛ. PLACEMENT: immediately after the focus (focus: ⲉⲧⲃⲉ- only?). No opposition between nexal and focal negation. TOPIC: affirmative [161].

---

[161] See §§2.5.1-2 for the negative topics, which seem to exclude a negated nexus or negative focus.

2.9.2.2   PATTERN (5): ⧣ *focus* → *circumstantial* ⧣. (*Wess. 9* 106a 7ff. parall. *P* 130² 71 ⲣⲡⲉ, see §2.9.2.4) ⲙⲏ ⲉⲧⲃⲉⲧⲙⲛⲧⲥⲧⲙⲏⲧˈ ⲁⲛ ⲉⲁⲛⲁⲓ ϫⲱⲕ ⲉⲃⲟⲗ ⲛⲍⲱⲃ ⲛⲓⲙ ⲉⲛⲁⲛⲟⲩϥ ⲏ ⲉⲧⲃⲉⲧⲙⲛⲧⲁⲧⲥⲱⲧⲙ ⲁⲛ ⲛⲧⲟϥ ⲉⲁ-ⲛⲉⲓⲕⲟⲟⲩⲉ ϫⲱⲕ ⲉⲃⲟⲗ ⲙⲡⲉⲓⲙⲏⲏϣⲉ ⲙⲡⲉⲧϩⲟⲟⲩ / (*A 1* 219) ⲙⲏ ⲉⲧⲃⲉⲛⲓϩⲃⲏⲩⲉ ⲣⲱ ⲁⲛ ⲉⲧⲛⲡⲗⲁⲥⲥⲉ ⲙⲙⲟⲟⲩ ϩⲙⲡⲉⲛϩⲏⲧ ⲙⲙⲓⲛ ⲙⲙⲟⲛ ⲁⲩⲱ ⲧⲉⲛⲙⲛⲧⲣⲉϥⲕⲁ-ϩⲧⲏⲛ ⲉⲣⲟⲛ ⲙⲁⲩⲁⲁⲛ ⲉⲁⲩϫⲟⲟⲥ ⲛϭⲓⲛⲉⲡⲣⲟⲫⲏⲧⲏⲥ ⲉⲧⲟⲩⲁⲁⲃ... ϫⲉ-.
Note (*A 1* 89) ϩⲓⲧⲛⲟⲩ ⲛⲉⲥⲛⲏⲩ ⲉⲁϩⲁϩ ⲣ-ϣⲙⲙⲟ ⲉⲣⲱⲧⲛ ⲙⲏ ϩⲓⲧⲛⲛⲛⲟⲙⲟⲥ ⲁⲛ.

NEGATOR: - ⲁⲛ. PLACEMENT: imm. following the focus (ⲉⲧⲃⲉ- only?). TOPIC: affirmative [161]. No opposition between nexal and focal negation.

2.9.2.3   PATTERN (6): ⧣ *focus* → ⲉ-*conj. form* (Sec. tense + circumstantial) [162]. (*A 2* 519) ⲉⲧⲃⲏⲏⲧ ⲁⲛ ⲉⲕⲛⲁϩⲩⲡⲟⲧⲁⲥⲥⲉ ⲛⲁⲓ ⲟⲩⲇⲉ ⲉⲧⲃⲏⲏⲧⲕ ⲁⲛ ⲉⲓⲛⲁϯ-ⲡⲙⲁ ⲛⲁⲕ ⲉⲣ-ϩⲱⲃ ⲛⲓⲙ / (*Ch.* 38.35ff.) ⲉⲣϣⲁⲛⲧⲃⲁϣⲟⲣ ⲁⲩⲕⲁⲕ ⲉⲃⲟⲗ ⲁⲛ... ⲉⲣⲉⲡⲙⲟⲩⲓ ⲧⲣⲣⲉ / (*A 1* 114) ⲙⲏ ϩⲱⲥⲁⲑⲏⲧ ⲁⲛ ⲉⲣⲉⲡⲁⲓ ⲧⲁⲙⲟ ⲙⲙⲟ / (*Wess. 9* 158a 30ff.) ⲉⲩⲙⲟⲥⲧⲉ ⲙⲙⲱⲧⲛ ⲁⲛ ⲉⲩϫⲱ ⲛⲏⲧⲛ ⲛⲛⲁⲓ ⲙⲛϩⲉⲛⲕⲟⲟⲩⲉ ⲉⲛⲁϣⲱⲟⲩ.

NEGATORS: - ⲁⲛ, ⲛⲛ- ⲁⲛ (rare). PLACEMENT: following or enclosing the focus. TOPIC: affirmative [161]. No opposition between nexal and focal negation.

2.9.2.4   ⧣ *focus* → *Basic Tense* ⧣ (§2.6.2): (*III* 16.3f.) ⲙⲏ ϩⲓⲧⲙⲡⲁϣⲁⲓ ⲁⲛ ⲙⲡⲉⲩϭⲱⲛⲧ ⲛⲉⲡⲣⲟⲫⲏⲧⲏⲥ ⲁⲩϫⲟⲟⲥ ϫⲉ-... / (*P* 130² 71 ⲣⲡⲉ) ⲙⲏ ⲉⲧⲃⲉⲧⲙⲛⲧⲥⲙⲛⲧ (sic) ⲁⲛ ⲁⲛⲁⲓ ϫⲱⲕ ⲉⲃⲟⲗ ⲛϩⲱⲃ ⲛⲓⲙ ⲉⲛⲁⲛⲟⲩϥ ⲏ ⲉⲧⲃⲉ ⲧⲙⲛⲧⲁⲧⲥⲱⲧⲙ ⲁⲛ ⲛⲧⲟϥ ⲁⲛⲉⲓⲕⲟⲟⲩⲉ ϫⲱⲕ ⲉⲃⲟⲗ ⲙⲡⲉⲓⲙⲏⲏϣⲉ ⲙⲡⲉⲑⲟⲟⲩ (parall. to *Wess. 9* 106a 7ff., see §2.9.2.2) / (*A 1* 124) ⲏ ⲉⲧⲃⲉϩⲉⲛⲡⲉⲑⲟⲟⲩ ⲁⲛ ⲙⲛϩⲉⲛϯ-ⲧⲱⲛ ⲁⲡⲕⲁϩ ⲟⲩⲱⲛ ⲛⲣⲱϥ ⲁϥⲱⲙⲕ ⲛⲛⲉⲧⲙⲙⲁⲩ / (*ibid.* 125) ⲉⲧⲃⲉ-ϩⲉⲛϩⲟⲙⲧ ⲁⲛ ⲏ ⲙⲁⲁⲃ ⲛϩⲁⲧ ⲁⲡⲉⲧⲙⲙⲁⲩ ⲡⲁⲣⲁⲇⲓⲇⲟⲩ ⲙⲡⲉⲛⲧⲁϥⲥⲟⲛⲧϥ / (*A 2* 80) ⲙⲏ ϩⲓⲧⲙⲡⲉϩⲟⲩⲟⲛⲟϭⲛⲉϭ ⲁⲛ ⲛⲧⲟϥ... ⲁⲓϫⲱ ⲙⲡⲉⲓϣⲁϫⲉ / (*A 1* 88) ⲉⲡϫⲓⲛϫⲏ ⲁⲛ ⲁⲕϫⲟⲟⲥ... (sim. 354, 366). For more exx., see §2.6.2.

2.9.2.5   PREDICATIVE MODIFIER NEGATED: ⧣ *modifier* - Ø ⧣ (§1.2.1.3.3). (*A 1* 158) ⲉⲛⲉ-ⲉⲧⲃⲉⲡⲉⲓϩⲱⲃ ⲁⲛ ⲛⲉⲟⲩⲛϣϭⲟⲙ ⲉⲧⲣⲉϩⲉⲛⲕⲟⲟⲩⲉ ⲧⲁⲙⲓⲟⲟⲩ ⲛⲁⲩ / (*III* 146.20ff.) ⲡⲗⲏⲛ ⲡϫⲟⲉⲓⲥ ϩⲙⲡⲉⲕϭⲱⲛⲧ ⲁⲛ... ⲟⲩⲧⲉ ⲉⲧⲃⲏⲏⲧ ⲁⲛ (cf. *Jer.* 10:24).

2.10   CONCLUDING NOTE ON THE FUNCTIONAL ESSENCE OF THE SECOND TENSE

In view of the data here presented, one can hardly consider the Second Tense an "unsatiated sign" (DRESSLER 1973:70) or a form "of incomplete predication" (Curme) in need of predicative complementation, but rather an index characterizing (a) a verb form as THEME (in the micro-syntactic extent) or THEME-TOPIC (in the macro-syntactic extent), (b) a verb lexeme or modifier as FOCUS. The distinction between (a) and (b) is resolved or signalled by the informational structure of the cotext: the identification of the focus, and therewith the determination of the function of the Second Tense itself, is effected by the isolation or non-isolation of a TOPIC in the extended environment of the converted conjugation form. I see the Second Tense, in association with other phenomena (word order, negation incidence, focusing modifiers and particles, suprasegmentals) as more of a focalizing than topicalizing agent. The functional category of which the Second Tense is but one of the exponents is the *characterization of a predicative syntagm for Functional (or Informational) Sentence Perspective and Communicative Dynamism* (i.e., thematic and generally cotextual boundness). This way of phrasing the functional essence of the form may appear banal: yet I believe it is preferable, highlighting the all-important macrosyntactic role of this conversion.

---

[162] Cf. KICKASOLA 1975:134ff. ("Affirmative Second Tense Containing Negative Patterns", "Affirmative Nexus with a Negated AdvP in Frontal Extraposition"). This is rather a Second Tense + circumstantial syncretism (§2.6). The use here of "extraposition" is unfortunate: the predicative modifier is not *extra*-, but *pre*-posed (see also Kickasola's p. 292f., where he refers to this "adverb" as a "predicative adjunct").

CHAPTER 3

THE SO-CALLED " DIRECT OBJECT " ADVERBAL EXPANSION:
PATTERNS, PARADIGMATICS AND DISTRIBUTION

3.0.1 DEFINITIONS: OBJECT, VALENCY, DIATHESIS.   The *object* is an expansion of the conjugated or extraconjugational verb lexeme, consisting of a pronoun (personal, indefinite, interrogative, demonstrative) or determinator expanded by a noun lexeme.   This object is either (a) preceded or (b) not preceded by a marker relating it to its verbal nucleus.   Obviously, this definition as it stands would subsume under (a) all prepositional-phrase expansions.   To narrow down and delimit that range of adverbal modification which is functionally a case apart and formally predictable — i.e. regulated — there is, I believe, no other way but that of applying the structural distinction between *rectional* (grammatically motivated, uncommutable — hence non-pertinent but a co-constituent of the verb) and *complementational* (optional, grammatically unmotivated, commutable — hence pertinent) modification (§1.1.2.1).   The traditional approximative, universalistic (yet inherently ethnocentric) conception of " direct " *vs.* " indirect " objects, of " transitive " *vs.* " intransitive " verbs, must not be uncritically imported into Coptic grammatical description (and then be post-hoc justified), but must be examined with a view to giving it structural meaning.

3.0.1.1   Trying to accommodate the conventional concept of (*in*)*transitivity* to the Coptic data, one can approach the problem at a semasiological angle [1], a *transformative-paradigmatic* angle (with an incidental morphologic aspect) [2], a *syntagmatic* (" constructional ") angle (again involving the morphosyntactic regulation of construct and pre-pronominal verb-lexeme allomorphs) or — and this is the usual practice — with a definition based on an unequal and individualistic admixture of all three [3].   The first approach, grouping some verb lexemes as transitive by semasiological criteria, would furnish a list partly coextensive with those lexemes selected by the other criteria, but this approach may be dismissed as essentially ungrammatical, also as largely subjective, arbitrary and uncontrollable.   The transformational approach would refer the transitive *active* in a relatively simple way to a *passive* transformation.   This assumes the existence in Coptic of a passive diathesis such as we know in Indo-European and Semitic, or at least the existence of a regular, clear-cut and predictable relationship: the transformation ' *actor* + *verb lexeme* + *direct object*' =>'*patiens*+*stative* + (*instrumental*) *actor*' [4] being symptomatic of transitives.

[1] CHERIX 1979:12f. SAUVAGEOT 1950:158f.; SCHMIDT 1973:118f. calls this an "unsyntactic" differentiation.   It is the basis of the generativist " subcategorization " and the structuralist *distinctive feature* in semasiological and morphologic functional analysis.

[2] Cf. SCHMIDT 1973:107, BUSSE 1974:124 n. 13, CALLENDER 1973a:65f.   For a different, original conception of transitivity as one of a set of options of information arrangement, one of several " networks of systems " (mood, theme, transitivity), see HALLIDAY 1967:37ff, 1968:212ff., 1972:146ff., 162ff.

[3] CHERIX' exposition (1979:7f.) is a typical one, that (untypically) gives some attention to the matter of definition. Cherix defines as transitive a verb that fulfils one of three conditions: (1) a verb that " has " (i.e. alternates in) construct and pronominal forms of the lexeme, (2) that " has " (i.e. is transformable into) a qualitative, the (grammatical) subject of the state expressed by which is identical (i.e. correferent) with the actor of the infinitive, (3) the N-/MMO⸗ object construction is added by Cherix as distinctive, primarily to cater for Greek-origin verbs and such native ones as "have" no qualitative or morphophonemic-alternation mechanism (without taking into account the possibility that the value of N- may differ here from that of N- alternating with the construct or pronominal forms; N-/MMO⸗ in pattern-oriented view does not enter into Cherix's definition).   See also QUECKE 1981:260f., 1982:285ff. and cf. SCHUCHARDT, SPITZER 1928:289, 295f.

[4] POLOTSKY 1960a:§9, FUNK 1978a:120f. (an excellent concise overview of the problem), QUECKE 1981:261.   The transformation ' *actor* + *verb lexeme* (infinitive, non-dur.)' => ' *actor* + *stative* (dur.)' is a possible criterion for *intransitives* (the opposition infinitive vs. stative is suppressed for intransitives in the Bipartite Pattern — i.e. it is maintained in the [rather limited] circumstances of *transitives* predicated in the Bipartite, with the functional opposition of durative action *vs.* statal passive).   This would mean that ⲈⲒⲠⲈ, while syntagmatically transitive, is resolvable into two paradigmatically (transformationally) transitive and intransitive-copular homonyms; for the latter, consider (*K* 9100) ⲚⲈⲦⲞ ⲚⲞⲨⲞⲈⲒⲚ ⲀⲨⲢ-ⲔⲀⲔⲈ / (*Wess. 18* 99.17ff.) ⲢⲰⲘⲈ ⲚⲒⲘ Ⲉ⳦Ⲟ ⲚⲈⲨⲤⲈⲂⲎⲤ... Ⲉ⳦ⲨⲀⲚⲢ-ⲀⲤⲈⲂⲎⲤ... / (*Ch.* 98.47ff.) ⲚⲈⲦⲞ ⲚⲢⲘⲘⲀⲞ ⲚⲀⲎⲦⲚ ⲦⲚⲎⲠ ⲈⲢ-ⲀⲎⲔⲈ / (*III* 48.28f.) ⲈⲨⲀⲨⲢ-ⲄⲰⲂ Ⲏ ⲤⲈⲞ ⲚⲄⲰⲂ.   There are still some problems here, esp. since the two lists, combinations and respective meanings have still to be established; witness such hairline oppositions as (*A 1* 289) ⲞⲨⲞⲚ ⲚⲒⲘ ⲈⲦⲞ ⲚⲀⲞⲦⲈ ⲀⲎⲦ⳦ ⲘⲠⲬⲞⲈⲒⲤ (" is fearful of...") *vs.* (*ibid.* 297) ⲞⲨⲞⲚ ⲚⲒⲘ ⲈⲦⲢ-ⲀⲞⲦⲈ ⲀⲎⲦ⳦ ⲘⲠⲬⲞⲈⲒⲤ (" fears "), *vs.* (*P* 131⁸ 94 ro) ⲠⲈⲀⲞⲞⲨ ⲈⲦⲞ ⲚⲀⲞⲦⲈ (" frightening ", "fearful"); (*Ch.* 21 *passim*) ⲚⲄⲢ-ⲀⲞⲞⲨⲦ ⲀⲚ ⲞⲨⲆⲈ ⲚⲄⲢ-ⲤⲀⲒⲘⲈ ⲀⲚ ⲚⲄⲢ-ⲘⲀⲤⲈ ⲀⲚ ⲞⲨⲦⲈⲀⲦⲞ ⲀⲒⲈⲒⲰ... ⲚⲄⲢ-ⲀⲞ⳦ ⲆⲈ ⲀⲚ ⲞⲚ ⲀⲒⲞⲨⲞⲞⲀⲈ... ⲚⲄⲢ-ⲂⲀⲢⲂⲀⲢⲞⲤ ⲀⲚ... "you do not *constitute*..." non-actual

However, this test can hardly be accepted as adequate on its own, in view of (a) the considerable group of lexemes for which a stative is not attested (which, on the other hand, cannot be said to constitute a separate class in any sense but this morphological one); (b) the important group of bivalent or trivalent (" one/two-expansion ") " intransitives ", such as ΝΑΥ or ᲒΑΡΕᲒ, stative-less, which are for all structural-functional purposes not different from " true " (by extra-Coptic standards) transitives; (c) the case of verb syntagms expanded by the prepositional phrase Ν-/ΜΜΟ⸗ (forming the subject matter of the present chapter); Ν- is, on the one hand, a direct-object marker after transitives under given conditions, yet on the other hand an " adverbial " i.e. modifier signal (§1.3.1), and is thus in fact an " inset " of the " in-direct " object as rection of transitives [5]; (d) the absence in Coptic of a single, unambiguous, predictable passive [6] corresponding symmetrically to the " active " ' actor + v. lexeme + object '. Moreover, this definition entails a subordinated, secondary treatment of the so-called " absolute ", object-less [7] transi-tives — which is unsatisfactory in a structural descriptive framework. Some of the foregoing objections will be touched on in the following pages. Cumulatively, they seem to rule out the transformational definition as greatly over-simplifying. The syntagmatic definition is hardly ever adopted independently, but usually appears as a not overly important component of a complex definition. Based on constructional data, including the compatibilities of the combinatory allomorphs of the verb lexemes, it is wanting in depth: it still lacks a *categorial* point of view, to account (*inter alia*) for the Ν-construction as a surrogate, alternant or variant direct-object expansion. On the whole, however, this approach can be said to be the vestibule to the one advocated here — namely, one of PATTERN and VALENCY STRUCTURE.

present (§3.1.2.1.1)?; (*A 1* 37) (the blessed mountain) ЕᲧΟ ΝΟΥΟΕΙΝ Η ЕᲧΡ-ΟΥΟΕΙΝ " is alight or sheds light ". On this issue, see CALLENDER 1970:248ff., 1973b:194 n. 2, 195, SHISHA–HALEVY 1976a:32. The recurring cases of *infinitives* of usually intransitive lexe-mes in durative environment (non-actual present? §3.1.2.1.1) weaken somewhat the distinctive value of the durative pattern for this purpose. Since it is conceivable that the burden of the functional opposition of *actual* vs. *non-actual* present falls on the formal opposition of *stative* vs. *infinitive* (intr.), we need yet an independent test for defining the intransitive.

    [5] Rectional Ν-/(ΜΜΟ⸗) being a " case " morpheme, it is really a constituent of the verb and does not belong, structural-analytically speaking, to the noun syntagm to which it is, by syntagmatic " accident ", prefixed (cf. BARRI 1977:29).

    [6] Verb diathesis is a pattern-related phenomenon, determined by the verb-actant(s) structure, rather than one related to the verb alone. This (well put by H. SCHUCHARDT, see *Brevier* 214f.) is almost a truism, but its ramifications are all too sel-dom fully realized. Consider the dependence of a " passive " value of the infinitive in Coptic on the presence of a (nominal, often pronominal) *object*: (*Ch.* 52.15ff.) ᲒΩΒ ΝΙΜ ЕΤЕΡЕΠΡΩΜЕ ΟΥΑᲧΟΥ ΑΝ ЕΛΛΥ ΝΑᲧ / (*P* 131[6] 44 ΡΙЕ) ЕᲧXЕ-ΤΝΟΥᲧᲧ ΔЕ ЕΤΜΚΡΙΝЕ ΜΜΟΝ " not to be judged " / (*Or.* 156.12ff.) (... ЕᲒΝΑΚ ΑΝ) ЕΝЕX-ΟΥΩΝЕ ΝΟΥΩΤ ЕΤΩΚ (i.e. into your well) "a stone to be thrown ", SHISHA–HALEVY 1975:473. Compare the famous *locus* (*Mt.* 22:30, Boh.) (ᲮЕΝ†ΑΝΑCΤΑCΙC) ΜΠΑΥᲮΙ ΟΥΔЕ ΜΠΑΥᲮΙΤΟΥ, corresponding to οὔτε γαμοῦσιν οὔτε γαμίζονται. Passive diathesis is nowhere explicitly defined for Coptic. The stative of transitive verbs furnish-es a morphologic statal passive form, predicatable (and occurring) only in the durative conjugation pattern (which in turn may be combined with the Tripartite-Conjugation categories by means of the periphrastic-suppletive conjugation with the use of the auxiliary ᲧΩΠЕ). A " *Vorgangspassiv* " does not exist in Coptic as a true category: in the construction ' CЕ-/-ΟΥ....... (ЕΒΟΛ) ᲒΙΤΝ- ', opposable to ' CЕ-/-ΟΥ..... ΝᲮΙ- ', the burden of the opposition lies on (ЕΒΟΛ) ᲒΙΤΝ-, which does no more than instrumen-tally introduce the noun-lexical or pronoun-lexical content of an indefinite personal pronoun. Consider the following striking instances: (*Wess. 9* 119a 27ff.) ΟΥΝΡΩΜЕ ЕΥXΩ ΜΜΟC ЕΡΟᲧ ᲒΙΤΝΝΡΩΜЕ XЕ-... / (*IV* 8.6) CЕΝΑΟΥЕΜ-ΘΗΥΤΝ ᲒΙΤΝΤΜΝΤΑΤΝΑᲒΤЕ / (*ibid.* 41.16f.) CЕΝΑΜЕΡΙΤΚ ᲒΙΤΜΠΝΟΥΤЕ ΜΝΝΡΩΜЕ / (*ibid.* 199.15f.) ΠΤΗΡᲧ ЕΥΡ-ᲒΜΜЕ ΜΜΟᲧ ᲒΙΤΜΠΤΩᲧ ΜΠΝΟΥΤЕ / (*K* 9292) ΝΑΙ ЕΤΟΥᲧΑXЕ ЕΡΟΟΥ ᲒΙΤΝΝЕΓΡΑΦΗ / (*Wess. 9* 143d 15ff.) ΠЕΝΤΑᲧΤΑΜΙΟΟΥ Η ΠЕΝΤΑΥΤΑΜΙΟΟΥ ЕΒΟΛ ᲒΙΤΟΟΤᲧ " who created them or by whom they were created ", cf. also *III* 170.27, *IV* 24.11, 66.21f., *Ch.* 88.35ff., 106.47f. etc. However, since, on the one hand, (ЕΒΟΛ) ᲒΙΤΝ- (" through the agency of ") is freely usable as a complement modifier phrase, and, on the other hand, the " indefinite " 3rd person plural pronoun is a fully privileged actor-expression in its own right — with no agentive specification — it is theoretically difficult to establish in Coptic a clear-cut " syntactic " passive category; consider such cases as (*IV* 28.5f.) ᲮЕΛΛΥ ΝᲒΩΒ ЕΝΑΝΟΥᲧ ЕΝΝΑᲧΑΑᲧ ΝΝЕΝЕΡΗΥ ЕΒΟΛ ᲒΙΤΜΠΝΟΥΤЕ / (*ibid.* 31.12) ΝΤЕΡΟΥΡ-ᲒΝΑΥ ЕΒΟΛ ᲒΙΤΜΠΝΟΥΤЕ / (*Ch.* 76.36f.) ᲧΤΑΚΟ ᲒΙΤΝΝΡΩΜЕ / (*III* 134.5f.) ΟΥΟЕΙ ΝΑΥ ЕΒΟΛ ᲒΙΤΜΠXΟЕΙC / (*ibid.* 47.14) ΚΑΛΩC ᲮЕ ЕΥΟΥЕᲧ-ΠΑᲧ ΝЕΒΙᲧ. Again it will be noted that it is the *object*, rather than the combination of 3rd plural and (ЕΒΟΛ) ᲒΙΤΝ-, that marks a construction as a " passive "-surrogate or translation equivalent — not a true passive transform. POLOTSKY (1957a:228f. = *CP* 230f.) accepts (in)transitivity as an intrinsic (lexematic) category in Coptic.

    [7] CHERIX 1979:9 (" absolut ", " moyen ").

3.0.1.2 To replace the three related imported dichotomies of transitive:intransitive verb, direct:indirect object, object:non-object (" adverbial ") expansion, I propose a dependency, *pattern* definition — the adaptation to Coptic of an analytic strategy which, although certainly not novel in any of its essential details, has found more and more adherents in the last three decades[8] (in Coptic grammatical description it has not been applied hitherto) — the pattern (i.e. syntagmatic/paradigmatic) compatibilities of the verb lexeme, leading to a non-dichotomous, gradient classification. In a simplified outline (see also §1.1.2.1):

(a) The *matrix*: The verb occupies a slot (" *Leerstelle* ") — a nuclear one — in a pattern or matrix in which other slots are occupiable by its actor and by rective expansions — " *actants* " in Tesnière's terminology. The actantial potential of the verb, its *valency*, can be conveniently stated by the number and nature of potentially or characteristically occupiable rective slots, i.e. the dependences the given lexeme can contract. Thus cⲱⲧⲡ (ⲛ-/-) (or rather *s-t-p*, with {ō/e/o} allomorphs of a relational archimorpheme), ⲛⲁⲩ (ⲉ-) are *bivalent* verbs, ⲙⲟⲩ2 (-/ⲛ- + ⲛ-), 2ⲱ (ⲉ- + ⲉ-), 2ⲁⲣⲉ2 (ⲉ- + ⲉ-) (*cf.* 2ⲁⲣⲉ2 ⲉⲣⲟⲟⲩ ⲉⲧⲙⲧⲣⲉⲩ- *IV* 56.6), ⲧⲥⲁⲃⲟ (-/ⲛ- + ⲉ-) are trivalent, while ⲛⲕⲟⲧⲕ, ⲉⲓ are univalent. This classification is distinctive: bivalent ϯ, ϭⲓⲛⲉ, ⲉⲓⲡⲉ, ⲙⲟⲩⲧⲉ (" give ", " find [following upon a search] ", " make ", " call ") are different from their trivalent homonyms (ϯ -/ⲛ- + ⲛ- " bring into a [given] state ", ϭⲓⲛⲉ -/ⲛ- + ⲛ- " discover in a [given] state or act ", ⲉⲓⲡⲉ -/ⲛ- + ⲛ- " make into... ", ⲙⲟⲩⲧⲉ ⲉ- + ϫⲉ- " name ") — different by the structural definition of identity. Transitive verbs are bi- or trivalent; intransitive ones, univalent (there are no zero-valents, like " it rains ", in Coptic). The zero-filled rection slot is very important: the case of ϯ ⲟⲩⲃⲉ-/(ⲉ2ⲟⲩⲛ) ⲉ- (etc.) or — syntagmatically — the zero-anaphora (§3.1.1.1.0.1).

(b) *Slot paradigms*, *object* vs. *complement*: some of the positions in the matrix are occupiable by one member only (or zero). These are conditioned, rectional or " case " expansions — a distinctive component of the verb lexeme (see n. 5). Since it is not opposed to another term, this satellite has no proper meaning, but contributes to the complex meaning of the verb syntagm (the preposition ⲉ- when noncommutable — i.e. after ⲛⲁⲩ or 2ⲁⲣⲉ2 — is as rectional, as devoid of meaning, as ⲛ-/ⲙⲙⲟ⸗ or the immediate object-construction cⲉⲧⲡ-, coⲧⲡ⸗). When a verb governs a paradigm of several rectional expansions — different prepositions, with an ensuing change of the overall meaning — we have *homonymy* of distinct verb lexemes, differing in meaning and rection-construction: cⲱⲧⲙ + Ø " lend an ear " (*Ch.* 154.42), cⲱⲧⲙ ⲉ- " listen to ", cⲱⲧⲙ -/ⲛ- " hear ", cⲱⲧⲙ ⲛcⲁ- " obey "[9]. When, however, the isolable meaning of the lexeme does not change as the modifiers commute (ⲉⲓ ⲉⲃⲟⲗ/ⲉ2ⲟⲩⲛ/ⲉ2ⲣⲁⲓ, 2ⲙⲟⲟc 2ⲓ-/2ⲛ-/ⲛcⲁ — but 2ⲙⲟⲟc ⲙⲛ-, rective) we have truly free (in the sense of " grammatically unmotivated ") substitutability, i.e. *non-rectional*, meaningful, extraneous (not verb-componential) *complement* expansion, Tesnière's " *circonstant* "[10]. A thorough study of Coptic verb valency and compatibilities, as also extensive and precise valency listing of all verb lexemes, awaits future scholarship; my concern in the following pages will be the distributional structure and role relationship of the two major rection types, *viz.* the mediate (ⲛ-/ⲙⲙⲟ⸗) and immediate object-constructions.

---

[8] Cf. Schuchardt 1905/6. Definitions in Tesnière 1965, Helbig 1971, Busse 1974, Baum 1976. I have in this paragraph relied heavily upon the illuminating exposition in Rosén 1977.

[9] Cf. Rosén 1977:168ff.

[10] The distinction between " object "-*actant* and " complement "-*circonstant* is difficult, practically and theoretically, and borderline or ambiguous cases abound. See (in addition to the reff. given in §1.1.2.1) the early discussions by von der Gabelentz (1869:383), Frobeen (1878:37f.), Paul (1920:§98). Frei's model does not distinguish between the two (1966:47), although he insists (1961:35f.) on their being kept distinct. Sauvageot (1960:348) relegates this distinction to an extra-grammatical level. See also Trubetzkoy 1939:77f., Mathesius–Vachek 1975:140.

3.0.2 Construction: relevant patterns and environments. Two constructions are in unstructured view rival and collateral [11]: (a) the *immediate* [12] construction: " *a* ", specified as " $a_{dur.}$ " (' *infinitive*$_{dur.}$ → *pronoun/noun syntagm* ') and " $a_{non\text{-}dur.}$ " (*infinitive*$_{non\text{-}dur.}$ → *pronoun/noun syntagm* ') and (b) the *mediate* [12] construction " *b* ", specified as " $b_{dur.}$ " (' *infinitive*$_{dur.}$ → N-*noun syntagm*/MMO-*pronoun* ') or " $b_{non\text{-}dur.}$ " (' *infinitive*$_{non\text{-}dur.}$ → N-*noun syntagm*/MMO-*pronoun* '). In the pattern code, the subscript refers to *environment* factor (of the nuclear verb): *durative*, the (in a sense) marked environment (almost only the present tense in the Bipartite Pattern) and *non-durative*, unmarked (for *Aktionsart* and in a sense morphosyntactically), the Tripartite Pattern and extra-conjugational infinitive. The expansion constituency includes the pronoun and noun syntagm [13]. The descriptive statements below refer to two kinds of structurally significant environments: (*a/b*) *neutralization* environment (§3.1), where patterns (*a*) and (*b*) are mutually unopposed and represented by either (*a*) (§3.1.1) or (*b*) (§3.1.2); (*a:b*) *opposition* environment (§3.2), where (*a*) and (*b*) are mutually opposed. I must concede in advance that these last statements are much less confident and decisive than the neutralization statements. My principal concern in this chapter is to examine the *functional load* of the opposition (*a:b*).

3.0.2.1 The morphophonemic alternation mechanism of the verb lexeme. As is well known, the Coptic verb lexeme may alternate in two pre-object allomorphs marked for syntactic dependence, often prosodically correlated as sandhi-forms (both are related to the syntactically unmarked " absolute " or dictionary form). These allomorphs signal the *verb* - (*satellite*) *noun* (" construct ") or *verb* - (*satellite*) *pronoun* (" pronominal ") syntagmatic links: (ЄΙΡЄ) Р-/ΛΛ⸗, (ϹШΠ) ϹЄΤΠ-/ϹΟΤΠ⸗. Both are specifically *non-final* (the " absolute " is unmarked in this respect). This mechanism, where available, provides the sole signalling of the *verb* - *object* interdependence in pattern (*a*). The sporadic absence (or rather graphemic " veiling ") of the construct allomorph is therefore noteworthy and must be correctly understood. This phenomenon, normal in Akhmimic and quite frequently encountered in Bohairic, is sporadic in Sahidic [14]; it is particularly common in Shenoute as far as literary Sahidic goes. The instances on my files are analyzed in the following table:

[11] The scarceness of a *varia lectio* fluctuation of both constructions ought on principle to prompt the question of some functional difference, be it ever so tenuous (such rare cases are *III* 72 n. 19, *A 1* 174 ΛΥΧΠЄ-ΝЄΥШΗΡЄ/ΛΥΧΠΟ ΝΝЄΥШΗΡЄ). Generally, on the construction of the object: Stern §§490, 491, 493; Schwarze–Steinthal 478-484; Steindorff 1951:§§389ff.; Till §261.

[12] I use " mediate " for an object-expansion marked by an extra-lexemic, post-adjunctal demarcative morpheme, " immediate " for a similar expansion marked *intra-lexemically* (by a segmental/modulation morpheme).

[13] This is in Coptic the meeting point *par excellence* of nominal and verbal syntagmatics. What expands the verb is in fact *the determinator* (a pronoun!), which is in turn expanded by a noun lexeme (§3.1.1.2.1 and Ch. 5).

[14] See Stern 1886:133, Andersson 1904:28ff., Erman 1915:187, Crum 1926:I 250, Sethe apud Kahle 1954:202f., 213f., Till 1928:§147a-b (also *ZÄS* 63:146f., 1928), Quecke 1972:45 with further reff., Shisha–Halevy 1976b:359f. This graphemic veiling is extended (in a comparable dialectological distribution) to the interlocutive (" independent ") personal pronoun when a proclitic subject in the bimembral Nominal Sentence: the atonic allomorph (functionally marked as non-predicative) ΛΝΓ-, ΝΤΚ- (etc.) is graphemically wanting, yet juncturally identifiable. This phenomenon is widespread in Shenoute (Shisha–Halevy 1976b:359): ΛΝΟΝ- (*Ch.* 65.23f., *IV* 19.22), ΛΝΟΚ- (*A 2* 70), ΝΤШΤΝ- (*Thompson* K 3 vo, *IV* 100.7).

Conjugation form (*non-dur.*)	Verb lexeme	Determination paradigms	Subsequent indication of juncture	Reference
perfect	ⲞⲨⲰⲚⲎ	ⲡ-	ⲚⲀⲚ ⲈⲂⲞⲖ	*Ch.* 112.16 ff.
fut. I	ⲞⲨⲰⲚⲎ	ⲡ-	ⲈⲂⲞⲖ	*Ch.* 103.7f.
fut. II	ⲞⲨⲰⲚⲎ	ⲡ-	ⲈⲂⲞⲖ	*Ch.* 65.10f., 78.13f.
perfect	ⲤⲰⲦⲘ	ⲡ-		*A 1* 109
infinit.	ⲞⲨⲰⲘ	ⲡ-		*Ch.* 104.40f.
conjunct.	ⲤⲰⲔ	ⲡ-	ⲈⲎⲢⲀⲒ	*IV* 168.7f.
-ⲦⲢⲈ-	Ⲱⲡ	ⲡ-		*Wess. 9* 173b 4ff.
perf.	ⲦⲰⲘ	ⲡ-		*P* 130⁴ 122 ⲖⲀ
jussive	ⲦⲰⲘ	ⲡ-		*P* 130⁴ 122 ⲖⲀ
aor.	ⲰⲰⲅⲈ	ⲡ-	ⲀⲚ	*IV* 94.3
fut. II	ⲦⲀⲬⲢⲞ	ⲡ-		*P* 131⁵ 43 Ⲣ
perf.	ⲤⲎⲀⲒ	ⲡ-		*IV* 72.20
conjunct.	ⲡⲰⲢⲬ	ⲞⲨ-		*III* 219.18f.
-ⲦⲢⲈ-	ⲬⲞⲞⲨ	ⲞⲨ-	ⲚⲀⲚ	*IV* 107.25
perf.	ⲰⲞⲢⲰⲢ	ⲞⲨ-		*IV* 19.13f. (A)
fut. I	ⲤⲔⲀⲒ	ⲞⲨ-		*A 2* 24
fut. III	ⲞⲨⲰⲘ	Ø-		*IV* 173.4,9
conjunct.	ⲬⲞⲞⲨ	(—)		*IV* 102.8
perf.	ⲤⲎⲀⲒ	(—)		*IV* 72.19
-ⲦⲢⲈ-	ⲡⲰⲎⲦ	(—)	ⲈⲂⲞⲖ	*IV* 100.2f.
fut. I	ⲞⲨⲰⲚⲎ	(—)	ⲈⲂⲞⲖ	*Ch.* 67.26ff.
(dur.)				
pres.	ⲞⲨⲰⲘ	Ø-		*III* 177.18 (A)
pres.	ⲞⲨⲰⲘ	Ø-		*A 2* 509
pres.	ⲞⲨⲰⲘ	Ø-	ⲎⲰⲰⳓ	*III* 202.19
pres.	ⲞⲨⲰⲰ	Ø-		*III* 145.28
pres.	ⲦⲰⳓ	Ø-	ⲘⲘⲎⲚⲈ	*III* 70.7
ⲢⲈⳓ-	ⳞⲰⲦⲂ	Ø-		*Ch.* 27.11f. (§3.4.1)
pres.	ⲰⳞⲤ	Ø-		*IV* 159.2f.
pres.	ⲦⲀⲨⲞ	Ø-		*IV* 159.2f.
pres.	ⲦⲀⲨⲞ	Ø-	ⲈⲂⲞⲖ	*III* 175.24 (A)

determination paradigms:

" ⲡ- "   incl. demonstratives

" ⲟⲩ- "   incl. ⲍⲉⲛ-

Ø-   zero determinator

(—)   indeterminables: ⲍⲁⲍ, ⲍⲟⲉⲓⲛⲉ

The three essential tell-tale features in this distributional picture are:

(a) *Determination complementary distribution*: ⲡ-determination is restricted to the non-durative infinitive, while for ($a_{dur.}$) only zero-determination of the noun is attested, this being reflected in the statements made in §§3.1.1.2.1, 3.1.2.1, 3.2.0.1.

(b) *Prosody*: in most instances we have clear indication of the close juncture of the *verb - object* link, while the rest do not counterindicate this.

(c) *Lexeme morphology*: the class distribution shows all principal lexemic patterns proportionately re-presented [15]. We may conclude that this phenomenon constitutes neither an infringement of the Stern-Jernstedt Rule (§3.1.2.1) nor a special zero-marked construction [16].

3.1   THE OPPOSITION MEDIATE VS. IMMEDIATE OBJECT-CONSTRUCTION SUPPRESSED

3.1.1   OPPOSITION REPRESENTANT: THE IMMEDIATE CONSTRUCTION

3.1.1.1   THE PRONOMINAL OBJECT IN NON-DURATIVE ENVIRONMENT. The following statement, found to be true: " unless contrary overruling factors are involved (§3.1.3.3), and when morphologically feasible, the pronominal direct object occurs exclusively in pattern ($a_{non-dur.}$), with the pronominal state of the verb lexeme expanded by a suffix pronoun ", extends the Stern-Jernstedt Rule (§3.1.2.1) to part of the non-durative environment " uncharted " in JERNSTEDT 1927 [17]. It hardly needs special exempli-fication, as the ($a_{non-dur.}$) pattern is attested on practically every other line in the corpus (many instances will be given *passim* in this chapter). A striking instance is the almost ubiquitous alternation of -ⲭⲱ ⲙⲙⲟⲥ (durative) with -ⲭⲟⲟⲥ (non-durative) — the neutric fem. pronoun -ⲥ-, the formal (" dummy ") object, is cataphoric to the subsequent ⲭⲉ-. This (and similar) alternation is clearly observable in such

---

[15] As a matter of fact we have no general statistics by which to evaluate or weight the class incidence of this phenom-enon. Striking is the high incidence of the biradicals (" ⲕⲱⲧ "; on ⲟⲩⲱⲙ cf. QUECKE 1972:45), also (relatively speaking) of ⲥⲍⲁⲓ, ⲥⲕⲁⲓ, and perhaps the low incidence of the causatives (cf., for Subakhmimic, NAGEL 1964:157-8).

[16] Cf. TILL 1928:§147a-b, EMMEL 1981:142f. (n. 5). For ⲭⲱⲱⲗⲉ ⲥⲙⲁⲍ ⲥⲙⲁⲍ, ⲕⲱⲧ ⲭⲁⲗⲉ ⲭⲁⲗⲉ ", see §1.3.3 above.

[17] Two letters from P. V. Jernstedt to W. E. Crum (Brit. Lib. Add. MS 45685, part II, ff. 302f., 379f.) prove that Jernstedt was well aware of this. He had started investigating the non-durative environment (using as corpus Budge's Martyrdom of Viktor; " Later on " — he writes — " I shall not forget Shenoute "). In his first letter, dated the 26.3.34, he announces his intention to extend the basic formulation of the rule, and reports his interim impression that (for ⲉⲧⲣⲉⲩⲥⲱⲧⲙ), although with a ⲡ-/ⲟⲩ-determinated object the mediate construction occurs as a rule, with the personal pronoun " the treatment is contrary to that in the praesentia ". In the second letter written five years later (1.3.39) Jernstedt, in a criticism of Chaîne's grammar, remarks on the rarity of the mediate construction with pronominals, stating this to be a fact of Shenoute's usage (and incidentally advocating the *Spezialgrammatik* approach). The existence of these letters was kindly brought to my attention by Prof. Bentley Layton.

cotextual configurations [18] as the following: (*A 1* 82-3) ...ЄΥΤΒΒΟ ΜΜΟΟΥ Η ЄΑΥΤΒΒΟΟΥ / (*Ench.* 66b) ЄΚЄΙΡЄ ΜΜΟС Η ΑΚΑΑС ΜΜЄΛΟС ΜΠΟΡΝΗ / (*III* 132.17f.) ЄΙΤЄ ΝЄΝΤΑΥСΟΥШΝЧ ЄΙΤЄ ΝЄΤЄΝСЄСΟΟΥΝ ΜΜΟЧ ΑΝ / (*IF* 108 apud *Dictionary* 742f.) ΝЄΤΖШΖ ΜΜΟС Η ΝЄΝΤΑΥΖΟΖС.

3.1.1.1.0.1 Cotext patterns: the anaphoric pronominal object - suffix vs. zero.

When a pronominal object is anaphoric to a noun syntagm [19] — and this is the usual case — it is observable that the form of the object varies and indeed alternates with the referate determinator (§5.1.1.0.1). This is fully in keeping with — indeed corroborative of — the general theory of the noun syntagm in Coptic (§5.1.1), according to which the determinator is the prime nucleus, the lexeme its first expansion: the referate of the anaphoric object is the article, not the noun lexeme:

(1) ' {п-}/{ΟΥ-}/∅- ΝΙΜ → *suffix pronoun* ': (*Ch.* 104.8f.) ЄΚШΑΝЄΙΡЄ ΜΠΖΑΠ ΜΗ ΝΤΑΚΑΑЧ ΝΑΚ / (158. 14ff.) ΟΥΟΝ... ЄΜΝΤΑЧ-ΠΟЄΙΚ ЄΟΥΟΜЧ / (*III* 38.3) ΠЄΙΖШΒ ΑΙΝΑΥ ЄΡΟЧ / (*ibid.* 34.28f.) ЄΥΛΟΒЄ ΝСΑΠΡΑΝ ЄΤ-ΡЄΥΧΙΤЧ ΑΥШ ΝСΑΝЄΖΒΗΥЄ ΑΝ ЄΛΑΥ / (*A 1* 256) ΧΙΝΤЄСΒШ ЄΤΝΑΝΟΥС ЄΧΟΟС ШΑΠΖΑΠ ΜΜЄ ЄΛΑЧ / (*III* 128.18) ΝЄΘΟΟΥ ΑΤЄΤΝΤΑΑΥ ΝΑΝ / (*ibid.* 25.3f.) ΖШΒ ΝΙΜ ЄΤЄΤΝΟΥΑШΟΥ ШΑΧЄ ΝΙΜ ЄΤЄΤΝΟΥΑШΟΥ ΧΟΟΥ ΑΥШ ΑΡΙ-СΟΥ / (*A 2* 468) ЧΙ ΜΠΡΟΟΥШ ΜΠЄΤΝΑΝΟΥЧ ΝΙΜ ЄΛΑЧ / (*ibid.* 396) ...ΟΥШΑΧЄ ЄΧΟΟЧ / (*A 1* 88) ΖЄΝΠЄΘΟΟΥ ЄΛΑΥ / (*ibid.* 45) ΑΠΝΟΥΤЄ ΤШШ ΝΑΚ ЄЄΙΡЄ ΝΖЄΝΖΒΗΥЄ ЄΥΝΑШΤ... ΜΠЧΤШШ ΝΑΚ ΧЄ-ΜΠΡΑΑΥ.

(2) ' ∅- determinator → -∅ object expansion ': (*A 2* 392) ЄΧΟΟС ΔЄ ΧЄ-ΜΠΟΥΧΙ-ΒΑΠΤΙСΜΑ ΝΙΜ ΠЄΤΟ ΜΜΝΤΡЄ ΧЄ-ΑΥΧΙ / (*ibid.* 59) ΝЄΝΖΒΗΥЄ ΓΑΡ ΝЄΤΤΡЄΝЄΙШΑΧЄ Τ-ΖΑΠ ЄΡΟΝ ΑΥШ ΝΑΝΟΥС ЄΥΤ / (*A 1* 39) ΑШ-ΑΖΟΜ ΑΥШ ΤШШ ΖШ ΝΜΜЄ / (*IV* 82.11) ШΑЧΤ-ΟСЄ ΝΖΟΥΟ ΝЧΤΡЄΖЄΝΚΟΟΥЄΤ / (*ibid.* 83.3) ...ЄΚΤ-ΖΙСЄ ΝΑΥ ЄΚΤ ΝΑΚ / (*Ch.* 113. 47ff.) ЄΥΧЄ-ΠΝΟΥΤЄ ΓΑΡ ΧΙ-ЄΟΟΥ ΖΝΝЄΥСЄΒΗС ЧΧΙ ΟΝ ΖΝΝΑСЄΒΗС / (*ibid.* 173-4) ЄΙС ШΟΜΤЄ ΝΡΟΜΠЄ ΤΝΗΥ ЄΙШΙΝЄ ΝСΑΚΑΡΠΟС ΖΝΤΒШ ΝΚΝΤЄ ΝΤ6ΙΝЄ ΑΝ ΖΙШШС / (*Ryl. Cat.* 32 No. 68 СΖ) ΜΝΤΟΥ-ΛΑΑΥ ΝΖШΒ ЄΧШ ЄΡΟΙ / (*Ch.* 91.17ff.) ...ЄΝΚШΤЄ ΝСΑΠЄΘΟΟΥ ЄЄΙΡЄ / (*P* 131[8] 105 ro) ΠЄΤ6Ν-ΑΡΙΚЄ ΓΑΡ ЄЧ6ΙΝЄ ΑΝ ЄΖΟΥΝ ЄΠЄΤШΑ-ΧЄ ΑΛΛΑ ЄΠΛΟΓΟС... / (*A 2* 153) ΝΤΑΝΙΜ ΝΡШΜЄ Ρ-ΔΙΚΑΙΟС ЄΝЄΖ ЄΤΒЄΠСΑ ΜΠΗΙ ... ΧЄ-ЄΝΝΑЄΙΡЄ ΑΝΟΝ [20] / (*III* 165.17) ΠЄΤΟΥШШ ЄΡ-ΑΤСШΤΜ ΜΑΡЄЧЄΙΡЄ / (*ibid.* 18.15f.) ΑΝΑШ ΜЄΝ ΜΠΟΥЄΙΡЄ (cf. 17.25) / (*K* 933) ΝСЄΝΑШΡ-ШΗΡЄ ΑΝ ЄΝЄΖ ΝΟΥЄΙШΤ... ЄΑΥЄΙΡЄ ΟΝ ΝΤΑΥЄΙΡЄ ЄΠΧΙΝΧΗ. This is a distinctive and favourite Shenoutean figure, of which the most frequently occurring instance is no doubt the constellation ' Ρ-ΝΟΒЄ → ЄΙΡЄ ' (*III* 16.24) ΝЄΤΝΑΡ-ΝΟΒЄ СЄΝΑЄΙΡЄ ΟΝ... / (*Ch.* 71.31ff.) ЄΙШΑΝΡ-ΝΟΒЄ Η ЄΙШΑΝΤΜЄΙΡЄ, also *ibid.* 65.14f., 66.7, 74.50ff., *III* 93.21, *P* 130[1] 37 ΠΝΖ, etc. *Anaphorically*, then, there is only a binary opposition of *zero:non-zero* determination, the equipollent opposition {п-}:{ΟΥ-}:∅- being simplified [21].

(3) In passing, let us look at two other noteworthy anaphora patterns: (a) (*A 1* 9) ...ЄΥΧШ ΜΜΟС ΧЄ-ЄΥΟ ΝΚΟΙΝΟΝΙΑ (sic) ΜΝΝЄΥЄΡΗΥ ΝСЄΟ ΑΝ ΖΝΟΥСΟΟΥΤΝ — anaphoric zeroing of a predicative-constituent modifier phrase [22] (' ΝСЄΟ ΑΝ ' in *thematic* status, the new rheme being ΖΝΟΥСΟΟΥΤΝ). This brings us to (b) the anaphoric zeroing of a lexeme-componential modifier: (*IV* 181.13) ΜΗΤΑΝΟЄΙ (sic) Ш ΠΡШΜЄ ЄΤ-

---

[18] Notably in the precising " *disjunctio Sinuthiana* " figure (Shisha–Halevy 1975:473, 1976a:37ff.).

[19] The *pronominal predicate* (of a "nominal Sentence "), anaphoric to ΟΥ-, ΖЄΝ-, is ΟΥΑ (ΠЄ)/ΟΥЄΙ (ΤЄ), ΖΟЄΙΝЄ (ΝЄ): (*A 2* 62) ΤЄСΖΙΜЄ ЄΤΧШ ΜΜΟС ΧЄ-ΑΝΓ-ΟΥΠΑΡΘЄΝΟС ЄΟΥЄΙ ΑΝ ΤЄ, *Or.* 159.45ff., 159-160 (von Lemm 1972a:12f., Shisha–Halevy 1976a:35). The predicate resumptive of (п-) is problematic — ΝΤΟЧ ΠЄ, an " illogical " extension of the " *c'est lui* " construction to cover the " *case vide* " of " *il l'est* "; e.g. *Or.* 157.27ff. (see Vergote, *BiOr* 13:226b, 1965); ΠΑΙ in (*A 1* 173) ЄΥΧШ ΜΜΟС ΧЄ-ΝЄΖΟΟΥ ΜΠΟΥΑ ΠΟΥΑ ΝЄ ЄΜΠΑΙ ΑΝ ΠЄ may be another way of expressing this but may on the other hand stand for the whole predication: " this is not the case ". ΖΟΙΝЄ in (*A 2* 254) (animals called) ' ΙШ ' (or) ' САΝΝЄΖ ' (Є)ΝΖΟΙΝЄ ΑΝ ΝЄ refers untypically to a lexemic zero form.

[20] Note that both " transitive " and " intransitive " Ρ- are here represented: see n. 4.

[21] п-, ΟΥ- are both excluded as immediate objects after the durative verb (see below); both are coordinated by ΜΝ-. An apparent exception to this anaphoric pattern: (*A 1* 154-5) ΤΟΡΓΗ Η ΠЄΜΚΑΖ ΝΖΗΤ ЄΤЄΡЄΠΝΟΥΤЄ ЄΙΝЄ Η ЄΤЧΝΑΝΤС ЄΧΝΝЄΤЧΝΟΥΧЄ Η ΝЄΤЧΝΑΝΟΧΟΥ ЄΒΟΛ is explicable by the special zeugmatic construction (yet another junctural link, §6.0.2).

[22] Cf. Tobler 1886:86ff.; see Dressler 1973:27f., 32ff. on (zero-)anaphoric constructions (with further reff.).

ⲙⲉⲉⲩⲉ ⲭⲉ-ⲁⲡⲛⲟⲩⲧⲉ ⲕⲱ ⲛⲁⲕ ⲉⲃⲟⲗ. ⲙⲡⲉⲭⲕⲱ / (*Ch.* 183.54ff.) ⲁⲩⲱⲁⲁⲧⲟⲩ ⲙⲉⲗⲟⲥ ⲙⲉⲗⲟⲥ ⲭⲉ-ⲉⲩⲛⲁⲕⲁ-ⲡⲛⲟⲩⲧⲉ ⲛⲥⲱⲟⲩ ⲁⲩⲱ ⲙⲡⲟⲩⲕⲁⲁⲩ / (*P* 130¹ 35 ⲣⲙⲅ) ...ⲛⲧⲉⲧⲉⲭⲙⲁⲧⲟⲩ ⲧⲏⲣⲥ ⲃⲱⲕ ⲉⲃⲟⲗ ⲍⲙⲡⲟⲩⲥⲱⲙⲁ ⲏ ⲥ̅ⲩⲁⲁⲧ ⲛⲃⲱⲕ (*IV* 67.7f.) ⲉⲩⲱⲁⲛⲕⲱⲗⲍ ⲉⲕⲗⲭ-ⲡⲁⲧ ⲉⲛⲛⲁⲕⲱⲗⲭ ⲧⲏⲣⲛ ⲉⲩⲱⲁⲛⲕⲱⲗⲍ ⲉⲧⲱⲟⲩⲛ ⲉⲍⲣⲁⲓ ⲉⲛⲁⲧⲱⲟⲩⲛ with both zero object and anaphorically zeroed modifier, proving their basic similarity. Also *A 2* 520 (ⲟⲩⲁⲍⲟⲩ ⲛ̅ⲥⲁ- → ⲟⲩⲁⲍⲟⲩ), 360 (ⲕⲁⲁⲩ ⲛ̅ⲥⲱⲭ → ⲕⲁⲁⲩ); compare (*P* 131⁷ 39 vo) ⲡⲉⲧⲙⲟⲕⲍ ⲛ̅ⲍⲏⲧ ⲙⲁⲣⲉⲭⲙⲕⲁⲍ (see n. 4).

3.1.1.1.0.2 THE OBJECTIVE PRONOUN PARADIGM. As may be gathered from §3.1.1.1.1, the suffix-pronoun paradigm, when expanding the verb, is *post-lexemic*. When, on the other hand, the pronominal object does not bound on the lexeme (and in isolated, morphologically peculiar cases where it does) we find an allomorphic paradigm — that of the *objective pronoun* (which, in contradistinction to the suffixes, is objective only). The objective pronoun occurs:

(a) After a (synchronic) suffix-pronoun in possessor role in the verboids ⲟⲩⲛⲧⲁ⸗, ⲙⲛⲧⲁ⸗ [23]. Here the objective pronoun is usually anaphoric to the antecedent (most often, substantivizing article) of the relative verboid: ' (ⲡ)ⲉⲧⲉⲟⲩⲛⲧⲁ⸗*suffix-pron.*⸗*objective pron.*' and therefore not as a rule found in the interlocutive persons [24]: *Singular*, *masc.*: -ⲭ, – ⲉⲧⲉⲟⲩⲛⲧⲁⲭⲭ (*A 1* 41), ⲙⲛⲧⲁⲕⲭ (*Or.* 158.2f.), – ⲉⲧⲉ-ⲟⲩⲛⲧⲁⲓⲭ (*A 2* 325), ⲟⲩⲛⲧⲁⲩⲭ, ⲙⲛⲧⲁⲩⲭ (*III* 172.18, 90.18), ⲟⲩⲛⲧⲁⲛⲭ (*A 2* 10, *P* 130¹ 132 ⲧⲕⲅ); *fem.*: -ⲥ, – ⲉⲙⲛ-ⲧⲁⲕⲥ (*P* 130⁴ 94 ⲥⲅ, 131⁶ 88 ro), ⲟⲩⲛⲧⲁⲭⲥ (*III* 85.14, 100.12, *Berl.* 1613 7 ⲥⲍ), – ⲉⲧⲉⲟⲩⲛⲧⲁⲓⲥ (*Mich. 550* 13 ap. *Dictionary* 563b), -ⲉⲧⲉⲟⲩⲛⲧⲁⲩⲥ (*P* 130⁴ 76 vo). *Plural*:-ⲥⲟⲩ (*Ch.* 23.48f., *K* 929), ⲟⲩⲛⲧⲁⲛⲥⲟⲩ (*III* 119.1).

(b) After an indefinite 3rd-person-plural suffix, diachronically in actor role, synchronically a semi-analyzable component of the lexeme: ⲭⲟⲟⲩ "send", ⲧⲛⲛⲟⲟⲩ "fetch", "send", (ⲧ)ⲧⲟⲟⲩ "make give" in *non-durative* environment (see Obs. (3) below)): *Singular, 1st person*: -ⲧ, ⲉⲩⲧⲙⲭⲟⲟⲩⲧ (*A 1* 465); *2nd pers. masc.*: -ⲕ, ⲁⲭⲧⲟⲟⲩⲕ (*IV* 193.10), ⲧⲛⲛⲟⲟⲩⲕ (*III* 38.21); *3rd person masc.*: -ⲭ, ⲭⲟⲟⲩⲭ (*IV* 88.18, *Ch.* 66.27), (ⲧ)ⲧⲟⲟⲩⲭ (*P* 131⁶ 44 ⲣⲓⲥ); *Plural, 3rd person*: -ⲥⲟⲩ, -ⲥⲉ, ⲧⲛⲛⲟⲟⲩⲥⲟⲩ (*III* 24.23), ⲭⲟⲟⲩⲥⲉ (very common: *III* 167.21f., *IV* 64.20, *Ch.* 40.23ff. etc.), (*III* 187.5).

(c) After ⲥⲍⲁⲓ (in variation with ⲥⲁⲍ⸗), ⲁⲡⲓ⸗ : *3rd pers. plur.* ⲥⲍⲁⲓⲥⲟⲩ (*Ch.* 94.15f., 185.23f., 160.2, *v.l.* ⲥⲁⲍⲟⲩ), ⲁⲡⲓⲥⲟⲩ (*III* 25.4): a case of ⲓ-final lexemes.

Observations: (1) Morphophonemically, most instances (excepting only ⲟⲩⲛⲧⲁⲕ⸗ (?), ⲁⲡⲓ⸗) could be phrased as "V$\underline{S}$-*pronoun*" ($\underline{S}$ = non-syllabic sonant, to include ⲭ).

(2) Only -ⲥⲟⲩ [25] is, properly speaking, a distinctive ecxlusive member of this paradigm: all others (and the list is probably incomplete) are homonymous with the corresponding suffixes or (ⲥⲉ) prefix.

(3) Some examples show the objective pronoun in case (b) to be in alternation with the mediate object-construction, viz. in *durative* environment: (*III* 150.7) ...ⲉⲉⲓⲭⲟⲟⲩ ⲙⲙⲟⲟⲩ / (*ibid.* 187.8) ...ⲉⲧⲉⲧⲛⲧⲛⲛⲟⲟⲩ ⲙⲙⲟⲟⲩ; like the suffix-pronoun, then, it is regulated by the Stern-Jernstedt Rule; in case (a), on the other hand, it is not commutable with ⲙⲙⲟ⸗.

3.1.1.2.1 NOMINAL/PRONOMINAL OBJECT: ZERO-DETERMINATED NOUN, SUBSTANTIVIZED RELATIVE, INDETERMINABLES. (1) The *zero-determinated* nominal object enters exclusively the constructions

---

[23] See STERN §§316, 342, STEINTHAL–MISTELI 1893:293.

[24] In (*A 1* 41) ⲡⲟⲩⲱⲱ ⲉⲧⲉⲟⲩⲛⲧⲁⲭⲉ ⲉⲍⲟⲩⲛ ⲉⲣⲟⲭ "the desire thou (fem.) hast for him" the order of elements may be conditioned (but in *Joh.* 4:18 [also *P* 130³ 10, not. Sh.] we do find (ⲡ)ⲉⲧⲉⲟⲩⲛⲧⲉⲉⲭ). Comparable cases are *Joh.* 16:15 (Chester Beatty and 3 of Horner's MSS) ⲉⲧⲉⲟⲩⲛⲧⲉⲥ-ⲡⲁⲉⲓⲱⲧ "which my Father has", *1 Joh.* 4:16 ⲧⲁⲅⲁⲡⲏ ⲉⲧⲉⲟⲩⲛⲧⲥ-ⲡⲛⲟⲩⲧⲉ "which God has" and *NHC XI* 16.10f. ⲟⲩⲛⲧⲉⲥ-ⲛⲏ "they have it" — all with a non-personal possessor.

[25] Discussed by Piehl (*ÄZ* 33:40ff. [1895]), Spiegelberg (*ÄZ* 53:133f. [1917]) and Till (*WZKM* 33:128 ff. [1926]), who typically considers these combinations "*unsinnig*".

($a_{dur.}$), ($a_{non-dur.}$) [26]: (*A 1* 256) ϨΟΙΝΕ ΜΕΝ ΕΥ†-ΚΑΡΠΟC ΝCΑϨΡΑΙ ϨΕΝΚΟΟΥΕ ΔΕ ΕΥ† ΜΠΕΥΚΑΡΠΟC ΝCΑΤΠΕ / (*A 2* 481) ΠΑΙ ΕΤϢΕΕΤ-ΡϢΜΕ ΝΟΥCΙΑ ΜΠΔΙΑΒΟΛΟC / (*ibid.* 352) ϤΡ-ΔΙΚΑΙΟCΥΝΗ / (*P* 130⁵ 34 ι) CΕΟΥΕϨ-ΒΑΡΟC ΔΕ ϨϢϢϤ ΕΧΜΠΡϢΜΕ / (*Ch.* 154.52ff.) ΕΥϢΑΝΟΥΕϨ-ΜΑΤΟΙ ΕΡΟΝ. In more precise rephrasing, this may be taken as a phenomenon of mutual exclusion between Ν-, the marker of construction (*b*), and the zero determinator which, as nucleus of the noun syntagm (§5.1.1), is really the object. This is a secondary statement, overruling others (§3.1.2); it does not invalidate them or constitute a deviation. It is absolutely essential here to define the zero for which this statement is true: it is only that zero which is commutable in a full paradigm with the two other determinators (§5.1.1.0.1), *viz.* {Π-}/{ΟΥ-}/Ø-, whereas a zero determinator in a paradigm not including either of the other two is not incompatible with Ν-, and hence does occur in construction (*b*). Consider the following: ΟΥ-*less paradigm*: -ΚΕ-/ΝΚΕ- (*III* 74.8, 19.5f.), —/Ν + *cardinal numbers* [27] (*III* 52.8, *IV* 124.7, *Berl.* 1613 5 vo [ΕΑΝΟΥϤΡ-ΜΑΑΒ/-Ρ-ϪΟΥϢΤ] *vs. III* 157.28, 112.1f., *IV* 103.6 — note *IV* 67.6 ΕΝΕΙΡΕ ΝΡϢΜΕ CΝΑΥ); Π-*less paradigm*: -ΛΑΑΥ/ΝΛΑΑΥ (*III* 94.1, *Ch.* 130.28f.), -ΟΥ/ΝΟΥ (interr.; *IV* 95.17, *A 2* 366 ΕΙΧΕ-ΟΥ *vs. III* 45.23, *Ch.* 166.1). *Indeterminables*, of course, do not count as zero-determinated, hence ought to be compatible with Ν-. I can, however, find examples of pattern (*b*) only for the indefinite ΡϢΜΕ [28]: (*IV* 80.18) ΝΝΕΡϢΜΕ ΠΡΟΤΡΕΠΕ ΝΡϢΜΕ. For ΝΙΜ (*Ch.* 78.46ff.), ΟΥΗΡ (*ibid.*, *III* 107.20f., *IV* 80.15), ϨΑϨ (*Ch.* 29.15ff., *III* 25.4f.), ϨΟΙΝΕ (*III* 139.4f.) I have only examples of the immediate construction.

(2) ΠΕΤ- (etc.), the substantivized relative syntagm, for which we distinguish (§5.2.3.1) two distinct patterns: (a) ΠΕΤ-/ΤΕΤ-/ΝΕΤ-, present, future, perfect etc. — not further determinable (i.e. Π-, the nuclear determinator, is always initial in this syntagm) and (b) ΠΕΤ-, further determinable: present tense only, Π- uncommutable (hence not a determinator, but a nominalizator morph). Determinators here include the definite (not feminine), indefinite (singular and plural), zero, Ø-... ΝΙΜ; see (3). Pattern (a) is compatible with the object marker Ν- (obligatory in the durative, §3.1.2.1): (*III* 15.23f.) ϨΜΠΤΡΕΚΤϢΡΠ ΝΝΕΤΕΝΟΥΚ ΑΝ ΝΕ / (*ibid.* 109.2f.) ΟΥΑΓΑΘΟΝ ΔΕ ΟΝ ΠΕ ΕΤΡΑϪϢ ΝΗΤΝ ΜΠΕΝΤΑΟΥΠΡΕCΒΥΤΕΡΟC... ϪΝΟΥΙ ΕΡΟϤ / (*ibid.* 205.4f.) ΤΕΤϬΑΙΟ ΝΝΕΤΡ-ΝΟΒΕ... ΤΕΚΡΙΝΕ ΝΝΕΤΝΗΥ ΝΕ / (*IV* 58.26)... ΝϤΟΥϢΜ ΜΠΕΤϤΝΑΟΥΟΜϤ / (*ibid.* 43.28) ΜΠΟΥ† ΜΠΕΤΕΡΟΟΥ / (*Ch.* 55.10ff.) ϪΕ-ΝΝΑϪϢ ΝΑϤ ΜΠΕΤΕϢϢΕ, but occurs also (in non-durative environment) in the immediate construction: (*III* 121.21f.) ΕϤϢΑΝΤΜΧΕ-ΠΕΤΕϢϢΕ / (*IV* 88.1) ΝΝΕΟΥΑ Η ϨΟΙΝΕ ΟΥΕΜ-ΝΕΤCΟΤΠ. Pattern (b) is, to my knowledge, found only in the immediate construction (incompatibility with Ν-?): *durative*: (*IV* 7.11) ΕΝΕΜΠΑΙ Ρ-ΠΕΘΟΟΥ ΑΝ / (*ibid.* 128.27, *Ch.* 63.9f.) — ΕΤΡ-ΠΕΘΟΟΥ, *non-durative*: (*III* 104.1) ΑϤΧΕ-ΠΕΘΟΟΥ / (*IV* 3.17f.) ΕΥϢΑΝΡ-ΠΕΤΝΑΝΟΥϤ / (*III* 150.21)) ΕΡ-ΠΕΤΝΑΝΟΥϤ etc.

(3) Ø-...- ΝΙΜ, the discontinuous determinator, and ... - ΝΙΜ, the postpositive determinator (§5.1.1.0.1) are distinct from zero determination, and are both compatible with Ν- [29]: (*Wess. 9* 179d 7f.) ΕΥΜΟCΤΕ ΜΠΕΘΟΟΥ ΝΙΜ / (*III* 20.5f.) ΕΝΕΙΡΕ ΝϨϢΒ ΝΙΜ ΝΑΓΑΘΟΝ / (*Ch.* 85.7f.) ΕΚΜΕ ΝϨΑΠ ΝΙΜ ΜΜΕ / (*III* 113.11) ΑΝCϢϢ ΝΝΟΒΕ ΝΙΜ / (*ibid.* 151.24) ...ΕΥΚϢ ΕΒΟΛ... ΝΑΡΙΚΕ ΝΙΜ. In the immediate construction: (*IV* 85.22) ϢΑΡΕ-ΠΕϤϨΗΤ ΤCΤΕ-ϨΝΟ ΝΙΜ ΕΒΟΛ.

---

[26] So explicitly in JERNSTEDT 1927:70, in terms of compatibility. It is interesting to note that the residual pre-object *nomina agentis* (construct participles, historically) have almost exclusively zero-determinated objects: ϤΑΙ-ΡΟΟΥϢ (*Ch.* 199.34f.), ΜΑΙ-ΝΟΥΤΕ (*III* 120.15), ΜΑΙ-ΤΟ ΝϨΟΥΟ (*Ch.* 110.10f.), ΜΑCΤ-ϨΗΚΕ (*Ch.* 104.25), ΜΑCΤ-ΡϢΜΕ (*III* 120.13), and so on. It may have been this generic, cliché-like or terminological application of these syntagms which was responsible for their survival into Coptic. (For the similar behaviour of the productive, remodelled analytic ΡΕϤ-, see §3.4.1.)

[27] See §5.1.1.0.1: ΟΥ- as the number "one" does belong in this paradigm.

[28] Pronominal ΡϢΜΕ "(any)one" is the animate counterpart of inanimate ΛΑΑΥ, and must be kept distinct from the determinable {Π-}/{ΟΥ-}/Ø-ΡϢΜΕ "a (usually male) human being", opposed to CϨΙΜΕ, ΝΟΥΤΕ, ΘΗΡΙΟΝ, etc. The incompatibility of Ν- with zero determination is not absolute. A (very rare) instance of the two morphs co-existing is *Mt.* 10:37 (Sah. and "Middle Egyptian").

[29] ΟΥΟΝ ΝΙΜ in (*Rossi 2/3* 13) ...ΕϤϪΝΟΥ ΝΟΥΟΝ ΝΙΜ is different in that ΟΥΟΝ is in Shenoutean Sahidic indeterminable.

3.1.1.2.2 Nominal / pronominal object: ογεϣ-/ογλϣ⸗, a unique lexicosyntactic overrule ογⲱϣ " desire ", " love " constitutes a well-known (though as yet unexplained) deviation from the Stern-Jernstedt Rule [30]. This lexeme enters the immediate construction only, even with non-zero-determinated nominal object: (*Ch.* 93.38f.) ...εϥϩορϣ ναϥ αγⲱ ενϥογαϣϥ αν / (*ibid.* 167-8) ...εγογεϣ-ⲡⲧⲃⲃⲟ ⲛⲛⲉγϣⲏⲣⲉ / (*K* 9040) ⲧογλϣⲕ ⲧⲱⲛⲉ / (*A 2* 153) ⲙⲏ ⲛⲉⲓⲟⲧⲉ ογεϣ-ⲛⲉγϣⲏⲣⲉ αν ⲏ ⲛϣⲏⲣⲉ ογεϣ-ⲛⲉγⲉⲓⲟⲧⲉ αν ⲏ ⲡⲣⲱⲙⲉ ογεϣ-ⲧⲉϥⲥϩⲓⲙⲉ αν ⲏ ⲧⲉⲥϩⲓⲙⲉ ογεϣ-ⲡⲉⲥϩⲁⲓ αν. When ογⲱϣ " wish " has an infinitival object, we find either the immediate construction or the " absolute " form of the lexeme expanded by (ε + *infinitive*): (*A 2* 238) ⲛⲓⲙ ϭⲉ ⲧⲉⲛογ ⲡⲉⲧογεϣ-ⲡ-ⲡⲓⲥⲧⲟⲥ αν, ⲛⲓⲙ ⲡⲉⲧογⲱϣ αν ⲉⲣ-ⲇⲓⲕⲁⲓⲟⲥ ⲛⲓⲙ ⲡⲉⲧογεϣ-ϩⲁⲣⲉϩ αν ⲉⲡⲉϥⲅⲁ-ⲙⲟⲥ ⲉϥογⲁⲁⲃ ⲛⲓⲙ ⲡⲉⲧογεϣ-ⲛⲁ αν... ⲛⲓⲙ ⲡⲉⲧογεϣ-ⲡ-ⲡⲉⲧⲛⲁⲛογϥ αν, ⲛⲓⲙ ⲡⲉⲧογⲱϣ αν ⲉⲕⲁ-ⲧⲉϥϩⲉⲗⲡⲓⲥ ϩⲓ-ⲡⲛογⲧⲉ / (*Ch.* 23.19ff.) ...ⲉⲕογεϣ-ⲙⲟογⲧϥ / (*ibid.* 68.28f.) ⲛⲧογεϣ-ϫⲟογ αν. Note the variation ⲉⲣⲉογεϣ-ⲧⲣⲁ-/ⲉⲣⲉογⲱϣ ⲉⲧⲣⲁ- in *A 2* 513.

3.1.1.2.3 A trend: the definite nominal object of deriving verbs. (1) The statement made in §3.1.1.2.1 is no doubt most pertinent for those syntagms of the form ' *construct verb-lexeme → Ø-noun lexeme* ' in which the verb has the formal-grammatical role of an auxiliary, noun-to-verb deriving element: ⲣ-ογⲟⲉⲓⲛ " shine ", ⲣ-ⲁⲛⲁϣ " swear ", ⲣ-ⲡⲟⲗⲉⲙⲟⲥ " fight ", ⲣ-ⲑγⲥⲓⲁ " sacrifice ", ⲧ-ⲉⲟογ " honour ", ϫⲓ-ϭⲟⲗ " lie " [31], ⲧ-ⲗⲟⲅⲟⲥ " report ", ϥⲓ-ⲣⲟογϣ " care for, be mindful of " and the like. This impression of the formal role of the nucleus verb is correlatable with the *semantic fusion* role — " univerbation " — in turn relatable to a systemic conception of its function: these are the denominal derived verbs, the Coptic answer to the Indo-European (notably Greek) derivational suffixes [32]: the verbal element is the marker of their verbal compatibilities (hence, the nucleus) and of their privileges of occurrence, while the zero-determined lexeme, providing the lexical content, is equivalent to the *root* constituent in the Indo-European derived stem, a " *forme base de motivation* " — accordingly, the zero determination is here operative [33]. Now it is my impression, which I offer here for what it is worth and which must still be confirmed or disproved empirically and on a statistical basis, that determination of the object in similar syntagms does not affect the construction — still ($a_{\text{non-dur.}}$), immediate — nor perceptibly the semantic univerbation; the only difference is that the nominal constituent is in this way accommodated to expandability and is characterized as (relatively) independent (a junctural indication). A few representative instances: -ⲣ-ⲡϩⲱⲃ (*Ch.* 103.24f.), -ⲣ-ⲛⲛⲟⲃⲉ (*Ch.* 57.57), -ⲣ-ⲡϩⲁⲡ, -ⲣ-ⲡⲉϥϩⲁⲡ (*Ch.* 86.42, 134.26f.), -ⲣⲑⲉ ⲛ- (*Ch.* 82.2,5, 182.54), with -ⲣ-ⲧⲉϥϩⲉ (*Ch.* 189.47f.) and -ⲣ-ⲧⲉⲓϩⲉ (*III* 177.6), -ⲣ-ⲡⲃⲟⲗ (*IV* 158.17)

---

[30] Jernstedt 1927:70. Nagel 1964:296f. attributes this aberrant property of ογⲱϣ to its " defectiveness ", insofar as what he terms a " personal passive " function (i.e. its intransitive reference in a non-durative environment) is concerned. I doubt that this reference is so much a property of the lexeme as a function of its environment, or that it is unique to ογⲱϣ (cf. ⲁϥογⲱⲛ ⲏ ⲁγογⲱⲛ ⲙⲙⲟϥ *A 1* 108 and Funk 1977:27ff., 30, 34) and that this accounts for this unusual phenomenon — the absence of a syntagmatically identifiable *durative infinitive*. It is true that ογⲱϣ, a " transitive " verb, is not opposed to a passive stative (ⲥⲉογⲁϣϥ ϩⲓⲧⲛ-, e.g. *Ch.* 106.47f. is suppletive), but neither are ⲙⲟⲥⲧⲉ " hate ", ϭⲓⲛⲉ " find ", ⲥⲱⲧⲙ " hear ", ϩⲓογⲉ " throw " (in Sah.) and quite a few others — all subject to the Stern-Jernstedt Rule. *Semasiological* incompatibility with durativity cannot be ruled out as the explanation (note the comparable exclusion of " verbs of perception and feeling " from the progressive category in English), but can only be inferred, not proven. We must for the present content ourselves with pointing out the special treatment of this lexeme — unless one accepts as " explanation " the parallel Demotic idiosyncrasy of *mr* (Parker 1961:183f., Johnson 1974:59, 61).

[31] For ϫⲱ we have four juncture grades (§6.0.2): ϫⲱ#, ϫⲉ-, ϫⲓ + (with a weakening link ε → ι), ϫⲟⲟ⸗ (cf. Steinthal–Misteli 1893:91f., 281 for a grading of the *verb-object* juncture).

[32] These too are probably nuclei in their syntagms (Barri 1977:29).

[33] Cf. Guillaume 1919:236f. (" mélange de mots " in " traitement zéro entre verbe et régime direct "); Dubois 1965: 150f., 154f. (" l'absence de l'article supprime l'existence du syntagme nominal "); Krámský 1972:36 (Collinson's definition), 58. The valency model of the compound verb is not straightforward; I suggest the assignment of the whole syntagm to the zero slot of the matrix: like ⲥⲱⲧⲡ $\overset{\text{ø}}{|}$ ⲙⲙⲟ⸗ $\overset{1}{,}$ ⲛⲁγ $\overset{ø}{|}$ ⲉⲣⲟ⸗ $\overset{1}{,}$ so ⲣϩⲁⲗ $\overset{ø}{|}$ ⲙⲙⲟ⸗ $\overset{1}{,}$ ⲣϩⲁⲡ $\overset{ø}{|}$ ⲉⲣⲟ⸗ $\overset{1}{}$ (see §§3.1.2.0.1 and 3.1.2.2.2 below).

and -P-ΠЄϤΒΟλ (*IV* 82.17), -P-ΤЄΥϬΟΜ (*III* 165.11, *IV* 159.9f.), -P-ΠΜЄЄΥЄ, -P-ΠЄϤΜЄЄΥЄ (*Ch.* 71.44f., *III* 146.31), -P-ΠϢΒϢ (*Ch.* 102.42, *IV* 49.9 ΤЄΟΒϢ) *vs.* ΑΡЄΡ-ΠϢΒϢ, -P-ΤΝΗCΤЄΙΑ (*Ch.* 101.11f.), -P-ΠΑΓΑΘΟΝ, -P-ΠΠЄΤΝΑΝΟΥϤ (*III* 115.25, *Ch.* 180.2f.), -P-ΠΟΥϢϢ -P-ΠЄϤΟΥϢϢ (*III* 134.3f., *Ch.* 49.53, 100.25f., 134.48f.), -P-ΠΠΟΝΗΡΟΝ (*Ch.* 105.50f.), -P-ΤCΥΝΑΖΙC (*IV* 155.25), -P-ΠЄϤΜΤΟΝ (*IV* 172.21, *Wess. 9* 154d 20ff.), -P-ΤΜЄ (*IV* 91.3), -P-ΤЄΙΑΝΟΜΙΑ (*IV* 114.1), -P-ΠЄΖΟΥΟ (*Ch.* 157.5f.), etc.; with indefinite determination: -P-ΟΥΑ-ΝΑϢ (*III* 16.12), -P-ΖЄΝΘΥCΙΑ (*III* 73.13), -P-ΟΥΝΑ (*IV* 114.20, *Ch.* 162.50f.); other auxiliary verbs: -ϬΝ-ΠΤΥΠΟC (*III* 114.13), -ϬΝ-ΟΥΝΑ (*Ch.* 104.13f., 118.31f.), -ϬΜ-ΠΟΥΟЄΙϢ (*Ch.* 101.5f., *III* 204.7), -ϬΝ-ΘЄ "find means" (*III* 99.6f., 25), -ϬΜ-Π(ЄϤ)ϢΙΝЄ (*IV* 49.5, 61.8), -ΧΙ-ΠΖΟ (*IV* 119.10; ΧΙ-ΖΟ *III* 39.22), ΧΙ- ΝϬΟΝC (*III* 123.7f., 138.6), etc. [34]

(2) The idea that this preference for construction (*a*) may be symptomatic of the close-juncture contour of these syntagms is perhaps corroborated by the verbs compounded with an "inalienable" noun (and its obligatory possessor-suffix), not all of which are subject to the Stern-Jernstedt Rule [35]: P-ΖΤΗ⸗ (*Ch.* 100.57f., *IV* 128.7, 155.7, *Ch.* 190.7, 191.3f.), ⲧ-ΖΤΗ⸗ (*IV* 94.20f., *III* 195.3) — all non-durative examples.

(3) P- as "verb of incomplete predication" (Curme), i.e. with essential adnexal ("predicative") complementation, "make... into" [36], enters, in non-durative environment predominantly, the immediate construction: (*III* 88.17f.) ΠΚΑΖ ΔЄ ΝΤΑΠΝΟΥΤЄ P-ΝЄΡϢΟΥ ΜΠΙCΤΟC ΝΧΟЄΙC ЄΡΟϤ / (*Ch.* 17.39ff.) ЄΝЄΜΠϤΡ-ΠCΑΤΑΝΑC ΝΑΤϬΟΜ / (*IV* 24.2) ΑΥΡ-ΠΔΙΑΒΟλΟC ΝΒΑλЄ / (*Ch.* 113.9ff.) ...ЄΡ-ΖΑΖ ΝΖΗΤ ΝΡϢΜЄ ΝΡΠЄ... / (*A 2* 293) ⲧΝΑΡ-ΠϢC ΝΟΥCΙϢЄ / note (*Wess. 9* 118a 23ff.) ΑΚΑΑΚ Ν- ... ΑΚΡ-ΖЄΝΚΟΟΥЄ ΝΜΜΑΚ with anaphoric zero (also *Ch.* 192.42f.).

(4) P- (often with predicative complementation) "spend (time)": *III* 28.5f., 42.25ff., 41.12, 132.22, *IV* 104.4 etc. also enters the immediate construction.

(5) So does P- "become" ("intransitive" P-, see n. 4): (*Ch.* 146.14ff.) ΑϤΡ-ΟΥΝΟϬ ЄΜΑΤЄ ΝΒϢ ΝЄ-λΟΟλЄ / (*III* 47.21) ϢΑϤΡ-ΠϢΟΥ / (*ibid.* 136.4f., 145.1) (—) ΑΥΡ-ΠЄΥΧΟЄΙC (cf. ΝЄΙΟ ΜΠΑΧΟЄΙC *ibid.* 145.3).

One plausible explanation for cases (3) to (5) is prosodic-junctural. Apparently, the whole '*incomplete-predication verb* + *nom. object* + *adnexal complement*' complex constitutes a functionally significant prosodic patterning, in which the close juncture of the first two elements — both of which together constitute the *theme* ("logical subject") to which the adnexal complement is the rheme ("logical predicate") — is a functional characteristic.

3.1.2 Opposition representant: the mediate construction

3.1.2.0.1 Ν-/ΜΜΟ⸗: a question of identity. Before proceeding to the core of the object-construction regulation — namely, the durative environment, in which construction (*b*) is the primary rule — let us briefly examine some verifiable facts regarding the characteristics of this construction, ($b_{\text{dur.}/\text{non-dur.}}$). As I see it, the synchronic question [37] to be posed cannot be one of *material* identity ("is Ν-/ΜΜΟ⸗ the

---

[34] ϤΙ-Π(ЄϤ)ΡΟΟΥϢ fluctuates with the mediate construction (ϤΙ ΜΠ(ЄϤ)ΡΟΟΥϢ), which may be due to the homonymy of the absolute and construct allomorphs of this lexeme (*IV* 166.3, 40.4, 19.6, 28.4,11, 36.1f., *Miss.* 283). Exceptions to the rule are relatively infrequent: -ЄΙΡЄ ΜΠΖΑΠ (*Ch.* 104.8f.), -ϬΙΝЄ ΝΟΥΝΑ (*III* 138.7), -ЄΙΡЄ ΜΠΤΥΠΟC (*IV* 156.4f) — all naturally in a non-durative environment.

[35] Cf. Polotsky 1960a:§23 Obs. 1, Layton 1981:258f.

[36] The picture for other verbs with adnexal complementation of their object is less clear. However, consider ΚΑ- in (*IV* 101.17) ...ΝCЄΚΑ-ΝΤΑλΑΙΠϢΡΟC ЄΥΤΑλΑΙΠϢΡЄΙ / (*Mun.* 177) ...ΝϤΚΑ-ΠЄϤΠΑΖΟΥ ЄϤϬΟλΠ, *Ch.* 88.15ff., 198.14ff.

[37] The fallacy that the (*per se* legitimate) diachronic scanning of Ν-/ΜΜΟ⸗ can somehow pass as a synchronic account is not entirely a matter of the past (Böhlig 1977). Similarly, the Indo-European-style case interpretation of Ν- (Steinthal-Misteli 1893:92, 293ff., Stern [see his index, under the various case-names], Till 237, etc.) cannot be considered adequate as a descriptive statement. (See Quecke 1981:260f. on the synchronic predicament.)

"same" lexical entity, throughout its adverbal occurrences?" — a question meaningless anyway as a structural-descriptive inquiry), but rather a taxonomic one of *role relationship*, i.e. of categorial (functional), tagmemic identity. It would advance our understanding to pause here and consider some typical positions and compatibilities:

(a) (*A 2* 107) ⲀⲦⲈⲦⲚⲈⲒⲢⲈ ⲚϨⲈⲚϪⲰϨⲘ / (*A 1* 463) ϨⲢⲀ (imp.) ⲘⲘⲞⲞⲨ / (*III* 114.9f.) ϤⲚⲀⲤⲈⲒ ⲚⲚⲈϤⲠⲞⲚⲎⲢⲞⲚ / (*Borg.* 247 ⲛ) ϤⲚⲀⲤⲒ ⲘⲘⲞⲤ ⲀⲚ / (*III* 96.11) ⲈⲒⲘⲈ ⲘⲘⲞⲔ / (*ibid.* 199.28) ⲘⲠⲞⲨⲀⲘⲀϨⲦⲈ ⲘⲘⲞ / (*Ch.* 71.3ff.) ⲞⲨ ⲠⲈϯⲚⲀϯ-ϨⲎⲨ ⲘⲘⲞϤ... ⲚⲤⲀⲦⲢⲀϯ-ⲞⲤⲈ ⲘⲘⲞⲒ ⲘⲀⲨⲀⲀⲦ / (*ibid.* 82.37ff.) ⲞⲨⲘⲚⲦⲀⲦⲤⲞⲞⲨⲚ ⲦⲈⲚⲦⲀⲤϢⲰⲠⲈ ⲘⲘⲞⲞⲨ / (*IV* 84.15) ⲚⲐⲈ ⲈⲦϤⲞ ⲘⲘⲞⲤ [38].

(b) (*IV* 82.28) ...ⲈϨⲞⲂⲤⲔ ⲘⲘⲞⲞⲨ / (*ibid.* 79.14) ϨⲘⲠⲈⲦⲞⲨⲀⲒⲦⲈⲒ ⲘⲘⲞⲞⲨ ⲘⲘⲞϤ / (*III* 166.22) ⲠⲀⲒ ⲠⲈ ⲠϢⲒ ⲈⲦⲞⲨⲚⲀϢⲒ ⲘⲘⲞϤ ⲚϨⲈⲚⲢⲰⲘⲈ / (*III* 66.21f.) ...ⲚⲤⲈⲦⲞϢϤ ⲚⲞⲨϨⲰⲂ / (*III* 171.20f.) ...ⲈⲦⲢⲈϤⲦⲘⲘⲞⲞⲨ ⲚϨⲈⲚⲀⲚⲀⲄⲔⲎ ⲀⲨⲰ ⲚϤⲦⲤⲞⲞⲨ ⲚϨⲈⲚⲬⲞⲖⲎ / (*A 1* 34) ⲦⲘⲘⲞⲞⲨ ⲚⲞⲨⲞⲈⲒⲔ [39] / (*Wess. 9* 139a 20f.) ⲘⲞⲢⲞⲨ ⲘⲘⲞϤ / (*Ch.* 94.51ff.) ⲠⲤⲘⲘⲈ ⲚⲦⲀⲔⲤⲘⲘⲈ ⲈⲢⲞⲒ ⲘⲘⲞϤ / (*A 2* 385) ⲠϢⲀϪⲈ ⲈⲒⲢⲈ ⲘⲘⲞϤ ⲚⲀⲦⲚⲞⲨⲦⲈ / (*IV* 173.1) ⲚⲐⲈ ⲈⲦⲞⲨⲞⲨⲀϢⲤ ⲘⲘⲞⲤ.

On the basis of this typology one might suggest the following two valency models with ⲛ-/ⲙⲙⲟ⸗ in the rectional slot(s):

	Ø	1	
(a)	V	ⲛ-/ⲙⲙⲟ⸗	
	Ø	1	2
(b)	V	ⲛ-/ⲙⲙⲟ⸗	ⲛ-/ⲙⲙⲟ⸗

Observe: (1) The obvious shortcoming of this scheme is (as far as the nucleus verb is concerned) that it is two-dimensional. The semasiological differences of nucleus — expansion relationship between "ⲥⲱⲧⲡ ⲙⲙⲟ⸗", "ⲁⲙⲁϩⲧⲉ ⲙⲙⲟ⸗", "ϣⲱⲡⲉ ⲙⲙⲟ⸗", "ⲟⲩⲉ/ⲟⲩⲏⲩ ⲙⲙⲟ⸗" and "ⲟ ⲙⲙⲟ⸗" are well substantiated by (and correlatable with) their respective paradigmatic properties (e.g., ⲥⲱⲧⲡ opposed to the stative — also with ⲛ-/ⲙⲙⲟ⸗ opposed to the immediate construction; ⲁⲙⲁϩⲧⲉ "with" no stative, no immediate construction; ϣⲱⲡⲉ with no imm. construction, but opposed to ϣⲟⲟⲡ; ⲟ (ⲛ-) alternating with ⲣ- in non-durative patterns). However, they are not reflected in the syntagmatic models, which do not display the substitution properties of the verbal nucleus (hence are not patterns in the true sense).

(2) In cases like ⲉⲃⲟⲗ ⲙⲙⲟ⸗ (*Ch.* 28.36f.), ⲉⲑⲏ ⲙⲙⲟ⸗ (*IV* 95.16), ⲙⲙⲟ⸗ is a secondary modifier of a modifier nucleus (§1.1.2.4.1), a hierarchy which can be reflected in a syntagmatic model.

(3) In cases like ⲟⲩⲛϭⲟⲙ ⲙⲙⲟ⸗ (*IV* 51.14f.), ⲡⲉⲧⲉⲣⲉⲛⲧⲛϩ ⲙⲙⲟϥ (*ibid.* 96.24), ⲙⲙⲟ⸗ is predicative (predicating "inalienable" possession, in the second position of the Bipartite pattern, §1.2.1.1) and thus not in the valency range of ⲟⲩⲛ.

(4) The fact that the second-slot ⲛ-/ⲙⲙⲟ⸗ remains constant in the case of a "passive transformation" (⟹ ϥϣⲁⲁⲧ ⲛ-/ⲙⲙⲟ⸗, ϥⲙⲉϩ ⲛ-ⲙⲙⲟ⸗) hardly invalidates this structural resolution (cf. Quecke 1981:261): (a) our matrix is a *non-dynamic* characteristic of the *active*, not the passive pattern; (b) on the contrary, the invariability of the second-slot ⲛ- is an important distinctive trait of it, adding a *paradigmatic* aspect to its differentiation from its first-slot homonym.

The above model resolves the identity of ⲛ-/ⲙⲙⲟ⸗ — "1st-slot ⲛ-/ⲙⲙⲟ⸗", "2nd-slot ⲛ-/ⲙⲙⲟ⸗") — which is adequate, from a structural viewpoint.

[38] Cf. Tobler 1908:1ff. ("De la manière dont nous sommes faits").

[39] With a zero-determinated object, we usually find the the prenominal allomorph (immediate construction): (*III* 106.18f.) ⲉⲧⲣⲉⲩⲧⲙⲙⲉϥ-ⲟⲉⲓⲕ ⲛⲑⲁⲓⲯⲓⲥ... ⲁⲩⲱ ⲛⲥⲉⲧⲥⲉϥ-ⲙⲟⲟⲩ ⲛⲑⲁⲓⲯⲓⲥ, but also (*ibid.* 104.13) ⲁⲩⲧⲥⲉϥ-ⲟⲩϩⲙⲝ (cf. Emmel 1981:136).

3.1.2.1 Nominal/pronominal object: pattern-symptomatic (categorial) neutralization: the " stern–jernstedt " rule. The core statement regarding the exclusion of the immediate object construction in durative environment was made by P. V. Jernstedt in clear, albeit non-structural terms (1927:70), in a true milestone of Coptic linguistic writing: " Der Gebrauch des Absolutus ist im Präsensstamm obligatorisch, a) wenn das Objekt, sei's äusserlich, sei's an sich determiniert ist, und b) wenn das Objekt mit unbestimmtem Artikel ist ". The two bound (pre-nominal and pre-pronominal) allomorphs of the verb lexeme are excluded before a non-zero-determinated noun or a pronoun, when this lexeme is predicated in the Bipartite pattern [40] (see §3.1.1.2.1.1 for an inverse exclusion before zero determination. Both cases mean neutralization of the opposition between constructions (*a*) and (*b*)).

3.1.2.1.1 This exclusion is a distinctive feature of the durative predicative verb lexeme, providing yet another vital diagnostic datum — a syntagmatic one — to formally define and distinguish between it and the homonymic non-durative (Tripartite and extraconjugational) one:

$$\text{(ч)сотп} \qquad vs. \qquad \text{(ач)сотп, (п)сотп}$$
$$\text{сотп}^{+} \qquad\qquad\qquad \text{сетп}^{-}$$
$$\qquad\qquad\qquad\qquad \text{сотп}^{=}$$

(subject to overruling, §§3.1.1.2.1-2) giving us a neat formal structural definition of " сотп$_{dur.}$ " and " сотп$_{non-dur.}$ ". I prefer not to take here a stand on the question — essentially speculative and non-descriptive — of whether this exclusion is a consequence or a symptom of the " adverbiality " of the Bipartite predicative verb-lexeme, the wherefore and rationale of this phenomenon [41]. As I see it, the present " durative infinitive " has nothing adverbial about it — it is not a modifier: it is adequately differentiated from its non-durative homonym by both paradigmatic and syntagmatic (pattern and expansion) properties. As far as synchrony goes, I find its structural assignment the only necessary, and quite satisfactory, " explanation ".

An all-important issue which is but marginally within the scope of the present discussion is the correlation of the expansion properties of the present-tense predicate with its two semasiological distinctive features, *durativity* and *actuality*. Under certain circumstances, functional suppression of the durativity feature takes place and is manifested in the invalidation (or overruling) of the Stern-Jernstedt Rule: Jern-

---

[40] Polotsky 1960a:§23 *Obs.* 1-4, Funk 1978a (III). This issue was treated by the early scholars: the outlines were first described by Stern (§490-40); Spiegelberg, *RT* 36:159f. (1912). The last to ignore the rule was Till (1928:§147f.).

[41] This aspect of the question has been treated by Jelanskaja (1970), with a diachronic-mentalistic bias (" How was the adverbial verbal predication *felt*? ") and by Schenkel (1978), who curiously denies the " verbal rection " capabilities of " adverbial " verb forms. The " adverbiality " of the Bipartite predicate *vs.* the " nominality " of the Tripartite predicate is not an explanation, but a tautology, or condensed restatement of pattern (esp. substitution) facts. I cannot see that the " adverbiality " of the durative infinitive is responsible for the exclusion of the immediate construction (where it is excluded): synchronically, the " adverbiality " of this predicate — and of the stative — are established only by substitution. (Moreover, I would not define [as does Schenkell the case of zero-determinated objects as a " *Paradebeispiel* " of *stehende Wendungen* [fixed expressions]): I doubt greatly (to return to the " adverbiality " question) that substitutability alone is sufficient to qualify the Bipartite verbal predicate as a modifier xecept in a vague, general manner of speaking. (Analogously, we would have to consider the predicate in нтеıзе пе [§1.2.1.2, as nominal!) Substitution alone is a notoriously unreliable, lopsided guide for grammatical definition, without the vital syntagmatic ordinate. Just as expansion properties are needed to resolve, e.g., the difference between " *he is trying* " (pres. progressive tense, historically " adverbial ") and " *he is trying* " (adjectival predication): " *he is very trying* ", vs. " *he is trying hard.* " — " *he is more trying than...* " vs. " *he is trying harder than...* ", in addition to the paradigmatic information " he is *trying/irksome/pestiferous* " vs. " he is *trying/attempting/doing...* ") — so in our Coptic case too we need the syntagmatic dimension, the expansion *differentiae specificae*, to reach a formal distinction. (The parallel between the English *-ing*, tense and gerund [historically, ' preposition + " nominal " infinitive '] with its superficial merger with the *nomen actionis*, and the Coptic " gerundial " infinitive, can be carried a long way.)

stedt 1927:70(3), ⲁϥⲟⲩⲱ ⲉϥ- [42]. Jernstedt himself attributed this to the "grammatical union" in the complex '*auxiliary + circumstantial present*', the conjugation base ("*Tempuscharakter*") of the auxiliary dictating the treatment of the lexically more important but grammatically subordinate auxiliate [43]. I find no evidence in Shenoute for this particular neutralization, but we do encounter the *Aufhebung* of durativity expressed in another, namely of the opposition *stative* vs. *infinitive* (for a lexeme with a "movement" sememe), overruling Polotsky 1960a:§9: (*Ch.* 189.32ff.) ⲡϫⲟⲉⲓⲥ... ⲛⲧⲁϥⲟⲩⲱ ⲉϥⲉⲓ ⲉϩⲣⲁⲓ ⲉⲛⲉϥϭⲓϫ (sim. *III* 105.6f., *Ryl. Cat.* 35 No. 70 ⲥⲙⲑ) [44]. It is an open question whether both exclusions — of the immediate object-expansion after transitives and of the infinitive with intransitives — are at all co-extensive, or whether either is symptomatic of any temporal-aspectual distinctive feature; if this is the case, we may glimpse here the syntagmatic-paradigmatic differentiation between an *actual*/durative and *non-actual* (atemporal, "aoristic") present, the latter yet to be empirically established and documented as a formal category [45]. Note, however, that until an independent unified definition of "intransitive" and (grammatically relevant) "movement sememe" is achieved, one runs here the risk of circularity, in basing a categorial definition on an exclusion feature: there are too many ambiguities [46], various componential-modification lexemes ('ⲉⲓ ⲉϩⲣⲁⲓ' 'ⲃⲱⲕ ⲉϩⲟⲩⲛ'), to assume an easily definable lexical "category" of this kind.

3.1.2.2 Nominal/pronominal object: morphological (lexemic) absence of morphophonemic alternation. The mediate construction is the sole one — *even in non-durative environment* — where the morphophonemic-alternation mechanism is not available [47].

3.1.2.2.1 Verbs of Egyptian origin, not compound: 1st-slot, rectional ⲙⲙⲟ⸗: ⲁⲙⲁϩⲧⲉ ⲙⲙⲟ⸗ "hold, grasp" (*III* 199.28, *IV* 86.4), ⲙⲁⲧⲉ ⲙⲙⲟ⸗ "reach, obtain" (*III* 100.22); ϩⲣⲁ ⲙⲙⲟ⸗ "drive off" (*Ming.* 322, *A 1* 463); ⲥⲱⲃⲉ ⲙⲙⲟ⸗ "mock, ridicule" (*III* 104.12); ϣⲟⲩϣⲟⲩ ⲙⲙⲟ⸗ "boast, pride oneself on..." (*III* 68.5f., *A 1* 330); ⲉⲣⲏⲧ ⲙⲙⲟ⸗ "pledge" (*III* 132.2f., 223.18), cf. (?) ⲱⲣⲕ ⲙⲙⲟ⸗ "swear by..." (*P* 130² 96 ⲣⲛⲁ); ⲣⲁϣⲉ ⲙⲙⲟ⸗ "rejoice in..." (*Mich. 550* 18); ⲉⲓⲙⲉ ⲙⲙⲟ⸗ "understand, know" (*III* 96.11);

[42] See also Jernstedt 1959:113 n. 8, and cf. Polotsky 1960a:§9 Obs. 1.

[43] It is only in the *perfective* ⲁϥⲟⲩⲱ ⲉϥ- (with ⲁ- ⲟⲩⲱ ⲉ- the discontinuous tense-morpheme of the *marked perfect* (*vs.* the unmarked ⲁϥ-) that we find this phenomenon; the negative correspondent here is ⲙⲡⲁⲧϥ- (Stern's "perfectum absolutum": ⲙⲡϥ- is unmarked). See Shisha-Halevy 1972, Quecke 1979:442f., Funk 1981:192ff. (Note that ⲁϥⲟⲩⲱ ⲉϥ- is the analytic "renewed" successor of ϩⲁϥ-, the original affirm. counterpart of ⲙⲡⲁⲧϥ- — Polotsky 1960a:§4 n. 1 (see now Funk 1981:191ff.). ⲟⲩⲱ is of course a descendant of the same *w3h* that is fused in ϩⲁϥ-. Thus, the familiar *analysis → synthesis → reanalysis* diachronic spiral is again in evidence.) Shenoutean exx. for this periphrastic tense: *III* 20.26, *IV* 108.15, *Ch.* 15.49f., 136.49ff. ⲟⲩⲱ in a Clause-Conjugation or post-eventive setting (ϣⲁⲛⲧϥ-, ⲉϥϣⲁⲛ-, ⲙⲛⲛⲥⲁⲧⲣⲉϥ-) has a different value: terminative *Aktionsart* ("have finished doing"), with ⲟⲩⲱ fully contributing lexically (e.g. *IV* 69.23, *Ch.* 133.8ff.).

[44] The case of ⲟⲩⲱ/ⲗⲟ ⲉϥϣⲱⲡⲉ (*III* 224,15, *Ch.* 175.35f.) may be different — a pertinent infinitive, expressing *ingression* and opposed to a stative expressing *state*.

[45] Shisha-Halevy 1976a:46 (cf. Young 1961:119f., and §7.2.4.1 below). According to Schenkel (1978:15) the present is generally "tempus-indifferent"; yet this is not strictly true, since, with its durative *Aktionsart* reference, it does have some absolute temporal systemic standing (unike the extratemporal ⲙⲛⲛⲥⲁ-/ϩⲙⲡⲧⲣⲉϥ- or atemporal Clause Conjugation forms). Historically, the category of non-actual present has yet to be traced. For Demotic, cf. Johnson 1974 exx. E44B and E46B; for LE, cf. *nty ḥr jjt* (and not *m jjt*), Wente 1959:96ff., 103ff., Černý-Groll §19.6 and reff. In (*III* 216.18f.) ⲛⲧⲟⲟⲩ ⲁⲛ ⲡⲉⲧⲧⲃⲃⲟ ⲙⲡⲣⲱⲙⲉ ⲟⲩⲧⲉ ϫⲁϩⲙⲉϥ the second infinitive is not a durative predicate, but hierarchically subordinate, an expansion; §6.0.2, link (5).

[46] The typically Shenoutean ⲥⲉⲣⲏⲥ ⲁⲩⲱ ⲥⲉⲣⲟⲉⲓⲥ (*A 1* 177, *III* 74.11, *IV* 24.20) juxtaposes the actual ⲥⲉⲣⲏⲥ "they are awake" and non-actual ⲥⲉⲣⲟⲉⲓⲥ "they are vigilant". Other candidates: (*III* 215.18) ⲛⲁϣⲉ-ⲛⲁⲱⲃϣ ⲉⲧϩⲉ ϩⲓⲧⲛⲛⲓⲧⲏⲩ "fall (as a natural fact)" / (*IV* 22.21) ⲛⲉⲧⲙⲟⲩ ⲧⲏⲣⲟⲩ ϩⲣⲁⲓ ⲛϩⲏⲧⲛ "those that should die" / (*Ch.* 22.49f.) ⲉⲕϩⲉ ⲉⲕⲧⲱⲟⲩⲛ "now and again" (but ⲉⲕⲡⲏⲧ in line 46!) / (*III* 44.1f.) ⲛⲉⲧⲉⲣⲉϩⲉⲛϫⲟ ϩⲉ ⲉϫⲱⲟⲩ ⲉⲩⲙⲟⲩ (observe the connection between this present and the determinated relative).

[47] Stern §§493, 495.

ΝЄ2ϹЄ ΜΜΟ⸗ "wake up" (*A 1* 75); ΝΟЄΙΝ ΜΜΟ⸗ "shake" (*III* 183.12); ΜΤΟΝ ΜΜΟ⸗ "rest oneself" (*III* 219.2f., *IV* 110.25), ϹϬΡΑ2Τ ΜΜΟ⸗ "rest oneself" (*IV* 69.22); ΚШΤЄ ΜΜΟ⸗ "turn" (no pre-object forms in Sh.? *A 1* 84, *Ch.* 44.49f.); ШШΠЄ ΜΜΟ⸗ "happen to..." (*III* 222.4); ΟΥШΝ ΜΜΟ⸗ "open" (*III* 206.18, *RE 10* 160a 14ff.); ϹШΚ ΜΜΟ⸗ (ΝΑΝΑ2) "impel, drag (by force)" (*IV* 79-80, 80.4f., see below for alternative explanations). The appraisal of this group is far from easy. Firstly, the existence or non-existence of pre-object allomorphs is after all often a subject for corpus-valid, not pan-Coptic (i.e. *Dictionary*-based) information: witness the case of ΚШΤЄ, ΟΥШΝ, ϹШΚ (?). Secondly, what about inconclusive, statistical *favouring* of the mediate construction (such as might be impressionistically pointed out for the 'ΚШΤ' class)? I have here employed the convenient expedient of syntagmatic consistency, not looking for a special meaning (i.e. pertinence) for 1st-slot, rectional ΜΜΟ⸗, since I treat only cases where it is unopposed to the immediate construction. Should an instance of such an opposition turn up, it would have to be referred to §§3.1.3.1ff. and scrutinized for pertinence. (With a nominal object after Ν⸗, the situation is even more complicated, not least due to the incomparably more extensive evidence. I have left whatever statement it is possible to make here, to §3.2 below.) Consequently, I do not assume what is often warranted diachronically, namely that ΜΜΟ⸗ has a different "meaning" after, say, ΑΜΑ2ΤЄ, after ϹШΒЄ after ϹΜΜЄ or ШШΠЄ (though here the Ν-rection of the stative, ШΟΟΠ ΜΜΟ⸗ [e.g. *III* 24.9, *IV* 99.8] points to a really distinct entity).

3.1.2.2.2 COMPOUND VERBS OF EGYPTIAN OR GREEK ORIGIN [48]:

Ρ-ΜΝΤΡЄ ΜΜΟ⸗ "testify" (*III* 17.10); Ρ-2ΑΛ ΜΜΟ⸗ "beguile" (*III* 221.28, *P* 130² 60 ob); Ρ-ΑΝΑШ ΜΜΟ⸗ "swear by" (*III* 19.3.11); Ρ-2ΜΜЄ ΜΜΟ⸗ "guide" (*IV* 82.2f., 199.15, both durative); -Ρ-ШΠΗΡЄ ΜΜΟ⸗ "be amazed at, wonder at" (*A 2* 319, dur.); Ρ-ΧΡΙΑ ΜΜΟ⸗ "need" (*IV* 56.5 [dur.], *A 2* 293); ΧΙ-ΗΠЄ ΜΜΟ⸗ "count" (*Ch.* 197.36f.); ΧΙ-ΚΒΑ ΜΜΟ⸗ "revenge oneself on" (*III* 26.11, 64.5f., *P* 130² 53 TIB, 131⁴ 151 M); ΧΙ-+ΒϹ ΜΜΟ⸗ "trip up" (*P* 130² 44 ΡΙΑ, 130⁵ 20 ro); ΧΙ-ΜΗϹЄ ΜΜΟ⸗ "take interest in" (*III* 65.26); +-ΟϹЄ ΜΜΟ⸗ "lose" (*Ch.* 71.6f.); +-2ΗΥ ΜΜΟ⸗ "gain" (*Ch.* 71.3ff., 97.6f.); +-ΝΑΑΚЄ ΜΜΟ⸗ "give birth to" (*A 2* 155 [dur.], *P* 131⁵ 65 vo); ΧΙ-ϹΝΟϥ ΜΜΟ⸗ "bleed", trans. (*III* 73.11); ΤΑШЄ-ΟЄΙШ ΜΜΟ⸗ "proclaim, preach" (*III* 75.20, *Wess. 9* 147a-b, d 21f.); ΚΑ-ΒΟΛ ΜΜΟ⸗ "vomit" (*Ch.* 27.42f.); ϹΜΝ-ϹΝΤЄ ΜΜΟ⸗ "found" (*A 2* 146, *III* 188.14f.); ΟΥЄ2-ϹΑ2ΝЄ ΜΜΟ⸗ "enjoin" (*III* 20.3, *IV* 43.1f.); ΜЄ2-ЄΙΑΤ⸗ ΜΜΟ⸗ "gloat over, look one's fill at" (*Ench.* 71a). At first sight, with the nominal object we face the difficulty of distinguishing *adverbal* Ν-/ΜΜΟ⸗ from *adnominal* Ν-ΜΜΟ⸗ (cf. §§1.0.2, 1.1.1, chapter 4) — the former expanding the verb syntagm, the latter its nominal component; but this distinction is irrelevant in this syntagm, where the two are neutralized.

3.1.2.2.3 VERBS OF GREEK ORIGIN (a specimen selection): ΑΠΟϹΤЄΡЄΙ ΜΜΟ⸗ (*III* 62.23); ϹΤΑΥΡΟΥ ΜΜΟ⸗ (*Ch.* 33.8f.); ΝΟΙ ΜΜΟ⸗ (*III* 204.27); ΔΟΚΙΜΑΖЄ ΜΜΟ⸗ (*Ch.* 13.16f.); ΚΟΛΑΖЄ ΜΜΟ⸗ (*IV* 7.19f.); ΑΠΑΤΑ ΜΜΟ⸗ (*III* 138.15); ΦΟΡЄΙ ΜΜΟ⸗ (*III* 100.4); and so on.

3.1.3 CONDITIONING (SELECTION) OF THE MEDIATE CONSTRUCTION (PRONOMINAL OBJECT, NON-DURATIVE ENVIRONMENT)

3.1.3.1 LEXEMES WITH PERTINENT ΜΜΟ⸗ RECTION. This group should be carefully kept apart from the non-alternating lexemes (§3.1.2.2.1): here we are concerned with verbs that do "have" a presuffixal

---

[48] STERN §509. Cf. §§3.0.1 and 1.1.2.1 (gen. obs., on their valency structuring Ρ-2ΑΛ $\overset{0}{|}$ ΜΜΟ⸗ $\overset{1}{}$).

allomorph and do enter construction (*a*), but also (*b*) (pronominal) — hence, have pertinent expansion (rection/complementation) properties. I am here concentrating on the pronominal object in non-durative environment (exceptions to the statement made in §3.1.1.1): ⲱϣ ⲙⲙⲟ⸗ "read in..." (*III* 192.20, 193.5); ϩⲱⲛ ⲙⲙⲟ⸗ "enjoin", in the following recurring fixed expression: "ⲛⲉⲛⲧⲟⲗⲏ/ⲛϣⲁϫⲉ/ϩⲱⲃ ⲛⲓⲙ/ⲛⲑⲉ/ⲡ /ⲛ- ...(ⲉ)ⲛⲧⲁⲛⲉⲛⲉⲓⲟⲧⲉ ϩⲱⲛ ⲙⲙⲟ⸗ ⲉ/ⲛ-ⲧⲟⲟⲧ⸗" (*III* 173.5, *IV* 65.3f.,10, 47.22f., 48.14f., 123.6,14f.,19, *Wess. 9* 173d 14ff., *A 2* 101, 500, *P* 131[6] 21 ro etc.) — a cliché reminiscent of (OT) Scripture idiom? Cf. *Ruth* 3:6, *I Sam.* 13:13, etc.; cf. also ⲟⲩⲉϩⲥⲁϩⲛⲉ ⲙⲙⲟ⸗, §3.1.2.2.1; ϩⲱⲧⲃ ⲙⲙⲟ⸗, ⲙⲟⲩⲟⲩⲧ ⲙⲙⲟ⸗ "slay" (intensive, deliberate, iterative, "augmentative" — occasionally conative?) (*Ch.* 28.7f., 121.27f., both infinitives: cf. *A 1* 167 ⲉⲩϣⲓⲛⲉ ⲛⲥⲁⲙⲟⲩⲟⲩⲧ ⲙⲡϫⲟⲉⲓⲥ, but *Ch.* 52.50f. ⲕⲱⲧⲉ ⲛⲥⲁⲑⲉ ⲙⲙⲟⲟⲩⲧϥ); so also ϣⲱⲱⲧ ⲙⲙⲟ⸗: (*A 2* 345) ...ⲉⲧⲣⲉⲩⲣϣⲣⲡ-ϣⲱⲱⲧ ⲙⲙⲟⲟⲩ, (*Leyd.* 328) ⲏ ⲛⲥⲉϣⲱⲱⲧ ⲙⲙⲟϥ ⲏ ⲛϥϣⲱⲱⲧ ⲙⲙⲟⲟⲩ; ϣⲱⲗ ⲙⲙⲟ⸗: (*III* 205.28 ...ⲉⲧⲣⲉⲩⲑⲗⲓⲃⲉ ⲙⲙⲟ ⲁⲩⲱ ⲛⲥⲉϣⲱⲗ ⲙⲙⲟ, but see §3.1.3.2.2-3 (also for ⲥⲱⲱϥ ⲙⲙⲟ⸗); ⲥⲱⲣ ⲙⲙⲟ⸗: (*A 2* 513) ϯⲁⲍⲓⲟⲩ ⲙⲡⲛⲟⲩⲧⲉ... ⲉⲧⲣⲁⲣ-ⲃⲟⲗ ⲉⲡϩⲁⲡ ⲛϯⲙⲛⲧⲛⲟⲩⲧⲉ ⲛⲛⲟⲩϫ ⲛⲧⲁⲣⲁⲣⲭⲉⲓ ⲟⲛ ⲛⲥⲱⲣ ⲙⲙⲟⲥ. ⲥⲱⲕ ⲛϫⲛⲁϩ (*IV* 79-80) and ⲥⲱⲕ (ⲛϫⲛⲁϩ understood, *IV* 80.7f.) have probably this rection only, differing from ⲥⲱⲕ alone (so too in the NT: *Luc.* 12:58, *Joh.* 6:44, 21:11, *Act.* 16:15 etc.).

3.1.3.2.1 Cotextual secondary selection of ⲙⲙⲟ⸗ ("non-reflexive object"). Here we encounter a secondary (ad hoc?) opposition or cotextual relevantization: a *non-reflexive* reference of ⲙⲙⲟ⸗, resolving the ambiguity of identical 3rd-person pronouns (the numbers indicate the personal reference of the pronoun): (*IV* 44.5) ...ⲉⲧⲣⲉϥ[1]ⲕⲱ ⲙⲙⲟϥ[2] ⲛⲁϥ[1] / (*Ch.* 44-5) ..ⲉⲧⲉⲧⲛⲧⲣⲉⲩ[1]ⲛⲟⲩϫⲉ ⲙⲙⲟⲟⲩ[2] ⲉⲡⲙⲟⲟⲩ / (*ibid.* 44.49f.) ...ⲉⲧⲣⲉⲩ[1]ⲕⲱⲧ ⲙⲙⲟⲟⲩ[2] / (*ibid.* 71.19f.) ...ⲉⲁϥ[1]ϥⲓ ⲙⲙⲟϥ[2] ⲛⲧⲙⲏⲧⲉ / (*IV* 89.1f.) ⲉⲩ[1]ⲛⲁϫⲟⲟⲩⲥⲟⲩ[2] ⲉⲡⲉⲓⲙⲁ ⲛⲥⲉ[1]ⲧⲱϩ ⲙⲙⲟⲟⲩ[2] ⲛⲥⲉ[1]ϯ ⲙⲙⲟⲟⲩ[2] ⲛⲁⲩ[3]. Here the rhythmic factor must be considered, §3.1.3.3.2.

3.1.3.2.2 Miscellaneous. (a) *Biblical reminiscence*: (*III* 56.1) ⲁⲧⲉϥⲁⲅⲁⲡⲏ ⲁⲛⲟⲕ ϫⲓ ⲙⲙⲟⲓ (*Cant.* 2:5) and (*IV* 79-80) ...ⲛϥⲥⲱⲕ ⲙⲙⲟⲓ ⲛϫⲛⲁϩ (reminiscence? of *Act.* 16:15): *III* 196-7 *passim*, ⲡⲱϩⲧ ⲙⲙⲟϥ/ ⲙⲡⲉϥϭⲱⲛⲧ etc., adaptation of *Ez.* 20:13.21, 36:18 (etc.).

(b) *Paradigmatic and cotextual association* (?): (*III* 196-7 *passim*) (-)ⲁⲙⲁϩⲧⲉ ⲙⲡⲉϥϭⲱⲛⲧ — (-)ⲡⲱϩⲧ ⲙⲙⲟϥ/ⲙⲡⲉϥϭⲱⲛⲧ, see (a) / (*III* 104.15) ⲁⲩⲛⲟϭⲛⲉϭ ⲙⲙⲟϥ by association with ⲥⲱⲃⲉ ⲙⲙⲟ⸗ (cf. *IV* 59.10 ⲉⲩ-ⲥⲱϥⲉ (sic) ⲏ ⲉⲩⲛⲟϭⲛⲉϭ); this may be a case of pertinent ⲙⲙⲟ⸗ (§3.1.3.1), but we need more evidence here.

(c) On *rhythmic-euphonic* motivations we know exceedingly little (§3.1.3.3.2). The wish to avoid a sequence of overshort forms and dissonance may explain (*III* 150.1) ...ⲛⲧⲛϯ ⲙⲙⲟⲟⲩ ⲉⲧⲟⲟⲧϥ ⲙⲡϫⲟⲉⲓⲥ, (*ibid.* 222.12) ⲙⲁⲣⲛⲙⲟⲕⲙⲉⲕ ⲙⲙⲟⲛ, and such cases. (*IV* 157.22f.) ⲛⲧⲁⲩⲧⲱϭⲉ ⲙⲙⲟϥ ⲛⲧⲟϥ; the presence of enclitic particles (§6.0.3) between two fully stressed units apparently constitutes a desirable rhythmic contour (§3.1.3.3.2); consider (*III* 163.22ff.) ⲉⲡⲙⲁ ⲉⲧⲣⲉⲩⲑⲃⲃⲓⲟⲩ... ⲉⲁⲩϫⲓⲥⲉ ⲇⲉ ϩⲱⲱϥ ⲙⲙⲟⲟⲩ.

(d) A residue of unaccountable instances: (*III* 38.14f.) ϩⲱⲥⲧⲉ ⲉⲧⲣⲁⲱϭⲧ ⲙⲙⲟϥ (cf. ⲟϭⲧ⸗ in *Dictionary* 540b): a case of "augmentative" construction (§3.1.3.1)? (*ibid.* 219.10f.) ...ⲛⲥⲉ[1]ⲧⲁϩⲟⲟⲩ[2] ⲉⲣⲁⲧⲟⲩ[2] ⲙⲡⲉϥⲙⲧⲟ ⲉⲃⲟⲗ ⲛϥⲡⲱⲣϫ ⲙⲙⲟⲟⲩ[2] ⲉⲃⲟⲗ ⲛⲛⲉⲩ[2]ⲉⲣⲏⲩ / (*RE 10* 162a 2f.) ⲡⲥⲱⲧⲏⲣ ⲛⲛⲉⲧⲙⲉ ⲙⲙⲟϥ ⲁⲩⲱ ⲉⲙⲛⲧⲁⲩⲥⲉⲓ ⲙⲙⲉ ⲙⲙⲟⲕ. Is this a case of assimilation to the construction of the durative predicate? Note that ⲙⲙⲟⲕ here expands an extra-conjugational infinitive (see next paragraph).

3.1.3.2.3 Possible morphophonematic/morphosyntactic combinatory conditioning of ⲙⲙⲟ⸗. One must here consider:

(a) instances of the *2nd person singular feminine* pronominal object after a lexeme of the biradical ('ⲕⲱⲧ') class in a case of a medial laryngal: (*III* 206.10) ⲁⲥⲱⲱϥ ⲙⲙⲟ (reflex.): contrast with (*A 2* 305)

ⲚⲦⲀϤⲤⲞϤϤ. Note the relatively high incidence of the ' ⲔⲰⲦ ' class [49] among instances of the pronominal mediate construction (preceding paragraphs), esp. with medial-laryngal lexemes: also ⲰϣⲰⲦ ⲘⲘⲞⲤ (*Leyd.* 328, *A 2* 345), ⲔⲰⲰⲤ ⲘⲘⲞⲤ (*IV* 83.23). More 2nd pers. fem. instances (also in other classes): (*III* 205.28) ...ⲚⲤⲈϢⲰⲖ ⲘⲘⲞ / (*P* 130² 67 ⲢⲞⲎ) ⲚⲦⲈⲢⲈⲡⲬⲀϪⲈ ϪⲞ ⲘⲘⲞ ⳜⲘⲡⲞⳞⲚⲦ ⲚⲀⲖⲀⲘ (" planted you ") ⲚⲈⲦⲈⲘⲡⲞⲨⲬⲞ ⲘⲘⲞ ⲢⲰ ϨⲞⲖⲰⲤ ⳜⲘⲡⲈⲨⲔⲀϨ.

(b) Alternatively (or conjointly) significant may be the many instances of ⲘⲘⲞⲤ expanding the *extra-conjugational infinitive* (esp. Ⲛ + inf.), (Ⲉ)ⲦⲢⲈ- or the conjunctive (*III* 150.1, 219.10f., *IV* 83.23, 89.2 twice, *Ch.* 62.42f.; see §7.1.3 for the structural affinities of the conjunctive with the Bipartite pattern); this construction is relatively rare in Sentence Conjugation infinitives.

These facts may prove to be no more than so many red herrings, but then they may well give glimpses of significant morphologic or morphosyntactic properties, providing an alternative explanation to that of §3.1.3.1.

3.1.3.3 NOMINAL OBJECT: DISCERNIBLE STYLISTIC MOTIVATION FOR THE SELECTION OF THE MEDIATE/ IMMEDIATE CONSTRUCTION. In the following paragraphs I indicate tentatively several factors of stylistic relevance that may possibly be responsible for the choice of the mediate or immediate construction. These are not statements of conditioning: contrary exx. are commonplace. Pending full empirical implementation, esp. statistical corroboration, let this be taken as a mere impressionistic record. (These elusive cases are by their very nature *explicable ad hoc* rather than *predictable*, at least until an explicit theory of Coptic literary stylistics is evolved, relating stylistic to syntactic function.)

3.1.3.3.1 (1) The MEDIATE construction *bracketing* two conjugation forms (with identical or semasiologically close lexemes — usually in the *disiunctio Sinuthiana*): ⲚⲈⲦϤⲒ Ⲏ ⲚⲈⲦⲚⲀϤⲒ Ⲛ- (*IV* 206-22), ⲚⲈⲦⲬⲰ Ⲏ ⲚⲈⲚⲦⲀⲨⲬⲰ Ⲛ- (*ibid.* 42.2), ⲚⲈⲦⲈⲒⲢⲈ Ⲏ ⲚⲈⲦⲚⲀⲈⲒⲢⲈ Ⲛ- (*III* 189.27f., *sim. Wess. 9* 111a 29ff.), ⲀϤⲬϢϢⲖⲈ Ⲏ ⲀϤⲔϢⲦϤ Ⲛ- (*III* 196.5f.); other exx.: *III* 193.12, *IV* 13.11, 170.25, *A 1* 88, etc. In (*IV* 44.2) ...ⲈⲀⲨⲢⲡⲔⲈⲘⲓϢⲈ Ⲏ ⲈⲀⲨⲢⲡⲔⲈⲤⲰϢ ⲚⲚⲈⲚⲦⲀⲨⲬⲚⲞⲨⲞⲨ ⲈⲢⲞⲞⲨ the mediate construction is *zeugmatic*.

(2) With two (or more) BRACKETED objects (one nuclear verb), we often encounter the IMMEDIATE construction: (*Ch.* 9.8ff.) ⲡⲈⲚⲦⲀϤⲦⲀⲘⲓⲈ-ⲦⲡⲈ ⲘⲚⲡⲔⲀϨ / (*ibid.* 69.45ff.) ⲡⲈⲦⲞⲨⲈϢ-ⲡⲰⲚϨ ⲀⲨⲰ ⲡⲞⲨⲞⲈⲒⲚ (§3.1.1.2.2) / (*IV* 113.19) ⲚⲚⲈⲨϢⲈϤⲦ-ⲡⲈⲨⲡⲢⲎϢ Ⲏ ⲦⲈⲨϨⲞⲒⲦⲈ Ⲏ ⲞⲨϨⲚⲀⲀⲨ, unless with lexemes where the prenominal allomorphs would, being short, upset the " rhythmic balance " (§3.1.3.3.2): (*III* 107.2f.) ⲀⲔⲬⲰ ⲚϨⲈⲚϢⲀⲬⲈ ⲈⲨⲤⲞⲨⲦⲰⲚ ⲀⲨⲰ ϨⲈⲚϨⲂⲎⲨⲈ ⲈⲨⲬⲎⲔ ⲈⲂⲞⲖ ⲘⲘⲚⲦⲘⲈ / (*ibid.* 113.9f.) ⲀⲚⲤⲰϢ ⲚⲦⲘⲚⲦⲀⲦⲤⲂⲰ ⲀⲨⲰ ⲦⲘⲚⲦⲀⲦⲤⲰⲦⲘ / (*ibid.* 113.1ff.) (Ⲉ)ⲚϢⲀⲚⲈⲒⲢⲈ ⲘⲪⲀⲡ ⲀⲨⲰ ⲡⲆⲒⲔⲀⲒⲞⲚ ⲀⲚⲦⲀⲒⲈ-ⲡϨⲀⲡ ⲘⲚ ⲡⲆⲒⲔⲀⲒⲞⲚ ⲀⲚⲤⲰϢ ⲘⲡⲬⲒⲚϬⲞⲚⲤ ⲘⲚⲡⲦⲰⲢⲡ / (*ibid.* 126.1ff.) ...ⲈⲦⲚⲀⲈⲒⲢⲈ ⲚϨⲈⲚⲡⲞⲢⲚⲒⲀ ⲘⲚϨⲈⲚⲬⲰϨⲘ ⲘⲚϨⲈⲚⲤⲰϢϤ... Also 186.2f., 155.8, 156.4 etc. We have an exception in (*IV* 40.21f.) ⲈⲢⲈⲡⲚⲞⲨⲦⲈ... ⲚⲦⲀⲦⲀⲔⲞ ⲚⲀⲮⲨⲬⲎ ⲘⲚⲡⲀⲤⲰⲘⲀ [50].

3.1.3.3.2 RHYTHMIC-EUPHONIC REGULATION [51]. Two basic principles seem to be relevant in this connection: (a) STRESS PATTERNING: the mediate construction constitutes two separate stress-units (verb-noun) of equal prosodic standing, whereas the immediate construction constitutes a single composite

---

[49] Statistics on the widespread Ⲛ-rection of this class are here essential.

[50] (*III* 113.5f.) (Ⲉ)ⲚϢⲀⲚⲢ-ⲢⲘⲢⲀϢ ⲀⲨⲰ ⲚϨⲀⲔ is a curious case of expanding (coordinating) the " object " of the intransitive Ⲣ- (note 4), marking it as predicative complementation by means of Ⲛ- (and not ϨⲒ-).

[51] The rhythmic factor in syntax is notoriously elusive, subjective and speculative, open to the pitfall of circularity and unverifiable. Nonetheless, it incontestably exists. Once again, we need first a full theory based on junctural-prosodic data, for which we hardly have even the rudiments (compare however CZERMAK 1928 and 1931: esp. 129ff., 156ff., 165ff.). On the rhythmic and similar factors and object constructions, see STERN: 319, SPIEGELBERG 1912:159f. (on motivation by the extent of the object), QUECKE 1979:447. For the ordering factor in + ⲚⲀⲤ Ⲛ- see EMMEL 1981 (esp. 139f.).

prosodic unit (probably with primary and secondary stress subunits). The MEDIATE object usually follows an unstressed (or relatively weakly stressed) element, thus forming a rhetorically effective, syllable-like rhythmic patterning or contour: ' stress - ⌣ - stress ' (' peak - dip - peak '). + ⲚⲀⲤ Ⲛ- is here especially striking [52] (e.g. *III* 33.24, 59.13, *Ch.* 70.55ff., 83.24ff., *IV* 74.27, 117.9f., 155.9f., 173.14, etc. etc.). Consider also: ⲬⲰ ⲚⲀⲤ Ⲛ- (*Ch.* 94.23ff.), ⲤⲰⲦⲠ ⲚⲀⲤ Ⲛ- (*Ch.* 75.40ff.), ⲔϣⲠⲈ ⲚⲀⲤ Ⲛ- (*III* 39.6f.), ⲔⲰ ⲚⲤⲰⲤ Ⲛ- (*IV* 117.28), ⲂϢⲀ ⲈⲂⲟⲗ Ⲛ- (*Ch.* 74.46ff.), ϤⲒ ⲘⲘⲀⲨ Ⲛ- (*Ch.* 108.37f., *Or.* 155.49ff.), ⲔⲰ ⲚⲀⲤ ⲈⲂⲟⲗ Ⲛ- (*III* 123. 14ff., 138.12f., *IV* 10.2f.), ϢⲠ ⲈⲢⲟⲤ Ⲛ- (*Ch.* 142.15f.) ϬⲒⲚⲈ Ⲛ2ⲎⲦⲤ Ⲛ- (*Ch.* 73.11f.), 2ⲰⲠ ⲈⲢⲟⲤ Ⲛ- (*III* 110.1), ⲘⲀⲦⲀ2ⲟ ⲈⲢⲀⲦⲞⲨ Ⲛ- (*Wess. 9* 126b 7f.), and so on.

A case in point is the interplay of (1) ' ⲞⲨⲚⲦ(Ⲁ)Ϥ + *noun* ⲘⲘⲀⲨ ' and (2) ' ⲞⲨⲚⲦⲀϤ ⲘⲘⲀⲨ Ⲛ + *noun* '; exx. for (1): *III* 71.23, *IV* 7.8, *Ch.* 120.7f., 125.20f., 152.27ff., etc.; for (2): *III* 45.7f., 34.16f., 52.9f., 58.8,11, 60.15 etc. With a *zero-determinated* object, this alternation is cancelled, only construction (1) being eligible (*III* 45.1f., 89.4f., 94.11f. etc.).

(b) A second principle seems to be that of RHYTHMIC BALANCING: the avoidance of overshort lexemic body (short, compared with the following — often complex — noun-syntagm and possibly the preceding conjugational framework). This may account for the frequent MEDIATE construction with (non-durative) ⲈⲒⲢⲈ, ϬⲒⲚⲈ, ⲈⲒⲚⲈ: (*III* 112-3) ⲈⲒⲢⲈ Ⲛ-: ⲦⲀⲒⲈ-, ⲘⲈⲢⲈ-, 9×/ (*III* 134.2) ⲈⲒⲢⲈ ⲘⲠⲞⲨⲰϢ ⲘⲠⲚⲞⲨⲦⲈ / (*A 2* 107) ⲀⲦⲈ-ⲦⲚⲈⲒⲢⲈ Ⲛ2ⲈⲚⲬⲰ2Ⲙ / (*Ch.* 105.55f.) ⲈⲒϢⲀⲚⲦⲘⲈⲒⲢⲈ ⲘⲠⲀⲀ2Ⲉ ⲦⲎⲢϤ... / (*III* 178.21) ⲚⲈⲚⲦⲀⲨⲈⲒⲢⲈ Ⲛ2ⲈⲚⲠⲞⲢⲚⲒⲀ ⲘⲚ2ⲈⲚⲔⲢⲞϤ / (*ibid.* 205.16f.) ⲀⲢⲈⲈⲒⲢⲈ Ⲛ2ⲈⲚⲠⲞⲢⲚⲈⲒⲀ ⲘⲚ2ⲈⲚⲤⲰϢϤ ⲘⲚ2ⲈⲚⲔⲢⲞϤ / (*III* 180.16) ⲚⲈⲦⲈⲢⲈⲠⲚⲞⲨⲦⲈ ⲚⲀⲈⲒⲚⲈ ⲚⲦⲈϤⲞⲢⲄⲎ ⲘⲠⲠⲈϤϬⲰⲚⲦ ⲈⲦⲂⲎⲎⲦⲞⲨ, consider also *III* 203.1, 126.1ff., 189.28, *IV* 4.9, 80.16f., *Wess. 9* 118a 15f., *III* 104.8 (ⲦⲰⲘ). The same may go for (non-durative) ⲬⲒ, +, ϤⲒ, although in this case the widespread mediate construction may also be preferred, as the only means to mark the verb-object interdependence. Since for these lexemes the absolute and construct allomorphs are homonymic, the functional burden falls on Ⲛ- (ⲬⲒ Ⲛ- *Ch.* 95.56, 107.14f., *III* 127.15, *IV* 3.19, 36.16f., etc.; ϤⲒ Ⲛ- *Wess. 9* 172d 23f., *III* 57.2f., *IV* 36.1f.,6,12, etc.; + Ⲛ- *III* 90.6,7, 117.30, *IV* 26.13, 122.5 etc.).

3.1.3.3.3 MISCELLANEOUS. (a) " Inner ", lexically cognate object (" *figura etymologica* "): *immediate construction*: (*Ch.* 27.13ff.) ⲚⲈⲦⲈⲘⲠⲞⲨⲦⲤⲠ ⲦⲈⲔ+ⲠⲈ / (*A 2* 80, cf. *A 2* 238) ⲘⲚⲚⲤⲀⲦⲢⲈⲨⲤⲞⲨⲚ-ⲠⲤⲟⲟⲨⲚ ⲦⲎⲢϤ — a recurring expression, cf. *P* 130[1] 36 ⲢⲚⲄ: ⲚⲈⲦⲚⲀⲦⲞⲗⲘⲀ ⲈⲢ-ⲚⲞⲂⲈ... ⲘⲚⲚⲤⲀⲦⲢⲈⲨⲤⲞⲨⲚ-ⲠⲤⲟⲟⲨⲚ, also *IV* 180.2 / (*A 2* 179) ⲘⲠⲞⲨⲦⲈⲠ-Ⲧ+ⲠⲈ / (*IV* 54.3) ⲈⲨⲚⲀⲦⲈϢ-ⲠⲈⲨⲦⲰϢ.

3.2 THE OPPOSITION MEDIATE VS. IMMEDIATE OBJECT-CONSTRUCTION MAINTAINED

The opposition environment is the *non-durative* infinitive and *nominal* object. Having considered possible motivations for selecting constructions (*a*) or (*b*), we are still left with an impressive bulk of evidence for both constructions, with no apparent *plan du contenu* aspect for their opposition. Without being able to correlate them with any functional difference, I would still like to put on record the following impressions of formal distribution in Shenoute: (a) the class most frequently favouring the *mediate* construction is the biradical (' ⲔⲰⲦ ') one, with ' ⲠⲰⲢⲬ ' (triradical, medial sonant) a close second. This impression is of course useless until it is weighted and evaluated against the relative frequency of morphologic classes and of the relevant syntagms for each class. (b) An *extralexemic* environmental factor which may be significant is the formal framework of the lexeme. There seems to be preference for the *mediate* object with (Ⲉ)ⲦⲢⲈ- and the extra-conjugational infinitive, although this is not pronounced enough to indicate different rectional properties in these cases.

---

[52] See LÖFSTEDT 1956:35-62, with further references on the question of " Wortform und Wortumfang ". In our case, " avoidance " may be too strong; " stylistic selection " is perhaps more apt.

3.3   The " Predication Mediators " [53]: Verb-Lexeme Premodifiers

These intriguing elements (Funk: " preverbals ", Layton: " preextensions " [54]) immediately precede the verb lexeme: ПⲒKⲈ- [55] " also, additionally, moreover ", Ⲣ2OYO/Ⲉ- " (even) more, rather ", (Ⲣ)-ϢⲢⲠ(N)- " early, first ". The mediators raise some serious analytic queries, from both syntagmatic and paradigmatic angles: What is their formal role? What " slot " positions do they occupy in the conjugation pattern, and how is it they do not disrupt it, the lexeme having precisely the same categorial definition (by commutation and expansion properties) as in the mediator-less conjugation pattern? [56] Indeed, this last phenomenon is, I am sure, the key to the mystery: these elements are VERB-LEXEME/STATIVE PREMODIFIERS — the only means in Coptic to modify unambiguously a verb lexeme alone [57], not the whole predication pattern (adpattern modification). The verb lexeme is the *nucleus* in this syntagm; the premodifier belongs, in IC terms, to the verb component [58]:

$$ ⲀY- \mid Ⲣ\text{-}ПKⲈ \parallel CϢTⲘ $$

nucl.   satellite

satell.(?)   nucl.

I query the satellital status of the lexeme/stative premodifiers, since we do not find elsewhere in Coptic the sequence ' *satellite → nucleus* ', inverse to the basic Coptic syntagmatic sequence, and because premodifiers (hence lexeme premodifiers?) are not adjuncts, properly speaking, but rather " presetting " modifiers (§1.1.2.2). Given this basic articulation, we must still bear in mind the following qualifications:

(a) The mediators are not (at least in part) mutually exclusive, and are therefore not a single category: (*Ch.* 105.3f.) TNПⲒKⲈⲢ2OYⲈ-+-6ϢNT. The lexeme ⲈⲒPⲈ (Ⲣ-) is compatible with the mediators.

(b) Except possibly for Ⲣ2OYO-, the commutation of the premodified durative infinitive does not exactly match that of the unmodified one: the *predicative modifier* does not occur after ПⲒKⲈ-, (Ⲣ)ϢⲢⲠ(N)- (mutual exclusion of essentially similar entities?).

(c) (Ⲣ)ϢⲢⲠ(N)- is quite rare in the durative pattern (probably for reasons of semasiological incompatibility); in Shenoute it does not, to the best of my knowledge, premodify a stative form. Consequently, it cannot really be tested for nuclearity. Shenoute's pronounced predilection for the mediators (QUECKE 1975/6:480f.) is a tangible distinctive stylistic trait. I cannot point in Shenoute to any other

[53] On these elements, see JERNSTEDT 1925; QUECKE 1962, 1970:380ff., 1975/6 (here treating Shenoutean usage); FUNK 1978a: 119, 1978b (with Shenoutean exx.); LAYTON 1979:191f.; BÖHLIG 1973; SHISHA-HALEVY 1975:473. Funk's study of this subject is undoubtedly the most penetrating and careful; Quecke's (and to an extent Funk's) is strikingly contrastive, regarding the mediators as translation-equivalents of Greek preverbs. (Whether or not they are " docile calques " remains outside the scope of an internal description.)

[54] I have used " conjugation mediators " (1975:473) only in the tagmemic sense of " zero slot " elements, i.e. elements that are not pattern constituents — have no formal, operative standing in the pattern — but transparent and phantom-like, manage to transmit the nexal or nucleus-satellite interdependences between the formal-grammatical (actor, conj. base, determinator...) and the lexical constituent.

[55] JERNSTEDT 1927:71 discusses this lexeme premodifier, concluding that it is " frozen ", Ⲣ- being no longer functional as a verb (as evidenced by the stative following it). He does not refer to the object construction after ПⲒKⲈ- + *infinitive*.

[56] JERNSTEDT 1925, FUNK 1978a:119, 1978b:105ff., SHISHA-HALEVY 1975:473. QUECKE 1970:380ff. raises unnecessary doubts as to the legitimacy of the ' mediator + stative ' construction with ϢⲢⲠ(N-). BÖHLIG 1973 considers the alternation of *infinitive/stative* after ϢⲢⲠ(N-) a variation, and thus misses the whole grammatical point. Layton (1979:191f.): " verbal preextensions... which somehow stand outside the conjugation ". (Cf. the transformationalist use of " preverb ".)

[57] FUNK 1978b:101.

[58] So explicitly FUNK 1978b:105f esp. §§4.2.2, 4.3.1), 1978a:119. The infinitive is not dependent on the modifier (*pace* QUECKE 1970:380).

mediator beside the three discussed here [59]: -ⲦⲢⲈ- [60], more of a conjugation-carrier (probably analyzable as Ⲧ- (nucl.) + ⲢⲈ-), ⲬⲠⲈ-/ⲬⲠⲒ-, -(Ⲉ)ⲩ-, and the future characteristic -ⲚⲀ-, are all nuclear in their respective syntagms, expanded by the " extra-conjugational " infinitive.

3.3.1 ⲢⲠⲔⲈ- (selective representative documentation for the premodified lexeme with object-expansion):

(a) *Non-durative* (rare): (1) *immediate* construction: (*III* 33.4) (2nd perf.) ⲚⲦⲀϤⲢⲠⲔⲈⲢ-ⲋⲦⲎϤ / (*Ch.* 149.27f.) ⲀⲨⲢⲠⲔⲈⲤⲟⲩϤϤ; (2) *mediate* construction: (*III* 57.2f.) ⲀⲨⲠⲀⲏⲄⲎ ⲘⲘⲟⲤ ⲈⲀⲨⲢⲠⲔⲈϤⲒ ⲘⲠⲈⲤⲢⲩⲱⲚ ⲚⲦⲟⲟⲦⲤ, also *IV* 44.2.

(b) *Durative* (this is the usual environment. Very often, we find here the circumstantial present; also exx. of the autofocal antithetic Second Present: " [not only...] but also "); (*Wess. 9* 119a 21 ff.) ⲤⲈⲢ- ⲠⲔⲈⲬⲱ ⲞⲚ ⲘⲘⲟⲤ / (*Ch.* 151.4ff. parall. *K*9294) ⲤⲈⲢⲠⲔⲈⲩⲞⲢⲩⲢ ⲚⲚⲈⲢⲠⲎⲨⲈ / (*A 2*486) ...ⲈⲨⲢⲠⲔⲈⲔⲱ ⲚⲋⲦⲎⲨ ⲈⲢⲟⲟⲨ (cf. POLOTSKY 1960a:§23 Obs. 1) / (*ibid.* 356) ...ⲈⲨⲢⲠⲔⲈⲔⲱⲦ ⲘⲘⲟⲟⲨ / (*Rossi 2/3* 27) ...ⲈⲨⲢⲠⲔⲈⲤⲟⲂⲦⲈ ⲚⲀⲨ ⲚⲦⲟϤ ⲚⲞⲨⲔⲢⲒⲘⲀ / (*ibid.* 34) ...ⲈϤⲢⲠⲔⲈⲋⲀⲬⲋⲈⲬ ⲘⲠⲈⲨⲱⲚⲋ / (*Or.* 160.43f.) ...ⲈⲨⲢⲠⲔⲈⲦⲀⲔⲟ ⲘⲠⲤⲱⲘⲀ, and so on. Note the frequent instances of -ⲢⲠⲔⲈ- premodifying the *stative*: (*A 1* 96) ⲤⲈⲢⲠⲔⲈⲟ ⲞⲚ ⲚⲬⲀⲬⲈ / (*Miss.* 284) ...ⲈϤⲢⲠⲔⲈⲟ ⲚⲞⲨⲀⲨⲠⲎ — contrast with the " intransitive " or copular -Ⲣ- in non-durative environment: (*P* 130² 137 ⲦⲀⲋ) ⲀϤⲢⲠⲔⲈⲢ-ⲬⲀⲬⲈ / (*Rossi 2/3* 77) ...ⲈϤⲢⲠⲔⲈⲘⲎⲚ ⲈⲂⲟⲀ ⲋⲚ- / (*A 2* 301) ...ⲈϤⲢⲠⲔⲈⲂⲎⲦ / (*ibid.* 322) ...ⲈⲒⲢⲠⲔⲈⲩⲀⲀⲦ. In (*IV* 80.9) ...ⲈⲤⲢⲠⲔⲈⲞⲨⲞⲬ ⲀⲚ Ⲉ- we have a rare *negatived* case (the only one known to me in Shenoute).

3.3.2 Ⲣ-ⲋⲟⲨⲟ/Ⲉ- (selective, representative object-expanded documentation):

(a) *Non-durative*: (1) *immediate* construction: (*A 2* 7-8) ⲘⲠⲞⲨⲢⲋⲟⲨⲟⲬⲟⲟⲨ, ⲀⲤⲢⲋⲟⲨⲈⲬⲀⲋⲘⲈⲤ / (*ibid.* 17) ⲘⲠⲩⲀⲬⲈ ⲚⲦⲘⲈ ⲚⲀⲢⲋⲟⲨⲈⲤⲟⲩϤ ⲀⲚ; (2) *mediate* construction: (*A 2* 10) ...ⲚϤⲦⲘⲢⲋⲟⲨⲈϤⲱⲦⲈ ⲘⲠⲈⲨⲢⲀⲚ.

(b) *Durative*: (*B. M. Cat.* 104 No. 230 ⲢⲘⲋ) ⲤⲈⲢⲋⲟⲨⲈⲬⲒ ⲘⲘⲟⲟⲨ ⲚⲄⲟⲚⲤ / (*A 1* 234) ⲠⲈⲦⲘⲟⲨⲋ ⲚⲦⲠⲈ ⲀⲨⲱ ⲈⲦⲘⲟⲨⲋ ⲘⲠⲔⲀⲋ ⲀⲨⲱ ⲈⲦⲢⲋⲟⲨⲈⲘⲟⲨⲋ ⲘⲠⲈϤⲎⲒ / (*ibid.* 304) ⲤⲈⲢⲋⲟⲨⲟⲬⲒⲤⲈ ⲘⲘⲟϤ / (*III* 76.12f., *Wess. 9* 154d 4f.) ⲈϤⲢⲋⲟⲨⲈⲘⲈ ⲘⲘⲟϤ / (*P* 130⁵ 17 Ⲣⲋ) ⲤⲈⲢⲋⲟⲨⲈⲬⲱⲔ ⲞⲚ ⲈⲂⲟⲀ ⲚⲚⲈϤⲈⲠⲒⲑⲨⲘⲒⲀ. Zero-determinated object: (*P* 131⁶ 30 ⲢⲘⲋ) ⲈⲢⲈⲠⲈϤⲋⲎⲦ ⲢⲋⲟⲨⲈⲦⲀⲨⲈ-ⲠⲞⲚⲎⲢⲟⲚ ⲈⲂⲟⲀ / (*Or.* 159.52f.) ...ⲈⲤⲢⲋⲟⲨⲈⲢ-ⲠⲈⲦⲚⲀⲚⲞⲨϤ ⲚⲒⲘ. The causative of -ⲢⲋⲟⲨⲟ- is illustrated by (*IV* 19.14f.) ...ⲚϤⲦⲢⲈⲨⲋⲟⲨⲞⲢ-ⲂⲢⲢⲈ. Note here again the stative premodified by -ⲢⲋⲟⲨⲟ-: (*A 2* 10) ϤⲢⲋⲟⲨⲈⲩⲞⲟⲠ (sim. *A 1* 204) / (*ibid.* 21) (ⲟ)ⲨⲋⲚⲀⲀⲨ ⲈϤⲢⲋⲟⲨⲈⲦⲤⲦⲎⲨ ⲈⲂⲟⲀ / (*ibid.* 331) ⲤⲢⲋⲟⲨⲈⲋⲟⲟⲨ / (*A 1* 155) ϤⲢⲋⲟⲨⲞⲦⲎⲦ ⲞⲚ ⲚⲋⲎⲦ / (*P* 130² 75 Ⲣⲟ) ϤⲞⲨⲟⲬ Ⲏ ϤⲢⲋⲟⲨⲞⲦⲂⲂⲎⲨ / (*A 1* 266) ⲠⲢⲱⲘⲈ ⲈⲦⲢⲋⲟⲨⲈⲤⲋⲟⲨⲞⲢⲦ (a recurring expression, also *A 1* 268, 269, 271, *A 2* 4, etc.) / (*B. M. Cat.* 79 No. 194,3) ⲤⲈⲢⲋⲟⲨⲈⲋⲟⲀⲅ / (*A 2* 527) ⲐⲈⲀⲠⲒⲤ... ⲈⲦⲢⲋⲟⲨⲟⲤⲚⲩ / (*Ch.* 195.21ff.) ⲠⲒⲚⲞⲂⲈ ⲋⲱⲱϤ ⲢⲋⲟⲨⲈⲚⲀⲩⲦ.

(c) Special cases of the non-durative lexeme. In the non-actual present (§3.1.2.1.1), etc. [61]: (*A 1* 276, collated) (Ⲉ)ⲚϤⲠⲎⲦ ⲀⲚ ⲚⲄⲒⲠⲈⲦⲈⲢ (sic) -ⲠⲟⲀⲀⲒⲘⲟⲤ (sic), ϤⲢⲋⲟⲨⲈⲠⲱⲦ ⲋⲱⲱϤ ⲚⲄⲒⲠⲘⲀⲦⲟⲒ / (*A 2* 245, collated) ⲈⲀⲨⲦⲘ-ⲠⲈⲨⲋⲎⲦ ⲈⲠⲀⲒ ⲬⲈ-ϤⲩⲟⲟⲠ ⲘⲠⲠⲈϤⲈⲒⲱⲦ ⲋⲀⲑⲎ ⲘⲠⲀⲦⲞⲨⲦⲀⲘⲒⲈ-ⲀⲀⲀⲨ, ⲈⲨⲢⲋⲟⲨⲈⲦⲚⲦⲱⲚⲞⲨ ⲈⲞⲨⲄⲀⲀⲈ ⲋⲚⲦⲈϤⲞⲨⲈⲢⲎⲦⲈ ⲤⲚⲦⲈ " having shut their hearts to the fact that He had been in existence with His Father

---

[59] Cf. FUNK 1978b:97ff., 101. I would not include -ⲦⲘ- under this heading: it is different formally and functionally. Its position is conditioned and is not always pre-lexemic (ⲈⲢⲩⲀⲚⲦⲘⲠⲢⲱⲘⲈ ⲤⲱⲦⲘ); it has a different systemic standing. (Note incidentally an instance — unique as far as I know — of -ⲦⲘ- negativing ⲦⲢⲈϤⲤⲱⲦⲘ *in conjugation* instead of (Ⲛ-) ⲀⲚ negativing the conjugation form: (*P* 130⁵ 98 Ⲣⲟ) ⲈⲒⲩⲀⲚⲦⲘⲋⲢⲟⲩ ϮⲚⲀⲦⲘⲦⲢⲈⲨⲤⲱⲦ ⲈⲩⲱⲠⲈ " Were I not long-suffering, I should not let them exist any longer ".)

[60] Although exceedingly rare in Sahidic, we find as close to Shenoute as Besa (ed. Kuhn, 101.17f.) an instance of durative ⲦⲢⲟ ⲘⲘⲟ⸗ Ⲉ- (cf. POLOTSKY 1939:111 = *CP* 375). Exx. like (*II Tim.* 1:6) ϮⲦⲢⲈⲔⲈⲒⲢⲈ ⲘⲠⲘⲈⲈⲨⲈ are not conclusive, although statistics may here prove illuminating.

[61] See QUECKE 1975/6:485f., FUNK 1978b:106 n. 68. In (*A 2* 376) ⲀⲀⲀⲀ ⲠⲈⲋⲢⲟⲟⲨ ...ⲢⲋⲟⲨⲈⲈⲒ ⲈⲂⲟⲀ collation with Zoega 246 ⲍⲅ shows that Amélineau omitted the perfect base.

before anything was created, they rather resemble a man crippled in both legs " — possibly an instance of an apodotic, Tripartite ·ЄЧСШТМ (Shisha–Halevy 1973) [62].

(d) The common -PⳐOYO ⳐN- could be taken as predicative modifier premodified by -PⳐOYO-: (*A 1* 110) OYCIϢЄ ПЄТⳐМПЄYⳐHT ЄЧPⳐOYO ⳐNTЄYѰYXH, also *Ch.* 33.43f., 104.51ff., *Or.* 160.41f. etc. Since however we find this also outside the present (*A 2* 396) ЧNАPⳐOYO ⳐМПССШВⳐ / (*IV* 86.3) МПPPⳐOYO ⳐШШК ⳐNNАI, we must perhaps conclude that P-ⳐOYO in this case is nuclear [63], a fully predicative verb syntagm (" abound ") complemented by ⳐN- [64]. That this is the copular (" intransitive ") P- is perhaps indicated by (*P 131⁵* 19 МГ) ЄТЄТNO NⳐOYO ⳐМПТШВⳐ: in that case -PⳐOYO- *in the durative* could be the mediator.

3.3.3 -PϢPП-/-PϢPПN-/-PϢOPПN-/-ϢPП- (selective object-expanded documentation):

(*a*) *Non-durative*: (1) the *immediate* construction: NϢАХЄ/КАТАΘЄ/П/(Є)NTАNϢPП ХOO⸗ — a recurring expression, very common: *A 1* 36, 152, *Wess. 9* 87b 28ff., 125a 15f., *III* 30.15, *IV* 7.24, 67.16f. etc. / (*Ch.* 56.28f.) АYPϢOPПNOPХN / (*ibid.* 123.18ff.) NTOC ГАP ПЄNTАCPϢOPПNP-MOYI ЄPOЧ / (*IV* 47.22ff.) NϢАХЄ ЄNTАYⳐШN ММOOY ЄТOOТN H NЄNTАYCАⳐOY NАN PϢPПТАМЄ-ТМINЄ NPШМЄ ЄТММАY...; (2) the *mediate* construction: (*A 2* 345) ...ЄТPЄYPϢPПYϢШТ ММOOY МАYААY / (*Wess. 9* 145a 11f.) ...ЄАYPϢPПNCOOYТN N-.

(*b*) *Durative* (rare): (*Wess. 9* 148b-c) ПЄТPϢPПYϢПЄ / (*IV* 194.1f.) NЄⳐВHYЄ ЄТЄPЄN△АIMON (sic) PϢPП-NЄIPЄ ММOOY.

3.4 Deverbative lexeme-carrying nominalizations and their object-expansion

PЄЧ-, the analytic, productive *nomen agentis* prefix, and АТ-, the " privative " deriving one, are both nuclei in relation to a following verb lexeme [65]. (They themselves, of course, expand a foregoing determinator.) A check of the object-expansion of their respective verbal components yields the following results:

3.4.1 PЄЧСШТМ [66], historically an *antecedent* + *adnominal present* syntagm, still reveals (with some exceptions) the expansion properties of a present tense (§3.1.2.1) for a nominal object, but of a non-durative pattern for a pronominal one (§3.1.1.1) and for especially close compound verbs (§3.1.1.2.3(2)):

Object construction	Ø-determ. object	Non-Ø-determ. object/subst. relat. (determinated) [67] /pron.
(a) *immediate*	PЄЧЧI-ѰYXH (*IV* 21.8) PЄЧТЄⳐМ-PШМЄ (*III* 61.6f.) PЄЧYMϢЄ-ЄI△ШΛON (*Ch.* 110.11ff.) PЄЧϯ-ⳐАП (*Ch.* 126.51f.)	ТЄYМNТPЄЧКА-ⳐТHY... (*IV* 42.4f., 116.8f.) ПPЄЧТNТШNЧ ЄПАГГЄΛOC (*Ch.* 204.13f.)

---

[62] Cf. Funk 1978b:107 n. 71.

[63] -ⳐOYЄ- is nuclear in {OY-}ⳐOYЄ + *noun* (*A 1* 400, *A 2* 12, 155, 402, *Wess. 9* 144d 29f.) {ПЄ-}ⳐOYЄ + *noun* (*A 2* 80, *P 130⁴* 119 КЄ) in relation to the following noun lexeme (it expands its determinator).

[64] This goes for (*Wess. 9* 142d 7ff.) АЧААY АYШ АЧPⳐOYO ЄPOOY and (*Ch.* 125.23f.) ПЄТP-ⳐOYO NАC.

[65] Cf. Funk 1978a:115f.

[66] Stern §172; Wiesmann 1914:130 (no PЄЧ- + *stative* is known to me in Shenoute), 1917:146; Till §§146, 260b, following Jernstedt 1927:70f. (4), who observes (without enlarging on this syntagm), that his rule does not fully apply here. Cherix 1979:11 (71, 75, 83 etc.) subsumes this under the Bipartite Pattern cases. For the opposition PЄЧMOY (aoristic, non-actual present) *vs.* PЄЧMOOYТ (actual statal present) see Funk 1976a:180 n. 1.

[67] See §5.2.3.1.

	РЕЧ2ШТВ-РШМЄ (*Ch.* 27.11f.)	
	РЄЧР-ПЄΘΟΟΥ (*III* 190.15)	
	РЄЧР-ϨΙΚ, РЄЧР-ПΑϨΡЄ, РЄЧΚΑ-ΟΥΝΟΥ (*III* 88)	
	РЄЧСЄШ-РШМЄ (*IV* 99.29)	
	РЄЧΧΙ-ΟΥΑ (*III* 78.13)	
	РЄЧР-ΟΥΟΕΙΝ (*III* 88.28)	
	РЄЧϬΝ-ΑΡΙΚЄ (*III* 121.23f.)	
	РЄЧΚЄТ-ΗΙ (*IV* 75.25)	
	РЄЧТΑΚЄ-ϨΗТ (*III* 121.15)	
	РЄЧСΚΡΚΡ-ШΝЄ ЄϨΡΑΙ (*P* 131⁶ 29 мⲟ)	
	РЄЧР-ϨШВ Є- (*Ch.* 35.32f.)	
	РЄЧПЄϨТ-СΝΟЧ ЄВΟΛ (*Ch.* 26.55ff.)	
	РЄЧΧΙ-ШΟΧΝЄ (*III* 123.22)	
(b) *mediate*		ТМΝТРЄЧТΑΚΟ ΝΜΜЄΛΟС (*Ch.* 67.32f.)
		МΝТРЄЧϬШШМЄ МПϨΑП (*Ch.* 52.2f.)
		ТЄΙРЄЧСШШ МПЄСΝΟΥТЄ (*Ch.* 149.7ff.)
		ПРЄЧТШРП ΝΝЄТЄΝΟΥЧ ΑΝ ΝЄ (*Ch.* 177.11ff.)
		ПРЄЧТШШ ΝΝЄТШΑΛΛЄΙ (*Ch.* 206.34f.)?
		РЄЧШП ЄΝΝСΙΟΥ (*III* 88.12)

3.4.2 ΑТ- [68]: here we have a different picture: (a) With a pronominal or non-zero-determinated nominal object, the construction is *mediate*: Р-/Ο Ν-ΑТСΟΟΥΝ ММΟ⸗ (*III* 212.8f., *IV* 2-3, 7.4f., *Ch.* 66.22f.) / (*P* 131⁷ 45 vo.) -Ο ΝΑТСΟΟΥΝ МПЄΥϨМΟТ. (ΘΕϮΙС ΝΑТТΑϨΟС [*III* 108.28] is quoted from Athanasius. Note ΑТСΟΟΥΝ Є- [*IV* 83.9, 100.5f.]; I know of no instance of *ΑТСΟΥΝ-). Is Р-ΑТСΟΟΥΝ ММΟ⸗ a case of ММΟ⸗-rection of a compound verb (§3.1.2.2.2)?

(b) We find the *immediate* construction with a zero-determinated object: (*IV* 42.12f.) ϨЄΝΑТШП-ϨМΟТ and with the compound verb Р-ϨТΗ⸗: (*IV* 49.12) ΝΑТР-ϨТΗΥ.

3.4.3 Miscellaneous. (a) With ШΟΥ- "worthy of..." we find the immediate construction of a nominal or pronominal object (the pronoun anaphoric-correferent with the determinator or nucleus of the syntagm): (*III* 64.6f., *IV* 23.20f., *P* 131⁶ 15 ro) — ΝШΟΥМЄСТШΟΥ / (*IV* 84.21) ΝШΟΥПΟΡШЧ / (*A 1* 269) ΝШΟΥСϨΟΥШΡΟΥ / (*IV* 157.12) ΘΟΙТЄ ΝШΟΥПΑϨС / (*III* 96.3) ΝШΟΥЧЄТ-ПЄΥР-ПМЄЄΥЄ ЄВΟΛ / (*Ch.* 205.48ff.) ТϨЄΙΚШΝ ΝШΟΥ-МЄΡΙТС / (*ibid.* 189.2ff.) ПΙШΟΥТМТΑΥЄ-ПЄЧРΑΝ / (*A 2* 84) ΝШΟΥΑШΟΥ (sic), ΝШΟΥМЄΡΙТΟΥ.

(b) With ϬΙΝ-, we find the immediate construction of a pronominal object, mediate/(immediate?) for the nominal one: (*A 2* 234) ТЄΝϬΙΝТΑΝϨΟΥТЧ/ (*A 1* 15) (of the friendly dog) ТϬΙΝΚΙМ ЄРОЧ (i.e. for his master) МПЄЧПΑϨΟΥ Η ПЄЧСΑТ МΝТϬΙΝЄΙРЄ ЄПЄСΗТ ΝΝЄЧМΑΑΧЄ.

(c) ...ЄЧΟ ММΑΙТΑЄΙΟЧ ЄВΟΛ ϨΙТΝΝΡШМЄ (*IV* 43.5).

---

[68] Stern §177; Jernstedt 1967, Funk 1976 are concerned mainly with the semantics and diathesis of this deverbative adjective (see §4.2.2.2.1).

CHAPTER 4

THE ADNOMINAL MODIFIER:
A DEFINABLE 'ADJECTIVE' CATEGORY IN COPTIC?

4.0.1 THE SO-CALLED "ADJECTIVE" IN COPTIC: A RESEARCH-HISTORICAL NOTE. Both early and current scholarly opinion speaks for the existence in Coptic of a grammatical category of "adjectives" *as well as* a syntactic device to form attributive syntagms [1], *viz.* the "*nota relationis*" N- (§§1.0.1.2, 1.1.1 spec. obs.). This amounts to a contradiction in terms, seeing that the so-called adjective is in fact such a syntagm [2]. Moreover, the grammars shed no light on the vital question of the '*nucleus - satellite*' arrangement or relative order, actually observing on the irrelevance of placement and non-existence of a significant order — hence, the variation status of {OY-}ΠΟΝΗΡΟC ΝΡѠΜΕ and {OY-}ΡѠΜΕ ΜΠΟΝΗΡΟC, the latter being nevertheless the "normal" (i.e. predominant) arrangement [3].

---

[1] TILL's unfortunate "Qualitätsgenitiv" (p. 70f.; 1928:§88a). Cf. STEINDORFF 1951:§§148, 156, STERN §§292ff. Stern's "attributive Relation" (§§185-8), distinct from "attributive Annexion" (§ 194, the case of -ѰΗΜ, -ΚΟΥΙ etc., considered by Stern in the same light as the *in fine compositi* elements, -O, -ѰΙΡΕ, -ΝΟΥϤΕ etc.).

[2] STERN §§168-9, 177, 185-8, 194 (Stern stresses the morphologic similarities of "adjective" and "substantive"); TILL §§114ff.; STEINDORFF 1951:§§148, 156. Most expositions (including Crum's in *Dictionary*, "adj" *vs.* "nn", "adj" usually corresponding to a Greek adjective, e.g. in p. 157a, 159b) have a definite ethnocentric flavour (so too GREGORIUS 1981). Stern, as usual, shows the most insight and offers the most pertinent discussion of this issue. Pre-Stern grammars are even less consistent. PEYRON (1841) calls ΝΑѰΕ- etc. "adiectiva quae distinguuntur ex suffixis" (33) or "quae utuntur suffixis" (74f.), ΕΤ-, ΕϤ- "adiectiva composita", "participia vel adiectiva" (34). (STEINDORFF 1951:§157 calls the augentia "Adjectiva mit Suffixen".) Modern treatments assume the existence of such a category and do not bother with definitions (so CHAÎNE 1933, STEINDORFF 1951, BÖHLIG 1979, GREGORIUS 1981, etc.) or evade the issue (so CHERIX 1979:14 "nom à valeur adjective, utilisé sans article, dans la construction attributive"). One often finds "adjective" and "attributive" (construction or noun) used as if synonymous.

[3] STERN §§186-8, STEINTHAL-MISTELI 1893:277, TILL §§114, 117-9, CHAÎNE 1933:§§181-226, STEINDORFF 1951:§156, MALLON-MALININE p. 73 ("Les adjectifs primitifs et derivés se placent soit avant, soit après les substantives"), GREGORIUS 1981:199, and so on.

4.0.2 THE PROBLEM: NOUN, SUBSTANTIVE, ADJECTIVE. Some or all of the following characteristics apply as a rule to — and indeed *define* — the Coptic nominal lexemic substitution group: (a) eligibility as expansions (satellites) of pronominal (determinators, §5.1.1.0.1) and semi-pronominal nuclei (ⲙⲛⲧ-, ⲣⲙ-, ⲁⲧ-); (b) eligibility (within noun syntagms) as expansions of verb lexemes (in the construct state, the immediate object construction, [§3.0.2); (c) the privilege (within noun syntagms) of occupying the actor slot in various conjugation patterns, often conditioning special base/converter allomorphs; also of occurring in variously appositive and extrapositive status (cf. §6.0.1); (d) compatibility with immediately preceding modifier markers (" prepositions "); (e) (morphologic) movability, irregular and extremely restricted (ⲥⲟⲛ: ⲥⲱⲛⲉ, ⲩⲏⲣⲉ: ⲩⲉⲉⲣⲉ, ⲍⲗⲗⲟ: ⲍⲗⲗⲱ, ⲥⲁⲃⲉ: ⲥⲁⲃⲏ)[4]; (f) (morphologic) countability, more or less regular, widespread but unpredictable (subject to regulation as yet obscure) (ⲥⲛⲟⲩ: ⲥⲛⲱⲱⲩ, ⲍⲗⲗⲟ: ⲍⲗⲗⲟⲓ, ⲥⲟⲛ: ⲥⲛⲏⲩ)[5]. Returning to (d), one notes the modifier and relator signal *par excellence*, the " nota relationis " ⲛ-, often discussed in the course of this work. Yet all these formal criteria do not warrant the differentiation in Coptic of *nomen substantivum* and *nomen adiectivum*, whatever the justification for this distinction in other languages[6] and for that matter pre-Coptic Egyptian[7]: the special " adjectival predicate " predication pattern is absent in Coptic, and the adnominal privilege is restricted to a closed lexical list of few members. This is not to say, however, that nominal subgrouping cannot be achieved on the strength of other formal criteria, for instance, the distinction of alienable and inalienable nouns (cf. §1.2.1.1, spec. obs.); nouns compatible with the determinators of one or both genders (§5.1.1.0.1), including cases of syntactic movability like ⲡ-/ⲧ-ⲍⲙⲍⲗ, ⲡ-/ⲧ-ⲛⲟ6, ⲡ-/ⲧ-ⲣⲙⲛ-; nouns compatible with ⲙⲛⲧ- (until evidence to the contrary is produced, one cannot assume that these constitute an open-ended list); -ⲟⲥ/-ⲟⲛ dual-ending Greek loan-adjectives (see below) or loan-substantives *vs.* all others; eligibility as " *in initio compositi* " or " *in fine compositi* " elements (for the unmarked, juxtaposed adnominal modifier, Stern's " attributive Annexion ", see below); verb lexemes, that is to say nouns privileged to occupy the predicate slots in certain verbal predication patterns, *vs.* all others. There are, of course, also many possible *semantic* subdivisions which are no less " formal " in the frame of reference of contextual compatibility. Yet none of these sub-categories can appropriately be termed " adjective ", to the exclusion of some or all of the others. (Note that all nouns, except for the few on the list of juxtaposed attribution, must be ⲛ-marked to occur adnominally; this applies also to Greek loan-adjectives: ⲡⲣⲱⲙⲉ ⲛⲁⲅⲁⲑⲟⲥ.) It is nonetheless the Greek loan-adjectives (ⲡⲟⲛⲏⲣⲟⲥ, ⲥⲟⲫⲟⲥ, ⲉⲗⲁⲭⲓⲥⲧⲟⲥ) — with some original two-ending compounds, like ⲁⲛⲟⲙⲟⲥ, ⲧⲁⲗⲁⲓⲡⲱⲣⲟⲥ —, that are implicitly taken as adjectives in Coptic[8] and constitute the core and major constituent of this vague class. Indeed, it is my impression that it is this considerable and prominent group grammarians have in mind when referring, with no formal or theoretical foundation,

---

[4] Unproductive, and of the same order as lexical motion (ⲉⲓⲱⲧ: ⲙⲁⲁⲩ).

[5] (*III* 157.11ff.) ⲉⲩⲉⲭⲟⲟⲥ ⲉⲡⲍⲗⲗⲟ ⲍⲁⲍⲧⲏⲛ ⲁⲩⲱ ⲉⲩⲉⲭⲟⲟⲥ ⲉⲑⲗⲗⲱ ⲍⲁⲍⲧⲛⲑⲩⲧⲛ ⲏ ⲛⲥⲉⲭⲟⲟⲥ ⲉⲛⲍⲗⲗⲟⲓ ⲉⲧⲍⲁⲧⲛⲑⲩⲧⲛ. An unpublished monograph by a student of mine, Ms. G. Rozyk, points to an individualizing-concretizing role of the lexemic plural in the Sahidic NT. — Incidentally, ⲟⲩⲥⲱⲛⲉ ⲛⲥⲍⲓⲙⲉ (*III* 94.12f., see *Dictionary* 343a) means here " wife-mate " (not " female sister ").

[6] A relatively late distinction in grammatical terminology (SCHOEMANN 1862:83ff. — mainly a semantic one). The usual adjectival syndrome, often converging with a conglomerate of specific morphs, is one of adnominal privilege of position, concord governability, morphologic grading (comparative, superlative, adequative, etc.), special semasiological characteristics, and (in some languages) syntactic or morphosyntactic peculiarities, such as special predication patterns, a distinction of attributive *vs.* predicative status, and so on.

[7] See SCHENKEL 1967:77ff.; the Egyptian adjective is primarily a syntactically definable category, yet neither the adnominal position (shared by the so-called " direct genitive ") nor the concord (shared by the appositive noun) are decisive. However, the special " adjectival predicate " pattern, lost between Demotic and Coptic, is. In Coptic this predication pattern is replaced cooperatively by the " adjective verbs ", the stative in the Bipartite conjugation, and the nominal sentence. Note esp. the pattern with zero-determinated predicate: (*Or.* 159.34ff.) (ⲉ)ⲃⲟⲧⲉ ⲡⲉ, (ⲉ)ⲥⲓⲱⲉ ⲡⲉ / (*III* 208.8) (ⲉ)ⲙⲟⲓⲍⲉ ⲡⲉ ⲛⲁⲩ... / (*IV* 23.22) ⲙⲕⲁⲍ ⲛⲍⲏⲧ ⲡⲉ ⲉⲥⲟⲧⲙ / (*Ch.* 183.23) ⲉⲣⲁⲱⲉ ⲡⲉ ⲛⲁⲩ... / (*B.L.Or.* 3581A 66, No. 198, f. 2 vo) ⲱⲓⲡⲉ ⲡⲉ ⲭⲉ-ⲛⲁⲓ.

[8] STERN §169; TILL §76, etc. See GREGORIUS 1981.

to Coptic " adjectives ". In the following pages I attempt to trace a way towards gaining a formal basis for a nominal sub-class, for which the name " adjective ", although still somewhat arbitrary, may not be amiss.

4.1 DETERMINATIVE-SUBORDINATIVE SYNTAGMATICS: ADNOMINAL EXPANSION; SYNTACTIC VS. SEMANTIC NUCLEUS AND SATELLITE

Let us first examine the syntagmatics of adnominal nominal modification. One (or more) N-marked noun syntagm following (in open juncture) another constitutes the Coptic attributive syntagm. But this is merely a special case in a whole paradigm of two-noun syntagms, where the formal changing factors are (a) the *determination* of either or both constituents, (b) the relator morph N- or NTE-. This corresponds, on the *plan du contenu*, to a semasiological spectrum ranging from possessive, through appurtenative, to attributive relationship [9] between the two consituents. Although the intricacies of this paradigm are, as yet, far from clear (see §1.1.1 spec. obs. for N-/NTE- distribution), it is certain that the *relative determination* of the constituents (or the determination contour of the complex) is a primary factor regulating the selection of their relator, and zero determination of the second constituent corresponds to an attributive connotation of the adnominal modifier [10]: the generic reference effected by the zero article (§5.1.1-2) for the second noun determines the qualificative relations between it and the first. The ' *noun → N + noun*' phrase is analyzable into nucleus and satellite (expansion) [11]. It is beyond controversy that the " *nomen relatum* " (TUKI's term [12]) or modifier noun is syntactically satellital, the expansion of the unmarked noun. The placement of the N-marked noun is fixed — invariably second in the syntagm. Since both constituents are nominal, the usual paradigmatic (" word-class ") test for identifying the nucleus cannot be applied here. However, it is the first term that carries the determinators (and subsequently relator morphs) for the whole complex syntagm (thus also the gender-number motivating factor: ΤϢΟΡΠΕ NCOTE [P 130² 67 vo]). It is nuclear also in accordance with the basic *nucleus → satellite* syntagmatic sequence in Coptic. But if this is so, one cannot but query the statement that ΠΠΟΝΗΡΟC NΡϢΜΕ and ΠΡϢΜΕ ΜΠΟΝΗΡΟC are mere variants: can nucleus and expansion (since the placement of the N-marked noun is fixed and non-pertinent), *determinatum* and *determinans*, really exchange status, with no correlated shift on the *plan du contenu*? In other words, what is the functional load of this arrangement opposition?

---

[9] Other languages employ a genitive-type morpheme to cover a similar semasiological range. This is striking in Romance, esp. French (cf. GUILLAUME 1919:125ff., ROTHENBERG 1970:238ff., 245ff.). But while in French one is concerned with an idiomatic, stylistically marked turn of phrase, in Coptic N-modification is the only systemic means to attribute the quality of one noun to another.

[10] Not the other way round, as is implied in Till's description; ΠΟΥΟΕΙΝ ΜΠΚΟCΜΟC, ΟΥΑΓΓΕΛΟC NΤΕΠΝΟΥΤΕ, ϨΕΝΝΟΥΤΕ NϢΕ, ΟΥΠΡΟΦΗΤΗC NΝΟΥϪ, ΟΥΤΡΟΦΗ NΕΛΑΧΙCΤΟΝ, ΟΥCϨΙΜΕ ΜΠΟΝΗΡΟC. The " closeness " of ' N-adjective' *vs.* the " looseness " of ' N-substantive ' (STEINTHAL–MISTELI 1893:276) is equally traceable to the different degree of determination. Incidentally, NTE- does not play a role in the " genitive ": attributive opposition (*pace* TILL §122 n. 3), since it is as a rule incompatible with the zero determination of the second noun.

[11] See §5.1.1-0.1; SEILER 1960:6f. The means of formal concatenation in Coptic are twofold: morphematic (N-, mark of satellital dependence) and tagmemic (word-order). This corresponds to pre-Coptic concord + order (see STEINTHAL–MISTELI 1893:275f.). Cf. SCHMIDT 1974:446f. for a typological-comparative approach to this issue.

[12] TUKI 84ff. and *passim*, in my opinion an excellent term. Elsewhere, Tuki defines N- as a " *littera coniunctiva* "; cf. STEINTHAL-MISTELI's " Nominalcasus " (1893:92), and see also SCHWARZE-STEINTHAL 459. The " *nomen relatum* " is in paradigm with other, verbal adnominal modifiers (relative, circumstantial, conjunctive, ΕΤΡΕϤ-; see Ch. 7 n. 31, §7.4). It syncretizes (neutralizes) the distinction between attributive and adnexal modification (§7.1.3): (*Wess. 9* 110a 5ff.) ΠϢΝΕ NϬΑΕΙΕ Η ΕΤΝΕϬϢϤ / (*III* 166.22f.) ϨΕΝΡϢΜΕ NΑΤCϢΤΜ... ΑΥϢ ΕΥΑΘΕΤΕΙ / (*P* 131⁵ 47 ro) ΝΕΥϨΒΗΥΕ ΕΤΝΑΝΟΥΟΥ ΑΥϢ NΔΙΚΑΙΟCΥΝΗ / (*A 2* 419-420, not Sh.) ΝΕΙΡΕϤϢΑϪΕ ΑΥϢ ΕΤΑCϢΟΥ / (*Mun.* 104) ΝΡΕϤϪΙΟΥΕ... ΜΝΝΡΕϤϪΙ-ϬΟΛ ΜΝΝΡΕϤϢΡΚ NΝΟΥϪ ΑΥϢ ΕΤΜΟΟϢΕ ϨΝΚΡΟϤ ΝΙΜ / (*A 2* 338) ϨΕΝΡΕϤΟΥΕΜ-ΡϢΜΕ ΝΕ ΑΥϢ ΝΡΕϤΠΕϨΤ-CΝΟϤ NϨΗΚΕ / (*RE 11* 16b 9f.) ΠΔΙΚΑΙΟC ΑΥϢ ΝΑΓΑΘΟC: in the last exx., N-/ΕΤ- introduce an *additional* expansion of the determinator (§5.1.1).

Note, however, that whereas the *syntactic* nucleus — the first noun — is always the first term, the *syntactic* satellite is always the second, it is otherwise with the non-grammatical " incumbents " in the ' (determinator) [ ] N- [ ] ' grammatical framework.   The change in placement means that the two noun lexemes turn or revolve symmetrically around the N-dependence mark (which, although in the scheme of Coptic juncture is attached to the second term, belongs as a matter of fact to the whole syntagm).   In this sense, there does take place a reversal of centre and periphery.   The SEMANTIC NUCLEUS (contextually essential, representing and integrating the syntagm in the semantic cotext; (OY-)PⱲME, (T-)ⱮⲨXH in OYPⱲME ⲘⲠOⲚHⲢOC and TAⲚOⲘOC ⲘⱮⲨXH [13]; belonging to a certain " meaning class ", cf. " form class " for the syntactic nucleus; often, but not necessarily the non-omissible component [14]) is placed first in OYPⱲME ⲘⲠOⲚHⲢOC, where it coincides with the syntactic nucleus, but second in OYⲠOⲚHⲢOC ⲚPⱲME, where SEMANTIC SATELLITE coincides with the syntactic nucleus.   In binary terms, the arrangement opposition is statable as one of *coincidence* vs. *non-coincidence* of syntactic and semantic constituents.   Put differently (but amounting to the same thing): a noun lexeme has a different *value* in syntactically nuclear or satellital status.   These are, in strict structural analysis, *non-identical homonymic signs*, and it is our task to find out under what (environmental) conditions the one or the other occurs [15].   This reformulation of the problem is, I believe, preferable to a formulation based on order — " usual ", inverted, motivated, etc. — which is more difficult to reduce to non-transformational, static opposition terms.   Instead of ARRANGEMENT opposition, we are dealing with opposition of PLACEMENT.

4.2 RELATIVE-ORDER (ARRANGEMENT) OPPOSITION: 'SEMANTIC NUCLEUS ⇄ SATELLITE', IN TERMS OF PLACEMENT OPPOSITION

The superficial impression that the arrangement in determinative-attributive groups is free or arbitrary is proved wrong by a careful sorting of the material.   In the first instance, we observe that place-

---

[13] Consider (*A 2* 486) ⲚEIⱲⲚE ⲚPⱲME (of hypocrites.   Amélineau: " ces hommes de pierre ", n. 4: " mot à mot: ces pierres d'hommes, c'est à dire: ces hommes insensibles ").   In cases of *proforma expansion* it is often difficult to assign the semantic roles: (*Mun.* 102) ⲚIPEⱮZIK ⲚPEⱮP-ⲠAZPE / (*Wess.* 9 105b 16ff., 24ff.) EYP-ⲆIKAIOC ⲚⲚAHT AYⱲ ⲚⱮAY ...EYP-ACEBHC ⲚATⲚA ⲚPEⱮXIⲚ6OⲚC AYⱲ ⲚⲚOEIK (*III* 95.15) OYXACIZHT ⲚKOIⲚAOϨOC / (*ibid.* 123.13f.) ⲚⱮAⲚZTHⱮ ⲚZAPⱮZHT ETEⲚAⱮEⲠEⱮⲚA / (*ibid.* 135.10f.) ZEⲚPEⱮXIⲚ6OⲚC ⲚE ⲚPEⱮP-ⲚOBE / (*Ch.* 108.15ff.) ...(E)ZEⲚⲚAHT ⲚE ⲚⱮAⲚZTHⱮ ⲘⲘAIPⱲME... and so on.   These cases are best understood as *additional expansions of a determinator*; see n. 12. (*A 2* 74) ZEⲚEⲖAXICTOⲚ ⲚⲚOYB ZIZAT / (*IV* 128.3) ⲠATⲚOYTE ⲚⲆIABOⲖOC / (*ibid.* 153.16) OYXAXE ⲚPⱲME, OYXAXE ⲚCZIⲘE / (*A 1* 76) TEIAⲐHT ⲚCZIⲘE; see also the exx. in §4.2.2.   Compare here the switch in position of *class* and *selector*, non-identical with (synt.) nucleus and expansion (SEILER 1960:19ff.), resulting in a role of *specification* (synt. nucleus = class, expansion = selector) or *characterization* (nucleus = selector, expansion = class).   Consider the following cases of specification: (*Ch.* 56.53f.) ⲠATⲚA ⲘⲘATOI " that soldier who is ruthless ", (*Rossi 2/3* 75) ⲠOⲚHⲢOC ⲚIⲘ ⲚPⱲME " every man that is wicked "; yet this is certainly not without exception in Coptic: (*P* 130[4] 97 ro) TEⱮKETAⲖAIⲠⱲPOC ⲘⱮⲨXH / (*A 2* 412) ⲠEBIHⲚ ⲚZEⲖⲖHⲚ / (*Wess.* 9 149d 20f.) ⲘⲠAPAⲚOⲘOC ⲚIOYⲆAI.

[14] Witness (*Miss.* 281) ⲠEⱮCⲚAY H ⲠEⱮⱲOⲘⲚT (scil. ⲚZOOY).   The so-called " reduction test " (" bad dogs " to " dogs"; SEILER 1960:6f.), leaves us in Coptic with the semantic, rather than syntactic nucleus.   The latter is identifiable mainly through the " centrifugal " basic syntagmatic sequence of Coptic (STERN §635: " Das selbständige und regierende steht vor dem angeknüpften und abhängigen "; see too SCHENKEL 1967:71, FUNK 1978a:117).

[15] For the extensive literature on the problem of adjective placement in various languages, see the bibliography in REINER 1968 (also the General Introduction).   This issue has been studied, with interesting and often varying results, exp. for French. WEIL 1879:53ff., WEINRICH 1966, BARRI 1975 suggest semantic union (adj. → N) *vs.* disunion or autonomy (N → adj.)   The inverse is asserted for English (BOLINGER 1972).   Teyssier (*Lingua* 20:236ff., 1961) distinguishes in English between qualifying and modifying placement; REINER 1968 suggests for French a distinction of " coappelative " *vs.* " (co)predicative ", " objectivation " (N → adj.) *vs.* subjective, impressionistic qualification (adj. → N).   The comparable opposition in German of *böse Húnde* vs. *bóse Húnde* is treated by SEILER 1960 (esp. 35f.) in terms of characterization *vs.* specification, respectively.   WEINRICH'S (1966) and BARRI'S (1975) approach to the French constructions is structuralist.   Weinrich rejects the " emotive " interpretation (covered in more detail below) as " mystification " (" les sentiments n'y sont pour rien ", p. 89) and advocates a distributional examination (p. 83f.); postposed adjectives are then found to be *distinctive*, while anteposed ones, morpheme-like, form a closer union with the following noun.

ment opposition obtains with a well-defined, restricted (even if extensive) list of noun lexemes (§4.2.2). For other nouns, the placement is fixed, i.e. non-pertinent, out of opposition, in our corpus — either invariably first-place (§4.2.1.1) or a second-place position (§4.2.1.2). In the latter case, a shift from second to first position entails a drastic shift — indeed, often a complete reversal — of the meaning of the syntagm: e.g., " a vessel of wood " becomes " vessel wood ", " women's passion " becomes " a woman of passion "; the interrelationship between the constituents is completely reversed. An " adjective " will be defined below as a nominal modifier for which a shift in placement (or rather replacement by a different-position homonymic alternant) does not bring about an *internal* semantic reversal of that order, but selects another member of an *externally* determinable paradigm, while the inter-constituent relationship remains constant. From another point of view, the *specificity contour* is different in the two cases: sharply rising or dipping in the non-adjectival postposed nom. modifier, it is moderate in the ⲣⲱⲙⲉ ⲙⲡⲟⲛⲏⲣⲟⲥ: ⲡⲟⲛⲏⲣⲟⲥ ⲛⲣⲱⲙⲉ paradigm. (Note that the distinction of semantic *vs.* syntactic nucleus and satellite is valid for both adjectives and modifier nouns, the only difference being that for the ' ⲡⲟⲛⲏⲣⲟⲥ ⲛⲣⲱⲙⲉ ' type of syntagm the nuclei and satellites are semantically on a par or commensurate, in partial equivalence [i.e. can be substituted for each other]; this is not the case with ⲟⲩⲍⲏⲧ ⲛⲱⲛⲉ, ⲟⲩⲛⲟⲃⲉ ⲙⲙⲟⲩ.)

4.2.1 THE PLACEMENT OPPOSITION SUPPRESSED (ORDER NEUTRALIZATION)

4.2.1.1 FIRST-PLACE-POSITION PARADIGM. This includes (beside determinators)[16]: (a) IDENTIFIERS: ⲍⲉⲛⲕⲟⲟⲩⲉ (*III* 59.27), ⲁⲩ, ⲟⲩ, ⲛⲓⲙ (*IV* 75.18f., *III* 108.1f., 137.1); (b) QUANTIFIERS: ⲛⲟϭ: (*A 1* 281) ⲟⲩⲛⲟϭ ⲏ ⲍⲉⲛⲛⲟϭ ⲙⲙⲏⲥⲧⲏⲣⲓⲟⲛ (sic) / (*Wess. 9* 131b 2ff.) ⲡⲓⲛⲟϭ ⲛⲍⲱⲃ ⲛⲃⲟⲧⲉ ⲁⲩⲱ ⲉⲧⲣ-ⲃⲟⲟⲛⲉ ⲉⲙⲁⲧⲉ / (*P* 131[6] 23 ⲡ) ⲧⲛⲟϭ ⲙⲡⲟⲗⲓⲥ / (*A 1* 65) ⲍⲉⲛⲛⲟϭ ⲛⲣⲱⲙⲉ... ⲍⲓⲛⲟϭ ⲛⲥⲍⲓⲙⲉ[17]; ⲕⲟⲩⲓ, ⲱⲏⲙ " a little ", " a small quantity/number " (ὀλίγος, *paucus*, *peu de*-; the second-place opposed homonym means " small, little ", μικρός, *paruus*): ⲍⲉⲛⲕⲟⲩⲓ ⲛⲱⲏⲛ, ⲍⲉⲛⲕⲟⲩⲓ ⲛⲟⲩⲟⲟⲧⲉ... (*Miss.* 231) / ⲉⲧⲙⲧⲣⲉϥⲉⲓⲣⲉ ⲛⲟⲩⲕⲟⲩⲓ ⲙⲡⲉⲧⲛⲁⲛⲟⲩϥ ⲭⲉ-ⲉϥⲉⲭⲓ ⲛⲟⲩⲛⲁ ⲕⲟⲩⲓ (*A 2* 502f.) / ⲍⲉⲛⲕⲟⲩⲓ ⲱⲏⲙ ⲙⲡⲉⲧⲛⲁⲛⲟⲩϥ (*K* 9028) / ⲛⲉⲓⲕⲟⲩⲓ ⲛⲍⲱⲟⲛ (*III* 45.27) / ⲍⲉⲛⲱⲏⲙ ⲛⲱⲉ (rare, *IV* 73.14f.); ⲍⲁⲍ, ⲍⲟⲉⲓⲛⲉ[17], ⲗⲁⲁⲩ, ⲟⲩⲏⲣ (*III* 108.5, 140.27, 107.20); *cardinal numbers* (from three onwards): *IV* 51.7, 54.29, *Ch.* 85.56f. With ⲥⲛⲁⲩ (masc.) the evidence is conflicting: we find both first-place (" a pair of... ") and the by far more common, historic appositive second-place position, with no detectable difference in meaning: (*Ch.* 86.50f.) ⲡⲓⲥⲛⲁⲩ... ⲛⲍⲱⲃ ⲛⲕⲉⲫⲁⲗⲁⲓⲟⲛ / (*Miss.* 283) ⲥⲛⲁⲩ ⲛⲣⲱⲙⲉ / (*P* 130[4] 93 vo) ⲥⲛⲁⲩ ⲙⲡⲉⲧⲛⲁⲛⲟⲩϥ, but (*P* 130[1] 36 ⲣⲛⲅ) ⲡⲓⲍⲱⲃ ⲥⲛⲁⲩ ⲛⲁⲛⲁⲅⲕⲁⲓⲟⲛ. For the feminine we find the first place: (*IV* 108.3) ⲕⲉⲛⲟϭ ⲥⲛⲧⲉ ⲛⲥⲍⲓⲙⲉ. *Ordinal numbers:* ⲱ(ⲟ)ⲣⲡ(ⲉ), ⲙⲉⲍ- (*Ch.* 86.45f., 174.11f., *III* 118.14), (*A 1* 33) ⲍⲉⲛⲙⲉⲍⲥⲛⲁⲩ ⲛⲏⲓ / (*ibid.* 92) ⲡⲙⲉⲍⲍⲟⲟⲩ ⲥⲛⲁⲩ ⲏ ⲡⲙⲉⲍⲱⲟⲙⲛⲧ ⲛⲍⲟⲟⲩ. ⲍⲁⲉ " last " (movable, countable) has accordingly first place: (*Ch.* 161.1f.) ⲛⲍⲁⲉⲟⲩ ⲛⲍⲟⲟⲩ / (*ibid.* 198.2f. = *Mt.* 5:26) ⲡⲍⲁⲉ ⲛⲕⲟⲇⲣⲁⲛⲑⲏⲥ, (17f.) ⲡⲍⲁⲉ ⲛⲗⲉⲡⲧⲟⲛ / (*A 2* 71) ⲑⲁⲏ ⲛⲁⲛⲧⲓⲗⲟⲅⲓⲁ / (*Rossi 2/3* 12) ⲡⲛⲟϭ ⲁⲩⲱ ⲡⲍⲁⲉ ⲛⲁⲅⲱⲛ / (*P* 130[1] 136 ⲧⲁⲥ) ⲡⲍⲁⲉ ⲛⲍⲟⲟⲩ (sim. *Rossi 2/3* 83) / (*IV* 208.10f.) ⲑⲁⲏ ⲛⲥⲁⲗⲡⲓⲅⲍ, etc.; but in certain temporal fixed expressions it occupies second place, namely after time-nouns, with a categorial (eschatological) reference (ⲍⲁⲉ, zero-determinated, is invariable here): ⲛⲉⲟⲩⲟⲉⲓⲱ ⲛⲍⲁⲉ (*III* 126.24, 164.20, 180.15,19f., 181.4f., *A 1* 90, 285, 290-1 etc.), ⲛⲉⲍⲟⲟⲩ ⲛⲍⲁⲉ (*IV* 76.15): " last days ", " latter days ".

---

[16] The determinators are really in " zero " or " pre-first " position; in fact, they constitute the prime nuclear paradigm, the initial boundary signal, the beginning of the concatenation of expansions. On the first-place paradigm see TILL §119, MALLON-MALININE §165, cf. STERN §187.

[17] In ⲍⲟⲉⲓⲛⲉ ⲉⲛⲛⲟϭ (sic), ⲍⲉⲛⲕⲟⲟⲩⲉ ⲉⲩⲥⲟⲃⲕ (*III* 27.10), ⲛⲟϭ is overruled by ⲍⲟⲉⲓⲛⲉ, due perhaps to the contrast figure. As distinct from ⲍⲉⲛⲛⲟϭ " some great ones ", this perhaps means " some (persons) who are great " (cf. *Man. Homilien* 27.15 ⲍⲁⲓⲛⲉ ⲛⲍⲁⲩⲧ, ⲍⲁⲓⲛⲉ ⲛⲥⲍⲓⲙⲉ, also in disjunctive contrast).

4.2.1.2.1 SECOND-PLACE-POSITION PARADIGMS (a). Here an inversion is possible, but entails a reversal of the interrelationship between nucleus and expansion (§4.2): this proves these cases to be *sociative* or appurtenative rather than attributive syntagms. Examples are of course ubiquitous, and the lists are open-ended; the following semasiological subgrouping is selective: (a) Ø-determinated, N-marked *abstracts* (incl. *nomina actionis*, infinitive), MNT-syntagms, individual lexemes: ME " truth ", NOYX, BOTE, KPOϤ, COΦIA, ΛOIMOC, ϢAY, MIϢE, ⲰN2 and so on; (b) noun lexemes with *generic-categoric* reference: 2OOYT, C2IME, PⲰME, ⲆAIMⲰN, CATANAC, ⲆIABOΛOC, ⲠNEYMA, 2HT, etc.; (c) noun-lexemes with *material-constituence* reference: ⲰNE, ϢE, CAPϪ, 2AT, NE2, OYOEIN, KAKE, and so on. This class is compatible with the first-place paradigm: (*IV* 156.19) ΛAAY N2ⲰB NNOBE MMOY / (*ibid.* 108.3) KENOϬ CNTE NC2IME / (*Ch.* 146. 15ff.) OYNOϬ EMATE NBⲰ NEΛOOΛE... and, unlike members of the latter, attributes in the second-place list can be compiled " freely ". They cannot therefore be taken as constituting a single paradigm but several, according to position and compatibility in a complicated system of semasiological principles (see footnote 19).

4.2.1.2.2 SECOND-PLACE-POSITION PARADIGM (b). Here we find the zero-determinated, dependence-unmarked, invariable [18] ϢHM and (rarely) KOYI: (*IV* 99.16) ⲠMA ϢHM NKA2 / (*Ch.* 103.35f.) 2EN2PHYE ϢHM MMNT2HKE / (*P* 131⁴ 141 vo, Sh.?) ΘH ϢHM MMAPIA / (*P* 130⁵ 69 ϪΓ) TKEϬICOYNOY ϢHM / (*Leyd.* 345) ⲠAPAⲠTⲰMA KOYI / (*III* 181.18f.) OYϬOⲠE KOYI MMOOY / (*A 2* 503) OYNA KOYI; ϢHM occurs in at least two fixed (lexicalized) syntagms, *viz.* ϢHPE/ϢEEPE ϢHM " boy ", " girl ", " child " (*IV* 61.27 2ENϢHPE ϢHM EYCOBK, *ibid.* 103.14, shows the the semantic weakening of ϢHM, in this compound-like syntagm: " small children "), and TCYNAΓⲰΓH ϢHM (*Berl.* 1611 7 TϪΘ). KOYI (perhaps more usually of *quantity* than mere size) and ϢHM are compatible [19]: 2ENKOYI ϢHM MⲠETNANOYϤ (*K* 9028) " a few small good (works) ", cf. 2ENKOYI MⲠETNA-NOYϤ (*Berl.* 1613 6 ro) " a few good (works) ". This curious, unique attributive syntagm is the last vestige of the pre-Coptic tagmemically marked attributive dependence — this marking being only partial, since in Coptic there is in this case no concord to (co-)mark this dependence.

4.2.1.2.3 CABE/H (" wise, clever ", *III* 22.21, 120.18, *IV* 82.9, etc.) and BPPE (" new ", *III* 65.10, 103.16, *Ch.* 44.45f. etc.) appear to have the privilege of only second-place position, although additional attestation is necessary; a glance at *Dictionary* 43a, 319a shows this is correct, with few exceptions, for Coptic generally [20].

4.2.1.3 In the case of MULTIPLE-ATTRIBUTE SYNTAGMS, the phrase loses its basic binary form, and N-symmetrical inversion is impossible. This probably means a neutralization of the arrangement factor. Consider the following examples: (*Ch.* 191.36ff.) OYPⲰME MⲠAPANOMOC NATNA NPEϤTⲰPⲠ NAKAΘAPTOC NKPOϤ N2EΛΛHN / (*III* 172.10f.) 2ENPⲰME NNAϢTEIME NXACI2HT NPEϤKⲰTE NCAⲠEΘOOY NIM / (*Ch.* 111.35ff.) OYEIⲰT NAΓAΘOC AYⲰ NCABE AYⲰ NEYCEBHC / (*Ch.* 199.37ff.) ⲠPⲰME NNAHT NϢAN2THϤ MMAI2HKE / (*III* 190. 14f.) ⲠPⲰME NPEϤP-ⲠEΘOOY NATMⲠϢA N2ⲰN E2OYN EⲠXOEIC / (*IV* 126.6f.) NE2BHYE MME AYⲰ NⲆIKAION / (*III* 121.23f.) 2ENPⲰME NATCⲰTM NPEϤKPMPM NPEϤϬN-APIKE. NB. A complex single attribute (" bracketed ", coordinated): (*Ch.* 79.31ff.) ΓENOC NIM N2EΛΛHN 2I2AIPETIKOC / (*III* 34.17) NE2BHYE NⲆIKAION AYⲰ NTBBO 2IME.

---

[18] Yet note 2ENϢEEPE ϢHME (*Wess.* 9 94a 1f., collated).

[19] I know of no other instance in Coptic of the compatibility of similar, paradigm-defined attributes (of the type " The Good Old Bad Old Days ", a programme on BBC Radio 4, 1979).

[20] -2OOYT (" wild ", ⲠIⲠIP2OOYT, ⲠIA2OOYT, *A 2* 104), -ME (" genuine ", NE2ME *III* 71.5), -OYHP (COYOYHP " dav such-and-such ", *IF* 232 *apud Dictionary* 489a), -BⲰⲰN " bad ", -NOYϤE " good ", -ϢIPE (" young ", in ϢHPEϢIPE *IF* 298, *Dictionary* 486a), -AC (" old ", HPⲠ AC *vs.* -NBPPE, *A 1* 194) are all in our corpus final (close-juncture?) constituents of compounds.

4.2.2 Placement opposition maintained: I define here the ADJECTIVE as any specific noun lexeme (N^x) featuring in both following paradigms: (α) ' N → N-N^x ' (parad. α); (β) ' N^x → N-N ' (parad. β), i.e. having the privilege of both first- and second-place positions; analytically speaking, the adjective comprises *two homonymic signs*, formally opposed and distinguishable by placement properties. Note that whereas in this class the conception of *a category or paradigm of two non-identical homonyms* — ⲢⲰⲘⲈ ⲘⲠⲞⲚⲎⲢⲞⲤ and ⲠⲞⲚⲎⲢⲞⲤ ⲚⲢⲰⲘⲈ — is feasible, this is not so with second-position modifier nouns (§4.2.1.2). There the total reversal of the constituent interrelationship brought about by a change in their arrangement, precludes their analysis as two different signs; a paradigmatic association of α- and β-sequences is not meaningful in that case.

ADJECTIVES comprise the following subgroups:
(a) Loan-adjectives of Greek origin. Various Greek morphologic types: -ⲚⲞⲤ, -ⲢⲞⲤ, -ⲓⲞⲤ, -ⲦⲞⲤ, -ⲔⲞⲤ, -ⲎⲤ. Also exocentric (ⲀⲚⲞⲘⲞⲤ, ⲌⲞⲘⲞⲞⲨⲤⲓⲞⲤ) and other two-ending Greek compounds (ⲠⲀⲢⲀⲚⲞⲘⲞⲤ, ⲦⲀⲖⲀⲓⲠⲰⲢⲞⲤ).

(b) Adjectives of Egyptian origin: prenominal *agent nouns*, non-analytic (Ⲁ-vocalized) (hist. " conjunct participles "): ⲰⲀⲚ-, ⲬⲀⲤⲓ-, ⲌⲀⲢⲰ-, ⲚⲀⲰⲦ-, ⲘⲀⲓ- as well as the analytic, productive agent nouns (really syntagms) in ⲢⲈϤ-; ⲀⲦ- " privative " syntagms [21]; ⲬⲀϪⲈ " inimical, hostile ".

(c) ⲌⲖⲖⲞ " old ", ⲰⲘⲘⲞ " alien "; ⲈⲂⲓⲎⲚ " miserable ", ⲘⲈⲢⲓⲦ " beloved ", ⲠⲈⲦⲞⲨⲀⲀⲂ " holy ".

DOCUMENTATION (representative; I am here illustrating the α paradigm):
(a) (*III* 41.2f.) ⲌⲈⲚⲰⲀϪⲈ ⲚⲈⲓⲢⲎⲚⲓⲔⲞⲚ, (49.2) ⲚⲈⲨⲤⲘⲞⲦ ⲘⲠⲞⲚⲎⲢⲞⲚ, (78.6) ⲠⲢⲰⲘⲈ ⲚⲀⲚⲞⲘⲞⲤ, (90.18) ⲠⲀⲈⲓⲰⲦ ⲚⲀⲄⲀⲐⲞⲤ, (154.15) ⲌⲈⲚⲞⲨⲰⲰ ⲚⲤⲀⲢⲔⲓⲔⲞⲚ, (*IV* 156.7) ⲢⲰⲘⲈ ⲚⲈⲨⲤⲈⲂⲎⲤ, (*Ch.* 12.19f.) ⲞⲨⲬⲢⲈⲓⲀ... ⲚⲀⲚⲀⲄⲔⲀⲓⲞⲚ, (14.13ff.) ⲞⲨⲢⲰⲘⲈ ⲘⲠⲚⲈⲨⲘⲀⲦⲓⲔⲞⲤ, (138.52ff.) ⲠⲚⲀ ⲚⲓⲘ ⲚⲀⲔⲀⲐⲀⲢⲦⲞⲚ;
(b) (*III* 50.3f.) ⲠⲈⲦⲚⲈⲓⲰⲦ ⲚⲚⲀⲰⲦⲌⲎⲦ, (57.7) ⲦⲈⲤⲠⲓⲤⲦⲓⲤ ⲚⲀⲦⲔⲓⲘ, (76.22) ⲌⲈⲚⲤⲚⲎⲨ ⲚⲀⲦⲤⲂⲰ, (70-1) ⲚⲈⲓⲢⲰⲘⲈ ⲚⲬⲀϪⲈ, (189.23,30) ⲠⲀⲄⲄⲈⲖⲞⲤ ⲚⲀⲦⲚⲀ, (*Ch.* 27.4ff.) ⲠⲓⲦⲰⲰ ⲚⲢⲈϤⲦⲀⲚⲌⲞ, (57.40ff.) ⲘⲀⲦⲞⲓ ⲚⲢⲈϤⲦⲰⲢⲠ, (77.51f.) ⲠⲢⲰⲘⲈ ⲘⲘⲀⲓⲚⲞⲂⲈ;
(c) (*III* 103.7f., 142.5f.) ⲠⲈⲚⲈⲓⲰⲦ/ⲚⲈⲠⲢⲈⲤⲂⲨⲦⲈⲢⲞⲤ ⲚⲌⲖⲖⲞ, (*IV* 172.16) ⲞⲨⲌⲎⲦ ⲚⲰⲘⲘⲞ, (*III* 62.22) ⲠⲈⲓⲢⲈϤ-Ⲣ-ⲚⲞⲂⲈ ⲚⲈⲂⲓⲎⲚ.

4.2.2.1 RECTION IN ' NOUN + ADJECTIVE ' SYNTAGMS: CONCORD. As has long ago been noted and often restated since [22], the Greek loan-adjectives have in Coptic partly kept their movability, alternating (extra- or sub-systemically in Coptic, though not of course in pre-Coptic Egyptian [23]) in a conditioning set of *animate* (common gender, ⲡ-/ⲧ- → -ⲞⲤ)/*inanimate* (sexual or natural neuter, ⲡ-/ⲧ- → -ⲞⲚ). Since this has never, to my knowledge, been put to the test in an extensive and homogenous corpus, let me specify here the nuclei governing each of these concord alternants in the Shenoutean texts. Note: (1) The *motivating element* is the *determinator* of the nucleus, the initiator and prime nucleus of the expansion concatenation. (2) The nucleus may be either singular or plural. (3) For the rection of personal pronouns and proper names, see below, §4.3; their expansion is *appositive*. (4) This concord rection operates in adnominal attributive adjectives. We need more evidence for *predicative* adjectives, namely ones expanding the predicate determinator in a Nominal Sentence pattern ('ⲞⲨⲠⲞⲚⲎⲢⲞⲤ ⲠⲈ', consider [*P* 131⁶ 88ro] ⲚⲦⲔ-ⲞⲨⲤⲀⲢⲔⲓⲔⲞⲚ ⲦⲎⲢⲔ), or Ⲛ-marked adnexally modifying ⲈⲓⲢⲈ/ⲟ (consider ⲤⲞ ⲚⲀⲢⲄⲞⲚ *III* 34.15f., ⲀⲀⲔ ⲚⲈⲖⲀⲬⲓⲤⲦⲞⲚ *IV* 41.9f., and ⲦⲈⲓⲀⲐⲎⲦ ⲚⲤⲌⲓⲘⲈ ⲈⲚⲦⲀⲠⲚⲞⲨⲦⲈ ⲀⲀⲤ ⲚⲰⲘⲘⲞ *A I* 76, indicating that the rules are different in this adverbal status). (5) This concord is observable in instances of the *postposed* (α) adjective;

---

[21] Cf. JERNSTEDT 1967, FUNK 1976b.

[22] STERN §169, STEINDORFF 1904:§172, TILL 1928:§88f., TILL §76, GREGORIUS 1981:199f.

[23] The very few movable Coptic adjectives (ⲌⲖⲖⲞ/Ⲱ, ⲰⲘⲘⲞ/Ⲱ, ⲤⲀⲓⲈ/Ⲏ, ⲤⲀⲂⲈ/Ⲏ) are better viewed as double-entry semi-analyzable lexemes, rather than true concord alternants.

exx. of concord in the anteposed (β) adjective are too few to be conclusive (see below). (6) - HC is invariable (animate only? *III* 182.3, 221.4, *IV* 156.7).

(a) -oc: *human beings and their parts*; *some special faculties*; *groupings*: ρωμε (ρεϥ- *IV* 3.20, ρμν- *III* 220.15); ϲϩιμε (*IV* 28.20); ειωτ (*IV* 29.18); ϣηρε, ϣεερε (*III* 173.14f., *Ch.* 169.31a.); ϲον (*IV* 32.21f., see obs. 1); ματοι (*Ch.* 70.37f.); ιουδαι (*Ch.* 143.25f.); ρρο (*IV* 29.22f.); αρχων (*III* 95.19); προφητης (*III* 171.14); δικαιος (*III* 28.5). *Note especially*: ϲνοϥ (only in the cliché 'ϲνοϥ νιμ νδικαιος', see obs. 2; *III* 166.18, 167.1f., *Ch.* 174.54f., *Thompson* A ϲμ); βαλ (in the cliché 'βαλ μπονηρος', see obs. 5; *IV* 88.10, *A 2* 527); μεεγε (*Ch.* 78.1f., *Wess. 9* 134a 3ff.); ϲπερμα (*III* 213.13f., *Ch.* 137.12f., 144.20f.; obs. 3); ψυχη (*Ch.* 140.17ff., obs. 4); γενος (*Ch.* 102.9ff.); λαος (*P* 131⁵ 21 vo); βιος (*A 2* 368: νϲεμνος, cliché); γαμος (*IV* 175.2f., obs. 6); ϲοου, ουοειϣ (only + ναρχαιος, obs. 7; *III* 164.12f., *A 2* 22, 247).

(b) -on: *inanimates*; *abstracts (incl. infinitives)*; *plants, non-human animates*: ϩνο, ϲκεγος (*Ch.* 193. 34f.), ϩωβ (*IV* 194.5), ϩρε, τροφη (*Ch.* 118.57f., *IV* 86.21, *P* 131⁶ 42 ro), ϲμοτ (*III* 49.2), πνεγμα (*Ch.* 20. 32ff.), δαιμων (*P* 131⁵ 56 ν), αγαθον (*III* 114.27), μτον (*IV* 116.14), ωνϩ (*III* 114.22f.), ουϣϣ (*Ch.* 73. 22f.,28f.), ϣοϫνε, επιβουλη (*Ch.* 33.10f., *III* 89.23), μοκμεκ (*Wess. 9* 131b 30f.), ϲω (*IV* 86.22), ερητ (*Ch.* 135.17f.), λογος, ϣαϫε (*III* 63.20f., 148.16), ϲβω (*A 2* 486), μντ-syntagms (*III* 155.16f., *P* 130² 10 ραθ, τενμντατϲοουν νϲαρκικον), αγαπη (*Ch.* 168.27f.), ϲυνηθεια (*III* 49.2f.), βιος (*A 2* 423, not Sh.), πραϫιϲ (*Ch.* 120.46ff., *A 1* 163), χρεια (*IV* 172.12f.), ροουϣ (*III* 100.25), ϩαπ, νομος (*Ch.* 85.4f.,39f.), λογιϲμος (*Ch.* 77.46ff.), ϲοειτ (*Ch.* 129.24f.), ϣδη (*Ch.* 207.3ff., Sh.?), τκας (*Ch.* 36.19f.), ϣϣνϥ (*Ming.* 318), εντηϭ (*A 2* 402), ϲοϭν (*Teza* 683). Note especially: βαλ (*III* 185.10, μπονηρον, obs. 5), ϲπερμα (*III* 208.12, μπονηρον, obs. 4, 8), ϲωμα (*III* 106.4f., *IV* 190.10, 191.12, obs. 8), ζωον (*K* 913, μπονηρον, obs. 8), ϣβηρ (*III* 30.8f., obs. 9), ϩητ (*Wess. 9* 172a 8f.).

Observations: (1) Occurs once (*IV* 84.2) with -on, perhaps to be taken as an ad-pattern modifier: ενεπεγειωτ πε η πεγϣηρε αγω τεγμααγ μντεγϲωνε η πεγϲον νϲαρκικον. Compare in this status (ν)καταϲαρϫ (*IV* 81.2f., 159.13).

(2) Only ϲνοϥ (νιμ) νδικαιος, excerpt quotation from *Mt.* 23:35.

(3) As against πνⲁ̄, list (b).

(4) For πεϲπερμα μπονηρον (*III* 208.12) cf. *Is.* 1:4, 14:20, 57:3-4, also in *A 2* 122 πεϲπερμα ... η μπονηρον αγω ννοεικ ϩιπορνη.

(5) -oc is the consensus in the source of this excerpt quotation (*Mt.* 6:23, 20:15, *Luc.* 11:34); ουβαλ μπονηρον (*III* 185.10) is an adaptation to the system of Shenoute.

(6) Only in πγαμος νϲγμνος (*IV* 175.2f.), a calque of σεμνὸς γάμος? Compare ουγαμος νϲεμνον (Bohairic, *Acta Martyrum* [edd. Balestri-Hyvernat] I 37.29), and see Drescher, *Le Muséon* 82:92f. (1969): also βιος νϲεμνος/νκοϲμικος (*A 2* 368).

(7) Only in νεουοειϣ/νεϩοου ναρχαιος " past times ", " days of old ". ναρχαιος appears to be an invariable modifier, " of old ", " of yore ", adverbal as well as adnominal [24]: (*P* 130⁴ 118 κγ) ναρχαιος αγω ον τενου, (*P* 131⁵ 23 [θθ]) εγϫε-μπεπνουτε ϯϲο επκοϲμος ναρχαιος, (*Or.* 166.42ff.) νθε νταϥααϲ ναρχαιος; consider also *III* 19.14, 66.21, 203.17 and (*A 1* 12) πνοϭ μπροφητης ϫιννααρχαιος.

(8) Influence of Greek gender?

(9) This would be difficult to explain without referring to *Act.* 10:14, where all Boh. MSS and Horner's "*a*" (Bodl. Hunt. 345) have νανανκαιον (αναγκεον) for ἀναγκαίους.

---

[24] Cf. Brugmann, *IF* 27:233ff. (1910), for a comparative study of the nominative masc. sgl. Greek adjective in " adverbial " status (esp. p. 240ff.). Incidentally, ἀρχαῖος does not occur (to the best of my knowledge) in this construction; however, we do find τἀρχαῖον (SCHWYZER I 620, II 617f.).

(10) Fixed, "imported complete", often technical, terms and collocations, with the original concord [25], include ΔΗΜΟϹΙΟΝ ΓΡΑΜΜΑ (*III* 23.22), ΤΕΠΛΑΤШΝΙΚΗ ΔΙΔΑϹΚΑΛΙΑ (*A 1* 15), ΤΚΑΘΟΛΙΚΗ ΕΚΚΛΗϹΙΑ (*Thompson* K 3 vo, *III* 61.1f., *Ch.* 146.50f. etc., very common), ΤΠΑΛΑΙΑ (ΑΥШ/ΜΝ-Τ-)ΚΑΙΝΗ ΔΙΑΘΗΚΗ (*Ch.* 175.32f., 186.52ff., *A 2* 244, *Duke 2* vo etc., very common); here we find the feminine form of Greek adjectives.

(11) The feminine occurs also in collocations which are Coptic in construction, but are still calques of Greek terminological and fixed clichés: (*A 2* 440, not Sh.) ΤΑΠΟΛΑΥϹΙϹ ΝϹШΜΑΤΙΚΗ, (*BMCat.* 77, No. 192 ϹΟΓ) ΝΕΙΠΑΡΘΕΝΟϹ ΝϹΕΜΝΗ. Otherwise, the feminine occurs only in in substantives, like ΠΟΡΝΗ " whore " (the quoted ΟΥϹϨΙΜΕ ΜΠΟΡΝΗ, *III* 97.14, where formally a modifier, is in appositive role), ΤϹΑΙΗ ΜΠΝΙΚΗ " the beautiful spiritual (woman) " (*Teza* 683).

4.2.2.2 DEFINITION OF THE OPPOSITION TERMS: UNMARKED (second-place-position adjectives) vs. MARKED (first-place-position adjectives). The paradigm of first-place-privileged adjectives, (β) is lexically and semasiologically much more restricted, and its functional value specifically definable: " *attribution* + *X* ", " *X* " being either (a) a detectable *affective or emotive charge*, or (b) a *contrastively distinctive* role (it is probable that (a) and (b) are but two aspects of one and the same semantic range; see n. 29). This characterization is unspecified (though not incompatible) with second-place (α)-adjectives. One is therefore led to regard (β)-adjectives as *marked*, and (α)-adjectives as *unmarked* members in a binary (privative) opposition: the first-place adjective is characterized, the second-place adjective, an uncharacterized or neutral term: " banal " attribution [26].

4.2.2.2.1 CONSTITUENCY: POSITION (β). First and foremost in all groups (§4.2.2) are *pejorative*, *degradatory* or *disapproving* attributes [27]: ΠΟΝΗΡΟϹ, ΑΚΑΘΑΡΤΟϹ, ΤΑΛΑΙΠШΡΟϹ, ϨΑΙΡΕΤΙΚΟϹ, ΑϹΕΒΗϹ, ΑΝΟΜΟϹ, ΠΑΡΑΝΟΜΟϹ, ΕΛΑΧΙϹΤΟϹ, ΑΚΕΡΑΙΟϹ, ΑΡΓΟϹ, ΕΒΙΗΝ, ΧΑΧΕ, ΧΑϹΙϨΗΤ, ΡΕϤΡΝΟΒΕ, ΡΕϤΚШϨ, ΑΤΝΑ, ΑΘΗΤ, ΑΤΝΟΥΤΕ, ШΜΜΟ; much less prevalent are non-pejorative ones (§4.2.2.2): ΑΓΑΘΟϹ, ΑΤΝΟΒΕ, ΡΕϤϢΜϢΕ-ΝΟΥΤΕ ΜΑΚΑΡΙΟϹ, ΧΡΗϹΤΟϹ, ϹΟϤΟϹ, ΜΕΡΙΤ.

4.2.2.2.2 FUNCTION (1): In the case of *pejorative attributes* [28] we are obviously faced with some attitudinal *differentia specifica* which, though hardly traceable formally in the context, is nevertheless inferable from the semasiological peculiarity of the adjectives themselves. This is, I believe, sufficient mark for some context-oriented property. Another, even more " formal ", is the frequent ΠΙ-determination [29] in this construction. Yet another, *relative* formal index may be the very high incidence of such indefinite or low-specificity semantic nuclei as ΡШΜΕ (very frequent), ϨШΒ, ϨΝΑΑΥ/ϨΝΟ, etc. The (β)-adjective may have been marked also by a special stress or intonation contour. " Affect " is as good a cover-term for this as any [30]: (*P* 130⁴ 97 ro) ΤΕϤΚΕΤΑΛΑΙΠШΡΟϹ ΜΨΥΧΗ (sim. *Ch.* 186.7) / (*Ch.* 123.48ff.) ΤΑΚΑ-

[25] GREGORIUS 1981:201.

[26] BERGSON's term (1960:62-98), opposed to " emphatic " (logically or affectively).

[27] In the unmarked term (postposed adjective) the proportion of pejorative *vs.* non-pejorative attributes is decidedly different. Obviously, both the subject-matter and Shenoute's stylistic temperament and predilections must be taken into account. All one can hope to establish is an inner consistency, a norm of usage proving the privileges of position to be more than whimsical variants.

[28] The usually pejorative (—) ΜΙΝΕ Ν- (" kind of... ") shares the marked (β) adjective paradigm: ΝΙΜΙΝΕ ΝΡШΜΕ ΝΑΡΓΟϹ (*Ch.* 62.3f.) / ΤΜΙΝΕ ΜΜΟΝΑΧΟϹ (*III* 92.10) / ΤΕΙΜΙΝΕ ΝΡШΜΕ ΝΑΘΗΤ (*A 2* 486), also *III* 82.7f., *IV* 42.3f., 47.24. Contrast this with the unmarked — ΝΤΕΙΜΙΝΕ (*III* 50.13, 110.19, 124.19f., 146.26, *IV* 59.7 etc.). Rare non-pejorative (neutral) instances, again with ΡШΜΕ the semantic nucleus (this seems to be significant): (*Ch.* 98.44f.) ΤΕΝΜΙΝΕ ΝΡШΜΕ / (*A 2* 398) ϨΕΝΚΕΜΙΝΕ ΝΡШΜΕ.

[29] POLOTSKY 1957a:229 (= *CP* 231). Observe that ΠΙ- too, like β-adjectives, is characterized both affectively and distinctively,

[30] Compare (among many other applications of this principle) WEIL 1879:36ff. (" l'ordre pathétique "); GAMILLSCHEG 1930:15. 25, 32 (affect including antithesis); REGULA 1951:179, 181d. (" Affektsyntax "); the " emotive order " in Firbas, *Časopis pro mod. filologii* 39:173 (1957); JONES 1977:63f. (" the emotive principle "); also REINER 1968: 225-244, 256. Other terms for approximately the same factor are " emphatic ", " subjective ", " impulsive ", " figured " order or syntax.

ⲑⲀⲢⲦⲞⲤ ⲚⲤⲨⲚⲀⲅⲰⲅⲎ / (*A 2* 73) ⲠⲒⲈⲖⲀⲬⲒⲤⲦⲞⲤ ⲚⲢⲰⲘⲈ (sim. *Wess.* 9 168b 13f.; — ⲚⲌⲰⲞⲚ *III* 47.15, — ⲚⲀϤ *ibid.* 82.28, — ⲚⲌⲚⲀⲀⲨ *A 2* 507, etc.) / (*IV* 82.1) ⲚⲔⲈⲀⲢⲅⲞⲤ ⲚⲢⲰⲘⲈ / (*Ch.* 147-8) ⲚⲒⲀⲐⲎⲦ ⲚⲢⲰⲘⲈ / (*A 2* 412) ⲠⲈⲂⲒⲎⲚ ⲚⲌⲈⲖⲖⲎⲚ (cf. *Cl. Pr.* 22 ⲦⲚⲌ: ⲠⲀⲈⲂⲒⲎⲚ ⲚⲢⲰⲘⲈ, appositive: " I, the miserable "; cf. §4.3) / (*Rossi 2/3* 75) ⲠⲞⲚⲎⲢⲞⲤ ⲚⲒⲘ ⲚⲢⲰⲘⲈ / (*Ch.* 56.53f.) ⲠⲀⲦⲚⲀ ⲘⲘⲀⲦⲞⲒ / (*A 1* 194) ⲠⲀⲦⲚⲞⲨⲦⲈ ⲘⲘⲀⲚⲒⲬⲀⲒⲞⲤ / (*P* 131[8] 109 vo) ⲌⲈⲚⲬⲀⲬⲈ ⲚⲢⲰⲘⲈ / (*III* 87.19) ⲚⲈⲒⲀⲤⲈⲂⲎⲤ ⲚⲢⲰⲘⲈ. Additional exx.: *Ch.* 63.55f., 142.39ff., 204.8ff., *Wess.* 9 149d 20f., 154a 17f., *A 1* 14 etc.

FUNCTION (2), with *non-pejorative* attributes (rather unusual): (a) In distinctive, antithetic role: (*IV* 127.25f.,29) ⲠⲀⲅⲀⲐⲞⲤ ⲚⲢⲰⲘⲈ, contrasting with ⲠⲠⲞⲚⲎⲢⲞⲤ ⲚⲢⲰⲘⲈ, ⲠⲢⲰⲘⲈ ⲚⲬⲀⲬⲈ in 11. 27, 28f., 30.

(b) Stylistic motivation (?) in the chiastic arrangement of (*A 1* 182-3) (ⲠⲰⲢⲬ) ⲚⲀⲠⲒⲤⲦⲞⲤ ⲚⲀⲦⲚⲞⲨⲦⲈ ⲈⲂⲞⲖ ⲚⲚⲢⲘⲚⲚⲞⲨⲦⲈ ⲘⲠⲒⲤⲦⲞⲤ (four-pole contrast: ⲀⲠⲒⲤⲦⲞⲤ: ⲠⲒⲤⲦⲞⲤ/ⲀⲦⲚⲞⲨⲦⲈ: ⲢⲘⲚⲚⲞⲨⲦⲈ).

(c) Polite clichés (devaluation of function 1): (*III* 15.14) ⲠⲈⲚⲘⲀⲔⲀⲢⲒⲞⲤ ⲚⲤⲞⲚ " our late brother " / (*III* 13.23 = 14.22) ⲠⲢⲈϤϢⲘϢⲈ-ⲚⲞⲨⲦⲈ ⲚⲤⲞⲚ / (*III* 25.8) ⲠⲀⲘⲈⲢⲒⲦ ⲚⲤⲞⲚ (sim. *Mun.* 92) / (*III* 13.15) ⲠⲈⲚⲘⲈⲢⲒⲦ ⲚⲈⲒⲰⲦ ⲈⲦⲤⲘⲀⲘⲀⲀⲦ (sim. *Mun.* 95) / (*III* 32.4f.) ⲞⲨⲘⲈⲢⲒⲦ ⲚϢⲂⲢ; compare with (*IV* 26.15) (ϢⲰⲠⲈ) ⲚⲞⲨϢⲎⲢⲈ ⲘⲘⲈⲢⲒⲦ, (*ibid.* 117.24) ⲌⲰⲤ-ⲤⲞⲚ ⲘⲘⲈⲢⲒⲦ (but also ⲚⲀⲤⲚⲎⲨ ⲘⲘⲈⲢⲀⲦⲈ, *III* 123.27f., probably appositive — Ⲙ- the definite article?); perhaps also (*III* 147.16) ⲌⲈⲚⲬⲢⲎⲤⲦⲞⲤ ⲚⲢⲰⲘⲈ "worthy persons", sim. *ibid.* 128.20f.

(d) A bracketing role, with multiple nuclei: (*III* 106.11f.) ⲌⲈⲚⲀⲦⲚⲞⲂⲈ ⲚⲀⲠⲞⲤⲦⲞⲖⲞⲤ ⲀⲨϢ ⲘⲠⲢⲞⲪⲎⲦⲎⲤ.

(e) Unexplained is still (*III* 213.9f.) ⲚⲤⲞⲪⲞⲤ ⲘⲠⲢⲞⲪⲎⲦⲎⲤ ⲚⲤⲀⲂⲈ ⲚⲢⲘⲚⲌⲎⲦ (cod. A only) — which may be stylistically motivated, with middle placement of the semantic nucleus.

FUNCTION (3)[?]: Although several examples seem to indicate an *inherent attribution* value for position (β) attributes (ⲠⲀⲦⲚⲀ ⲘⲘⲀⲦⲞⲒ *Ch.* 56.53f.), *vs.* an *incidental attribution* value for the unmarked placement (Ⲛ- being the non-predicative counterpart of -Ⲟ Ⲛ-), I have not been able to follow this lead through to achieve a comprehensive description.

4.3 DETERMINATIVE AND APPOSITIVE SYNTAGMS: SUPPLETIVE NEUTRALIZATION FOR PRONOMINAL AND PROPER-NAME NUCLEI

Proper names and personal pronouns, neither determinable, since both are extreme on the scale of specificity (the pronoun of maximal specificity and maximal phoric applicability, the proper name of maximal specificity, minimal phoric applicability [31]) are as a rule nuclei of an *appositive* attributive syntagm, i.e. are expanded by a ' determinator (definite article) + adjective ' syntagm and not by an Ⲛ-marked modifier adjective or substantive [32]. Thus it is the satellite that carries the overt determination, when the nucleus does not. Here are some examples for this allosyntagm of the attribution syntagmeme:

Proper names (adjectives occupy here first or second-place positions; ⲚⲞϬ always precedes the nucleus [33]): ⲤⲒⲚⲞⲨⲐⲒⲞⲤ ⲠⲒⲈⲖⲀⲬⲒⲤⲦⲞⲤ (*Mun.* 92, 95, *III* 13.19, 14.15 etc.) / ⲠⲀⲒⲔⲀⲒⲞⲤ ⲀⲂⲈⲖ, ⲠⲀⲒⲔⲀⲒⲞⲤ ⲚⲰⲌⲈ (*P* 130[2] 105 ⲦⲘⲀ) / ⲀⲂⲈⲖ ⲠⲀⲒⲔⲀⲒⲞⲤ (*III* 173.10, *P* 130[2] 53 ⲦⲒⲀ, etc.) / ⲠⲀⲒⲔⲀⲒⲞⲤ ⲒⲰⲂ (*Ch.* 38.10f., *A 2* 367, 478) / ⲠⲚⲞϬ ⲀⲂⲢⲀⲌⲀⲘ (*RE 10* 162a 10) / ⲠⲚⲞϬ ⲚⲀⲢⲬⲀⲅⲅⲈⲖⲞⲤ ⲘⲒⲬⲀⲎⲖ (*Ch.* 33.37ff.) / ⲠⲚⲞϬ ⲘⲘϢⲨⲤⲎⲤ ⲒⲎⲤⲞⲨ

---

[31] See KURYŁOWICZ 1960:182. The present writer is preparing a monographic study of the syntax of the proper name in Coptic.

[32] Cf. CALLENDER 1970:297f.: " a proper noun cannot form part of an attribution but may form part of an apposition ". (The modals " cannot ", " may " would be out of place in a descriptive statement. Callender uses " attribution " in a more restricted sense than I do; the construction in point, while syntactically appositive, is functionally still attributive.)

[33] ⲠⲚⲞϬ... ⲚⲄⲀⲂⲢⲒⲎⲖ (*A 2* 376, collated) is a rare instance of an Ⲛ-marked proper name semantic nucleus. Under certain contextual conditions, a proper name may be determinated: ⲞⲨⲒⲞⲨⲆⲀⲤ (ⲚⲞⲨϢⲦ), ⲌⲀⲚⲒⲞⲨⲆⲀⲤ, ⲚⲀⲒⲒⲞⲨⲆⲀⲤ, in De Vis, *Homélies coptes de la Vaticane* I 64f — the proper name is thus " de-specified ", marked as appellative.

ⲚⲀⲨⲎ (*Ch.* 76.3ff.) / ⲠⲘⲀⲓⲢⲰⲘⲈ ⲗⲓⲃⲈⲢⲓⲟⲥ (*Ch.* 200.2f.) / ⲠⲀⲤⲈⲃⲎⲤ ⲤⲀⲦⲀⲚⲀⲤ [34] (*Ch.* 148.14f.) / ⲠⲓⲀⲚⲟⲘⲟⲤ ⲚⲀ-ⲃⲞⲨⲬⲞⲆⲞⲚⲞⲤⲤⲞⲢ (*Ch.* 49.17ff.) / ⲓⲰⸯⲀⲚⲚⲎⲤ ⲠⲘⲈⲢⲓⲦ (*P* 131[6] 23 ⲡ). With *pronouns*, the nucleus invariably precedes the appositive attribute: ⲀⲚⲞⲚ ⲚⲓⲦⲀⲗⲀⲓⲠⲰⲢⲞⲤ (*A 1* 175, *Ch.* 99.2f., etc.) / ⲀⲚⲞⲔ ⲠⲓⲈⲗⲀⲭⲓⲤⲦⲞⲤ (*A 1* 16) / ⲚⲦⲰⲦⲚ ⲚⲀⲦⲤⲃⲰ, ⲚⲦⲰⲦⲚ ⲚⲢⲈ4ⲔⲢⲘⲢⲘ (*III* 144.1.16). (For the '*pronoun + noun*' apposition to a preceding personal pronoun, see §6.1.3.3.) Note that ⲠⲚⲞⲨⲦⲈ usually behaves like a proper name [35]: ⲠⲚⲞⲨⲦⲈ ⲠⲀⲄⲀⲐⲞⲤ (*Ch.* 13.31, *A 1* 154, etc.) / ⲠⲚⲞⲨⲦⲈ ⲠⲰⸯⲀⲚⲥ̄ⲦⲎ4 (*A 2* 178) / ⲠⲚⲞⲨⲦⲈ Ⲡⲥ̄ⲀⲢⲰⲥ̄ⲎⲦ (*III* 123.13) / NB. ⲠⲚⲞⲨⲦⲈ ⲠⲚⲀⲎⲦ ⲚⲰⸯⲀⲚⲥ̄ⲦⲎ4 Ⲛⲥ̄ⲀⲢⲰⲥ̄ⲎⲦ ⲠⲀⲄⲀⲐⲞⲤ (*A 1* 87, uncollated) / ⲠⲀⲄⲀⲐⲞⲤ ⲠⲚⲞⲨⲦⲈ ⲚⲰⸯⲀⲚⲥ̄ⲦⲎ4 (*IV* 34.7f.) / ⲠⲘⲀⲓⲢⲰⲘⲈ ⲠⲤⲰⲦⲎⲢ ⲠⲚⲞⲨⲦⲈ (*III* 23.21). So too do ⲠⲬⲞⲈⲓⲤ and of course ⲓ̄ⲥ̄: ⲠⲬⲞⲈⲓⲤ ⲠⲀⲄⲀⲐⲞⲤ (*A 2* 287) / ⲠⲬⲞⲈⲓⲤ ⲠⲰⸯⲀⲚⲦⲥ̄ⲦⲎ4 (*A 1* 103) / ⲓ̄ⲥ̄ ⲠⲰⸯⲀⲚⲥ̄ⲦⲎ4 ⲚⲚⲀⲎⲦ (*A 1* 105, uncollated). ⲠⲀⲤⲬⲀ is apparently not considered a proper name: ⲠⲔⲈⲚⲞ6 ⲘⲠⲀⲤⲬⲀ (*Ch.* 44.52f.).

---

[34] ⲤⲀⲦⲀⲚⲀⲤ is a common appellative in (*Ch.* 65.31f.) ⲠⲞⲨⲰⲚⲰⲩ ⲠⲤⲀⲦⲀⲚⲀⲤ or else, like ⲠⲚⲞⲨⲦⲈ, part of a proper name with innate determination.

[35] Cf. ⲠⲚⲞⲨⲦⲈ ⲠⲰⸯⲀⲈⲚⲈ2 (*Teza* 684). (*A 2* 411) ⲘⲎ ⲀⲗⲗⲞ-ⲠⲢⲰⲘⲈ ⲀⲚ ⲚⲀⲄⲀⲐⲞⲤ... ⲀⲗⲗⲞ-Ⲡ2ⲚⲞ ⲚⲀⲄⲀⲐⲞⲚ... ⲀⲗⲗⲞ-ⲠⲚⲞⲨⲦⲈ ⲞⲚ ⲚⲀⲄⲀⲐⲞⲤ ⲀⲨⲰ ⲠⲈ4ⲰⸯⲎⲢⲈ ⲚⲀⲄⲀⲐⲞⲤ (uncollated) may be a contrary example; others are (*A 1* 130) ⲠⲚⲞⲨⲦⲈ ⲚⲚⲀⲎⲦ (uncollated) / (*A 2* 376) ⲠⲚⲞⲨⲦⲈ ⲘⲘⲈ.

CHAPTER 5

EXCURSUS: NEUTER GENDER AS A SYNTAGMATICALLY MANIFESTED, PARADIGMATICALLY DEFINED CATEGORY

5.1 COPTIC GENDER

The observation of gender in Coptic [1] provides the occasion for a study in structural description with several interesting theoretical aspects, the more specific ones being those of environment (conditioning, rection) and neutralization, the more general and basic ones being gender exponence, option and selection, as well as the definition of a category in general. The relevance of this study to our examination of Coptic modifiers lies in its contribution to an understanding of the *nucleus - satellite* nominal/adnominal syntagmatics, in a classic illustration of the advantages of a structuralist approach to a difficult grammatical issue.

5.1.1 EXPONENTS; SYNTAGMATICS. It is well known that Coptic gender is syntagmatic and pronominal rather than lexematic or morphematic (FUNK 1978a:110): the article-pronoun or determinator is, insofar as it is marked for gender, the primary exponent or carrier of this category. The noun lexeme (a satellite expanding the article nucleus, see below) does not usually carry any intrinsic mark of gender. Of course, the question of concord does not yet arise here, within the ' *article → noun* ' minimal noun syntagm, but only when this is further expanded, in cotext patterns involving other pronouns in cohesion with the article (§5.1.1.1) [2]. The interdependence of the article and its expansion I see as one of *mutual selection*, i.e. the compatibility of a lexeme with either — or both [3] — of the two singular definite articles,

---

[1] Some conventional discussions of Coptic gender: STERN §§302, 487; TILL §§75f., 79; MALLON-MALININE p. 44ff.

[2] Meillet (" Le genre grammatical ", 1919, in *Linguistique historique et linguistique générale* p. 206) calls these movable pronouns " débris de genre "; English, he says, " a profité de la destruction totale de la fin de mot où figurait la marque du genre pour écarter une distinction inutile ". The " usefulness " of any grammatical distinction may be arguable, but in Coptic — and, in a different way, in English — the pronouns have proved staunch custodians of the historic category.

[3] Fodor's general definition of gender (1959) as " the concord between a variable and an invariable " is hardly applicable

п-, т-. The question of " where " the gender is, is not one of descriptive relevance; the article is the concord motivant. The general thesis of the so-called inherence of grammatical (i.e. *signifié*-less) gender in the lexeme itself [4] is therefore nowhere put to the test in Coptic. The few instances of " nomen mobile ", the sex-referable residue of a pre-Coptic system (CON: ϢⲰⲚⲈ, ⲌⲀⲖⲞ: ⲌⲀⲖⲰ, ϢⲎⲢⲈ: ϢⲈⲈⲢⲈ, see §4.0.1), synchronically only semi-morphological and unproductive, — as also are the lexical pairs (ⲈⲒⲰⲦ: ⲘⲀⲀⲨ, ⲢⲰⲘⲈ: ⲤⲌⲒⲘⲈ) — are not really marked for gender, but stand in semasiological-paradigmatic opposition, which must grammatically be related to the same pronoun-compatibility or mutual selection.

5.1.1.0.1 DETERMINATORS. It is the articles or gender-characterized determinators that carry the gender mark for the minimal noun syntagm. This is by no means a novel observation or one peculiar to Coptic [5], but it is certainly not banal or trivial, since it opens our eyes to a crucial fact, namely the *nuclear status* of the article in the noun syntagm, with the noun lexeme its satellite (expansion). This analytic statement, although by no means *communis opinio* as far as general and European linguistics is concerned, is upheld by some eminent syntacticians [6], and constitutes in fact the major and most noteworthy contribution of Jernstedt's study of Coptic determination (1949) [7]. To be exact, he asserts this of the *indefinite* articles, pointing to a subordination relationship between them and their nouns not unlike that between a noun and its attribute: " one (of the category...) "; see JERNSTEDT 1949 *passim*, esp. §§10,14, 18, 20ff., 25. The same is true, however, of all determinators [8]: the article is the prime nucleus, the initial boundary signal and beginning of the concatenation of adnominal modification (Ch. 4). Indications that this analysis is correct abound in many constructions involving the noun syntagm, a model

of which (after FREI 1965:44f.) would be
$$\begin{matrix} \text{П-} \\ \text{ОⲨ-} \\ \text{Ø-} \end{matrix} \diagdown \underset{\text{ⲢⲰⲘⲈ}}{\diagup} $$
It is the determinators that establish

here, where we have two lists, a very short one (a) of determinators (п-, т-) and a much longer one (b) of noun lexemes, with a member from (b) compatible and coupled with either one or both members of (a). It is possible to describe this in terms of *presupposition* — a given member of (a) presupposing a certain member of (b), or vice versa — i.e. as determination or rection (BAZELL 1949:8ff.).

[4] Cf. Hamp, *Archiv Orientální* 40 (1972) 344 (on Western Iranian dialects): " The gender is inherent in the noun and is transplanted to pronominals... by a simple but far-reaching concord rule "; cf. also DAMOURETTE–PICHON §303: " L'article reçoit la sexuisemblance et ne la confère pas... elle leur [i.e. to substantives] est donnée en dehors de lui par l'acte mental, qui conçoit la substantialité ". Jernstedt, whose study of Coptic gender-determination phenomena is by far the most penetrating, says (1949:§4): " Gender is a lexical characteristic of the noun " — with which it is difficult to differ; but when he claims (*ibid.*) to know that the determinator " agrees in gender with the determined noun ", he risks circularity, for the gender of the determinated noun is made manifest only by, and in, the determinator. Moreover, when he says (§25) that the article " overrules the inherent gender of the noun ", he is again begging the question. Generally speaking, the major flaw in Jernstedt's discussion lies in its overemphasis of the mentalistic and dynamic aspects of concord phenomena, this making many of his statements (esp. in §§13, 19) hard to accept. I also disagree with his assertion (§23) that the lexeme embodies both (abstract) property and (concrete) substance; it contains neither, except as a potentiality realized and resolved in syntagm with the *actualisateur* pronoun.

[5] See, for instance, BALLY 1950:§139, DUBOIS 1965:56 (the article opposition " met en évidence la marque du genre "). In Gaelic bardic-grammatical terminology, *innsgne* covers both " gender ", " person " and " pronoun-article " (O'Cuiv, *Transact. Philol. Soc.* 1965:152, Adams, *FL* 4:160 [1970]). Cf. KURYŁOWICZ 1964:210f., KERN 1888:100, 103n., and, the earliest instance to my knowledge of this approach, the Stoic definition of the article (Diocles ap. SCHMIDT 1839:39) ἄρθρον ἐστί στοιχεῖον λόγου πτωτικὸν διορίζων τὰ γένη τῶν ὀνομάτων καὶ τοὺς ἀριθμούς "; see too ROBINS 1951:31.

[6] See SEILER 1960:12ff.; FREI 1956:163-5, *idem* 1968:§3.2.3.1, 3.3.2.1; BARRI 1975a:75-83. We find this idea expressed by GUILLAUME as early as1919 (p. 25), though in a somewhat different sense: " L'article est quelque chose qui ' emploie ' le nom ".

[7] The same view is held by SCHENKEL 1966:129. See also (for Egyptian) Edel, *BiOr* 25 (1968) 36. This has an immediate bearing on the morphology:syntax " levelling " issue: the " word-internal " interdependence between article and noun is only juncturally different from that between the two-word nucleus and satellite (cf. Hjelmslev, *Prolegomena* 26). Incidentally, the distinction between *syntactic* and *semantic* nucleus is as valid for noun-syntagm analysis as it is for the ' NS + expansion ' one (§4.1).

[8] Probably also of other prefixed morphs in the minimal syntagm, like ⲀⲦ- and ⲘⲚⲦ- (FUNK 1978a:116); the *izâfet* dependence is synchronic in Coptic too (*pace* NAGEL 1980:89f.).

the class status ("nominal" syntax) for the whole syntagm; it is to them that anaphoric reference is made [9]. This analysis conforms to the basic non-predicative syntagmatic sequence in Coptic: nucleus → satellite. Only thus can we account (and account elegantly) for instances of apparent inconsistency [10]. like ⲡⲥⲩⲗⲗⲁⲃⲏ "the (book) of the syllable, syllabary" (*BL Or.* 8800 4 vo.) [11]; ⲡϭⲟⲙ ⲧⲏⲣϥ "he who is all power" (*RE 10* 161a 27f.); ⲡⲙⲟⲓⳅⲉ ⲧⲏⲣϥ "he who is all wonder" (*ibid.* 28); ⲡⲙⲟⲓⳅⲉ (*ibid.* 163a 33) [12]; ⲡⲙⲉ ⲙⲁⲩⲁⲁϥ (*Ch.* 59.20f.) [13] "he who alone is of truth". This seems to prove that (a) it is not the lexeme which selects the gender; (b) the determinator/noun dependence is a mutual one of *compatibility*, rather than of rection: ⲙⲟⲓⳅⲉ can in principle expand both "masculine" and "feminine" determinator pronouns, just (from the point of view of syntagmatic compatibility) as ⳅⲙⳅⲁⲗ or ⲉⲃⲓⲏⲛ can, and with precisely the same internal relationship. The same, of course, applies to the indefinite determinators, which, however, are either unmarked or indirectly marked for gender (see below): ⲟⲩⲙⲟⲓⳅⲉ ⲡⲉ ⲡⲛⲟⲩⲧⲉ "A wondrous one is God" (*P* 130[2] 46 ⲥⲕ) / ⲟⲩⲙⲉ ⲡⲉ ⲡⲛⲟⲩⲧⲉ ⲁⲩⲱ ⲟⲩⲙⲉ ⲡⲉ ⲡⲉⲛ ⲭⲟⲉⲓⲥ (*P* 130[5] 22 ⲫⲛ) / the common ⳅⲉⲛⲙⲛⲧ- "phenomena characterized by the quality of..." (e.g. *III* 206.1-5) / ⳅⲉⲛⲥⲁⲣ ⲛⲉⲓⲱ ⳅⲓ ⳅ ⲧⲟ (*P* 130[2] 86 ro, not Sh.?) "(persons) characterized by ass and horse-flesh", and so on. Although it is true that the above are isolated, rare instances — lexemes have their "usual" (i.e. statistically prevalent) compatibilities with either ⲡ- or ⲧ-, hence "are" masculine or feminine —, it is important to remember that the rarer compatibility is an open possibility [14], a productive procedure.

Paradigmatically, I would suggest the following scheme as the structured inventory of the main determinators, all quintessentially nuclear, expandable by noun lexemes [15]:

determinators proper				*quantifiers*	
ⲡ-ⲧ-/ⲛ-	"the-"		ⲕⲉ-	"other-"	
ⲟⲩ[m]-/ⲟⲩ[f]-/ⳅⲉⲛ-	"a-"		ⲟⲩ[m]-/ⲟⲩ[f]-	"one-"	
∅-	"-"		∅- ... ⲛⲓⲙ	"any, every-" (discontinuous)	
— ⲛⲓⲙ	"all"				

Observations: ⲡ-/ⲧ-//ⲛ- — masc. sgl./fem. sgl./masc. + fem. pl. — represent the whole demonstrative and possessive series.

[9] See below §5.2.1, and §3.1.1.1.0.1. The Nominal Sentence is a striking case in which the advantages of this conception are clear, it being really a pronominal predication pattern: ⲟⲩ-/ⲡ- + ⲡⲉ. This analysis, as Jernstedt himself points out, would account for syntagms like (a) ⲟⲩ-/ⳅⲉⲛ-ⲧⲉⲓⲙⲓⲛⲉ (*A 2* 417, 421 [not Sh.], *RE 11* 16a 10), an instance of hyperdetermination, where ⲧⲉⲓ-, in commutation with the bare noun, expands the indefinite articles; (b) ⳅⲉⲛⲧⲕⲁⲥ ⲛⲉ ⳅⲓϭⲱⲛⲧ ⳅⲓⲡⲉⲓⲣⲁⲥⲙⲟⲥ (*A 2* 435, not Sh.), ⲡⲉⲙⲕⲁⳅ ⲛⳅⲏⲧ ⳅⲓⲗⲩⲡⲏ ⳅⲓⲁⲯⲁⳅⲟⲙ (*A 1* 77), (ⲯⲯⲧ ⲙ)ⲡⲟⲉⲓⲕ ⳅⲓⳅⲟⲉⲓⲧⲉ (*III* 205.23f.). Note ⳅⲉⲛⲙⲟⲓⳅⲉ ⲉ ⲭ ⲛⲙⲟⲓⳅⲉ ⲛⲉ ⲛⲉϥⳅⲃⲏⲩⲉ (*Cat.* 43.29) "His works constitute wonder upon wonder" — for ⲙⲟⲉⲓⳅⲉ ⲉ ⲭ ⲛⲙⲟⲉⲓⳅⲉ, here expanding ⳅⲉⲛ-, see §1.2.1.1; the articles here bracket ⳅⲓ-coordinated, zero-determinated nouns (see POLOTSKY 1957a:233f. = *CP* 233). (Incidentally, in BM 991 ro - *BMCat.* 411, collated) we find the remarkable ⲡⲉⲓⲗⲟⲅⲟⲥ ⲡⲁⲛⲯⲏⲣⲉ... ⲁⲛ ⲙⲁⲩⲁⲁⲩ ⲡⲉ ⲁⲩⲱ ⲯⲉⲉⲣⲉ.)

[10] One suspects that a misunderstanding of the true nature of the article-noun relationship underlies "fluctuating gender" in CRUM's *Dictionary* (e.g. in ⲙⲟⲉⲓⳅⲉ, ⲯⲡⲏⲣⲉ, ϭⲟⲟⲛⲉ), and also the so-called "overrule" of the "inherent gender" by the article (JERNSTEDT 1949:§25). See further instances in KAHLE 1954:250 (sub b); ⲧⲡⲗⲁϭⲉ *Luc.* 5:36 (Palau Rib. ed. Quecke, see BROWNE 1979b:201); ⲡⲧⲁⲗⲉⲡⲱⲣⲓⲁ in (Boh.) *Ps.* 11:6, 13:3, 39:3; *Rom.* 3:16, must be accounted for differently.

[11] SHISHA-HALEVY 1976a:33. The translation in *Enchoria* 5 (1975) 98 should be modified accordingly.

[12] Cf. ⲡⲉⲯⲡⲏⲣⲉ *Dan.* 9:4 (and other exx. in CRUM 581a).

[13] Cf. ⲡⲙⲉ *Apoc.* 3:7, 19:11. Again, these cases may be viewed as instances of *hyperdetermination* (definite article before zero-determination).

[14] There may be a connection between the compatibility of a lexeme with both masculine and feminine articles and its occurrence as zero-determined predicate in a Nominal Sentence (see Ch. 4, n. 7).

[15] It is amazing that a hundred years after Stern's *Grammatik* we have no adequate account of noun determination in Coptic. (KRÁMSKÝ's facts [1972:89] are either over-simplified or inaccurate; so, for that matter, are his Greek and Celtic systems. This is of course a constant danger in this genre of linguistic reporting, and yet the difference in the quality of the information given by modern typologists and that found in nineteenth-century studies such as STEINTHAL-MISTELI is truly staggering.) I see the major obstacle here in the too narrow patterning, the scrutiny of the noun syntagm alone — at best with some offhand contextual consideration — in an attempt to isolate the function of what is a macrosyntactically operative element *par excellence*. See NAGEL 1980:77f., LAYTON 1981:261 for recent brief expositions.

OY-: in a juncturally different way, all *numbers* are pronominal nuclei of their noun syntagm.

KE-: the plural of KEOYA is ZENKOOYE, just as that of OYA is ZOINE; cf. *IV* 88.1f.

Ø-: see below, §5.2.0.1. It is not strictly true (LAYTON 1981:261) that zero and OY- share the same privileges of occurrence: OY- (not ZEN-) is excluded before KE-, Ø- isn't; Ø- is compatible as immediate expansion of the durative verbal predicate, OY- is not.

— NIM, Ø- NIM: (discontinuous): NIM, like zero determination, suppresses (overrules) the gender-number category, and is accordingly incompatible with gender-number-explicit determinators [16]. As a rule, though with not infrequent deviations, — NIM expresses *universal*, Ø- NIM *distributive*, THP⸗ (§6.1.1) *integral* totality [17].

5.1.1.1 PHORICS AND CONCORD. When the minimal noun syntagm is in any way expanded or included, there may arise the occasion of a cohesive secondary exponent of gender, usually in the form of an amalgamate person-gender-number pronoun — third-person -ч-/-c-/-OY- — but also by a non-personal demonstrative, by OYA/OYEI/ZOINE [18], or, more rarely, zero [19]. This linear reference may be either resuming, ANAPHORIC (§5.2.1) to a determinator [20], or assuming, CATAPHORIC (§5.2.2) [21]. In either case, but especially in the former, *concord ruling* between the referent (pronoun) and referate (determinator) constitutes an important feature, a junctural link (§6.0.2) in the cotext pattern: concord exists here in the sense of *rection* only in the ultra-noun-syntagm extent:

(a)	п-	motivates (governs)		masc. + sgl.
	т-	"	"	fem. + sgl.
	N-	"	"	(masc. + fem.) + pl.
(b)	OY^m-	"	"	masc. + sgl.
	OY^r-	"	"	fem. + sgl.
	ZEN-	"	"	(masc. + fem.) + pl.
(c)	Ø-	"	"	suppression of the
	Ø- NIM	"	"	gender-number
	ØKE-	"	"	distinction (§5.2)

(a) In the case of the gender-explicit referate, the concord is resolute and comparatively straightforward:

' п ⪯ PWME..... -ч- ' (etc.)

(b) With OY- we have a superficial syncretism-neutralization of OYA/OYEI in the nuclear syntagm (JERNSTEDT 1949:§§4, 13) to be resolved in the sequence [22].

---

[16] See QUECKE 1979:447. I know of two Sah. instances of NIM in compatibility with non-zero determinators: OYZOOYT NIM (*Ex.* 12:48 Bodmer) and пВАРОС NIM (NHC VII 11.10) — insufficient evidence to modify the above structure (more Boh. exx. in CRUM 225b).

[17] See BRØNDAL 1943:25ff.

[18] See JERNSTEDT 1949:§2, v. LEMM 1972a:12f. (1899).

[19] See §5.2.1.5 and §§3.1.1.1.0.1, 6.0.2 (delimitations) for zero resumptions.

[20] Two typologically important points of consideration are the *redundance of gender signals* in the noun syntagm (cf. DUBOIS 1965:64ff.), comparatively low in Coptic, and the *cohesive value* of the respective resumptions (*ibid.* 87f.).

[21] See DRESSLER 1973:§12.4, pp. 20ff., 57, with further literature on "phorics" in general; also PALEK (1968), HALLIDAY-HASAN (1976) for English. The cataphoric direction of reference is called by GUILLAUME (1919:224f.) "extension anaphoric prospective".

[22] A nice question is, what motivates the gender when the OY-determinated noun syntagm is the predicate of a Nominal

(c) It is pre-eminently in patterns with the zero-determination referate that one observes the masc. ~ fem. fluctuation, indicating a neutralization which I propose to call "neuter gender" (§§5.2.0.1, 5.2.1).

5.1.2 CATEGORIAL STRUCTURE. I suggest the following categorial model (after KURYŁOWICZ 1964: Ch. 1 §10 and BRØNDAL 1943:15ff.) as a convenient summary diagram for displaying the paradigmatic (role) relationship within this category:

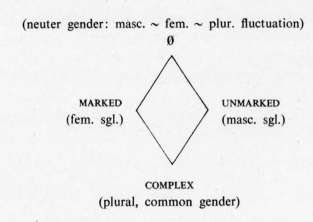

(neuter gender: masc. ~ fem. ~ plur. fluctuation)

Ø

MARKED (fem. sgl.)　　　　UNMARKED (masc. sgl.)

COMPLEX
(plural, common gender)

Observations: (a) The masculine:feminine opposition in Coptic is really *equipollent*, but some of its former characteristics of privative opposition still survive (§5.2).

(b) -ɪ-, +- and ⲀⲚⲞⲔ represent the one case where the animate class overrules the category of gender; elsewhere, the inverse is true: animate-inanimate is a transsecting distinction in Coptic.

5.2 GENDER NEUTRALIZATION ENVIRONMENT: NEUTER GENDER

It is mainly in two phoric patterns — the anaphora to a zero article (Ø-, Ø- ⲚⲒⲘ, Ø-ⲔⲈ-) and the cataphora to a verbal nominalization, content clause, adnexal complementation etc. — that a masc./fem. neutralization takes place. This I now propose to define as a NEUTER GENDER ARCHIMORPHEME[23] neutralization, as defir̃ed by Trubetzkoy: replacement of a feature (in our case, gender) by zero in a given environment. Needless to say, the neutralization takes place in the expansion, not in the nominal nucleus itself. This neutralization is in favour of the masculine term of the opposition, that is to say, no zero-determinated noun with masculine-article compatibility is resumed by a feminine pronoun, whereas the contrary is true (exx. below). Thus the masculine reveals itself as the *unmarked* term or node in a

---

Sentence with the gender-explicit ⲦⲈ the pronominal subject. In §12, JERNSTEDT (1949) suggests that ⲦⲈ is the motivant; in §10 his analysis hints at the following descriptive order: (1) ⲦⲈ resolves ⲞⲨ-, (2) ⲞⲨ- motivates the sequence (Ⲉ)Ⲥ-; in §25 he states explicitly that "ⲞⲨ- 'underlies' the concord and overrules the gender".

[23] Naturally, taking the term not in its usual morphologic Indo-European-oriented sense, but as a descriptive designation of a syntagmatic-paradigmatic phenomenon. Some delving into the original purport and tortuous terminological history of "neuter" may here prove rewarding: Protagoras' σκευή, the Stoics' οὐδέτερον, Aristotle's μεταξύ ("indifferent", acc. to H. M. Hoenigswald, "Media, Neutrum u. Zirkumflex", in *Festschrift A. Debrunner*, Bern 1954, 209-212) — see ROBINS 1951:22. The connection between neuter gender and masc./fem. neutralization is not unknown outside Coptic, notably in Rumanian (with a complementary distribution, masc. in the sgl. and fem. in the pl., see Rosetti, "Sur la catégorie du neutre", *Proc. 9th Intern. Congr. Ling.*, 1964, 779ff., criticised by R. H. Hall, *Word* 21:421ff. [1965]). One ought however to make a distinction between the *diachronic* issue — the transition from a morphologic 3-gender to a 2-gender system — and the purely synchronic one.

privative opposition of gender [24]. This is fully in agreement with pre-Coptic morphology. This zero or "neuter" node of the categorial structure is realized through "*flottement*", a fluctuation between masc. and fem. of which the *signifié* is gender indifference, "neither" gender, *Ungeschlechtigkeit* — not to be confused with the *complex* node, common gender, conflating *both* masculine and feminine. The apparent choice between masc. and fem. resumption is but a false option, since it does not entail a corresponding change on the *plan du contenu* — insofar as one can judge by contextual information.

Without enlarging on the semantics of the zero article, the referate of this neutralization, one cannot but note that its *deindividualizing* effect [25] corresponds, as far as gender is concerned, to an *ageneric* (as well as anumeric) functional standing of the noun syntagm: a negation of all noun categories, pronominally and adnominally manifested in Coptic.

5.2.0.1 Synopsis of reference cotext patterns

CATAPHORIC	ANAPHORIC
infin. prep. =ч ~ c → xe- є(тре)- circ. conv. (the pron.: *object expansion*) §5.2.2.1 f.	' Ø-Noun^fem. → =ч ~ c ~ oy ' §5.2.1.1
# ч ~ c + conj. form → xe- є(тре)- # conjunctive (the pron.: *gramm. subject*) §5.2.2.1 f.	' Ø-Noun^fem. + NIM → ч ~ c ~ oy ' §5.2.1.2
# oy-Noun → пє → ‖ xe- є(тре)- ‖ # §5.2.2.2.1	' Ø-кє-Noun^fem. → ч ~ c ~ oy ' §5.2.1.3
' пац → ‖ xe- ' єтрє- ‖ §5.2.2.2.2	' Ø-Noun^masc. / Ø-Noun^masc. + NIM / Ø-кє-Noun^masc. → ч ~ oy ' §5.2.1.4

[24] In French too we observe the neutric use of the masculine, unmarked term of a privative opposition (Dubois 1965:52, 57; see S. Lampach, "La relation des genres dans le système de pronoms de la 3e personne en français"; *Word* 12:51ff. [1956]; S. A. Schane, "The Notion of Markedness and its Morphosyntactic Consequences", *Proc. 10th Intern. Congr. Ling.* II, 757ff.; critically, C. E. Bazell, "The Correspondence Fallacy in Structural Linguistics", in E. P. Hamp *et al.*, *Readings in Linguistics* II, Chicago 1966, p. 276ff.). In Coptic the unmarkedness of the masc. gender is semasiologic rather than morphologic: "masculine gender" *means* "masc. + indifferent", while "feminine gender" means "feminine". Feminine-oriented gender neutralization does occur in Coptic: a well-known instance is єісэннтє "behold", where the feminine, originally anaphoric, synchronically — f at all analyzable — cataphoric, is normal, although both masc. and pl. marked alternants are frequent. Crum has an impressive collection of exx. for тє as an "invariable" subject or occasionally copula in Nominal Sentence patterns (391b): these must be further examined and classified before they can be appreciated. On the whole, however, it is the masculine that is the "freezing" gender: beside the phoric cases discussed here, consider the particles эωωч, нточ (originally phoric too - §§6.1.2.3, 6.1.3.4 - synchronically "phoric" in a macrosyntactic sense, back to a preceding context).

[25] See Guillaume 1919:62, 233ff., 241f., 303f.; Dubois 1965:149ff. ("L'absence de tout référent supprime toute forme d'actualisation"), 154f. (the absence of the article suppresses and negates the existence of the noun syntagm, giving the noun ad-

5.2.1 COTEXT PATTERNS: ANAPHORIC REFERENCE TO A ZERO ARTICLE

5.2.1.1 REFERATE: Ø-Noun[fem.]; REFERENT (a): *masculine singular* (always 3rd person; all referents actor-expressions in adnominal circumstantial forms)[26]: (*III* 205.17f.) ⲀⲄⲀⲠⲎ ... ⲈⲨⲬⲎⲔ ⲈⲂⲞⲖ / (87.2) ⲔⲀⲒⲈ (ⲈⲨⲢⲎⲦ / (93.10) ⲤⲂⲰ ⲚⲀⲘⲈ ⲈⲨⲬⲎⲔ ⲈⲂⲞⲖ / (195.2ff.) ⲘⲚⲦⲬⲀⲬⲈ ⲈⲨⲢ-ⲚⲞⲨⲢⲈ / (*IV* 154.22) ⲈⲦⲠⲰ ⲈⲨⲞⲢⲰ / (*Ch* 144.10f.) ⲈⲔⲒⲂⲈ ⲈⲨⲞ ⲘⲠⲨⲢⲄⲞⲤ / (*A* 2 242) ⲌⲈⲖⲠⲒⲤ ⲈⲨⲰⲞⲨⲈⲒⲦ / (289) ⲠⲒⲦⲈ ⲈⲨⲬⲞⲖⲔ Ⲏ ⲈⲨⲬⲎⲔ / (*Wess.* 9 141d 6f.) ⲤⲂⲰ ⲈⲨⲄⲞⲞⲘⲈ / (*Or.* 160.4f.) ⲌⲎⲆⲞⲚⲎ ⲈⲨⲌⲞⲞⲨ / (*P* 130² f.6, ⲠⲌ-ⲠⲎ) ⲤⲨⲚⲀⲄⲰⲄⲎ ⲈⲨⲢ-ⲄⲢⲰⲌ ⲈⲨⲤⲞⲨⲘ.

REFERENT (b): *feminine singular* (actor-expression, object expansion of adnominal constructions; reflexive object in adverbal modification): (*III* 76.6f.) ⲞⲨⲚⲤⲌⲒⲘⲈ ⲞⲚ ⲈⲚⲈⲘⲠⲞⲨⲢⲰⲢⲠⲢ-ⲚⲞⲈⲒⲔ ⲈⲢⲞⲤ ⲚⲈⲤⲚⲀⲠⲈⲒⲐ. ⲀⲚ ⲠⲈ / (*IV* 15.8f.) ⲘⲚⲤⲚⲨⲈ ⲚⲀⲄⲘ-ⲄⲞⲘ ⲈⲠⲞⲞⲚⲈⲤ ⲈⲂⲞⲖ... / (*Or.* 153.8f.) ⲞⲨⲚⲤⲌⲒⲘⲈ ⲈⲨⲀⲤⲄⲰⲨⲦ... / (159.51f.) ⲞⲨⲚⲤⲌⲒⲘⲈ ... ⲈⲤⲢⲌⲞⲨⲈⲢ-ⲠⲈⲦⲚⲀⲚⲞⲨⲨ / (160.47ff.) ⲞⲨⲚⲤⲌⲒⲘⲈ ⲈⲤⲠⲞⲢⲚⲈⲨⲈ...

Obviously, this evidence[27], which is quantitatively weaker than that for the masc. referent, raises the possibility that in fact the masculine is the normal anaphoric referent in this case. Moreover, one cannot gainsay the possible argument that in cases of Ø-ⲤⲌⲒⲘⲈ *sex* may be overruling *gender* (in Shenoute I do not recall any instance of Ø-ⲤⲌⲒⲘⲈ with a masc. anaphora).

REFERENT (c): *plural* (actor-expression or object expansion, possessor in adnominal constructions): (*Or.* 160.50ff.) ⲞⲨⲚⲤⲌⲒⲘⲈ ⲞⲚ ⲞⲨ ⲘⲞⲚⲞⲚ ⲬⲈ-ⲚⲤⲈⲦ-ⲖⲀⲀⲨ ⲚⲀⲨ ⲀⲚ ... ⲀⲖⲖⲀ ⲚⲔⲈⲌⲒⲤⲈ ⲞⲚ ⲘⲠⲈⲤⲌⲀⲒ, ⲠⲈⲦⲞ ⲚⲚⲞⲈⲒⲔ ⲈⲢⲞⲤ ⲈⲨⲀⲤⲨⲘⲨⲎⲦⲨ ⲚⲌⲎⲦⲞⲨ " There are women who not only do not receive anything, but even serve those who commit adultery with them, with the products of their husbands' toil "; note the progressive transition from plur. to fem. sgl.; the inverse is evident in (*P* 130² 5-6 ⲠⲌ-ⲠⲎ) ⲞⲨⲚⲤⲨⲚⲀⲄⲰⲄⲎ ⲞⲚ ⲈⲨⲢ-ⲄⲢⲰⲌ... ⲀⲨⲰ ⲈⲨⲨⲒ ⲌⲀⲌⲈⲚⲐⲖⲒⲮⲒⲤ... ⲞⲨⲚⲤⲨⲚⲀⲄⲰⲄⲎ ⲞⲚ ⲈⲨⲤⲞⲨⲘ... ⲈⲨⲨⲞⲨⲌ.

5.2.1.2 REFERATE: Ø-Noun[fem.] + ⲚⲒⲘ; REFERENT (a): *masculine singular*; no exx. in Shenoute[28].

REFERENT (b): *feminine singular* (possessor in adnominal circumstantial construction or Nominal Sentence): (*Wess.* 9 132a 4f.) ⲤⲂⲰ ⲚⲒⲘ ⲈⲘⲚⲦⲀⲤ ⲘⲘⲀⲨ ⲚⲦⲤⲞⲪⲒⲀ ⲚⲦⲠⲈ / (*Zoega* 603.18) ⲄⲈⲚⲈⲤⲒⲤ ⲚⲒⲘ ⲦⲈⲤⲌⲀⲈ ⲠⲈ ⲠⲦⲀⲔⲞ.

REFERENT (c): *plural*[29] (object-resumption of the extraposed zero-determinated noun): (*Thompson* H 3 ro) ⲤⲀⲢⲌ ⲚⲒⲘ ⲤⲈⲚⲀⲬⲞⲔⲢⲞⲨ.

---

jectival status and affiliating it to the verb syntagm: " une tarte maison ", " il est médecin "). See too TOBLER 1908: 81ff., 1894:96-112, KRÁMSKÝ 1972:23. Note that the zero-form of the Coptic lexeme does not show the ' lexemic plural ' (ⲌⲰⲂ : -ⲌⲂⲎⲨⲈ), which seems in fact to have a concretizing/individualizing value.

[26] See JELANSKAJA 1965:108, 1967, where she places the phenomenon in its right context, the ageneric function of zero-determination. Jelanskaja was the first to interpret this remarkable construction correctly (see also CRUM 1926 I 189 n. 1, 250). As a rule, editors have either emended (so occasionally, though not always, Leipoldt) or ignored the masc. readings without further deliberation. Some non-Shenoutean exx. on my files: *Deut.* (Budge) 22:11 (ⲌⲂⲤⲰ), 25:14 (ⲞⲒⲠⲈ), *Joh.* 15:13 (ⲀⲄⲀⲠⲎ), *Tit.* 2:3 (ⲤⲂⲰ), *Sir.* 36:29 (ⲤⲌⲒⲘⲈ), *Clem.* 26.1 (Schmidt, Akhm. ⲠⲒⲤⲦⲒⲤ), *Apoc. El.* 7.10 (Steindorff, Akhm., ⲤⲈⲈⲦⲈ); Crum, *Short Texts* 189 (ⲄⲞⲞⲨⲚⲈ), 289 (ⲀⲄⲀⲠⲎ), *BMCat.* 511 f. 1 (Fay., ⲒⲰⲦ); Chassinat, *Papyrus médical* 48, 73, 159 (ⲚⲞⲨⲚⲈ, ⲂⲚⲚⲈ, ⲀⲢⲦⲘⲈⲤⲒⲤ); *Wess.* 18 5.20 (ⲂⲚⲚⲈ), *Zoega* 629f. (ⲔⲀⲢⲞⲈⲒⲀ, ⲂⲀⲨⲞⲨⲨ, ⲔⲰⲔⲔⲞⲦⲀⲪⲚⲎ); *NHC* II 128.19f. (Layton, *BASP* 14:72f., 1977: ⲂⲞⲎⲐⲈⲒⲀ), VII 74.18f. (ⲦⲈⲬⲚⲎ); Crum-Steindorff, *Rechtsurkunden* 92.35 (ⲈⲌⲞⲨⲤⲒⲀ), 10.32 (ⲠⲢⲀⲤⲒⲤ); Till, *Osterbrief* (Akhm.) A 80 (ⲌⲞⲘⲒⲖⲒⲀ), B III 4 (ⲌⲢⲎⲢⲈ). *Deut.* 22:5 (Budge) " ⲤⲔⲈⲨⲎ... ⲈⲠⲀ-ⲠⲈ " raises an interesting question: are we to read here σκευή (fem. sgl.) or σκεύη (neut. pl. — so apparently understood by Rahlfs, Swete, also Hatch-Redpath)? The former seems preferable: the uniqueness of the Coptic adnominal construction here as regards gender must be weighed against the difficulty of assuming a Greek construction (neut. pl. + sgl. verb) *with* a Greek plural noun in the Coptic text.

[27] Also uncommon outside Shenoute: Allberry, *Man. Psalm Book* 151.18 (Subakhm., ⲔⲚⲌⲈ).

[28] This is a provisional and probably erroneous statement, to judge by the ample non-Shenoutean evidence: *Lev.* 7:21 (ⲂⲞⲦⲈ), *Act.* 23:1 (ⲤⲨⲚⲈⲒⲆⲎⲤⲒⲤ), *Tit.* 2:10 (ⲠⲒⲤⲦⲒⲤ), Athanasius (Lefort) 2.23 (ⲤⲘⲎ), Besa (Kuhn) 35.15 (ⲈⲒⲞⲠⲈ), Pachom (Lefort) 55.24f. (ⲮⲨⲬⲎ); Polotsky, *Kephalaia* (Subakhm.) 84.27f. (ⲤⲀⲢⲌ), 139.2ff. (ⲄⲀⲘ), 150.26 (ⲀⲚⲀⲄⲔⲎ); Crum, *Epiphanius* 110.8f., 247.11 (ⲀⲢⲈⲦⲎ); Budge, *Homilies* 88.6 (ⲌⲒⲎ); *NHC* VII 91.23 (ⲄⲚⲰⲘⲎ); Crum-Steindorff, *Rechtsurkunden* 23.10 (ⲠⲢⲞⲌⲀⲒⲢⲈⲤⲒⲤ), 75.53 (ⲄⲞⲘ), 82.37 (ⲮⲨⲬⲎ, ⲈⲌⲞⲨⲤⲒⲀ), 104.42f. (ⲈⲌⲞⲨⲤⲒⲀ).

[29] Outside Shenoute: *Lev.* 21:11 (ⲮⲨⲬⲎ)), 23:29 (ⲮⲨⲬⲎ), *Jud.* 21:11 (ⲤⲌⲒⲘⲈ). See STERN §486. I cannot find a correlation between the number of the referent and the kind of totality expressed by ⲚⲒⲘ. On the other hand, ⲚⲒⲘ in the quantifier paradigm is usually expanded by the adnominal circumstantial, not the relative (SHISHA–HALEVY 1972:105f.).

5.2.1.3 REFERATE: Ø-ⲔⲈ(ⲤⲈ)-Noun^fem. (usually after ⲞⲨⲚ-, ⲘⲚ-); REFERENT (a): *masculine singular* (actor-expression in adnominal constructions) [30]: (*III* 92.6f.) ⲘⲚⲄⲈⲀⲚⲞⲘⲒⲀ ⲈⲨⲌⲞⲞⲨ / (*Ch.* 125.38ff.) ⲘⲘⲚ-ⲤⲈⲌⲈⲖⲠⲒⲤ ⲚⲌⲰⲂ ⲚⲀⲄⲀⲐⲞⲚ ⲬⲈ-ⲚⲨϢⲞⲞⲠ ⲚⲀⲤ ⲀⲚ / (*Rossi 2/3* 12) ⲔⲈⲄⲚⲘⲒϢⲈ ⲈⲨⲞ ⲚⲚⲞϬ.

REFERENT (b): *feminine singular* (actor expression in adnominal circumstantial): (*Cat.* 42.26f.) ⲔⲈ-ⲘⲚⲦⲘⲚⲦⲢⲈ ⲈⲤⲚⲌⲞⲦ ⲀⲨⲰ ⲈⲤⲞ ⲚⲚⲞϬ ⲈⲠⲈⲌⲞⲨⲞ.

REFERENT (c): *plural* (actor expression or object in adnom. constructions; for adnominal ⲬⲈ-clauses see §7.4): (*A 1* 215) ⲞⲨⲚⲔⲈⲈⲔⲔⲖⲎⲤⲒⲀ ⲈⲀⲨⲢ-ⲠⲀⲒ / (*A 2* 33) ⲘⲎ ⲞⲨⲚⲄⲈϢⲀⲒⲢⲈ ⲬⲈ-ⲘⲠⲞⲨⲠⲞⲢⲬⲞⲨ / (*Ryl. Cat.* p. 31 No. 67) ⲘⲚⲄⲈⲠⲀⲢⲀⲪⲨⲤⲒⲤ ⲬⲈ-ⲘⲠϤⲖⲀⲀⲨ / (*P* 130^5 15 ro) Ⲏ ⲞⲨⲚⲔⲈⲄⲢⲀⲪⲎ ⲬⲈ-ⲘⲠⲈⲚⲤⲰⲦⲘ ⲈⲢⲞⲞⲨ.

5.2.1.4 REFERATES: Ø-Noun^masc., Ø-Noun^masc. + ⲚⲒⲘ, Ø-ⲔⲈ-Noun^masc.; REFERENTS: *masculine singular*; *plural*. The masculine referent *per se* is not as significant as is the absence of a feminine variant i.e. the absence of fluctuation. This definitely means that the neutralization is masculine-oriented. Where it not for the (scant) evidence of feminine variants and the cataphoric referents (see below), one could conclude that the masculine term is the sole exponent of neuter gender. The exemplification is selective:

(1) Ø-Noun^masc.: (*A 2* 16) ⲢⲰⲘⲈ ⲘⲠⲞⲚⲎⲢⲞⲤ ⲈϤⲠⲎⲦ ⲚⲤⲀⲢⲰⲘⲈ ⲘⲠⲞⲚⲎⲢⲞⲤ / (*IV* 85.6) ⲌⲚⲞ ⲈϤⲚⲀⲞⲨⲞⲘϤ / (*P* 130^5 95 vo) ⲠⲀⲌⲢⲈ... ⲈϤⲬⲒ-ⲌⲘⲬ / (*A 1* 72) ⲘⲀⲦⲞⲒ ⲈⲚⲀⲚⲞⲨϤ / (*IV* 17.9f.) ⲢⲰⲘⲈ ⲈⲞⲨⲚⲦⲤ-ⲚⲈⲤⲌⲒⲞⲞⲨⲈ ⲚⲂⲰⲔ ⲈⲌⲞⲨⲚ ϢⲀⲢⲞⲨ / (*A 1* 226) ⲞⲨⲚϢⲎⲢⲈ ϢⲎⲘ ⲈϢⲀⲨϢⲞⲚϤ ... ⲞⲨⲚϢⲎⲢⲈ ⲆⲈ ⲞⲚ ϢⲎⲘ ϢⲀⲨⲔⲖⲎⲢⲞⲚⲞⲘⲈⲒ.

(2) Ø-Noun^masc. + ⲚⲒⲘ: (*IV* 73.8f.) ϢⲰⲚⲈ ⲚⲒⲘ ⲚⲦⲈⲒⲌⲈ ⲈϤⲞⲨⲞⲚⲌ ⲈⲂⲞⲖ / (*Ch.* 161.19ff.) ⲢⲰⲘⲈ ⲚⲒⲘ ⲈⲦⲈⲢⲈⲒⲤ̄ ⲚⲀⲞⲨⲞϢϤⲞⲨ ⲌⲀⲢⲀⲦϤ.

(3) Ø-ⲔⲈ-Noun^masc.: (*III* 201.16) ⲔⲈⲌⲰⲂ ⲈⲀⲢⲀⲀϤ ⲚⲦⲈϢⲠ ⲘⲘⲞϤ ⲀⲚ ⲬⲈ-ⲞⲨⲚⲞⲂⲈ ⲠⲈ / (*Ch.* 21.3ff.) ⲔⲈⲌⲚⲞ ⲈϢⲀⲔⲢ-ⲠⲞⲖⲈⲘⲞⲤ ⲚⲌⲎⲦϤ / (*P* 130^5 59 vo) ⲘⲘⲚⲄⲈⲞⲤⲈ ⲀⲨⲰ ⲘⲘⲚⲄⲈⲘⲔⲀⲌ ⲚⲌⲎⲦ ⲈϤⲞ ⲚⲚⲞϬ... / (*BMCat.* 81, No. 196) ⲘⲚⲄⲈⲌⲰⲂ ⲬⲈ-ⲚϤϪⲎⲔ ⲀⲚ ⲈⲂⲞⲖ ⲚⲌⲎⲦⲞⲨ ⲦⲎⲢⲞⲨ.

5.2.1.5 SOME REMARKABLE ANAPHORIC CONSTRUCTIONS

(a) Anaphora to a non-specific referate — either the preceding context comprehensively or any unboundable component thereof: REFERENTS: *feminine singular*: ⲘⲚⲚⲤⲰⲤ "thereafter" (*IV* 200.21, *Ch.* 18.24f. etc.), ⲚⲤⲬⲒ ⲈⲢⲞⲒ ⲀⲚ "this does not concern me" (*A 1* 52), -ⲤⲈ ⲈⲢⲞⲤ "discover this, arrive at this conclusion" (*IV* 64.18f., *Ch.* 12.6, *A 1* 135.6). Note that these cases are easily mistaken for *non-phoric*; the pronouns, however, are invariably referents in a linear sense.

(b) Anaphora to an extra-(pre-)posed, topicalized verbal ("preinclusion") nominalization. REFERENTS: *masculine/conditioned feminine/zero* (see §2.7.1.4.2 for further exx.): (*A 1* 199) ⲈⲂⲰⲔ ⲘⲈⲚ ⲈⲚ-ⲦⲞⲠⲞⲤ ⲚⲘⲘⲀⲢⲦⲨⲢⲞⲤ ⲈϢⲀⲎⲖ ⲈϢϢ ⲈϢⲀⲖⲖⲈⲒ ⲈⲦⲂⲂⲞⲔ ⲈϤⲒ-ⲦⲈⲠⲢⲞⲤⲪⲞⲢⲀ ... ⲚⲀⲚⲞⲨϤ; ⲈⲬⲰ ⲆⲈ ⲈⲞⲨⲰⲘ ⲈⲤⲰ ⲈⲤⲰⲂⲈ, ⲘⲀⲖⲖⲞⲚ ⲆⲈ ⲈⲠⲞⲢⲚⲈⲨⲈ ⲀⲨⲰ ⲈⲌⲦⲂ-ⲢⲰⲘⲈ... ⲞⲨⲀⲚⲞⲘⲒⲀ ⲦⲈ / (*A 2* 443, not Sh.) ⲌⲞⲦⲈⲒ ⲆⲈ ⲬⲈ-ⲠⲈⲌⲞⲨⲞ ⲘⲠⲈⲚϢⲚⲌ... ⲈϢⲀⲨⲔⲀⲦⲞⲢⲐⲞⲨ ⲘⲘⲞϤ ⲌⲒⲦⲚⲦⲈⲒⲠⲀⲢⲀⲐⲎⲢⲎⲤⲒⲤ ⲚⲦⲈⲒⲘⲒⲚⲈ, ⲞⲨⲞⲚ ⲚⲒⲘ ⲤⲞⲞⲨⲚ ⲘⲠⲀⲒ / (*A 1* 405-6) ⲈⲬⲞⲞⲤ ⲆⲈ ⲬⲈ... ⲈⲈⲒⲘⲈ ⲈⲠⲀⲒ ⲞⲨⲀⲦϬⲞⲘ ⲠⲈ / (*IV* 64.15f.) ⲈⲬⲞⲞⲤ ⲆⲈ ⲬⲈ-ⲚⲀϢ Ⲛ?Ⲉ Ⲏ ⲚⲒⲘ ⲠⲈⲚⲦⲀϤϢⲞⲬⲚⲈ... ⲈⲘⲘⲚⲢⲰⲘⲈ ⲤⲞⲞⲨⲚ (sim. *Wess. 9* 148b 16ff.).

(c) The case of anaphoric-cataphoric concord "conflict": see §5.2.2.3.3.

5.2.2 "SENTENCE PRONOMINALIZATION": CATAPHORIC REFERENCE TO A VERBAL NOMINALIZATION, "THAT"-CLAUSE, ADNEXAL COMPLEMENTATION

5.2.2.1 REFERENTS: *masculine ~ feminine* (ϥ ~ Ⲥ). These pronouns herald and represent the referate noun (-equivalent) in the nuclear verb syntagm, and cannot be replaced by it — that is, they are

---

[30] Outside Shenoute: *Marc.* 12:31 (ⲈⲚⲦⲞⲖⲎ), with fem. variae lectiones.

in an exclusively syntagmatic relationship with it; this is the formal cohesion-factor of the pattern. The ' *pronoun → noun* ' discontinuous component may be considered the distinctive grammatical feature here (and in fact the kernel of the typological correspondence with the Indo-European " impersonals ", to which this pattern is in part the Coptic answer):

(a) *feminine*: OBJECT-EXPANSION: TAA⸗C (NA⸗) E(TPE)- (*III* 191.25f., *Ench.* 79a); COTⲠ⸗C (NA⸗) E- (*A 1* 275, *III* 39.17f.); CMNT⸗C E(TPE)- (*III* 20.2f.); TOϬ⸗C (EPO⸗) XE- (*A 2* 50); XOO⸗C XE-[31] (*passim*); OⲠ⸗C XE- (*A 2* 44); KAA⸗C ⲌMⲠEϤ2HT E- (*P* 130² 100 ro); ⲌE EPO⸗C + circumstantial (*A 2* 543, *Wess. 9* 159a 8ff., *P* 130² 107 ro)[32]; ϬNT⸗C + circumstantial (*P* 131⁶ 13 vo); ACTOR EXPRESSION: (NE)NANOYC E(TPE)-/XE-/circumstantial/conjunctive[33] (*A 2* 380, *Ryl.* 69 NZ, *Wess. 9* 174d 25ff., 158b 24ff.); (E)CMOK2 (NA⸗) E-, (E)CMOTN (NA⸗) E- (*Rossi 2/3* 63, *A 2* 266, *Ch.* 13.49ff.); -C-ⲰⲠE (CNAⲰⲠE, EC Ⲱ ANⲰⲠE, NNEC-ⲰⲠE) ETPE-/conjunctive[33] (*III* 164.5f., *IV* 102.7) CⲠPEⲠEI ETPE- (*A 2* 258); CTO ETPE- (*A 2* 103, 258); CKH E2PAI ETPE- (*IV* 91.16f.); NCP-NOϤPE AN E(TPE-) (*IV* 98.23); NCP-XPIA AN N- (*Miss.* 233); NCXI EPO⸗ AN E(TPE)- (*IV* 103.12); ECNCⲰ⸗ E- (*Ch.* 65.13ff.); CEPO⸗ E- (*III* 22.22); ACPANA⸗ ETPE- (*IV* 96.10f.).

(b) *masculine*: OBJECT-EXPANSION: ϬNT⸗Ϥ EϤCH2 XE- (the second pronoun is non-pertinent [conditioned]; *III* 21.18, *P* 130¹ 137 TⲀH); KAA⸗Ϥ (NA⸗) E(TPE)- (*IV* 63.1f., 66.12); CA2⸗Ϥ XE- (*IV* 108.15f.); CⲰTM EPO⸗Ϥ XE- (*IV* 39.4ff., *P* 131⁶ 42 ro-vo), OⲠ⸗Ϥ XE- (*A 2* 256); ACTOR EXPRESSION: (E)ϤCH2 XE- (*passim*); ϤO NPOOYⲰ (⸗ PPOOYⲰ) (NA⸗) XE-/2A-/ETBE- (*III* 34.9, *Miss.* 279); ϤⲰOOⲠ NPOOYⲰ E- (*Ming.* 325); ϤO MMOI2E XE- (*A 2* 537); ϤOBⲰ EPO⸗ XE- (*A 2* 454); ϤPⲰⲰE E- (*Wess. 9* 140c 2f.); ϤOYON2, ϤNAOYⲰN2 (EBOⲖ) XE- (*IV* 8.17); Ϥ2MⲠEN2HT, NEϤ2MⲠEN2HT AN, MⲠEϤBⲰK E2MⲠA2HT... XE- (*IV* 18.4f., *A 2* 151, *RE 10* 159b 30ff., *Mun.* 176)[34]; NANOYϤ, Ϥ2OⲖϬ ETPE- (*A 1* 227)[34]; ϤP-ⲰAY + ϤPANA⸗ ETPE- (*IV* 167.15f.).

5.2.2.1.1 Analysis of the distributional structure of the above patterns, carried out on the basis of the classification shown below, reveals several unmistakable combinatory features (the symbol (*) means a very rare or unique attestation):

	masculine referent		fem. referent		masc./fem. referent	masc.	fem.
OBJECT EXPANSION:	CA2⸗	XE-	TAA⸗	E(TPE)-	OⲠ⸗	XE- (*)	XE- (*)
	(*) KAA⸗	E(TPE)-	COTⲠ⸗	E(TPE)-			
	CⲰTM EPO⸗	XE-	CMNT⸗	E(TPE)-			
	ϬNT⸗ EϤCH2	XE-	XOO⸗	XE-			
			(*) TOϬ⸗	XE-			
			ⲌE EPO⸗	circ.			

---

[31] Outside Shenoute, one encounters XOOϤ, exclusively or alongside XOOC. See KAHLE 126:1 233ff., 252; CRUM 1954:150f.; STERN p. 310. The object-pronoun here is obligatory, hence purely formal (unless it is lexicalized by Ⲡ Ⲱ AXE or sim.); XⲰ " sing " is therefore a different lexeme.

[32] A similar instance of circumstantial adnexal complementation after a neutric cataphoric referent is XEKAAC + circ. Future III (POLOTSKY 1957:233 = *CP* 233), although it is doubtful whether XEKAAC is synchronically at all analyzable.

[33] The conjunctive too is an adnexal modifier, in paradigm with the circumstantial: see §7.1.3.

[34] Possibly not cataphoric, at least not purely so: NANOYϤ AYⲰ Ϥ2OⲖϬ ENOYHP (sic) ETPENP-MⲠ Ⲱ A 2EIOYCOⲠ (sic)... ETPENCⲰOY2 EⲠEIMA. Cf. earlier on the same page ⲠETNANOYϤ AYⲰ ⲠETNOTM, and (p. 257) Ϥ2OⲖϬ AYⲰ NANOYϤ (Ϥ here *anaphoric*, referring to the inside of the fruit). *NB*: (*P* 130² KB, not Sh.?) NANOYC ΔE E6M-Ⲡ Ⲱ INE NNECNHY ET2HⲰ N2ENⲰⲰNE... NANOYϤ AYⲰ ϤP-NOϤPE NN2M2AⲖ MⲠNOYTE: the second pronoun group is ana-, not cataphoric.

	masculine referent		fem. referent		masc./fem. referent		
						masc.	fem.
ACTOR EXPRESSION:	=CH2	ϪE-	=TO	ETPE-	NANOY= (?)	ETPE- (*) (?)	E(TPE)-/ϪE-/ circ./conj.
	=O NPOOYϢ	ϪE-	=KH EϨPAI	ETPE-			
	=O MMOIϨE	ϪE-	=P-NOЧPE	E-			
	=OBϢ EPOЧ	ϪE-	=P-XPIA	N-			
	=OYϢNϨ EBOΛ	ϪE-	=PANA=	E(TPE)-	=ϨMΠEЧ ϨHT	ϪE- (*)	E(TPE)-
	(*) =PϢϢE	E-	=MOTN	E-			
	(*) { =ϨOΛϬ }		=MOKϨ	E-			
	(?) { NANOY= }	ETPE-	=ΠPEΠEI	ETPE-	=PANAЧ	ETPE- (*)	ETPE-
	=BϢK EϪMΠAϨHT	ϪE-	=COTΠ	E(TPE)-			
	=P-ϢAY	ETPE-	=ϪI EPOЧ	ETPE-			
			=EPOЧ	E-			
			=NCϢЧ	E-			

The *feminine* referent points most often to a following *infinitive* referate (ε + inf., N + inf., ETPE-), whereas the *masculine* regularly assumes the sequence of ϪE-: this impression is enhanced by a quantitative consideration of the evidence, since, barring ϪOO= and NANOY= for the fem., KAA= for the masculine, all deviations from the alternation C → E(TPE)-/Ч → ϪE- are extremely rare. Now it is precisely in the case of ϪOOC, NANOYC, KAAЧ that the different functions of E(TPE)- and ϪE- are most clearly observable and (after NANOYC) even paradigmatically opposed: ETPE- for a *marked prospective* reference, ϪE- for an unmarked general inclusion of various constructions (notably the Nominal Sentence, Second Tense and tense-marked predications). It may therefore be stated as a general rule that C- is used to herald *prospective expansions of the nuclear syntagm* whereas the masculine pronoun assumes the sequence of an included clause in general. However, this statement cannot well be reconciled with the feminine in ϪOOC (ϪE- only), NANOYC ϪE- or the (rare) KAAЧ ETPE-, OΠC ϪE- etc. where we have true neutric fluctuation (neutralization) [35].

5.2.2.2 REFERENTS: ΠE, ΠAI: masculine only.

5.2.2.2.1 ΠE, the pronominal subject in a Nominal Sentence of the pattern ⧺ Predicate → Subject ⧺, may serve to represent formally a following noun or noun equivalent; in the latter case, we may have instances in which the masculine gender of ΠE must be cataphoric, since it can hardly be anaphoric to a predicate which is either feminine or not gender-characterized:

(a) REFERATE ϪE-: (*A 1* 150) OYMOIϨE ΠE ϪE- / (*A 2* 465-6) OY ΠE ϪE-' ϨIΠAϨOY MMOOY ' H ϪE-' ϨIΘH MMOOY ' ' ϨIΠAϨOY ' ΠE ϪE-, ' ϨIΘH ' ΠE ϪE-. In the answer we have a different (Subject → Predicate) pattern, with ΠE copular and of unclear phoric standing (so too *A 2* 491 ' COKЧ EΠAϨOY ' ΠE ϪE-).

(b) REFERATE E(TPE)-: (*A 1* 307) OYATϢϢΠE ΠE ETPEЧ- / (*IV* 89.14) NTEIϨE ON ΠE... ETPEY- (§1.2.1.2) / (*A 2* 148) OYΘΛIΦIC ΠE ETPEY- (5) TEIϨE ϢHM ΠE KAΠMA NTOPΓH...

(c) REFERATE *non-specific*: (*Wess. 9* 90b 13ff.) NΘE ΓAP ETEOYNOϬ MMNTACEBHC ΠE EϨPAI EϪMΠETNA-ϪOOC... ϪE-..., TAI ON TE ΘE EYNOϬ MMNTACEBHC TE EϨPAI EϪNNETNAϪOOC... ϪE...

[35] Note that the conjunctive shares a paradigm with E(TPE)- after the feminine-neutric cataphora, as an adnexal-subcoordinative modification of the verb, not expansion of the pronoun: §§7.2.4(a), 7.3.2, 7.4.

We see that when the predicate is marked for gender, the subject-pronoun may concord anaphorically with the predicate — or, to put it differently, the anaphora may overrule the cataphora as regards gender (see §5.2.2.3.3): (*IV* 166.3f.) ⲧⲉⲭⲣⲓⲁ ⲧⲉ ⲉ- / (*A 2* 61) ⲧⲉⲓⲍⲉ ⳝⲏⲙ ⲧⲉ ⲉⲧⲣⲉ - / (*K* 9298) ⲧⲙⲟⲓⲍⲉ ⲧⲉ ⲭⲉ- / (*III* 183.28) ⲟⲩⲙⲟⲓⲍⲉ ⲧⲉ ⲭⲉ- / (*A 2* 3) ⲟⲩⲙⲛⲧⲁⲑⲏⲧ... ⲧⲉ ⲉ- (7) ⲟⲩⲁⲛⲟⲙⲓⲁ ⲧⲉ ⲉⲧⲣⲉ- / (*III* 26.4) ⲟⲩⲁⲛⲟⲙⲓⲁ... ⲧⲉ ⲭⲉ- / (*III* 184.2) ⲟⲩⳝⲡⲏⲣⲉ ⲧⲉ ⲉ⳺ⳝⲁⲛ-... which brings home to us that in this pattern neither the phoric status nor the concomitant concord are predictable. In a manner of speaking, ⲡⲉ/ⲧⲉ are Janus-faced, with either face apt to take concord precedence with no discernable environmental conditioning or consequence. When the predicate bears a masculine gender mark, it is of course impossible to refer the gender of ⲡⲉ: (*A 1* 181) ⲟⲩⲁⲅⲁⲑⲟⲛ ⲡⲉ ⲉⲧⲣⲉ- (the lexeme morphologically marked) / (*A 1* 1) ⲡⲉⲧⲉⲍⲛⲁⲓ ⲁⲛ ⲡⲉ ⲉⲧⲣⲉ- / (*A 2* 432, not Sh.) ⲙⲡⲁⲣⳝⲙⲉ ⲅⲁⲣ ⲛⲓⲙ ⲁⲛ ⲡⲉ ⲉⲧⲣⲉ⳺-, ⲡⲉ possibly anaphoric to a non-phoric (§5.2.3) " neuter " pronoun ⲡⲁ- — or are ⲡⲁ- (and ⲡⲉ) cataphoric to ⲉⲧⲣⲉ-? / (*A 1* 307) ⲟⲩⲁⲧⳝⳝⲡⲉ ⲡⲉ ⲉⲧⲣⲉ⳺- / (*Ch.* 76.23ff.) ⲟⲩⲁⲧⳓⲟⲙ ⲡⲉ ⲉⲧⲣⲉ-.

5.2.2.2.2 ⲡⲁⲓ is cataphoric to an appositive ⲭⲉ-clause or ⲉⲧⲣⲉ-, serving apparently to accommodate ⲭⲉ-/ⲉⲧⲣⲉ- in various syntactical positions: modifying verbs (ⲥⲟⲟⲩⲛ, ⲥⳝⲧⲙ, ⲙⲉⲉⲩⲉ), governed by prepositions, in actor status, appositive subject in a Nominal Sentence pattern, etc.: ⲡⲁⲓ ⲭⲉ- (*Ch.* 174.22f., *III* 128.23, *IV* 2.20, 112.20, *A 1* 161, 230, *A 2* 371, *Wess.* 9 164d 20ff.); ⲡⲁⲓ ⲟⲩⲟⲛⲍ ⲉⲃⲟⲗ ⲭⲉ- (*P* 131⁵ 152 ro); ⲡⲁⲓ ⲉⲧⲣⲉ- (*Ch.* 123.2f., *III* 61.8, *IV* 104.9f. ⲡⲉⲓⲕⲉⲟⲩⲁ ⲉⲧⲣⲉ-, 107.19f.).

5.2.2.3 SOME REMARKABLE CATAPHORIC CONSTRUCTIONS

5.2.2.3.1 Major types and representative examples of a *zero cataphoric referent* — thus no explicit cohesion with the ⲭⲉ-/ⲉⲧⲣⲉ- referate:

(a) ⲧⲛⲛⲟⲟⲩ ⲭⲉ- (*III* 26.22); (b) ⲙⲡⳝⲣ ⲉⲧⲣⲉ- (*A 1* 213, *Ming.* 92); (c) ⲕⲁⲧⲁⲑⲉ ⲉⲧⲥⲏⲍ ⲭⲉ- (*III* 118.20) and similar cases where ⲉⲧ-, marking the adnominal status of the verb syntagm, also occupies the actor slot of the Bipartite pattern [36], leaving no room for an exponent of cohesion with ⲭⲉ-; (d) Greek loan-elements: the 3rd person sgl. of finite verbs, treated as if containing a Coptic pronominal element: (ⲟⲩⲕ) ⲉⳉⲉⲥⲧⲓ ⲉ + infinitive (*III* 30.16, *IV* 4.12): note that ⲉⳉⲉⲥⲧⲓ is partly conversible in Coptic, thus assimilated as a predication form; ⲅⲉⲛⲟⲓⲧⲟ + conjunctive, ⲙⲏ ⲅⲉⲛⲟⲓⲧⲟ ⲉⲧⲣⲉ-, ⲁⲗⲗⲟ — ⲁⲗⲗⲟ conj./ⲧⲣⲉ-: see §7.3.3.

(e) Unconjugated lexemes, the valency of which includes, or consists of ⲉⲧⲣⲉ- or ⲭⲉ- (as first or second modification: §1.1.2.0.1): ⲍⳝ ⲉⲣⲟ⳺ ⲉⲧⲣⲉ- (*A 1* 67, 205), ⲍⳝ ⲭⲉ- (*Ryl.* 70 ⲥⲛⲅ), ⲍⲁⲡⲥ ⲉⲧⲣⲉ- (*A 2* 378); compare the contentualization of noun lexemes, usually in predicative status, by means of ⲉⲧⲣⲉ- (ⲧⲁⲛⲁⲅⲕⲏ... ⲉⲧⲣⲉ- *IV* 69.16f., (ⲡ)ⲕⲁⲓⲣⲟⲥ... ⲉⲧⲣⲉ- *III* 74.14, perhaps (ⲟⲩⲛ/)ⲙⲛⳓⲟⲙ ⲉⲧⲣⲉ- *III* 145.11 — here ⲉⲧⲣⲉ- is in paradigm with the conjunctive: see §§7.3.2, 7.4), and of course the numerous verb lexemes (ⲟⲩⳝⳝ, ⲟⲩⲉⲍ-ⲥⲁⲍⲛⲉ, ...) modifiable by ⲉⲧⲣⲉ-, where the cohesion factor is inherent in the valency spectrum.

(f) In (*III* 107.6) ⲛⲛⲁⲍⲣⲁⲓ ⲍⳝⲥ ⲉⳝⲭⲉ-ⲛⲟⲩⲏⲍ ⲛⲥⲁⲟⲩⲥⲁ... " It seems to me as if we live apart... " a zero cataphoric referent may be postulated, coinciding with the zero subject of the predicative ⲍⳝⲥ ⲉⳝⲭⲉ- (§1.2.1.3.3), but it may be preferable to take ⲛⲛⲁⲍⲣⲁⲓ as the subject, with no cataphora at all.

5.2.2.3.2 Rare instances of an invariable masculine referent -⳺, the formal obligatory exponent of inalienable possession (cf. §1.2.1.1, spec. obs. 1), expanded by a noun syntagm (even fem. or plural) and really part of a discontinuous possessor morph {⳺ + Noun} (§6.0.1.2.3): ⲍⲏⲧ⳺ ⲛⲛⲉⲍⲓⲟⲙⲉ (*Ench.* 66a) / ⲡⲧⲁⲍⲟ ⲉⲣⲁⲧ⳺ ⲛⲁⲣⲉⲧⲏ ⲛⲓⲙ (*A 2* 442-3, not Sh.) / ⲡⲕⲁⲕⲉ ⲉⲧⲛⲗⲓⲕⲧ⳺ ⲛⲧⲉⲛⲡⲣⲟⲍⲁⲓⲣⲉⲥⲓⲥ (*P* 130⁵ 50 ⲥⲕⲁ), cf., not Shenoutean but emulating his idiom, (*BLOr.* 8811 17 ⲥⲗⲏ) ⲕⲟⲩⲛ⳺ ⲛⲧⲉⲥⲍⲓⲙⲉ [37].

---

[36] POLOTSKY 1960a:§12.
[37] See POLOTSKY 1930:874 (= *CP* 343).

5.2.2.3.3 Anaphora *vs.* cataphora in a single syntagm: an interesting instance of *varia lectio* reflecting a conflict of anaphoric and cataphoric references: (*A 2* 169) ογcοπ ΑΝ πεΝΤΑΙϪΟΟc Ϫε- (*Borg.*, -c- cataphoric) *vs.* ογcοπ ΑΝ πεΝΤΑΙϪΟΟγ Ϫε- (*Ryl.* with -γ- seemingly resuming π-); however, this is not the substantivizing pronominal nucleus (§5.2.3.1) but the formal subject/glose marker, which does not usually motivate anaphoric reference, and here anaphora is by no means the rule: (*A 1* 365) ΝΤωΤΝ πεΤεΡεπϢΑϪε εΤcΗϩ Ϫω ΜΜΟc εΤΒεΤΗγΤΝ Ϫε-, with two other symptoms of the non-phoricity of π-: the masc. sgl. after a plural *vedette* and the resumption by a 2nd person plural pronoun. As a rule, the anaphora to substantivizing π- overrules a cataphora in such cases of conflict; consider (*Ench.* 67b) πεΤεΡεΤεΓΡΑΦΗ Ϫω ΜΜΟγ Ϫε-, or (*Ch.* 29.55f.) πεΝΤΑΝϪΟΟγ Ϫε-.

5.2.2.3.4 In a case like (*RE 11* 16b 20) ΝΟγΚ Ϭε Νε ΧΑΡΙcΜΑ ΝΙΜ, the concord is cataphoric, regressively motivated.

5.2.3 Non-phoric environment. Here neuter gender is realized by a " freezing ", i.e. a greater or lesser degree of *incommutability* of the masculine pronoun.

5.2.3.1 In the nuclear π- expanded by a relative conversion (πεΤ-, πεΝΤΑγ-, etc.) [38]. The analysis of this difficult syntagm is by no means straightforward [39]. In brief, one notes here two different patterns: (a) πεΤ-/ΤεΤ-/ΝεΤ- (etc.): any conjugation-form; " definite ", i.e. not further determinable, so really *outside* the determination category; π- is the determinator; (b) πεΤ-: present(-equivalent) only, invariable, unmotivating, of " zero determination " status, i.e. further determinable [40]; π- is a substantivator morpheme. Pattern (b) is paradigmatically restricted as regards both the conjugation-form and its predicate constituency (NAGEL 1973:120). Now it is difficult to see what the invariability of π- in pattern (b) could mean, unless it is the same indifference to gender that we have called " neuter "; note, however, that this πεΤ- is compatible only with masculine-marked or unmarked determinators: ππεΤ-, πιπεΤ-, ϩεΝπεΤ-, excluding *Τ-πεΤ- (NAGEL op. cit. 118f.); that is to say, the gender-explicit, *marked* feminine nucleus Τ- is incompatible with the substantivator (homonymic with the unmarked masculine determinator): this is, I daresay, a case of systemic, not haphazard non-attestation. In instances of pattern (a) like (*IV* 112.20) πεΤεΙΝΑϪΟΟγ / (*A 1* 1) πεΤεϩΝΑΙ / (*IV* 107.19) πεΤπΡΗπεΙ (sic) / even (*III* 119.28) πεΤcΗϩ, it would perhaps be rash to interpret π- as neutric, as anything but masculine gender, be its associative connection with any specific masculine noun lexeme (ϢΑϪε, ΛΟΓΟc, ϩωΒ...) doubtful as it may; the opposition of this πεΤ- to ΤεΤ- and ΝεΤ- is sufficient grounds, as the only pertinent, necessary and sufficient datum for a definition of gender in Coptic.

5.2.3.2 In the *glose* segment πεΤ- (etc.) of a Cleft Sentence with (pro)nominal *vedette* (POLOTSKY 1962:§1f.); although this π- can be traced to the pronominal subject πε, it is in the crystallized Cleft Sentence pattern not the anaphoric pronoun, referring to a specific identifiable nominal or pronominal element, but the formal, non-phoric mark of the logical subject: ΝΤΟc Νϩογο πεΤεΡε+πΡΟΦΗΤεΙΑ ϪΗΚ εΒΟΛ εϩΡΑΙ εϪωc Ϫε- (*Ch.* 143.44ff.) [41].

---

[38] πεΤ- *can* be anaphoric, in such cotext patterns as (*Wess. 9* 179b 30ff.) ΝΑcεΒΗc ΝΤΑγΜΟγ Η ΝεΤΝΑΜΟγ, also *III* 126.20ff.

[39] See NAGEL 1973, SHISHA-HALEVY 1976c:134 n. 1, QUECKE forthcoming.

[40] See NAGEL 1973b, QUECKE forthcoming (" *determinierbar* " vs. " *undeterminierbar* "), id. 1981:261f. Consider ϩεΝπεθΟΟγ (*A 1* 103), ΚεπεΤΝΑΝΟγγ (*Ch.* 88.16f.), ογπεΤεϢϢε (*A 2* 256), ΝΙπεΤϢΟγεΙΤ (*Wess. 9* 141b 21f.), Μπεθ Ηπ (*III* 165.13), ΝεγπεΤΝΑΝΟγογ (*A 2* 471), πεΤΝΑΝΟγγ ΝΙΜ (*A 1* 133), cΝΑγ ΜπεΤΝΑΝΟγγ (*P* 130⁴ 93 vo), ϩεΝΚΟγΙ ΜπεΤΝΑΝΟγΟγ (*III* 206.21) which shows the non-motivating nature of π-.

[41] A basically similar case is πΝΑγ πε, πΚΑΙΡΟc πε, πεΟγΟεΙϢ πε (*III* 224.20f., *IV* 29.26, *Ch.* 167.47f.), for which the " not yet " form is ΜπΑΤγΡΝΑγ (*Ch.* 107.32f.) In a cotextually conditioned alternant pattern occurring in the sequence of a Cleft Sentence, πε is anaphoric and represents the whole *glose*: (*Ch.* 103.31ff.) ΜΜΟΝΑϪΟc... ΝεΤΗπ εΡ-ΝΗcΤΙΑ ϪΝ-ΝΤΟΚ πε / (*III* 68.14ff.) ΝΙΜ πεΤεΡεπϪΟεΙc πΝΟγΤε ΝΑϪΝΟγγ... / (SHISHA-HALEVY 1976a:55) ΑΝΟΚ πε Η ΚεΟγΑ ΝΤΑϩε, ϩεΝΚεΡρϢΟγ Νε...

5.3 A CONCLUDING NOTE: PRONOUNS, CONJUGATION BASES AND THE TYPOLOGY OF COPTIC

We have seen that the prime nucleus in the noun syntagm and noun phrase is the determinator pronoun (" article "). Indeed, in Coptic grammar, so to speak, the pronoun reigns supreme: with the possible exception of the stative, the entire grammatical system may be phrased in terms of a pronominal core and an indispensable yet inessential (indeed *satellital*) lexemic periphery: the patterns are formulable for the nuclear pronoun, which is given a lexical content by lexemic expansion. Within this frame of reference the " pronouns " in verbal syntagmatics are the CONJUGATION BASES. They (with their pronominal actor) are the nuclei of the verb syntagm, representing the verb in the system and incorporating it in the discourse [42]. Like the determinators, they are of necessity expanded (by verb lexemes: these are also privileged to occur after the determinators, and prove the noun syntagm to be — in this respect at least — hierarchically different from the verb syntagm. While both noun and verb lexemes are " nominal ", only the verb-lexeme subdivision features in verb syntagms). Allowing for the difference in semasiological categories, ΑϤ-[ⲤⲰⲦⲘ] is no different, analytically speaking, from ⲠⲈϤ-[ⲤⲞⲚ]. In a final reckoning, then, in Coptic we are left with verb/noun lexemes and pro-verbs/pronouns to " grammaticalize " and actualize [43] them. (The stative — neither a lexeme nor a grammeme, but a typically pre-Coptic " synthetic " blending of both — does not fit in this scheme: neither do the " adjective-verbs ", another piece of " historical left-over " in Coptic.)

---

[42] Cf. already Aug. Schleicher (*Zur Morphologie der Sprache*, 1859, p. 21) who, at a time when the Coptic conjug. bases were conventionally termed ' Tempuscharakteristik ' or ' Tempuszeichen ', suggested they were ' original demonstratives '. For a comparable conception of a lexically empty auxiliary verb as a grammaticalized substitute (' *verbum vicarium* ', ' verbal pronoun ') see BALLY 1950:87, TESNIÈRE 1965:73, 91, DUBOIS 1965:96f.

[43] To my knowledge, only Vergote uses " actualisateur " in this connection (*Grammaire copte* I a, Louvain 1973, p. 84); see BALLY 1950:§119.

THE AUGENS, AN ANAPHORIC-COHESION MODIFIER OF PRONOMINAL REFERENCE. SYNTACTIC PROSODY

6.0.0.1 TERMINOLOGY AND DEFINITION. The pronoun-containing group of modifiers has had scant special attention hitherto, and nowhere can I find a discussion of its functions, compatibilities or paradigms. The prosodic properties of the augens (né " Verstärker ") have in part been the topic of an important paper by Polotsky (1961), yet with no functional or categorial definition; other discussions are scattered, meagre and inadequate [1]. Polotsky's " Verstärker " is in fact the only cover-term for this group. This I propose to replace by the Celtological " augens ", which is earlier, more cosmopolitan and in the general run of grammatical terminology, and, from the functional point of view, remarkably apt [2].

---

[1] STERN §§256-8 (the felicitous " adjunctive pronomina "), SCHWARZE–STEINTHAL §§345-6, 468-9 (" Pronominalstämme "), TILL §§194-6, p. 390.

[2] " Nota augens " was coined by Zeuss (Grammatica Celtica, 1853, 332ff., 341, 344f.), for the Gaelic (old Irish) -se/su/som, etc., the Cymric " reduplicated " and especially the " conjunctive " pronouns (mod. Welsh minnau/tithau/yntau, etc.). However, his terminology is not uniform: he employs in a similar sense " nota amplians ", " positio ampliata ", " ampliatio " (347), " augmentum " (344), " amplificatio " (379ff.), " emphatica forma " (of the Breton pronoun, 375). The primary pronoun is " auctum " or " ampliatum ". His main statement runs as follows (332): " Comitantur saepissime in utraque quoque lingua [i.e. in Gaelic

The augens is by no means a single category, in the strict sense of the word; it is here used as a common cognomen for the class of modifier morphs, typically of secondary prosodic status, that include or constitute a secondary pronominal element, in cohesion with a primary (pro)nominal segment, in a specific prosodic-syntagmatic extent. Functionally, the augens does not precisely "strengthen" or "emphasize"[3] the primary (pro)noun. It expands it, and modifies it in a structurable range of semasiological nuances, including that of "insistence": see below. The prosodic properties of the augens, related to its functional ones, call for a brief and selective preliminary investigation of *sentence-prosodic features*, before we proceed to introduce the data and their paradigmatic/syntagmatic structuring: this will be but a sketch, aiming at the boldest simplification.

6.0.1   APPOSITION, EXTRAPOSITION; WORD-ORDER AND THE PLACEMENT OF THE NOMINAL ACTOR

6.0.1.1 FRONTAL EXTRAPOSITION[4]. A noun syntagm or independent pronoun may be followed in the same pattern extent, by a pronominal resumption or representation. This is known (from a formal point of view) as (*frontal*) *extraposition* of the primary (pro)noun[5] or as *segmentation*[6] of the sentence (cf. the rhetorical-stylistic "anticipation", "prolepsis", "nominativus pendens", "casus absolutus"). Prosodically, the extraposed element is shown by what segmental criteria we have to be an *independent colon* (§6.0.3; see STERN §§484, 635; SCHWARZE-STEINTHAL 465f., 487 on the construction): (*A 1* 333) ⲚⲦⲞϤ ⳔⲈ ⲠⲖⲞⲅⲞⲤ ⲠⲈⲚⲦⲀϤⲢ-ⲤⲀⲢⳅ / (*Ch.* 50.20ff.) ⳅⲀⳅ ⲘⲈⲚ ⲚϢⲀⳈⲈ ⲀⲨϢ ⲚⳅϢⲂ ⲀⲓⳈⲞⲞⲨ / (*III* 18.15f.) ⲀⲚⲀϢ ⲘⲈⲚ ⲘⲠⲞⲨⲈⲓⲢⲈ[7] / (*III* 86.4) ⲚⲦϢⲦⲚ ⲆⲈ ⲘⲠⲈⲦⲚⲤⲞⲨϢⲚϤ / (*P* 130² 54 ⲦⲓⲆ) ⲀⲚⲞⲚ ⲆⲈ ⳅϢϢⲚ ⲘⲀⲢⲚ⳨-ⲤⲂϢ ⲚⲀⲚ ⲘⲀⲨⲀⲀⲚ / (*III* 197.6f.) ⲚⲀϢ ⲚⳅⲈ ⲚⲈⲨⲤϢϢⲈ ⲘⲚⲚⲈⲨⲎⲓ ⲀⲨϢ ⲚⲈⲨⳅⲓⲞⲘⲈ ⳅⲓⲞⲨⲤⲞⲠ ⲀⲨⲢ-ⲚⲀⳅⲈⲚⲔⲞⲞⲨⲈ. A *functional* analysis must regard the thematic structure of the whole pattern. This is a case of TOPICALIZATION, very typical of Coptic, a topic-prominent language (§2.0.2.1), or *theme prominence* ("thematic foregrounding", Halliday's "marked theme")[8]. This relative functional and structural autonomy of the extraposed segment matches, and is correlatable with, its prosodic one.

---

and Cymric] pronomina personalia ad maiorem emphasin primitus, ut videtur, idque tam absoluta quam infixa vel suffixa, notae quaedam, orta plerumque ex ipsis pronominibus, quas dicere poterimus notas ampliantas vel augentes; atque pronomina ipsa, si occurrunt vel sine his notis vel cum iisdem, sunt aut formae simplices vel aucta aut ampliata ". It was Pedersen (*Vergl. Grammatik*, 1913, II 137ff.) who modified Zeuss' term into " *Augens* ", pointing out that it is a pronoun in its own right, an enclitic " pronominal " which follows the " pronomhaltige Betonungseinheit ", emphasizing the " durch die Verbalendung, das infigierte oder suffigierte Pronomen oder die verbundene Genitivform ausgedrückte Begriff ". For the functional attribute of the augens, Pedersen applies the vague though ubiquitous " Hervorhebung " (cf. §§2.0.2.1-2); the native Irish term is *treise* (" force ", " emphasis "). For some classic discussions, see E. Lewy, *ZCPh* 27:10-13 (1957); Greene, *Ériu* 24:121-133 (1973); O'Briain, *ZCPh* 14:311-315 (1923); Pokorny, *ZCPh* 18:233ff. (1930); Hull, *Lg.* 16:12-16 (1940).

[3] See §§2.0.2.1-2. The idea is that of the " *nachdrücklicher Hinweis* " kind of emphasis (HOFMANN 1936:37); " *renforcement* " (MÜLLER-HAUSER 1943:116f.: " lui + même, seul..., pron. personal tonique "). POLOTSKY's " Verstärker " (1961:294 n. 1 = *CP* 398) is an adaptation of the Arabic " corroborative strengthener ", *at-taʾkīd* (Wright II 282).

[4] " Front " and " rear " correspond to the initial and final boundaries of the sentence, respectively.

[5] Cf. JESPERSEN 1937: Ch. 12.

[6] BALLY 1950:§§79-99, cf. SATZINGER 1976:7ff.; see REGULA 1966:131ff., HINTZE 1952:281ff., SCHENKEL 1967, esp. 116ff., and our §2.0.2.1.

[7] See §3.1.1.1.0.1 for this " zero " resumption of a zero article; §2.7.1.4.2 and note 130 there for the resumptions of extraposed ⳅⲞⲦⲓ (ⳈⲈ-) and ⲈⳈⲞⲞⲤ; for resumption generally as an exponent of cohesion, see §6.0.2.1; for concord issues, §5.2.1. In ⲀⲚⲀϢ ⲘⲈⲚ ⲘⲠⲞⲨⲈⲓⲢⲈ (*III* 18.15f.) we witness the only way of focalizing the lexical component of a compound verb, an idiomatic native equivalent of the " tautological infinitive " (GOLDENBERG 1971).

[8] HALLIDAY 1967:213f., 219, 237, 242; GRIMES 1975:342, 344.

6.0.1.2 Rear extraposition [4] refers to a different set of patterns, in which a noun syntagm or independent pronoun [9] expands, refers back to and as a rule *lexicalizes* a nuclear pronoun. These patterns give one a recurrent typologic impression that in Coptic the minimal patterns of grammar are all " custom-built " for the pronoun: the grammar may be phrased in terms of a system in which the pronoun rules supreme. The pronoun is grammatically essential, nuclear; the noun (which as a matter of fact is actualized in the *parole* as a noun syntagm by its determinator, yet another pronoun) is not essential, but expands the pronoun or is substituted (i.e. in syntagmatic or paradigmatic relation) for it [10].

6.0.1.2.1 *Rear extraposition marked by* ⲛϭⲓ-: this is a well-known construction, often quoted as a typological showpiece [11]. ⲛϭⲓ- marks an expansion of a third-person " suffix "-pronoun nucleus. This is usually a formal actor, with a verbal predicate: (*III* 160.22f.) ...ⲉⲧⲣⲉⲩϣⲱⲡⲉ ⲛϭⲓⲛⲉⲧⲙⲙⲁⲩ ⲉⲩⲟ ⲛⲁⲧⲕⲁⲣⲡⲟⲥ / (*Ch.* 78.2ff.) ⲙⲁⲣⲉϥϫⲟⲟⲥ ⲛⲁⲓ ⲛϭⲓ- / (*ibid.* 141.31f.) ⲡⲉϫⲁⲥ ⲛϭⲓ- / (*ibid.* 162.7f., *A 1* 167) ⲛⲁϣⲱⲟⲩ ⲛϭⲓ-, *vs.* ⲛⲁϣⲉ- 176.16f. etc. Here Shenoute agrees with Gnostic Sah. usage (cf. *NHC* VI 28.28). This extraposition is as a rule placed after other expansions (rectional and complementational) of the verb syntagm: (*A 2* 396) ⲉϥⲛⲁⲧⲃⲃⲟ ⲧⲏⲣϥ ⲛⲟⲩⲏⲣ ⲉⲃⲟⲗ ϩⲛⲣⲱⲙⲉ ⲛⲓⲙ ⲛϭⲓⲡⲉⲧⲟⲩⲃⲁⲡⲧⲓⲍⲉ ⲙⲙⲟϥ / (*ibid.* 449, not Sh.) ⲡⲁⲓ ϩⲱⲱϥ ⲟⲛ ⲛⲧⲁϥⲛⲟⲓ ⲙⲙⲟϥ ⲙⲡⲉⲓⲙⲁ ϩⲛⲟⲩⲱⲛϩ (sic) ⲉⲃⲟⲗ ⲛϭⲓⲡⲛⲟϭ ⲛⲉⲕⲕⲗⲏⲥⲓⲁⲥⲧⲏⲥ / (*IV* 5.26ff.) ⲛⲓⲙ... ⲛⲉⲧⲟⲩⲛⲁⲙⲟⲩϩ ⲁⲛ ⲛⲟⲣⲅⲏ ⲉϩⲟⲩⲛ ⲉⲣⲟⲟⲩ ⲛϭⲓⲧⲏⲡⲉ ⲧⲏⲣⲥ ⲛⲛⲇⲓⲕⲁⲓⲟⲥ / (*ibid.* 206.27ff.) ⲉⲩⲉⲉⲓ ⲉϩⲣⲁⲓ ⲉϫⲱⲟⲩ ϩⲙⲡⲉⲟⲩⲟⲉⲓϣ ⲉⲧⲙⲙⲁⲩ ⲏ ⲛⲧⲟϥ ⲧⲉⲛⲟⲩ ⲛϭⲓⲛⲉⲓⲥⲁϩⲟⲩ ⲧⲏⲣⲟⲩ / (*IV* 68.17f.) ⲛϥⲙⲉⲉⲩⲉ ⲁⲛ ⲉⲃⲟⲗ ⲉⲗⲁⲁⲩ ⲙⲡⲉⲑⲟⲟⲩ ⲉⲡⲧⲏⲣϥ ⲛϭⲓ-. Note too the distribution of two appositional constructions with a Second-Tense focalization pattern: (*theme/topic* → *focus*) ⲛϭⲓ- (*III* 116.6, 169.23, 183.3f.) and (*theme/topic* ⲛϭⲓ-) → *focus* (*III* 117.28f., 133.11f., *IV* 127.4f.), where the type of focality plays a role (§2.8.2). Rarely, the nucleus may be the *possessor*, in the possession verboid or possessive determinator: (*Ch.* 192.31ff.) ⲙⲛⲧⲁϥ-ⲥⲓ ⲅⲁⲣ ⲟⲩⲧⲉ ϣⲓ ⲛϭⲓⲡϫⲓ-ⲕⲃⲁ / (*IV* 45.24f.) ⲛⲑⲉ ⲟⲛ ⲉⲧⲉⲩⲥⲩⲛⲏⲑⲉⲓⲁ ⲧⲉ ⲧⲁⲓ ϫⲓⲛⲧⲉⲩⲁⲣⲭⲏ ⲛϭⲓ- / (*A 1* 90) ⲧⲉϥϭⲓⲛⲕⲱ ⲉⲃⲟⲗ ⲛⲛⲉⲛⲛⲟⲃⲉ... ⲛϭⲓⲡⲛⲟⲩⲧⲉ (compare ⲧⲉⲩϭⲓⲛⲉⲓ ϣⲁⲣⲟⲟⲩ ⲕⲁⲗⲱⲥ ϩⲓⲧⲛⲛⲁⲅⲅⲉⲗⲟⲥ, *Wess. 9* 161c 11ff., where ϩⲓⲧⲛ- introduces a non-appositive " new " nominal actor). The appositive noun syntagm may be indefinite: (*A 2* 449, not Sh.) ⲁϥⲉⲓ ⲛϭⲓⲟⲩⲟⲩⲟⲉⲓϣ, but is usually ⲡ- (or equivalently) determinated.

6.0.1.2.2 Cases of *zero-marked rear extraposition* in special circumstances:

(a) An appositive noun introduced — *mediated* — by an appositive independent pronoun (all persons): (*III* 60.4f.) ϥϫⲱ ⲅⲁⲣ ⲙⲙⲟⲥ ⲛⲧⲟϥ ⲡϫⲟⲉⲓⲥ ϫⲉ- (see §6.1.3.3).

[9] Here we come up against the difficulty of distinguishing (with the segmental data at our disposal) between pronominal apposition and the augens: §3.1.3.3.

[10] Cf. Steinthal–Misteli 1893:50, and see §5.3 above.

[11] The only monographic discussion of ⲛϭⲓ- is by Morenz (1952), who looks to Shenoute for his source material. What Morenz has in mind, however, is the rhetorical or stylistic motivation for the selection of this construction, rather than its structural definition and function. Considerations like the alleged " inelegance " (" unschön ", pp. 4f., 7) of an inserted extensive nominal " subject " (i.e. actor) which has therefore to be deferred until after the completion of the conjugation form are rather dubious. Even if such considerations were true, this cannot constitute a descriptive statement, particularly since (on the one hand) ⲛϭⲓ- can introduce the shortest appositive actor-expressions (consider ...ⲛϭⲓ-ⲛⲉⲧⲙⲙⲁⲩ *RE 10* 163a 27, ...ⲛϭⲓ-ⲛⲁⲓ *III* 160.22, ...ⲛϭⲓ-ⲡϫⲟⲉⲓⲥ *III* 117 28), while, on the other hand, very long complex nominal phrases are found in mid-conjugation actor position (witness the constructions in §6.0.2.1, link 6). Nor is the " Betonung " (p. 5ff.) of the " subject " an independently determinable and controllable factor. It is rather the tendency of the language to separate (" isolate ") the lexical from the grammatical which underlies the widespread incidence of this construction (cf. Steinthal–Misteli 1893:50, 284, and see §5.3 above). Typologically speaking, one recalls the " *complément explicatif* " of Berber dialects (cf. Galand, *CFS* 21:33-53, 1964, esp. pp. 43ff.; *ead.*, " Relations du verbe et du nom dans l'énoncé berbère ", in: *LACITO-documents* [EURASIE, 2], Colloque: Relations Prédicat-Actant(s), I, Paris: SELAF, 1979, 131-146, esp. 132ff.) completing the purely grammatical information of the person index and localizing it in the " infinite " (so Galand, meaning " long out of all comparison ", but of course closed) list of the lexicon. Here, too, Celtic supplies a striking parallel (studies by O'Nolan, Pokorny, MacCana and others). I believe the " Hellenizing " interpretation of the Shenoutean phenomenon (Weiss 1972: n. 112) is as doubtful as the stylistic one.

(b) Nominal apposition to a *delocutive* (third person) pronoun in object status: (*BMCat.* 83, No. 199 ⲧϫⲁ) ⲛⲁϣ ⲛⲍⲉ ⲛⲧⲱⲧⲛ ⲧⲉⲧⲛⲁⲣ-ⲃⲟⲗ ⲉⲣⲟⲥ ⲧⲟⲣⲅⲏ ⲉⲧⲛⲏⲩ / (*Ch.* 43.38ff.) ⲛⲧⲉⲣⲉⲓⲙⲟⲩⲧϥ ⲛⲕⲉⲥⲟⲡ ⲡⲉⲕⲏⲓ ⲙⲡⲓ-ϭⲛ-ⲗⲁⲁⲩ ⲛⲉⲓⲇⲱⲗⲟⲛ ⲛⲍⲏⲧϥ / (*III* 21.19) ⲁⲩⲕⲱⲧ ⲙⲙⲟϥ ⲡⲡⲩⲣⲅⲟⲥ ⲉⲧⲙⲙⲁⲩ / (*ibid.* 88.27) ⲧⲛⲁⲧⲣⲉⲧⲛⲥⲟⲩⲱⲛⲟⲩ ϭⲉ ⲛⲉⲣⲱⲟⲩ / (*Ench.* 66b) ⲕⲧⲁⲕⲟ ⲙⲙⲟⲥ ⲛⲧⲟϥ ⲑⲓⲕⲱⲛ ⲙⲡⲛⲟⲩⲧⲉ ⲍⲛⲛⲃⲟⲧⲉ ⲛⲧⲁⲕⲁⲁⲩ. In (*IV* 36.21f.) ⲁϥⲧⲣⲉⲩ-ϣⲱⲡⲉ ⲧⲏⲣⲟⲩ ⲙⲡⲏⲩⲉ ⲙⲛⲡⲕⲁⲍ, the apposition is to the actor exponent in the causative infinitive; cf. exx. in §6.0.1.2 (a).

(c) Nouns in " vocative " or addressing role, esp. in post-imperative position: (*P* 130² 7 ϥ) ⲙⲡⲣϣⲱⲡⲉ ⲧⲥⲩⲛⲁⲅⲱⲅⲏ ⲉⲣⲉ-... / (*A 1* 464) ⲏ ⲉⲕⲛⲁⲭⲟⲟⲥ ⲡⲃⲁⲃⲉⲣⲱⲙⲉ...

(d) Nominal apposition to the " actor " (third-person pronoun) of a modifier predicate (Bipartite pattern): (*III* 15.21f.) ⲛϥⲍⲁⲧⲛⲧⲏⲩⲧⲛ ⲁⲛ ⲡⲥⲁⲧⲁⲛⲁⲥ. Here probably belongs the regular construction ⲉϥⲧⲱⲛ + *noun* (*III* 31.13, 107.15, *Ch.* 200.43, 48f., 206.31ff., etc.) where (1) no real opposition obtains with a mid-conjugation nominal actor (a rare example of this is *A 1* 212: ⲉⲣⲉⲛⲉⲛⲕⲉⲉⲥ ⲧⲱⲛ), which means that the pronominal " actor " is a mere " slot filler ", a cataphoric index with no nominal substitution; (2) ⲉϥ-ⲧⲱⲛ ⲛϭⲓ- does occur, as a rare variant (e.g. *A 2* 336, collated: ⲉⲥⲧⲱⲛ ⲧⲁⲛⲟⲙⲓⲁ... ⲉⲩⲧⲱⲛ ⲇⲉ ⲛⲥⲁⲣϫ... ⲏ ⲉⲩⲧⲱⲛ ⲛϭⲓⲛⲉⲧⲟⲩⲟⲩⲱⲙ ⲍⲛⲧⲉⲩⲧⲁⲡⲣⲟ).

6.0.1.2.3 The ⲛ-*marked nom. modifier in apposition to a suffix pronoun* is of yet more restricted distribution [12].

(a) A cataphoric pronominal representation of a *nominal possessor* after one of a closed list of inalienable nouns as *possessum* (cf. §1.2.1.1 spec. obs.). This is again a case where no noun is substitutable for the pronoun, which is thus a formal obligatory slot-filler " heralding " the subsequent noun: ' -ϥ → ⲛ+*noun*' is structurally the possessor expression [13]: ⲭⲱϥ ⲙⲡⲕⲁⲍ (*RE 10* 163a 17f.), ⲣⲱⲥ ⲛⲧⲁⲛⲟⲙⲓⲁ (*A 1* 298), but generally as components of prepositions: ⲍⲁⲣⲁⲧϥ ⲛ- (*III* 38.10), ⲛⲁⲓⲕⲧϥ ⲛ- (*K* 9067, *P* 130⁵ 50 ⲥⲕⲁ), ⲉⲧⲟⲟⲧⲟⲩ ⲛ- (*III* 48.3), ⲉⲍⲟⲩⲛ ⲉⲍⲣⲁⲩ ⲛ- (*P* 130¹ 139 ⲧⲙⲥ), ⲍⲏⲧϥ (a preposition in itself) ⲛ-, (*BLOr.* 3581A 159, No. 253 ⲛⲥ), ⲍⲓⲧⲟⲩϣϥ ⲛ- (*III* 52.16) etc.; the ⲛ-mark of dependence is thus complementary (allomorphic) to the immediate (markless) government of non-compound prepositions [14]. Some examples of this kind hint at a tendency to " fossilizing ", i.e. immutability of the pronominal exponent in the masc. sgl. [15]: ⲍⲏⲧϥ ⲛⲛⲉⲍⲓⲟⲙⲉ ⲉⲧⲉⲉⲧ (*Ench.* 66a).

(b) ⲙⲡⲉⲥⲛⲁⲩ " ... the two ", " both/either of... ", not in opposition to ⲛϭⲓ-; the nuclear plural (second, third persons) pronoun is in different roles (not however in actor status?): (*A 2* 403) ⲧⲛⲁⲡⲓⲑⲉ ⲙⲙⲱⲧⲛ ⲙⲡⲉⲥⲛⲁⲩ / (*Miss.* 283) ⲛⲛⲉⲍⲟⲟⲩ ⲉⲣⲉⲛⲉⲍⲃⲏⲩⲉ ϫⲓ ⲙⲙⲟⲟⲩ ⲉⲣⲟⲟⲩ ⲁⲛ ⲙⲡⲉⲥⲛⲁⲩ... ⲡⲥⲟⲡ ⲉⲧⲟⲩⲛⲁϫⲓⲧⲟⲩ ⲉⲣⲟⲟⲩ ⲁⲛ ⲙⲡⲉⲥⲛⲁⲩ / (*Or.* 160.27f.) ϥⲥⲍⲟⲩⲟⲣⲧ ⲛϭⲓⲡⲉⲧⲛⲟⲩϣϣ ⲙⲡⲉⲥⲛⲁⲩ / (*A 2* 443-4, not Sh.) ⲡⲍⲱⲃ ⲇⲉ ⲟⲩⲟⲛⲍ ⲉⲃⲟⲗ ⲍⲓⲧⲟⲟⲧⲟⲩ ⲙⲡⲉⲥⲛⲁⲩ (sim. *ibid.* 436, 445); NB. (*III* 39.11f.) ⲉⲓⲥⲛⲉ ⲙⲡⲉⲥⲛⲁⲩ ⲁⲩⲟⲩⲱⲛⲍ ⲉⲃⲟⲗ ⲧⲁⲭⲩ, where ⲙⲡⲉⲥⲛⲁⲩ must be appositive to ⲛⲉ, itself with the same reference as the actor-suffix.

6.0.1.3 WORD ORDER; THE PLACEMENT OF THE NOMINAL ACTOR, A PARADIGMATIC EVALUATION. Turning our attention to placement rules for individual pattern components, we find they combine a conditioning by a great many factors in several parameters [16] and are by nature mutual and relative, i.e.

---

[12] LAYTON 1981:§6.2 (I would prefer " restricted " to " anomalous ").

[13] Cf. the Semitic " extended construct state " (cf. Rosén, *JAOS* 81:25, 1961).

[14] Some non-compound (unanalyzable) prepositions use this mediate manner of governing a noun: ⲍⲁⲣⲟϥ ⲙⲡⲁⲓ (*P* 130² 115 ⲓⲍ), ⲍⲁⲣⲟⲥ ⲛⲧⲡⲉ (*P* 131⁵ 20 ⲣⲡⲍ, *A 2* 360, *III* 96.21, *Ch.* 195.46 — " ⲍⲁⲧⲡⲉ " not attested? — also ⲍⲁⲣⲟϥ ⲙⲡⲣⲏ *P* 131⁵ 20 ⲣⲡⲍ, all after *Eccl.* 3:1, 1:3 etc.), ⲉⲣⲟϥ ⲛ- (only in the sense of " to the debit of... ": *Ryl. Cat.* 34, No. 69 ⲛⲥ, *A 2* 59, *Ch.* 102.9f., *Rossi* 2/3 58 ⲉⲣⲟϥ ⲛⲛⲍⲏⲕⲉ, uncollated: -ϥ immutable?), ⲟⲩⲧⲱϥ ⲛ- (*IF* 163 apud *Dictionary* 495a).

[15] See §5.2.2.3.2 above, with reff.

[16] See for instance §2.6.3-4.

influenced by other rules regarding the placement of other elements in a given extent. This calls for a multivariate analysis for which I doubt that Coptic grammatical research is yet ready. Generally speaking, one assumes word order is not " free "; it involves either taxemes, i.e. features of arrangement, or a distinctive feature of placement (for example, with the adjective: see Ch. 4). In either case, a change in order entails a corresponding change (often too subtle to be detected by the linguist or to be transposed into another language) on the *plan du contenu*. What we can supply, however, are (1) statements on the relative placement of isolated pattern constituents (modifiers, Chs. 1 and 4; the augens, particles, see below). (2) Statements on the relative placement of constituent *groups* (theme/topic and focus, Ch. 2). This is obviously not adequate by any standard, when the call is for a " general theory of Coptic word order ". It is nevertheless an indispensable stage in evolving such a theory: the individual placement-consideration of individual constituent categories. Word-order statements are the aftermath and culmination of the description process, not an early phase of it, nor an issue to be resolved on its own. In Coptic, where the mobility of most of the basic constituents of patterns is low or nil, this approach is even more requisite; here one can hardly concur with Dionysius of Halicarnassus' dictum[17] that " the order of words is more significant than their selection ".

Among unmistakable circumstances with greater or lesser bearing on the arrangement of constructions and placement of elements, we note (a) the typologically significant " *Grundrichtung* " or basic syntagmatic phrase sequence, *nucleus* → *satellite* (*determinatum* → *determinans*)[18], (b) the sequence in the predication and focalization patterns, (c) a cotext-oriented *thematic* sequence[19], (d) the prosodic contour(s) of the utterance, correlated with (c) and mapped on (a) and (b), and (e) motivation of a rhetorical, stylistic, rhythmic-euphonic order[20], mapped whenever required and possible onto (a), (b), (c) and (d). This is a notoriously slippery ground, where the dangers of circular statement are plain to see, since we do not have any working knowledge of these factors; they constitute mere post-analysis judgements of interpretation, not pre-analysis principles. All (a) to (e) factors concur to give the actual arrangement and placements; we cannot hope to resolve these into its several sets of conditioning, except in a very imperfect, approximative and always speculative manner.

As regards the placement of the nominal actor (" grammatical " and, unless there is some signa-to the contrary, " logical " subject, i.e. theme/topic, §2.0.2.0.1) of a verbal predication, we note the following ternary (double-binary) paradigm and opposition (the Tripartite is chosen as representative):

(a) " ⲡⲣⲱⲙⲉ ⲥⲱⲧⲙ "

— — — — — — — — — — — — —

(b) " ⲡⲣⲱⲙⲉ ⲁ4ⲥⲱⲧⲙ "

(c) " ⲁ4ⲥⲱⲧⲙ ⲛ6ⲓ-ⲡⲣⲱⲙⲉ "

In one analysis, the less common member (a), far from being *synchronically* the unmarked " neutral " term (which is historically the case), is revealed as being marked by the synthesis of lexical and grammatical components. Members (b) and (c) are opposed to (a) as " isolating " (see n. 11) and analytic, and mutually opposed in their thematic structure. I would say that (c), strictly speaking a case of " delayed theme " and secondary information point[21], is here unmarked, while (b) is the marked member, in which

---

[17] *Apud* WEIL 1879:2.

[18] Cf. STEINTHAL–MISTELI 1893:275ff. Although this issue has never been properly treated, it constitutes an essential part of the scholar's *Sprachgefühl* (cf. P. de Lagarde's " unkoptische Stellung ", " kein Kopte stellt so ", in *Aus dem deutschen Gelehrtenleben*, Göttingen 1881, pp. 44, 50, 59).

[19] WEIL 1879:11ff., 76ff., 83ff.; MATHESIUS 1941, and subsequently often in Prague School treatments of this question (see §2.0.2.0.1 ff.).

[20] Note the case of a chiastic placement of nominal actors, (b)-(c) below, also the chiastic arrangement of topic and focus, §2.6.3.1.2: (Z 306 CNZ) ⲍⲙⲡⲁⲓ ⲟⲛ ⲛⲧⲁ4ⲭⲟⲟⲥ ⲛ6ⲓⲡⲁⲡⲟⲥⲧⲟⲗⲟⲥ ⲡⲁⲩⲗⲟⲥ ⲭⲉ-... ⲛⲧⲁⲡⲭⲟⲉⲓⲥ ⲭⲟⲟⲥ ⲟⲛ ⲉⲧⲃⲉⲡⲁⲓ ⲭⲉ-...

[21] HALLIDAY 1967:239ff.

the thematicity of the actor is specially signalled by segmentation, the thematic structure of the clause being thus made transparent: ογπνᾱ ΝΑΚΑΘΑΡΤΟΝ ΑϤΡ-ΟΥΔΡΑΚШΝ ΑΥШ ΟΥ2ΟϤ ΜΝΟΥΟΙΤ, ΑΥШ ΟΥΟΥШΝϤ ΑϤΡ-ΟΥΒΑϢΟΡ (*RE 10* 160a 27ff.). In another view, it is (a) which is unmarked *vis à vis* (b) and (c), in which the thematic structure is overt.

6.0.2 JUNCTURE (COHESION) FEATURES. BOUNDARIES. THE COPTIC WORD. Any two segments and elements of an utterance join each other in a way that is gradable on a scale exposing the gradient or parameter of cohesion. As criteria for the hierarchic assignment of inter-segment cohesion, we isolate juncture (cohesion) features: LINKS [22] and their negation, DELIMITATIONS [23], the former amounting to measure points of *closeness*, the latter of openness or non-closeness, of " looseness ". By links and delimitations, phonological or ultra-phonemic, we can characterize any given syntagmatic constellation: the more links there are, the closer the attachment — the more delimitations, the more open. Links are symptoms of the *extent of validity*, while delimitations give us *juncture boundaries* [24]. I do not offer here a systematic scale-related gradation of juncture. This must be done as part of a special study, preferably based on examination of homogenous MSS. I simply give selective lists of the more striking cohesive patterns: links and delimitations. Note that these are no more than *relative indexes*, exponents of the parameter or level of juncture (even the apparently absolute junctural dichotomies, *initial:final*, *close:open*, are deceptively so, and in fact equally relative [25]).

6.0.2.1 LINKS: (*morphophonemic* [26], *morphemic*) (Ø) " A short vowel is maintained in an open syllable ", valid only in the extent of the lexemic unanalyzable " word ": ΟΟΤΠ, ΟΕΤΠ-, ϢΟΡΠ, ΟΡΧ, ϤΟΤ⸗Ν, ΚΟΤ⸗Ϥ.

(1) " A labializable [27] nasal constituting part or the whole of a prefixed morph is assimilated to an immediately following primary (i.e. unconditioned) non-syllabic [28] labial ", validity extent: the segment ' *prefix + noun syntagm* '; progressive dependence (allophonic allomorph): ϬΜ-ΟΥΟΕΙϢ (*A 2* 117), ΕΡΜ-ΠΧΟΕΙΟ (*A 2* 165), ϢΑΝΤϤΜ-ΠΡШΜΕ (*IV* 101.16, *Ryl. Cat.* 34f. No. 70 ΟΜΔ) [29], ΤΕΤΜΜΝΤΑΘΗΤ (*Wess. 9* 141a 17), ΠΟΑ ΒΒΟΛ (*III* 196.28f.), ΕΜΠΕΤΝΑΝΟΥΟΥ (*III* 203.13) [30], ΑΧΜΠ2ΛΛΟ (*IV* 113.5), ΝΤΜΠΧΟΕΙΟ (*IV* 33.22).

(2) " A ' suffix-paradigm ' pronoun is selected as actor expression by an immediately preceding converter morpheme ", validity extent: the converted conjugation form; regressive dependence (allomorph): ΕΙΟШΤΜ (ΑΝ) (closer than ΕΝϮΟШΤΜ ΑΝ [31], delimitation 2).

---

[22] I adopt here Rosén's terminology of 1964, but extend the notion of juncture to be coterminous with " cohesion ". Rosén 1964:160: " A dependence that exists between two parts of the same order if they occur in a segment not exceeding their arrangement, but which does not exist if they occur in separate utterances ".

[23] Rosén 1964:163: " A dependence that exists between two parts of the same order if they occur in two different utterances, but which does not exist if they occur in a segment not exceeding their arrangement ".

[24] Rosén 1964:§45.

[25] The only special study of this subject is Erman 1915, a contrastive Sahidic:Bohairic listing of environments (see Shisha-Halevy 1981:317f.).

[26] Not (to the best of my knowledge) attested in Shenoute is the Coptic case of Trubetzkoy's " *corrélation prosodique de gémination* ", like ΟΥΜΕΕ ΠΕ (*Deut.* 13:14, see Polotsky 1957c:348f. = *CP* 390f.).

[27] Not, for instance, the Ν in ΜΝ-, 2ΕΝ-, ΧΙΝ-. Another link:delimitation opposition is signalled by the syllabic:non-syllabic status of the plural definite article before the initial (stressed:unstressed) vowel of a noun lexeme, regularly at least for native lexemes. Cf. Polotsky, *OLZ* 59:253 n. 1, 1964 (note omitted by mistake in *CP*).

[28] Not in ΝΜΟΑ2 (*Wess. 9* 139a 27).

[29] Not in *Chassinat* (Ν-ΠΟΟΕ, *Ch.* 56.50f.). Cf. for this phenomenon Kahle 1954:98ff.

[30] But ΕΝΠΕΘΟΟΥ (*III* 202.5f.), ΝΝΒΑΑΜΠΕ (*ibid.* 219.12).

[31] Polotsky 1960a:§28 (obs.).

(3) " A prenominal converter allomorph is selected by an immediately following nominal actor expression ", validity extent: the converted conjugation form; progressive dependence (allomorph): ЄРЄ/ НЄРЄ/ЄТЄРЄПРШМЄ СШТМ (АН) (closer than ЄМПРШМЄ СШТМ АН [32], delimitation 3).

Syntactic: (4) ' Determinator {*noun-lexeme* + ²¹- *noun-lexeme*} ' juncture between the noun lexemes closer than in '*determinator* + *noun lexeme* + АΥШ/МН- *determinator* + *noun lexeme*' (delimitation 4); progressive bracketing: 2ЄНТКАС НЄ 2І6ШНТ 2ІПЄІРАСМОС (sic) (*A 2* 435, not Sh.) / ПЄМКА2 Н2НТ 2ІΛΥПΗ 2ІАШΑ2ΟΜ 2ІНО6НЄ6 2ІΟΥШΛС Н2НТ (*A 1* 77).

(5) (a) # *converter* + *conjugation base* [33]/*converter* + *actor* {*verb lexeme* + *verb lexeme* + *verb lexeme* [34]...} #; (b) # *converter* {(*conj. base* + *verb lexeme*) + (*conj. base* + *verb lexeme*) + (*conj. base* + *verb lexeme*)} # (perfect tense only); (c) # {(*conjugation base*/*converter* + *actor*) + (*conj. base*/*converter* + *actor*) + (*conj. base*/*converter* + *actor*)...} *verb lexeme* #. Cases of progressive (a-b) or regressive bracketing [35], closer than the juncture of repeated (coordinated, disjoined) (*base*/*converter* + *verb lexeme*) unit (delimitation 5).

Examples: (a) АПКА2 ΟΜΚΟΥ Н СΟΟΥ (*IF* 268, apud *Dictionary* 318a-b) / НЄНТАΥΡ-ПАІ АΥШ СВТЄ-2ЄН-СΟΤВЄЧ НАΥ (*A 2* 341) / ЄΥШΑΝΧΝΟΥΚ Н ΧΝΟΥΤΝ (*ibid.* 528) / ННЄРШМЄ СЄК-ТЄЧ2ΟІТЄ Є2РАІ... Н ΜΜΟΝ НТС... (*IV* 95.10f.) / МПЧСШМС АΥШ ЧШТЄ ЄВΟΛ (*Wess.* 9 87a 31ff.) / НТШШ... НТАПНΟΥТЄ ΧΟΟΥ Н ΛΑΥ (*Ench.* 72b) / ЄРЄ ПЄЧ2НТ ПΟΟНЄ Н КТНΥ ЄПΑ2ΟΥ (circ., *A 2* 24) / НЄТЄРЄПЄЧНЄ2 ТΟ2С ΜΜΟΟΥ Н ΟΥΟΝ2 ЄВΟΛ 2ІШΟΥ (*ibid.* 529) / ...ПЄТТВВΟ МПРШМЄ ΟΥΔЄ ΧΑ2МЄЧ, v. 1. ΟΥТЄ ЄТΧШ2М ΜΜΟЧ (*A 1* 327; note the non-susceptibility of the second infinitive to the Stern–Jernstedt Rule, §3.1.2).

(b) НЄНТАΥΧІ-СΟТЄ Н АΥШΟΟ6ΟΥ (*III* 69.14f., *v.l.* МННЄНТАΥШΟΟ6ΟΥ) / ΟΥΟΝ НІМ ЄНТАЧСШТМ АΥШ АЧΧІ-СВШ (*ibid.* 173.18f.) / ...НТАΥПІСТЄΥЄ ЄПНΟΥТЄ АΥШ АΥ2ЄΛПІΖЄ ЄПЄЧΧ͞С (rel., *RE 11* 17a 12f.) / НТАЧТСАВΟ АΥШ АЧΡ-2НМЄРΟС 2ІТМ- (Sec. Perf., *III* 28.25f.) / ЄНТАПЄІШАΧЄ 6ШΛП ЄРΟІ АІЄІМЄ ЄРΟЧ ТЄНΟΥ 2НТЄІРΟМПЄ ТАІ (Sec. Perf., *ibid.* 219.3f.).

(c) base + *zero-determinated* actor (МПЄ- repeated 26 times, *A 2* 383; 7 times, *A 1* 80; 9 times, *Ch.* 26-7; МЄРЄ- 5 times, *A 2* 25); ЄН2ΟСΟΝ ЄМНА66ЄΛΟС ЄММНАРΧΗ ЄММН6ΟМ НАΥ6М-6ΟМ ЄПΟΡΧΝ... (*A 2* 381) / ΟΥΝ-МАТΟІ ΓΑΡ... ΟΥΝΡЄЧΧΙΝ6ΟΝС, ΟΥΝΝΟЄΙΚ, ΟΥΝΠΟΡΝΟС, ΟΥΝΑΚΑΘΑΡΤΟС НРШМЄ 2ΜΟΟС... (*Ch.* 57.40ff.).

(6) # (*conjugation base*/*converter*) + (*interposition*) + (*pred. verb-lexeme*) #, closer than # (*conj. base*/*converter* + *nom. actor*) + (*interposition*) + (*conj. base* + *anaphoric pronoun* + *pred. verb-lexeme*) # (delimitation 6) [36]. Examples: МПЄТЄККΛΗСІΑ МПЄΧ͞С ПΛΑΟС НВРРЄ НТАΥПІСТЄΥЄ ЄРΟЧ, ЄІТЄ... ЄІТЄ... ЄІТЄ

[32] Polotsky 1960a:§28.

[33] -ТРЄ(ЧСШТМ) behaves in this respect like a conjugation base (it is a *conjugation carrier*): АНТІТРЄΥШΡΧ Н ТШМ ЄРΟΟΥ (*A 2* 505), ЄТМТРЄΥЄІ... АΥШ ЧΟТΝ ЄВΟΛ (*ibid.* 529), ΧЄ-ЄЧНАТРЄΝΙΜΝΗШЄ СΟΥШΝΝ АΥШ МЄΡΙТΝ Н2ΟΥΟ (*III* 107-8), also *A 1* 173, *A 2* 81 So does (*base* + *mediator* [lexeme premodifier §3.3]): АΥШΡП-НАΥ ΟΝ Н ЄΙМЄ (*A 2* 97), ННЄΥЄШЄІ ШΑΡΟΟΥ... Н ЄВШΚ ЄТЄΥМΝТРШМЄ (*IV* 61.7f.). Likewise the future characteristic НА: ЄΝΑΘΛΙВЄ АН Н2ЄΝΑТ6ΟМ Н 6ΟТПΟΥ ЄВΟΛ (*A 2* 505-6), НЄТНАΚΛΑΥ НСШΟΥ... Н КΟΜШΟΥ, ПΛΟΓΟС МПНΟΥТЄ НАТ6ΛЄΙΟΟΥ Н СΟШΟΥ (*P* 130² 9 СΛΗ), and МН-/ΟΥΝ-: ЄΝЄМΝΠΡШМЄ НΚΟТΚ Н ТΑ2Є (*IV* 180.3). Consider also the rare bracketing # *base* [(*actor* + *v. lexeme*) + (*actor* + *v. lexeme*)] # ННЄРШМЄ 2РАІ Н2НТΝ СЄШЧ-2ΝΟ Н ПЄЧ2НТ ΟΥΑШЧ АН (*IV* 85.6f.), and the variation ШΑΥΘΜΚΟЧ Н2ΟΥΟ ΧЄ-ННАΧΟΟС ΧЄ-МΟΟΥТЧ (*A 1* 241).

[34] Є + infinitive, ЄТРЄ- occur as bracketed verbal predicates: *IV* 94.27f., 61.7f., 20f. (see *Ch.* 7 n. 63).

[35] Pattern (b) with the relative converter corresponds to Jespersen's " exhausted relative ". See Wiesmann 1927:67f., Till §483, Shisha–Halevy 1976a:51; for Egyptian, cf. De Buck, *JEA* 23:162 (1937). See §2.8.4 for the analogous pattern with the Second-Tense converter.

[36] Cf. Steinthal–Misteli 1893:50; Till 1928:§202e; Nagel 1969:465ff.; Browne 1976:231; Quecke 1977:77f. The construction is especially common, on the one hand, in Gnostic texts, on the other in late Sahidic ones. Note that a juncture contour *noun syntagm......noun syntagm* usually characterizes the " Trimembral " # *subject* + *copula* + *predicate* # Nominal Sentence pattern (also the *Wechselsatz* # N_1 ПЄ N_2 #), in contrast to the # *predicate* + *pron. subject* + *nominal* (*lexical*) *subject* # one: ПШШЧ НТЄΨΥΧΗ Н2ЄНРШМЄ ЄΥΑΡΧЄΙ МННЄТΟΥΑΡΧЄΙ ЄΧΟΥ ПЄ ΧΟΟС... (*A 2* 76) / АРА ПΟΥΝΟЧ НΟΥШΗΡЄ ЄВΟΛ 2НТМΝТРММΑΟ ЄНТАПЄЧЄΙШТ ТΑΑС НАЧ ПЄ ΟΥ2ΟΟΥ (*ibid.* 364) / ПΑНЄΡШΟΥ ΔЄ 2ШШЧ НΔΙΚΑΙΟС НТАПНΟΥТЄ + НТСНЧЄ Є2РАІ ЄТΟΟТΟΥ ПЄ ПΧΙ-КВΑ ΜΜΟΟΥ (*III* 90.5f.). Note the punctuation in: 2ЄНШΗΡЄ АΥШ 2ЄНШЄЄРЄ ЄРЄПСШ ТΟ 2ІШΟΥ' НЄ 2ЄНРШМЄ ЄΥΧШ ΜΜΟС ΧЄ... (*Or.* 153.27ff.)

OYON NIM NTAYXI NTAⲰⲢEA MⲠEⲠNA ETOYAAB KOTOY (*Ch.* 150.42ff.) / EⲢENETOYH2 2NNEITOⲠOC MAⲀⲀON ⲀE NⲢⲰME NTAYTAN2OYTOY O MMNTⲢE (*IV* 84.15ff., circ.) / NTOⲠOC NTAⲠCOEIT MⲠONHⲢON NNET+ OYBENEYEⲢHY ETBE2AⲢⲠAZE MⲠⲢAN 2ANOYB ⲠⲰ2 EMAY (*III* 35.2ff.) / MH EⲢENⲰHⲢE MⲠKAKE MNⲠ6OCM NTAYⲠⲰT N0E N2EN-BAⲰOⲢ EYⲠHT 2AⲠ2O NMMOYI NAXOOY... (*ibid.* 87.22ff.). Also *III* 128.19f., 221.24ff., *IV* 46.8f., 108.2f., 163.7f., 56.11f., 17.9ff., *A 1* 150-1, etc.

(7) ' XEKAAC EYE-/(E)NNEY- ', closer than ' XEKAAC + (interposition) + *conjunctive* (delimitation 7; see §7.2.6.1 [c]).

(8) '(*pro*)*noun* [→ (resumption)]' (in various constructions), closer than '(*pronoun* [→ (no resumption)]' (delimitation 8). Examples: OYⲰAXE... ENANOYY EXOOY (*A 2* 462) / 2A2 MEN NⲰAXE AYⲰ N2ⲰB AIXOOY (*Ch.* 50.20ff.) / ⲠAI ETMMAY AYⲰ NEIKOOYE ⲠNOYTE NAKⲢINE 2NTMHTE MⲠAI MNNAI ETMMAY (*III* 130. 7f.) / AⲰ MⲮYXH... NETYMMAY AN N6IⲠCATANAC (*ibid.* 211.8f.) / ENMHHⲰE NTAKXOOC XE-CEXI-2NAAY NAY (*Ch.* 41.12ff.) / NTOK ⲠETOYXⲰK EBOⲀ N2HTK NNEYⲠA0OC (*ibid.* 21.18ff.) / NTOⲠOC NTAⲠCOEIT MⲠONHⲢON... ⲠⲰ2 EMAY (*ibid.* 129.23ff.). There is no doubt a need to refine further the gradation of cohesion (e.g. by kind and "strength" of anaphoric exponents; consider [*Ench.* 74-5] NETEⲢEⲠAI XⲰ NHTN NNAI) and relate it to anaphoric concord, which similarly displays allomorphic "assimilation" conditioning: the derelevantization in a given environment of a morphological opposition that is elsewhere pertinent.

Additional links discussed elsewhere (see n. 26): the compatibility and ordering of enclitics (see §6.0. 3.2); negative syncategorization and personal maintenance between the nucleus and the conjunctive (adnexal modifier), see §7.1.2.2.

6.0.2.2 DELIMITATIONS. (∅) Devalidization of link (∅); ensuing boundary: *lexeme stem* (TAMⲰ-TN)

(1) Labializable morpheme or morpheme-part not labialized before a secondary (conditioned) labial (cf. link 1); ensuing boundary: *prefix*] [*assimilated prefix*. 2NMMOOY (*Wess. 9* 91a 27f.), NMMOYI (*A 2* 383), NMⲠOⲀIC (*III* 132.15).

(2) Negation of link (2). Ensuing boundary: *converter*] [N-AN *negatived Bipartite* (pronominal actor).

(3) Negation of link (3). Ensuing boundary: *converter*] [N-AN *negatived Bipartite* (nominal actor) [37].

(4) Opposition to link (4). Ensuing boundary: *determinator*] [*several coordinated noun lexemes*.

(5) Opposition to link (5). Ensuing boundary: (*several*) *base/converters*] [(*several*) *predicative verblexemes*.

(6) Opposition to link (6). Ensuing boundary: *base/converter* + *nominal actor*] [*pred. verb lexeme*; examples: A-... AY- (*IV* 205.15ff.), NTA-... ENTAY- (Sec. Perf., *III* 90.8f.), EⲢⲰAN-... EYⲰAN- (*Ch.* 41.11ff., parall. *III* 80.15f.), EⲢE-... EY- (Sec. Pres., *III* 209.13ff.), ENEⲢE- ... ENEY- (*RE 10* 164b 12ff.) [38]. The extended intervening segment in this case is symptomatic of the open(er) juncture. A similarly telltale phenomenon is the intercalability of the parenthetic — ⲠEXAY — "said he" [39]: *antecedent*] [*rel. form* (*A 1* 228, *A 2*

EⲰXE-0E NNETEⲢETOⲢⲄH NAEI EXⲰOY EBOⲀ XE-MNTAY-IC̅ MMAY XE...· TE 0E ON ETOYNAXⲰAX... (*Ch.* 185.8ff.; also *A 1* 131, 234, *III* 223.10f.). One could formulate the distinction also by postulating two {ⲠE} morphemes, differing in prosodic properties (see §1.1.2.3, spec. obs.). — Note the punctuation in (*Besa* 48.7f.) TETN2E· TE TN2E, NETN2BHYE· NE NEN2BHYE, vs. lack of punctuation in other types of Nom. Sentence (42.23, 48.17, 42.17, 51.13).

[37] One may include here the second person feminine singular: EⲢECⲰTM AN ({ere-∅-sôtm an}) *vs.* ENTECⲰTM AN, perhaps also more open than EYCⲰTM AN. Cf. ROSÉN 1964:182: "Two segments apparently adjacent, but separated by a zero segment, join in a different degree of juncture than either of them would join with a medium segment that was not zero".

[38] See YOUNG 1969:400. Note other cases of morpheme resumption: N- ... NYNA- AN (*IV* 11.15f.), MH EⲢⲰAN-... MH PⲰ + apodosis (*A 2* 26), EⲰXE- ... EⲰXE- (*IV* 28.16ff.).

[39] Cf. Kiecker's well-known discussion of the "*Schaltesatz*" in various languages, *Glotta* 11:179-183 (1921); also *IF* 30: 145-185 (1912), *IF* 32:7-23 (1913). For the "vocative" as a parenthetic prosodic indicator, consider (*P* 130² 6 ⲠH) 2Ⲱ 6E EⲢO TCYNAⲄⲰⲄH EⲢEYI NNETⲰOXⲠ THⲢOY NE; cf. — NTOK in §6.1.3, and E. FRAENKEL 1965, HINTZE 1950:135ff. (on parenthesis generally).

192), *extraposed noun*] [*main pattern* (ⲠⲢⲢⲞ — ⲠⲈⲬⲀϤ — ϤⲚⲀⲦⲀⲔⲞ *A 2* 335, *RE 10* 159a 10f.; NB. ⲀⲚⲞⲔ ⲌⲰ — ⲠⲈⲬⲀϤ — +ⲚⲀⲤⲰⲦⲠ *III* 17.20f. / ⲠⲈⲦⲠⲎⲦ ⲄⲀⲢ — ⲠⲈⲬⲀϤ — ⲀϤⲔⲀⲦⲞⲞⲦϤ ⲈⲂⲞⲖ *P* 130⁴ 102 vo), *conj. carrier*] [*verbal lexeme* (ⲌⲘⲠⲦⲢⲈⲦⲀⲮⲨⲬⲎ — ⲠⲈⲬⲀϤ — ⲰⲦⲞⲢⲦⲢ *III* 199.5f.), *Second-Tense theme*][*focal modifier* (*Wess. 9* 174d 29ff. / ⲚⲦⲀⲓⲰⲰⲠⲈ ⲄⲀⲢ ⲀⲚ — ⲠⲈⲬⲀϤ — ⲘⲠⲞⲚⲎⲢⲞⲤ ⲚⲔⲈⲞⲨⲀ *A 2* 431), *nominal predicate* (+ augens)] [*pronominal subject* (ⲌⲈⲚⲰⲀϤⲦⲈ ⲦⲎⲢⲞⲨ — ⲠⲈⲬⲀⲨ — ⲚⲈ *III* 118.15f.), *cataphoric referent*] [*referate* (ⲚⲀⲰ ⲚⲌⲈ ⲔⲬⲰ ⲘⲘⲞⲤ — ⲠⲈⲬⲀϤ — ⲬⲈ- *A 2* 430, also *ibid.* 432-3 [all not Sh.], 453), *verbal nucleus*] [*expansion* (*III* 99.8f., *Wess. 9* 140a 15ff. / ⲌⲰ ⲄⲀⲢ — ⲠⲈⲬⲀϤ — ⲈⲠⲈⲞⲨⲞⲈⲓⲰ ⲚⲦⲀϤⲞⲨⲈⲓⲚⲈ *P* 131⁶ 20 ⲔⲀ; between two co-ordinated clauses, — ⲠⲈⲬⲀϤ· ⲀⲨⲰ — *Wess. 9* 161d 10ff.), and, surprisingly, *rel. converter* (prenominal!)] [*conv. Nominal Sentence* (ⲦⲀⲓ ⲦⲈ ⲐⲈ ⲈⲦⲈⲢⲈ — ⲠⲈⲬⲀϤ — ⲞⲨⲠⲈⲦⲰⲞⲨⲈⲓⲦ ⲠⲈ... *A 2* 435 [not Sh.], collated). Yet another symptom, still in need of being refined, is the prosodic slot open for enclitics (§6.0.3, and note the position of enclitics in the exx. quoted above).

(7) Opposition to link (7). Ensuing boundary: ⲬⲈⲔⲀⲀⲤ] ["*eventual*"-*apodotic conjunctive*.

(8) Absence of resumption[40] of a (pro)noun (stylistically, anacoluthic construction[41]): (*IV* 108.17f.) ⲀⲚⲞⲚ ⲌⲰⲰⲚ ⲌⲰⲂ ⲚⲓⲘ ⲈⲦⲚⲀⲌⲈ ⲚⲀⲨ ⲌⲀⲌⲦⲎⲚ ⲚⲚⲀⲤⲌⲀⲓ ⲚⲎⲦⲚ / (*III* 24.10f.) ⲠⲈⲦⲈⲢⲈⲠⲌⲎⲦ ⲄⲈ ⲘⲠⲞⲨⲀ ⲠⲞⲨⲀ ⲚⲀⲰⲞⲠϤ... ⲠⲈⲦϤⲚⲀⲰⲬⲞⲞϤ ⲚⲦⲰⲦⲚ ⲈⲦⲤⲞⲞⲨⲚ / (*Ch.* 85.1ff.) ⲚⲐⲈ ⲈⲦⲔϤⲓ-ⲢⲞⲞⲨⲰ ⲌⲀⲠⲤⲞⲞⲨⲦⲚ / (*IV* 26.13) ⲦⲀⲓ ⲦⲈ ⲐⲈ ⲚⲦⲀ-ⲠⲬⲞⲈⲓⲤ + ⲚⲞⲨⲰⲎⲢⲈ ⲚⲀⲂⲢⲀⲌⲀⲘ / (*III* 21.13f.) ⲚⲌⲞⲞⲨ ⲈⲦⲈⲤⲞⲞⲨⲚ Ⲏ ⲈⲦⲈⲦⲚⲤⲞⲞⲨⲚ ⲬⲈ-ⲰⲀⲓⲈⲓ ⲰⲀⲢⲰⲦⲚ / (*IV* 80.1f.) ⲠⲈⲌⲞⲞⲨ Ⲏ ⲠⲚⲀⲨ ⲈⲧⲚⲀⲦⲰⲰ ⲀⲚ ⲈⲞⲨⲰⲘ / (*IV* 34.9f.) ⲦⲀⲢⲬⲎ ⲚⲦⲀϤⲤⲰⲚⲦ ⲘⲠⲢⲰⲘⲈ / (*III* 68.2f.) ⲠⲔⲀⲓⲢⲞⲤ ⲈⲚⲦⲀⲚ-ⲂⲀⲢⲂⲀⲢⲞⲤ ⲰⲰⲖ / (*P* 131⁷ 45 ⲅⲟ) ⲠⲘⲀ ⲈⲦⲈⲰⲀⲨⲢ-ⲌⲰⲂ ⲈⲠⲚⲈⲌ / (*III* 138.26ff.) ⲠⲈⲓⲰⲀⲬⲈ ⲤⲚⲀⲨ +ⲚⲀⲦⲞⲖⲘⲀ ⲚⲦⲀⲬⲞⲞⲤ ⲘⲠⲈⲘⲦⲞ ⲈⲂⲞⲖ ⲚⲚⲀⲤⲚⲎⲨ... ⲬⲈ-...

Additional delimitations, treated elsewhere[42]: *topicalized quotation*] [*focus* (§2.7.2.4, (b) topic: ' Basic Tense + interrogative modifier ', more open than ' Second Tense + interr. modifier '.

6.0.2.3 The question of the definition and delimitation of the WORD, far from being banal or trivial is as perplexing in Coptic as it is in other languages or in general linguistics. The futility of the attempt to apply universally any of the criteria currently suggested was admitted as early as 1949 (at the Sixth International Congress of Linguists, Oslo)[43]. Different " words " — semantic, lexical, prosodic, syntactic, morphologic, paradigmatic — are not coextensive; such properties as autonomy, separability, bondage, semasiological or prosodic weight are gradient and relative. The definition, tacitly accepted unanimously — " minimal free form " (originally Bloomfield's) — cannot be uncritically accepted, since " minimal ", " free ", even " form " all beg the question, being values that are questionable, relative or in need of definition (" minimalness ", also in Martinet's " *signe minimum* ", is as illusory as contextual independence; " freedom " and prosodic weight vary with the pattern; " form " is just an empty terminological head-word). Often, a vague conception of the word is carried over from languages for which it has in some way been crystallized and as it were legitimized and perpetuated in word-dividing print, to serve as a model for unwritten languages and generally exotic ones. This is, however, hardly relevant

---

[40] To be distinguished from *zero* resumption, §3.1.1.1.0.1.

[41] One might aim at a general cohesional definition of anacoluthia, e.g. in cases like (*III* 104.23ff.) ⲬⲈⲔⲀⲤ ⲚⲦⲞⲔ ⲌⲰⲰⲔ ... ⲈⲔⲚⲀ- ⲀⲚ (opener juncture than for ⲬⲈⲔⲀⲤ ⲈⲚⲚⲈⲔ), or (*Ch.* 88.22ff.) ⲈⲢⲰⲀⲚⲞⲨⲀ ⲆⲈ ⲬⲞⲞⲤ ⲬⲈ-+ⲘⲈ ⲘⲠⲬⲞⲈⲓⲤ ⲠⲚⲞⲨⲦⲈ ⲌⲘⲠⲈϤⲌⲎⲦ ⲦⲎⲢϤ ⲘⲚⲦⲈϤⲮⲨⲬⲎ ⲦⲎⲢⲤ... where the 3rd-person pronoun is an exponent of cohesion that would be absent in the 1st person; in the case of (*A 1* 137) ⲈⲚⲈⲠⲈⲚⲈⲓⲰⲦ Ⲏ ⲦⲈⲚⲘⲀⲀⲨ ⲚⲈⲦⲌⲀⲦⲎⲚ ... ⲚⲦⲚⲚⲀⲰⲚ-ⲌⲦⲎⲚ ⲀⲚ ⲌⲀⲢⲞⲞⲨ, the protasis - apodosis juncture is looser than in the " orthodox " ⲈⲚⲈ-, ⲚⲈ- ⲚⲀ (ⲠⲈ) *irrealis* complex.

[42] Juncture would distinguish the two seams — and eventually the two morphs — in ⲈⲚⲈ + *conjugation form*; interrogative ⲈⲚⲈ is followed by more open juncture: ⲈⲚⲈ ⲀⲢⲀ ⲈⲨⲰⲞⲞⲠ ⲌⲚⲦⲈⲓⲞⲨⲤⲓⲀ ⲚⲞⲨⲰⲦ (*P* 130⁵ 66 ⲟⲅ), not affecting the actor pronoun by " converting " it from the prefix to the suffix paradigm: (Ⲭ)ⲈⲚⲈ+- (*Ch.* 95.33f.); consider also ⲈⲚⲈⲀϤ- (*IV* 184.2, *vs.* ⲈⲚⲈⲚⲦⲀϤ- for the converter), ⲈⲚⲈ + Sec. Tense (*BMCat.* p. 79 No. 194 f. 4).

[43] See MATTHEWS 1974:Chs. 2, 5, 9; BARRI 1977, for some discussions and further reff. to the extensive literature on this subject (and the related issue of morphology/syntax stratification).

to Coptic, where *scriptio continua* is the rule, and no length of intimate contact with Greek could change this; indeed, other than the isolated instances of syllable-division marking, this is almost the only consistent piece of evidence we have reflecting native grammatical theory. As a matter of fact, word-division in . Coptic texts has ever been a pseudo-issue, purely the preoccupation of Western scholarship, rather than a meaningful issue of grammar [44]. In Coptic, we have SYNTAGMS — patterns of ordered categories, with distinctively varying juncture contours:

ⲁ = ϥ = ⲥⲱⲧⲙ	*vs.*	ⲁ = ⲡⲣⲱⲙⲉ ‿ ⲥⲱⲧⲙ
ⲁⲛⲅ = ⲟⲩⲣⲱⲙⲉ	*vs.*	ⲟⲩⲣⲱⲙⲉ ‿ ⲡⲉ
-ⲥⲉⲧⲡ = ⲡⲣⲱⲙⲉ	*vs.*	ⲥⲱⲧⲡ ‿ ⲙⲡⲣⲱⲙⲉ
ϥ = ⲥⲱⲧⲙ	*vs.*	ⲡⲣⲱⲙⲉ ‿ ⲥⲱⲧⲙ

Unless we use " word " as synonymous with these patterns, I cannot see that the term is called for by the system. Of the precise role of manuscript *punctuation* we are still ignorant. Both its purpose (rhetorical, dictional?) and system(s), probably idiotextual or idiosyncratic with every scribe, must be decided for every text separately [45], in conjunction with its grammatical norm. Punctuation marks, far from being " *sinnlos gesetzt* ", " *nicht eben wichtig oder nothwendig, sondern der Übersichtlichkeit eher hinderlich* " [46], where not reading instructions, may be optional signals of junctural boundaries of different levels. ⲛⲉⲕ-ⲛⲁⲣⲟⲩ ⲡⲉ (*Ch.* 13.42f.) is opposed to -ⲣ'ⲁⲧⲛⲟⲩⲧⲉ (*ibid.* 17.15) and -ⲣ'ⲡⲟⲗⲉⲙⲟⲥ (*ibid.* 21.28); the comma *before* ⲡⲉ (*ibid.* 25.23, 59.13) indicates prosodic characteristics of a distinct Nominal Sentence pattern; commas mark the opening and closing of a parenthesis (*Or.* 161.40f.), and so on. (Attention is drawn *passim* to punctuation in connection with syntactical issues.)

6.0.3 SUB-SENTENCE PROSODIC UNITS: THE COLON; ENCLISIS, HIERARCHIES AND PLACEMENTS. Beyond information on the parameter of cohesion inside patterns, the placement of certain kinds of element supplies us with data on the boundaries of prosodic units which make up, as constituent elements, the prosodic structure of the whole: the COLA. These are more easily isolated than defined in a dead language where we are in the dark regarding phonetic realities, and can see only their traces. We must content ourselves with those that are objective, non-circular and striking enough even to " syntaktisch unbewaffnete

[44] Cf. STEINTHAL–MISTELI 1893:290 (on " looseness " and independence of elements). There is to date no theoretical discussion of the Coptic word; various proposals for word-division systems have been a poor substitute (we do not even have a passable working definition of the " word " in Coptic). Initially devised with a practical view to facilitating the analysis of the text, these systems have acquired through time and use a kind of theoretical authority and significance, although none are based on a preliminary set of theoretical principles. Often, technical and grammatical considerations are inextricably mixed. To mention the main systems proposed or in use: STERN 1886 is the most reflective of all, and combines junctural-prosodic, semasiological and functional considerations, none quite consistent with the others: ϫⲉ is separated (cf. ὅτι), so are ⲟⲩⲛ, ⲡⲥⲟⲩⲉⲛ ϥ†, ⲉⲧⲉ ⲡⲁⲓ ⲡⲉ (*vs.* ⲉⲧⲥⲱⲧⲙ). MISTELI's (1893) has maximal separation, employing the hyphen to mark some (not all) special cases of close juncture: ⲉⲙⲡⲉ-ⲓ ⲛⲁⲩ ⲉ ⲟⲩ ⲇⲓⲕⲁⲓⲟⲥ ⲉ ⲁ ⲡ-ϫⲟⲉⲓⲥ ⲕⲁⲁ-ϥ ⲛⲥⲱ-ϥ/ⲥ-ⲛⲉⲙⲏ-ⲓ/ⲙⲡⲉ ϩⲁⲓ ⲛⲁⲩ. TILL 1941 offers two arbitrary contrasting lists — his aim is clearly diacritic and practical. " Lexical " units are separated, " grammatical " ones are not: ⲙⲉⲣⲉ-ⲡⲉⲓⲱⲧ *vs.* ⲙⲉⲣⲉ (love) ⲡⲉⲓⲱⲧ; ⲛⲟⲩϫⲱⲱⲙⲉ *vs.* ⲛ (bring) ⲟⲩϫⲱⲱⲙⲉ; ⲛⲧⲉⲡⲛⲟⲩⲧⲉ — *vs.* ⲛⲧⲉ (of) ⲡⲛⲟⲩⲧⲉ; ⲛⲧⲉⲧⲛ- (conj.) *vs.* ⲛⲧⲉⲧⲛ ⲛⲁϣⲃⲏⲣ. So too in TILL 1960: here the professed motivation is to " enhance the perspicuity of the text "; whatever combination is juncturally close *may* be written as a single stretch, but is divided to eliminate ambiguities: ⲟⲩⲛⲧⲉ ⲡⲉⲓⲱⲧ ⲡⲱⲛϩ, † (inf.) ϩⲓⲥⲉ, ⲛⲁ ⲛⲁⲉⲓⲟⲧⲉ, ⲁϥⲣ ϩⲁϩ ⲛⲛⲟⲃⲉ, ⲙⲛ (" with ") ⲧⲉϥⲙⲁⲁⲩ, ⲁϥϣ (" can ") ϣⲡ. KASSER 1965 introduces — together with separation of words — the apostrophe, thus applying a native Coptic division mark, albeit without precise statement of its role in MSS. It is used in close and open junctures alike: ⲡⲁ' ⲉⲧ ⲛⲁ' ⲡⲉϥ'; ⲡⲁⲓ' ⲡⲉ' ⲡⲗⲟⲅⲟⲥ ⲉⲛⲧⲁ' ⲡⲉⲛ'ⲉⲓⲱⲧ ⲉⲧ'ⲟⲩⲁⲃ ⲙ'ⲡⲣⲟⲫⲏⲧⲏⲥ ⲁⲡⲁ ϣⲉⲛⲟⲩⲧⲉ ϫⲟⲟϥ. ⲛⲓⲙ' ⲡⲉⲧ'ⲛⲁ'ϩⲱⲡ ⲛ'ⲛⲉⲧ'ⲣ'ⲛⲟⲃⲉ... See also Amélineau, *Schenoudi*, I, p. xxxviii and *Sphinx* 17:177-207 (1913), 18:1-30 (1914-5).
[45] In Shenoute, cf. SHISHA–HALEVY 1972:§4.6.1 (for Chassinat), 1975:482-4 (for *BLOr.* 8664).
[46] STERN §§4, 635; cf. PEYRON §9, SCHWARZE–STEINHAL I §§46-50; POLOTSKY 1959:457 (= *CP* 236). For the junctural significance of the Boh. Djinkim, cf. POLOTSKY 1949.

Augen " [47], and we must bear in mind that they are probably phantom-images of a colon, definable as " an expiratory complex with a main stress unit " [48]. One cannot say what the significance of our written cola is, in terms of " real " prosody (intonation, stress, pauses), just as no syntaxization can be really valid without suprasegmental data; yet these textual hints must be exploited for what they are worth.

6.0.3.1 Foremost among the syntactic phenomena indicative of colon boundaries is the placement of the so-called " enclitics " — the amorphous class of words which are found to occupy the *second position* in the sentence [49]. Yet this is thin ground, and we must walk with care, for it is after all by means of these self-same enclitics that the first (initial) position is defined. The circularity of the definition and the inadequacy of the conception of " sentence " as a prosodic unit become apparent once we extend our attention to *native* Coptic particles. On the basis of examples (a selection of which is given in §6.0. 3.1.1) we arrive at the following statements: (a) enclitics are *indexes* of some prosodic articulation, following the distinction of an immobile Greek-origin core (ⲘⲈⲚ, ⲆⲈ, ⲄⲀⲢ) and a mobile native-origin periphery (ⲄⲈ, ⲢⲰ, ⲞⲚ, ⲚⲦⲞⳓ, ⲌⲰⳉ, certain augentia). (b) Enclitics ride (not unlike corks on water) the (to us otherwise imperceptible) prosodic scheme. They are " floated " by the suprasegmental contour, and their actual placement is a co-product of their segmental relationships and this contour [50]; this placement is neither secondary nor shifted. (c) Enclitics are placed as (1) COLON-SECOND, (2) COLON-FINAL (as *colon-boundary signals* [51]; in a different view, this amounts to *intercolary* placement, the enclitics being disjunctors, signalling something like a musical " rest "). (d) The following syntactical units (as isolated by enclitics) occur as separate cola: conjugation forms (+ expansion); Nominal Sentence patterns; noun syntagms, extraposed noun syntagms, expanded noun syntagms; modifiers, incl. coordinatives or disjunctives: ⲀⲨⲰ, Ⲏ, ⲞⲨⲦⲈ, ⲀⲖⲖⲀ; in focalization patterns, the theme, focus or both together may constitute a colon.

6.0.3.1.1 A representative selection of examples — colon boundaries for which I believe there is segmental signalling — are indicated (see also §6.0.2.2 (6), for — ⲠⲈⲬⲀⳓ — as intercolary boundary marker): ⲀⲚⲞⲚ ⲆⲈ ⲌⲰⲰⲚ | ⲞⲨ ⲠⲈⲦⲚⲚⲀⳄⲞⲞⲨ (*III* 29.10) / ⲘⲀⲢⲈⲠⲞⲨⲀ ⲄⲀⲢ | ⲠⲞⲨⲀ ⲘⲞⳉⲦⳓ (*ibid.* 110.6f.) / ⲌⲞⲦⲀⲚ ⲆⲈ | ⲠⲈⲚⲤⲞⲚ | ⲈⲢⳉⲀⲚ- (*ibid.* 101.11f.) / ⲚⲀⲒ ⲄⲀⲢ ⲦⲎⲢⲞⲨ | ⲈⲢⳉⲀⲚⲠⲚⲞⲨⲦⲈ Ⲣ-ⲌⲚⲀⳓ | ⲤⲈⲚⲀⲠⲀⲢⲀⲔⲈ (*ibid.* 31.6f.) / ⲌⲘⲠⲈⲒⳉⲀⳅⲈ ⲄⲀⲢ | ⲚⲦⲀⲠⲀⲒ ⲈⲦⲘⲘⲀⲨ ⳓⲈⲒ... (*IV* 164.9f.) / ⲀⲚⲞⲚ-ⲌⲈⲚⲢⲰⲘⲈ ⲄⲀⲢ | (*ibid.* 155.1f.) / ⲈⲚⲚⲀ†-ⲌⲎⲨ ⲄⲀⲢ | ⲚⲞⲨ (*ibid.* 184.7) / ⲀⲢⲬⲈⲖⲀⲞⲤ ⲆⲈ ⲞⲚ | ⲠⲈⲠⲒⲤⲔⲞⲠⲞⲤ ⲌⲰⳉ ⲚⲔⲀⲢⲬⲀⲢⲒⲤ | Ⲁⳓ- (*III* 109.4f.) / ⲌⲚⲞⲨⳉⲤⲚⲈ ⲆⲈ | ⲌⲰⲤ ⲈⳅⲬⲈ-ⲚⲦⲀⲨⲠⳉⳉⳅ ⲚⲌⲎⲦ | ⲚⲦⲀⲨⲠⳉⳉⳅ ⲄⲀⲢ | ⲠⲌⲞⲞⲨⲦ ⲘⲈⲚ | ⲚⲦⲀⳓ† ⲘⲠⲈⳓⲚⲒ ⲚⲞⲨⳉⲘⲘⲞ... (*ibid.* 96.24f.) / ⲚⳉⲈⲈⲢⲈ ⲆⲈ | ⲦⲞⲨⲈⲒ ⲘⲈⲚ | ⲀⲤ†-ⲠⳉⲤ ⲌⲰⳉⲤ ⲞⲚ | (*ibid.* 97.1f.) / ⲞⲨⲚⲌⲈⲚⲀⳓ ⲄⲀⲢ | ⳉⲞⲞⲠ | ⲤⲞⲠ ⲘⲈⲚ | ⳉⲀⲨ- | ⲤⲞⲠ ⲆⲈ ⲞⲚ | ⳉⲀⲨ- (*ibid.* 48.6ff.) / ⲈⲠⲒⲆⲎ | ⲀⲔⳅⲞⲞⲤ ⲆⲈ ⲞⲚ | ⲌⲚⲚⲈⲔⳉⲀⳅⲈ ⲚⲈⲠⲢⲀ (*ibid.* 81.12) / ⲈⲂⲞⲖ ⲄⲀⲢ ⲀⲚ | ⲬⲈ-ⲈⳓⲞ ⲈⲠⲀⲒ ⲚⲦⲞⳓ | ⲚⳓⲒ- (*ibid.* 66.2f.) / ...ⲚⳓⲠⳉⲌ ⲆⲈ ⲞⲚ | ⳓⲠⲎⲌ ⲢⲰ | (*ibid.* 113.13f.) / ⲚⲈⲦⲈⲚⲞⲨⳓ ⲚⲈ ⲆⲈ | ⲚⲈ ⲚⲈⲬⲎⲢⲀ ⲘⲚⲚⲞⲢⳘⲀⲚⲞⲤ (*ibid.* 93.18f.) / ⲌⲈⲚⲈⲂⲞⲖ ⲦⲰⲚ ⲄⲈ | ⲚⲈ (*v.l.* ⲌⲈⲚⲈⲂⲞⲖ ⲄⲈ | ⲦⲰⲚ | ⲚⲈ, *ibid.* 216.17) / †ⲚⲀⳓ-ⲠⳉⲀⲦ ⲄⲀⲢ | (*Leyd.* 311) [52] / ⲀⲒⳅⲈ-ⲠⲒⳉⲀⳅⲈ ⲠⲀⲒ ⲞⲚ | ⲘⲘⲀⲢⲔⲈⲖⲒⲚⲞⲤ (*III* 31.27) / ⲈⲦⲢⲈⲨ†-ⲚⲀⲠⲢⲢⲞ | ⲘⲠⲢⲢⲞ ⲞⲚ (*ibid.* 88.18) / ⲚⲦⲞⳓ ⲠⲈ ⲀⲚⲞⲚ | ⲌⲘⲠⲈⲦⲚⲈⲒⲢⲈ ⲘⲘⲞⳓ (*Ch.* 90.8ff., if ⲚⲦⲞⳓ is taken as an augens and not as a term in an identify-

---

[47] E. FRAENKEL 1964a:73. Fraenkel's classic studies (1964a-c, 1965), with those of WACKERNAGEL 1892 and POLOTSKY 1961, have been the main source of inspiration for the present discussion; see also J. J. FRAENKEL 1947.

[48] E. FRAENKEL 1964c:135ff., 138; cf. CZERMAK 1928 and 1931:79f.

[49] WEIL 1879:90ff.; WACKERNAGEL 1892; LAUER 1959; E. FRAENKEL 1964, 1965; HELLWIG 1974, esp. p. 160ff. For Egyptian-Coptic, see CZERMAK 1931:129ff.; POLOTSKY 1961. FECHT 1964 and SÄVE-SÖDERBERGH 1949 are motivated rather by metric and not essentially syntactic considerations: "stress" and "accentuation" have within this frame of reference a connotation different from (though certainly related to) that of non-metric sentence prosody. (For further references, see POLOTSKY 1961: 313 n. 2.)

[50] Cf. HELLWIG 1974:164ff.

[51] Cf. POLOTSKY 1961:esp. 295ff., 303ff. Polotsky's " *Spitzenwort* " is often, if not always, a whole colon; cases like ⲚⲐⲈ ⲄⲀⲢ ⲚⲚⲢⲰⲘⲈ... (*III* 181.3) are possibly instances of colon-second placement, although even here we may have colon-final or intercolary placement.

[52] See EMMEL 1981: esp. 137ff.

ing Wechselsatz "ⲚⲦⲞⳐ ⲠⲈ ⲀⲚⲞⲚ") / ⲞⲨⲞⲈⲒ ⲆⲈ | ⲚⲀⲚ ⲚⲦⲞⳐ | ⲈⲢⳤⲀⲚ — (*III* 174.15,28). Instances of " Kurz-kolon " [53]: ⲘⲎ ⲄⲀⲢ | ⲘⲚⲢ⳰ⲘⲈ... (*IV* 180.12) / ⲞⲨⲦⲈ Ⲣ⳰ | ⲘⲚⲌⲎⲨ (*A 1* 46) / ⳘⲘⲠⲈⲞⲨⲞⲈⲒⳤ ⲈⲦⲘⲘⲀⲨ | Ⲏ ⲞⲚ ⲦⲈ-ⲚⲞⲨ (*IV* 205.10f.) / Ⲏ Ⲣ⳰ | ⲀⲠⲦⲀⲔⲞ ⲞⲨ⳰ ⲈⳐⲈⲒ (*III* 105.6) / ⲚⲒⲘ ⲚⲦⲞⳐ | ⲠⲈⲦⲤⲞⲞⲨⲚ (*III* 200.22) / ⲈⲒⲘⲈ ⲚⲦⲞⳐ | Ⳣ ⲚⲢ⳰ⲘⲈ ⲚⲀⲦⲤ⳰ⲦⲘ (*ibid.* 165.19) / ⲀⲖⲖⲀ | ⲈⲂⲞⲖ ⲚⲦⲞⳐ | Ⳉⲉ- (*P* 130[1] 139 ⲦⲘⲈ) / ⲧⲚⲀⲠⲈⲒⲐⲈ ⲘⲘ⳰ⲦⲚ ⲘⲠⲈⲤⲚⲀⲨ | ⲀⲨ⳰ ⲦⲎⲢⲚ | ⲦⲚⲚⲀⲢⲀⳤⲈ (*A 2* 403) / ⲀⲨ⳰ ⲚⲦⲞⳐ | ⲬⲢⲎⲤⲒⲠⲠⲞⲤ (*III* 32.1f.) / ⲀⲔⳤ ⲘⲠⲀⲦⲂⲚ̄Ⲏ | Ⲏ ⲚⲦⲞⳐ | ⲔⲈⲌ⳰Ⲃ (*ibid.* 62.25f.) / ⲀⲨ⳰ Ⳉⲉ | ⲘⲠⲈⲦⲚⳉⲉ-ⲖⲀⲀⲨ (*ibid.* 185.3) / ⲚⲦⲞⳐ ⲄⲀⲢ | ⲀⲨ⳰ ⲠⲈⳐⲈⲒ⳰Ⲧ | ⲞⲨⲀ ⲚⲈ (*RE 11* 17a 2) / ⲈⲚⲘⲈⲈⲨⲈ | ⲈⲞⲨ Ⳉⲉ ⲦⲈⲚⲞⲨ | (*IV* 183.7) / ⲀⲚⲞⲚ Ⲍ⳰ⲞⲚ | ⲤⲈⲔ⳰ⲦⲈ ⲞⲚ | ⲚⲤⲀ- (*III* 142.18f.) / ⲀⲖⲖⲀ | ⲚⲀⲘⲈ ⲠⲈ | ⲠⲈⳐⲞⲨⳤⳤ ⲠⲈ | ⲈⲦⲢⲈ- (*ibid.* 131.15f., cod. B; see §6.0.3.3).

6.0.3.2 ENCLITICS: RELATIVE PLACEMENT AND COMPATIBILITIES. As suggested above, the place-ment of any member of a pattern is a facet of its categorial, i.e. functional essence. A study of the com-bined and relative placement of *enclitics*, however, is instructive of their *prosodic hierarchy* and *relative en-cliticity*. Observe in the following table: (1) Since factors of semasiological as well as prosodic compatibility are at play here, it is extremely difficult to classify non-attestation in this case as significant (systemic) or accidental. However, presumably accidental (provisional) non-occurrence is indicated by parentheses: (—). (2) One must remember that this presentation is extremely simplified, ignoring (for the sake of convenience) (a) the interdependence of word and pattern prosodic properties, (b) the possible influence of various prosodic patterns transcending the syntactic ones, (c) the influence of the environment in general, and neighbouring particles in particular, and (d) the possibility, not to be ignored, of mobility — flexible placement — of individual enclitics.

TABLE I

→	ⲘⲈⲚ	ⲄⲀⲢ	ⲆⲈ	Ⲣ⳰	Ⳉⲉ₁	ⲚⲦⲞⳐ	ⲀⲚ	ⲞⲚ	Ⲍ⳰ⳤⳐ	Ⳉⲉ₂	ⲠⲈ
ⲘⲈⲚ	×	+	—	(—)	+	(—)	+	(—)	(—)	(—)	(—)
ⲄⲀⲢ	—	×	—	(—)	(—)	(—)	+	+	+	(—)	+
ⲆⲈ	—	—	×	(—)	(—)	+	+	+	+	(—)	+
Ⲣ⳰	—	—	—	×	(—)	+	+	(—)	(—)	(—)	+
Ⳉⲉ₁	—	—	—	—	×	+	+	+	+	—	+
ⲚⲦⲞⳐ	—	—	—	—	—	×	+	(—)	—	(—)	+
ⲀⲚ	—	—	—	—	—	+	×	+	+	+	+
ⲞⲚ	—	—	—	—	—	+	—	×	(—)	(—)	+
Ⲍ⳰ⳤⳐ	—	—	—	—	—	—	+	+	×	(—)	+
Ⳉⲉ₂	—	—	—	—	—	—	—	(—)	(—)	×	(—)
ⲠⲈ	—	—	—	—	—	—	—	—	—	—	×

DOCUMENTATION: ⲘⲈⲚ ⲄⲀⲢ: *P* 131[4] 158 ro (DENNISTON 67) [54]: ⲘⲈⲚ ⲄⲀⲢ — ⲆⲈ — ⲆⲈ —, — ⲄⲀⲢ relating the whole complex to the preceding cotext, ⲘⲈⲚ cataphorically to the ⲆⲈ-related sequence. ⲘⲈⲚ Ⳉⲉ: *Ench.* 77b. ⲘⲈⲚ ⲀⲚ: *III* 33.16f., 34.19, 94.25. ⲄⲀⲢ ⲀⲚ: *III* 55.14, 66.2. ⲄⲀⲢ ⲞⲚ: *III* 85.13f. ⲄⲀⲢ Ⲍ⳰ⳤⳐ: *P* 131[5] 65 ro. ⲄⲀⲢ ⲠⲈ: *III* 32.22, 66.4. ⲄⲀⲢ ⲀⲚ ⲠⲈ: *Or.* 168.10f. ⲆⲈ ⲀⲚ: *A 2* 4, *IV* 71.13f. ⲆⲈ ⲚⲦⲞⳐ: *III* 46.5f.,

---

[53] Cf. LAUER 1959:70.

[54] Other ready-imported Greek particle amalgams are ⲀⲢⲀⲄⲈ (DENNISTON 43; *A 2* 334. To be related in some way to the very common ⲀⲢⲀ Ⳉⲉ — *IV* 179.2, 193.8, *III* 71.23, 220.15f., *Ch.* 11.9f., 164.18ff. ?); ⲞⲨⲔⲞⲨⲚ (both οὐκοῦν and οὔκουν, *III* 24-5, 66.17, 93.14f., *Wess. 9* 142b 28ff.); ⲘⲎ ⲀⲢⲀ (Ⳉⲉ) (*III* 80.25f., *IV* 129.8, 193.8, *Ch.* 110.26f.); ⲔⲀⲒⲦⲞⲒⲄⲈ (DENNISTON 564; *Ch.* 81.5f., 138.5f., 158.11f., *Wess. 9* 131b 15f.) and ⲔⲀⲒⲦⲞⲒ (*IV* 38.1f.); ⲔⲀⲒⲄⲀⲢ (καὶ γάρ, DENNISTON 108ff.; *III* 32.18, 461f., 135.29, *IV* 19.16, 92.19, 184.11f.).

145.12f. ⲆⲈ ⳞⲰⳜ: *III* 65.16; this is ⲆⲈ marked as adversative. ⲆⲈ ⲞⲚ: *III* 37.4; ⲆⲈ marked as additive or non-adversative. An extremely common combination, more frequent than ⲆⲈ alone (ⲆⲈ in its various combinations is the most frequent of all Greek-origin particles in Shenoute). ⲆⲈ ⲠⲈ: *III* 60.29, 110.20; rather rare, the usual form being ⲆⲈ ⲞⲚ ⲠⲈ (in *III* 52.18, 53.25 we have ⲆⲈ preceding the *copular*, not pronominal ⲠⲈ). Ⲣⳍ ⲚⲦⲞⳞ: *Ch.* 42.10ff. Ⲣⳍ ⲀⲚ: *A 2* 87, *III* 22.19, 211.17, 215.2f. Ⲣⳍ ⲠⲈ: *Ch.* 17.4f., *III* 164.9f. ⳪₁ ⲀⲚ: *Ch.* 157.28ff. ⳪₁ ⲞⲚ: *Wess. 9* 88a 14f., *III* 199.10. ⳪₁ ⳞⲰⳜ: *Ch.* 112-3, *Young* 15. ⳪₁ ⲠⲈ: *III* 216.17, *Mun.* 177, *Ench.* 94a. ⲚⲦⲞⳞ ⲀⲚ: *A 1* 135 ⲚⲦⲚⲞⲨⲀⳟ ⲚⲦⲞⳞ ⲀⲚ / *Ch.* 52.37ff. ⳞⲰⳅ ⲈⲞⲨⲢⳟⲘⲈ ⲚⲦⲞⳞ ⲀⲚ ⲠⲈ / *ibid.* 198.45ff. ⲘⲎ ⲈⲨ+ⲤⲂⳎ ⲚⲀⲚ ⲚⲦⲞⳞ ⲀⲚ. ⲚⲦⲞⳞ ⲠⲈ: *III* 105.24f., 145.12f. ⲀⲚ ⲚⲦⲞⳞ: *only in rhetorical questions* (usually introduced by Ⲏ, ⲘⲎ): *III* 105.24f. Ⲏ ⲀⲢⲚⲀ ⲀⲚ ⲚⲦⲞⳞ ⲠⲈ... / *P* 130² 71 ⲢⲠⲈ... Ⲏ ⲈⲦⲂⲈⲦⲘⲚⲦⲀⲦⲤⳎⲦⲘ ⲀⲚ ⲚⲦⲞⳞ ⲀⲚⲈⲒⲔⲞⲞⲨⲈ ⳘⲰⲔ ⲈⲂⲞⲖ... / *A 1* 125 ⲘⲎ ⲈⲦⲂⲈⲞⲨⳞⲢⲈ ⲀⲚ ⲚⲦⲞⳞ ⲚⲤⲀⲢⲔⲒⲔⲞⲚ... ⲀⲚ ⲞⲚ: *Wess. 9* 120a 24f. [55]. ⲀⲚ ⳞⲰⳜ: *Mun.* 177. ⲀⲚ ⳪₂ "not anymore": *Ch.* 80.32ff., *Ench.* 85b, *BLOr.* 3581A 93 (No. 209 2 vo). ⲀⲚ ⲠⲈ: *IV* 157.15f. ⲞⲚ ⲚⲦⲞⳞ "at least": *III* 93.24. ⲞⲚ ⲠⲈ: *III* 42.23, *A 1* 250. ⳞⲰⳜ ⲞⲚ: *III* 65.16. ⳞⲰⳜ ⲠⲈ: *IV* 207.3.

Needless to say, this *exposé* covers no more than a paragraph in some future comprehensive work on Coptic prosody, written to integrate " particles " with other pattern constituents (especially modifiers). One can nonetheless make out at least seven prosodic paradigms (or fillers of prosodic slots) on a *scale of decreasing encliticity* (no compatibility within each group, only commutation). In syntagm, the particle higher on the list precedes the lower:

    (1) ⲘⲈⲚ
    (2) ⲄⲀⲢ, ⲆⲈ
    (3) Ⲣⳍ, ⳪₁
    (4) ⲀⲚ
    (5) ⲚⲦⲞⳞ, ⳞⲰⳜ
    (6) ⳪₂, ⲞⲚ
    (7) ⲠⲈ

Note: These compatibilities are valid only within *a single-colon-extent*, and thus constitute a link (§6.0.2.1). Consider (*III* 93.18) - ⲚⲞⲨⳞ ⲚⲈ | ⲆⲈ ⲚⲈ / (*III* 97.1f.) ⲚⳟⲈⲈⲢⲈ ⲆⲈ | ⲦⲞⲨⲈⲒ ⲘⲈⲚ | / (*A 1* 123) ⲞⲨⳟⲠⲎⲢⲈ ⲠⲈ | ⲚⲦⲞⳞ | ⲈⳞⳟⲀⲚ (for the compatibility and relative placement of particles and augentia see §6.1.0.1). Group (6) is closest to the modifier hypercategory. (To this group may be assigned the " particular " ⲦⲈⲚⲞⲨ, see §1.3.4.) ⳪₁: ⳪₂: (3:6), based on ⲀⲚ ⳪₂ "not... anymore" *vs.* ⳪₁ ⲀⲚ "not... then ". ⲠⲈ is not a particle but an enclitic pronoun in the Bimembral Nominal Sentence pattern (see §1.1.2.3 and note 36). ⳪₂ and ⲠⲈ are the only absolutely final particles; as such, they form *final boundary signals* of the relevant junctural extent (colon). ⲚⲦⲞⳞ (5) can probably be resolved into ⲚⲦⲞⳞ₁ " on the other hand ", " just ", grade (3), and ⲚⲦⲞⳞ₂ " at least ", " only ", grade (6), before ⲠⲈ — on the strength of the opposition ⲀⲚ ⲚⲦⲞⳞ₂: ⲚⲦⲞⳞ₁ ⲀⲚ (for ⲚⲦⲞⳞ and ⳞⲰⳜ see also §§6.1.2.3, 6.1.3.4).

6.0.3.3 " ⲦⲎⴹ ⴹⲀⲊⴹ Ⲟⴼ ⲦⲎⴹ ' ⴼⲞⲢⴹⴹⲎⴹⲆⴹⴹⲆ ⴹⲚⴹⲖⴹⲦⴹⴹ ' ". One of the most intriguing phenomena to do with the linear behaviour of enclitics is their occasional *double simultaneous occurrence* in a single syntactic unit — once in the colon-second/final conditioned " secondary " (or better in the prosodic-structure overrule) position, and again in the constructional syntactic-structure (" primary ") position. This provides us with a neat junctural index confirming the colon delimitation [56]. I find the following enclitics with this property:

[55] See LAYTON 1979:173ff.

[56] Cf. (for the Greek ἄν) WACKERNAGEL 1892:394, 396ff., 399ff. and E. Fraenkel, *Beobachtungen zu Aristophanes* (Rome, 1962) pp. 89ff., 216 (on μɛ, ἐμοί, τι, τις). For Coptic, this phenomenon has not (to the best of my knowledge) been discussed; it is usually discredited by the editors and " buried " in apparatuses. Outside Shenoute, I note (Bohairic) *Acta Martyrum* (CSCO, edd. Balestri-Hyvernat) I 106.26 cod. A, 143.20f., 144.20, all exx. of ⲠⲈ; II 246.5f, (ⲞⲚ), 351.24f., 17.26 (ⲆⲈ), 323.16 (ⲄⲀⲢ), 306.9f. (ⲚⲀ⸗); (Bohairic) *Gen.* 43:32 (ⲠⲈ; see ANDERSSON 1904:39). See *Dictionary* 256a for two exx. of " repeated " ⲞⲚ.

(a) ⲡⲉ, by far the most common: (*IV* 52.27) ⲁⲩⲱ ⲡⲥⲟⲟⲩ ⲛⲥⲟⲡ ⳉⲓⲣⲟⲩⳅⲉ ⲡⲉ ⲱⲟⲙⲧ ⲛⲥⲟⲡ ⲡⲉ (*subject, predicate-*ⲡⲉ) / (*A 2* 447, not Sh.) ⲟⲩⲙⲩⲧⲣⲟⲛ (sic) ⲡⲉ ⲛⲕⲟⲓⲛⲟⲛ ⲡⲉ (*predicate-*ⲡⲉ) / (*A 2* 111) ⲙⲏ ⲛⲛⲁⲓ ⲁⲛ ⲛⲉ ⲛⲉⳉⲡⲓⲟ ⲙⲛ ⳅⲉⲛⲕⲟⲟⲩⲉ ⲉⲛⲁⲱⲟⲩ ⲛⲉ ⲛⳉⲡⲓⲟ (*predicate* - ⲡⲉ, *subject*) / (*IV* 104.9 cod. A) ⲟⲩⲁⲛⲁⲅⲕⲁⲓⲟⲛ ⲇⲉ ⲟⲛ ⲡⲉ ⲛⲧⲉⲓⲕⲉⳅⲉ ⲡⲉ ⲡⲉⲓⲕⲉⲟⲩⲁ (*predicate* - ⲡⲉ, *subject*) / (*A 2* 196, parall. *III* 131.15f. cod. B) ⲁⲗⲗⲁ ⲛⲁⲙⲉ ⲡⲉ ⲡⲉⳇⲟⲩⲱⲱ ⲡⲉ ⲉⲧⲣⲉⳇ- (*subject* - ⲡⲉ - *predicate*; Amélineau's note: "lisez: ⲁⲗⲗⲁ ⲛⲁⲙⲉ ⲡⲉⳇⲟⲩⲱⲱ ⲡⲉ; le mot ⲛⲁⲙⲉ s'employant comme adverbe et ne comportant pas la présence d'un enclitique qui se trouve d'ailleurs après le mot suivant, comme il doit s'y trouver d'après la grammaire.") / (*Mun.* 103) ⲉⲧⲉⲛⲉⲛⲧⲁⲩ ⲱⲡⲉ ⲙⲙⲁⲗⲁⲕⲟⲥ ⲛⲉ ⳉⲣⲁⲓ ⲛⳉⲏⲧⲉ ⲛⲉ (*rel.- predicate -* ⲡⲉ). Perhaps also *III* 22.12ff., 75.16f., both alternatively interpretable as instances of the ⧺ *modifier-*ⲡⲉ ⧺ predication, §1.2.1.2. Compare also instances of (ⲛⲉ) ⲉⲓⲥⲡⲉ ⲁⳇ— ⲡⲉ in irrealis apodoses, e.g. (*A 1* 95) ⲉⲛⲉⲩⳉⲛⳅⲉⲛⲕⲉⲙⲁ... ⲛⲉⲩⲛⲁⲕⲟⲛⲥⲟⲩ ⲏ ⲛⲉⲉⲓⲥⲡⲉ ⲁⲩⲕⲟⲛⲥⲟⲩ ⲡⲉ, also ibid. 107.

(b) ⲁⲛ: (*A 2* 475) (ⲧⲗⲟⲓⳅⲉ) ⲧⲁⲓ ⲛⲧⲁⲛⲉⲧⲟⲩⲁⲁⲃ ⳃⲟⲟⲥ ⲁⲛ ⲉⲧⲃⲏⲏⲧⲟⲩ ⲁⲛ ⲁⲗⲗⲁ ⲉⲧⲃⲏⲏⲧⲛ ⳃⲉ... (cf. 476, with a single negator; §2.9.1.1-2) / (*ibid.*) ⲟⲩⲧⲉ ⲡⲕⲟⲥⲙⲟⲥ ⲁⲛ ⲛⲛⲉⳃⲏⲩ ⲉⲧⲁⲱⲉ ⲉⲣⲟⲟⲩ ⲛⲁⲱⲛⲁⳅⲙⲟⲩ ⲁⲛ ⲉⲱⲙⲥ.

(c) ⲟⲛ (*IV* 150.4, not Shenoute) ⲁⲩⲱ ⲟⲛ ⲛⳇⲥⲙⲟⲩ ⲟⲛ ⲛⳉⲓⲡⳃⲟⲉⲓⲥ.

(d) ⲛⲧⲟⳇ (*A 1* 295, quot. from *Deut.* 31:27) ⲛⲁⲱ ⲛⲧⲟⳇ ⲛⳅⲉ ⲙⲛⲛⲥⲁⲡⲁⲙⲟⲩ ⲛⲧⲉⲧⲛ+-ⲛⲟⲩ⳿ⲥ ⲛⲁⳇ ⲁⲛ ⲛⲧⲟⳇ.

6.0.3.4 Polar placement. Another intriguing placement phenomenon, which I cannot integrate in a broad theory, is the polar placement of the augens ⳉⲱⲱⳇ in the Nominal Sentence pattern. The augens is *colon-*(or at least pattern-)*final* when referable to a pronoun *inside* the pattern, but *colon-second* when its referate follows the pattern (differently Polotsky 1961:306 [+ n. 4] = *CP* 410): (*Wess. 9* 171c 15f.) ⲟⲩⲛⲟⲃⲉ ⲛⲁⲓ ⲡⲉ ⳉⲱ' / (*III* 179.13f.) ⲡⲉⲧⲛⲙⲡⲱⲁ ⲅⲁⲣ ⲡⲉ ⳉⲱⲧⲧⲏⲩⲧⲛ, vs. (*III* 187.12) ⲧⲁⲓ ⳉⲱⲧⲧⲏⲩⲧⲛ ⲧⲉ ⲧⲉⲧⲛⳉⲉ / (*P* 130¹ 140 ⲧⲙⳅ-ⲏ) ⲛⲉⲡⲉⲧⲉⲱⲱⲉ ⳉⲱⲱⲥ ⲟⲛ ⲡⲉ ⲉⲧⲣⲉⲩⲧⲁⲁⲩ ⲛⲁⲥ / (*RE 11* 18a 24f.) ⳅⲉⲛⲓⲟⲩⲇⲁⲓ ⳉⲱⲟⲩ ⲛⲃⲣⲣⲉ ⲛⲉ / (*A 1* 260) ⲧⲁⲓ ⳉⲱⳇ (sic) ⲧⲉ ⲑⲉ ⲙⲡⲇⲓⲁⲃⲟⲗⲟⲥ / (*A 2* 45) ⳅⲉⲛⲡⲣⲟⲇⲟⲧⲏⲥ ⳉⲱⲟⲩ ⲛⲣⲉⳇⳃⲓⲟⲩⲉ ⲁⲩⲱ ⲛⲁⲡⲟⲥⲧⲁⲧⲏⲥ ⲛⲉ.

6.1.0.1-3 The augens: paradigms and compatibilities, a synoptic preview

In the following tables, " + " signifies normal (strong) documentation, " (+) " significantly weak documentation, " — " significant non-attestation, " (—) " (probably) accidental non-attestation.

6.1.0.1 Minimal combinatory (reference) patterns (augens/referate framing)

TABLE II

REFERATE			THP⸗	ⳉⲱⲱ⸗	{ⲛⲧⲟ⸗}	ⲙⲙⲓⲛ ⲙⲙⲟ⸗	ⲙⲁⲩⲁⲁ⸗
DETERMINATOR		def.	+	+	+	(+)	+
	Sgl.	indef.	+	—	—	—	+
		∅	—	—	—	—	+
	Pl.	def.	+	+	+	—	+
		indef.	+	(+)	—	—	+
ACTOR PRONOUN		1	—	+	+	—	+
	Sgl.	2	(+)	+	+	—	(—)
		3	(+)	+	+	—	+
	Pl.	1	+	+	+	—	+
		2	+	+	+	—	(—)
		3	+	+	+	—	+

REFERATE			THP⸗	ⲌⲰⲰ⸗	{ⲚⲦⲞ⸗}	ⲘⲘⲒⲚ ⲘⲘⲞ⸗	ⲘⲀⲨⲀⲀ⸗
OBJECT PRONOUN (or actor + obj.)	*Sgl.*	1	—	+	+	+	+
		2	—	+	+	+	+
		3	—	+	+	+	+
	Pl.	1	—	+	+	+	+
		2	—	+	+	+	+
		3	+	+	+	+	+
ⲡⲉⲧ-			(+) §6.1.1.1(d)	(—)	+	—	(—)
ⲛⲉⲧ-			+	+	+	—	+
Noun + ⲉⲧ-			(+) §6.1.1.1(d)	(+)	(—)	—	+
IMPERATIVE (+ expansion)	*Sgl.*	1	—	(—)	(—)	(+)	—
		2	—	+	+	—	—
	Pl.	1	—	(+)	(—)	—	—
		2	+	+	+	—	—
ZERO REFERATE			+ §6.1.1.1(e)	—	—	—	+ §6.1.4.1.3
ⲡⲱϥ, ⲡⲉϥ-	*Sgl.*	1	—	+	—	(+)	+
		2	—	+	+	(+)	+
		3	—	+	—	+	+
	Pl.	1	+	+	—	(+)	+
		2	(—)	+	+	(+)	+
		3	+	+	—	+	+
INDEPENDENT PRONOUN	*Sgl.*	1	—	+	—	—	(—)
		2	—	+	—	—	+
		3	—	+	—	—	+
	Pl.	1	—	+	—	—	+
		2	(+)	+	—	(+)	(—)
		3	+	+	—	(+)	+
PRONOMINAL SUBJECT in Nom. Sent.	*Sgl.*	1	—	—	—	—	—
		2	—	—	+	—	—
		3	(+)?	—	—	—	—
{ⲡⲉ}	*Pl.*	1	—	—	—	—	—
		2	—	—	—	—	—
		3	+	+	+	—	+

6.1.0.2   Augens placement: Table III

augens placement		THP=	2ШШ=	{NTO=}	MAYAA=	MMIN MMO=
post-referate:	immediate	+	+	+	+	+
	non-immediate	(+)	+	+	(—)	(—)
pre-referate:	immediate	(+)	+	+	—	—
	non-immediate	(+)	+	+	—	—

Non-immediate placement: the augens is separated from its nucleus (referate) by an element (or elements), which is not a grammatical entity, nor an enclitic, nor a simple expansion. Two prosodic groups emerge: on the one hand, 2ШШ= and NTO=; on the other hand, MAYAA= and MMIN MMO=; THP= occupies an intermediate position. (The paradigmatic affinity of 2ШШ= with NTO= on the one hand, and of MAYAA= with MMIN MMO= and THP= on the other hand, is also corroborated by the data presented in Table IV.)

6.1.0.3   Augens/augens and augens/enclitic: compatibilities and arrangement
Table IV

	THP=	2ШШ=	{NTO=}	MAY-AA=	MMIN MMO=	ΔЄ	ΓAP	AN	ON	GЄ	PШ	{ΠЄ}
THP=	×	—	—	—	—	—	—	+	+	—	—	+
2ШШ=	+	×	+	+	+	—	—	—	+	—	—	+
{NTO=}	—	—	×	—	—	—	—	+	—	—	—	+
MAYAA=	—	—	+	×	+	—	—	+	—	—	—	+
MMIN MMO=	—	—	—	—	×	—	—	—	—	—	—	—
ΔЄ	+	+	+	+	(—)							
ΓAP	+	—	—	(—)	(—)							
AN	+	—	+	+	+							
ON	+	—	+	—	—							
GЄ	+	+	—	—	—							
PШ	—	—	+	—	—							
{ΠЄ}	—	+	—	—	+							

See Table I

(§6.0.3.2)

DOCUMENTATION: THP⸗ ⲀN: *Wess. 9* 143b 4ff., *A 2* 238-9, *Ch.*52.53ff.; THP⸗ ON: *III* 73.2; THP⸗ {ⲡⲈ}: see §6.1.1.2.4. ⲌⲰⲰ⸗ ON (very common): *III* 66.8, *P* 130¹ 139 ⲦⲘⲈ, etc.; ⲌⲰⲦⲦⲎⲨⲦⲚ ⲚⲦⲰⲦⲚ: *A 2* 468; ⲌⲰⲰ⸗ | {ⲚⲦⲞ⸗} + Noun (§ 6.1.3.3): *Ch.* 56.30ff., *A 1* 16 ⲈⲌⲞⲨⲚ ⲈⲞⲨⲞⲚ ⲚⲒⲘ ⲀⲨⲰ ⲈⲌⲞⲨⲚ ⲈⲢⲞⲒ ⲌⲰ ⲀⲚⲞⲔ ⲠⲈⲒⲈⲖⲀⲬⲒⲤⲦⲞⲤ; ⲌⲰⲰ⸗ ⲘⲘⲒⲚ ⲘⲘⲞ⸗ *A 1* 261; ⲌⲰⲰ⸗ ⲦⲎⲢ⸗ *A 1* 373; ⲌⲰⲰ⸗ {ⲡⲈ} see §§6.0.3.4 and 6.1.2.2c. {ⲚⲦⲞ⸗} ⲀN: *Ch.* 156.1ff., *III* 65.8; {ⲚⲦⲞ⸗} {ⲡⲈ}: §6.1.3.2 (c), *Wess. 9* 147d 28f., *IV* 207.7. ⲘⲀⲨⲀⲀ⸗ ⲘⲘⲒⲚ ⲘⲘⲞ⸗: *III* 146.24f. (cf. ⲘⲀⲨⲀⲀ⸗ + ⲘⲘⲒⲚ ⲘⲘⲞ⸗, §6.1.4.4); ⲘⲀⲨⲀⲀⲦⲚ ⲀⲚⲞⲚ + Noun: *A 2* 31; ⲘⲀⲨⲀⲀ⸗ {ⲡⲈ}: *Wess. 9* 125b 18f., *IV* 207.6. ⲆⲈ ⲌⲰⲰ⸗: *A 1* 374, *III* 65.16 (ⲆⲈ ⲌⲰⲞⲨ ON), *A 1* 261 (ⲆⲈ ⲌⲰⲰⲨ ⲘⲘⲒⲚ ⲘⲘⲞⲨ); {ⲆⲈ ⲚⲦⲞ⸗}: *Ch.* 86.3f., 15.28f., *A 1* 192, *IV* 12.7; ⲆⲈ ⲦⲎⲢ⸗: *A 1* 289, *III* 46.10f.; ⲆⲈ ⲘⲀⲨⲀⲀ⸗: *III* 46.12. ⲄⲀⲢ ⲦⲎⲢ⸗: *III* 31.6 *Ch.* 165.44ff., *A 2* 546, *P* 131⁶ 20 ⲔⲀ. ⲀⲚ {ⲚⲦⲞ⸗}: *IV* 207.7, *A 2* 78, *A 1* 74, 205, *III* 211.17, *IV* 38.21, 193.15; ⲀⲚ ⲦⲎⲢ⸗: *A 2* 151, *IV* 20.20f.; ⲀⲚ ⲘⲀⲨⲀⲀ⸗: *Wess. 9* 144c 24ff.; ⲀⲚ ⲘⲘⲒⲚ ⲘⲘⲞ⸗: *A 2* 459. ON ⲦⲎⲢ⸗: *Wess. 18* 140b 8ff.; ON ⲀⲚⲞⲚ: *P* 130² 65 vo. ⲄⲈ ⲦⲎⲢ⸗: *A 2* 520; ⲄⲈ ⲌⲰⲰ⸗: *III* 67.17f., 107.14. ⲢⲰ {ⲚⲦⲞ⸗}: *III* 188.18f., *Ch.* 42.10ff., *Wess. 9* 95a 20f. {ⲡⲈ} ⲘⲘⲒⲚ ⲘⲘⲞ⸗: *III* 202.27ff., *Wess. 9* 156a 4ff.

We note that (a) ⲄⲀⲢ, ⲆⲈ, ⲄⲈ, ⲢⲰ all precede the augens, (b) some augentia ({ⲚⲦⲞ⸗}, ⲦⲎⲢ⸗, ⲘⲀⲨⲀⲀ⸗) precede {ⲡⲈ}, ⲘⲘⲒⲚ ⲘⲘⲞ⸗ follows it, while ⲌⲰⲰ⸗ occurs in both positions, under a special conditioning (§6.0.3.4) [57]; (c) the placement oppositions: ⲀⲚ ⲦⲎⲢ⸗ : ⲦⲎⲢ⸗ ⲀⲚ, ⲀⲚ {ⲚⲦⲞ⸗}: {ⲚⲦⲞ⸗} ⲀⲚ, ⲀⲚ ⲘⲀⲨⲀⲀ⸗ : ⲘⲀⲨⲀⲀ⸗ ⲀⲚ are all formally definable as the difference between *adjunctal negation* of the augens ('augens→ⲀⲚ') and *augential modification of a locally negated (pro)noun* (' ⲀⲚ→augens '). {ⲚⲦⲞ⸗} ⲀⲚ is much less common than ⲀⲚ {ⲚⲦⲞ⸗} (the former occurs in focalization patterns). ⲦⲎⲢ⸗ ⲀⲚ too occurs in focalization patterns, while ⲀⲚ ⲦⲎⲢ⸗ is characteristic of *rhetorical questions*. I cannot find any regulation for ⲘⲀⲨⲀⲀ⸗ ⲀⲚ *vs.* ⲀⲚ ⲘⲀⲨⲀⲀ⸗.

6.1.1 " ALL ", " ENTIRE(LY) " (*totus, universus* [58]): GROUP or UNITARY TOTALITY (INTEGRALITY).

6.1.1.1 ⲦⲎⲢ⸗ IN COHESION WITH PRONOMINAL REFERATES IN VERB SYNTAGMS. (a) *Actor suffix-pronouns*: (*A 1* 48) ⲦⲚⲘⲞⲔⲌ ⲚⲌⲎⲦ ⲦⲎⲢⲚ ⲌⲒⲞⲨⲤⲞⲠ / (*Ch.* 155.27f.) ⲦⲀⲒ ⲦⲈ ⲐⲈ ⲈⲦⲈⲦⲚⲠⲎⲦ ⲦⲎⲢⲦⲚ / (*A 1* 381) ⲀⲨⲦⲢⲈⲨⲰⲰⲠⲈ ⲦⲎⲢⲞⲨ (sim. *A 2* 355, *IV* 36.21, *RE 10* 161b 1) / (*IV* 207.4f.) ⲚⲈⲚⲦⲀⲨⲘⲞⲨ ⲦⲎⲢⲞⲨ ⲤⲈⲞ ⲚⲨⲘⲘⲞ ⲈⲠⲚⲞⲨⲦⲈ Ⲏ ⲚⲈⲦⲞⲚⲌ ⲤⲈⲎⲠ ⲦⲎⲢⲞⲨ ⲈⲠⲚⲞⲨⲦⲈ / (*Ch.* 90-1) ⲀⲚⲰⲰⲠⲈ ⲚⲐⲈ ⲚⲚⲒⲀⲔⲀⲐⲀⲢⲦⲞⲤ ⲦⲎⲢⲚ / (*A 1* 302) ⲚⲤⲈⲬⲎⲔ ⲈⲂⲞⲖ ⲀⲚ ⲦⲎⲢⲞⲨ. Additional exx.: *III* 87.17, 140.2, *IV* 67.7, 109.16, 191.7f., *Ch.* 97.10, 133.53ff., 162.44ff., etc.

(b) *Object (expansion) suffix-pronouns*: (*A 2* 238-9) ⲈⲚⲚⲀⲰⲬⲞⲞⲨ ⲦⲎⲢⲞⲨ ⲀⲚ (sim. *Ch.* 52.53ff., 11.9f.) / (*Ch.* 197-8) ...ⲦⲀⲢⲚⲦⲀⲀⲨ ⲦⲎⲢⲞⲨ / (*III* 45.28) ⲠⲀⲨ ⲚⲈⲂⲒⲰ ⲠⲈⲦⲤⲞⲦⲠ ⲚⲌⲎⲦⲞⲨ ⲦⲎⲢⲞⲨ (cf. ibid. 144.14f. ⲌⲰⲂ ⲚⲒⲘ ⲈⲦⲈⲒⲢⲈ ⲘⲘⲰⲦⲚ ⲚⲀⲒ ⲚⲌⲘⲌⲀⲖ ⲚⲌⲎⲦⲞⲨ ⲦⲎⲢⲞⲨ) / *IV* 36.5f., 49.16f., 5.20f., *Mun.* 161: ⲚⲌⲎⲦⲞⲨ ⲦⲎⲢⲞⲨ, a recurring collocation, tending to the final position / (*IV* 20.20f.) ⲘⲎ ⲘⲠⲚⲞⲨⲦⲈ Ⲟ ⲚⲚⲞⲄ ⲈⲢⲞⲞⲨ ⲀⲚ ⲦⲎⲢⲞⲨ.

(c) *Determinators; nuclei of relative forms/nuclei + anaphoric pronoun*: (*A 1* 87) ⲚⲈⲦⲞⲨⲎⲌ ⲦⲎⲢⲞⲨ ⲌⲢⲀⲒ ⲚⲌⲎⲦⲈ / (*Ch.* 18.19f.) ⲚⲈⲦⲈⲚⲞⲨⲨ ⲦⲎⲢⲞⲨ (zero subject, but in 19.4f. ⲚⲈⲦⲈⲚⲞⲨⲨ ⲦⲎⲢⲞⲨ ⲚⲈ) / (*A 2* 360) ⲚⲈⲦⲰⲞⲞⲠ ⲚⲀⲨ ⲦⲎⲢⲞⲨ / (*Ch.* 17.28f.) ⲚⲈⲦⲦⲰⲞⲨⲚ ⲦⲎⲢⲞⲨ ⲈⲌⲢⲀⲒ ⲈⲬⲰⲞⲨ / (*Wess. 9* 129a 6f.) ⲚⲈⲦⲌⲚⲘⲠⲎⲨⲈ ⲦⲎⲢⲞⲨ / (*P* 130⁴ 156 ⲦⲌⲀ) ⲚⲈⲦⲈⲰⲰⲈ ⲈⲖⲀⲀⲨ ⲦⲎⲢⲞⲨ) / (*P* 130² 7 ⲡⲞ) ⲚⲈⲦⲈⲬⲒ ⲘⲘⲞⲞⲨ ⲦⲎⲢⲞⲨ ⲈⲢⲞ / (*A 1* 121) ⲚⲈⲚⲦⲀⲨⲀⲀⲨ ⲚⲈ ⲦⲎⲢⲞⲨ / (*RE 10* 163a 38) ⲚⲈⲦⲚⲌⲎⲦⲞⲨ ⲦⲎⲢⲞⲨ (ambiguous; sim. *IV* 36.22) / (*A 1* 266) ⲚⲈⲚⲦⲀⲨⲂⲞⲦⲞⲨ ⲈⲂⲞⲖ ⲦⲎⲢⲞⲨ. Note that here we find only *plural referates*. Additional exx.: *Ch.* 130.5f., *A 1* 388, 446, *RE 10* 161b 20.

(d) ⲦⲎⲢ⸗ with *adverbal* reference, in merely formal cohesion with an actor pronoun or nucleus of a relative form (here also singular): (*RE 10* 162a 1f.) ⲠⲈⲦⲌⲞⲖⲄ ⲦⲎⲢⲨ / (*A 1* 14) ⲠⲈⲦⲎⲠ ⲈⲰⲰⲠⲈ ⲦⲎⲢⲨ / (*Ch.* 70.43f.) ⲠⲀⲒⲘⲰⲚ ⲈⲦⲞⲨⲞⲰⲨ ⲦⲎⲢⲨ (sim. *IV* 175.11f. ...ⲚⲄⲞⲨⲰⲰⲨ ⲦⲎⲢⲔ) / (*A 2* 396) ⲈⲨⲚⲀⲦⲂⲂⲞ ⲦⲎⲢⲨ ⲚⲞⲨⲎⲢ

---

[57] {ⲚⲦⲞ⸗} follows {ⲡⲈ} when they belong to different cola: ⲌⲰⲤ ⲈⲨⲬⲈ-ⲚⲦⲞⲨ ⲡⲈ | ⲀⲚⲞⲚ | ⲌⲘⲠⲈⲦⲚⲈⲒⲢⲈ ⲘⲘⲞⲨ (*Ch.* 90.9f.).

[58] Cf. EBELING 1905:51-87 (" Tutto 'lauter' "), Løfstedt, *Vermischte Studien zur lateinischen Sprachkunde und Syntax*, Lund 1936, 209ff. (*toti* = *omnes*), BRØNDAL 1943: 125-132, Hofmann, " Die lateinischen Totalitätsausdrücke ", in *Mélanges... Marouzeau*, Paris 1948, 283-290.

/ (*IV* 193.6f.) ⲧⲉⲯⲩⲭⲏ ⲛⲥⲟ6 ⲉⲧⲍⲟⲟⲩ ⲧⲏⲣⲥ / (*Ch.* 22.3f.) ⲡ2ⲛⲟ ⲉⲧ6ⲁⲙ̅ⲗⲟⲙⲧ ⲧⲏⲣ4 / NB. (*A 1* 463) ⲛⲥⲁ2ⲟⲩ ⲧⲏⲣⲟⲩ ⲉⲧⲥⲏ2 ⲧⲏⲣⲟⲩ.

(e) *Post-imperatival* ⲧⲏⲣ⸗: (*A 1* 70) ⲕⲁⲧⲁⲗⲁⲗⲉⲓ 6ⲉ ⲛⲥⲱⲓ ⲧⲏⲣⲧⲛ. Cf. ⲙⲓⲱⲧⲛ ⲧⲏⲣⲧⲛ (*III* 25.18). ⲡⲭⲱⲕ ⲁⲉ ⲉⲃⲟⲗ ⲡⲉ ⲣ⁻ⲟⲩ2ⲏⲧ ⲛⲟⲩⲱⲧ ⲧⲏⲣⲧⲛ (*Wess. 9* 115b 5ff.) is a quotation (*I Pet.* 3:8). ⲧⲏⲣ⸗ here has a zero referate, and "finitizes" the infinitive (cf. §7.2.5 for the conjunctive in a similar function). Similarly, the post-imperatival augens explicates and specifies the gender/number category neutralized (syncretized) in the imperative form.

6.1.1.2 ⲧⲏⲣ⸗ IN COHESION WITH PRONOUNS OUTSIDE VERB SYNTAGMS

6.1.1.2.1 *Determinators.* (a) *Plural* (definite article, demonstratives, possessive articles): (*A 2* 247) ⲛⲉⲛⲉⲓⲟⲧⲉ ⲧⲏⲣⲟⲩ ⲛⲁⲣⲭⲁⲓⲟⲥ / (*A 1* 373) ⲁⲛ2ⲁⲓⲣⲉⲧⲓⲕⲟⲥ 2ⲱⲟⲩ ⲧⲏⲣⲟⲩ ⲉⲧⲭⲓ-ⲟⲩⲁ... ⲉⲓ ⲉⲃⲟⲗ / (*Ch.* 179.10ff.) ⲛⲣⲉ4-ⲣ-ⲛⲟⲃⲉ ⲧⲏⲣⲟⲩ ⲙⲡⲕⲁ2 / (*Wess. 18* 140b 8ff.) 2ⲛⲛⲁⲓ ⲟⲛ ⲧⲏⲣⲟⲩ ⲉⲙⲡⲉⲩ2ⲏⲧ 6ⲛ-ⲁⲣⲓⲕⲉ ⲉⲣⲟⲟⲩ ⲁⲛ / (*III* 118.11f.) ⲛⲱⲁⲭⲉ ⲧⲏⲣⲟⲩ ⲛⲭⲡⲓⲟ ⲁⲩⲱ ⲛⲥⲁ2ⲟⲩ ⲧⲏⲣⲟⲩ ⲉⲧⲉⲣⲉⲡⲁⲓ ⲭⲱ ⲙⲙⲟⲟⲩ ⲛⲧⲁ4ⲭⲟⲟⲩ ⲧⲏⲣⲟⲩ ⲉⲧⲃⲏⲏⲧⲛ / (*A 1* 289) ⲛⲉⲡⲣⲟⲫⲏⲧⲏⲥ ⲁⲉ ⲧⲏⲣⲟⲩ ⲙⲛⲛⲁⲡⲟⲥⲧⲟⲗⲟⲥ ⲧⲏⲣⲟⲩ ⲙⲛⲛⲉⲧⲟⲩⲁⲁⲃ ⲧⲏⲣⲟⲩ... / (*III* 215.24f.) ⲱⲁⲛⲧⲉⲛⲉⲓⲣⲓⲕⲉ ⲧⲏⲣⲟⲩ ⲱⲱⲡⲉ.

(b) 2ⲉⲛ- ⲧⲏⲣⲟⲩ "all sorts of... ", especially frequent after 2ⲉⲛⲕⲉ- " all kinds of other... ": (*Wess. 9* 172d 6ff.) 2ⲉⲛⲕⲉ2ⲃⲏⲩⲉ ⲧⲏⲣⲟⲩ ⲉⲛⲁⲱⲱⲟⲩ (sim. *IV* 30.28f.) / (*IV* 14.21f.) 2ⲉⲛⲕⲟⲟⲩⲉ ⲧⲏⲣⲟⲩ ⲛⲧⲉⲓ2ⲉ (sim. *ibid.* 115.10) / (*A 1* 114) ⲛⲧⲟ ⲡⲉⲧⲛⲁⲉⲓⲣⲉ 2ⲉⲛⲡⲉⲑⲟⲟⲩ ⲧⲏⲣⲟⲩ " all sorts of evil " (Amélineau's translation, " tous les maux ", is wrong) / (*A 2* 504) ⲧⲉⲓⲣⲉ ⲛ2ⲉⲛⲡⲉⲧⲛⲁⲛⲟⲩⲟⲩ ⲧⲏⲣⲟⲩ ⲙⲡⲉⲕⲙⲧⲟ ⲉⲃⲟⲗ.

(c) *Numbers* + ⲧⲏⲣⲟⲩ " whole ", " complete ": (*IV* 57.22f.) ...ⲉⲟⲩⲛ2ⲟⲩⲟ ⲉⲟⲩⲟⲉⲓⲕ ⲛⲟⲩⲱⲧ ⲛⲧⲟⲟⲧⲟⲩ ⲏ ⲥⲛⲁⲩ ⲏ ⲱⲁⲱⲟⲙⲧ ⲧⲏⲣⲟⲩ " three whole (loaves) " / (*ibid.* 71.4f.) ⲙⲛⲛⲥⲁⲟⲩⲉⲃⲟⲧ ⲏ ⲥⲛⲁⲩ ⲏ ⲱⲟⲙⲧ ⲧⲏⲣⲟⲩ.

(d) *Singular definite article*: unitary totality: " the whole ", "all of the...": (*P* 131⁶ 108 ro, *III* 168.5, *A 2* 108) ⲡⲙⲟⲩ ⲧⲏⲣ4 " all that is of death " / (*Ch.* 99.21f.) ⲑⲉⲗⲡⲓⲥ ⲧⲏⲣⲥ ⲙⲡⲁⲃⲓⲟⲥ / (*A 2* 238) ⲓ̅ⲥ̅ ⲡⲉⲭ̅ⲥ̅ ⲡⲉ2ⲗⲟ6 ⲧⲏⲣ4 " all (that is) of sweetness " / (*Ryl. Cat.* 35 No. 70 ⲥⲙ⊖) ⲧⲟⲣⲅⲏ ⲧⲏⲣⲥ / (*III* 184.8) ⲧⲉⲱⲏⲣⲉ ⲧⲏⲣⲥ ⲧⲉ... / (*P* 130⁵ 52 vo) ⲡⲉⲓⲕⲉⲥⲙⲟⲧ ⲧⲏⲣ4... ⲛⲁⲓⲕⲁⲓⲟⲥ ⲧⲏⲣⲟⲩ, ⲛⲉⲧⲟⲩⲁⲁⲃ ⲧⲏⲣⲟⲩ... ⲛⲕⲟⲟⲩⲉ ⲧⲏⲣⲟⲩ... ⲛⲉⲥⲟⲟⲩ ⲧⲏⲣⲟⲩ / (*RE 10* 161a 27ff.) ⲕⲥⲙⲁⲙⲁⲁⲧ ⲡ6ⲟⲙ ⲧⲏⲣ4 ⲁⲩⲱ ⲡⲭⲱⲱⲣⲉ ⲧⲏⲣ4 ⲡⲙⲟⲓ2ⲉ ⲧⲏⲣ4... ⲡⲟⲩⲟⲉⲓⲛ ⲧⲏⲣ4 "(thou) who art all might and all strength, all wonder... all light " [59] / Note the recurring idiomatic ⲛⲧⲉⲓ2ⲉ ⲧⲏⲣⲥ " so much " (*IV* 162.6, *Ch.* 42.2f., *P* 130⁴ 48 vo, etc.), cf. Hebrew *kol-kax*. Additional exx.: *Ch.* 133.42f., 140. 17ff., *IV* 64.11, 163.4, *III* 37.20, 185.24f., etc.

(e) *Singular indefinite* ⲟⲩ- ⲧⲏⲣ⸗ " a whole... ", " a complete... ": (*IV* 153.23f.) ⲟⲩⲡⲁⲱⲉ ⲛⲟⲩⲟⲩⲛⲟⲩ ⲏ ⲟⲩⲟⲩⲛⲟⲩ ⲧⲏⲣⲥ / (*A 1* 204) ⲥⲛⲁⲣ-ⲟⲩⲟⲩⲱⲏ ⲛⲣⲟⲉⲓⲥ ⲧⲏⲣⲥ / NB. (*A 2* 16) ⲟⲩⲥⲩⲛⲁⲅⲱⲅⲏ ⲛⲣⲉⲙ2ⲉ (sic) ⲧⲏⲣⲟⲩ " a congregation of people who are all freemen ".

6.1.1.2.2 *The possessor exponent in the possessive article* (*uncommon*): (*A 2* 315) ⲡⲉⲛⲁⲱⲕⲁⲕ ⲧⲏⲣⲛ / (*III* 43.26) ⲡⲉⲩⲥⲛⲟ4 ⲧⲏⲣⲟⲩ. Also *ibid.* 13.3, *IV* 34.5f. Plural only, most often 1st person plural.

6.1.1.2.3 *Independent pronoun* (rare): (*Ch.* 165.44ff.) ⲛⲧⲱⲧⲛ ⲅⲁⲣ ⲧⲏⲣⲧⲛ ⲛⲧⲉⲧⲛ-ⲛⲱⲏⲣⲉ ⲙⲡⲟⲩⲟⲉⲓⲛ / (*III* 139.21) ⲛⲧⲱⲧⲛ ⲧⲏⲣⲧⲛ ⲙⲙⲉⲣⲁⲧⲉ / (*P* 131⁶ 88 ro) ⲛⲧⲕ-ⲟⲩⲥⲁⲣⲕⲓⲕⲟⲛ ⲧⲏⲣⲕ.

6.1.1.2.4 *Pronominal subject of a Nominal Sentence.* Note the conditioned placement. The predicate noun syntagm is indefinite: (*Ch.* 22.18f.) 2ⲉⲛⲫⲁⲛⲧⲁⲥⲓⲁ ⲧⲏⲣⲟⲩ ⲛⲉ / (*III* 217.11) 2ⲉⲛⲉⲃⲟⲗ ⲁⲛ ⲛⲧⲡⲉ

---

[59] See §5.1.1.0.1 for the significance of such cases of '*masc. determinator* + " *feminine* " *noun lexeme*'. For the sense of the modified syntagm (" he is all heart and no brain "), cf. EBELING 1905:52f., 57ff.

ⲧⲏⲣⲟⲩ ⲛⲉ *vs.* (215.10) ⲥⲉⲛⲉⲃⲟⲗ ⲁⲛ ⲛⲉ ⲥⲙⲡⲕⲁⲥ ⲧⲏⲣⲟⲩ: ⲥⲙⲡⲕⲁⲥ interposes between the referate and ⲧⲏⲣ⸗; otherwise, the pre-referate placement is constant / (*A 2* 16) ⲥⲟⲓⲛⲉ ⲧⲏⲣⲟⲩ ⲛⲉ; ⲥⲟⲓⲛⲉ is anaphoric to the determinator in the preceding ⲥⲉⲛⲱⳉ "thieves" / (*P* 130² 2 ⲡ) ⲟⲩⲕⲣⲟϭ ⲧⲏⲣϥ ⲡⲉ / (*P* 130⁵ 22 ⲫⲙⲑ) ⲥⲉⲛⲉⲃⲟⲗ ⲧⲏⲣⲟⲩ ⲛⲉ ⲥⲙⲡⲉⲥⲡⲉⲣⲙⲁ ⲙⲡⲉⲛⲉⲓⲱⲧ / (*RE 10* 159b 7) ⲟⲩⳉⲗⲟϭ ⲧⲏⲣϥ ⲡⲉ.

6.1.1.3 PECULIARITIES OF PLACEMENT [60]. ⲧⲏⲣ⸗ *colon-(or sentence-)final*: pre-referate: ⲥⲉⲛⲡⲟⲛⲏⲣⲟⲛ ⲧⲏⲣⲟⲩ ⲛⲉ (*Ch.* 32.48f., §6.1.1.2.4) / ⲉⲓⲥ ⲏⲏⲧⲉ ⲧⲏⲣⲟⲩ ⲥⲉⲥ ⲏⲥ... (*III* 61-2, sim. *ibid.* 89.11f.) / ⲥⲉⲛⲁⲩ ⲉⲣⲟϥ ⲥⲙⲡⲉⲓ-ⳉⳉ ⲛⲟⲩⲱⲧ ⲧⲏⲣⲟⲩ (*Ch.* 61.5ff.) / ⲛⲉⲛⲧⲁⲩⲃⲱⲕ ⲉⲡⲉⲥ ⲏⲧ ⲉⲣⲟⲥ ⲧⲏⲣⲟⲩ (*P* 131⁶ 81 ro).

6.1.2 ⲥⲱⲱ⸗ "INCLUSIVE/SEQUENTIAL CONFRONTATION" ("he too", "he... in his turn", "he, for his part"); the *second term* is characterized (§6.3).

6.1.2.0.1 MORPHOLOGICAL. *1st person sgl.* ⲥⲱ/ⲥⲱⲱⲧ, in variation (variant readings in *III* 168.15). *2nd fem. sgl.* ⲥⲱⲱⲧⲉ (*III* 194.16, *Or.* 157.8). *2nd plur.* ⲥⲱⲧ-ⲧⲏⲛⲉ (*IV* 60.28) is Akhmimoid [61] (ⲥⲱⲱⲧ-ⲧⲏⲩⲧⲛ in *A 1* 366, collated). *3rd plur.* ⲥⲱⲱⲟⲩ (*IV* 105.22, collated). ⲥⲱⲧ-ⲧⲏⲩⲧⲛ and ⲥⲱⲟⲩ are normal.

6.1.2.1 *Post-referate* placement.

6.1.2.1.1 In cohesion with *pronominal* referates: *immediate* post-referate placement.

6.1.2.1.1.1 Referate in *verb syntagms*: (a) *Actor pronoun*: (*A 1* 39) ⲁⳉⲁⲥⲟⲙ ⲁⲩⳉ ⳇⳉⳉ ⲥⲱ ⲛⲙⲙⲉ / (*IV* 60.27f.) ⲕⲁⲧⲁⲑⲉ ⲉⲧⲟⲩⲉⲓⲣⲉ ⲙⲙⲟⲥ ⲥⲁⲧⲏⲛ ⲉⲧⲉⲧⲛⲁⲁⲁⲥ ⲥⲱⲧⲧⲏⲛⲉ / (*Ch.* 43.2ff.) (ⲉⲕⳉⲱ ⲙⲙⲟⲥ... ⳉⲉ-...) ⳇⲛⲁ ⳉⲟⲟⲥ ⲥⲱⳉⲧ ⲛⲧⲉⲓ ⲥⲉ... ⳉⲉ- / (*ibid.* 51.2f.) ⳉⲁⲛⲙⲉⲉⲩⲉ ⲥⲱⲱⲛ ⲉⲡⲁⲓ, "we too" / (*III* 19.23f.) ⲧⲛⲛⲁⲃⲱⲕ ⲉⲣⲁⲧϥ ⲙⲡⲛⲟⲩⲧⲉ ⲥⲉⲛⲁⲃⲱⲕ ⲥⲱⲟⲩ / (*ibid.* 24.12f.) ⳇⲛⲏⲩ ⲉⲥⲣⲁⲓ ⲉⲛⲉⳉϭⲓⳉ ⲁⲩⳉ ⲧⲉⲧⲛⲛⲏⲩ ⲥⲱⲧⲧⲏⲩⲧⲛ. Additional exx.: *III* 53 *passim*, 54.2, 64.28-65.3, *RE 11* 15a 8f., etc.

(b) *Actor noun-syntagm (determinator)*; *nucleus of relative*; *demonstrative*: (*III* 63.21ff.) ⲉⳉⳉⲉ-ⲡⲃⲁⲗ ⲙⲡⲣⲱⲙⲉ... ⲙⲉ ⳉ ⲥⲉⲓ... ⲉⲓⲉ ⲁⲙⲛⲧⲉ ⲥⲱⲱϥ... ⲉ ⳇⲛⲁⲥⲉⲓ ⲏ ⲉ ⳇⲛⲁⲙⲟⲩⲥ ⲛⲁⳉ ⲛⲥⲉ / (*A 2* 491) ⲉⲣⳉⲁⲛ ⲧⲉⳉⲩⳉⲏ ⲇⲉ ⲧⲟⲃⲥ ⲉⲡ ⳉⲟⲉⲓⲥ ⳉⲁⲣⲉⲡⳉⲟⲉⲓⲥ ⲥⲱⲱϥ ⲛⲁ ⲁⲩⳉ ⲛ ⳇⲙⲉⲣⲓⲧⲥ... / (*IV* 105.22) ⲁⲡⲉⲧⲙⲙⲁⲩ ⲙⲉⲛ ⲛⲧⲟⲩ ⲥⲛⲟⲩⲥⲟⲟⲩⲧⲛ, ⲁⲛⲁⲓ ⲥⲱⲱⲟⲩ (sic) ⲛⲧⲟⲩ ⲥⲛⲟⲩⲥⲟⲟⲩⲧⲛ / (*A 1* 77) ⲥⲉⲛⲁⲥⲁⲣⲉⲥ ⲉⲣⲟϥ ⲉϥⲥⲟⲟⲩⲥ... ⳉⲁⲛⲧⲟⲩⲧⲁⲁϥ ⲕⲟⲩⲓ ⲕⲟⲩⲓ ⲛⲧⲟⲟⲧⲟⲩ ⲛ ⲥⲉⲛ-ⲕⲟⲟⲩⲉ ⲛⲧⲉⲛⲉⲧⲙⲙⲁⲩ ⲥⲱⲟⲩ ⲟⲛ ⲛⲟ ⳉϥ ⲉⲥⲉⲛ ⲥⲛⲁⲁⲩ / (*III* 45.5f.) ⲉⳉ ⳉⲉ-ⳉⲁⲣⲉ ⲡⲥⲁⲓⲣⲉⲧⲓⲕⲟⲥ ϭⲉ ⲙⲛⲡⲥⲉⲗⲗⲏⲛ ⲡⲱⲣⳉ ⲉⲃⲟⲗ ⲛⲛⲉⲩϭⲓⳉ... ⲉⲓⲥ-ⲛⲥⲁⲗⲗⲁⲧⲉ ⲥⲱⲟⲩ ⲉⲓⲣⲉ ⲙⲡⲁⲓ ⲛⲥⲁⲥ ⲛⲥⲟⲡ. Also: *III* 65.12,16, *A 1* 373-4.

(c) *Object pronoun (expansion pronoun)*: (*A 2* 462) ⲛⲉⲧⲛⲁⳉⲟⲡⲥ ⲇⲉ ⲉⲣⲟⲟⲩ... ⲥⲛⲁⳉⲟⲡⲟⲩ ⲥⲱⲟⲩ ⲉⲣⲟⲥ / (*A 2* 358) ⲡⲉⲧⲛⲁⲧⲱⲙⲧ ⲉⲡⲁⲑⲏⲧ ⲉⲓⲉ ⳇⲛⲁⲧⲱⲙⲧ ⲉⲣⲟⲓ ⲥⲱ / (*III* 144.28f.) ⲁⲩⲁⲁⲧ ⲥⲱⳉⲧ ⲛ ⳇⲙⲙⲟ ⲛⲥⲁⲥ ⲛⲥⲟⲡ ⲥⲙⲡⲁⲥ ⲏⲧ / (*IV* 108.21) ⲡⲉⲥⲥⲁⲓ ⲅⲁⲣ ⲛⲁⲛ ⲁⲩⳉ ⲛⲏⲧⲛ ⲥⲱⲧⲧⲏⲩⲧⲛ ⲡⲉ / (*III* 162.9) ⳇⳉⲱ ⲙⲙⲟⲥ ⲛⲏⲧⲛ ⲁⲩⳉ ⲛⲁⲓ ⲥⲱ ⲟⲛ / (*A 1* 16) ...ⲉⲥⲟⲩⲛ ⲉⲟⲩⲟⲛ ⲛⲓⲙ ⲁⲩⳉ ⲉⲥⲟⲩⲛ ⲉⲣⲟⲓ ⲥⲱ.

(d) Post-imperatival ⲥⲱⲱ⸗ (cf. *independent* pronoun + ⲥⲱⲱ⸗ + *imperative*, below): ⲥⲱⲱ⸗ is gender/number characterizing: (*P* 130¹ 132 ⲧⲕⲍ) ⲉⲓⲙⲉ ⲥⲱⲧⲧⲏⲩⲧⲛ / (*IV* 86.8) ⲉⲣ ⳉⲁⲛⲧⲙⲡⲉⲧⳉⳉⲛⲉ ⲛⲁⲙⲉ ⳉⲓⲧϥ ⲛ ⳉⲛⲁⲥ ⲉⲟⲩⲉⲙ-ⲟⲩⲥⲛⲁⲁⲩ, ⳉⲁⲣⲉⲡⲉϥⲥⲏⲧ ⲱⳉ; ϭⲱ ⲥⲱⲱⲕ ⲛⲟⲩⲉ ⳉⲛⲟⲩⲱⲙ / NB. (*Ch.* 182.57f.) ⳉⲟⲟⲥ ⲥⲱⲱⲛ (*inclusive* 1st person plural, = "1st + 2nd pers."; cf. *P* 131⁶ 44 ⲣⲓⲉ: ⲕⳉ ⲉⲃⲟⲗ ⲛⲛⲉⲛⲉⲣⲏⲩ).

6.1.2.1.1.2 *Determinators*; ⲡ- etc.: (*III* 17.6) (The empty sealed tomb is full of bones and impurities) ⲡⲣⲱⲙⲉ ⲥⲱⲱϥ ⲉⲧⲣ-ⲛⲟⲃⲉ... ϥ ⳉⲟⲩⲉⲓⲧ, ϥⲙⲉⲥ ⲇⲉ ⲟⲛ ⲙⲙⲟⲕⲙⲉⲕ ⲙⲙⲛⲧⲁⲕⲁⲑⲁⲣⲧⲟⲥ /(*Cat.* 41 .5f.) ⲟⲩⳉⲁⳉⲉ ⲛⲥⲱⲃⲉ ⲡⲉ ⲡⲁⲓ ⲛⲛⲓⲟⲩⲇⲁⲓ ⲥⲱⲟⲩ "for the Jews too". ⲥⲉⲛ-: (*A 2* 19) ⲉⲧⲃⲉⲟⲩ ⲛ ⳉⳉⲉ ⲁⲛ ⲉⲣ-ⲥⲉⲛⲣⲱⲙⲉ ⲛⲥⲛⲟϥ ⲥⲱⲟⲩ...

---

[60] Cf. POLOTSKY 1961:308f. (= *CP* 412f.).
[61] SHISHA–HALEVY 1976b:358.

ⲛⲩⲙⲙⲟ ⲉⲛⲥⲩⲛⲁⲅⲱⲅⲏ ⲙⲡⲛⲟⲩⲧⲉ (as did the people and Josua in the case of Achan) / (*Wess. 9* 151c 1ff.)
ⲟⲩⲛ2ⲉⲛⲇⲓⲕⲁⲓⲟⲥ ⲛⲁⲓ ⲉⲩⲛⲁⲧⲁ2ⲟⲟⲩ ⲛ6ⲓⲡ2ⲱⲃ ⲛⲛⲁⲥⲉⲃⲏⲥ, ⲁⲩⲱ ⲟⲩⲛ2ⲉⲛⲁⲥⲉⲃⲏⲥ 2ⲱⲟⲩ ⲉⲩⲛⲁⲧⲁ2ⲟⲟⲩ ⲛ6ⲓ-
ⲡ2ⲱⲃ ⲛⲛⲇⲓⲕⲁⲓⲟⲥ (or is this pre-referate placement?) / (*RE 10* 160a 16ff.) (2ⲉⲛⲡⲩⲅⲏ ⲙⲙⲟⲟⲩ, when blocked,
are opened up with proper tools) 2ⲉⲛⲙⲁⲁⲭⲉ 2ⲱⲟⲩ ⲉⲁⲩⲧⲱⲙ... ⲟⲩ ⲡⲉⲧⲛⲁⲟⲩⲱⲛ ⲙⲙⲟⲟⲩ ⲛⲥⲁⲡⲗⲟⲅⲟⲥ ⲙⲡⲛⲟⲩⲧⲉ.

6.1.2.1.1.3   *The possessor exponent of the possessive article or pronoun*: (*A 2* 280) ⲉⲧⲃⲉⲡⲣⲟⲟⲩⲩ ⲛ-...
ⲁⲩⲱ ⲉⲧⲃⲉⲡⲉⲧⲛⲣⲟⲟⲩⲩ 2ⲱⲧⲧⲏⲩⲧⲛ / (*III* 97.2) (ⲡ2ⲟⲟⲩⲧ ⲙⲉⲛ ⲛⲧⲁ4+ ⲙⲡⲉ4ⲏⲓ ⲛⲟⲩⲩⲙⲙⲟ) ⲡⲩⲉⲉⲣⲉ ⲇⲉ ⲧⲟⲩⲉⲓ ⲙⲉⲛ
ⲁⲥ+-ⲡⲱⲥ 2ⲱⲱⲥ ⲟⲛ / (*IV* 50.20) ⲉⲩⲛⲁⲥ2ⲁⲓ ⲙⲡⲉⲩ2ⲱⲃ 2ⲱⲟⲩ ⲛⲟⲉ ⲛⲛⲉⲥⲛⲏⲩ ⲧⲏⲣⲟⲩ / (*Ch.* 186.40f.) (Everyone's
shadow) ⲁⲩⲱ ⲟⲛ ⲧⲱⲛ 2ⲱⲱⲛ / (*A 1* 464) ⲛⲟⲉ ⲛⲧⲁⲡⲙⲟⲟⲩ ⲛⲉⲃⲣⲓⲉⲓⲙ ⲩⲱⲡⲉ ⲉⲩⲩⲟⲩ2, ⲧⲉⲕⲥⲃⲱ 2ⲱⲱⲕ ⲙⲛⲛⲉⲕⲩⲁⲭⲉ... ⲛⲁⲩⲱⲡⲉ ⲉⲩⲩⲟⲩ (2ⲱⲱⲕ "illogically" modifying ⲧⲉⲕ-, instead of ⲧⲉⲕⲥⲃⲱ ⲙⲛⲛⲉⲕⲩⲁⲭⲉ).

6.1.2.1.1.4   *Independent pronoun* (very common): (*A 1* 61) ⲁⲛⲟⲕ ⲁⲩⲱ ⲛⲧⲟⲟⲩ 2ⲱⲟⲩ ⲁⲛ- / (*P* 130[5]
133 ro) ⲁⲩ+-ⲉⲟⲟⲩ ⲛⲁⲓ, ⲁⲛⲟⲕ 2ⲱⲱⲧ +ⲛⲁ+-ⲉⲟⲟⲩ ⲛⲁⲩ / (*III* 29.10) (the foal can be bridled and tamed) ⲁⲛⲟⲛ
ⲇⲉ 2ⲱⲱⲛ ⲟⲩ ⲡⲉⲧⲛⲛⲁⲭⲟⲟ4 / (*ibid.* 38.19f.) ⲉⲩⲭⲉ-ⲛⲧⲕ-ⲟⲩⲡⲛⲁ̄ ⲏ ⲟⲩⲁⲅⲅⲉⲗⲟⲥ ⲉⲁ4ⲉⲓ ⲉⲃⲟⲗ 2ⲓⲧⲙⲡⲛⲟⲩⲧⲉ, ⲁⲛⲟⲕ
2ⲱⲱⲧ ⲁⲛⲅ-ⲡⲉ42ⲙ2ⲁⲗ / (*Or.* 153-5, *passim*) ⲉⲩⲭⲱ ⲙⲙⲟⲥ ⲛⲁⲕ ⲱ ⲡⲣⲱⲙⲉ ⲁⲩⲱ ⲛⲧⲟ 2ⲱⲱⲧⲉ ⲧⲉⲥ2ⲓⲙⲉ... ⲁⲭⲓⲥ ⲉⲣⲟⲓ
ⲁⲩⲱ ⲛⲧⲟⲕ 2ⲱⲱⲕ ⲙⲁⲧⲁⲙⲟⲓ... / (*A 2* 382-3) ⲉⲩⲭⲉ-ⲛ+ⲣⲓⲙⲉ ⲛⲁⲓ ⲁⲛ... ⲉⲓⲉⲛⲧⲱⲧⲛ 2ⲱⲧⲧⲏⲩⲧⲛ ⲙⲡⲣⲣⲓⲙⲉ ⲛⲏⲧⲛ /
(*A 2* 293f.) ⲙⲡⲥ+-2ⲧⲏⲥ ⲙⲡⲁⲩⲁⲭⲉ, ⲁⲛⲟⲕ 2ⲱ +ⲛⲁⲕⲱ ⲛⲛⲟⲩⲥ ⲛⲛⲁ2ⲣⲁⲓ ⲛⲟⲉ ⲛⲟⲩⲛⲕⲁ ⲉⲣⲉⲑⲁⲧⲏⲩ 4ⲓ ⲙⲙⲟ4 ⲉⲡⲟⲩⲉ.
ⲁⲥⲛⲟⲩⲭⲉ ⲛⲛⲁⲩⲁⲭⲉ 2ⲓⲡⲁ2ⲟⲩ ⲛⲧⲉⲥⲙⲛⲧⲁⲧⲥⲱⲧⲙ, ⲁⲛⲟⲕ 2ⲱ +ⲛⲁⲩⲱⲡ ⲉⲣⲟⲥ ⲙⲡⲉⲓⲙⲉⲣⲟⲥ... ⲁⲥⲗⲩⲡⲉⲓ ⲙⲙⲟⲓ, ⲁⲛⲟⲕ
2ⲱ +ⲛⲁⲧⲁⲁⲥ ⲉⲧⲟⲟⲧ4 ⲙⲡⲉⲙⲕⲁ2 ⲛ2ⲏⲧ / (*P* 130[2] 1 oz) ⲕⲟ ⲙⲡⲭⲟⲉⲓⲥ ⲙⲡⲉⲕ2ⲱⲃ, ⲁⲛⲟⲕ 2ⲱⲱⲧ +ⲟ ⲙⲡⲭⲟⲉⲓⲥ ⲙⲡⲁ2ⲱⲃ
/ (*A 2* 519), an especially illuminating example: ⲛⲁⲩ ⲛ2ⲉ ⲁⲛⲟⲕ ⲉⲓⲛⲁⲉⲓⲣⲉ ⲛⲟⲩ2ⲱⲃ ⲉⲭⲱⲕ, ⲛⲧⲟⲕ 2ⲱⲱⲕ ⲙⲡⲕ-
ⲣ-ⲗⲁⲁⲩ ⲉⲭⲱⲓ ⲟⲩⲇⲉ 2ⲁⲣⲟⲕ ⲙⲁⲩⲁⲁⲕ.   Additional exx.: *III* 29.27f., 94.15, 124.22, 176.20f., *IV* 56.5f., 108.5,
Ch. 39.8f., 62.38ff., *Or.* 157.50ff., 158.14ff., 165.20ff., etc.

6.1.2.1.2   *Non-immediate* post-referate placement (relatively rare).   Referate: *noun* syntagm: (*A 1*
76) ⲛⲟⲉ ⲉⲛⲧⲁⲧⲉⲓⲁⲑⲏⲧ ⲛⲥ2ⲓⲙⲉ ⲉⲛⲧⲁⲡⲛⲟⲩⲧⲉ ⲁⲁⲥ ⲛⲩⲙⲙⲟ ⲉⲣⲱⲧⲛ ⲭⲟⲟⲥ 2ⲱⲱⲥ ⲟⲛ ⲭⲉ- / (*ibid.* 87) ⲉⲩⲭⲉ-+ⲛⲁⲭⲓ-
ⲡⲁ2ⲡⲓⲟ... ⲁⲩⲱ ⲛⲧⲉⲧⲙⲡⲁⲓ ⲏ ⲛⲁⲓ ⲣ-ⲃⲟⲗ 2ⲱⲟⲩ ⲉⲡⲉⲭⲡⲓⲟ... / (*ibid.* 104) ⲙⲛ6ⲟⲙ ⲙⲙⲟⲓ ⲉ4ⲓ 2ⲱ ⲛⲟⲉ ⲛⲧⲁⲥⲩⲱⲡⲉ ⲙⲙⲟⲓ
(*even* in the present predicament, let alone if God bring down upon me the retribution or malediction of
this oath...).

6.1.2.2   *Pre-referate* placement [62], 2ⲱⲱ= *colon-final* (*intercolary*):   (a) Following ⲛⲟⲉ, ⲕⲁⲧⲁⲑⲉ,
ⲧⲁⲓ (ⲧⲉ ⲑⲉ), ⲛⲧⲉⲓ2ⲉ [63]: (*A 1* 41) ⲡⲟⲩⲱⲩ ⲉⲧⲉⲟⲩⲛⲧⲁ44 ⲉ2ⲟⲩⲛ ⲉⲣⲟ ⲛⲟⲉ 2ⲱⲱⲧⲉ ⲙⲡⲟⲩⲱⲩ ⲉⲧⲉⲟⲩⲛⲧⲁ4ⲉ ⲉ2ⲟⲩⲛ
ⲉⲣⲟ4 / (*ibid.* 297) (they sinned) ⲛⲟⲉ 2ⲱⲱⲛ ⲟⲛ ⲧⲉⲛⲟⲩ ⲉⲧⲛⲣ-ⲛⲟⲃⲉ / (*Wess. 9* 162c 15ff., parall. *III* 136.28f.)
...ⲕⲁⲧⲁⲑⲉ 2ⲱⲟⲩ ⲉⲧⲉⲛⲁⲩⲉⲡⲟⲩⲱⲩ ⲛⲛⲉⲧ+-ⲥⲃⲱ ⲛⲁⲩ... / (*A 2* 468) ⲛⲧⲉⲓ2ⲉ 2ⲱⲧⲧⲏⲩⲧⲛ ⲉⲧⲉⲧⲛⲩⲁⲛⲧⲙⲁⲓⲉ-ⲡⲗⲟⲅⲟⲥ
ⲙⲡⲛⲟⲩⲧⲉ... ⲧⲟⲧⲉ ⲧⲉⲧⲛⲁⲩⲱⲡⲉ ⲙⲙⲁⲕⲁⲣⲓⲟⲥ / (*Borg.* 194 ⲓⲥ) ⲛⲧⲉⲓ2ⲉ 2ⲱⲱⲧⲧⲏⲩⲧⲛ, ⲱ ⲡ2ⲉⲗⲗⲏⲛ ⲙⲛⲛ2ⲁⲓⲣⲉⲧⲓⲕⲟⲥ, ⲛⲧⲉ-
ⲧⲛⲁⲩⲣ-ⲡⲡⲉⲧⲛⲁⲛⲟⲩ4 ⲁⲛ.   Also *III* 48.24f., 150.28, *IV* 36.1, *Ch.* 105.6ff., *A 1* 61, 366, etc.   Compare also
the recurring, idiomatic (post-referate) ⲛⲧⲁ2ⲉ 2ⲱⲱⲧ ⲟⲛ "like me (too)" (e.g. *III* 150.23, 162.22, 168.15,
171.10, 184.24, *P* 130[1] 139 ⲧⲙⲉ etc.).

(b) Following ⲭⲉⲕⲁ(ⲁ)ⲥ [64]: (*A 2* 49) ...ⲭⲉⲕⲁⲥ 2ⲱⲱⲛ 2ⲛ2ⲁⲣⲉ2 ⲛⲓⲙ ⲉⲛⲛⲁ2ⲁⲣⲉ2 ⲉⲡⲉⲛ2ⲏⲧ / (*A 1* 461)
...ⲭⲉⲕⲁⲥ 2ⲱⲱⲕ ⲛⲛⲉⲟⲩⲁ ⲩⲡ-2ⲙⲟⲧ ⲛⲧⲟⲟⲧⲕ ⲉⲛⲉ2 / (*Wess. 9* 115b 8ff.) ⲭⲉⲕⲁⲥ 2ⲱⲟⲩ ⲉⲣⲉⲡⲉⲩ2ⲏⲧ ⲙⲧⲟⲛ, sim.
(*P* 130[1] 134 ⲧⲗⲁ) ⲭⲉⲕⲁⲥ 2ⲱⲱⲛ ⲉⲣⲉⲡⲉⲛ2ⲏⲧ ⲙⲧⲟⲛ.   Compare also the recurring ⲭⲉ(ⲕⲁⲥ) ⲉⲕⲛⲁⲕⲱ/ⲉ4ⲉⲕⲱ
2ⲱ ⲛⲁⲓ ⲉⲃⲟⲗ ⲛⲛⲁⲛⲟⲃⲉ (*III* 135.28f., *A 1* 87, *P* 130[1] 139 ⲧⲙⲉ).   Additional exx.: *III* 104.9f., *IV* 7.16, 194.12f.,
P 130[1] 133 ⲧⲗ.

---

[62] POLOTSKY 1961:295ff. (= *CP* 399ff.).

[63] POLOTSKY 1961:301, 304ff. (= *CP* 405, 408ff.). Polotsky treats ⲛⲟⲉ with other antecedents; in Shenoute, — ⲑⲉ —
clearly has a special standing.

[64] POLOTSKY 1961: 304f., 307 (= *CP* 408f., 411).

(c) Following a (plural, mostly indefinite) predicative noun syntagm, in a Nominal Sentence: (*RE 11* 18a 24f.) ϨⲈⲚⲒⲞⲨⲆⲀⲒ ⲌⲰⲞⲨ ⲚⲂⲢⲢⲈ ⲚⲈ / (*IV* 90.18) ϨⲈⲚⲢⲈϤϨⲈⲦⲂ-ⲮⲨⲬⲎ ⲚⲢⲰⲘⲈ ⲌⲰⲞⲨ ⲚⲈ / (*A 2* 12) ϨⲈⲚϨⲞⲨⲈⲢⲈϤ-ϪⲒ-ϬⲞⲗ ⲌⲰⲞⲨ ⲚⲈ / (*P* 130¹ 137 ⲦⲗⲎ) ⲚⲈⲚⲤⲚⲎⲨ ⲌⲰⲞⲨ ⲚⲈ. Also: *III* 31.15f., *IV* 52.7, 91.5, *A 2* 511, etc. For (*III* 187.12) ⲦⲀⲒ ϨⲰⲦⲦⲎⲨⲦⲚ ⲦⲈ ⲦⲈⲦⲚϨⲈ [65], see §6.0.3.4.

(d) Miscellaneous cola: *Imperatives*: (*A 2* 320) Ⲣ-ⲞⲨⲞⲈⲒⲚ ϬⲈ ϨⲰⲰⲚ ⲈⲠⲈⲚϨⲎⲂⲤ / (*P* 131⁶ 30 ⲢⲘⲈ) ⲤⲞⲞⲨⲚ ϨⲞⲞⲨ (sic) ⲚⲚⲈⲚⲦⲀⲠϪⲞⲈⲒⲤ ⲠⲚⲞⲨⲦⲈ ⲀⲀⲨ / (*P* 130² 24 ϤⲚⲆ) ⲀⲢⲈⲔⲰⲚⲤ ⲆⲈ ⲞⲚ ⲈⲚⲈϨ ⲘⲠϨⲞϤ... ⲔⲰⲚⲤ ϨⲰⲰϤ ⲘⲠⲚⲞⲂⲈ ϨⲚⲦⲈⲚⲦⲞⲗⲎ. *Conjugation-forms* (+ expansion): (*IV* 205.18f.) ⲀⲨϬⲰϢⲦ ϨⲰⲰⲚ ⲈϨⲢⲀⲒ ⲈϪⲰⲚ / (*ibid.* 105.29) ⲤⲈⲈⲒⲢⲈ ⲚϨⲈⲚϨⲂⲎⲨⲈ ⲚⲤⲰⲂⲈ ϨⲰⲞⲨ ⲚⲘⲘⲀⲨ " with them too ". (*Pre*)*modifiers*: (*A 2* 76) ⲈⲨϪⲈ-ⲈⲦⲂⲈⲞⲨⲔⲦⲞ ⲈⲠⲀϨⲞⲨ ⲘⲘⲀⲦⲈ ⲀⲦϨⲒⲘⲈ ⲚⲗⲰⲦ ⲠϢⲰⲚⲈ... ⲈⲦⲂⲈⲞⲨϨⲨⲠⲞⲔⲢⲒⲤⲒⲤ ϨⲰⲰⲔ ⲚⲢⲰⲘⲈ ⲘⲠⲦⲢⲈⲦⲈⲔⲮⲨⲬⲎ ⲠϢⲰⲚⲈ / (*Wess.* 9 156a 18ff.) ...ⲈⲦⲢⲈⲬⲞⲞⲤ ϨⲰⲦⲦⲎⲨⲦⲚ ⲈⲢⲰⲦⲚ ⲚⲦⲈⲒϨⲈ.

6.1.2.3 The non-commuting, non-phoric ϨⲰⲰϤ: a "particle", exponent of interclausal cohesion [66]: " on the contrary ", " on the other hand ", " rather ", " actually ". The " particle " ϨⲰⲰϤ can be distinguished from the phoric (within clause extent) ϨⲰⲰ⸗ in the 3rd person sgl. masculine by criteria of contextual semantics: it is often adversative, and as a rule not inclusive; by its prevalence in certain configurations (mostly interrogative): (*A 1* 113, *A 2* 298) ⲈⲦⲂⲈⲞⲨ ϨⲰⲰϤ / (*III* 103.7) ϨⲒⲦⲚⲚⲒⲘ ϨⲰⲰϤ / ⲚⲒⲘ ϨⲰⲰϤ ⲠⲈⲦⲚⲀ- (*RE 10* 164a 2f., *Young* Ⲓⲅ, etc.) / (*RE 11* 15b 1) ⲞⲨ ϨⲰⲰϤ ⲠⲈ ⲠⲈⲔⲀϨⲈ; of course, also by the significant absence of concord (Polotsky 1961:304 n. 2 = *CP* 408): (*III* 161.13) ⲚⲐⲈ ϨⲰⲰϤ ⲚϨⲈⲚⲘⲀ ⲚⲈⲗⲞⲞⲗⲈ / (*ibid.* 163.19f.) ⲈⲠⲘⲀ ⲈⲦⲢⲈⲨⲈⲒⲢⲈ ⲘⲠⲀⲄⲀⲐⲞⲚ ⲀⲨⲈⲒⲢⲈ ϨⲰⲰϤ ⲘⲠⲠⲞⲚⲎⲢⲞⲚ / (*ibid.* 51.20) ⲔⲞⲨⲰϢ ϨⲰⲰϤ ⲈⲚⲀⲨ ⲈⲠϨⲎⲦ / (*ibid.* 56.10) (the deviation and evil of the Jewish congregation) ⲘⲚⲦⲀⲒⲞ ϨⲰⲰϤ ⲚⲦⲀⲒ (i.e. of the Christian one) / (*ibid.* 202.18f.) ⲦⲈϢⲒⲞⲈⲒⲔ ... ⲦⲈⲞⲨⲰⲘ-ⲚⲞⲂⲈ ϨⲰⲰϤ. Nevertheless, there is considerable overlapping between the augential, sequential (" ... in his turn ") and non-commutable ϨⲰⲰϤ. In many instances, the opposition between the macro-syntactic signal (interclausal relator, " anaphoric-regressive conjunct ", referring in a sense to the whole preceding cotext as to a nucleus) and its augential, clause-extent phoric homonym (referring to a noun or 3rd pers. sgl. masc. pronoun) cannot be maintained unless by subjective semasiological interpretation. Some such ambiguous instances: (*Ch.* 169.22ff.) ⲞⲚⲦⲰⲤ ⲞⲨⲀⲐⲎⲦ ϨⲰⲰϤ ⲀⲨⲰ ⲞⲨϢⲀϤⲦⲈ ⲠⲈ / (*ibid.* 77.41ff.) (ⲠⲀⲠϪⲀϪⲈ ⲠⲈ ⲚⲞⲨϪⲈ...) ⲠⲀⲠⲢⲰⲘⲈ ϨⲰⲰϤ ⲠⲈ ⲚⲈϪ- / (*III* 52.7) (ⲠⲘⲞⲞⲨ ⲈⲨϢⲀⲚⲦⲀϨϤ ⲘⲚⲠⲎⲢⲠ ϢⲀϤⲢ-ⲞⲨⲀ ⲚⲞⲨⲰⲦ) ⲠⲢⲰⲘⲈ ⲆⲈ ϨⲰⲰϤ ⲘⲠⲚⲞⲨⲦⲈ, ⲈϤϢⲀⲚⲘⲈⲦⲈⲬⲈ ⲈⲠⲈⲠ̄Ⲛ̄Ⲁ̄ ⲈⲦⲞⲨⲀⲀⲂ ϢⲀϤⲢ-ⲞⲨⲀ ⲚⲞⲨⲰⲦ ⲚⲘⲘⲀϤ / (*A 1* 162) ⲠⲈⲦⲈⲢⲈⲠⲢⲰⲘⲈ ⲘⲈⲈⲨⲈ ⲈⲢⲞϤ ϪⲈ-ⲞⲨⲤⲞⲨⲞ ⲠⲈ ⲈⲞⲨⲦⲰϨ ϨⲰⲰϤ ⲚϨⲞⲨⲞ ⲠⲈ.

6.1.3 {ⲚⲦⲞ⸗}: " non-inclusive (often exclusive) non-sequential symmetric confrontation " (" he, for one ", " he insofar as he is concerned ", " he, however " [66]) or reinforcement [67]; the *second* term is characterized.

6.1.3.1 *Post-referate* (immediate, non-immediate) placement.

6.1.3.1.1 Referate in *verb syntagm*: (a) *Actor pronoun* (more rarely, actor noun syntagm): (*A 2* 298) ⲈⲦⲂⲈⲞⲨ ϨⲰⲰϤ ⲈϤⲢⲒⲘⲈ ⲚϬⲒⲠⲀⲒ Ⲏ ⲈⲢⲈⲢⲒⲘⲈ ⲚⲦⲞ / (*ibid.* 267) (they say what they do not know will or will not

---

[65] Cf. Polotsky 1961:301 (= *CP* 405).

[66] Cf. Amélineau, *Schenoudi* II p. xciii (on " ⲘⲀⲦⲀⲘⲞⲔ Ⲏ ⲘⲀⲢⲒⲦⲀⲘⲞⲔ ⲀⲚⲞⲔ "): " Cette tournure de phrase est assez souvent employée par Schenoudi, et c'est une manière de parler tout à fait primitive: *les deux personnes y sont toujours opposées l'une à l'autre au sens contraire* " (my italics). As a matter of fact, the actual semantics depend on contextual factors, the address tone and interpersonal environment. This is especially striking in the case of the post-imperatival ⲚⲦⲞⲔ (see below).

[67] This is the " Verstärker " *par excellence* (Schwarze–Steinthal 466 " Verstärkung ", Stern §255 " Hervorhebung "; Czermak 1931 " dynamisch gestärkt ", and so on). Here is indeed the nearest thing to *bona fide* reinforcement, or better *insistence*, since here a true pronoun — prosodically marked as modifier — corroborates another. For pre-Coptic, cf. Hintze 1952: 290f. (" pronominale Hervorhebung "). (Incidentally, in LE — gr *ntf* (etc.) [Erman 1933:§682] " he too " is a striking *clause-final* construction of this augens.)

happen) +ⲚⲀⲦⲀⲘⲞⲔ ⲈⲠⲈ+ⲤⲞⲞⲨⲚ ⲀⲚⲞⲔ ⲈⲢⲞϤ (sim. *ibid.* 382, 521, *III* 128.19f., a recurring expression) / (*ibid.* 292) ⲘⲎ ⲀⲀⲆⲀⲘ +-ⳞⲎⲨ ⲚⲀⲀⲀⲨ ⲬⲈ-ⲀϤⲤⲰⲦⲘ ⲚⲤⲀⲠⲈⳞⲢⲞⲞⲨ ⲚⲦⲈϤⳞ̇ⳞⲒⲘⲈ, Ⲏ ⲀⲤ+-ⳞⲎⲨ ⲚⲦⲞⲤ ⲚⲀⲀⲀⲨ ⲬⲈ-ⲀⲤⲤⲰⲦⲘ ⲚⲤⲀⲠⲈⳞⲢⲞⲞⲨ ⲘⲠϤⲞϤ / (*ibid.* 153) ⲚⲦⲀⲚⲒⲘ ⲚⲢⲰⲘⲈ Ⲣ-ⲆⲒⲔⲀⲒⲞⲤ ⲈⲚⲈⳞ ⲈⲦⲂⲈⲠⲤⲀ ⲘⲠⲎⲒ ... ⲬⲈ-ⲈⲚⲚⲀⲈⲒⲢⲈ ⲀⲚⲞⲚ / (*ibid.* 374) ⲞⲨⲞⲒ ⲚⲀⲚ ⲬⲈ-ⲀⲚⲀⲘⲈⲀⲈⲒ, ⲈⲚⲀⲒⲀⲦⲞⲨ ⲚⲦⲞⲞⲨ ⲚⲚⲈⲦⲞⲨⲀ̇ⲀⲀⲂ ⲦⲎⲢⲞⲨ / (*P* 130² 6 Ⲡ̄Ⳓ-Ⲡ̄Ⲏ) ⲈⲢⲈⲤⲞⲦⲠ ⲚⲦⲞ ⲈⲚⲒⲘ... ⲘⲎ ⲈⲢⲈⲞⲨⲞⲦⲂ ⲚⲦⲞ ⲈⲦⲀⲒ... Ⲏ ⲈⲢⲈⳘⲰⲂⲈ ⲚⲦⲞ ⲈⲦⲀⲒ... ⲘⲎ ⲈⲚⲈⲤⳠ ⲚⲦⲞ ⲈⲦⲀⲒ... / (*III* 21.9f.) ⲈⳠⲬⲈ-ⲘⲠⲈⲤⲞⲨⲰⲚⲦ ⳘⲀ-ⲠⲞⲞⲨ, ⲀⲒⲤⲞⲨⲰⲚⲈ ⲀⲚⲞⲔ / NB., in *text-initial* position (*III* 44.18) ⧺ ⲈⲒⳞⲘⲞⲞⲤ ⲀⲚⲞⲔ ⳞⲒⳬⲚⲞⲨⲦⲞⲞⲨ / (*ibid.* 208.5) ⧺ ⲀⲒⲚⲀⲨ ⲀⲚⲞⲔ ⲈⲞⲨⲀ / (*A 1* 122) ⲈⲢⲈⲤⲞⲞⲨⲚ ⲦⲰⲚ Ⲏ ⲈⲢⲈⲈⲒⲘⲈ ⲦⲰⲚ Ⲏ ⲈⲒⲚⲀⲈⲒⲘⲈ ⲦⲰⲚ ⲀⲚⲞⲔ ⲬⲈ- / (*Cat.* 42.32) God said: ⲘⲀⲢⲚⲦⲀⲘⲒⲞ ⲚⲞⲨⲢⲰⲘⲈ, and not: +ⲚⲀⲦⲀⲘⲒⲞ ⲀⲚⲞⲔ / (*III* 156.16) (those who curse their neighbours) ⲈⲨⲈⳘⲰⲠⲈ ⲚⲦⲞⲞⲨ ⲈⲨⳞⲞⲨⲞⲢⲦ. Additional exx.: *IV* 38.21, *Wess. 9* 95a 20f., *RE 10* 163a 27, *Ch.* 117.8, 156.1ff., 183.57f., *A 1* 123, *A 2* 18, 78, *P* 130² 65 vo, *III* 65.8, 144.1, 201.9, 211.17 and many more; this is undoubtedly the commonest construction of this augens.

(b) *Post-imperatival* {ⲚⲦⲞ⸗}, more patently than in the case of other augentia, supplies gender-number characterization of the imperative form. Accordingly, the augens is here evidently different in syntactic status and the ensuing function: it is often indistinguishable from the *extraposed independent pronoun* (§6.1.3.3) [68]. (*P* 130¹ 35 Ⲣ̄Ⲙ̄Ⲅ̄) ⲔⲰ ⲚⲤⲰ ⲚⲦⲞ ⲘⲠⲀⳘⲀⲬⲈ / (*Cat.* 42.33) God said: ⲘⲀⲢⲚⲦⲀⲘⲒⲞ ⲚⲞⲨⲢⲰⲘⲈ, not: ⲦⲀⲘⲒⲞ ⲚⲦⲞⲔ / (*III* 88.11,14f.) ⲘⲠⲢⲢ-ⳞⲞⲦⲈ ⲚⲦⲰⲦⲚ, ⲘⲠⲢⲦⲢⲈⲨⲀⲚⲀⲔⲢⲒⲚⲈ ⲘⲘⲞⲞⲨ ⲚⲦⲰⲦⲚ / (*ibid.* 145.10) ⲘⲠⲢⲈⳠ-ⲔⲀⲔⲈⲒ ⲚⲦⲰⲦⲚ / (*IV* 86.8f.) ⳞⲔⲞ ⲚⲦⲞⲔ ⲀⲘⲀⳞⲦⲈ ⲚⲦⲞⲔ ⲈⲦⲘⲠⲞⲢⳘⲔ ⲈⲂⲞⲀ / (*ibid.* 189.3) ⳘⲰⲠⲈ ⲚⲦⲞⲔ ⲘⲠⲒⲤⲦⲞⲤ ⲈⳠⲞⲨⲀⲀⲂ / (*A 1* 78) +ⲚⲀⲬⲰ Ⲏ ⲬⳠ ⲚⲦⲞⲔ... +ⲚⲀ+ Ⲏ + ⲚⲦⲞⲔ.

6.1.3.1.2 The referate: *expansion suffix-pronoun* (no " direct object "?): (*IV* 119.20f., also 120.4, *P* 130² 61 ⲞⲄ) ⳞⲀⲦⲎⲚ Ⲏ ⳞⲀⲦⲚⲦⲎⲨⲦⲚ ⲚⲦⲰⲦⲚ, a recurring expression / (*P* 131⁵ 23 ro-vo) (if God did not spare the ancients), ⲈⲒⲈ ⲈϤⲚⲀ+-ⲤⲞ ⲈⲢⲞⲚ ⲀⲚⲞⲚ... / (*Ch.* 57.44ff.) Ⲏ ⲈⲢⲈⲚⲀⲘⲚⲦⳘⲀϤⲦⲈ ⳞⲎⲠ ⲈⲢⲞⲒ ⲀⲚⲞⲔ', — note the punctuation / (*Wess. 9* 147d 28f.) ⲞⲨ ⲈⲢⲞⲔ ⲚⲦⲞⲔ ⲠⲈ ⳘⲒⲚⲈ...

6.1.3.1.3 The referate: *possessor exponent* in the possessive-pronoun syntagm: (*A 1* 69) ⲠⲀⲚⲦⲰⲤ ⲘⲠⲈⲠⲈⲤⳘⲀⲬⲈ Ⲣ-ⳘⲀⲨ ⲚⲈ, Ⲏ ⲘⲠⲈⲠⳘ Ⲣ-ⳘⲀⲨ ⲚⲀⲤ ⲚⲦⲞ, sim. (*A 1* 122) ⲘⲠϤⳞⲀⳞ̇ⲈⲢⲀⲦϤ ⲈⳬⲘⲠⳘ ⲚⲦⲞ *your* temple, vs. the old Temple / (*IV* 207.6f.) ⲠⲀ-ⲚⲈⲦⲞⲚⳞ ⲘⲀⲨⲀⲀⲨ ⲠⲈ... ⲠⲀ-ⲚⲈⲦⲘⲞⲞⲨⲦ ⲀⲚ ⲚⲦⲞⲞⲨ ⲠⲈ. In the two last constructions, the incidence of {ⲚⲦⲞ⸗} is remarkably rarer than for ⳞⲰⳘ⸗. So too, in the case of the next one.

6.1.3.1.4 The referate: *noun syntagm* (in extraposition): (*III* 109.19ff.) ⲚⲈⲒⲀⲦⳘⲠ-ⳞⲘⲞⲦ ⲆⲈ ⲚⲦⲞⲞⲨ ⲀⲨⲰ ⲚⲈⲒⲀⲦⲘⲠⳘⲀ ⲘⲠⲈϤⲦⲀⲀⲤ ⲚⲀⲨ ⲈⲈⲒⲘⲈ ⲈⲘⲘⲨⲤⲦⲎⲢⲒⲞⲚ.

6.1.3.1.5 The referate: *pronominal subject of interrogative Nominal Sentence* (see also §6.1.3.2), interlocutive person only? ⲚⲦⲔ-ⲚⲒⲘ ⲚⲦⲞⲔ (*Cat.* 42.14, 43.8) / ⲚⲦⲔ-ⲞⲨⲞⲨ ⲚⲦⲞⲔ (*A 1* 210). The augens appears to be here a rhetoricity marker (no answer expected).

6.1.3.2 *Pre-referate placement* [69]: {ⲚⲦⲞ⸗} colon-second or intercolary. (a) Following ⲚⲐⲈ: (*A 2* 307) ⲚⲐⲈ ⲚⲦⲞⲔ ⲈⲦⲔⲤⲞⲞⲨⲚ / (*IV* 112.19) ⲚⲐⲈ ⲀⲚⲞⲔ ⲚⲦⲀⲒⲈⲒⲘⲈ / (*Ch.* 144.2f.) ⲚⲐⲈ ⲚⲦⲞⲤ ⲈⲦⲤⳬⳠ ⲘⲘⲞⲤ.

(b) Following the focus modifier in interrogative (focus-initial) focalization patterns (§2.6): (*A 2* 519) ⲚⲀⳘ ⲚⳞⲈ ⲀⲚⲞⲔ ⲈⲒⲚⲀⲈⲒⲢⲈ ⲚⲞⲨⳞⲰⲂ ⲈⳬⲰⲔ / (*ibid.* 11) ⲈⲦⲂⲈⲞⲨ ⲚⲦⲞⲞⲨ ⲞⲨⲞⲒ ⲚⲀⲨ ⲀⲚ / (*P* 130⁵ 24 Ⲣ̄Ⲡ̄Ⲁ̄) ⲈⲦⲂⲈⲞⲨ ⲀⲚⲞⲚ ⲚⲦⲚⲞⲨⲰⳘ ⲀⲚ ⲈⳬⲞⲞⲤ / (*Ch.* 169.7f.) ⲚⲀⳘ ⲚⳞⲈ ⲚⲦⲞⲞⲨ ⲈⲨⲚⲀⲢ-ⲂⲞⲀ..., vs. ⲚⲀⳘ ⲚⳞⲈ ⲈⲨⲚⲀⲢ-ⲂⲞⲀ ⲚⲦⲞⲞⲨ, e.g. *III* 75.12. See §6.1.3.3 on the *augens: extraposed indep. pronoun* issue.

[68] Cf. the post-imperatival dependent pronoun in Middle Egyptian (Gardiner §337) and of course comparable constructions in numerous old and modern languages.

[69] Polotsky 1961:310ff. (= *CP* 414 ff.).

(c) The referate: 3rd person *pronominal subject in the Nominal Sentence*: (*A 1* 108) ΠΛϬΕ ΠΛϬΕ ΝΤΟΟΥ ΝΕ.

(d) Following various predications (augens or extraposed pronoun?): (*Ch.* 90.8ff.) ⲌⲰⲤ ⲈⲨⲬⲈ-ⲚⲦⲞⳤ ΠⲈ ⲀⲚⲞⲚ ⲌⲘⲠⲈⲦⲚⲈⲒⲢⲈ ⲘⲘⲞⳤ / (*A 1* 61) ⲘⲚⲌⲦⲞⲢ ⲚⲦⲞⲞⲨ ⲈⲢⲞⲞⲨ / (*A 1* 113) ⲈⲂⲞⲖ ⲬⲈ-ⲘⲚⲌⲀⲠ ⲈⲠⲀⲒ... Ⲏ ⲬⲈ-ⲘⲚⲌⲀⲠ ⲚⲦⲞⲞⲨ ⲈⲚⲈⲦⲘⲘⲀⲨ.

6.1.3.3 {ⲚⲦⲞ⸗}: *augens* vs. *independent pronoun, extraposed*[70]. On the face of it, the independent pronoun — the prosodically full (or unmarked) pronoun *lexeme*[71] — is conspicuous in that, like a noun syntagm, it may constitute a whole colon or be the initial component of one. The *augens* {ⲚⲦⲞ⸗}, on the other hand, being prosodically marked as dependent (as a modifier?) can only join (or "fasten onto") and boundary-mark an existing colon. In the reality of the written *parole*, however, there are few cases in which this difference can be detected or formally determined in the text (the more so since the pronoun, like the post-referate augens, occurs as an expansion — an apposed pronominal lexeme, lexicalizing suffix-pronouns). Two especially striking such cases are the appositive phrases '*indep. pron.* + *noun*'[72] and '*indep. pron.* + ⲀⲨⲰ/ⲘⲚ + *noun*/*indep. pron.*'. In the former we find (a) the pronoun serving to introduce a nominal apposition — in complementary distribution with ⲚϬⲒ-: the *interlocutive* persons are here prevalent, 'ⲚⲦⲞⳤ + *noun*' being uncommon; (b) 'ⲚⲦⲞⲔ + vocative noun'. For the latter, we find naturally only interlocutive persons. Both cola tend to be sentence-final. Polotsky's "rule of thumb"[73], according to which an augential {ⲚⲦⲞ⸗} occupies second position, whereas the independent pronoun does not, assumes that the augens, like Greek-origin enclitics, is invariably colon-second (*pronoun*: ⲚⲀⲰ ⲚⲌⲈ ⲚⲦⲞⳤ — vs. *augens*: ⲚⲀⲰ ⲚⲦⲞⳤ ⲚⲌⲈ —). Since I believe the augens can (like other enclitics) be colon-final, marking the colon boundary, as well as colon-second; and since the augens (like other native enclitics) may have properties different from the "core" group of Greek-origin ones (§6.0.3), it is questionable whether this distinction is really so tangible. It may imply no more than the variability of the prosodic contour of ⲚⲀⲰ ⲚⲌⲈ. Incidentally, I find in Shenoute no clear instance of ⲚⲀⲰ ⲚⲦⲞⳤ ⲚⲌⲈ - (augens), while we do find some of ⲚⲀⲰ ⲚⲌⲈ ⲚⲦⲞⳤ with ⲚⲦⲞⳤ, the invariable "particle" (§3.1.3.4), evidently enclitic. It is of course not to be taken for granted that {ⲚⲦⲞ⸗} and ⲚⲦⲞⳤ share the same prosodic properties.

Examples: (a) '*indep. pron.* + *noun*': (*P* 130[1] 136 ⲦⲖⲈ) ⲈⲚⲦϬⲀⲒⲎⲨ ⲚⲞⲨⲎⲢ ⲀⲚⲞⲚ ⲚⲈⲒⲀⲦⲤⲰⲦⲘ / (*P* 131[5] 36 ⲤⲘⲂ) ⲠⲀⲒ ⲚⲦⲀⳤ⬚Ⲭ Ⲓ-ⲤⲀⲢⳅ ⲈⲦⲂⲎⲎⲦⲚ ⲀⲚⲞⲚ ⲚⲈⲢⲰⲘⲈ (sic) / (*A 1* 74) ⲚⲦⲚⲎⲠ ⲀⲚ Ⲏ ⲚⲦⲈⲚⲠ ⲀⲚ ⲚⲦⲞ ⲦⲤⲨⲚⲀⲄⲰⲄⲎ / (*III* 137.25) ...Ⲏ ⲈⲒⲰⲀⲚⲬⲞⲞⲤ ⲀⲚⲞⲔ ⲠⲒⲈⲂⲒⲎⲚ... / (*ibid.* 13.13f.) ⲠⲀⲈⲂⲒⲎⲚ (i.e. "my humble person") ⲀⲨⲰ ⲚⲈⲚⲈⲂⲒⲎⲚ ⲌⲒⲞⲨⲤⲞⲠ ⲀⲚⲞⲚ-ⲚⲈⲔⲌⲘⲌⲀⲖ ⲚⲈⲤⲚⲎⲨ / (*Ch.* 56.29ff.) ⲠⲀⲚⲦⲰⲤ' ⲞⲨⲚⲦⲀⲚ-ⲦⲈⲚϬⲞⲢϬⲤ ⲌⲰⲰⲚ' ⲀⲚⲞⲚ' ⲘⲘⲞⲚⲀⲬⲞⲤ ⲀⲨⲰ ⲚⲞⲨⲎⲎⲂ (note the colon-boundary punctuation; also that ⲌⲰⲰ⸗ and the *augens* {ⲚⲦⲞ⸗} are not attested as compatible) / (*III* 60.4f.) ⳤⲬⲰ ⲄⲀⲢ ⲘⲘⲞⲤ ⲚⲦⲞⳤ ⲠⲬⲞⲈⲒⲤ ⲬⲈ-. Additional exx.: *III* 68.9, 70.17f., 96.9f., 134.25, *A 2* 31, etc.

(b) 'ⲚⲦⲞⲔ + voc. noun': (*III* 47.4f.) ⲆⲒⲔⲀⲒⲰⲤ ⲈⲨⲘⲞⲤⲦⲈ ⲘⲘⲰⲦⲚ... ⲚⲦⲰⲦⲚ Ⲱ ⲚⲌⲀⲒⲢⲈⲦⲒⲔⲞⲤ.

(c) '*indep. pron.* + ⲀⲨⲰ/ⲘⲚ + *indep. pron.*/*noun*: (*III* 185.6f.) ⲀⲚⲰⳘⲚ ⲌⲚⲞⲨⲘⲔⲀⲌ ⲚⲌⲎⲦ ⲀⲚⲞⲚ ⲀⲨⲰ ⲚⲦⲰⲦⲚ / (*A 1* 131) ⲦⲰⲔ ⲚⲌⲎⲦ ⲚⲦⲞⲔ ⲀⲨⲰ ⲚⲦⲰⲦⲚ / (*ibid.* 71) ⲈⲚⲚⲀⲨⳤⲒ-ⲠⲢⲞⲞⲨⳘ ⲘⲠⲈⲒⲌⲰⲂ ⲚⲞⲨⲰⲦ ⲘⲚⲚⲈⲚⲈⲢⲎⲨ ⲚⲀⲰ ⲚⲌⲈ ⲀⲚⲞⲚ ⲀⲨⲰ ⲚⲦⲞ / (*IV* 38.17f.) ⲈⲦⲂⲈⲞⲨ ⲚⲄⲚⲀⲈⲒ ⲀⲚ ⲈⲠⲀⲒⲠⲚⲞⲚ ⲚⲦⲞⲔ ⲀⲨⲰ ⲚⲦⲞⲤ / (*Ch.* 159-160) ...ⲀⲖⲖⲀ ⲌⲚⲚⲈⲚⲔⲈⲎⲒ ⲞⲚ ⲀⲚⲞⲚ ⲘⲚⲚⲈⲚⳘⲎⲢⲈ ⲀⲨⲰ ⲚⲈⲚⲈⲒⲞⲦⲈ / (*ibid.* 42.14ff.) ...ⲌⲚⲚⲞⲂⲈ ⲚⲀⲒ ⲈⲦⲔⲞ ⲚⲞⲨⲞⲈⲒⲈ ⲈⲢⲞⲞⲨ... ⲚⲦⲞⲔ ⲘⲚⲚⲈⲦⲈⲒⲚⲈ ⲘⲘⲞⲔ / (*III* 37.12ff.) ⲞⲨⲤⲘⲞⲨ ⲚⲀⲰ ⲚⲀⲈⲒⲎⲤ ⲠⲈⲦⲌⲒⲬⲰⲚ ⲀⲚⲞⲚ ⲘⲚⲚⲈⲚⲈⲒⲞⲦⲈ ⲘⲚⲚⲈⲚⳘⲎⲢⲈ... / (*ibid.*

---

[70] Polotsky 1961:295 (= *CP* 399), 309f. (= *CP* 413f.), 311 (= *CP* 415) n. 2.

[71] In Brøndal's term (1943:103), {ⲚⲦⲞ⸗} is the "*forme substantielle*" of the pronoun, *vs.* the "*formes fonctionnelles*" {-ⳤ}, {ⳤ-}, {ⲀⲚⲄ-}, {ⲠⲈ} and the augens (modifier pronoun) {ⲚⲦⲞ⸗}.

[72] Czermak 1931:§259.

[73] 1961:§17.

157.2) ...ⲀⲨⲰ ⲚⲦⲀⲦⲘⲈⲒⲘⲈ ⲀⲚⲞⲔ ⲞⲨⲦⲈⲠⲌⲀⲖⲞ ⲞⲨⲦⲈ ⲚⲌⲀⲖⲞⲒ...   Cases like (*III* 88.11f.) ⲈⲒⲤⲌⲎⲎⲦⲈ ⲀⲚⲞⲔ ✝✝ ⲞⲨⲂⲈ- or (*ibid.* 36.24f.) ⲰⲀⲚⲦⲈⲞⲨ... ⲰⲰⲠⲈ ⲀⲚⲞⲚ ⲘⲠⲚ- are ambiguous, as are in my opinion ⲚⲀⲰ ⲚⲌⲈ ⲚⲦⲞⲴ (etc., §6.1.3.2).

6.1.3.4   Non-commuting (non-phoric) ⲚⲦⲞⳓ is a " particle "[74], an inter-clausal relator, often (like ⲌⲰⲰⳓ, §6.1.2.3) accompanied by ⲀⲖⲖⲀ or ⲆⲈ. Indeed, its synchronic relation to the commuting (i.e. analyzable) augens {ⲚⲦⲞⲴ} is analogous to that of the particle ⲌⲰⲰⳓ to the augens ⲌⲰⲰⲴ. On the formal level, this is a case of "freezing" or fossilization of the pronoun component, which is the cohesion (within clause-extent) or segment-reference factor, in the unmarked gender, namely the masculine (3rd person sgl.)[75]. This cancels its segment-reference, its phoricity (a cancelling evident in instances of discord). On the functional level, this entails a shift from *intra*-clausal modification to *inter*-clausal relation[76]. Some typical and instructive cases of the particle, distinguishable from the augens (3rd pers. sgl. masc.) mainly by discord and sometimes by placement: (*A 1* 123) ⲞⲨⲰⲠⲎⲢⲈ ⲠⲈ ⲚⲦⲞⳓ... | ...ⲈⳓⲰⲀⲚ- / (*A 2* 540) ⲚⲀⲰ ⲚⲌⲈ ⲚⲦⲞⳓ... | ...ⲚⲈⲚⲦⲀⲚⲰⲀⲬⲈ ⲈⲦⲂⲎⲎⲦⲞⲨ... ⲈⳓⲚⲀ✝-ⲤⲞ ⲈⲢⲞⲞⲨ (also *III* 153.10; *vs.* ⲚⲀⲰ ⲚⲦⲞⳓ ⲚⲌⲈ *IV* 195.2; in *A 1* 295 ⲚⲀⲰ ⲚⲦⲞⳓ ⲚⲌⲈ ⲘⲚⲚⲤⲀⲠⲘⲞⲨ ⲚⲦⲈⲦⲚ✝-ⲚⲞⲨⳓⲤ ⲚⲀⳓ ⲀⲚ ⲚⲦⲞⳓ, the augens (post-referate) and particle occur in one clause[77]) / (*Rossi 2/3* 27) ⲀⲖⲖⲀ ⲈⲨⲢⲠⲔⲈⲤⲞⲂⲦⲈ ⲚⲀⲨ ⲚⲦⲞⳓ ⲚⲞⲨⲔⲢⲒⲘⲀ / (*III* 174-5 *passim*) ⲞⲨⲞⲈⲒ ⲆⲈ ⲚⲀⲚ ⲚⲦⲞⳓ | ⲈⲚⲰⲀⲚ—, a recurring expression / (*ibid.* 76.15f.) ⲠⲔⲀⲒⲢⲞⲤ ⲈⲦⲞⲨⲘⲈⲈⲨⲈ ⲚⲦⲞⳓ ⲈⲠⲀⲒ ⲈⲦⲰⲀⲬⲈ ⲬⲈ-. Note the following indicative cases of the particle in construction with other elements: ⲀⲨⲰ ⲚⲦⲞⳓ, Ⲏ ⲚⲦⲞⳓ " and moreover ", " or even " and the like: *III* 32.1, 62.26, *IV* 80.20, 206.28, 207.25f. etc. (contrast with Ⲏ ⲔⲈⲞⲨⲀ ⲚⲦⲞⳓ, *IV* 46.29); — ⲞⲚ ⲚⲦⲞⳓ " at least ", *III* 93.24; — ⲆⲈ ⲚⲦⲞⳓ is of course ubiquitous (e.g. *III* 145. 13); ⲈⲂⲞⲖ ⲀⲚ ⲬⲈ-... ⲀⲖⲖⲀ ⲈⲂⲞⲖ ⲚⲦⲞⳓ ⲬⲈ-, *III* 19.8, 186.5, *A 1* 71, *P* 130¹ 139 ⲦⲘⲈ, 130² 10 ⲤⲀⲐ etc.; — ⲀⲚ ⲚⲦⲞⳓ in rhetorical questions, *A 1* 125, 152, *Wess. 9* 106a 11ff. Consider also the following striking instances of the particle: (*III* 192.19f.) (ⲘⲠⲢⲬⲞⲞⲤ ⲌⲚ ⲦⲈⲒⲈⲠⲒⲤⲦⲞⲖⲎ ⲬⲈ-) ⲀⲖⲖⲀ ⲰⲰ ⲘⲘⲞⲤ ⲚⲦⲞⳓ ⲬⲈ- / (*IV* 12.10f.) (ⲘⲠⲢⲰⲘⲈ ⲀⲚ ⲠⲈⲦⲔⲦⲞ ⲘⲘⲞⲤ...) ⲚⲦⲞⲤ ⲚⲦⲞⳓ ⲠⲈⲦⲔⲦⲞ ⲘⲠⲢⲰⲘⲈ / (*ibid.* 13.9) (this is not the occasion to discuss these things) ⲀⲖⲖⲀ ⲈⲬⲰ ⲚⲦⲞⳓ ⲌⲚⲞⲨⲘⲈⲢⲞⲤ / (*ibid.* 15.5) (not in order to slay sinner and innocent alike) ⲀⲖⲖⲀ ⲈⲦⲢⲈⲤ✝ ⲚⲦⲞⳓ ⲚⲚⲈⲚⲦⲀⲨⲢ-ⲚⲞⲂⲈ ⲈⲦⲞⲞⲦⳓ ⲘⲠⳉⲒ-ⲔⲂⲀ / (*ibid.* 16.18f.) ⲈⲰⲀⲨⲬⲞⲢⲤ ⲀⲚ ⲌⲒⲦⲚⲌⲈⲚⲔⲞⲞⲨⲈ, ⲀⲖⲖⲀ ⲈⲰⲀⲨⲬⲈⲢ-ⲤⲚⳓⲈ ⲚⲒⲘ ⲚⲦⲞⳓ | ⲈⲂⲞⲖ ⲌⲒⲦⲞⲞⲦⲤ / (*ibid.* 157.21ff.) ⲀⲚ✝ⲦⲢⲈⲨⲠⲰⲢⲈⲔ (sic) ⲘⲠⲈⲒⲈⲚⲦⲎⳓ... ⲚⲦⲀⲨⲦⲰⳓⲈ ⲘⲘⲞⳓ ⲚⲦⲞⳓ / (*III* 165.19) ⲈⲒⲘⲈ ⲚⲦⲞⳓ | Ⲱ ⲚⲢⲰⲘⲈ ⲚⲀⲦⲤⲰⲦⲘ: post-imperatival particle (" *doch* ", " *donc* ", with an additional " rest " prosodic signalling role?). The augens/particle are variant readings in (*IV* 103.1) ⲈⲚⲦⲰⲢⲠ ⲘⲘⲞⲞⲨ ⲀⲚ, ⲈⲨⲦⲰⲢⲠ ⲘⲘⲞⲚ ⲚⲦⲞⳓ/ⲚⲦⲞⲞⲨ.

6.1.4   ⲘⲀⲨⲀⲀⲴ, ⲘⲘⲒⲚ ⲘⲘⲞⲴ, ⲞⲨⲀⲀⲴ

6.1.4.1   ⲘⲀⲨⲀⲀⲴ: Polemic, contrastive, exclusive, (less usually) reflexive modification: " ... alone ", " only... ", " ... (him)self- (by [his] own agency, with no one's intervention) "[78] (μόνος/ μόνον, ἐμ-/σε-/ἑαυτοῦ, κατ' ἰδίαν).

---

[74] Cf. Polotsky 1961:304 (= *CP* 408), 309f. (= *CP* 413f.), Stern §598, *Dictionary* 232-3.

[75] Compare §5.1.2 above.

[76] Cf. the illuminating parallel in Old and Middle Egyptian, namely *r.f, r.k, r.i*... the analyzable augens and modifier, where *r*- is the modification, and *-f* the cohesion exponent, *vs. jrf/rf* (the latter, at least in the *Coffin Texts*, a prosodically included alternant), an unanalyzable, invariable particle, " frozen " in the unmarked gender and non-phoric within clause-extent but signalling inter-clausal relation. Celtic parallels are Irish *leis* (3rd sgl. masc. form of the preposition *le*-) and Welsh *ynteu* (old 3rd sgl. masc. " conjunctive " pronoun).

[77] Cf. (particle *vs.* augens/extraposed pronoun) ⲚⲀⲰ ⲚⲦⲞⳓ ⲚⲌⲈ ⲠⲤⲰⲘⲀ Ⲏ ⲠⲢⲰⲘⲈ ⲦⲎⲢⳓ ⲚⲀⳓⲘⲒⲚⲈ... ⲚⲀⲰ ⲚⲌⲈ ⲚⲦⲞⲔ ⲈⲔⲚⲀⲢ-ⲰⲀⲨ... (*BLOr.* 3581A 71, No. 202 ⲢⲠⲀ).

[78] Stern §257, Schwarze–Steinthal 345f., 468 (" *allein* " → " *selbst* ").

6.1.4.1.0.1　1st sgl. ⲘⲀⲨⲀⲀⲦ, 2nd sgl. fem. ⲘⲀⲨⲀⲀⲦⲈ. Two fluctuating bases, ⲘⲀⲨⲀⲀ= (with all persons, sgl. and plural) and ⲘⲀⲨⲀ(Ⲁ)Ⲧ= (all *plural* persons, but also 3rd sgl. masc. and fem.; 2nd plur. ⲘⲀⲨⲀ(Ⲁ)Ⲧ-ⲐⲎⲨⲦⲚ); acc. to *Dict.* 198a, ⲘⲀⲨⲀⲦ- is Shenoutean.

6.1.4.1.1　ⲘⲀⲨⲀⲀ= in cohesion with a *verb syntagm* (or verb lexeme). (a) With a *single pronominal referate* (NB. This construction is not attested with ⲘⲘⲒⲚ ⲘⲘⲞ=); "adverbal". *Reflexive*: (*Ch.* 71.6ff.) ⲞⲨ ⲠⲈⲦⲚⲀⲦ-ⲌⲎⲨ ⲘⲘⲞϤ... ⲚⲤⲀⲦⲢⲀⲦ-ⲞⲤⲈ ⲘⲀⲨⲀⲀⲦ / (*ibid.* 132.15ff.) ⲚⲔⲈⲘⲈⲖⲞⲤ ⲚⲦⲀⲚⲦⲀⲔⲞⲞⲨ ⲘⲀⲨⲀⲀⲚ. "Only": (*A 2* 429, not Sh.) ⲌⲰⲤ ⲈⲠⲈⲦⲈϢϢⲈ ⲠⲈ ⲔⲀⲦⲀⲠⲤⲰⲘⲀ ⲈⲦⲢⲈϤⲘⲞⲨ ⲘⲀⲨⲀⲀϤ ⲚϬⲒⲠⲠⲞⲚⲎⲢⲞⲤ / (*III* 109.16) (ⲦⲈⲤⲂⲰ ⲘⲘⲈ) ⲦⲀⲒ ⲚⲦⲀⲨϬⲘ-ϬⲞⲘ ⲘⲀⲨⲀⲀⲨ ⲚϢⲞⲠⲤ ⲈⲢⲞⲞⲨ ⲚϬⲒⲚⲈⲚⲦⲀⲨⲦⲀⲀⲤ ⲚⲀⲨ ⲈⲈⲒⲘⲈ... *Non-reflexive*, "alone", "on one's own", "by oneself (also = with no outside help)": (*RE 10* 163a 36f.) ⲚⲈⲦϬⲈⲈⲦ ⲘⲀⲨⲀⲀⲨ (cf. *IV* 91.22 ⲠⲈⲦⲞⲨⲈϢ-ϬⲰ ⲘⲀⲨⲀⲀϤ, 156.6, etc.) / (*III* 159.12) ...ⲈⲨⲌⲘⲞⲞⲤ ⲘⲀⲨⲀⲀⲨ / (*RE 10* 164b 31f.) ⲈⲚⲈⲚⲦⲀⲠⲚⲞⲨⲦⲈ ⲞⲨⲰϢ ⲈⲦⲢⲈϤⲘⲞⲨ ⲘⲀⲨⲀⲀϤ, opp. to line 33 ⲠⲚⲞⲨⲦⲈ ⲠⲈⲚⲦⲀϤⲘⲞⲞⲨⲦϤ; *cf.* ⲀⲤⲘⲞⲞⲨⲦⲤ ⲘⲀⲨⲀⲀⲤ *III* 97.19, 204.10 etc. / (*IV* 161.19) ⲚⲚⲈⲢϢⲘⲈ ϤⲒ-ⲠⲔϢϢⲤ ⲘⲀⲨⲀⲀϤ / (*ibid.* 103.15f.) ⲚⲚⲈⲨⲔⲀⲀⲨ ⲘⲀⲨⲀⲀⲨ / (*A 2* 31) ⲈⲚⲈⲚⲞⲨⲀⲀⲂ ⲘⲀⲨⲀⲀⲦⲚ "had we alone been pure". More exx.: *IV* 107.26, 157.28, *A 1* 135, *A 2* 110 (ⲚⲦⲈⲦⲚϢⲒⲠⲈ ⲀⲚ ⲘⲀⲨⲀⲀⲦⲐⲨⲦⲚ "you are not ashamed of yourselves"), 535, etc.

(b) With a double (identical) referate; here the overlapping with ⲘⲘⲒⲚ ⲘⲘⲞ= is more in evidence. Reflexive (contrastive, often "with no outside help"): (*P 130² 54 ⲦⲒⲀ*) ⲘⲀⲢⲚⲦ-ⲤⲂⲰ ⲚⲀⲚ ⲘⲀⲨⲀⲀⲚ / (*A 2* 190) Ⲏ ⲈⲢⲈⲒϢⲌⲀⲚⲚⲎⲤ ⲚⲀⲀⲢⲚⲀ ⲘⲘⲞϤ ⲘⲀⲨⲀⲀϤ / (*Miss.* 284) ...ⲈϤⲞⲨⲈϢ-ⲘⲞⲞⲨⲦϤ ⲘⲀⲨⲀⲀϤ (also *A 2* 93, 509) / (*A 2* 70) ⲀⲨⲤⲞⲨⲰⲚⲞⲨ ⲘⲀⲨⲀⲀⲨ (but not the things they had come for; also *IV* 188.12) / (*A 2* 110) ⲀⲦⲈⲦⲚ-ⲘⲈⲤⲦⲈ-ⲐⲎⲨⲦⲚ ⲘⲀⲨⲀⲀⲦⲐⲨⲦⲚ / (*ibid.* 398) ⲈⲔⲈⲒⲢⲈ ⲘⲘⲞⲔ ⲘⲀⲨⲀⲀⲔ ⲚⲦⲀⲖⲀⲒⲠⲰⲢⲞⲤ / (*A 2* 501, 503) ⲘⲠⲢϢⲰⲠⲈ ⲈⲔⲈⲒⲢⲈ ⲘⲘⲞⲔ ⲚⲆⲒⲔⲀⲒⲞⲤ ⲘⲀⲨⲀⲀⲔ/ⲚϤⲤⲨⲚⲌⲒⲤⲦⲀ ⲘⲘⲞϤ ⲘⲀⲨⲀⲀϤ ⲌⲰⲤ ⲆⲒⲔⲀⲒⲞⲤ/ⲈϤⲦⲀⲘⲒⲞ ⲘⲘⲞϤ ⲘⲀⲨⲀⲀϤ ⲌⲰⲤ ⲆⲒⲔⲀⲒⲞⲤ / (*RE 10* 164a 27f.) ...ⲈⲚⲦ ⲘⲘⲞⲚ ⲈⲌⲢⲀⲒ ⲈⲠⲚⲞⲂⲈ ⲘⲀⲨⲀⲀⲚ / (*Cl. Pr. 21* f.b ro) ⲠⲈⲨⲬⲠⲒⲞ ⲈⲦⲈⲢⲈⲠⲞⲨⲀ ⲠⲞⲨⲀ ⲬⲠⲒⲞ ⲘⲘⲞϤ ⲚⲌⲎⲦϤ ⲘⲀⲨⲀⲀϤ / (*III* 35.20 parall. *Ch.* 130.30ff.) ⲈⲒⲦⲀⲒⲞ ⲀⲚ ⲘⲘⲞⲒ ⲘⲀⲨⲀⲀⲦ / (*A 2* 510) ⲚⲈⲤⲞⲞⲨ... ⲚⲈⲦⲞ ⲚⲞⲨϢⲚϢ ⲈⲢⲞⲞⲨ ⲘⲀⲨⲀⲀⲨ / (*ibid.* 529) ...ⲈⲒⲌⲘⲞⲞⲤ ⲈⲒϢⲀⲬⲈ ⲚⲘⲘⲀⲒ ⲘⲀⲨⲀⲀⲦ / (*ibid.* 384) ⲀⲚⲞⲚ ⲠⲈⲦⲠⲎⲦ ⲚⲤⲰⲚ ⲘⲀⲨⲀⲀⲚ; note the recurring expression "ⲦⲘⲚⲦⲢⲈϤⲔⲀ-ⲌⲦⲎ= ⲈⲢⲞ= ⲘⲀⲨⲀⲀ=" (*III* 176.5f., *IV* 42.4f., 116.8f., *Mun.* 163, *A 1* 219, etc.). This is a very common construction; additional exx. are *III* 168.1f., 221.21f., *IV* 32.12f., 92.6f., *Ch.* 180.15ff., *Wess. 9* 87a 9f., *A 2* 118, 372, 519, etc.

6.1.4.1.2　ⲘⲀⲨⲀⲀ= in cohesion with a *pronoun/noun syntagm*, mostly as a co-focusing modifier referring to the predicate of a Nominal Sentence/Cleft Sentence:

(a) Referate: ⲡ-, demonstrative, proper noun: (*A 2* 298) ⲔⲀⲒⲄⲀⲢ ⲠⲚⲞⲨⲦⲈ ⲀⲚ ⲘⲀⲨⲀⲀϤ... ⲠⲈⲦⲞ ⲘⲘⲚⲦⲢⲈ / (*ibid.* 32) ⲀϢⲎⲔ ⲠⲒⲆⲞⲨⲘⲀⲒⲞⲤ ⲘⲀⲨⲀⲀϤ ⲀⲚ ⲠⲈⲚⲦⲀϤⲘⲈⲢⲈ-ⲚϢⲀⲬⲈ... / (*A 1* 250) ⲦⲘⲚⲦⲀⲦⲤⲰⲦⲘ ⲘⲀⲨⲀⲀⲤ ⲦⲈ (scil. ⲦⲈⲦϢⲞⲞⲠ ⲘⲠⲆⲀⲒⲘⲰⲚ ⲈⲦⲘⲘⲀⲨ) / (*ibid.* 251) ⲚⲀⲒ ⲆⲈ ⲘⲀⲨⲀⲀⲨ ⲀⲚ ⲚⲈⲦⲚⲘⲘⲀϤ / (*Ryl. Cat.* 32 No. 67 ⲦϤⲐ) ⲚⲦⲞⲔ ⲠⲈ ⲠⲚⲞⲨⲦⲈ ⲘⲘⲈ ⲘⲀⲨⲀⲀⲔ: # *subject-copula-predicate* #: "You are the only true God" (perhaps a solemn pro-/acclamatory ["anacletic"] "theological" Nominal Sentence pattern [the ἐγώ εἰμι, σὺ εἶ-type], with both terms of equal informative weight; is ⲚⲦⲞⲔ the referate? see (d) below with more exx.); compare the recurring ⲠⲚⲞⲨⲦⲈ ⲘⲘⲈ ⲘⲀⲨⲀⲀϤ (*Wess. 9* 161b 10f., *A 2* 547, *P 131⁶* 105 ro), ⲠⲘⲈ ⲘⲀⲨⲀⲀϤ "the only true One", "the only One who is of truth" (*Ch.* 59.29ff.; for the masc. determinator see §5.1.1.0.1), ⲠⲞⲨⲀ ⲘⲀⲨⲀⲀϤ ⲠⲚⲞⲨⲦⲈ (*P 130⁵* 35 vo) / (*IV* 184.8) ⲦⲤⲨⲚⲀⲄⲰⲄⲎ ⲚⲚⲒⲞⲨⲆⲀⲒ ⲘⲀⲨⲀⲀⲨ (and not ours) / NB. (*A 2* 354) ⲚⲀ-ⲚⲈⲦⲘⲠϢⲀ ⲘⲀⲨⲀⲀⲨ ⲚⲈ, sim. (ⲦⲀ-ⲚⲈⲦⲘⲠϢⲀ ⲘⲀⲨⲀⲀⲦⲞⲨ) *A 1* 193. More exx.: *Ch.* 95.11ff., *Wess. 9* 143a 9ff, *A 2* 489, 503, etc. Note here the striking prevalence of adjunctal negation ("not only...", see §6.1.4.1.4), and the very common and typically Shenoutean ⲈⲒⲘⲎⲦⲒ Ⲉ-/ⲈⲢⲞ= ⲘⲀⲨⲀⲀ= "but for X alone" (with pronoun: *III* 90.3, *Wess. 9* 147b 22f., 162a 9f.; with noun syntagm: *III* 186.28, *IV* 62.11ff., 171.15, 205.21f., *Ch.* 99.55ff., *Wess. 9* 162b 14ff.); this has a native Coptic equivalent in ⲚⲤⲀ- ⲘⲀⲨⲀⲀ= (*Ch.* 60.40f., 109.24ff.) and ϢⲀⲦⲚ- ⲘⲀⲨⲀⲀ= (*ibid.* 18.51f.).

(b) Referate: ⲞⲨ-/ⲌⲈⲚ- "only...", "a mere..."; again, usually referring to the predicate of a Nom. Sentence/Cleft Sentence: (*A 2* 167) ⲞⲨⲚⲀ ⲘⲀⲨⲀⲀϤ ⲠⲈⲦⲌⲘⲠⲈⲤⲌⲎⲦ / (*ibid.* 408) ⲞⲨⲢⲀⲚ ⲘⲀⲨⲀⲀϤ ⲠⲈⲦⲈⲦⲚⲦⲀⲨⲞ

ⲘⲘⲞϤ " a name, no more " — "ⲠⲚⲞⲨⲦⲈ ⲚⲦⲠⲈ" / (*ibid*. 303) ⲈⲚⲈϨⲈⲚϢⲎⲢⲈ ϢⲎⲘ ⲘⲀⲨⲀⲀⲨ ⲚⲈ, ⲚⲈⲞⲨⲔⲞⲨⲒ ⲚⲚⲞϬ-ⲚⲈϬ ⲠⲈ / (*III* 212.14f.) ϨⲈⲚⲂⲀⲀⲈ ⲚϨⲞⲞⲨⲦ ⲘⲚϨⲈⲚϨⲞⲞⲨⲦ ⲀⲚ ⲘⲀⲨⲀⲀⲨ ⲚⲈⲦⲘⲞⲞϢⲈ... / (*Ch*. 196.32ff.) ⲞⲨϨⲢⲈ ⲘⲠⲚⲈⲨⲘⲀⲦⲒⲔⲞⲚ ⲀⲨⲰ ⲞⲨϨⲢⲈ ⲀⲚ ⲚⲤⲰⲘⲀⲦⲒⲔⲞⲚ ⲘⲀⲨⲀⲦⲤ / (*IV* 107.7f.) ⲞⲨϨⲞⲞⲨⲦ ⲀⲚ ⲘⲀⲨⲀⲀϤ, ⲀⲖⲖⲀ ϨⲈⲚϨⲒⲞⲘⲈ ⲞⲚ.

(c) Referate: the *possessor exponent in the possessive article*; unlike ⲘⲘⲒⲚ ⲘⲘⲞ⸗, not only with a double identical referate. This construction, much rarer than that with ⲘⲘⲒⲚ ⲘⲘⲞ⸗, seems to be restricted to *inalienable nouns* (see §1.2.1.1 spec. obs. 1). ⲠⲈⲚϨⲦⲞⲢ ⲘⲀⲨⲀⲀⲚ (*A 2* 143) / ⲚⲈⲦⲞⲨⲰⲘ ⲚⲚⲈⲨⲤⲀⲢϩ ⲘⲀⲨⲀⲀⲨ (*A 1* 239) / (ϪⲒ-Ⲙ/ⲘⲀⲒ-)ⲠⲈⲨⲘⲦⲞⲚ ⲘⲀⲨⲀⲀⲨ (etc.), a recurring expression (*III* 127.15, *IV* 153.13f., 172.21, *P* 130² 2 ⲡ: ⲞⲨⲘⲀⲒⲠⲈϤⲘⲦⲞⲚ ⲘⲀⲨⲀⲀϤ ⲠⲈ ⲀⲨⲰ ⲞⲨⲘⲀⲒⲠⲈⲘⲦⲞⲚ ⲀⲚ ⲠⲈ ⲘⲠⲈⲦϨⲒⲦⲞⲨⲰϤ) / ⲦⲈⲨⲮⲨⲬⲎ ⲘⲀⲨⲀⲀⲨ (*IV* 165.10, *Ch*. 56.51f., *III* 193.22, *Wess. 9* 145d 17ff., 171c 31f.) / ⲠⲈⲨⲦⲀⲔⲞ ⲘⲀⲨⲀⲀⲨ (*Ch*. 73.11ff., *Wess. 9* 171b 30f., *P* 130⁴ 141 ro) / ⲚⲈⲔⲘⲈⲈⲨⲈ ⲘⲀⲨⲀⲀⲔ (*A 1* 46) / ⲠⲈⲨⲞⲨⲰϢ ⲘⲀⲨⲀⲀⲨ (*III* 98.4f., *IV* 84.8) / ⲦⲀⲘⲚⲦϨⲎⲔⲈ ⲘⲀⲨⲀⲀⲦ (*Ch*. 99.30f.) also ⲦⲈⲔⲆⲒⲔⲀⲒⲞⲤⲨⲚⲎ (*III* 90.8f.), ⲦⲈϤⲈϨⲞⲨⲤⲒⲀ (*IV* 89.17f.), ⲠⲈⲚⲞⲨϪⲀⲒ (*A 2* 248).

(d) Referate: *independent pronoun*: (*A 2* 99) Ⲱ ⲚⲦⲞⲔ ⲘⲀⲨⲀⲀⲔ ⲠⲚⲞⲨⲦⲈ ⲈⲦⲈϨⲈⲚⲘⲈ ⲚⲈ ⲀⲨⲰ ϨⲈⲚϨⲀⲠ ⲘⲘⲈ ⲚⲈ ⲚⲈϤϨⲂⲎⲨⲈ ⲦⲎⲢⲞⲨ — a pattern hybrid, of a vocative with a Nominal Sentence (predicating ⲚⲦⲞⲔ — or both terms in an acclamatory Nominal Sentence — yet without a formal pronominal subject or copula). Compare *ibid*. 173 ⲚⲦⲞⲔ ⲠⲚⲞⲨⲦⲈ ⲘⲀⲨⲀⲀⲔ, v. 1. ⲚⲦⲞⲔ ⲠⲈ... See exx. for " ⲚⲦⲞϤ ⲠⲈ ⲠⲚⲞⲨⲦⲈ ⲘⲀⲨⲀⲀϤ " and sim., under (a) above; consider (*RE 10* 161a 30) ⲚⲦⲞⲔ ⲠⲈ ⲠⲚⲞⲨⲦⲈ ⲘⲀⲨⲀⲀⲔ / (*Wess. 9* 160c 24ff.) ⲚⲦⲞϤ ⲠⲈ ⲠⲚⲞⲨⲦⲈ ⲘⲘⲈ ⲘⲀⲨⲀⲀϤ / (*RE 11* 16b 9f.) ⲚⲦⲞⲔ ⲚⲀⲘⲈ ⲘⲀⲨⲀⲀⲔ ⲠⲈ ⲠⲆⲒⲔⲀⲒⲞⲤ ⲀⲨⲰ ⲚⲀⲅⲀⲐⲞⲤ / (*A 1* 283) Ⲏ ⲚⲦⲞϤ ⲘⲀⲨⲀⲀϤ ⲀⲚ ⲠⲈⲚⲦⲀϤⲈⲢ-ⲠⲠⲞⲚⲎⲢⲞⲚ / (*A 2* 16) ⲚⲦⲞⲞⲨ ⲘⲀⲨⲀⲀⲨ ⲀⲚ ⲈⲦϨⲘⲠⲠⲀⲢⲀⲆⲒⲤⲞⲤ / (*III* 13.8).

6.1.4.1.3 *Zero referate*: ' when on (one's) own " — "adnominal-circumstantial modification": (*Wess. 9* 125b 18ff.) (ⲦϬⲒⲚϢⲀⲎⲖ ⲈⲦⲘⲘⲀⲨ) ⲦⲀ-ϨⲈⲚⲘⲀ ⲘⲀⲨⲀⲀⲚ ⲦⲈ ⲈⲚⲤϬⲢⲀϨⲦ (parall. *IV* 67-8) / (*IV* 52.21f., 116.22) ⲈⲦⲢⲈⲨϢⲀⲎⲖ ⲚⲤⲀⲞⲨⲤⲀ ⲘⲀⲨⲀⲀⲨ (cf. *ibid*. 146.16, not Shenoute: ϨⲚⲞⲨⲤⲀ ⲘⲀⲨⲀⲀⲨ) / prob. also (*Wess. 9* 113a 27f. after *Mt*. 14:13) — ϨⲚⲞⲨⲘⲀ ⲚϪⲀⲒⲈ ⲘⲀⲨⲀⲀϤ. Compare ⲞⲨⲘⲀ ϨⲀⲢⲒϨⲀⲢⲞ⸗ ⲘⲀⲨⲀⲀ⸗ (§6.1.5.1 below).

6.1.4.1.4 *The affinity of* ⲘⲀⲨⲀⲀ⸗ *with the negator*: the ⲀⲚ adjunctal negation of ⲘⲀⲨⲀⲀ⸗ (ⲘⲀⲨⲀⲀ⸗ ⲀⲚ, see §2.9.1.2.3) is extremely common, as a kind of native Coptic equivalent for ⲞⲨ ⲘⲞⲚⲞⲚ (§1.3.11.2.1): " not only ", " not just " [79]; ⲘⲀⲨⲀⲀ⸗ here is, as a rule, ad(pro)nominal. Like its non-cohesive (non-pronominal) counterpart ⲘⲘⲀⲦⲈ [80], ⲘⲀⲨⲀⲀ⸗ may occur *after* ⲀⲚ, which then negates not the augens but, locally, a sentence constituent including its referate. This analytic difference is however not cor-relatable to any perceivable difference in meaning. Compare the contrast of ⲘⲀⲨⲀⲀ⸗ ⲀⲚ (augens neg. as adjunct: ⲈⲨⲞⲨⲞⲚϨ ⲈⲠⲚⲞⲨⲦⲈ ⲘⲀⲨⲀⲀϤ ⲀⲚ *III* 209.14f., - ⲀⲚⲞⲚ ⲘⲀⲨⲀⲀⲚ ⲀⲚ *ibid*. 13.8) *vs.* ⲀⲚ ⲘⲀⲨⲀⲀ⸗ (augens modifying a neg. sentence constituent: - ⲚⲂⲀⲀⲈ ⲀⲚ ⲘⲀⲨⲀⲀⲨ *Wess. 9* 145b 2ff.), with that of ⲘⲘⲀⲦⲈ ⲀⲚ (- ⲚⲦⲈⲒϨⲈ ⲘⲘⲀⲦⲈ ⲀⲚ *RE 11* 18a 4f.) *vs.* - ⲀⲚ ⲘⲘⲀⲦⲈ (ϢⲀⲢⲈⲠϢⲰⲤ ⲈⲨⲪⲢⲀⲚⲈ ⲀⲚ ⲘⲘⲀⲦⲈ ⲈϪⲚ- *ibid*. 16b 17f.).

6.1.4.2 ⲘⲘⲒⲚ ⲘⲘⲞ⸗ " - *own* ", " - *self* ", REFLEXIVE, NON-CONTRASTIVE, NON-EXCLUSIVE (αὐτός, ἑαυτοῦ, ἴδιος) [81].

6.1.4.2.0.1 MORPHOLOGY. The form ⲘⲘⲒⲚⲈ ⲘⲘⲞ⸗ is attested in Shenoute (e.g. *A 2* 17), and could give us an etymological clue (no etymology is suggested for this augens): *Young* ⲒⲀ, *P* 130⁵ 40 Ⲙⲅ; in one MS (Borg. 189) we find ⲘⲘⲈⲒⲚⲞⲨ ⲘⲘⲞ⸗ (*A 1* 233, 239, 241, 271) beside the normal ⲘⲘⲒⲚ.

6.1.4.2.1 ⲘⲘⲒⲚ ⲘⲘⲞ⸗ in cohesion with *actor + expansion* pronoun in a verb syntagm — more rarely, *subject + expansion* in a Nom. Sentence. Double identical referate (contrast §6.1.4.1.1): (*A 2* 302) ϤⲤⲞⲞⲨⲚ ⲄⲀⲢ ⲘⲘⲞϤ ⲘⲘⲒⲚ ⲘⲘⲞϤ / (*ibid*. 108) ⲀⲦⲈⲦⲚϨⲈⲦⲂ-ⲐⲎⲨⲦⲚ ⲘⲘⲒⲚ ⲘⲘⲰⲦⲚ / (*A 1* 204-5) ⲈⲢⲈϢⲒⲚⲈ ⲚⲤⲀ-

---

[79] Cf. DAUMAS 1952:128f.
[80] Cf. KICKASOLA 1975:301 and reff. there; our §1.3.1.1.(b).
[81] STERN §298 (ⲘⲘⲒⲚ " Adverb der Hervorhebung eines Suffixes ").

ⲣⲓⲙⲉ ⲉⲟⲩⲥⲱⲛⲉ ⲛⲧⲉⲧⲟⲉⲓⲧ ⲉⲣⲟ ⲙⲙⲓⲛ ⲙⲙⲟ / (*Young* ⲓⲁ) ⲙⲛⲅⲟⲙ ⲁⲉ ⲙⲙⲟⲛ ⲉⲧ-ⲡⲱⲛ (i.e. ⲡⲉⲛⲥⲱⲙⲁ) ⲍⲁⲣⲟⲛ ⲙⲙⲓⲛⲉ ⲙⲙⲟⲛ / (*A 2* 373) ⲁⲛⲥⲟⲧⲡⲥ ⲛⲁⲛ ⲉⲩⲣⲩⲱⲣⲛ ⲙⲙⲓⲛ ⲙⲙⲟⲛ / (*III* 170.22f.) ⲟⲩⲛⲍⲁⲍ ⲧ-ⲥⲃⲱ ⲉⲃⲟⲗ ⲍⲓⲧⲟⲟⲧⲟⲩ ⲙⲙⲓⲛ ⲙⲙⲟⲟⲩ / (*A 2* 99) ⲛⲧⲁⲩⲥⲟⲕⲟⲩ ⲉⲭⲱⲩ ⲙⲙⲓⲛ ⲙⲙⲟⲩ / (*RE 10* 162a 8f.) ...ⲉⲩⲉⲓⲣⲉ ⲙⲙⲟⲩ ⲛⲁⲩ ⲙⲙⲓⲛ ⲙⲙⲟⲩ / (*ibid.* b 14f.) ⲡⲉⲛⲧⲁⲩⲧⲁⲁⲩ ⲙⲙⲓⲛ ⲙⲙⲟⲩ ⲍⲁⲣⲟⲛ / (*A 2* 159) ⲙⲟⲣⲕ ⲙⲙⲓⲛ ⲙⲙⲟⲕ ⲍⲛⲍⲉⲛⲙⲣⲣⲉ ⲛⲱⲛⲍ / (*P* 130⁵ 40 ⲙⲅ) (those who wish) ⲉⲱⲙⲥ ⲙⲡⲭⲟⲓ ⲍⲁⲣⲟⲟⲩ ⲙⲙⲓⲛⲉ ⲙⲙⲟⲟⲩ / (*III* 117.5f.) ⲁⲛⲅ-ⲟⲩⲕⲁⲧⲁⲣⲱⲧⲛ ⲁⲛ ⲁⲗⲗⲁ ⲁⲛⲅ-ⲟⲩⲕⲁⲧⲁⲣⲟⲓ ⲙⲙⲓⲛ ⲙⲙⲟⲓ. (Rarely, the referate of ⲙⲙⲓⲛ⸗ ⲙⲙⲟ⸗ is included solely in an agentive phrase: [*A 2* 104] ⲍⲉⲛⲍⲟⲧⲃⲥ ⲛⲉ ⲉⲃⲟⲗ ⲍⲓⲧⲛⲧⲏⲩⲧⲛ ⲙⲙⲓⲛ ⲙⲙⲱⲧⲛ [and not by others, *contrastive* - an exception] / [*ibid.* 341] ...ⲍⲙⲡⲧⲣⲉⲍⲉⲛⲧⲱⲍ ⲩⲱⲡⲉ ⲉⲃⲟⲗ ⲛⲍⲏⲧⲟⲩ ⲙⲙⲓⲛ ⲙⲙⲟⲟⲩ). Additional exx.: *A 2* 370, 373, *III* 64.10f., 202.27f., *IV* 15.11, *Ch.* 97.6ff., 136.8ff., *Wess. 9* 117b 4ff., 131b 6ff., *RE 10* 162b 14f., *Rudnitzky* A 20ff., etc.

6.1.4.2.2   Referate: pronoun/noun syntagm: (a) the *possessor exponent* in the possessive article or pronoun: " (his) own "; as a rule, with a double referate; almost exclusively in delocutive (third) persons; as a rule, with *inalienable nouns*: (*A 1* 112) ⲉⲩⲛⲁⲥⲟⲣⲩ ⲉⲃⲟⲗ (the net) ⲉⲛⲉⲩⲟⲩⲉⲣⲏⲧⲉ ⲙⲙⲓⲛ ⲙⲙⲟⲩ / (*ibid.* 97) ⲍⲙⲡⲧⲣⲉⲩⲧⲁⲁⲩ ⲉⲍⲣⲁⲓ ⲉⲛⲉⲩⲟⲩⲩ ⲙⲙⲓⲛ ⲙⲙⲟⲩ / (*ibid.* 213) ...ⲉⲩⲣⲡⲕⲉⲍⲱⲛ ⲉⲧⲃⲉⲡⲉⲩⲥⲱⲙⲁ ⲙⲙⲓⲛ ⲙⲙⲟⲟⲩ / (*IV* 1.2f.) ⲥⲉⲟⲩⲏⲍ ⲍⲛⲛⲉⲩⲡⲟⲗⲓⲥ ⲙⲙⲓⲛ ⲙⲙⲟⲟⲩ / (*A 2* 368) ⲁⲩⲩⲓ-ⲡⲉⲩⲣⲟⲟⲩⲩ ⲙⲙⲓⲛ ⲙⲙⲟⲩ / (*RE 10* 164b 35f.) ⲩⲣⲍⲟⲩⲉⲥⲟⲟⲩⲛ ⲛⲛⲉⲍⲃⲏⲩⲉ ⲙⲡⲉⲙⲩⲟⲩ ⲙⲙⲓⲛ ⲙⲙⲟⲩ / (*III* 187.10f.) ⲁⲩⲍⲉ ⲍⲛⲧⲉⲩⲧⲁⲡⲣⲟ ⲙⲙⲓⲛ ⲙⲙⲟⲩ. A marginal overlapping with ⲙⲁⲩⲁⲁ⸗ (§6.1.4.1.2c) is evident here. This is the case with ⲍⲧⲟⲣ (ⲙⲁⲩⲁⲁ⸗, *A 2* 143; ⲙⲙⲓⲛ ⲙⲙⲟ⸗, *ViK* 908 ⲥⲛⲅ, *IF* 203 ap. *Dictionary* 727); ⲯⲩⲭⲏ (ⲙⲁⲩⲁⲁ⸗, *IV* 165.10 ⲙⲙⲓⲛ ⲙⲙⲟ⸗, *ibid.* 51.17f.). Other examples: *A 1* 233 (ⲡⲉⲩⲏⲓ), 276 (ⲧⲉⲩⲡⲣⲟⲍⲁⲓⲣⲉⲥⲓⲥ), *Ch.* 175.23f. (ⲡⲉⲩⲥⲛⲟⲩ); note also ⲉⲃⲟⲗ ⲛⲍⲏⲧⲟⲩ ⲙⲙⲓⲛ ⲙⲙⲟⲟⲩ (*A 1* 292-3, *A 2* 341).

(b) Referate: *determinators*; *independent pronouns* (predicated in Nom. Sentence/Cleft Sentence): extremely rare, compared with the incidence of the exclusive ⲙⲁⲩⲁⲁ⸗ (§6.1.4.1.2): (*A 2* 49) ⲧⲛⲁⲭⲱ ⲁⲉ ⲙⲡⲓⲩⲁⲭⲉ ⲛⲧⲕⲉⲍⲉ, ⲉⲛⲉⲓⲛⲉ ⲙⲡⲭⲟⲓ ⲉⲭⲙⲡⲣⲱⲙⲉ ⲙⲙⲓⲛ ⲙⲙⲟⲩ (" comparing the ship to man himself ") / (*Wess. 9* 156a 4ff.) (ⲡⲏⲣⲡ ⲛⲛⲉⲕⲃⲱ ⲛⲍⲉⲣⲙⲁⲛ) ⲉⲧⲉⲛⲧⲱⲧⲛ ⲡⲉ ⲙⲙⲓⲛ ⲙⲙⲱⲧⲛ / (*III* 177.5) ⲛⲧⲟⲟⲩ ⲙⲙⲓⲛ ⲙⲙⲟⲟⲩ ⲛⲉⲧⲛⲁⲥⲉⲓ ⲛⲛⲉⲩⲕⲁⲣⲡⲟⲥ.

6.1.4.3   ⲟⲩⲁⲁ⸗ " only... ", " ... alone " [82] is relatively very rare in Shenoute, functionally overlapping ⲙⲁⲩⲁⲁ⸗, compatible (in cotext patterns, §6.1.4.4) with ⲙⲙⲓⲛ ⲙⲙⲟ⸗, but not with ⲙⲁⲩⲁⲁ⸗ (to which ⲟⲩⲁⲁ⸗ is etymologically related). The forms of this augens on my files are ⲟⲩⲁⲁ⸗ (3rd person sgl. and plur.), ⲟⲩⲁⲁⲧ⸗ (3rd sgl., 2nd plur.) and ⲟⲩⲁⲧ⸗ (2nd plur.).

(a) *Double referate in verb syntagms* (+ expansion): (*A 1* 73) ⲁⲧⲉⲧⲛⲩⲱⲡⲉ ⲛⲭⲣⲟⲡ ⲛⲏⲧⲛ ⲟⲩⲁⲁⲧⲧⲏⲩⲧⲛ / (*III* 184.15) ...ⲉⲁⲧⲉⲧⲛⲉⲙⲥ-ⲧⲏⲩⲧⲛ ⲟⲩⲁⲧⲧⲏⲩⲧⲛ / (*IV* 117.4f.) ⲛⲉⲧⲟ ⲛⲥⲁⲃⲉ ⲛⲁⲩ ⲟⲩⲁⲁⲩ / (*A 2* 503) ...ⲉⲩⲧⲁⲓⲟ ⲙⲙⲟⲩ ⲟⲩⲁⲁⲩ / (*P* 130² 52 ⲧⲑ) ⲧⲁⲓ ⲉⲧⲧⲁⲕⲟ ⲙⲙⲟⲩ ⲟⲩⲁⲁⲩ / (*B.L.Or.* 8800 18 ⲛⲍ, this line skipped in error in *Ench.* 72, to follow line 38) ⲙⲏ ⲛⲧⲱⲧⲛ ⲁⲛ ⲁⲧⲉⲧⲛⲧⲁⲕⲉ-ⲧⲏⲩⲧⲛ ⲟⲩⲁⲁⲧⲧⲏⲩⲧⲛ.

(b) Referate: *noun, indep. pronoun* (predicative): (*III* 35.6, parall. *Ch.* 129.36f.) ⲣⲁⲕⲟⲧⲉ ⲁⲛ' ⲟⲩⲁⲁⲧⲩ, ⲏ ⲉⲫⲉⲥⲟⲥ / (*Ench.* 71a-b) ⲛⲧⲱⲧⲛ ⲟⲩⲁⲁⲧⲧⲏⲩⲧⲛ ⲁⲧⲉⲧⲛⲥⲃⲧⲉ-ⲧⲏⲩⲧⲛ ⲍⲛ ⲍⲉⲛⲍⲃⲏⲩⲉ ⲛⲗⲟⲓⲙⲟⲥ.

6.1.4.4   Cotext patterns: ' ⲙⲙⲓⲛ ⲙⲙⲟ⸗ + ⲙⲁⲩⲁⲁ⸗ ', ' ⲙⲙⲓⲛ ⲙⲙⲟ⸗ + ⲟⲩⲁⲁ⸗ '. The frequent co-textual pairing collocation of ⲙⲁⲩⲁⲁ⸗, ⲙⲙⲓⲛ ⲙⲙⲟ⸗ and (rarely) ⲟⲩⲁⲁ⸗ is a striking stylistic-rhetorical device, one that can be put to diagnostic use. The prevalent arrangement, more than twice as common as the other, is ' ⲙⲁⲩⲁⲁ⸗ → ⲙⲙⲓⲛ ⲙⲙⲟ⸗ ': (*A 1* 55) ⲙⲡⲛⲩⲛ-ⲍⲧⲏⲛ ⲍⲁⲣⲟⲛ ⲙⲁⲩⲁⲁⲛ ⲉⲣ-ⲧⲙⲉ, ⲉⲛⲭⲓ ⲙⲙⲟⲛ ⲛⲅⲟⲛⲥ ⲙⲙⲓⲛ ⲙⲙⲟⲛ / (*A 2* 67) ⲩⲁⲧⲛⲁⲩ ⲉⲛⲥⲱⲩ ⲙⲙⲟⲛ ⲙⲁⲩⲁⲁⲛ ⲁⲩⲱ ⲉⲛⲥⲱⲩ ⲙⲙⲟⲛ ⲙⲙⲓⲛ ⲙⲙⲟⲛ / (*ibid.* 241) ⲉⲩⲭⲉ-ⲡⲣⲉⲩⲣ-ⲛⲟⲃⲉ ⲛⲁⲧⲁⲕⲟⲩ ⲙⲁⲩⲁⲁⲩ ⲛⲑⲉ ⲉⲧⲥⲏⲍ, ⲡⲣⲉⲩⲣ-ⲡⲉⲧⲛⲁⲛⲟⲩⲩ ⲟⲛ ⲛⲁⲥⲙⲛⲧⲩ ⲙⲙⲓⲛ ⲙⲙⲟⲩ / (*ibid.* 458 [not Sh.], *III* 224.9f.,17f.) ⲟⲩⲍⲏⲩ ⲡⲉ ⲉⲩⲩⲁⲛⲥⲟⲩⲱⲛⲩ ⲙⲁⲩⲁⲁⲩ. ⲙⲡⲁⲧⲉⲧⲉⲕⲧⲏⲥⲓⲥ ⲅⲁⲣ ⲥⲟⲩⲱⲛⲥ ⲙⲙⲓⲛ ⲙⲙⲟⲥ /

---

[82] Stern §257, Schwarze-Steinthal 346.

(*IV* 6.18f.) ⲈⲨϬⲞⲚⲦ ⲈⲢⲞⲞⲨ ⲘⲀⲨⲀⲦⲞⲨ ⲚⲞⲨⲎⲢ… ⲀⲨⲰ ⲈⲨⲤⲀϨⲞⲨ ⲈⲢⲞⲞⲨ ⲘⲘⲒⲚ ⲘⲘⲞⲞⲨ / (*Ench.* 85a) ⲚⲈⲚⲦⲀⲨ⳨-ϪⲢⲞⲠ ⲚⲀⲨ ⲘⲀⲨⲀⲀⲨ ⲀⲨⲰ ⲈⲀⲨⲰϢⲠⲈ ⲚⲀⲨ ⲚⲤⲔⲀⲚⲆⲀⲖⲞⲚ ⲘⲘⲒⲚ ⲘⲘⲞⲞⲨ. In (*III* 146.24f.) ⲀⲒϪⲒⲦ ⲚϬⲞⲚⲤ ⲘⲀⲨⲀⲀⲦ ⲘⲘⲒⲚ ⲘⲘⲞⲒ we have true clause-internal compatibility. Additional exx : *III* 162.11f.,14ff., 165.16ff., 176.6f., *IV* 51.16ff., *A 1* 305.

' ⲘⲘⲒⲚ ⲘⲘⲞ⸗ → ⲘⲀⲨⲀⲀ⸗ ': (*A 1* 219) ⲚⲒϨⲂⲎⲨⲈ ⲈⲦⲚⲠⲖⲀⲤⲤⲈ ⲘⲘⲞⲞⲨ ϨⲘⲠⲈⲚϨⲎⲦ ⲘⲘⲒⲚ ⲘⲘⲞⲚ ⲀⲨⲰ ⲦⲚⲘⲚⲦ-ⲢⲈϤⲔⲀ-ϨⲦⲎⲚ ⲈⲢⲞⲚ ⲘⲀⲨⲀⲀⲚ / (*A 2* 345) ⲠⲈⲦⲦⲰⲂⲈ ⲘⲘⲞⲞⲨ ⲠϪⲀϪⲈ ⲈϨⲞⲢⲞⲨ ⲈⲢⲞⲞⲨ ⲘⲘⲒⲚ ⲘⲘⲞⲞⲨ ⲈⲦⲢⲈⲨⲢϢⲢⲠ-ϢⲰⲰⲦ ⲘⲘⲞⲞⲨ ⲘⲀⲨⲀⲀⲨ / (*Wess.* 9 176a 22ff.) ⲀⲨⲦⲰⲞⲨⲚ… ⲈϨⲢⲀⲒ ⲈϪⲰⲞⲨ ⲘⲘⲒⲚ ⲘⲘⲞⲞⲨ ⲈⲀⲨⲦⲞⲨⲚⲞⲤ ⲈⲘⲀⲦⲈ ⲈϨⲢⲀⲒ ⲈϪⲰⲞⲨ ⲘⲀⲨⲀⲀⲨ ⲚϨⲰⲂ ⲚⲒⲘ ⲈϤϨⲞⲞⲨ / (*P* 130² 1 oz) ⲈⲨϪⲒ ⲘⲘⲞⲞⲨ ⲚϬⲞⲚⲤ ⲘⲘⲒⲚ ⲘⲘⲞⲞⲨ ⲈⲂⲞⲖ ϨⲒⲦⲞⲞⲦⲞⲨ ⲘⲀⲨⲀⲀⲦⲞⲨ. Other exx.: *A 1* 17, *A 2* 45, *RE 10* 164b 21ff.

' ⲞⲨⲀⲀ⸗ → ⲘⲘⲒⲚ ⲘⲘⲞ⸗ ': (*A 2* 504) ⲀϤⲔⲦⲞ ⲚⲚⲈϤϢⲀϪⲈ ⲈϨⲞⲨⲚ ⲈⲢⲞϤ ⲞⲨⲀⲀϤ ⲈⲀϤⲦⲘⲀⲒⲞϤ ⲘⲘⲒⲚ ⲘⲘⲞϤ.

Note also the cotextual combination of the two augentia in the following instances: ⲠⲈⲨⲘⲦⲞⲚ ⲘⲘⲒⲚ ⲘⲘⲞⲞⲨ: ⲠⲈⲨⲘⲦⲞⲚ ⲘⲀⲨⲀⲀⲨ (*A 1* 9.4:7); ⲀⲚⲄ-ⲞⲨⲔⲀⲦⲀⲢⲞⲒ ⲘⲘⲒⲚ ⲘⲘⲞⲒ: ⲚⲦⲈⲦⲚ-ϨⲈⲚⲔⲀⲦⲀⲢⲰⲦⲚ ⲘⲀⲨⲀⲦⲦⲎⲨⲦⲚ (*III* 117.6:11); ⲈⲦⲢⲈⲚⲢ-ϨⲎⲂⲈ ⲚⲀⲚ ⲘⲀⲨⲀⲀⲚ: ⲈⲢϢⲀⲚⲦⲘⲠⲢⲰⲘⲈ ⲘⲔⲀϨ ⲚϨⲎⲦ ⲈϪⲰϤ ⲘⲘⲒⲚ ⲘⲘⲞϤ (*ibid.* 213.14:16f.).

6.1.5   Bᴏʀᴅᴇʀ-ʟɪɴᴇ ᴀᴜɢᴇɴᴛɪᴀ: ϨⲀⲢⲒϨⲀⲢⲞ⸗, ⲚⲀ⸗ are adjunctal prepositional modifiers pronominally cohesive (" reflexive "), with greater or lesser regularity and predictability of this cohesion. On the whole, however, they are *adverbal* (ad-lexemic) rather than ad(pro)nominal modifiers (although this distinction is gradient, not dichotomic, to judge by " true " augentia).

6.1.5.1   ϨⲀⲢⲒϨⲀⲢⲞ⸗ " apart ", " on one's own " (*Dictionary* 634). (a) *Adverbal* (*ad-lexemic*) - usually *intransitive verbs*: (*III* 210.9) …ⲈϤⲚⲀ ⲈϤⲚⲎⲨ ⲈϤⲔⲒⲘ ϨⲀⲢⲒϨⲀⲢⲞϤ / (*ibid. ibid.* 18f.) (of the soul) ⲠⲈⲤⲠⲰⲦ Ⲏ ⲠⲈⲤ-ⲔⲰⲦⲈ ⲈϨⲢⲀⲒ ϨⲀⲢⲒϨⲀⲢⲞⲤ (*v.l.* ϨⲀⲢⲞⲤ) / (*ibid.* 117.6f.) …ⲈⲦⲢⲀϬⲰ ϨⲀⲢⲒϨⲀⲢⲞⲒ ⲈⲈⲒⲘⲞⲔϨ ⲚϨⲎⲦ (also *IF* 95 apud *Dictionary* 643b) / (*P* 131⁷ 45 ro) ⲚⲈϨⲂⲎⲨⲈ ⲈⲦⲈⲨϢϢⲈ ⲈⲀⲀⲨ ϨⲀⲢⲒϨⲀⲢⲞⲚ / (*P* 131⁵ 16 vo) ⲈⲨϪⲈ-ⲞⲨⲚⲞⲨⲀ ⲆⲈ ϪⲰ ⲘⲘⲞⲤ ϪⲈ-⳨ⲦⲂⲂⲎⲨ ϨⲀⲢⲒϨⲀⲢⲞϤ (note the partial personal concord with the referate — " mixed " concord, an inverse kind of " style indirect libre " or " erlebte Rede "). Additional exx.: *A 2* 14, *Ch.* 42.26ff., *P* 130¹ 135 ⲦⲀⲈ.

(b) *Adnominal* (" apart "): (*Wess.* 9 176a 3ff.) (they sinned against him, every one in his own way) ⲦⲤⲨⲚⲀⲄⲰⲄⲎ ⲚⲔⲞⲢⲈ ϨⲀⲢⲒϨⲀⲢⲞⲤ… ⲚⲈⲚⲦⲀⲨⲠⲞⲢⲚⲎⲨⲈ ϨⲀⲢⲒϨⲀⲢⲞⲞⲨ, ⲚⲈⲚⲦⲀⲨⲈⲠⲒⲐⲨⲘⲈⲒ ⲈⲨⲈⲠⲒⲐⲨⲘⲒⲀ ϨⲀⲢⲒϨⲀⲢⲞⲞⲨ ⲀⲨⲰ ⲚⲔⲞⲞⲨⲈ ⲦⲎⲢⲞⲨ ϨⲀⲢⲒϨⲀⲢⲞⲞⲨ / (*IV* 167.18f.) (every one to his job), ⲚⲈⲦⲢ-ϨⲘⲘⲈ ϨⲀⲢⲒϨⲀⲢⲞⲞⲨ, ⲚⲈⲦⲤϨⲀⲒ ⲞⲚ ϨⲀⲢⲒϨⲀⲢⲞⲞⲨ, ⲘⲚⲚⲔⲞⲞⲨⲈ ⲦⲎⲢⲞⲨ ⲔⲀⲦⲀⲦⲀⲌⲒⲤ.

(c) An instance of *zero referate*? (*IV* 91.14f.) ⲈⲨⲚⲀϢⲰⲠⲈ ⲚⲞⲨⲘⲀ ϨⲀⲢⲒϨⲀⲢⲞⲞⲨ ⲘⲀⲨⲀⲀⲨ (compare §6.1.4.1.3).

6.1.5.2   ⲚⲀ⸗ [83] is a componential modifier of the verb lexeme (*intransitives*, mostly verbs of movement or posture; note one instance of ⲞⲨⲰⲘ intransitivized by ⲚⲀ⸗), which occurs as a rule as *imperative*; ⲚⲀ⸗ signals here a special *address tone*, corresponding (in non-imperatives) to a *self-centered* mode of action (*Aktionsart*); this often amounts to perfective-aspect characterization. Note that, like other augentia, ⲚⲀ⸗ here also supplies the gender-number characterization [84]. (*A 1* 73) ⲀⲚⲀϪⲰⲢⲈⲒ ⲚⲎⲦⲚ / (*A 2* 224) ⲤⲈⲒ ⲚⲎⲦⲚ ⲚⲚⲈⲦⲚϨⲎⲆⲞⲚⲎ ⲚϪⲰϨⲘ / (*ibid.* 398) ⲘⲞⲞϢⲈ ⲚⲀⲔ ⲈⲂⲞⲖ / (*III* 192.1, *Ench.* 67a) ⲘⲞⲞϢⲈ ⲚⲀⲔ ⲈϨⲢⲀⲒ / (*Wess.* 9 139d 12f., 26f.) ⲂⲰⲔ ⲚⲎⲦⲚ ⲈⲢⲀⲦⲞⲨ… ⲂⲰⲔ ⲚⲎⲦⲚ ⲈⲘⲀⲨ / (*IV* 104.1) ⲈⲨⲚⲀⲚⲔⲞⲦⲔ ⲚⲀⲨ ⲘⲘⲀⲨ, jussive. Rarely, we find non-imperative verb-forms: ⲠⲰⲦ ⲚⲀ⸗ " run *away* " (*IV* 121.27, 171.2f.) and ⲞⲨⲰⲘ ⲚⲀ⸗ " eat *away* " (*Quot.* (2) ⲦⲈⲯⲨⲬⲎ ⲦϢⲞⲨⲚ ⲚⲦⲈⲞⲨⲰⲘ ⲚⲈ ⲈⲂⲞⲖ ϨⲘⲠⲈⲚⲦⲀⲢⲈⲈⲠⲒⲐⲨⲘⲈⲒ ⲈⲢⲞϤ).

---

[83] Sᴛᴇʀɴ §503. For the prosodic affinity of ⲚⲀ⸗ with the augens see Pᴏʟᴏᴛsᴋʏ 1961:313 (= *CP* 417), Eᴍᴍᴇʟ 1981 (esp. 137f.).

[84] On the so-called " ethical dative " in Egyptian — a term singularly infelicitous — see Hɪɴᴛᴢᴇ 1950:82ff., with further literature.

6.2 THE AUGENS AND MODIFICATION

Beyond the paradigmatic identity of the augens, by itself amply indicative of its modifier status (as are also, without exception, the respective etymologies), we have encountered several instances where, even if formally in ad(pro)nominal cohesion, the augens nevertheless modifies the verb syntagm as a whole or its lexemic component. Two augentia have pronoun-less kindred and functionally close or concurrent associates: ⲘⲘⲀⲦⲈ for ⲘⲀⲨⲀⲀ⸗ (A 2 18 ⲚⲦⲀⲨⲘⲞⲞⲨⲦϤ ⲀⲚ ⲈⲦⲂⲈ ⲚⲈϤⲚⲞⲂⲈ ⲘⲘⲀⲦⲈ Ⲏ ⲚⲦⲀⲨⲌⲰ ⲈⲢⲞϤ ⲘⲀⲨⲀⲀϤ, the negation to be referred to both clauses / III 209.1f. ...ⲈⲨⲞⲨⲞⲚⲌ ⲈⲠⲚⲞⲨⲦⲈ ⲘⲀⲨⲀⲀϤ ⲀⲚ ⲀⲖⲖⲀ ⲈⲚⲔⲈⲢⲰⲘⲈ ⲞⲚ, ⲞⲨⲦⲈ ⲚⲦⲈⲨϢⲎ ⲀⲚ ⲘⲘⲀⲦⲈ ⲦⲈⲦⲞ ⲘⲘⲚⲦⲢⲈ ⲚⲚⲈⲨⲘⲚⲦⲀⲤⲈⲂⲎⲤ, ⲀⲖⲖⲀ ⲠⲈⲌⲞⲞⲨ ⲞⲚ) and ⲚⲞⲨⲰⲦ "singly", adnominal, which is (as unit-defining) quite different semantically from ⲞⲨⲀⲀ⸗. (ⲚⲞⲨⲰⲦ, like the adnominal ⲘⲀⲨⲀⲀ⸗, is also a focusing adjunct.) [85]

6.2.1 FOCALIZABILITY.

Most augentia occur in focalization patterns (Ch. 2), where they either co-mark the focus or, more rarely, constitute together with their referate a complex (*pronoun + augens*) focus; this is common with ⲘⲘⲓⲚ ⲘⲘⲞ⸗, ⲘⲀⲨⲀⲀ⸗ and ⲞⲨⲀⲀ⸗ (where I would impressionistically say this accounts for about a third of all occurrences): (A 2 238-9) ⲈⲚⲚⲀϢⲬⲞⲞⲨ ⲦⲎⲢⲞⲨ ⲀⲚ / (ibid. 99) ⲚⲦⲀϤⲤⲞⲔⲞⲨ ⲈⲬⲰϤ ⲘⲘⲓⲚ ⲘⲘⲞϤ / (ibid. 403) ⲚⲈϤⲚⲀϢⲀⲬⲈ ⲀⲚ ⲌⲀⲢⲞϤ ⲀⲖⲖⲀ ⲈϤⲚⲀϢⲈ-ⲠⲈⲦϤⲚⲀⲤⲞⲦⲘⲈϤ / (ibid. 547) ⲈⲔⲚⲀⲔⲰ ⲈⲂⲞⲖ ⲈⲦⲂⲈⲠⲈⲔⲢⲀⲚ ⲘⲀⲨⲀⲀϤ / (A 1 305) ⲘⲎ ⲈϢⲀⲨⲔⲈⲦ-ⲠⲎⲒ ⲈⲦⲂⲎⲎⲦϤ ⲘⲀⲨⲀⲀϤ / (ibid. 239) ⲈⲨⲢ-ⲚⲞⲂⲈ ⲈⲢⲞⲞⲨ ⲘⲀⲨⲀⲀⲨ / (Wess. 9 144c 24ff.) ⲈⲦⲂⲈⲠⲈϤϬⲂⲂⲒⲞ ⲀⲚ ⲘⲀⲨⲀⲀϤ ⲚⲦⲀϤⲬⲞⲞⲤ... / (A 2 473) ⲈϤⲤϢ ⲀⲚ ⲘⲠⲚⲞⲨⲦⲈ ⲀⲖⲖⲀ ⲈϤⲤϢ ⲘⲘⲞϤ ⲞⲨⲀⲀϤ. More exx.: III 78.23f., 165.16ff., IV 38.22f., 96.13,17, RE 11 17a 1, Ch. 28.32ff., 72.49ff., 76.52ff., 109.36ff., Wess. 9 110b 7ff., etc. [86]. Compare also the same augentia as co-focal in the "nominal" Cleft Sentence (§§6.1.4.1.2, 6.1.4.2.2): (A 1 251) ⲚⲀⲒ ⲆⲈ ⲘⲀⲨⲀⲀⲨ ⲀⲚ ⲚⲈⲦⲚⲘⲘⲀϤ / (III 177.5) ⲚⲦⲞⲟⲨ ⲘⲘⲓⲚ ⲘⲘⲞⲞⲨ ⲚⲈⲦⲚⲀⲤⲈⲒ ⲚⲚⲈⲨⲔⲀⲢⲠⲞⲤ.

6.3 CONCLUDING NOTE: ON THE FUNCTIONAL ESSENCE OF THE AUGENS

To be precise, one must distinguish between the roles of the *pronominal* and *lexemic* components of the augens: the former serves the purpose of cohesion, gender-number characterization (after the imperative and zero referates) — this component is *syntagmatically* operative. The lexemic component, on the other hand, is paradigmatically assignable [87]:

distinctive confrontation: EXCLUSIVE		*distinctive confrontation*: INCLUSIVE	
marked (+)	ⲘⲀⲨⲀⲀ⸗		ⲌⲰ⸗
neutral (∅)	ⲘⲘⲓⲚ ⲘⲘⲞ⸗		{ⲚⲦⲞ⸗}

totality: INTEGRAL	
marked (+)	ⲦⲎⲢ⸗
neutral (∅)	— ⲚⲒⲘ (?)

{ⲚⲦⲞ⸗} is, beyond doubt, the most interesting of the group. In the first place, its pronominal and lexemic components *coincide* — it is after all the pronominal lexeme. (Or is ⲚⲦⲞ- to be taken as a lexemic isolable constituent? This would still leave us with the unanalyzable first persons.) Secondly, it alone

---

[85] Consider however NHC VII 125.6 vs. line 25f. ⲚⲦⲔ-ⲞⲨⲠⲚⲈⲨⲘⲀ ⲞⲨⲀⲀϤ ⲀⲨⲰ ⲈϤⲞⲚⲌ vs. ⲚⲦⲔ-ⲞⲨⲠⲚⲈⲨⲘⲀ ⲚⲞⲨⲰⲦ ⲈϤⲞⲚⲌ. Note also "adverbial" ⲌⲰ⸗ in Rom. 11:21 (translating κατὰ φύσιν); see Dictionary 651b.

[86] On the other hand, ⲌⲰ⸗ occurs as adjunct to the theme/topic: (IV 195.4) ⲘⲎ ⲈⲨϢⲀⲬⲈ ⲌⲰⲞⲨ ⲚⲦⲈⲒⲌⲈ ⲀⲚ / (Ch. 106.25ff.) ⲈⲒⲞⲚⲌ ⲌⲰϢⲦ' ⲈⲦⲈⲢⲈ ⲚⲘⲘⲞⲚⲀⲬⲞⲤ, but also co-focally: (III 56.14) ⲚⲦⲞⲤ ⲌⲰⲰⲤ ⲈⲤⲘⲈ ⲘⲘⲞϤ, foc. pattern (3), §2.3.2.

[87] The prevalence of - ⲌⲰ⸗ ⲞⲚ - compared with -ⲆⲈ {ⲚⲦⲞ⸗} is instructive for the semantics of the augens; so also is the fact that whereas ⲌⲰ⸗ is invariably the *second term* in the cotextual patterning, {ⲚⲦⲞ⸗} is either first or second (although as the second term — in anaphoric contrast — it is undoubtedly more frequent).

of all augentia serves to mark a *prominent topic* (§2.0.2.1) [88]: like other well-known syntactic phenomena, augential modification (esp. by {NTO⸗}) constitutes an *option of staging* (§2.0.2.0.1) and a means of information structuring. The augens is essentially a dialogue, not narration element (first-person egocentric " reporting " narration excepted). It is not *per se* " emphasizing " (§2.0.2.2), although it does often play a contributive part in focalization: *confrontation* does after all cover a considerable section of the spectrum of inter-clausal cotextual relations, for which *focalization* is in a way the archetypal functional category.

---

[88] The prominent topic — also marked by extraposition (§6.0.1) — should be kept distinct from the marked logical predicate (rheme/focus), *pace* CALLENDER 1970:186ff.

CHAPTER 7

THE CONJUNCTIVE: AN N-MARKED CONJUGATED ADNEXAL MODIFIER

7.0.1 RESEARCH-HISTORICAL: GRAMMATICAL OPINION

The conjunctive is, I believe, the most intriguing of Coptic verb forms: with the circumstantial (§7.1.3) it is probably the most important systemically. While its general semasiological value is fairly well understood, we are in the dark regarding its true nature, its syntagmatic and paradigmatic relationships, a comprehensive theory to cover all its functions. We know approximately *what* the conjunctive does environmentally; we do not understand its mechanism, nor its own value. Whereas the pre-Coptic (esp. Late Egyptian) conjunctive has had to date no less than *nine* monographs devoted to it (by Gardiner, Mattha, Černý, Wente, Sauneron, Lichtheim, Volten, Callender and Borghouts, in that order), not to mention lengthy grammar and textbook discussions, we have had none for Coptic. This is unfortunate and redolent of the prevailing complacency about " familiar " Coptic grammatical categories. One suspects that giving the form a traditional " Indo-European name" has to some extent blunted the need for a fresh, unbiased examination, as well as prejudiced the appreciation of the function of this form, unconsciously and perhaps inevitably (witness the *modal* overtones rashly attributed to the Coptic conjunctive). In Egyptian, on the other hand, the strangeness has not been so damped (" conjunctive " in Egyptian is second- or third-hand terminological transference). Whoever hopes to find a consistent, integral systemic picture in the grammarians' descriptions [1] is due for a disappointment. He will have to become reconciled to the unaccounted-for, functionally dual nature of the form — " conjunctival " (" continuing ") and " subjunctival " roles; to statements in terms of ellipsis, of various whims of this peculiar form, not to mention the fragmentated account: no taxonomy or descriptive statements in terms of functional load, compatibilities and generally *système de valeur* can be found. Corpus-specific statements are rare. Stern's account is, as usual, the most careful and reliable, and his presentation of the data is precise and cannot be faulted, even if his interpretation of them is sometimes open to objection. A paraphrase (in the original terminology) of the average impression would run as follows (no criticism is offered at this point): the conjunctive is a subordinated-clause form, serving as a coordinated (" copulative ") continuation of preceding verb forms — it can be introduced by such conjunctions as ⲀⲨⲰ, Ⲏ, ⲞⲨⲦⲈ, ⲀⲖⲖⲀ. Being too weak to constitute an autonomous sentence, it connects mostly subject-identical sentences to the main verb-form. In Bohairic, and to a lesser degree in Sahidic, it also has a " subjunctive " role [2]. It may have various modal values (" subjective ", final-consecutive, with or without suitable conjunctions). In independent status, it expresses modal, deliberative or futuric nuances of will or obligation. It can also be dependent upon a Nominal Sentence [3]; it can be adnominal [4]. Callender's pan-chronic remarks (1973a:69ff) call for special attention. In the framework of a generative model, he says, the conjunctive can be handled in a " natural " way (" a natural explanation ", p. 72). This is by no means a *description*, let alone a categorial or role appraisal, but one possible schematization of conjunctive constructions (meant to illustrate the advantages of a generative model). Although helpful (if one subscribes to, and deems instructive, " deep structure " realities), this presentation does not in any way add to our understanding of the Coptic system of grammar.

While I do not offer here a critical appraisal of the above statements — my own stand will be made clear in the course of the following paragraphs — I must point out that a careful examination of the examples on which they are based leads one to reject the modal functions alleged for the conjunctive. Moreover, there is no doubt that a dialect-internal, or better corpus-based investigation would make for better insight into the issues of ⲀⲨⲰ - *vs.* Ø-, ⲦⲀ⁻ *vs.* ⲚⲦⲀ⁻ in the 1st person sgl., and the functioning and compatibilities [5] of the form.

---

[1] Stern §§440ff., 595; Steindorff 1951:§§366-372, 386; Till §§321ff., 366, 401, 416, 485, etc.

[2] On this " subjunctive " role (mainly in the 1st person) see Stern §§442-6, Till 1928:§139d, Steindorff 1951:174, Till §421, Nagel 1969b:§55b; often it is obvious that the alleged modal value stems from misinterpretation of the construction or from the " quicksands of translation ".

[3] Till 1928:§139d.

[4] A most important observation (see §7.3.2 below). However, the sole example offered by Till and Steindorff (*Job* 10:21 ⲘⲠⲀϮⲂⲰⲔ ⲈⲠⲘⲀ ⲚⲦⲀⲦⲘⲤⲞⲦⲦ) is not conclusive, since the conjunctive may be taken (in sense, even if not formally) to continue ⲘⲠⲀϮ⁻ (cf. the Hebrew בטרם אלך ולא אשוב, Greek ὅθεν οὐκ ἀναστρέψω).

[5] Most present-tense examples turn out to be either of the *protatic* circ. present (our §7.2.4) or non-actual, non-temporal or futuric (predicating ⲚⲎⲨ). Stern's one example of the conjunctive continuing past tense (*Act.* 27:33) is emended into the circ. present (so Thompson); the conjunctive in Steindorff's example (*Joh.* 12:5) is *apodotic* rather than continuative (our §7.2.6). Nagel's exx. of the " independent " conjunctive in *NHC* II (1969b:453) may all be interpreted as apodotic or governed by Ⲏ (our §7.3.1.1; on the issue of the " independent " conj., cf. Polotsky 1962b:479 = *CP* 270). His " final " conjunctive (p. 455) is in fact part of the discontinuous ' ⲬⲈⲔⲀⲀⲤ... *conjunctive* ' syntagm. The conjunctive allegedly continuing the perfect (p. 455) is not conclusive, and can be referred to Ⲛ+*infinitive*.

7.0.2 A MORPHOLOGICAL NOTE ON THE SHENOUTEAN CONJUNCTIVE. But for occasional instances of transmission of a phonetic actualization of the conjunctive, with the supralinear stroke in its base replaced by the vowel ε: ΝΕϤϹϢΤΜ (e.g. in *IV* 60.22), Shenoute's conjunctive has the classical Sahidic morphology. For the first person singular [6], ΝΤΑ- is by far the more common form (over thirty occurrences in *Ch.* and *L*); ΤΑ- is attested almost exclusively in the post-imperative paradigm (§7.2.1.1.1) where the conjunctive has assumed part of the functional load of the classical ΤΑΡΕϤϹϢΤΜ (§7.2.1.1.5); ΤΑ- is thus specialized, at the overlap point of the two post-imperatival categories [7], while ΝΤΑ- has been generalized; at any rate, the two are not mere variants in Shenoute [8].

7.1 CATEGORIAL AND MACRO-SYNTACTIC CHARACTERIZATION OF THE CONJUNCTIVE

7.1.1 A NON-INITIAL, INHERENTLY SATELLITAL VERB-FORM: A MODIFIER. The Coptic conjunctive is a non-autonomous finite Tripartite Clause conjugation form. Non-initial by nature, it is a specific modifier verb expanding (a) a verbal nucleus (§7.1.2, 7.2), (b) a non-verbal nucleus (other modifiers or nouns, often in predicative status; §§7.1.3, 7.3). The homonymity of its base (Ν-, prenominal and pre-zero allomorph ΝΤΕ-) with Ν-, the modifier marker *par excellence*, is in all probability meaningful (its pre-Coptic forms notwithstanding [9]); so is its synchronically peculiar personal morphology (the only Tripartite Conjugation base not followed by a " suffix "-paradigm pronoun). Except for the 1st person singular, this is homonymic with the Bipartite Pattern pronominal actor. This, no less than the base of the conjunctive, must be a constituent part of its distinctive feature, symptomizing its functional speciality as an *inductible*, *categorizable* form. More on the correlation of its formal composition and functional value — *adnexal modification* — see §7.1.3 below.

7.1.2 THE VERBAL NUCLEUS: THE CONJUNCTIVE A CATEGORIZABLE, ATEMPORAL, AMODAL FORM; GROUP CATEGORIZATION; MICRO-/SUB-COORDINATION; ΑΥϢ VS. Ø-; COMPATIBILITIES; TEXT-GRAMMATICAL PROPERTIES; PARADIGMS

7.1.2.1 The conjunctive is a *categorizable verb-form*, that is not only retro-dependent but impressed with the characteristics of the nuclear form expressed by a conjugation base, converter or any other formal indications of tense, mode or syntactic status. Of its own, the conjunctive has only (beside the ability to predicate a verb lexeme) the exponents of person (nom. and pronominal actors) and negation categories; yet even for those the conjunctive may still be induced by the nuclear verb: this is signalled by the negative fact of non-assertion (zero) of negation, by the junctural linkage of pronominal-personal concord. By the assertion of negation (ΤΜ in its proper slot [10]), or by the disruption of the said concord for the (pro)nominal actor, the conjunctive is auto-categorized for negation and person respectively. The conjunctive is not tense/mode-indifferent, but " co-qualifiable " [11]. By itself *unmarked* for these categories, it is marked *cotextually*, with the effect of constituting, together with its nuclear verb, a specific

---

[6] See POLOTSKY 1944:10f. (= *CP* 115f.).

[7] POLOTSKY 1944:1ff. (= *CP* 106ff.), 1950:87ff. (= *CP* 222ff.).

[8] Variation status for ΝΤΑ-/ΤΑ- in Shenoute immediately identifies the non-Shenoutean grammatical system of quotation (*III* 56.10f., 111.14f., *IV* 26.22f., *Ch.* 193.7ff. etc.).

[9] Diachronically, the original form of the conjunctive (acc. to Gardiner's thesis), *ḥnʿ-ntf-sḏm*, is analyzable as a preposition governing an (*actor* + *verb*) nexus, with its modifier status evident (*ḥnʿ* features in all reconstructions. See BORGHOUTS 1979 notes 2 and 9).

[10] I have no example of the *nucleus - conjunctive* dependency being adjunct-negated by ΑΝ (cf. §2.9.1.2.3 for other clause-conjugation adjuncts. In *I Cor.* 4:19, ΑΝ negates another modifier).

[11] Cf. GONDA 1957:19.

closely knit subtextual unit, its cohesion signalled by syncategorization [12]: the conjunctive represents [13] the nuclear verb in the linear sequence, with reduced characterization. The conjunctive extends, evolves, unravels and contentualizes the nuclear notion, or attaches [14] and often serializes additional verbal notions, in a construction that is paradigmatically related to (and in contrastive analysis is comparable with) a *coordinated* complex.

7.1.2.2 The '*verb - conjunctive*' dependence does not strictly fit the usual narrow definition of coordination (cf. DIK 1972:25ff.: " the coordinated terms are equivalent as to grammatical function and bound together at the same level of grammatical hierarchy " [15]) since the two terms are syntactically not on a par. Moreover, their attachment may be either paratactic-asyndetic (juxtaposed) or syndetic, with ΑΥШ, H (NTOЧ), ΑΛΛΑ " mediating " between them. (These elements are hierarchically in the conjunctive immediate-constituent: they are its premodifiers [§1.1.2.2]. The pre-modification of the conjunctive is not less free than for other verb clauses; it may be fairly extensive, making it — together with intercalations and expansions of the nucleus — often difficult at first sight to refer the conjunctive to its nucleus. Some striking exx. are *IV* 74.4ff., 92.10ff. Particles too, like ΔЄ/MЄN and NTOЧ clearly belong in the conjunctive clause. Whatever the hierarchic status of coordinators in other languages [16], I cannot see any cogent reason for assigning the Coptic ones as a separate IC in the analytic model; ΑΥШ, even if regularly used in a coordinating role, is for all that a premodifier [§1.3.10] [17].) The opposition between syndetic and asyndetic conjunctives is complicated, being regulated by numerous juncture-significant parameters: concord/discord of person, of negation; extent of intercalation between nucleus and conjunctive. In the main paragraphs below, I shall adduce specific data on the distribution of both constructions. However, it is possible to present the - ΑΥШ - vs. -Ø- opposition in the *nucleus - conjunctive* syntagm as a binary privative one, and, by referring to its paradigmatic relationship with the real coordinative-syntagm ('*verb* + ΑΥШ + *verb*'), resolve its function: MICRO-COORDINATION (hereafter symbolized ←→; - ΑΥШ - , - H - , - ΑΛΛΑ - etc.; also *variant*, non-significant absence [–] of ΑΥШ) vs. SUBCOORDINATION (+→, Ø-, ΑΥШ excluded): the former *non-vectorial*, undirected, symmetric - reciprocal, antithetic, accumulative, reversible [18], synonymous (here we find the figure-like repetition of lexemes) and serializing [19]; the latter *vectorial*, directed, irreversible [20]. Whereas

---

[12] Among comparable " *Gruppenflexion* " (or " suspended affixation ") cases in other languages, one recalls the Turkish (Altaic) gerund or *converb* (esp. the *-ip* gerund, called by Kononov the " conjunctive gerund "); it is, however, not finite — with the progressive reduction in characterization being more drastic — and cannot be concatenated in a series of converbs; the *Amharic* gerund, being finite, is perhaps a closer parallel (see LOHMANN 1965:225ff.; G. Goldenberg, *BSOAS* 40:489ff., 1977 for the terminological history of the Ethiopian forms). Compare also the well-known " narrative infinitives " in various languages (Latin, Romance languages [cf. REGULA 1951:157ff.], Celtic languages, Semitic languages).

[13] " *Ablösend* " (" continuing + replacing ", " relieving ") seems to have been a keyword in the early descriptions (STERN §447, p. 277, STEINTHAL–MISTELI 1893:298f.); cf. TOBLER 1886:216ff. (on direct speech relieving indirect: " [ein Modus] der den Gedanken fortsetzt und weiterführt und, besonders wenn das Subjekt dasselbe bleibt, sämmtliche Verbalformen ablösen kann ").

[14] Cf. STEINTHAL–MISTELI's " *adjunctiv* " (1893:298f.).

[15] Cf. SANDMANN 1954:208ff. (" interchangeability, morphological uniformity, common relationship to a third element "). The '*verb* + *conjunctive*' complex does enter BALLY's broader definition of coordination (1950:§68f.).

[16] Cf. DIK 1972:52ff. for the two views on the hierarchic structure of coordination. I cannot see how one can be dogmatic on this point in general, seeing this is a decided language-specific issue. On English *and*, though, I would agree with Wells, De Groot and others (against Blümel, Bloomfield and others, incl. Dik himself) assigning *and* in " *he huffed and he puffed* " to the second IC, rather than regarding it as a third intermediating constituent (see reff. in DIK *loc. cit.*).

[17] Compare in Late Egyptian *ḥr* and *m-mjtt* preceding the conjunctive (BORGHOUTS 1979:16 n. 19). Note that the junction of nucleus and conjunctive is by no means the same as between two conjunctives in a series — even though ΑΥШ, H etc. do occur in both slots. I concentrate here on the former; the latter is comparatively uninteresting, not differing (acc. to my analysis) from coordinated adjuncts.

[18] Cf. the Sanskrit *itaretayoga* and *samuccaya* dependencies (GONDA 1957:59f.).

[19] Not catalogic, but rather as " *enumerative Redeweise* " (HAVERS 1931:15, 114, 154, 203; *IF* 45:229-251, 1927) breaking the action up into stages and presenting them one by one.

the former differs from true coordination only in terms of closer juncture realized by the link of syncategorization [21], the latter may express logical nuances of purpose, consequence, circumstance and content, which would (in contrastive consideration) correspond to a *hypotactic* rather than paratactic manner of expression [22].

In the following pages, we shall observe the varying *categorization contour* of the individual patterns, displaying data regarding *personal maintenance* (i. e. pronominal concord [23]), *negation syncategorization* (negative → affirmative), *negation encategorization* (affirmative/negative nucleus → negative conjunctive, not resuming the nuclear negation) [24], *negation maintenance* (neg. nucleus → neg. conjunctive, resuming the nuclear negation) and the special *personal encategorization* (§7.2.5, *infinitive + conjunctive*). All must be correlated with the formal/functional distinction - ΑΥⲰ - *vs.* -Ø- (←→ *vs.* +→) [25]; this information in fact constitutes the distinctive " profile " of each pattern.

7.1.2.3 *Compatiblities.* The nucleus verb may consist of (a) an *extratemporal* [26] or merely contextually temporal verb-form (ⲈⲀⲈⲀ-/ⲙⲈⲈⲀ-, ⲈⲀⲀⲚⲦⲈⲀ-, ⲙⲠⲀⲦⲈⲀ-, protatic syntagms, infinitive, ⲈⲦⲢⲈⲈⲀⳓⲰⲦⲙ) or (b) *modal* verb-forms (imperatives, optative [alias " Third Future "]) or (c) the present-based " imminent " future (— ⲚⲀ-), a complex temporal function or (d) the perfect and present tenses in certain *non-temporal* roles. The conjunctive is compatible only with a transcending, temporally non-specific, equivocal, non-actual, uncharacterized or irrelevant frame of reference.

7.1.2.4 On the text-grammatical level, the conjunctive (again, compatible with [rhetorical] dialogue and exposition, not with narrative texture and its catalogic, time-axis serialization) constitutes with its nucleus a specific subtextual unit, comparable (esp. in the case of a concatenation of multiple conjunctive

---

[20] Not necessarily in cases of " irreversible binomial " collocations (MALKIEL 1959) like " live and die ", " eat and drink " (see §7.2.1.1.1 and *passim* for the latter collocation in Coptic).

[21] Other comparable types of the group-categorization link (§6.0.2): the narrative ⲚⲦⲀ- (rel.) Ⲁⳓ- (*IV* 40.3), ⲚⲦⲀⲠⳊⲞⲈⲒⲤ ⲄⲀⲢ (Sec. Perf.) ⳊⲞⲞⲤ ⲀⲨⲰ ⲀⲀⲚ ⲚⲘⲠⲈⲀ... (*III* 73.5f.), ⲚⲈⲦⲢⲞⲈⲒⲤ ⲀⲨⲰ ⲈⲦⲀ ⲀⲢⲈⳊ (*IV* 21.10); they are paradigmatically relatable to the ' verb + *conjunctive* ' syntagm.

[22] The " subjunctive " function of the conjunctive, diachronically regarded (by STEINTHAL–MISTELI 1893:298) as the last phase of a transition from a coordinative " adjunctive " to a subordinative role, as a " parataxis " (in the sense of " conjunctionless hypotaxis ").

[23] Not necessarily simple concord: in cases like (ⲠⲞⲨⲀ ⲠⲞⲨⲀ ⲘⲘⲞⲚ) → ⲚⲦⲚ- (*IV* 32.14f.) or (ⲀⲀⲀⲨ ⳊⲢⲀⲒ ⲚⳊⲎⲦⲚ Ⲏ ⳊⲀⲦⲚⲦⲎⲨⲦⲚ ⲚⲦⲰⲦⲚ) → ⲚⳓⲈ- (*ibid.* 35.27f.) the concord is no less in evidence than in a straighforward repetition of the pronoun.

[24] *Affirmative* encategorization is marked by premodifiers such as ⲀⲀⲀⲀ (e.g. *III* 31.4f.).

[25] A frontal extraposition to the actor of the conjunctive as a rule conditions ⲀⲨⲰ, overruling and neutralizing the *micro-: subcoordination* opposition (e.g. *III* 139.17f., *IV* 66.8ff.). This reduces the tridimensional opposition (a) to a bidimensional one (b) (consider however the construction in *A 1* 135-6, *III* 220.2ff.).

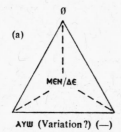

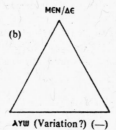

[26] KOSCHMIEDER 1965:13ff.25, 31 (of the Turkish aorist). Cf. POLOTSKY 1959:460 (= *CP* 237) n. 1.

forms) with our (Western) paragraph — a polyarthric unit with unmistakable initial and terminal signals and exponents of cohesion, which (at the thematic level) sets forth and " embroiders " [27] a specific topic.

7.1.3 THE NON-VERBAL NUCLEUS. It is somewhat more difficult to conceive of the conjunctive as expanding any element but the verb; yet this construction is most important, a key pattern furnishing a clue to the functional mystery of the form. On first analysis, here too the nucleus is predicative (in its limited extent): a predicate noun (ⲔⲈⲔⲞⲨⲒ (ⲠⲈ), ⲞⲨⲘⲞⲒⲌⲈ (ⲦⲈ) etc.) with the conjunctive both an expansion and (in the larger complex) a sentence-constituent in its own right; a modifier (mostly of Greek origin; ⲘⲞⲄⲒⲤ, ⲌⲰⲤⲦⲈ, ⲈⲒⲘⲎⲦⲒ, ⲔⲀⲚ, ⲘⲚⲚⲤⲰⲤ etc.) — here the conjunctive may be taken to expand (also contentualize) the modifier, predicative in a single-term clause (# *modifier*-∅ #, §1.2.1.3.2) [28] — yet also having a role of sentence-constituent in the larger extent of *modifier + conjunctive;* a modifier in another predicative pattern (ⲠⲀⲣⲀⲔⲈⲔⲞⲨⲒ (ⲠⲈ), §1.2.1.2); other predicative (sometimes modifier-equivalent) syntagms or expressions: ⲘⲈϢⲀ⸗(Ⲕ) " perhaps ", " (you) do not know "; ⲀⲗⲗⲞ‒ " it is something else... ", ⲘⲎ ⲄⲈⲚⲞⲒⲦⲞ " God forbid ", ⲌⲀⲘⲞⲒ " would that ", (ⲚⲈ)ⲚⲀⲚⲞⲨⲤ (ⲠⲈ) " it (were) better ". (The individual nuclei will be studied in paradigmatic detail below, with the paradigms of substitutables for the conjunctive.)

7.1.3.1 As noted, all these nuclei can be shown to be, *in their own extent*, predicative. In terms of overall *information-structure*, however (FSP, §2.0.2.3) careful evaluation shows them to be essential first-position sentence constituents — *themes* — with the conjunctive the second, *rhematic* constituent; the relationship between the nucleus and the conjunctive is *nexal* in addition to its being *expansional*. This analysis is, I believe, equally applicable to the adverbal conjunctive: the *verb - conjunctive* dependency is complex, twofold, combining a *nexal* relationship with a *satellital* (expansional) one. That the two dependencies are not by any means incompatible [29] is amply illustrated by the other important *adnexal* modifier sentence-form in Coptic, namely the CIRCUMSTANTIAL [30] — in fact, the conjunctive is often in paradigmatic association with the circumstantial, both adnominally [31], adverbally, and occasionally in ad-modifier status. Both circumstantial and conjunctive are " *wortbezogen* ", participial (μετοχή-) forms, in the sense of " sharing ", " participation ", " cooperative union " (" Teilhabe eines Vorgangs oder Zustands an einem anderen " [32]) of two predication-carrying clauses in an ultraclausal predication com-

---

[27] BORGHOUTS 1979:16, 24.

[28] This is TESNIÈRE's analysis (1965:188f.) of such French constructions as " *heureusement que...* ", " *probablement que...* " (see TOBLER 1886:51-4, 102f., for two comparable *que*-constructions in Old French). Comparable are Israeli Hebrew *še*-clauses after " impersonals " (ROSÉN 1977:113-5; a special part of speech, definable by this pattern as a " predicative constituent of a sentence nucleus ": *kᵉdáy še-* " it is advisable that... ", *mutár/asúr še-* " it is allowed/forbidden... "; the *še-* clause is the personal alternant of the infinitive). See also ROSÉN 1979:462f.). I would not term the Coptic nuclei " impersonal ", which has a specific morphological and morphosyntactic Indo-European connotation, but rather define them as " non-verbal elements adnexally expanded by the conjunctive ".

[29] Cf. Ch. 2 (p. 81) on *III* 191.21ff. (cf. BARRI 1978).

[30] SHISHA–HALEVY 1972:§0.4 and *passim*, 1976a:47, 1976c:134 n. 3.

[31] The interesting *adnominal paradigm*, which has yet to be further investigated, is:

	relative (attributive) ⎫
	circumstantial (adnexal) ⎬ neutralized after non-ⲡ determination
(NOUN SYNTAGM)	*conjunctive* (adnexal, micro/subcoordinating, contentualizing)
	ⲈⲦⲣⲈϤ‒ (contentualizing)
	ϪⲈ‒ (generic, " such... as ")

See further in §7.4 below.

[32] LOHMANN (1965:224ff.) studies this category in languages of different type.

plex (*Satzgefüge*). Beyond the basic semasiological differences [33] between the two verbal modifiers, we note the following interrelated structural ones:

CIRCUMSTANTIAL	CONJUNCTIVE
(a) " Converter ": a " vertical ", transsecting syntactic category; self-characterizing for grammatical categories.	Non-transsecting. Unmarked for most grammatical categories.
(b) With no significant syncategorization.	In syncategorization cohesion.
(c) Also initial.	Non-initial.
(d) Focalizable. Characteristically predicative complementation.	Non-focalizable. Uncharacteristically pred. complementation.

Notes. (b) The circumstantial *is* syncategorized (for person) when it is a predicative complement of auxiliary " descriptive " verbs (ⲀϤⲖⲟ ⲈϤ-, ⲀϤⲟⲨⲱ ⲈϤ-), in suppletive periphrases (ⲀϤϣⲱⲡⲈ ⲈϤ-) [34] or generally after verbs " of incomplete predication ". (c) It is an open question whether the conjunctive can occur in absolutely initial position (i.e. after ⲬⲈ- or in text-initial position). The view that it is found initially is held by most grammarians: I do not share this view, which is not corroborated by Shenoutean usage. (d) I do not know of any unequivocal instance of the conjunctive focalized by the Second Tense or any other topicalization form, yet some exx. indicate that the conjunctive can complement verbs " of incomplete predication ", in paradigm with the more usual circumstantial (ⲤⲚⲀϣⲱⲡⲈ/ⲈⲤϣⲀⲚϣⲱⲡⲈ + *conjunctive*, exx. below).

Needless to say, point (a) subsumes the elementary difference between a *converted* syntagm and a " basic " (i.e. unconverted — but, in our case, *unconvertible*) " conjugation-form " syntagm; this distinction makes for others, in the negativing procedure and other syntactic phenomena. But in this respect it will not do to be too dogmatic: one realizes, with some surprise, that here the morphological oddity of our form somehow falls into place. Historically, this is the only Tripartite Pattern form the base of which does not go back to an auxiliary-verb nucleus or to *jw-*. Synchronically, it is the only Tripartite Pattern form in which the actor-expression is not a suffix pronoun, but a paradigm coincident with that of the prefix pronouns (except for the 1st person sgl. which, it may be argued, is " heteroclitic ", suppletively imported from ⲦⲀⲢⲈϤⲤⲱⲦⲘ). Putting two and two together, it may perhaps not be rash to make the following suggestions:

(a) The conjunctive characteristic Ⲛ/ⲚⲦⲈ occupies an intermediate position between a conjugation base and a converter (in the micro- and macro-syntactic sense) [35].

(b) Whereas the first IC-analysis of all other Tripartite Pattern forms is

$$\underbrace{\overbrace{conjugation\ base + actor\ suffix}}_{(n\ u\ c\ l\ e\ u\ s\ [``\ pro\text{-}verb\ ";\ \S5.4])}\ \Big]\ \begin{array}{c} verb\ lexeme\ (``\ infinitive\ ")\\ (s\ a\ t\ e\ l\ l\ i\ t\ e) \end{array}$$

---

[33] These are as a matter of fact not as pronounced as might be expected: the circumstantial too is often " coordinative " (consider ⲈϤ- *III* 13.15, 203.19f., and especially ⲈⲀϤ- *Ch.* 54.58, 93.30f., *III* 18.3, 113.18, *Cat.* 42.39), while the conjunctive may express various " subordinative " shades of meaning (cause, effect, result, content).

[34] SHISHA–HALEVY 1972:§1.3 (pp. 57-66).

[35] See §2.0.1.1 above.

— or, in the thematic structure, *actor* ⎤ [*base* + *verb lexeme*]
(theme) ⎦ (discontinuous rheme) —

that of the conjunctive is different:

N ⎤ [*actor* + *verb lexeme*]
(NTε) ⎦ (theme) (rheme)

and is to a degree analogous to the structure of a converted conjugation form: N-, the syntactically signal-ling " *nota relationis* " is a full constituent, not in the same IC as the actor exponent. Thus, we cannot claim full material identity of the converter-like base of the conjunctive with the prepositional — adjunctal, but often also adnexal — N-, but the similarity in form and function cannot be ignored. I see the conjunc-tive base N- as the signal or exponent of a specific syntactic status: NϤCШTM is the *representative* of the whole class of verbal predications in the modifier-conversion form. Just as the *nota relationis* N- is the modifier-mark *par excellence* (§1.0.1 and *passim*), so is NϤCШTM the quintessential verbal modifier — and this is correlatable with its present-like bipartite # *theme - rheme* # schematic structure [36].
(c) Following the base, the rest of the conjunctive form — noun-syntagm/prefix-like pronoun + verb lexeme — must be further IC-analyzed (second analysis) as two pattern constituents of equal syntagmatic standing: *theme* + *rheme*, and *not* in terms of a nucleus - satellite dependency. This returns us to the Bipartite Pattern, and this ties in with the functional " indifference " or unmarkedness of the conjunctive with regard to most temporal-modal categories [37]. (Incidentally, -TM- — characteristic of all Clause Con-jugations, POLOTSKY 1960a:§27 — is the verbal-modifier negation in Coptic, apart from its use to negative the infinitive.)

7.2 COTEXT PATTERNS AND PARADIGMS

7.2.1 # MODAL PREDICATION + CONJUNCTIVE

7.2.1.1 THE IMPERATIVE SYSTEM

7.2.1.1.1 THE IMPERATIVE

(a) *Subcoordination* (+→): nuclear verb affirmative/negatived; conjunctive affirmative; personal mainte-nance disrupted; negation syncategorization [38] (*III* 181.10) TШOYN NTNMETANOI, inclusive 1st person plural: " you and us " / (*A 1* 206) OYШM NΓCШ — " irreversible binomial ", cf. *ibid.* εOYШM ΑYШ εCШ, ΑYOYШM ΑYШ ΑYCШ. Howeνεr, in the light of (*A 2* 437) NIM ΠεTNΑOYШM ΑYШ NϤCШ ΑXNTϤ, (*RE 11* 18a 11ff.) MΑ-ΡεϤOYШM ΑYШ NϤCШ, (ΠεTOYШM ΑYШ εTCШ, εϤOYШM ΑYШ εϤCШ), (*IV* 66.17) MΠΑTOYOYШM ΑYШ NCεCШ, etc., one must conclude that subcoordination is not the rule in Coptic in this case. / (*III* 210.15f.,19f.) ΑMOY NΓNΑY εTεIΨYXH εNTΑΠCΑTΑNΑC ΑΑC NBΑΛH / (*ibid.* 16.12, 18.1) KΑΑT TΑTΡεNεCNHY Ρ-OYΑNΑϢ NΑI [39] / (*IV*

---

[36] The non-actual, non-durative present (§3.1.2.1.1) being tense-unmarked, is here called to mind.

[37] This analysis (already suggested in outline by SCHWARZE, SCHWARZE–STEINTHAL 451: " die Verbindung des Relativs... mit den Verbal-Präfixen des Präsens ") is here advocated for Sahidic (and " Middle Egyptian ") only. The Akhmimic con-junctive (and some other non-literary forms) in which the pronominal form is truly homonymic with the present, might be sim-ilarly analyzed, although the zeroing of the N- must be accounted for. In Bohairic, the conjunctive base + actor seems a veritable " pro-verb " (§5.3). See KAHLE 1954:160ff. for an interesting analysis of N-zeroed forms of the conjunctive in various dialects. Incidentally, this approach ties in with Mattha's reconstruction of the conjunctive as ḫnꜥ ntt-jw.f ḥr sḏm (*BIFAO* 45:43-55, 1947; rejected by Černý, *JEA* 35:25-30, 1949; see VOLTEN 1964:79f.).

[38] Cf. Sauneron, *BIFAO* 61 (1962) 59-67.

[39] KΑΑT TΑ-, not attested in the Sahidic New Testament, occurs in the Old Testament (*Job* 10:20), Bohairic (XШ NHI NTΑ-, XΑT NTΑ-), and especially (?) in Akhmimic (cf. TILL 1928:§139c).

1.14) ⲥⲱⲧⲙ ⲧⲁⲧⲁⲙⲟⲕ ⲉⲙⲙⲛⲧⲩⲁⲛⲥⲧⲏϥ ⲙⲡⲉⲧϫⲟⲥⲉ. Note that both instances of the 1st person sgl. are causative (lexically or grammatically): see §7.2.1.1.4 / (*Ch.* 185.48ff.) ϭⲱⲩⲧ ⲉϪⲛⲛⲉⲕⲥⲁⲣⲍ ⲛⲅⲛⲁⲩ Ϫⲉ-ⲟⲩ ⲡⲉ ⲡⲓⲕⲙⲟⲙ ⲛⲩⲩⲃⲍ (cf. *IV* 200.14) / (*Ch.* 72.25ff.) ⲕⲁ-ⲛⲟⲩⲩⲛⲩ ⲛⲥⲉⲟⲩⲁⲍⲟⲩ ⲛⲥⲁⲛⲟⲩⲩⲛⲩ / (*ibid.* 102.5ff.) ⲙⲡⲣⲥⲱⲧⲙ ⲛⲧⲟϥ ⲉⲣⲟⲓ ⲉⲓϪⲱ ⲛⲛⲁⲓ ⲛⲧⲉⲧⲛⲉⲃⲩ-ⲑⲏⲩⲧⲛ ⲉⲛⲍⲟⲟⲩ ⲛⲛⲏⲥⲧⲉⲓⲁ ⲉⲧⲧⲏⲩ, consecutive. Syncategorized negation / (*P* 131⁷ 25 ro) ⲗⲟⲓⲡⲟⲛ ⲙⲡⲣⲣ-ⲁⲙⲉⲗⲏⲥ ⲛⲥⲉⲩⲧⲁⲙ ⲉⲣⲱⲛ ⲉⲙⲡⲣⲟ (sic) ⲙⲡⲙⲁ ⲛϪⲓ-ⲡⲁⲍⲣⲉ / (*RE 10* 160a 32f.) ⲃⲩⲕ ⲛⲧⲉⲧⲛϪⲟⲟⲥ... / (*III* 29.26) ⲩⲗⲗ ⲉϪⲱⲛ ⲛⲧⲛⲉⲓⲣⲉ ⲕⲁⲧⲁⲛⲉⲛⲧⲁⲕϪⲟⲟⲩ ⲉⲣⲟⲛ / (*ibid.* 63.20f.) +-ⲍⲧⲏⲕ ⲁⲉ ⲍⲱⲱϥ ⲉⲡⲗⲟ-ⲅⲟⲥ... ⲛϥϪⲱ ⲛⲁⲕ... / (*P* 130⁵ 83 ⲣⲓⲁ) ⲁⲙⲟⲩ ⲛⲩⲟⲣⲡ ⲉⲃⲟⲗ ⲍⲛⲛⲉⲕⲁⲕⲁⲑⲁⲣⲥⲓⲁ, ⲧⲟⲧⲉ ⲛⲅϪⲟⲟⲥ Ϫⲉ "ⲡⲁⲥⲱⲧⲏⲣ": the temporal sequence is explicitated; not so in (*Ch.* 55.4ff.) ⲧⲁⲗⲟ ⲉⲣⲟϥ ⲛⲅⲧⲟⲃⲥϥ ⲛⲅⲃⲱⲕ ⲉⲍⲣⲁⲓ ⲛⲅⲉⲓ " Mount it (your horse), and spur it, and go up (to the sky) and come away ".

(b) *Microcoordination* (←→) is here less usual. Nuclear verb —affirmative only; conjunctive: affirmative/negative (very rare); personal maintenance; negation syncategorization (very rare): (*Ch.* 164.19ff.) +-ⲍⲧⲏⲧⲛ ⲁⲩⲱ ⲛⲧⲉⲧⲛⲣⲟⲉⲓⲥ ⲛⲧⲉⲧⲛⲩⲗⲏⲗ / (*IV* 41.9f.) ⲁⲁⲕ ⲛⲉⲗⲁⲭⲓⲥⲧⲟⲛ ⲍⲙⲡⲩⲁϪⲉ ⲛⲧⲉⲕⲧⲁⲡⲣⲟ ⲛⲅⲁⲁⲕ ⲛⲁⲧⲛⲟⲉⲓ ⲍⲛⲧⲙⲏⲧⲉ ⲛⲛⲥⲁⲃⲉⲉⲩ (cf. *III* 91.4ff. ⲁⲛⲁⲩ... ⲛⲧⲉⲧⲛⲛⲁⲩ ⲁⲉ ⲍⲱⲱϥ) / (*III* 193.3f.) ⲩⲓⲛⲉ ⲛⲥⲁ+ⲣⲏⲛⲏ ⲛⲅⲡⲱⲧ ⲛⲥⲱⲥ / (*ibid.* 63.9ff.) ⲥⲱⲟⲩⲍ ⲁⲉ ⲉⲍⲟⲩⲛ... ⲛⲅⲧ[ⲙⲩⲩ]Ϫⲡ ⲉⲡⲁⲍⲟⲩ.

7.2.1.1.2 The rhetorical jussive ⲙⲁⲣⲉϥ-/ⲙⲡⲣⲧⲣⲉϥ-. This form, in Scripture Coptic the *causative imperative*, functionally coextensive with the *jussive* (" third-person imperative ")⁴⁰, has in Shenoute a different standing. As a jussive, it is curtailed in function, specialized and marked for rhetorical and " figurative " jussive mode, while for the objective, " real ", usually preceptive and generally unmarked jussive the *autofocal Second Future* ⲉϥⲛⲁⲥⲱⲧⲙ (§§2.1.3, 7.2.1.1.3) is used (with ⲛⲛⲉϥ-, a suppletive negative form, apart from the rare ⲉϥⲛⲁ- ⲁⲛ and perhaps ⲙⲡⲣⲧⲣⲉϥ-): ⲙⲁⲣⲉϥⲥⲱⲧⲙ and ⲉϥⲛⲁⲥⲱⲧⲙ are to be regarded as *allo-forms*, in rhetorical and preceptive/unmarked environment respectively.

(a) (+→): Nuclear verb: affirmative/negative; conjunctive: affirmative only; neg. syncategorization; personal maintenance disrupted (note that as a pronominal actor we find only the 3rd person plural): (*III* 149.19) ⲙⲁⲣⲟⲩⲉⲓ ⲛⲥⲉⲛⲉϪ-ⲡⲁϭⲥⲉ ⲉⲍⲟⲩⲛ ⲉⲍⲣⲁⲛ, also *ibid.* 201.12 / (*ibid.* 18.24ff.) ⲙⲁⲣⲉⲛⲉⲧⲛⲁⲡⲁⲣⲁⲃⲁ ⲙⲡⲧⲩⲩ... ⲟⲩⲉⲍ-ⲛⲟⲃⲉ ⲉϪⲛⲛⲉⲩⲛⲟⲃⲉ ⲛⲧⲉⲡⲣⲁⲛ ⲙⲡⲛⲟⲩⲧⲉ ⲩⲱⲡⲉ ⲉϥⲟⲩⲁⲁⲃ / (*IV* 39.4ff.) ⲙⲡⲣⲧⲣⲉⲟⲩⲁ ⲥⲱⲧⲙ... Ϫⲉ-... ⲛⲥⲉ-ⲙⲉⲉⲩⲉ... Ϫⲉ-..., subcoordination of *consequence*; neg. syncategorization / (*ibid.* 37-8) ⲙⲡⲣⲧⲣⲉⲩⲡⲣⲟⲥⲉⲭⲉ ⲉⲣⲟⲛ ⲍⲓⲧⲛⲛⲉⲧⲧⲱⲍⲙ... ⲛⲥⲉⲅⲛⲧⲛ ⲉⲣⲉⲛⲉⲛⲍⲏⲧ ⲙⲛⲛⲉⲛⲯⲩⲭⲏ ⲩⲟⲩⲉⲓⲧ, neg. syncategorization. Note the discontinuous actor exponence (for a passive-equivalent form), remarkable for ⲧⲣⲉ-, -ⲩ- + ⲍⲓⲧⲛ- + ⲥⲉ-.

(b) (←→): Nuclear verb: affirmative/negative; conjunctive: affirmative only; neg. syncategorization; personal maintenance. (*Ch.* 163.31ff.) ⲙⲁⲣⲟⲩⲁⲓⲥⲑⲁⲛⲉ ⲁⲩⲱ ⲛⲥⲉⲥⲱⲧⲙ ⲉⲡⲉⲧϪⲱ ⲙⲙⲟⲥ Ϫⲉ- / (*ibid.* 165.22f.) ⲙⲁ-ⲡⲛⲣⲟⲉⲓⲥ ⲛⲧⲛⲛⲏϥⲉ / (*RE 11* 18a 11ff.) ⲙⲁⲣⲉϥⲟⲩⲱⲙ ⲁⲩⲱ ⲛϥⲥⲱ: see under §7.2.1.1.1(a) / (*P* 130⁵ 22 ⲫⲛ) ⲁⲛⲟⲛ ⲍⲱⲱⲛ ⲱ ⲛⲉⲥⲛⲏⲩ ⲙⲁⲣⲛⲣ-ⲧⲙⲉ ⲁⲩⲱ ⲛⲧⲛϪⲱ ⲛⲧⲙⲉ... ⲁⲩⲱ ⲛⲧⲛⲣ-ⲙⲡⲩⲁ ⲙⲡⲛⲟⲩⲧⲉ... / (*IV* 5.21ff.) ⲙⲡⲣⲧⲣⲉⲛⲁⲁⲛ ⲛⲩⲙⲙⲟ ⲉⲡⲛⲟⲩⲧⲉ... ⲁⲩⲱ ⲛⲧⲛⲩⲱⲡⲉ ⲛϪⲁϪⲉ... — neg. syncategorization.

7.2.1.1.3 The preceptive/unmarked jussive: ⲉϥⲛⲁⲥⲱⲧⲙ/ⲛⲛⲉϥⲥⲱⲧⲙ. This is the form intruding (in diachronic view) into the neat Scriptural suppletive imperative paradigm *imperative*/ⲙⲁⲣⲉϥ-, disturbing its equilibrium and acting to confine the classical jussive ⲙⲁⲣⲉϥⲥⲱⲧⲙ to its specialized rhetorical value. Note the following distinctive characteristics of this cotext pattern: (a) The opposition *microcoordination*: *subcoordination* is here virtually neutralized, as pertinent ⲁⲩⲱ does not occur here at all⁴¹, and the conjunctive as a rule specifies the actual (logico-temporal) sequence of phases in the execution of the instructions. (b) Personal maintenance is here usual. (c) The textual distribution is in this case understandably

---

⁴⁰ A (typically non-classical?) case like (*IV* 114.18f.) ⲙⲁⲣⲓⲙⲡⲩⲁ ⲛⲛⲁⲩ ⲉⲣⲟϥ... ⲁⲩⲱ ⲙⲁⲣⲉϥⲕⲟⲗⲁⲍⲉ ⲙⲙⲟⲓ proves the rhetoricity of the Shenoutean ⲙⲁⲣⲉϥⲥⲱⲧⲙ.

⁴¹ Barring the overruling conditioning of ⲁⲩⲱ before a frontal extraposition to the actor of the conjunctive, see n. 25.

limited: almost all instances occur in non-rhetorical "*Vita Monachorum*"-type textual stretches (a single instance in *Chassinat*). Nuclear verb: affirmative/negative; conjunctive: affirmative/negative; personal maintenance (see below); neg. syncategorization, encategorization. (*IV* 93.1f.) ЄΥΝΑΝΑΥ ЄΠЄΤΟΥΝΑΧΙΤЧ ЄΡΟΟΥ ΝΟЄΙΚ... ΝСЄΧΙΤΟΥ ΝΑΥ ЗΜΠϹΗΥ ΜΠΤШϬ / (*ibid.* 61-2) ЄΥΝΑЄΙ ΝϬΙΝЄСΝΗΥ ΝСЄΨΑΛΛЄΙ ЄΡΟΟΥ ΝСЄΤΟΜСΟΥ / (*ibid.* 160.2f.) ЄΥΝΑСЗΑΙСΟΥ ΝСЄΤΝΝΟΟΥСΟΥ ΝΑΥ ΝСЄΝΑΥ ЄΠЄΤЄΨШЄ ЄΛΑЧ / (*ibid.* 161.21f.) ЄΥΝΑΘΝЄ-ΠЄ-ϬΛΟϬ ЄΠСШΜΑ ЄΤΜΟΟΥΤ ΝΤЄЗЄΝΝΟϬ ΝΡШΜЄ ЧЄΙ ЗΑΧШЧ ΑΥШ ЗΑΡΑΤЧ... ЄΡЄ-ΠЄΤЧЄΙ ЄЗΡΑΙ ΝΑΝ-ΤЄЧΝΑЗΒЄ ЄΒΟΛ ΝΤЄΠЄΤΝΑЧЄΙ †-ΤШЧ ЄЗΟΥΝ / (*ibid.* 83.14f.) ЄΥΝΑΨΑΛΛЄΙ ΝЧΟΜΤ ΝСΟΠ... ΝСЄΨΛΗΛ ΝЧΟΜΝΤ ΝСΟΠ... A solitary instance of the personal maintenance disrupted is rhetorical (*Ch.* 187.2ff.) ЄΥΝΑ†-ЗΤΗΥ ΧЄ-ЄΡЄΝЄΓΡΑФΗ ΧЄ-ΟΥ ΑΥШ ΧЄ-ΟΥ ΝЄΝΤΑΥСЗΑΙСΟΥ... ΑΥШ ΝΤΝΜΤΟΝ ΜΜΟΝ ЗΝΝЄΥШΑΧЄ ΝΟΥΟЄΙΝ (although here the 1st person person plur. may be taken to resume anacoluthically the preceding ΡШΜЄ ΝΙΜ). Additional exx.: *IV* 46.5f., 50-1, 66.2ff.,7ff., 83.12f.,17f.,20f., 111.9f.,14f., etc.

The negative counterpart of jussive ЄЧΝΑСШΤΜ appears to be ΝΝЄЧСШΤΜ, syncategorizing the conjunctive: (*IV* 73.10ff.) ΝΝЄΛΑΑΥ... ΧЄЧ-ΚШЗΤ ЄΛΑΑΥ ΜΜΑ ΜΜΟΟΥ... Η ΝСЄΧΙ-СΝΟЧ ΜΜΟΟΥ / (*ibid.* 88.1ff.) ΝΝЄΟΥΑ Η ЗΟΙΝЄ ΟΥЄΜ-ΝЄΤСΟΤΠ... ΝΤЄΚЄΟΥΑ Η ЗЄΝΚΟΟΥЄ ΟΥЄΜ-ΝЄΤϬΟΧΒ Η ΝЄΤСΟШЧ / (*ibid.* 103.5f.) ΝΝЄΡШΜЄ ΝЗΗΤΝ ϬШ ΝЧΤΜΒШΚ ЄΠΟΥШΜ — a striking case of subcoordination: the neg. conjunctive does not maintain the negation of ΝΝЄ-, but contentualizes ϬШ; consider the variant reading ϬШ ΝΟΥЄШΝΒШΚ and the parallel in (*IV* 66.24f.) ϬШ ЄΤΜΒШΚ.

7.2.1.1.4 ЄЧЄСШΤΜ, properly speaking the *optative* (§7.2.1.2), is also used as a polite or restrained imperative and jussive [42]: (*IV* 43.23) ЄЧЄШΑΧЄ ΜΝΝЄΤΝΑΧΙ ΤΗΡΟΥ ΝЧ2ШΝ ЄΤΟΟΤΟΥ ЄΤΡЄΥ-... / (*ibid.* 62. 15f.,24) ЄΤЄΤΝЄΜΟΟШЄ ЗΙΠΑЗΟΥ ΝΝЄСΝΗΥ ΝΤЄΤΝϬШ ЄΤЄΤΝΟΥΗΥ ΜΜΟΟΥ... ЄΤЄΤΝЄШШ ΝΤЄΤΝШΛΗΛ / (*III* 157. 11f.) ЄΥЄΧΟΟС ЄΠЗΛΛΟ ЗΑΤΗΝ ΑΥШ ЄΥЄΧΟΟС ЄΘΛΛШ ЗΑЗΤΝΤΗΥΤΝ Η ΝСЄΧΟΟС ЄΝЗΛΛΟΙ ЄΤЗΑΤΝΤΗΥΤΝ... / (*IV* 207.26) ЄΥЄΟΥШШΒ ΝСЄΧΟΟС ΧЄ-... (more exx.: *III* 157.21, *IV* 43.9ff.).

7.2.1.1.5. THE POST-IMPERATIVE PARADIGM: MEMBERS AND FUNCTIONS

	ΤΑΡЄЧСШΤΜ	rhetorical, affective; archaistic-Biblical stylistically marked; ensured desirable result (§7.2.1.1.5.1)
imperative	ΑΥШ + *fut. I*	unmarked, not purposeful consequence [43]: *III* 21.2ff., 116.4f., *Ch.* 152.49ff., *IV* 40.5ff., 41.3ff.
' СШΤΜ '	Ø + *fut. I*	*III* 17.2, *Wess. 9* 139a 20ff.
' ΜΠΡСШΤΜ '	ΑΥШ + *imperative*	coordination of reciprocally symmetric or mutually independent imperatives [44]:
	ΑΥШ + *rhet. jussive*	*III* 25.4, *IV* 162.10f.
	conjunctive	micro-/subcoordination
	ЄΤΡЄЧ-	deliberate purpose

---

[42] POLOTSKY 1950:84ff. (= *CP* 219ff.).

[43] Cf. POLOTSKY 1944:7f. (= *CP* 112f.). In Shenoute, the future is not restricted to the 1st person singular.

[44] Compare (*A 1* 57) ЗΑΡЄЗ ΜΠΡΤΡЄΥΤΑЗШΤΝ ΟΥΤЄ ΜΠΡΤΡЄΛΑΑΥ ЄΙΜЄ, *ibid.* 234 СШΤΜ ΑΥШ ΜΑΡЄΝΡ-ЗΟΤЄ.

rhetorical jussive	ⲁⲨⲱ + *fut. I*	unmarked consequence: *Ch.* 37.10ff.
' ⲘⲀⲢⲈⲨⲤⲰⲦⲘ '	ⲁⲨⲱ + *rhet. jussive*	two coordinated jussives: mutually independent (*IV* 38.6ff., 114.18f.),
' ⲘⲠⲢⲦⲢⲈⲨⲤⲰⲦⲘ '		or reciprocally symmetric (*IV* 156.7, *Ch.* 165.30ff.)
	conjunctive	micro-/subcoordination
	ⲈⲦⲢⲈⲨ-	deliberate purpose
	ⲦⲀⲢⲈⲨⲤⲰⲦⲘ	stylistically marked consequence (§7.2.1.1.5.1)
preceptive jussive	ⲁⲨⲱ + *prec. jussive* (very rare)	mutually independent, non-sequential coordination: two separate enjoinments; reciprocal symmetry (*III* 157.11f., *IV* 58.15, 99.17f.)
' ⲈⲨⲚⲀⲤⲰⲦⲘ '		
' ⲈⲨⲈⲤⲰⲦⲘ '	ⲁⲨⲱ ⲈⲨⲈⲤⲰⲦⲘ (rare)	
	conjunctive	sequential micro-coordination
	ⲦⲀⲢⲈⲨⲤⲰⲦⲘ (rare)	§7.2.1.1.5.1

7.2.1.1.5.1 Like ⲘⲀⲢⲈ-, ⲦⲀⲢⲈⲨⲤⲰⲦⲘ, the classical " Future Conjunctive ", is in Shenoute restricted and shifted in value compared with its role in the Scripture idiom [45] — the post-imperatival apodotic form with a promissive overtone. In Shenoute, it is not the conjunctive (with which ⲦⲀⲢⲈⲨ- has synchronically the satellital status in common — the same kind of modification dependency in relation to the nuclear verb [46]) that has encroached on its territory, but rather the coordinative ⲁⲨⲱ + *future I*. Generally speaking, three statements (illustrated below) may be made on the Shenoutean ⲦⲀⲢⲈⲨⲤⲰⲦⲘ: (a) It is *stylistically marked* as rhetorical, affective, redolent of archaic-Biblical overtones and typical of passages in which this atmosphere (often conveying an authoritative aura) must be effected, or in otherwise stylistically striking stretches. (b) The distribution of ⲦⲀⲢⲈⲨ - has been extended to post-interrogative [47] and generally final environments (inside the imperative system, we find ⲦⲀⲢⲈⲨ- following the jussives ⲘⲀⲢⲈⲨ- and ⲈⲨⲚⲀ-); the " promissive " semantic component of ⲦⲀⲢⲈⲨ- has been greatly weakened. (c) Where it is opposed to other final constructions in cases (a) and (b), ⲦⲀⲢⲈⲨ- seems to convey the sense of *final desirable result* rather than downright deliberate purpose.

(a) *Stylistic effect*: (1) *archaic-Biblical simulation*: (*III* 84.14ff., parall. *Ch.* 48.28ff.) ⲰⲚ-ⲌⲦⲎⲔ ⲄⲈ ⲌⲀⲠⲈⲔⲖⲀⲞⲤ ⲚⲄⲤⲞⲞⲦⲞⲨ... ⲦⲀⲢⲞⲨⲤⲢⲨⲈ ⲈⲈⲒⲘⲈ ϪⲈ-ⲘⲚⲄⲈⲚⲞⲨⲦⲈ ⲚⲂⲀⲖⲀⲔ, addressed to God; an argumentative application of *Ps.* 45:11. Similarly, *III* 84.20ff. (parall. *Ch.* 48.52ff.) ⲦⲰⲘ ⲄⲈ ⲈⲢⲚⲀⲚⲞⲘⲒⲀ ⲚⲒⲘ ⲘⲚϪⲒ ⲚⲄⲞⲚⲤ ⲚⲒⲘ... ⲦⲀⲢⲈⲚⲈⲦⲤⲞⲞⲨⲚ ⲘⲘⲞⲔ ⲤⲢⲨⲈ ⲈⲢ-ⲌⲘⲌⲀⲖ ⲚⲀⲔ. Indeed, ⲦⲀⲢⲈⲨ- is an unmistakable sign of a Biblical quotation or reminiscence in the Shenoutean texture: *A 2* 228 (*Prov.* 7:2), *Cl. Pr.* 22 ⲦϪⲀ (*Ps.* 36:37), *A 2* 388 (*Ps.* 68:33), *A 2* 235 (*Rom.* 11:35), *III* 112.20f. (*Prov.* 7:1a), *A 2* 189 (*Mt.* 11:3) and many more.

---

[45] POLOTSKY 1944:1ff. (= *CP* 102ff.), 1950: 87ff.(= *CP* 222ff.).

[46] Consider (*Ch.* 198.44ff.) ⲘⲎ ⲈⲨⲦ-ⲤⲂⲰ ⲚⲀⲚ ⲚⲦⲞⲨ ⲀⲚ ⲚⲦⲈⲒⲌⲈ ⲌⲒⲦⲘⲠⲒⲔⲈⲰⲀϪⲈ ⲦⲀⲢⲠⲚⲔⲰ ⲚⲤⲰⲚ ⲚⲦⲈⲚⲘⲚⲦⲀⲦⲚⲀⲌⲦⲈ, where ⲦⲀⲢⲈⲨ- is focalized by a Second Present, showing itself to be a true modifier-clause.

[47] POLOTSKY 1944:5f., §3B (= *CP* 110f.).

(2) Ponderous, turgid categoric style (similar to (1)? Note the high incidence of ⲉⲓⲙⲉ or its paraphrases, which may be indicative of a certain tone of address): (*A 2* 64) ⲙⲟⲩⲧⲉ ⲛⲧⲟ ⲧⲡⲁⲣⲑⲉⲛⲟⲥ ⲛⲥⲟϭ ⲕⲱⲧⲉ ⲛⲛⲟⲩ-ⲍⲛⲁⲁⲩ ⲧⲏⲣⲟⲩ ⲧⲁⲣⲉⲉⲓⲙⲉ ⲭⲉ-... / (*ibid.* 121) ⲕⲱ ⲇⲉ ⲛⲁⲕ ⲍⲱⲱⲕ ⲛⲧⲙⲉ ⲧⲁⲣⲉⲡϣⲁⲭⲉ ⲭⲟⲟⲥ ⲛⲁⲕ ⲭⲉ-... / (*A 1* 234) ⲥⲱⲧⲙ ⲁⲩⲱ ⲙⲁⲣⲉⲛⲣ-ⲍⲟⲧⲉ ⲍⲏⲧϥ ⲙⲡⲉⲧⲙⲟⲩⲍ ⲛⲧⲡⲉ ⲁⲩⲱ ⲉⲧⲙⲟⲩⲍ ⲙⲡⲕⲁⲍ ⲁⲩⲱ ⲉⲧⲣⲍⲟⲩⲉⲙⲟⲩⲍ ⲙⲡⲉϥⲏⲓ ⲧⲁⲣⲉⲛⲉⲓⲙⲉ... ⲭⲉ- / (*A 2* 72) ⲡⲛⲟⲩⲧⲉ ⲉⲙⲙⲛⲧϣⲁⲛⲍⲧⲏϥ (sic) ⲛⲓⲙ ⲉϥⲛⲁⲁⲁⲛ ⲛⲙⲡϣⲁ ⲙⲡⲉⲓⲍⲱⲃ ⲥⲛⲁⲩ ⲧⲁⲣⲛⲙⲉⲧⲉⲭⲉ ⲉⲡⲧⲏⲣϥ / (*P* 131⁶ 13 vo) ⲉϣⲱⲡⲉ ⲛⲧⲕ-ⲟⲩⲍⲏⲕⲉ ⲁⲙⲟⲩ ⲉⲧⲉⲕⲕⲗⲏⲥⲓⲁ ⲁⲩⲱ ⲕⲛⲁϣⲱⲡⲉ ⲛⲣⲙⲙⲁⲟ ⲍⲛⲛⲁⲡⲛⲟⲩⲧⲉ; ⲉϣⲱⲡⲉ ⲇⲉ ⲟⲛ ⲛⲧⲕ-ⲟⲩⲣⲙⲙⲁⲟ ⲁⲙⲟⲩ ⲉⲧⲉⲕⲕⲗⲏⲥⲓⲁ ⲧⲁⲣⲉⲡⲛⲟⲩⲧⲉ ⲥⲙⲟⲩ ⲉⲣⲟⲕ ⲍⲛⲧⲉⲕⲙⲛⲧⲣⲙⲙⲁⲟ. ⲉϣⲱⲡⲉ ⲟⲛ ⲉⲙⲛⲧⲁⲕ-ϣⲏⲣⲉ ⲙⲙⲁⲩ, ⲁⲙⲟⲩ ⲉⲧⲉⲕⲕⲗⲏⲥⲓⲁ ⲁⲩⲱ ⲕⲛⲁϣⲱⲡⲉ ⲛⲉⲓⲱⲧ ⲛⲟⲩⲙⲏⲏϣⲉ ⲛϣⲏⲣⲉ — suppletion of ⲁⲩⲱ + *future I* for the 2nd person?

(3) A special rhetorical effect or figure: ⲧⲁⲣⲉϥ- repeats the imperative verb: (*A 2* 224-5) ⲥⲉⲓ ⲛⲏⲧⲛ ⲛⲛⲉ-ⲧⲛⲍⲏⲇⲟⲛⲏ ⲛⲭⲱⲍⲙ ⲍⲓⲥⲱⲱϥ... ⲧⲁⲣⲉⲧⲉⲧⲛⲥⲉⲓ ⲟⲛ ⲙⲡⲣⲱⲕⲍ ⲙⲛⲡⲕⲱⲍⲧ ⲉⲧⲉⲙⲉϥϣⲱⲙ / (*ibid.* 461) ϣⲟⲡⲥ ⲉⲣⲟⲕ (i.e. the Kingdom) ⲍⲙⲡⲉⲓⲙⲁ ⲧⲁⲣⲉⲥϣⲟⲡⲕ ⲉⲣⲟⲥ ⲍⲱⲱⲥ ⲍⲙⲡⲙⲁ ⲉⲧⲙⲙⲁⲩ (cf. 462: ⲛⲉⲧⲛⲁϣⲟⲡⲥ ⲉⲣⲟⲟⲩ... ⲥⲛⲁϣⲟⲡⲟⲩ ⲍⲱⲟⲩ ⲉⲣⲟⲥ) / compare here (*Ch.* 98.21f., 199.8ff.) ⲛⲁ ⲧⲁⲣⲟⲩⲛⲁ ⲛⲏⲧⲛ, ϯ ⲧⲁⲣⲟⲩϯ ⲛⲏⲧⲛ̄ and (*P* 131⁶ 43 ro) ⲛⲁ ⲧⲁⲣⲟⲩⲛⲁ ⲛⲁⲕ, ϣⲉⲛ-ⲍⲧⲏⲕ ⲧⲁⲣⲟⲩϣⲉⲛ-ⲍⲧⲏⲩ ⲍⲁⲣⲟⲕ, ⲕⲱ ⲉⲃⲟⲗ ⲧⲁⲣⲟⲩⲕⲱ ⲛⲁⲕ ⲉⲃⲟⲗ, adaptations of *Luc.* 6:37-8.

(b) ⲧⲁⲣⲉϥⲥⲱⲧⲙ in other environments than post-imperative: (1) as a rhetoric post-interrogative apodosis ("that he may..."): (*A 2* 510) ⲉϥⲧⲱⲛ ⲡⲟⲩϣⲛϣ ⲧⲁⲣⲉⲡϣⲱⲥ ⲡⲱⲧ ⲛⲥⲱϥ / (*Ch.* 197-8) ⲟⲩ ⲡⲉⲧϣⲟⲟⲡ ⲛⲁⲛ ⲧⲁⲣⲛⲧⲁⲁⲩ ⲧⲏⲣⲟⲩ... ⲛⲧⲛⲧⲁⲁⲩ ⲛⲧⲛⲣ-ⲃⲟⲗ (note the conjunctive subcoordinated to ⲧⲁⲣⲛⲧⲁⲁⲩ).

(2) Following final constructions: (*P* 131⁵ 43 ρ) ⲉⲓϣⲁⲭⲉ ⲛⲙⲙⲏⲧⲛ ⲭⲉⲕⲁⲥ ⲉⲧⲉⲧⲛⲁⲧⲁⲭⲣⲟ-ⲡϣⲁⲭⲉ ⲙⲡⲛⲟⲩⲧⲉ ⲛⲍⲏⲧⲧⲏⲩⲧⲛ ⲧⲁⲣⲉⲧⲉⲛϯ-ⲍⲏⲩ ⲛⲟⲩⲕⲟⲩⲓ / (*Thompson* K 3 vo) ⲛⲉⲧⲛⲁ ⲉⲃⲟⲗ... ⲉⲩⲡⲏⲧ ⲛⲥⲱⲧⲛ ⲉⲩⲧⲁⲩⲟ ⲉⲡⲉⲥⲏⲧ ⲛⲛⲉ-ⲧⲛⲛⲟⲩⲧⲉ ⲉⲩⲟⲩⲱϭ ⲙⲙⲟⲟⲩ ⲉⲡⲟⲩⲱⲛⲍ ⲉⲃⲟⲗ ⲙⲡⲉⲧⲛϣⲓⲡⲉ ⲧⲁⲣⲉⲧⲉⲧⲛⲉⲓⲙⲉ ⲭⲉ-ⲟⲩⲕⲣⲙⲉⲥ ⲡⲉ ⲡⲉⲧⲛⲍⲏⲧ. Compare in the post-interrogative paradigm the apodotic-retrospective conjunctive (§7.2.7) (*III* 148.25ff.) ⲉⲩⲧⲱⲛ ⲛⲉⲛϣⲃⲉⲉⲣ... ⲉⲧⲙⲟⲩⲧⲉ ⲉⲣⲟⲛ ⲭⲉ-ⲁⲅⲅⲉⲗⲟⲥ ⲛⲥⲉⲛⲁⲩ ⲉⲛⲉⲛⲕⲁⲕⲓⲁ [48].

7.2.1.2 The optative (ⲉϥⲉⲥⲱⲧⲙ/ⲛⲛⲉϥⲥⲱⲧⲙ) [49] is relatively rarely expanded by a subcategorized conjunctive (there is not a single instance in *Ch.*). Multiple ⲉϥⲉ-periods are more common as nuclei· Personal maintenance is the rule; ⲁⲩⲱ is not attested; negation is syncategorized or encategorized; nucleus/ conjunctive affirmative or negative.

(a) (+→): (*III* 179.11f.) ⲡⲛⲟⲩⲧⲉ ⲉϥⲉⲥⲙⲟⲩ ⲉⲣⲱⲧⲛ ⲛϥⲁⲩⲭⲁⲛⲉ ⲛⲏⲧⲛ ⲛⲛⲉⲧⲛⲍⲓⲥⲉ ⲛϥⲑⲙⲕⲟ ⲙⲡⲭⲁⲭⲉ ⲛⲛⲁⲍⲣⲏⲧⲛ / (*III* 20.16, *IV* 40.19f.) ⲉϣⲱⲡⲉ ⲉⲓϣⲁⲛⲡⲁⲣⲁⲃⲁ ⲙⲡⲉⲛⲧⲁⲓⲍⲟⲙⲟⲗⲟⲅⲉⲓ ⲙⲙⲟϥ, ⲉⲓⲉⲛⲁⲩ ⲉⲧⲙⲛⲧⲉⲣⲟ ⲙⲡⲛⲟⲩⲧⲉ ⲛⲧⲁⲧⲙ-ⲃⲱⲕ ⲉⲍⲟⲩⲛ ⲉⲣⲟⲥ, oath formula; neg. encategorization (adversative sense): "... may I see the Kingdom... but not enter it".

(b) (←→), very rare: (*IV* 50.9f.) ⲛⲛⲉⲡⲉⲩⲍⲏⲧ ⲧⲁⲕⲟ... ⲛⲥⲉⲣ-ⲡⲱⲃϣ ⲭⲉ-ⲛⲉⲟⲩⲛ ⲟⲩⲥⲭⲏⲙⲁ ⲣⲱ ⲙⲙⲟⲛⲁⲭⲟⲥ ⲧⲟ ⲍⲓϣⲟⲩ.

7.2.1.2.1 The post-optative paradigm includes in addition to the conjunctive also the *coordinated optative* (- ⲁⲩⲱ ⲉϥⲉⲥⲱⲧⲙ): (*IV* 116.4f.) ⲡⲛⲟⲩⲧⲉ ⲉϥⲉⲥⲙⲟⲩ ⲉⲣⲟⲟⲩ ⲁⲩⲱ ⲉϥⲉⲍⲁⲣⲉⲍ ⲉⲣⲟⲟⲩ ⲁⲩⲱ ⲉϥⲉϯⲙⲧⲟⲛ ⲛⲁⲩ / (*ibid.* 171.3f.) ⲉϥⲉϣⲱⲡⲉ ⲉϥⲥⲟⲩⲟⲣⲧ ⲁⲩⲱ ⲉⲩⲉⲉⲓ ⲉⲍⲣⲁⲓ ⲉⲭⲱϥ ⲛϭⲓⲛⲉⲓⲥⲁⲍⲟⲩ ⲧⲏⲣⲟⲩ / (*III* 131.5f.) ⲡⲛⲟⲩⲧⲉ

---

[48] Yet another member of the post-interrogative paradigm is ⲙⲁⲣⲉϥⲥⲱⲧⲙ: (*III* 149.16ff.) ⲉⲩⲧⲱⲛ ⲛⲉⲧⲟⲩⲙⲟⲩⲧⲉ ⲉⲣⲟⲟⲩ ⲭⲉ-ⲍⲉⲛⲣⲉϥⲣ-ⲛⲟⲃⲉ ⲛⲉ... ⲙⲁⲣⲟⲩⲉⲓ ⲛⲥⲉⲛⲉⲭ-ⲡⲁϭⲥⲉ ⲉⲍⲟⲩⲛ ⲉⲍⲣⲁⲛ/ (*P* 131⁴ 160 ⲙ) ⲉⲩϣⲟⲟⲡ ⲧⲱⲛ ⲧⲉⲛⲟⲩ ⲙⲁⲣⲟⲩⲧⲁⲙⲟⲛ. Post-imperatival ⲙⲁ-ⲣⲉϥⲥⲱⲧⲙ is perhaps more common in Bohairic, e.g. *Mt.* 13:30, *Luc.* 7:7 (codd.), *Joh.* 18:8, corresponding to Sah. conjunctive, ⲙⲁⲣⲉϥ-, ⲉⲧⲣⲉϥ- (Horner) / ⲧⲁⲣⲉϥ- (Chester Beatty A, B). Cf. Kahle 1954:190 for the post-imperatival and final paradigm (featuring also ⲉⲧⲣⲉ-, ⲭⲉ-final constructions, 190ff. for ⲧⲁⲣⲉϥ- as the apodotic component of oath formulae).

[49] Polotsky 1950:84ff. (= *CP* 219ff.). I use the term not as a name for a *mood* (in the Indo-European or Semitic sense, of a regularly transsecting morphological subsystem) but for a specific conjugation-form pair, affirmative and negative "Future III".

ЄЧЄСШТМ ЄРООУ ΑΥШ ЄЧЄΝΑ2ΜΟΥ Є2ШВ ΝΙΜ ЄЧ2ΟΟΥ ΝЧ+-6ΟΜ ΝΑΥ 2Ν2ШВ ΝΙΜ — the second optative is micro-coordinated to a conjunctive (with the common theme " resisting everything "); so too in (*IV* 207.28ff.) ЄΡЄΠΧΟЄΙΟ ЄΙΝЄ Є2ΡΑΙ ЄΧШΟΥ ΜΠΟΑ2ΟΥ ΑΥШ ЄΡЄΠΧΟЄΙΟ ΜΟΥΡ ΝΤΟΡΓΗ ΜΠЄΨ6ШΝΤ Є2ΡΑΙ ЄΡΟΟΥ 2ΜΠЄ2ΟΟΥ ΝΤΟΡΓΗ ΝЧΝΟΧΟΥ Є2ΡΑΙ ЄΤЄ2ΡШ ΝΚШ2Τ — the conjunctive *specifies* (contentualizes) the second term of the optative coordination.

7.2.1.3 FINAL/CONSECUTIVE CONJUNCTIONAL SYNTAGMS. Here we encounter the well-known difficulty of determining the opposition between ΧЄΚΑΑΟ *vs.* ΧЄ-ЄЧЄСШТМ and ΧЄ *vs.* ΧЄΚΑΑΟ ЄЧΝΑСШТМ — an opposition the functional resolution of which must await some future study [50]. The conjunctive expands all constructions [51]. Note that ΑΥШ-microcoordination is here incomparably more frequent than with the post-imperatival conjunctive.

(a) (←→), usually with ΑΥШ: (*III* 158.28ff.) ЄΥЄΤΑΜΟΝ 2ΝΟΥΜΝΤΜЄ ЄΠЄΝΤΑΥΝΑΥ ЄΡΟЧ ΧЄΚΑΟ ЄΥЄШШΠЄ ЄΥ-СМАМААТ 2ΝΝЄΥ2ΒΗΥЄ ΤΗΡΟΥ ΑΥШ ΝΟЄЄΙ Є2ΡΑΙ ЄΧШΟΥ Ν6ΙΝЄΟΜΟΥ ΤΗΡΟΥ ЄΤΟΗ2 / (*ibid.* 40.27f.)... ΧЄ-ЄΡЄ-2ЄΝΨΥΧΗ ΝΑ+-2ΗΥ ΑΥШ ΝΤЄ2ЄΝΨΥΧΗ ΒШΚ ЄΡΑΤЧ ΜΠΝΟΥΤЄ 2ΝΤΒΒΟ ΝΙΜ / (*IV* 18.16f.) ...ΧЄ-ЄΟΝΑЄΙΝЄ ΝΟΥΝΑ Є2ΡΑΙ ЄΧШΟΥ ΑΥШ ΝΟΡ2ΟΥЄΤΑΑΥ ЄΤΟΟΤЧ ΜΠΝΑ / (*ibid.* 21.3f.) ...ΧЄ-ΝΝЄЧΠΑΤΑΟΟЄ ΜΜΟΥ ΑΥШ ΝЧΜΟΟΥΤΟΥ. Additional exx.: *III* 78.19f., 99.6ff., 122.3f., 194.18f. Without ΑΥШ: (*IV* 155.11ff.) ...ΧЄ-ЄΝЄΧΙ ΝΟΥΒЄΚЄ ΜΠΙΟΤΙΟ... ΝΤЄΝΧΙ ΜΠΤШШΒЄ ΝΜΠΟΝΗΡΟΝ ΝΤΑΝΑΑΥ. Also *Ch.* 18-19, 101.44ff.

(b) (+→), considerably less common: (*III* 119.7ff.) ОЄЄΠΙΤΙΜΑ ΝΑΝ ЄΤΜΚΑΤΑΛΑΛЄΙ ΟΥΔЄ ЄΤΜΚΡΜΡΜ... ΧЄ-ΝΝЄΠΝΟΥΤЄ 6ШΝΤ ЄΡΟΝ ΝЧΤΑΚΟ ΝΝЄΝ2ΒΗΥЄ / (*Ch.* 148.47ff.) ...ΧЄ-ЄΟΝΑΑΥ2ΑΝЄ ΝΤЄΝЄΟЄΚΙΒЄ ΑΥ2ΑΝЄ ΝΜΜΑΟ. Also *IV* 51.8f.

7.2.2 EXTRATEMPORAL PREDICATIONS

7.2.2.1 ШΑЧСШТМ (and conversions): I know of no certain instance of МЄЧСШТМ subcategorized by the conjunctive. Conjunctive: affirmative only. Personal maintenance is the rule (only 3rd persons, sgl. and plur.).

(a) (←→) (ΑΥШ very rare): (*III* 110.2f.) ШΑЧΤΟΑΒΟΟΥ ЄΡΟΟΥ ΑΥШ ΝЧЄΥΦΡΑΝЄ ΜΜΟΟΥ Ν2ΗΤΟΥ / (*ibid.* 176.3) ΝΘЄ ΔЄ ЄΤЄШΑΥШΟΟΥЄ ΝΟЄШШΠЄ ΝΑΤΚΑΡΠΟΟ / (*IV* 24.19f.) ΝЄΤЄШΑΥΜΟΥΟΥΤ ΜΠΟШΜΑ ΑΥШ ΝΟЄΜΟΥΟΥΤ ΜΠΝΟΒЄ Ν2ΗΤΟΥ — repeated lexeme / (*ibid.* 38.29) ΟΥΝ2Α2 ΟΝ ΝΟ2ΙΜЄ ЄШΑΥΡ-ΧШШΡЄ ΚΑΤΑΚΑΙΡΟΟ ΑΥШ ΝΟЄΧΡΟ — etymologically related lexemes / (*ibid.* 82.11) ШΑЧ+-ΟΟЄ Ν2ΟΥΟ ΝЧΤΡЄ2ЄΝΚΟΟΥЄ + — repeated lexeme / (*Ch.* 80.21ff.) ШΑΥΠΑΡΑΙΤЄΙ ΜΠΟΥШШ ЄΤ2ΟΟΥ ΝΟЄΟШΤΠ ΝΑΥ ΜΠΑΓΑΘΟΝ — antonyms / (*P* 131⁴ 157 vo) ΠΟΥΟЄΙΝ ΠЄШΑЧЧΙ ΜΜΑΥ ΜΠΚΑΚЄ ΝЧΑΑЧ ΝΘЄ ΜΠЄΤЄΝЄЧШΟΟΠ ΑΝ — paraphrase. Also *III* 45.3ff., 152.24f., 163.14f., *IV* 94.3ff.

(b) (+→): doubtful, perhaps (*IV* 25.25f.) ШΑΡЄΝΟΟΟΝЄ ЄΙ ΝΟЄΟΥΛΑ ΜΜΟЧ ΝΟЄЧΙ ΜΠЄЧΧΡΗΜΑ ΤΗΡЧ / (*ibid.* 70.17ff.) ШΑΥЄΓΚΡΑΤЄΥЄ ΜΜΟΟΥ... ΝΟЄΤШΟΥΝ ЄΥ2ΚΑЄΙΤ ΝΟЄЄΙ ЄΒΟΛ ΝΟЄΟΥШΜ / (*III* 31.9) ШΑЧΚΤΟЧ ΟΝ ΝЧ-ΟΥШΝ2 ЄΒΟΛ. Also *III* 179.2ff., *IV* 26.4 (a rare case of the personal maintenance disrupted), 113.6f.

7.2.2.2 ШΑΝΤЧСШΤΜ: affirmative conjunctive only; no pers. maintenance.

(a) (←→): (*IV* 24.13f.) ΝЄΥΝΑΝЄΧЄ ΜΜΟΟΥ ΑΝ ΠЄ ШΑΝΤΟΥΝΟΧΟΥ Є2ΡΑΙ ЄΠΚШ2Τ ΑΥШ Є2ΡΑΙ ЄΠΜΟΟΥ ΑΥШ ΝΟЄ-ΡΑ2ΤΟΥ ЄΠΚΑ2 / (*Ch.* 121.6ff.) (ΑΟ2ΜΟΟΟ Є2ΡΑΙ ΜΠΔΙΑΒΟΛΟΟ ΑΥШ 2ΑΡΑΤΟΥ ΝΝΔΑΙΜШΝ) ШΑΝΤΟΥΠΛΗΓЄ

---

[50] See STERN §611-2, STEINDORFF 1951:§440-3, etc. WILSON 1970:23-51 is no help. Note that the distribution of the four terms of this complex category varies from one Shenoute text to another: *Chassinat* clearly favours ΧЄ-syntagms (ЄЧΝΑ-syntagms appear to be rather more frequent — less specialized? — in Shenoute than in the Scriptures).

[51] For Shenoutean instances of ΧЄΚΑΑΟ resumed by the conjunctive — a typical New Testament construction — see §7.2.6.1 (3) below.

ⲘⲘⲞⲤ ⲀⲨⲰ ⲚⲤⲈⲨⲀⲀⲢ ⲈⲢⲞⲤ / (*Wess. 9* 96b 16ff.) ⲚⲒⲘ ⲡⲈⲚⲦⲀⲨⲀⲬⲈ ⲘⲚⲠⲞⲨⲰⲚⲨ ⲨⲀⲚⲦⲨⲠⲰⲦ ⲚⲨⲂⲰⲔ... / (*P 131*[6] 31 vo) ...ⲨⲀⲚⲦⲞⲨⲨⲰⲠⲈ ⲚⲦⲈⲖⲒⲞⲤ ⲚⲀⲘⲈ ⲚⲤⲈⲨⲰⲠⲈ ⲚⲬⲀⲨⲘⲞⲈⲒⲦ — same lexeme.

(b) (+→): (*Ch.* 45.55ff., parall. *III* 82-3) ...ⲈⲦⲢⲈⲨⲤⲀⲚⲞⲨⲨⲞⲨ ⲨⲀⲚⲦⲞⲨⲢ-ⲚⲞϬ ⲚⲦⲈⲦⲚⲨⲒⲦⲞⲨ / (*III* 143.7f.) ⲘⲠⲈ-ⲚⲈⲦⲘⲘⲀⲨ ⲈⲒ ⲨⲀⲚⲦⲈⲠⲚⲞⲨⲦⲈ ϬⲰⲚⲦ ⲈⲢⲞⲞⲨ ⲚⲨⲦⲢⲈⲨⲂⲰⲔ ⲈⲠⲈⲤⲎⲦ ⲈⲀⲘⲚⲦⲈ ⲈⲨⲞⲚⳈ / (*A 1* 77) (of honey) ...ⲨⲀⲚⲦⲞⲨ-ⲦⲀⲀⲨ ⲔⲞⲨⲒ ⲔⲞⲨⲒ ⲚⲦⲞⲞⲦⲞⲨ ⲚⳈⲈⲚⲔⲞⲞⲨⲈ ⲚⲦⲈⲚⲈⲦⲘⲘⲀⲨ ⳈⲰⲞⲨ ⲞⲚ ⲚⲞⳉⲨ...

7.2.2.3 ⲘⲠⲀⲦⲨⲤⲰⲦⲘ (rare): (a) (←→): (*IV* 66.16ff.) ⳈⲀⲘⲞⲒ ⲞⲚ ⲈⲚⲈⲨⲆⲞⲔⲒⲘⲀⳅⲈ ⲘⲘⲞⲞⲨ ⲚⲨⲞⲢⲠ ⲠⲈ ⲘⲠⲀ-ⲦⲞⲨⲰⲘ (sic) ⲈⲂⲞⲖ ⳈⲘⲠⲞⲈⲒⲔ ⲀⲨⲰ ⲚⲤⲈⲤⲰ ⲈⲂⲞⲖ ⳈⲘⲠⲀⲠⲞⲦ.

(b) (+→): (*IV* 97.11f.) ⲘⲈⲨⲀⲔ ⳁⲚⲀⲢ-ⲠⲀⲒ ⲚⲞⲨⲨⲎⲢⲈ ⲨⲎⲘ ⲘⲠⲀⲦⲨⲢ-ⲦⲈ ⲚⲦⲈⲠⲈⲨⲔⲢⲒⲘⲀ ⲨⲰⲠⲈ ⳈⲒⳉⲰⲨ.

7.2.3 THE PRESENT-BASED FUTURE (ⲨⲚⲀⲤⲰⲦⲘ and conversions)

7.2.3.1 *Basic Tense*: ⲨⲚⲀⲤⲰⲦⲘ.

(a) (←→): nuclear verb/conjunctive: affirmative, negative; negation syncategorization/encategorization; no personal maintenance. Note the frequent *prophetic style*: (*III* 124.5) ⲀⲨⲰ ⲠⲈⲨⲦⲞⲢⲦⲢ ⲘⲚⲠⲠⲰⳉⲤ ⲚⳈⲎⲦ ⲘⲚⲦⲖⲨⲠⲎ ⲘⲚⲠⲀⲨⲀⳈⲞⲘ... ⲚⲀⲢ-ⳉⲞⲈⲒⲤ ⲈⲢⲞⲞⲨ ⲚⲤⲈⲨⲰⲠⲈ ⲚⲀⲨ ⲚⳈⲘⳈⲀⲖ / (*ibid.* 219.8ff.) ⲦⲞⲦⲈ ⲨⲚⲀⳈⲘⲞⲞⲤ ⲈⳈⲢⲀⲒ ⲈⳉⲘⲠⲈⲨⲐⲢⲞⲚⲞⲤ... ⲚⲤⲈⲤⲰⲞⲨⳈ ⲈⳈⲞⲨⲚ ⲚⲄⲈⲚⲞⲤ ⲚⲒⲘ... ⲚⲤⲈⲦⲀⳈⲞⲞⲨ ⲈⲢⲀⲦⲞⲨ ⲘⲠⲈⲨⲘⲦⲞ ⲈⲂⲞⲖ... ⲚⲨⲠⲰⲢⳉ ⲘⲘⲞⲞⲨ; also with coordinated ⲀⲨⲰ + *future* subunits: (*III* 101.14ff.) ⲦⲞⲦⲈ ⲔⲚⲀⲚⲞⲒ ⲚⲚⲈⲦⳈⲎⲚ ⲚⲦⲈⲠⲈⲔⳈⲎⲦ ⲀⲨⲰ ⲔⲚⲀ-ⲨⲰⲠⲈ ⲚⲢⲈⲨⲢ-ⳉⲞⲈⲒⲤ ⳈⲚⲚⲈⲔⲘⲈⲈⲨⲈ ⲚⲦⲈⲠⲔⲰⳈⲦ ⲘⲠⲈⲠⲚⲀ ⲢⲰⲔⳈ ⲚⲚⲈⲔⳈⲨⲖⲎ ⲀⲨⲰ ⲠⳈⲎⲂⲤ ⲘⲠⲚⲞⲨⲦⲈ ⲚⲀⲢ-ⲞⲨⲞⲈⲒⲚ ⲈⲢⲞⲔ. Compare also *IV* 104.12 (Biblical style, characteristic of quotations; consider *III* 123.6f.,12f., 173.20ff., 195.18ff., *IV* 8.5f., 9.11f.) / (*III* 125.18ff.) ⲞⲨⲚⳈⲀⳈ ⲚⲀⲢ-ⲨⲘⲘⲞ ⲈⲠⳉⲞⲈⲒⲤ Ⲓ͞Ⲥ ⳈⲢⲀⲒ ⲚⳈⲎⲦⲚ ⲈⲒⲦⲈ ⳈⲞⲞⲨⲦ ⲈⲒⲦⲈ ⲤⳈⲒⲘⲈ ⲚⲤⲈⲢ-ⳈⲀⲈ ⲈⲂⲰⲔ ⲈⳈⲞⲨⲚ ⲈⲠⲘⲀ ⲚⲘⲦⲞⲚ... / (*ibid.* 158.7f.) (apodotically) ⲦⲚⲚⲀⲢ-ⲂⲞⲖ ⲠⲈ ⲈⳈⲈⲚⲚⲞϬ ⲚⲔⲢⲒⲘⲀ ⲈⲂⲞⲖ ⳈⲒⲦⲘⲠⲚⲞⲨⲦⲈ ⲚⲦⲚⳉⲒ ⲚⳈⲈⲚⲤⲘⲞⲨ ⲀⲨⲰ ⲦⲚⲚⲀϬⲘ-ϬⲞⲘ ⲠⲈ ⲈⳈⲢⲀⲒ ⲈⳉⲘⲠⲤⲀⲦⲀⲚⲀⲤ / (*IV* 97.22ff.) ⲞⲨⳈⲎⲦ ⲄⲀⲢ ⲈⲨⲘⲈⳈ ⲚϬⲞⲖ ⲚⲀⲨⲢ-ⲠⲘⲈⲈⲨⲈ ⲀⲚ ⲚⳈⲈⲚⳈⲂⲎⲨⲈ ⲚⲖⲞⲒⲘⲞⲤ ⲈⲀⲀⲨ ⲚⲨⲢ-ⲠⲘⲈⲈⲨⲈ ⲚⲚⲈⳈⲂⲎⲨⲈ ⲈⲦⲈⲢⲈⲠⲚⲞⲨⲦⲈ ⲚⲀⲀⲀⲨ ⳈⲘⲠⲈⳈⲞⲞⲨ ⲚⲦⲞⲢⲄⲎ — repeated lexeme: neg. syncategorization? / (*Ch.* 94.10ff.) ⳁⲚⲀⲦⲀⲘⲰⲦⲚ ⲈⲚⲈⲚⲦⲀⲨⳉⲒ-ϬⲞⲖ ⲈⲢⲞⲚ ⲚⳈⲎⲦⲞⲨ ⲀⲨⲰ ⲚⲦⲀⲦⲤⲀⲂⲰⲦⲚ ⲈⲚⲈⲚⲦⲀⲚⲤⳈⲀⲒⲤⲞⲨ ⲚⲀⲨ — synonyms. Other exx.: (repeated lexeme) *III* 115.17f., *Ch.* 107.14ff.

(b) (←→): no personal maintenance; negation syncategorized, affirmation encategorized. (*III* 123.27) ⳁⲚⲀⲦⲞⲖⲘⲀ ⲆⲈ ⲚⲦⲀⳉⲰ ⲘⲠⲈⲒⲨⲀⳉⲈ / (*ibid.* 36.17f., parall. *Ch.* 132.9ff.) ⲈⲦⲂⲈⲞⲨ ⲚⲦⲚⲚⲀⲀⳅⲒⲞⲨ ⲘⲘⲞⲨ ⲀⲚ ⲚⲨⲐⲈ-ⲢⲀⲠⲈⲨⲈ ⲈⲚⲂⲀⲖ ⲘⲠⲈⲚⳈⲎⲦ / (*Ch.* 49.8ff.) ⲚⲤⲈⲚⲀϬⲘ-ϬⲞⲘ ⲄⲀⲢ ⲀⲚ ⲈⲢ-ⳈⲘⳈⲀⲖ ⲚⲀⲔ (and so) ⲚⲤⲈⲢ-ⳈⲘⳈⲀⲖ ⲚⲚⲢⲈⲨⳉⲒⲚ-ϬⲞⲚⲤ, addressed to God; affirmative encategorization / (*IV* 3.18f.) ⲤⲈⲚⲀⲔⲀⲀⲨ ⲠⲀⲚⲦⲰⲤ ⲚⲤⲈⲂⲰⲔ / (*Ch.* 83.13ff.) ⲈⲦⲂⲈⲞⲨ ⲚⲈⲤⲞⲞⲨ ⲚⲀⲤⲞⲨⲚ-ⲠⲈⳈⲢⲞⲞⲨ ⲀⲚ ⲘⲠⲨⲰⲤ ⲘⲘⲈ... ⲚⲤⲈⲠⲰⲦ ⲈⲢⲀⲦⲨ / (*ibid.* 93.22ff.) ⲤⲚⲀⲨⲰⲠⲈ ⲚⲦⲈⲦⲚⲘⲈⲤⲦⲰⲒ / (*A 1* 135-6) Ⲏ ⲚⲤⲚⲀⲨⲰⲠⲈ ⲀⲚ ⲠⲈⲦⳉⲰ ⲚⲚⲀⲒ Ⲏ ⲠⲈⲦⲘⲞⲔⲘⲈⲔ ⲈⲢⲞⲞⲨⲚⲤⲈⳈⲈ ⲈⲢⲞⲤ... ⲈⲨⲞ ⲚⲢⲈⲨⳉⲒ-ϬⲞⲖ / (*P 130*[5] 56 NB) ⲞⲨⲚⲞⲨⲞⲈⲒⲨ ⲄⲀⲢ ⲚⲀⲨⲰⲠⲈ ⲚⲦⲈⲚⲈⲞⲨⲞⲈⲒⲈ ⲰⳈⲤ ⲚⲚⲈⲨⲤⲰⲨⲈ (see §7.2.3.6 below).

7.2.3.2 *Circumstantial future*: uncommon. Usually adnominal (or open to attributive adnominal interpretation) although a *protatic* role is not excluded (in fact, both functions are neutralized in the adnominal syntactic slot). No negation; no - ⲀⲨⲰ -: subcoordination only? (*Ch.* 190.31ff.) ⲞⲨ ⲠⲈⲦⲦⲀⲒⲎⲨ ⲈⲠⲘⲞⲨ ⲚⲞⲨⲢⲰⲘⲈ ⲈⲨⲚⲀⲈⲒ ⲈⲂⲞⲖ ⳈⲘⲠⲤⲰⲘⲀ ⲚⲨⲂⲰⲔ ⳈⲀⲦⲘⲠⳉⲞⲈⲒⲤ ⲀⲨⲰ ⲚⲨⲨⲰⲠⲈ ⲘⲚⲠⳉⲞⲈⲒⲤ ⲚⲞⲨⲞⲈⲒⲨ ⲚⲒⲘ, cf. *ibid.* ibid. 52ff. ⲈⲨⲨⲀⲚⲈⲒ ⲈⲂⲞⲖ / (*IV* 162.2ff.) ...ⳈⲞⲤⲞⲚ ⲀⲠⲀⲒ ⳁ-ⲦⲰⲨ ⲈⳈⲞⲨⲚ, ⲚⲦⲀⲠⲀⲒ ⲈⲚ-ⲦⲰⲨ ⲈⲂⲞⲖ. ⲀⲨⲰ ⳈⲞⲤⲞⲚ ⲈⲢⲈ-ⲠⲀⲒ ⲚⲀⲈⲒ ⲈⲂⲞⲖ, ⲚⲦⲈⲠⲀⲒ ⳁ-ⲦⲰⲨ ⲈⳈⲞⲨⲚ. The construction here is difficult, although the sense is clear: (talking of the pall-bearers) "As soon as one puts his (shoulder) in (under the pall), the other takes his (shoulder) out (from under the pall); and as soon as one withdraws, the other puts his (shoulder) in". More specifically, difficult here are (a) the past tense in a preceptive context, (b) the apparent parallelism in the interdependence of, on the one hand, ⳈⲞⲤⲞⲚ Ⲁ- and ⲚⲦⲀ- (Second Perfect), and, on the other hand, ⳈⲞⲤⲞⲚ

ⲉⲡⲉ- ⲛⲁ- and the conjunctive; while the former is well understandable as a circumstantial clause (ⲍⲟⲥⲟⲛ
ⲁ-) focalized by a Second Tense, in the sense of " no sooner... than... " (§2.7.1.1), the latter seems anacoluthic, conflating a subcoordinative role (actual sequence, preceptive stage sequence) with a main-
clause (jussive?) one. The juxtaposition of perfect and future tenses makes perhaps for vividness and
a scenic dramatic effect in portraying the desired execution of this instruction.

7.2.3.3 *Second Future.* Cases of the conjunctive subcategorized by a thematic (topical) future in
a focalization pattern — foc. patterns (2), (6), §§2.2, 2.6.1; the conjunctive is impressed also with the thematicity category. Note that in pattern (2) the conjunctive *follows the focus*, and is thus a case of the *dis,
continuous multiple theme* figure (§2.7.1.3.3). Negation syncategorization (by the nexus negator - ⲁⲛ
not the negated theme), negation encategorization.

(1) (←—→): (*Ch.* 85.26ff.) ⲉⲣⲉⲡⲭⲟⲉⲓⲥ ⲡⲉⲭⲥ ⲛⲁⲥⲙⲟⲩ ⲉⲣⲟⲟⲩ ⲛⲟⲩⲏⲣ ⲁⲩⲱ ⲛϥ+-ⲉⲟⲟⲩ ⲛⲁⲩ / (*III* 65.3f.) ⲉⲧⲃⲉⲟⲩ ⲉⲕ-
ⲛⲁⲡⲣⲟⲥⲉⲭⲉ ⲉⲡⲉⲛⲧⲁⲙⲱⲩⲥⲏⲥ ⲭⲟⲟϥ ⲭⲉ-..., ⲛⲅⲧⲙ+-ⲍⲧⲏⲕ ⲛⲧⲟϥ ⲉⲡⲉⲛⲧⲁⲓⲉⲍⲉⲕⲓⲏⲗ ⲭⲟⲟϥ ⲭⲉ- — neg. encategorization / (*ibid.* 123.7f.) ⲛⲁⲱ ⳓⲉ ⲛⲍⲉ ⲧⲉⲛⲟⲩ ⲉⲓⲛⲁⲭⲓ-ⲛⲁⲓ ⲉⲧⲙⲙⲁⲩ ⲛⳓⲟⲛⲥ ⲏ ⲛⲧⲁⲑⲙⲕⲟⲟⲩ ⲉⲡⲭⲓⲛⲭⲏ. Also: *IV*
14.4ff., 76.20f., 161.12ff. (jussive ⲉϥⲛⲁ-?).

(b) (+—→): (*III* 188.20f.) ⲉⲣⲉⲡⲉⲧⲱⲁⲭⲉ ⲛⲙⲙⲉ ⲛⲁⲕⲱ ⲁⲛ ⲛⲍⲉⲛⲙⲁⲧⲟⲓ ⲍⲁⲣⲁⲧϥ ⲛϥⲕⲱⲗⲉ ⲛⲛⲉⲧⲥⲱⲧⲡ ⲛⲁⲩ ⲙⲡⲙⲟⲩ
ⲛⲍⲟⲩⲟ ⲉⲡⲱⲛⲍ / (*IV* 101.15ff.) ⲉⲣⲉⲡⲟⲩⲁ ⲡⲟⲩⲁ ⲛⲁⲙ-ⲡⲉϥⲙⲁⲕⲍ ⲁⲛ ⲉⲃⲟⲗ ⲍⲁⲡⲛⲁⲍⲃⲉϥ ⲉⲧⲃⲉⲟⲩⲣⲁⲛ ⲛⲥⲉⲕⲁ-ⲛⲧⲁⲗⲁⲓ-
ⲡⲱⲣⲟⲥ ⲉⲩⲧⲁⲗⲁⲓⲡⲱⲣⲉⲓ — neg. syncategorization.

7.2.3.4 The *preterite future*, ⲛⲉϥⲛⲁⲥⲱⲧⲙ: always apodotic to an *irrealis* protasis (ⲡⲉ, when present,
immediately precedes the conjunctive). No ⲁⲩⲱ-microcoordination; negation syncategorization, affirmation encategorization. (*III* 88.25ff.) ⲉⲛⲉⲧⲉⲧⲛⲥⲟⲟⲩⲛ ⲛⲛⲉⲣⲱⲟⲩ ⲛⲉⲧⲉⲧⲛⲁⲣ-ⲍⲟⲧⲉ ⲁⲛ ⲡⲉ ⲛⲧⲉⲧⲛⲁⲓⲥⲑⲁⲛⲉ ⲉⲍⲟⲩⲛ
ⲉⲡⲛⲟⲩⲧⲉ: the negative syncategorization does not extend to the conjunctive (= affirmation encategorization) but this depends on the sense of ⲁⲓⲥⲑⲁⲛⲉ ⲉⲍⲟⲩⲛ ⲉ- (as far as I know, a unicum; cf. αἰσθάνεσθαι
ἐπί, with an adversative sense of " feel against "? This could suit a neg. syncategorization) / (*IV* 42.3ff.)
...ⲛⲉⲣⲉⲧⲉⲓⲙⲓⲛⲉ ⲛⲣⲱⲙⲉ ⲛⲁⲱⲙⲥ ⲛⲥⲉⲟⲙⲥⲉ ⲛⲙⲙⲁⲩ... ⲛⲉⲩⲛⲁⲣ-ⲁⲧⲱⲁⲩ ⲡⲉ ⲛⲥⲉⲁⲁⲧⲉ ⲛⲁⲧⲱⲁⲩ ⲛⲙⲙⲁⲩ / (*IV* 96.25)
([ⲉ]ⲛⲉⲩⲟ ⲅⲁⲣ ⲁⲛ ⲛⲁⲧⲥⲟⲟⲩⲛ) ⲛⲉⲩⲛⲁⲍⲙⲟⲟⲥ ⲁⲛ ⲛⲥⲉⲱⲁⲭⲉ ⲉⲣⲟⲓ ⲛⲭⲓⲟⲩⲉ.

7.2.3.5 The *relative future* ⲉⲧ-ⲛⲁ- only in the following two cases:

(1) the " substantivized " relative ⲡⲉⲧ-ⲛⲁⲥⲱⲧⲙ (i.e. ⲉⲧⲛⲁ- expanding the determinator series ⲡ-);
ⲉⲧⲛⲁ- expanding *indefinite pronominal* nuclei (ⲟⲩⲟⲛ ⲛⲓⲙ, ⲣⲱⲙⲉ (ⲛⲓⲙ)) — paraphrasing the foregoing case —,
temporal nouns (ⲡⲉⲍⲟⲟⲩ) paraphrasing a conjunctional construction. Note here the affinity with the
various specific protatic or " *fallsetzend* " (case-presenting) conditional, relative or temporal syntagms
(§7.2.4) and with cases of the hypothetic non-actual/non-narrative present/perfect (§7.2.4.1), as nuclei
of the conjunctive. (←—→)/(+—→) not in opposition. As with the protatic nucleus, we find here too frequent negation encategorization. (*III* 74.3f.) ⲟⲩⲟⲉⲓ ⲇⲉ ⲛⲛⲉⲧϥⲛⲁⲧⲙⲍⲟ ⲁⲩⲱ ⲛϥⲭⲉⲣⲟ... ⲛϥⲧⲙⲟⲱⲙⲉϥ / (*ibid.*
154.27f.) ⲛⲉⲧⲛⲁⲭⲱ ⲇⲉ ⲛⲟⲩⲱⲁⲭⲉ ⲏ ⲟⲩⲍⲱⲃ ⲉϥⲍⲟⲟⲩ ⲍⲣⲁⲓ ⲛⲍⲏⲧⲛ... ⲁⲩⲱ ⲛⲥⲉⲧⲙⲧⲁⲍⲟ ⲉⲣⲁⲧϥ ⲙⲡⲱⲁⲭⲉ ⲏ ⲡⲍⲱⲃ... —
neg. encategorization / (*IV* 113.5f.) ⲡⲉⲧⲛⲁⲍⲁⲣⲉⲍ ⲉⲍⲉⲛⲕⲟⲩⲓ ⲛϥⲱⲱⲡⲉ ⲉϥⲉⲛⲍⲟⲧ ⲉⲣⲟⲟⲩ / (*ibid.* 171.1f.) ⲡⲉⲧ-
ⲛⲁⲣ-ⲛⲟⲃⲉ ⲍⲛⲟⲩⲥⲱⲡ... ⲁⲩⲱ ⲛϥⲧⲙⲭⲱ ⲙⲡⲉⲛⲧⲁϥⲁⲁϥ — neg. encategorization / (*Ch.* 25.39ff.) ⲍⲙⲡⲉⲍⲟⲟⲩ
ⲉⲧⲉⲣⲉⲧⲟⲣⲅⲏ... ⲛⲁⲥⲉⲍⲥⲱⲕ ⲛⲑⲉ ⲛⲟⲩⲕⲣⲙⲉⲥ ⲁⲩⲱ ⲛⲥⲍⲓⲧⲕ ⲛⲥⲱⲁⲱⲕ ⲉⲃⲟⲗ ⲍⲛⲁⲙⲛⲧⲉ, also *IV* 182.3f., 208.11f.
Additional exx.: *IV* 122.5ff. (ⲛⲉⲧⲛⲁ-, ⲟⲩⲟⲛ ⲛⲓⲙ ⲉⲧ- ⲛⲥⲉⲧⲙ-), 125.20f., 126.8ff., 166.21f., 169.11, 207.27f.,
Ch. 34.34ff.

(2) ⲡⲉⲧⲛⲁ-, the *glose* constituent in a rhetorical-interrogative Cleft Sentence[52]. Frequent negation encategorization (a rhetorical figure); neg. syncategorization.

(a) (←——→): (*III* 33.26f.) ⲡⲁⲓ ⲡⲉⲧⲛⲁϯ-ϣⲓⲡⲉ ⲛⲧⲙⲛⲧⲣⲉϥϫⲓ-ⲅⲟ ⲛϥⲉⲩⲫⲣⲁⲛⲉ ⲙⲡⲛⲟⲩⲧⲉ / (*IV* 4-5) ⲛⲓⲙ ⲅⲁⲣ ⲡⲉⲧⲛⲁⲕⲗⲏ-ⲣⲟⲛⲟⲙⲉⲓ ⲛⲧⲙⲛⲧⲉⲣⲟ ⲛⲙⲡⲏⲩⲉ ⲛⲥⲉⲧⲙⲱϣⲡⲉ ⲉⲩⲟ ⲛⲣⲣⲟ / (*ibid.* 32.19ff.) ⲛⲓⲙ ⲛϣⲏⲣⲉ ⲛⲣⲙⲛϩⲏⲧ ⲛⲉⲧⲛⲁⲉⲡⲓⲑⲩⲙⲉⲓ ⲁⲛ ⲉⲣ-ϩⲱⲃ ⲉⲛⲉϩⲃⲏⲩⲉ ⲉⲧⲉⲣⲉⲡⲉⲩⲉⲓⲱⲧ ⲉⲧϩⲛⲙⲡⲏⲩⲉ ⲣ-ϩⲱⲃ ⲉⲣⲟⲟⲩ... ⲁⲩⲱ ⲛⲥⲉⲟⲩⲁϩⲟⲩ ⲛⲥⲁⲡⲉⲥⲙⲟⲧ ⲛⲛⲁⲅⲅⲉⲗⲟⲥ (sim. *III* 200.14ff.) / (*Ch.* 56.46ff.) ⲁⲩ ⲙⲙⲁ ⲛⲉⲧϥⲛⲁⲡⲁⲅⲉ ⲙⲙⲟⲟⲩ ⲏ ⲛϥⲃⲱⲕ ⲉϩⲟⲩⲛ ⲉⲣⲟⲟⲩ ⲛϥⲧⲙⲛ-ⲡⲟⲥⲉ ⲛⲧⲉϥⲯⲩⲭⲏ — second conjunctive subcoordinated, neg. encategorized. Additional exx.: *III* 186.24f., *IV* 88.10f., 164.13f., *Ch.* 203.20ff.

(b) (+——→) (*A 2* 240) ⲛⲓⲙ ⲡⲉⲧⲛⲁⲥⲱⲧⲙ ⲉⲛⲁⲓ ⲛϥⲧⲙⲕⲱ ⲛⲁϥ ⲛⲛⲉⲥⲃⲟⲟⲩⲉ ⲛⲛⲉⲅⲣⲁⲫⲏ — neg. encategorization / (*IV* 74.25) ⲡⲛⲟⲩⲧⲉ ⲛⲧⲟⲕ ⲉⲧⲛⲁⲕⲟⲧⲕ ⲛⲅⲧⲁⲛϩⲟⲛ / (*ibid.* 156.19f.) ⲛⲓⲙ ⲡⲉⲧⲛⲁⲡⲣⲟⲥⲉⲭⲉ ⲁⲛ ⲭⲉ-ⲉϥⲟⲩⲱⲙ ⲛⲁϣ ⲛϩⲉ ⲛⲧⲉⲧⲙⲛⲉϩⲃⲏⲩⲉ ⲉⲣ-ϩⲟⲩⲟ ϩⲣⲁⲓ ⲛϩⲏⲧϥ ⲡⲁⲣⲁⲟⲩⲭⲉⲣⲥⲟⲥ "so that... not": negation maintenance / (*Ch.* 120.25ff.) ⲛⲓⲙ ⲛⲉⲧⲛⲁⲕⲁⲁϥ ⲛⲁⲩ ϩⲙⲡⲉⲩϩⲏⲧ ⲛⲥⲉϭⲱ ϩⲛϯⲙⲛⲧϭⲱⲃ ⲧⲏⲣⲥ "and still...".

7.2.3.6 Paradigm

ϥⲛⲁⲥⲱⲧⲙ	ⲁⲩⲱ ϥⲛⲁⲥⲱⲧⲙ
	conjunctive

Observations: (1) ⲁⲩⲱ + *future* is very common in *prophetic*, *promissory* or *threatening* textual stretches (e.g. *III* 114.9f., 89.7f., 136.22ff., 198.18ff., *IV* 104.11f., *Ch.* 178.31ff., 103.1ff., 128.36ff., 148.10ff.).

(2) For ⲁⲩⲱ + *future* in post-imperatival status, see §7.2.1.1.5.

(3) I have found no evidence in Shenoute for the conjunctive following a futuric - ⲛⲏⲩ present predicate (cf. *I Cor.* 4:19, *II Tim.* 4:4).

(4) Following ⲥⲛⲁϣⲱⲡⲉ, the paradigm is joined by ⲉⲧⲣⲉ-, a "that"-form heralded by -ⲥ- (§5.2.2.1).

(5) *Circumstantial future*. I have found no example of any form or construction in opposition to the conjunctive after this nucleus.

(6) *Second Future*. I have found no example of coordinated *thematic* Sec. Future units (as distinct from *jussive* Sec. Future, §7.2.1.1.3) opposed to the conjunctive here.

(7) A rare example of coordinate *irrealis* apodoses (with no common thematic denominator calling for microcoordination): (*IV* 157.15f.) ⲛⲉⲣⲉⲡⲛⲟⲩⲧⲉ ⲛⲁⲥϩⲟⲩⲉⲣ-ⲕⲁⲉⲓⲛ ⲁⲛ ⲡⲉ ⲁⲩⲱ ⲛⲉϥⲛⲁⲉⲛ-ⲡⲙⲟⲩ ⲁⲛ ⲡⲉ ⲉϫⲛⲁ-ⲛⲁⲛⲓⲁⲥ ⲙⲛⲥⲁⲡⲡⲓⲣⲁ ⲧⲉϥⲥϩⲓⲙⲉ.

(8) ⲡⲉⲧⲛⲁ- ⲁⲩⲱ ⲡⲉⲧⲛⲁ- is extremely rare[53] (*III* 198.14ff. ⲡⲉⲧⲛⲁϫⲓⲟⲩⲉ ⲕⲁⲧⲁⲗⲁⲁⲩ ⲛⲥⲙⲟⲧ ⲁⲩⲱ ⲡⲉⲧⲛⲁϥⲓ ⲉⲃⲟⲗ ϩⲛⲛⲛⲕⲁ ⲛⲧⲇⲓⲁⲕⲟⲛⲓⲁ); so is ⲉⲧⲛⲁ- ⲁⲩⲱ ⲉⲧⲛⲁ- (*III* 137.19f. ⲟⲩⲟⲛ ⲛⲓⲙ ⲉⲧⲛⲁⲣ-ⲃⲟⲗ ⲙⲡϣⲓ ⲁⲩⲱ ⲉⲧ-ⲛⲁϥⲉϭ-ⲡⲉϥⲥⲟⲛ paraphrases and transforms *I Thess.* 4:6 ...ⲉⲧⲙⲣ-ⲃⲟⲗ ⲙⲡϣⲓ ⲁⲩⲱ ⲉⲧⲙϥⲉϭ-ⲡⲉϥⲥⲟⲛ).

7.2.4 Conditional and temporal protatic syntagms[54].

The frequent negative and affirmative encategorization here is stylistically distinctive (a figure). Distinction between (←——→) and (+——→) is difficult, perhaps not warranted.

---

[52] The two syntagms, ⲡⲉⲧ- ("substantivized relative") and ⲡⲉⲧ-/ⲡⲉ ⲉⲧ-/ⲉⲧ- (*glose*) are diachronically and synchronically to be kept apart, as regards both external and internal relationships. However, they coincide as nuclei of the conjunctive. See Polotsky 1962, esp. §6, and Quecke forthcoming.

[53] In (*IV* 204.21ff.) ⲟⲩⲟⲛ ⲛⲓⲙ ⲉⲧⲛⲁ- ...ⲏ ⲛⲉⲧⲛⲁ- *two categories* of persons are enumerated. ⲁⲩⲱ ⲉⲧⲛⲁ-/ⲡⲉⲧⲛⲁ- is coordinated to a relative *present* (*III* 198.10f., *IV* 49.1, 90.13) as a rhetorical figure (the relative present is mainly subcategorized as (ⲡ)ⲉⲧ- ⲁⲩⲱ ⲉⲧ-, e.g. *III* 21.10, 74.11f., 93.17f., 127.16f.); with *glose-forms*: *III* 46.6f.13, 215.14f., *Ch.* 27.32ff., 95.13ff., *Wess. 9* 108a 13ff.; cf. Shisha-Halevy 1972: 114ff. For the perfect, we find (ⲡ)ⲉⲛⲧⲁϥ- (ⲁⲩⲱ) ⲁϥ-/ⲉⲁϥ-, cf. *III* 69.14f., 177.24f., *Ch.* 29.37ff., 40.18ff. etc.

[54] Cf. Erman 1933:§584, Hintze 1952:271f., Spiegelberg 1925:§145, cf. §495, Johnson 1974:288ff.

(1) The *Conditional*: ЄϤϢⲀⲚⲤⲰⲦⲘ unvested or vested [55] with ⲔⲀⲚ, ϨⲞⲦⲀⲚ, ⲈϢⲰⲠⲈ. Note the following data regarding the categorization contour: frequent *negation encategorization* (ЄϤϢⲀⲚ- (ⲀⲨⲰ) ⲚϤⲦⲘ-), the neg. conjunctive signifying " the next (negative) stage ", " and not... ", " so that... not ", " even though... not... ", " nevertheless/but/still... not... " (*III* 158.10f., *IV* 3.17f.; *III* 121.8f., *IV* 85.3, *Ch.* 45. 16ff., 72.12ff.). *Negation syncategorization* (ЄϤϢⲀⲚⲦⲘ- (ⲀⲨⲰ) ⲚϤ-, *IV* 106.5f.); *negation maintenance*, (ЄϤϢⲀⲚⲦⲘ- ⲀⲨⲰ ⲚϤⲦⲘ- *III* 65.25f., 131.20ff.); *affirmation encategorization* (ЄϤϢⲀⲚⲦⲘ- + conjunctive + ⲀⲨⲰ ⲀⲖⲖⲀ, ⲆⲈ, *III* 19.4ff., *A 1* 88).

(a) (←→), personal maintenance: (*III* 19.4ff.) ЄⲨϢⲀⲚⲦⲘⲢ-ⲀⲚⲀϢ ⲘⲠⲢⲀⲚ ⲘⲠⲚⲞⲨⲦⲈ ⲚⲤⲈⲈⲒⲢⲈ ⲆⲈ ⲚⲔⲈⲀⲚⲀϢ—affirm. encategorization / (*ibid.* 125.14ff.) ⲈϢⲰⲠⲈ ⲈⲚϢⲀⲚⲦⲘⲤⲰⲦⲘ ⲚⲤⲀⲠⲚⲞⲘⲞⲤ... ⲀⲨⲰ ⲚⲦⲚⲦⲘϮ-ϨⲦⲎⲚ ⲈⲘⲠⲀⲢⲀⲆⲞⲤⲒⲤ ⲚⲚⲈⲚⲈⲒⲞⲦⲈ — neg. maintenance / (*IV* 3.17f.) ЄⲨϢⲀⲚⲢ-ⲠⲈⲦⲚⲀⲚⲞⲨϤ ⲚϨⲎⲦⲞⲨ Ⲏ ⲚⲤⲈⲦⲘⲈⲒⲢⲈ — neg. encategorization / (*ibid.* 106.5f.) ЄⲨϢⲀⲚⲦⲘⲤⲰⲦⲘ ⲀⲨⲰ ⲚⲤⲈϪⲒ-ⲤⲂⲰ — neg. syncategorization / (*Ch.* 117.14ff.) ⲔⲀⲚ ЄⲨϢⲀⲚⲨϢⲰⲦ ⲚⲚⲨϨⲚ ⲚⲦⲈⲬⲰⲢⲀ ⲚⲦⲀⲨⲂⲰⲔ ⲈⲢⲞⲤ ⲀⲨⲰ ⲚⲤⲈϢⲞϤⲤ / (*A 1* 88) ⲈϢⲰⲠⲈ ⲈⲢϢⲀⲚⲦⲘⲠⲞⲨⲀ ⲘⲘⲞⲚ ⲘⲈⲦⲀⲚⲞⲒ ⲀⲖⲖⲀ ⲚⲦⲚⲤⲰⲦⲠ ⲚⲀⲚ... — affirm. encategorization. Additional exx.: *III* 36.8f., 110.17f., 153.23 (repeated lexeme), 183.7f., *IV* 56.15ff., 94.4f., 102.18f. (repeated lexeme), *Ch.* 28.44ff., 82.50ff., 88-9, 166.2ff., etc.

(b) (+→) (?), no personal maintenance: (*III* 65.24ff.) ⲈϢⲰⲠⲈ ⲢⲰ ⲈϤϢⲀⲚⲦⲘⲚ-ⲦⲘⲎⲤⲈ ⲈϨⲞⲨⲚ ⲚϤⲦⲘⲀⲀⲤ (*v.l.* Cod. Ⲁ ⲚϤⲀⲀⲤ) ⲚⲞⲨⲔⲈⲪⲀⲖⲀⲒⲞⲚ ⲚϤϪⲒ-ⲘⲎⲤⲈ ⲞⲚ ⲘⲘⲞⲤ — variant reading neg. syncategorization/maintenance / (*ibid.* 16.22f.) ⲔⲀⲚ ⲈⲢϢⲀⲚⲠⲚⲞⲨⲦⲈ Ⲓ̅Ⲥ̅ ⲞⲨⲰⲚϨ ⲈⲂⲞⲖ... ⲚⲤⲈⲢ-ⲀⲚⲀϢ ⲘⲘⲞϤ ⲈⲨⲚⲀⲨ ⲈⲢⲞϤ (" and so... ") / (*ibid.* 220.2ff.) ⲈⲨϢⲀⲚⲠⲞⲢϪⲞⲨ ⲈⲂⲞⲖ ⲚⲚⲈⲨⲈⲢⲎⲨ ⲚⲈⲤⲞⲞⲨ ⲘⲈⲚ ⲚⲤⲈⲘⲦⲞⲚ ⲘⲘⲞⲞⲨ ϨⲚⲚⲈⲨⲘⲀ ⲘⲘⲞⲞⲚⲈ ⲚⲂⲀⲀⲘⲠⲈ ⲆⲈ ⲚⲤⲈϨⲢⲀ ⲚⲤⲰⲞⲨ ⲈϨⲈⲚⲘⲀ ⲚϪⲀⲈⲒⲈ... / (*IV* 69.13, *A 1* 136 etc.) ⲈⲤϢⲀⲚϢⲰⲠⲈ... ⲚⲦⲈ- — the conjunctive sharing this slot with ⲈⲦⲢⲈ- after the cataphoric -Ⲥ- (§5.2.2.1). Peculiarly, - ⲀⲨⲰ - occurs here in cases of *actual sequence*: (*III* 150.14f.) ⲈⲒϢⲀⲚⲦⲰⲞⲨⲚ ⲈⲒϨⲘⲞⲞⲤ... ⲀⲨⲰ ⲚⲦⲀⲈⲒ ⲈⲂⲞⲖ.

PARADIGM: complete coordinated sets of *protasis* + *apodosis* excepted, " concurrent " constructions are here rare. For ЄϤϢⲀⲚ- ⲀⲨⲰ ЄϤϢⲀⲚ- I have very few examples; one (*IV* 155.14ff.), in ponderous rhetorical style, with relatively independent protases: ⲈⲒϢⲀⲚⲤϨⲞⲨⲰⲢⲈⲦ ⲘⲀⲨⲀⲀⲦ... ⲀⲨⲰ ⲈⲒϢⲀⲚⲤⲘⲚⲦⲤ ⲈⲦⲘⲞⲨⲈⲘ-ⲞⲈⲒⲔ...; another (*III* 121.8ff.) with protases too incommensurate to be microcoordinated: ⲈϢⲬⲈ-ⲈⲨϢⲀⲚ-...ⲀⲨⲰ ϨⲞⲦⲀⲚ ⲈⲚϢⲀⲚⲦⲘ-...

(2) ⲈϢⲬⲈ, ⲈϢⲰⲠⲈ:

ⲈϢⲬⲈ-		ⲀϤ-	ⲈϢⲰⲠⲈ		Ⲉ-　　　 see under (3)
		ⲞⲨⲚ-			ЄϤϢⲀⲚ-, ЄϤⲦⲘ-
		ⲚⲦⲀϤ- (§2.1.5)			ⲞⲨⲚⲦⲀ⸗
					ⲘⲘⲞⲚ
					ⲚⲦⲀϤ-

(a) (←→): neg. encategorization/maintenance; no personal maintenance. (*III* 139.18) ⲈϢⲬⲈ-ⲞⲨⲚϨⲞⲈⲒⲚⲈ... ⲈⲨⲔⲢⲘⲢⲘ... ϪⲈ-ⲈⲒϪⲒ ⲘⲘⲞⲞⲨ ⲚϬⲞⲚⲤ ⲀⲨⲰ ⲚⲦⲞⲞⲨ ⲚⲤⲈⲦⲘⲦⲀⲘⲞⲒ... — neg. encategorization / (*A 1* 99) ⲈϢⲬⲈ-ⲚⲦⲀⲠⲀⲒ ϪⲞⲞⲤ ϨⲘⲠⲚⲞϬⲚⲈϨ ⲚⲦⲈϤⲮⲨⲬⲎ ϪⲈ-'ⲘⲀⲢⲒⲘⲞⲨ ⲚⲦⲈⲚⲀⲒ ⲰⲚϨ' ⲀⲨⲰ ⲚⲤⲈⲘⲞⲨ... / (*Wess. 9* 122d 11ff.) ⲈϢⲰⲠⲈ ⲞⲨⲚⲦⲎⲦⲚ-ⲞⲨϨⲰⲂ ⲘⲚⲚⲈⲦⲚⲈⲢⲎⲨ ⲚⲦⲈⲦⲚⲚⲀⲨ ⲈⲨⲦⲨⲠⲞⲤ ⲚⲈⲒⲢⲎⲚⲎ... / (*Ch.* 195.8ff.) ⲈϢⲬⲈ-ⲀⲠⲈⲦⲈⲞⲨⲚⲦⲀϤ-ⲤⲞⲨ ϬⲘ-ϬⲞⲘ ⲈⲦⲀⲀⲨ ⲚⲀⲔ ⲚϤⲦⲘϬⲘ-ϬⲞⲘ ⲆⲈ ⲚⲦⲞⲔ... ⲈⲦⲀⲀⲨ ϨⲀⲠⲤⲰⲦⲈ ⲚⲦⲈⲔⲮⲨⲬⲎ... — neg. encategorization. Also *A 1* 97, *P* 130⁴ 111 ⲪⲚⲄ (ⲈϢⲰⲠⲈ ⲚⲦⲀⲨ- ⲀⲨⲰ ⲚⲦⲞⲤ ⲚⲤ-), *Ch.* 85-6.

(b) (+→) (?): (*IV* 101.8) ϪⲈⲔⲀⲤ ⲈⲨⲈⲈⲒⲘⲈ ϪⲈ-ⲤⲈⲞⲨⲰϢ ⲈϨⲀⲢⲈϨ ⲈⲢⲞⲤ; ⲈϢⲰⲠⲈ ⲘⲘⲞⲚ ⲚⲤⲈⲦⲘϪⲒⲦⲞⲨ... (i.e. the applicants to join the community. The neg. conjunctive [neg. maintenance] contentualizes ⲘⲘⲞⲚ).

---

[55] SHISHA-HALEVY 1972:§0.3, Ch. 3.

(3) *Circumstantial-converter* protases (unvested or vested [55] with ⲈϢⲰⲠⲈ, ⲔⲀⲚ, ⳅⲀⲘⲞⲒ):

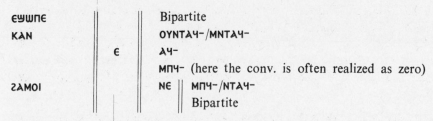

(a) (←→): characteristic frequent neg. encategorization; neg. syncategorization/maintenance; no personal maintenance. (*III* 157.1f.) (ⳅⲈⲚⳅⲂⲎⲨⲈ ⲚⲤⲈϢⲞⲞⲠ ⲀⲚ) Ⲏ ⲚⲦⲞϤ ⲈⲨϢⲞⲞⲠ ⲚⲦⲀⲦⲘⲈⲒⲘⲈ ⲀⲚⲞⲔ ⲞⲨⲦⲈ ⲠⳅⲀⲗⲞ... — neg. encategorization / (*ibid.* 40.20ff.) ⲔⲀⲚ ⲈⲒϢⲗⲎⲗ ⲚⲘⲘⲀⲨ ⲔⲀⲚ ⲈⲨϢⲗⲎⲗ ⲚⲘⲘⲀⲒ ⲔⲀⲚ ⲈⲒⲞⲨⲈⲘ-ⲞⲈⲒⲔ ⲚⲘⲘⲀⲨ ⲈⲨ-ⲞⲨⲰⲘ ⲚⲘⲘⲀⲒ Ⲏ ⲈⲣⲈⲦⲞⲞⲦ ⲀⲨⲰ ⲦⲞⲞⲦⲞⲨ ⳅⲘⲠⲈⲒⲭⲞⲠ ⲚⲞⲨⲰⲦ ⳅⲒⲦⲈⲒⲦⲣⲀⲠⲈⳅⲀ ⲀⲨⲰ ⲚⲤⲈⲦⲞⲗⲘⲀ ⲈⲦⲀⲔⲞ ⲚⲚⲦⲀⲘⲒⲞ ⲘⲠ-ⲚⲞⲨⲦⲈ... / (*ibid.* 139.25ff.) ...ⲈⲦⲈⲦⲚⲤⲞⲞⲨⲚ ⲚⲀⲘⲈ ⲭⲈ-ⲀⲒⲭⲒ-ⳅⲞⲈⲒⲚⲈ ⲚⳕⲞⲚⲤ... ⲀⲨⲰ ⲚⲦⲰⲦⲚ ⲚⲦⲈⲦⲚⲦⲘⲦⲀⲘⲞⲒ... — neg. encategorization / (*P* 130² 41 ⲢⲤ) ⲈϢⲰⲠⲈ ⲞⲨⲈⲒⲰⲦ ⲘⲚⲞⲨⲘⲀⲀⲨ ⲈⲞⲨⲚⲦⲀⲨ ⲘⲘⲀⲨ ⲚⳅⲈⲚϢⲎⲢⲈ ⲘⲚⳅⲈⲚϢⲈⲈⲢⲈ ⲀⲨⲰ ⲚⲦⲈⳅⲀⳅ ⲚⳅⲎⲦⲞⲨ ⳅⲈ ⲈⳅⲣⲀⲒ ⳅⲚⲞⲨϢⲤⲚⲈ... / (*IV* 31.3ff.) ⳅⲈⲚⲢⲰⲘⲈ ⲈⲘⲚⲦⲀⲨ ⲘⲘⲀⲨ ⲚⳅⲈⲚϢⲎⲢⲈ Ⲏ ⲚⲦⲞϤ ⲈⲨⲚⲦⲀⲨ ⲚⲤⲈⲀⲠⲞⲦⲀⲤⲤⲈ ⲘⲘⲞⲞⲨ ⲘⲚⳅⲈⲚⳅⲨⲠⲀⲢⲭⲞⲚⲦⲀ ⲈⲚⲀϢⲞⲨ... / (*ibid.* 196.14f.) (ⲈϢⲭⲈ-ⲞⲨⲚⳅⲞⲈⲒⲚⲈ... ⲚⲤⲈⲞⲨⲰϢ Ⲁ̀Ⲛ ⲈⳕⲰ ⲚⲞⲨⲈϢⲚⲞⲨⲰⲘ...) Ⲏ ⲚⲦⲞϤ ⲔⲀⲚ ⲈⲀⲨⲞⲨⲰⲘ ⲚⲤⲈⲦⲘⲤⲀⳅϢⲞⲨ ⲈⲂⲞⲗ ⲘⲘⲞⲞⲨ... (i.e. from the victuals) — neg. encategorization / (*ibid.* 98.14f.) ...ⲈⲀⲨⲦⲰϢⲔ ⲈⳅⲈⲚⳅⲂⲎⲨⲈ ⲘⲠⲚⲈⲨⲘⲀⲦⲒⲔⲞⲚ ⲚⳕⲦⲰⳅ ⳅⲚⳅⲈⲚⳅⲂⲎⲨⲈ ⲚⲤⲰⲘⲀⲦⲒⲔⲞⲚ... / (*Ch.* 63.12ff.) ⲞⲨⲀⲦⳕⲞⲘ ⲠⲈ ⲈⲦⲢⲈⲠⲆⲒⲀⲂⲞⲗⲞⲤ ⲦⲢⲈⲢϢⲘⲈ Ⲣ-ⲚⲞⲂⲈ ⲘⲠⲈϤⲞⲨⲰϢ Ⲣ-ϢⲞⲢⲠ ⲈⲠⲘⲈⲈⲨⲈ ⲘⲠⲆⲒⲀⲂⲞⲗⲞⲤ Ⲏ ⲚϤⳅⲞⲦⲢ ⲚⲘⲘⲀϤ / (*ibid.* 195.53ff.) (" Will our heart be capable of receiving love towards our neighbour) ⲘⲠⲚϢⲞⲨⲰϤ ⲚϢⲞⲢⲠ ⲈⲂⲞⲗ ⳅⲚⲘⲘⲚⲦⲘⲀⲒⳅⲞⲘⲦ ⲀⲨⲰ ⲚⲦⲚⲈⲒⲀⲀϤ ⲈⲂⲞⲗ ⳅⲘⲠⲈⲤⲗⲰϢⲘⲈ ⲦⲎⲢϤ... / (*P* 130² 75 ⲢⲞ) ⲚⲒⲘ ⲠⲈⲦⲚⲀⲢ-ⲚⲀⲒ ⲈⲘⲠⲈⲠⲚⲞⲨⲦⲈ ⲢϢⲠⲤⲀⳅⲈ-ⲠⲈϤⳅⲞ ⲈⲂⲞⲗ ⲘⲘⲞⲞⲨ ⲀⲨⲰ ⲚϤⲀⲀⲨ ⲚϢⲘⲘⲞ ⲈⲠⲈϤⲠⲚⲀ... / (*A* 2 357) (" What is his worth") ⲔⲀⲚ ⲈⲘⲠϤⲔⲀ-ⲔⲈⳅⲚⲀⲀⲨ ⲭⲈ-ⲘⲠϤⲦⲢⲈⲨϢⲰⲠⲈ ⲚⲀϤ... ⲀⲨⲰ ⲚϤⲢ-ⲢⲘⲘⲀⲞ ⲚⳅⲎⲦⲞⲨ... — affirm. encategorization / (*Wess.* 9 88b 11ff.) ⲈⲚⲈⲘⲠⲈⳅⲎⲦ ⲚⲚⲈⲦⲞⲨⲎⳅ ⳅⲚⲐⲒⲗⲎⲘ ⲘⲠⲒⲞⲨⲞⲈⲒϢ ⲤⲀⳅⲰϤ ⲈⲂⲞⲗ ⲘⲘⲞϤ ⲀⲨⲰ ⲚⲦⲈⲦⲈⲨⲯⲨⲭⲎ ⲢϢⲢⲠⲚϢⲰⲠⲈ ⲘⲘⲀ ⲚⲆⲀⲒⲘⲰⲚ... ⲚⲈⲨⲚⲀⲀⲒⲭⲘⲀⲗⲰⲦⲒⳅⲈ ⲀⲚ ⲠⲈ ⲘⲠⲒⲎ̄ⲗ̄ / (*Zoega* 200 ⲦⲒⲀ) ⲈⲚⲈⲘⲠⲈⲘ-ⲠⲀⲢⲀⲫⲨⲤⲒⲤ ⲦⲰⲘ ⲚⲂⲀⲗ ⲚⲤⲈⲦⲰⲘ ⲘⲠⳅⲎⲦ ⲚⲚⲈⲦⲈⲒⲢⲈ ⲘⲘⲞⲞⲨ... / (*A* 1 202) ⳅⲀⲘⲞⲒ ⲈⲚⲈⲨϢⲞⲞⲠ ⲚⲘⲘⲀⲚ ⲦⲈⲚⲞⲨ ⲚⲤⲈ-ⲦⲘⲠⲈⳅ-ⲚⲈⲚⳅⲞⲈⲒⲦⲈ ⳅⲒⲭⲰⲚ... — neg. encategorization / (*K* 928) (ⲔⲀⲈⲒⲚ) ⳅⲀⲘⲞⲒ ⲈⲚⲈⲘⲠϤⲢ-ⲗⲀⲀⲨ ⲚⲀⲅⲀⲐⲞⲚ ⲈⲚⲈⳅ ⲚϤⲦⲘⲘⲞⲨⲞⲨⲦ ⲆⲈ ⲞⲚ ⲚⲞⲨⲀⲦⲚⲞⲂⲈ. (ⲒⲞⲨⲆⲀⲤ) ⳅⲀⲘⲞⲒ ⲈⲚⲈⲘⲠϤⲢ-ⲀⲠⲞⲤⲦⲞⲗⲞⲤ ⲈⲚⲈⳅ ⲚϤⲦⲘⲠⲀⲢⲀⲆⲒⲆⲞⲨ ⲞⲚ ⲘⲠⲭⲞⲈⲒⲤ. (ⲔⲀⲒⲫⲀⲤ) ⳅⲀⲘⲞⲒ ⲈⲚⲈⲘⲠϤⲢ-ⲞⲨⲎⲎⲂ ⲈⲚⲈⳅ ⲚϤⲦⲘⲭⲒ-ϢⲞⳍⲚⲈ ⲞⲚ ⲈⲘⲞⲨⲞⲨⲦ ⲘⲠⲭⲞⲈⲒⲤ — neg. maintenance / (*IV* 9.18f.) ⳅⲀⲘⲞⲒ ⲈⲚⲈⲚⲦⲀⲨⲘⲞⲨⲢ ⲚⲞⲨⲰⲚⲈ ⲚⲤⲒⲔⲈ ⲈⲠⲈⲨⲘⲀⳅⳅ ⲚⲤⲈⲞⲘⲤⲞⲨ ⳅⲘⲠⲠⲈⲗⲀⳕⲞⲤ ⲚⲐⲀⲗⲀⲤⲤⲀ. Also: *IV* 123.20ff. (ⲈϢⲰⲠⲈ ⲈⲚ- Ⲏ ⲈⲚ- Ⲏ ⲚⲦⲞϤ ⲈⲚ- ⲀⲨⲰ ⲚⲦⲈ-), 163.2f. (ⲘⲠⲞⲨ- ⲚⲤⲈ-), *Ch.* 165.16ff. (ⲈⲚⲈⲘⲠⲞⲨ- ⲀⲨⲰ ⲚⲤⲈ-), *Wess.* 9 119b 9ff. (ⳅⲀⲘⲞⲒ ⲈⲚⲈⲘⲠⲞⲨ- ⲚⲤⲈⲦⲘ-).

(b) (+→) (?): (*III* 111-2) ⳅⲀⲘⲞⲒ ⲈⲚⲈⲚⲦⲀⲒⳕⲒⲚⲈ... ⲚⲚⲒⲚⲞⲨⲦⲈ ⲚⳅⲀⲦ ⳅⲒⲚⲞⲨⲂ... ⲘⲀⲗⲒⲤⲦⲀ ⲐⲒⲔⲰⲚ ⲚⲚⲞⲨⲂ ⲦⲀⲒ ⲈⲦⲒⲢⲈ ⲚⲤⲈ ⲘⲘⲀⳅⲈ ⲚⳅⲒⲤⲈ ⲀⲨⲰ ⲤⲞⲞⲨ ⲚⲞⲨϢϢⳋ ⲚⲦⲀⳕⲈⲦⳕⲰⲦⲤ Ⲏ ⲚⲦⲀⳕⲈⲦⳕⲰⲦⲞⲨ / (*A* 2 526) ⲠⲘⲀⲈⲒⲚ ⲠⲈ ⲠⲀⲒ ⲘⲠⳅⲎⲦ ⲈⲦⲤⲞⲞϤ ⲚⲀⲔⲀⲐⲀⲢⲦⲞⲤ ⲘⲠⲢⲰⲘⲈ ⲈϤⲚⲀⲨ ⲈⲨⲘⲈⲗⲞⲤ ⲚⲦⲈⲠⲈϤⲤⲰⲘⲀ ⲚϤⲢ-ⲀⲦϢⲀ[Ⲩ] ⳅⲚⲚⲈϤⲘⲈⲈⲨⲈ.

PARADIGM: ⲈⲚⲈ - ⲀⲨⲰ ⲈⲚⲈ- (rare): (*Ch.* 36.11ff.) ⲈⲚⲈⲞⲨⲚⳕⲞⲘ ⲅⲀⲢ ⲘⲘⲞⲔ, ⲀⲨⲰ ⲈⲚⲈⲦⲂⲞⲎⲐⲈⲒⲀ ⲀⲚ ⲦⲈ ⲘⲠⲈⲭ̄Ⲥ̄... — incommensurate protases (the second non-verbal).

7.2.4.1 Atemporal, generic verb forms: (*non-actual*) *relative-protatic present, parabolic (non-narrative) perfect*. We encounter here either (a) the present form with no actual or durative reference [56],

---

[56] See §3.1.2.1.1. Cf. Young 1961:115-8 (past reference of the present), 118f. (esp. 118 n. 17, on the present as a habitual tense). For the conjunctive after the pres., Polotsky 1960a:§23 Obs. 4 (= *CP* 248), Browne 1979a:40; earlier, Stern §280f. (f). For pre-Coptic correspondents, see Erman 1933:§583, Spiegelberg 1925:§144, Johnson 1974:291f. (E528-9).

OYN- or the verboid OYNTA⸗, or (b) the non-narrative, gnomic-parabolic perfect tense [57] — as a rule in relative and adnominal-circumstantial conversion, the equivalents of a *generic relative clause* (" such... as...") or of a gnomic suppositive hypothetic protasis (" supposing...", " should it ever happen that...") [58]. (Note the frequent negation encategorization, cf. §7.2.4.)

(1) *Present*: (a) (←→): (*Ch.* 26.12f.) ΝΕΚΣШШЧ ΕΤΕΟΥΝ6ΟΜ Ν2ΕΝШΗΡΕ ШΗΜ ΕΣΟΥΝΟΥ ΑΥШ ΝΣΕΤΜ2ШΠ ΕΝΕΤΚШΜШ ΜΜΟΚ — neg. encategorization / (*IV* 122.5ff.) ΝΕΤΝΑ+ ΔΕ ΟΝ ΜΠΕΥΟΥΟΕΙ Ε2ΟΥΝ ΕΡΟΝ ΕΤΡΕΥΟΥШ2 ΝΜΜΑΝ... ΟΥΟΝ ΝΙΜ ΕΤΟ ΝΚΟΙΝШΝΟΣ ΝΜΜΑΝ... ΝΣΕΤΜΑΠΟΤΑΣΣΕ ΝΝΚΑ ΝΙΜ ΕΤШΟΟΠ ΝΑΥ... — here the conj. is probably microcoordinated to the substantivized future / (*Leyd.* 355) ΠΕΤΣШΤΕ ΜΜΟΝ ΝЧ2ΥΠΟΜΙΝΕ (sic) 2ΙΟΥΜΝΤΡΕЧ2Ι-ΛΑ / (*IV* 156.9ff.) (ΟΥΡШΜΕ Η ΟΥΣ2ΙΜΕ) ΕΥΑΜΕΛΕΙ ΕΤΑ2ΟΟΥ ΕΡΑΤΟΥ ΑΥШ ΝΣΕШΙΠΕ ΑΝ 2ΗΤΟΥ ΝΝΕΣΝΗΥ ΝΕΓΚΡΑΤΗΣ ΝΑΜΕ ΑΥШ ΕΤ2ΟΣΕ... ΑΥШ ΝΣΕΤΜΣШΤΜ ΝΑΥ ΕΡ-ΠΕΥΣШΜΑ ΝΑΥ Ν2Μ2ΑΛ... / (*Cairo* 8007) ΟΥΝΡШΜΕ ΕΥΟΥΕШ-ΤΡΕЧΤШΟΥΝ ΜΠΑΤЧ2ΜΟΟΣ, ΝΣΕΟΥΕШ-ΤΡΕЧ 2ΜΟ[ΟΣ...].

(b) (+→): (*III* 41.5) ΝΕΤΣΟΟΥΝ ΕΝΕΥ2ΒΗΥΕ ΝΣΕ2ШΠ Ε2ШΟΥ — lexical equivalence of neg. encategorization: " ...and (should they) not tell " / (*Ch.* 195.1f.) ΠΕΤΕΟΥΝΤΑЧΣΟΥ ΝЧΤΜΝΑ Ν2ΗΤΟΥ — neg. encategorization [59] / (*IV* 120.3f.) ΟΥΟΝ ΝΙΜ 2ΡΑΙ Ν2ΗΤΝ ΕΥΡ-ΝΟΒΕ Η ΕΥΝΑΡ-ΝΟΒΕ... ΑΥШ ΝΣΕΤΜΧΕ-ΠΝΟΒΕ ΝΤΑΥΑΑЧ — ΝΑ- nucleus? / (*Wess.* 9 94b 10ff.) ΝΙΜ ΠΕΤΣΟΟΥΝ ΑΝ ΧΕ-Ν2ΑΛΑΤΕ ΜΝΝΤΒΝΟΟΥΕ ΑΥШ ΠΚΕΣΕΕΠΕ Ν2ШΟΝ ΣΕΜΕ ΝΝΕΥΕΡΗΥ ΝΤΝΤΜΡ-ΠΜΕΕΥΕ ΑΝΟΝ ΜΠΤШΠ ΕΝΕΝΕΡΗΥ — neg. encategorization, the conjunctive expanding the generic present ΣΕΜΕ — or better neg. maintenance, with ΠΕΤΣΟΟΥΝ ΑΝ the nucleus (ΤШΠ Ε- " be familiar with ").

(2) *Perfect*: (*A 2* 363-4) ΟΥΡШΜΕ ΠΕΝΤΑΠΝΟΥΤΕ + ΝΑЧ " There was a man to whom God had given...") ΝΟΥΜΝΤΡΜΜΑΟ ΜΝ2ΕΝ2ΥΠΑΡΧΟΝΤΑ ΑΥШ ΟΥΕΟΟΥ ΑΥШ ΝΤΕΤΜΠΝΟΥΤΕ +-Ε2ΟΥΣΙΑ ΝΑЧ ΕΟΥШΜ ΕΒΟΛ Ν2ΗΤΣ... ΟΥ-ΡШΜΕ ΕΑΠΝΟΥΤΕ + ΝΑЧ ΝΟΥΜΝΤΡΜΜΑΟ 2ΙΧΜΠΚΑ2 ΝЧΤΜΑΑЧ ΝΜΠШΑ Ν+-6ΟΜ ΝΑЧ ΝΡ-ΠΕΤΝΑΝΟΥЧ Ν2ΗΤΣ — neg. encategorization / (*III* 204.12ff.) ΝΘΕ ΓΑΡ ΝΟΥΡШΜΕ ΕЧ2ΝΝΕЧΠΕΘΟΟΥ ΕΑЧΕΙ ΜΠΟΥΕ ΕΤΡΕЧ6Μ-ΠΟΥШΙΝΕ ΑΥШ ΝΤΕΧΟΟΣ ΝΑЧ ΧΕ-'ΤΒΒΟΚ ΕΒΟΛ 2ΝΝΕΚΠΕΘΟΟΥ' ΕΡΕШΟΟΠ ΝΤΟ 2ΡΑΙ 2ΝΝΟΥΠΕΘΟΟΥ. Very striking, with the whole *protasis-apodosis* complex hypothetic, is (*A 2* 453, not Sh.) ΟΥΚΟΥΝ ΕШШΠΕ ΛΟΥΑ ΛΑЧ ΜΜΙΝ ΜΜΟЧ ΝШΗΡΕ ΜΠΝΟΥΤΕ 2ΙΤΝΤΑΡΕΤΗ ΕΑЧΧΙ ΝΤΕΙΕ2ΟΥΣΙΑ ΝΤΕΙΓΕΝΙΑ (sic) ΤΑΙ ΑΠΑΙ ΣΟΥΝ-ΠΚΑΙΡΟΣ ΝΤΝΛΑΚΕ ΕΤΝΑΝΟΥΣ ΑΥШ ΝЧΡΑШΕ.

7.2.5 APERSONAL/PERSONAL VERB NOMINALIZATIONS: the infinitives

7.2.5.1 The apersonal (non-causative) infinitive, in varying syntactic statuses and the full range of meaning nuances [60], is expanded by the conjunctive.

(1) The infinitive in *adjunct* status (expanding another verb: ' (Ε)СШТМ '):

(a) (←→): ΑΥШ-microcoordination is the rule. Personal maintenance; negation syncategorization. (*III* 40. 14f.) ...ΕЧ2ΑΡΕ2 ΕΤΜΠΑ2ΤЧ ΝΟΥΔΑΙΜΟΝΙΟΝ ΑΥШ ΝЧШШΠΕ 2ΑΤΕ2ΟΥΣΙΑ ΝΟΥΠΝΑ... / (*ibid.* 143.23f.) ΕΙΑΝΑΓ-ΚΑΖΕ ΜΜШΤΝ ΕΣΑ2ΕΤΗΥΤΝ ΕΒΟΛ ΜΠΝΟΥΤΕ ΑΥШ ΝΤΕΤΝΡ-ΘΥΣΙΑ ΝΝΕΙΔШΛΟΝ. Also: *III* 92.8ff., *IV* 38.12f. (here Leipoldt emends the text unnecessarily to Ε + inf.).

(b) (+→): personal maintenance; neg. encategorization. (*A 2* 405) ΜΗ ΟΥΝ6ΟΜ ΝΟΥΕΙΔШΛΟΝ ΕШΒΤЧ Η ΕΠΟΟΝΕЧ ΕЧΟ ΝШΕ ΝЧΑΑЧ ΝΟΥШΝΕ Η ΝΤΟЧ ΝЧΑΑЧ ΝΟΥ2ΑΤ ΑΝΤΙ2ΟΜΝΤ — the first conj. premodified by the circumstantial present / (*P 130⁵* 38 vo) ΝΑΝΟΥΣ ΝΑΝ ΕΡ-ΣΟΦΟΣ ΝΤΝΚΛΗΡΟΝΟΜΕΙ ΜΠΕΟΟΥ Ν2ΟΥΟ ΕΡ-ΑΘΗΤ ΝΤΝ-ΣШΤΠ ΝΑΝ ΝΟΥΣШШ ΕЧΧΟΣΕ... ΝΑΝΟΥΣ ΝΑΝ ΕΘΒΒΙΟΝ ΝΤΝΧΙ ΝΟΥ2ΜΟΤ ΕΒΟΛ 2ΙΤΜΠΝΟΥΤΕ Ν2ΟΥΟ ΕΡ-ΧΑΣΙ2ΗΤ

---

[57] Compare (pre-Coptic Egyptian) HINTZE 1952:61f., ERMAN 1933:§582, BORGHOUTS 1979:20ff. (" ' thematic ' rather than temporal ", " non-witnessed acts ", " hearsay ", " non-objective sequence ", " inferential ", " customary, habitual, non-point past " [Wente]); SPIEGELBERG 1925:§147 Anm., JOHNSON 1974:291, 293.

[58] Cf. the similar role of ΕШШΑΝ- (+ conjunctive), e.g. *Ch.* 190.49ff., or of ΕШΧΕ-ΟΥΝ- (+ conjunctive), e.g. *IV* 24-5.

[59] Cf. (Bohairic) *Jac.* 4:17 ΦΗ ΕΤΣШΟΥΝ ΝΟΥΠΕΘΝΑΝΕЧ ΕΑΙЧ ΟΥΟ2 ΝΤΕЧШΤΕΜΑΙЧ.

[60] See RUDNITZKY 1956:48ff.

ⲛⲧⲉⲡⲛⲟⲩⲧⲉ + ⲟⲩⲃⲏⲛ / (*III* 118.25f.) ⲉⲱⲝⲉ-ⲱⲱⲉ ⲉⲱⲓⲡⲉ ⲍⲏⲧⲟⲩ ⲛⲛⲉⲛⲉⲓⲟⲧⲉ ⲉⲛⲧⲁⲩⲛⲕⲟⲧⲕ ⲛⲧⲛⲍⲩⲡⲟⲙⲓⲛⲉ — an instance of " generic " personalization (encategorization of person), see under (2). Also *III* 135-6, 140. 13ff., *IV* 196.11.

(2) The infinitive in *subject/predicate* status. In this case we find the *generic personalization* of the infinitive (i.e. person encategorization): for the *generic* (rhetorical) *person* [61], Coptic uses the 3rd person sgl. masc., the 2nd person sgl. masc. or the 1st plural. (*III* 65-6) ⲟⲩⲙⲛⲧⲙⲁⲕⲁⲣⲓⲟⲥ ⲡⲉ + ⲙⲡⲍⲏⲕⲉ ⲛⲩⲧⲙⲝⲓ ⲛⲧⲟⲟⲧⲩ, ⲏ ⲉⲁⲕⲝⲓ ⲟⲛ ⲛⲅⲍⲱ ⲉⲣⲟⲕ ⲉⲧⲱⲃⲃⲉⲓⲱ ⲛⲛⲉⲛⲧⲁⲕⲧⲁⲁⲩ ⲛⲁⲩ / (*Ch.* 104.28ff.,39ff.) ⲟⲩⲛⲟⲃⲉ ⲡⲉ ⲟⲩⲱⲙ-ⲡⲟⲉⲓⲕ ⲛⲟⲩⲣⲱⲙⲉ ⲛⲅⲧⲙⲣ-ⲡⲉⲩⲍⲱⲃ — here the non-generic (anaphoric) 3rd person precludes its use as a generic person / (*A I* 37) ⲛⲁⲛⲟⲩ-ⲱⲓⲛⲉ ⲧⲁⲣⲛⲅⲓⲛⲉ ⲛⲟⲉ ⲉⲧⲥⲏⲍ — reminiscence of *Mt.* 7:7 (etc.) / (*Ming.* 89) ⲡⲱⲛ ⲇⲉ ⲍⲱⲱⲛ ⲡⲉ ⲝⲓⲧⲟⲩ ⲏ ⲉⲕⲁⲁⲩ ⲍⲓⲱⲱⲩ ⲛⲧⲛⲧⲙⲩⲓⲧⲟⲩ ⲙⲙⲁⲩ ⲍⲓⲝⲱⲩ — neg. encategorization. Cotextual categorization of person / (*III* 67.5ff.) ⲙⲡⲝⲱⲕ ⲁⲛ ⲉⲃⲟⲗ ⲙⲡⲛⲟⲙⲟⲥ ⲡⲉ ⲙⲉⲣⲉ-ⲡⲉⲧⲍⲓⲧⲟⲩⲱⲕ ⲛⲅⲙⲉⲥⲧⲉ-ⲡⲉⲕⲝⲁⲭⲉ... ⲁⲗⲗⲁ ⲡⲝⲱⲕ ⲉⲃⲟⲗ ⲙⲡⲛⲟⲙⲟⲥ ⲡⲉ ⲙⲉⲣⲉ-ⲛⲉⲕⲝⲁⲭⲉ ⲛⲅⲱⲗⲏⲗ [...] — the infinitive is the predicate constituent in the Copular (# *subject-copula-predicate* #) Nominal Sentence pattern (reminiscence of *Mt.* 5:43-4 with *Rom.* 10:4, 13:10).

7.2.5.2   The causative infinitive (ⲉ-)ⲧⲣⲉⲩ-ⲥⲱⲧⲙ

(1) In *adverbal adjunctal* status (incl. object expansion): ⲉⲧⲣⲉⲩⲥⲱⲧⲙ

(a) (←→) very common; as a rule, personal maintenance: (*III* 36.5ff., parall. *Ch.* 131.24ff.) ⲁⲩⲉⲣⲏⲧ ⲛⲁⲩ ⲟⲛ ⲉⲧⲣⲉⲩⲟⲩⲱⲙ ⲛⲥⲉⲥⲱ ⲛⲙⲙⲁⲩ ⲍⲓⲝⲛⲧⲉⲩⲧⲣⲁⲡⲉⲍⲁ, cf. *ibid.* 202.4 ...ⲉⲧⲣⲉⲩⲟⲩⲱⲙ ⲁⲩⲱ ⲛⲥⲉⲥⲱ, see §7.2.1.1.1 / (*ibid.* 31.3ff.) +ⲡⲁⲣⲁⲕⲁⲗⲉⲓ ⲛⲧⲉⲧⲛⲙⲛⲧⲣⲙⲛⲍⲏⲧ ⲉⲧⲙⲧⲣⲉⲧⲉⲧⲛⲍⲟⲙⲉⲗⲉⲓ ⲛⲍⲏⲧⲟⲩ, ⲁⲗⲗⲁ ⲛⲧⲉⲧⲛⲝⲓ-ⲍⲣⲏⲧⲛ ⲉⲛⲱⲁⲝⲉ ⲉⲧ-ⲟⲩⲁⲁⲃ — affirmative encategorization / (*ibid.* 112.24f.) (ⲛⲱⲁⲝⲉ ⲉⲧⲟⲩ+-ⲥⲃⲱ ⲛⲁⲛ ⲛⲍⲏⲧⲟⲩ) ⲉⲧⲣⲉⲛⲙⲉⲥⲧⲉ-ⲡⲡⲉ-ⲑⲟⲟⲩ ⲛⲧⲛⲙⲉⲣⲉ-ⲡⲡⲉⲧⲛⲁⲛⲟⲩⲩ / (*IV* 65.6ff.) (ⲛⲉⲧⲟⲩⲱⲱ) ⲉⲧⲣⲉⲡⲛⲟⲩⲧⲉ ⲡⲝⲟⲓⲥ ⲓ̅ⲥ̅ ⲥⲙⲟⲩ ⲉⲣⲟⲟⲩ ⲁⲩⲱ ⲛⲩⲕⲱ ⲙⲡⲩⲡ̅ⲛ̅ⲁ̅ ⲍⲓⲝⲱⲟⲩ... ⲁⲩⲱ ⲛⲩⲍⲁⲣⲉⲍ ⲉⲣⲟⲟⲩ... / (*Ch.* 33.16ff.) (ⲛⲉⲧⲁⲍ̅ⲓⲟⲩ) ⲉⲧⲣⲉⲓ̅ⲥ̅ ⲧⲁⲕⲟⲕ ⲁⲩⲱ ⲛⲩⲩⲟⲧⲕ ⲉⲃⲟⲗ / (*P* 131[5] 65 vo) ...ⲉⲧⲣⲉⲩⲩⲱⲡⲉ ⲉⲃⲟⲗ ⲛⲍⲏⲧⲧⲏⲩⲧⲛ ⲁⲩⲱ ⲛⲧⲱⲧⲛ ⲛⲧⲉⲧⲛ+-ⲛⲁⲁⲕⲉ ⲙⲙⲟⲩ. Additional exx.: *III* 106.18f., *IV* 30.25ff., 176.2f., *Ch.* 51.7ff., 86.21ff., etc.

(b) (+→) rarer: (*IV* 56.6f.) ⲛⲧⲟⲟⲩ ⲍⲱⲟⲩ ⲉⲩⲍⲁⲣⲉⲍ ⲉⲣⲟⲟⲩ ⲉⲧⲙⲧⲣⲉⲩⲁⲡⲁⲧⲁ ⲙⲙⲟⲟⲩ ⲛⲥⲉⲥⲱ ⲛⲍⲟⲩⲟ / (*ibid.* 122. 15f). ...ⲉⲧⲣⲉⲩⲕⲧⲟⲩ ⲛⲩⲁⲣⲛⲁ ⲛⲩⲕⲱⲧⲉ ⲛⲥⲁⲑⲉ ⲛⲝⲓⲧⲟⲩ ⲛⲕⲉⲥⲟⲡ / (*Ch.* 189.18ff.) ...ⲉⲧⲣⲉⲩⲟⲩⲉⲅⲡ-ⲛⲉⲩⲕⲉⲉⲥ ⲛⲥⲉ-ⲣⲟⲕⲍⲟⲩ ⲉⲩⲟⲛⲍ: actual sequence - irreversible.

(2) *Adnominal, ad-modifier*, assorted adjunctal roles: ⲉⲧⲣⲉⲩⲥⲱⲧⲙ ·(*III* 211.2f.) ⲁⲩⲉⲓⲛⲉ ⲛⲟⲩⲛⲟⲥ ⲛⲕⲉ-ⲣⲁⲩⲛⲟⲥ ⲉⲝⲱⲟⲩ... ⲍⲱⲥⲧⲉ ⲉⲧⲣⲉⲩⲕⲟⲛⲥⲟⲩ ⲍⲛⲛⲥⲱⲙⲁ ⲉⲧⲟⲩⲛⲍⲏⲧⲟⲩ ⲁⲩⲱ ⲛⲩⲕⲛⲥ-ⲛⲥⲱⲙⲁ ⲛⲙⲙⲁⲩ — microcoordination / (*IV* 187.9ff.) ⲙⲏ ⲍⲛⲩⲁⲝⲉ ⲏ ⲍⲛⲍⲃⲏⲩⲉ ⲛⲉ ⲛⲁⲓ ⲉⲧⲣⲉⲛⲥⲱⲧⲙ ⲉⲣⲟⲟⲩ ⲛⲧⲟⲩⲩⲍ ⲉⲧⲟⲟⲧⲛ ⲉⲣ-ⲛⲟⲃⲉ ⲁⲩⲱ ⲛⲧⲛⲧⲙ-ⲝⲟⲟⲥ ⲛⲁⲩ ⲝⲉ — neg. encategorization of a second conjunctive (coordinated by - ⲁⲩⲱ -). For adnominal ⲉⲧⲣⲉ- see §7.4 below.

(3) In *subject/predicate* status: ⲉⲧⲣⲉⲩⲥⲱⲧⲙ

(a) (←→): no ⲁⲩⲱ; personal maintenance. (*III* 182.20ff.) ...ⲟⲩⲧⲉ ⲟⲩⲁⲛⲟⲙⲓⲁ ⲁⲛ ⲧⲉ ⲉⲧⲣⲉⲛⲙⲉⲗⲉⲧⲁ ⲛⲛⲱⲁⲝⲉ ⲧⲏⲣⲟⲩ ⲛⲛⲉⲅⲣⲁⲫⲏ... ⲛⲧⲛⲩⲱⲡⲉ ⲇⲉ ⲍⲱⲱⲩ ⲍⲛⲍⲉⲛ+-ⲧⲱⲛ... ⲛⲧⲙⲉⲧⲁⲛⲟⲓⲁ ⲁⲛ ⲧⲉ ⲉⲧⲣⲉⲛⲣ-ⲍⲉⲛⲛⲏⲥⲧⲉⲓⲁ ⲙⲛⲍⲉⲛⲱⲗⲗ ⲙⲙⲁⲧⲉ ⲛⲧⲛⲩⲱⲡⲉ ⲍⲱⲱⲩ ⲛⲕⲣⲟⲩ ⲍⲣⲁⲓ ⲍⲛⲍⲱⲃ ⲛⲓⲙ ⲉⲩⲍⲟⲟⲩ / (*Ch.* 160.15ff.) (ⲕⲉⲍⲱⲃ) ⲉⲧⲉⲡⲁⲓ ⲡⲉ ⲉⲧⲣⲉⲛⲣ-ⲍⲟⲧⲉ ⲍⲏⲧⲩ ⲛⲧⲛⲩⲓⲡⲉ ⲇⲉ ⲟⲛ ⲍⲏⲧⲟⲩ ⲛⲛⲉⲩⲁⲅⲅⲉⲗⲟⲥ.

(b) (+→): (*III* 104.19f.) ⲙⲏ ⲟⲩⲗⲁⲁⲩ ⲛⲁⲩ ⲡⲉ ⲉⲧⲣⲉⲡⲕⲁⲍ ⲡⲱⲍ ⲛⲩⲱⲙⲕ ⲛⲧⲥⲩⲛⲁⲅⲱⲅⲏ ⲙⲡⲟⲛⲏⲣⲟⲥ / (*ibid.* 150.18ff.) ⲉⲡⲉⲧⲉⲱⲱⲉ ⲡⲉ ⲉⲧⲣⲉⲛⲉⲓ ⲉⲃⲟⲗ ⲍⲓⲧⲛⲛⲁⲓ ⲉⲧⲛⲏⲩ ⲛⲁⲛ ⲍⲓⲃⲟⲗ ⲉⲛⲙⲟⲕⲍ ⲛⲍⲏⲧ ⲉⲧⲃⲏⲏⲧⲟⲩ... ⲛⲧⲉⲛⲉⲓ ⲉⲍⲟⲩⲛ ⲉⲧⲥⲩⲛⲁⲅⲱⲅⲏ ⲛⲧⲛⲣⲁⲱⲉ — actual sequence.

---

[61] Another case in which personalization is called for is the object-slot of a reflexive infinitive: (*A I* 199) ⲉⲃⲱⲕ ⲙⲉⲛ ⲉⲛ-ⲧⲟⲡⲟⲥ ⲛⲙⲙⲁⲣⲧⲩⲣⲟⲥ ⲉⲩⲍⲛⲁ ⲉⲱⲩ ⲉⲩⲁⲗⲗⲉⲓ ⲉⲧⲃⲃⲟⲕ... ⲛⲁⲛⲟⲩⲩ; consider also (*P* 131[6] 13 vo) ⲙⲡⲣⲧⲣⲉⲛⲃⲱⲕ ⲉⲣⲁⲧⲛ ⲍⲛⲟⲩⲕⲣⲟⲩ... ⲛⲅⲛⲧⲥ ⲉⲣⲉⲡⲱⲁⲝⲉ ⲙⲡⲛⲟⲩⲧⲉ ⲡⲟⲣⲱ ⲉⲃⲟⲗ. For the " generic person " see Jespersen, *Philosophy of Grammar* (1924) 215ff.

(4) Conjugation carrier in the *coeventive* (ⲍⲙⲡⲧⲣⲉϥⲥⲱⲧⲙ) and *posteventive* (ⲙⲛⲛⲥⲁⲧⲣⲉϥⲥⲱⲧⲙ) forms: -ⲧⲣⲉϥⲥⲱⲧⲙ (Nuclear verb affirmative only). Only (←→); personal maintenance disrupted; neg. encategorization. (*III* 169.12ff.) ⲙⲛⲛⲥⲁⲧⲣⲉⲕϯ-ⲥⲃⲱ ⲛⲁⲩ ⲛⲟⲩⲥⲟⲡ ⲁⲛ ⲟⲩⲧⲉ ⲥⲛⲁⲩ ⲁⲛ ⲁⲗⲗⲁ ⲛⲍⲁⲍ ⲛⲥⲟⲡ ⲉⲙⲁⲧⲉ ⲁⲩⲱ ⲛⲥⲉⲧⲙⲣ-ⲍⲛⲁⲩ ⲉⲥⲱⲧⲙ (also *IV* 52.6, 156.11) / (*A* 2 403) ⲍⲙⲡⲧⲣⲉϥⲣ-ⲟⲩⲁ ⲛⲟⲩⲱⲧ ⲙⲛⲡⲉⲡⲛⲁ ⲉⲧⲟⲩⲁⲁⲃ ⲁⲩⲱ ⲛⲧⲉⲡⲉⲡⲛⲁ ⲉⲧⲟⲩⲁⲁⲃ ⲣ-ⲟⲩⲁ ⲛⲟⲩⲱⲧ ⲛⲙⲙⲁϥ / (*III* 134.3f.) ⲙⲛⲛⲥⲁⲧⲣⲉⲩⲃⲱⲕ ⲉⲃⲟⲗ ⲉⲡⲙⲁ ⲉⲧⲟⲩⲙⲉⲉⲩⲉ ⲉⲣ-ⲡⲟⲩⲱⲯ ⲙⲡⲛⲟⲩⲧⲉ ⲛⲍⲏⲧϥ ⲁⲩⲱ ⲛⲥⲉⲉⲓⲣⲉ ⲍⲱⲱϥ ⲍⲙⲡⲙⲁ ⲉⲧⲙⲙⲁⲩ ⲛⲛⲉⲩⲟⲩⲱⲯ ⲛⲍⲏⲧ ⲉⲑⲟⲟⲩ. Also *III* 49.1ff., *Ch.* 66.18ff.

(5) *Personal infinitive* after prepositions: -ⲧⲣⲉϥⲥⲱⲧⲙ: (*Wess. 9* 118b 11ff.) ⲁⲛⲧⲓⲧⲣⲉⲛⲣ-ⲙⲟⲉⲓⲍⲉ ⲉⲭⲛⲛⲧⲁⲙⲓⲟ ⲙⲡⲛⲟⲩⲧⲉ ⲙⲛⲛⲉϥⲙⲉⲗⲟⲥ ⲧⲏⲣⲟⲩ ⲛⲧⲛϯ-ⲉⲟⲟⲩ ⲛⲁϥ ⲁⲕⲧⲣⲉⲍⲁⲍ ⲣ-ⲙⲟⲉⲓⲍⲉ ⲉⲭⲙⲡⲧⲁⲕⲟ / (*Ch.* 178-9) ⲡⲉⲍⲟⲟⲩ ⲡⲉ ⲛⲧⲣⲉⲩⲡⲁⲣⲁⲅⲉ ("they" - heaven, earth and its inhabitants) ⲛⲧⲉⲙⲡⲩⲗⲏ ⲛⲙⲡⲏⲩⲉ ⲟⲩⲱⲛ... ⲛⲥⲉⲃⲱⲕ ⲉⲍⲟⲩⲛ ⲛⲍⲏⲧⲟⲩ — actual, dramatic succession of apocalyptic events. All these are apparently subcoordination instances.

(6) ⲧⲣⲉϥⲥⲱⲧⲙ *causative*, predicated in a conjugation form — very rarely expanded by the conjunctive (subcoordination only?): (*III* 131.20) ⲉⲓⲯⲁⲛⲧⲙⲧⲣⲉⲡⲕⲁⲍ ⲟⲩⲱⲛ ⲛⲣⲱϥ ⲛϥⲟⲙⲕⲟⲩ — neg. syncategorization; sim. (*Ch.* 114-5) ⲛⲉϥⲛⲁⲧⲣⲉⲁⲙⲛⲧⲉ ⲟⲩⲱⲛ ⲛⲣⲱϥ ⲛϥⲟⲙⲕⲟⲩ ⲍⲛⲑⲁⲏ.

7.2.5.3 PARADIGMS: It is striking that, whereas coordination of multiple infinitives is much more common for the simple infinitive than micro-/subcoordination by the conjunctive, the inverse ratio is observable for the causative-personal infinitive ⲉⲧⲣⲉϥ-, where micro-/subcoordination is more usual by far than coordination of terms.

(a) ⲉⲥⲱⲧⲙ ⲛⲥⲱⲧⲙ ⲡⲥⲱⲧⲙ	ⲁⲩⲱ ⲉⲥⲱⲧⲙ	(1) adverbal adjuncts: coordinated series of co-nuclear adjuncts (e.g. *III* 122.7f., *IV* 37.11, *Ch.* 87.19ff., 107.25ff., etc.; very frequent) (2) neg. infinitive coordinated to a homolexemic affirm. one (*IV* 75.29ff., 163.16, *Ch.* 65.14f.). (3) adjuncts expanding extraconjugational infinitives [62] (*III* 94.12, 114.13f., *IV* 38.21, 95.2, *Ch.* 197.8ff.).
(b) in-conjugation -ⲥⲱⲧⲙ	ⲁⲩⲱ ⲥⲱⲧⲙ	*III* 107-8, 215.7f., *Ch.* 165.30ff.
(c) ⲛⲥⲱⲧⲙ	ⲁⲩⲱ ⲉⲧⲣⲉϥ-	*Ch.* 203.24ff. [63]
(d) ⲉⲧⲣⲉϥ-	ⲁⲩⲱ ⲉⲧⲣⲉϥ-	independent coordinated adjuncts (*III* 86.9f., *IV* 33. 16ff., 183.9f., *Ch.* 67.17ff.).
(e) ⲉⲧⲣⲉϥ-	ⲁⲩⲱ ⲉⲥⲱⲧⲙ	*IV* 91.2f.
(f) ⲙⲛⲛⲥⲁⲧⲣⲉϥ-	ⲁⲩⲱ ⲙⲛⲛⲥⲁⲧⲣⲉϥ-	*III* 169.10ff. (3×)
(g) ⲍⲙⲡⲧⲣⲉ-	ⲁⲩⲱ ⲍⲙⲡⲧⲣⲉ-	*III* 138.8ff.

[62] ⲁⲩⲱ ⲉ + *infinitive* coordinated to abstract nouns: *Ch.* 41.43ff. (parall. *III* 80.24f.), 98.45ff.

[63] An even more radical cohesive syncategorization (reduction of categories) than with the conjunctive. This is a very close junctural *link* in paradigm with constructions of looser juncture (§6.0.2.1). RUDNITZKY 1956:56-8 quotes many instances of a "conjunctive" role of ⲉ + *infinitive*/ⲉⲧⲣⲉϥ-. Upon examination, these are classifiable as follows:

7.2.6 THE RHETORICAL APODOTIC-RETROSPECTIVE ROLE OF THE CONJUNCTIVE; POORLY DOCUMENTED OR INADEQUATELY ESTABLISHED FUNCTIONS

7.2.6.1 The *rhetorical apodotic-retrospective-eventual role* of the conjunctive [64]

(1) The conjunctive as a non-initial rhetorical question or asseveration, following a formal or logical rhetorical protasis (" given that... ", " in view of this... "): (*IV* 195.6ff.) ⲈϢϪⲈ-ⲞⲨⲚⲢⲰⲘⲈ ⲈⲨⲖⲨⲠⲎ (sic) ⲀⲨⲰ ⲈⲢⲈⲠⲈⲨϨⲎⲦ ϬⲚ-ⲀⲢⲒⲔⲈ ⲈⲢⲞⲞⲨ ⲈⲨⲤⲰⲦⲘ ⲈⲠⲚ̄ⲦⲀⲠⲀⲠⲞⲤⲦⲞⲖⲞⲤ (sic) ϪⲞⲞⲥ... ⲈⲒⲈ-ⲚⲄⲞⲨϪⲀⲒ ⲚⲦⲞⲔ ⲈⲦⲞⲢⲄⲎ ⲈⲔⲀⲠⲀⲦⲀ ⲀⲨⲰ ⲈⲔⲞⲨⲰⲘ ⲈⲂⲞⲖ ϨⲚ̄ⲦⲈⲦⲢⲀⲠⲈⲌⲀ ⲚⲚ̄ⲆⲀⲒⲘⲞⲚⲒⲞⲚ... Ⲏ ⲚⲄⲂⲰⲔ ⲈϨⲞⲨⲚ ⲈⲦⲘⲚ̄ⲦⲈⲢⲞ (Leipoldt's suggested emendation, adding - ⲀⲚ, is I believe unacceptable) / (*ibid.* 100.2ff.) Ⲏ ⲈϢϪⲈ-ⲠⲀⲢⲀⲔⲈⲔⲞⲨⲒ ⲚⲤⲈⲦⲢⲈⲨⲠⲰϨⲦ-ϨⲀϨ ⲚⲤⲚⲞϤ Ⲛ̄ϨⲎⲔⲈ ⲈⲂⲞⲖ... ⲚⲤⲈϮ-ⲤⲞ ⲈⲤⲈϢⲦ-ⲐⲎⲨⲦⲚ ⲚⲦⲰⲦⲚ (for ⲠⲀⲢⲀⲔⲈⲔⲞⲨⲒ + *conj.* see §7.3.1 below) / (*Ch.* 15.14ff.) ⲘⲎ ⲠⲀⲎⲢ Ⲣ-ⲞⲨⲞⲈⲒⲚ ⲀⲚ ϨⲘ̄ⲠⲈϨⲞⲞⲨ Ⲏ ⲚⲦⲚ̄ϬⲰϢⲦ ⲀⲚ ⲚϨⲀϨ ⲚⲤⲞⲠ... ϢⲀϨⲢⲀⲒ ⲈⲦⲠⲈ ... ⲀⲨⲰ ⲚⲦⲚ̄ⲚⲀⲨ ⲀⲚ ⲈⲖⲀⲀⲨ ⲀⲚⲞⲚ ⲠϢⲀⲚϨⲦⲎϤ ⲞⲚ ⲚϤⲦⲘ̄ⲦⲤⲀⲂⲈ-ⲚⲈⲚⲈⲂⲒⲎⲚ — negation maintenance: the conjunctive realizes the ⲘⲎ (" *nonne* ") rhetorical question after the protasis-equivalent circumstances expressed by the preceding present forms: " Isn't the air full of light in daytime, and do we not often look up at the sky, and still do not see anything, nor does God enlighten us miserable ones " / (*B.M.Cat.* 82, No. 198 f.1 vo) ⲀⲨⲚⲈϪ-ⲠⲤⲀⲦⲀⲚⲀⲤ ⲈⲂⲞⲖ ϨⲚ̄ⲦⲠⲈ ϪⲈ-ⲀϤⲔⲰⲦⲈ ⲚⲤⲀⲐⲈ ⲚⲢ-ⲚⲈϤⲂⲞⲦⲈ, ⲚⲄⲀⲀⲨ ⲆⲈ ϨⲰⲰⲔ ⲀⲨⲰ ⲚⲄϪⲞⲔⲞⲨ ⲈⲂⲞⲖ; " ... and wilt thou too do and carry out these abominations? " / (*A 1* 210) ⲠⲈϪⲀⲨ ϪⲈ-ⲈⲚⲤⲞⲂⲦⲈ ⲚⲦⲀⲠⲀⲚⲎ ⲘⲠⲂⲰⲖ ⲈⲂⲞⲖ ⲘⲠⲠⲀⲤⲬⲀ, Ⲏ ⲚⲄⲦⲘ̄ϪⲰⲔⲘ ϨⲚ̄ⲞⲨⲘⲞⲞⲨ ⲀⲨⲰ ⲚⲄⲦⲘ̄ⲦⲀϨⲤⲔ ⲚⲞⲨⲚⲈϨ Ⲏ ⲚⲄϪⲞⲔⲘⲈⲔ ⲀⲨⲰ ⲚⲄⲦⲀϨⲤⲔ ⲘⲠⲔⲀϨ ⲦⲎⲢϤ ⲘⲠϪⲀϪⲈ; / (*Ch.* 167-8, parall. *III* 74.14ff.) ⲠⲔⲀⲒⲢⲞⲤ ⲠⲈ ⲈⲦⲢⲈⲞⲨⲈⲒⲰⲦ ⲀⲨⲰ ⲞⲨⲘⲀⲀⲨ ϢⲰⲠⲈ ⲚⲐⲈ ⲚⲞⲨⲂⲀⲢⲂⲀⲢⲞⲤ ⲈⲚⲈⲨϢⲎⲢⲈ ⲀⲨⲰ ⲚⲈⲨϢⲈⲈⲢⲈ... ⲚⲦⲈⲒϨⲈ ⲞⲚ ⲠⲈ ⲞⲨⲞⲚ ⲚⲞⲨⲞⲚ ⲀⲨⲰ ⲞⲨⲤⲰⲚⲈ ⲚⲞⲨⲤⲰⲚⲈ. ⲀⲢⲀ ⲚⲦⲈⲞⲨⲞⲨϪⲀⲒ ϢⲰⲠⲈ Ⲛ̄ϨⲀϨ; " ' ... and may this perhaps mean that salvation of many will ensue? " — an ironic-sceptical question [65] / (*ibid.* 13.8ff.) ⲚⲦⲞⲔ ϨⲰⲰⲔ ⲦϬⲞⲘ ⲘⲠⲈⲔⲤⲰⲘⲀ ϢⲞⲞⲠ ⲚϨⲎⲦⲔ, ⲘⲘⲚ̄ϢⲰⲚⲈ, ⲘⲘⲚ̄ⲦⲔⲀⲤ, ⲘⲘⲚ̄ⲠⲈⲒⲢⲀⲤⲘⲞⲤ ⲚⲢⲰⲘⲈ... ⲀⲨⲰ ⲚⲄⲦⲘⲈϢϮ ⲞⲨⲂⲈ-ⲠⲚⲞⲂⲈ; " ... and still thou canst not fight against sin? " / (*ibid.* 58.15ff.) ⲈⲦⲂⲈⲞⲨ ⲈⲒⲚⲀⲢ-ⲚⲒⲠⲀⲢⲀⲪⲨⲤⲒⲤ ⲘⲘⲚ̄ⲦⲀⲤⲈⲂⲎⲤ; ⲞⲨ ⲘⲞⲚⲞⲚ ϪⲈ-ϮϨⲰⲚ ϪⲈ-' ⲘⲠⲢⲀⲀⲨ ', ⲀⲖⲖⲀ ϪⲈ-' ⲤⲈⲢϨⲞⲨⲈⲤϨⲞⲨⲞⲢⲦ ⲚϬⲒⲚⲈⲦⲈⲒⲢⲈ ⲘⲘⲞⲞⲨ ', ⲚⲦⲀⲦⲘ̄ϢⲰⲠⲈ ⲀⲚⲞⲔ ⲈⲒⲤϨⲞⲨⲞⲢⲦ ⲈⲒϢⲀⲚⲀⲀⲨ; / (*Wess. 9* 139a 24ff.) ⲤⲰⲦⲘ ⲈⲚⲈⲒⲘⲚ̄ⲦⲀⲤⲈⲂⲎⲤ. ϨⲈⲚⲒⲈⲒⲂ ⲚⲂⲀϢⲞⲢ . ϨⲈⲚⲀⲠⲈ Ⲛ̄ϨⲞϤ. ϨⲈⲚⲚⲀⲀϪⲈ ⲚⲘⲤⲀϨ... ⲚⲦⲈⲚⲢⲰⲘⲈ ⲔⲀ-ϨⲦⲎⲨ ⲈⲢⲞⲞⲨ ϪⲈ-ⲈⲨⲚⲀⲘⲦⲞⲚ ⲈⲦⲂⲎⲎⲦⲞⲨ... — a case of rhetorical dependent exclamatory asseveration (overlapping the adnominal adnexal role of the conjunctive, §7.3.2): " foxes' nails, snakes' heads, crocodiles ' teeth, and people should trust them to allay (their pains)! ". Compare here the use of the conjunctive (and of ⲦⲀⲢⲈϤⲤⲰⲦⲘ) following a rhetorical interrogative. See exx. in §7.2.1.1.5 — e.g. *III* 148.25ff. ⲈⲨⲦⲰⲚ ⲚⲈⲚϢⲂⲈⲈⲢ... ⲈⲦⲘⲞⲨⲦⲈ ⲈⲢⲞⲚ ϪⲈ-ⲀⲄⲄⲈⲖⲞⲤ ⲚⲤⲈⲚⲀⲨ ⲈⲚⲈⲚⲔⲀⲔⲒⲀ.

(2) The conjunctive non-rhetorical, following a formal or logical temporal protasis: (*A 1* 204f.) ⲈⲢⲈ-ϢⲒⲚⲈ ⲚⲤⲀⲢⲒⲘⲈ ⲈⲞⲨⲤⲰⲚⲈ ⲚⲦⲈⲦⲞⲈⲒⲦ ⲈⲢⲞ ⲘⲘⲒⲚ ⲘⲘⲞ (" ... and you end up by... ") / (*A 2* 505) ϨⲘ̄ⲠⲈϨⲞⲞⲨ ⲈⲦⲞⲨ-

---

(a) Following *jussive* ⲚⲚⲈϤ- (*IV* 110.19ff.), ⲈϤⲚⲀ- (*IV* 93.1ff.), neg. imperative (*IV* 104.22): here ⲈⲦⲢⲈϤ- apparently serves as a *jussive* form (by virtue of its " that "-form nature?), while ⲉ + *infinitive* is a true subcategorization form. The jussive context (as Rudnitzky rightly observes) is here probably the primary factor; but see a case of *initial* jussive ⲉ + inf./ⲈⲦⲢⲈϤ-: (*IV* 68.10ff.) ⲀⲨⲰ ⲈⲠⲞⲢϢⲞⲨ... ⲈϤⲒⲦⲞⲨ ϨⲢⲀⲒ ϨⲚⲞⲨⲘⲚ̄ⲦϢⲞⲨϢⲞⲨ ⲀⲨⲰ ⲞⲚ ⲈⲦⲘ̄ϢⲰ ⲈⲂⲞⲖ... ⲞⲨⲆⲈ ⲞⲚ ⲈⲦⲘ̄ⲦⲢⲈⲚϢⲰⲠⲈ ⲚⲐⲈ ⲚⲚⲈⲒⲦⲂⲚⲎ...

(b) ⲉ + *infinitive* as a subcategorization form after ⲠⲈⲦⲚⲀ- (*IV* 90.7ff.).

(c) ⲈⲦⲢⲈϤ- anacoluthically coordinated to another verb: (*III* 181.18ff.) ϨⲚ̄ⲚⲈⲞⲨⲞⲈⲒϢ ⲈⲦⲈⲚⲤⲈⲚⲀⲠⲰⲦ ⲀⲚ ⲚⲞⲨϬⲞⲠⲈ ⲔⲞⲨⲒ ⲘⲘⲞⲞⲨ ⲈϨⲢⲀⲒ ⲈϪⲰⲞⲨ ⲀⲖⲖⲀ ⲈⲦⲢⲈⲨϮ-ϬⲞⲘ ⲚⲦⲞϤ Ⲛ̄ϨⲞⲨⲞ ⲘⲠⲰⲀϨ ⲘⲠⲔⲰϨⲦ ⲈⲦⲘⲘⲀⲨ.

(d) ⲈⲦⲢⲈϤ- coordinated to ⲉ + *infinitive*: (*IV* 80.24ff.).

(e) ⲈⲦⲢⲈϤ- anacoluthically *expanding* another verb (*III* 179.20ff., the nucleus ⲘⲠϢⲀ). I do not include here the frequent occurrence of this construction in Leipoldt's No. 76 (not Shenoute; *IV* 133.17ff., 136-7 *passim*, 146 *passim*, 149.17ff. etc.). Compare also *Dictionary* 52a (III: " (ⲉ + *inf.*) coordinating a 2nd verb ") and 430a (" elliptical jussive use of ⲈⲦⲢⲈ- ").

[64] Cf. CRUM 1926:I 250f., II 373. For earlier stages of Egyptian, see ERMAN 1933:585; HINTZE 1952:272f., FRANDSEN 1974: 148-152; SPIEGELBERG's instances of the " independent " conjunctive are all open to this interpretation (1925:§§152-3); VOLTEN 1964:65f.; LICHTHEIM 1964:3f. expresses some doubts concerning this function (however, the alleged " independent injunctive " role is far from established for Coptic).

[65] Cf. DENNISTON 46 (ἄρα): " a sceptical tone ", " leaving the question open ", or even presupposing a negative answer. Or do we here have the *inferential* ἄρα in initial position (BLOMQUIST 1969:128f.)?

ⲚⲀϢⲒⲚⲈ ⲚⲤⲀⲚⲈⲨⲌⲂⲎⲨⲈ ⲚⲤⲈⲦⲘϬⲚⲦⲞⲨ, Ⲏ ⲈⲀⲨϬⲚⲦⲞⲨ ⲞⲚ ⲚⲤⲈϪⲒ-ϢⲒⲠⲈ ⲈϪⲰⲞⲨ / (*IV* 60.2ff.) ⲤⲈⲤⲞⲦⲠ ⲚⲚⲀⲌⲢⲘⲠⲚⲞⲨⲦⲈ ⲚϬⲒⲚⲈⲚⲦⲀⲨϪⲞⲞⲤ ϪⲈ-' ⲦⲚⲚⲀⲞⲨⲰⲘ ' (on an eating day)... ⲀⲨⲰ ⲚⲤⲈⲦⲘⲞⲨⲰⲘ, ⲚⲌⲞⲨⲞ ⲈⲠⲈⲚⲦⲀⲨϪⲞⲞⲤ ϪⲈ- ' ⲚⲦⲚⲚⲀ-ⲞⲨⲰⲘ ⲀⲚ ' ⲌⲘⲠⲈⲌⲞⲞⲨ ⲚⲦⲀⲨϪⲞⲞⲤ ϪⲈ ' ⲚⲦⲚⲚⲀⲞⲨⲰⲘ ⲀⲚ ⲚⲌⲎⲦϤ ' ⲀⲨⲰ ⲚⲤⲈⲞⲨⲰⲘ — the conjunctive with an *eventual* sense: " ... and (they) finished by eating/not eating ".

(3) A few instances of ' ϪⲈⲔⲀⲀⲤ + *conditional/circumstantial* + *conjunctive* ', where the conjunctive is both apodotic and resumptive-constitutive of the final clause. This famous construction, frequent in the New Testament, has been studied by LEFORT (1948a): he concludes that the " adverbial " (really pro-tatic) interposition is not the conditioning factor for the conjunctive, which must have here a special (" volitive ") modal value and stand in a " *liaison grammaticale vague* ", and anacoluthic syntax, with ϪⲈⲔⲀⲀⲤ. Nevertheless, he does not entirely renounce the interpretation of the conjunctive as " cop-ulative " — which raises the question: To what is the conjunctive coordinated? The construction is uncommon in Shenoute; it can here be interpreted as an *apodotic-resuming* role, or (less probably, I think) as the conjunctive in construction with and adnexal to ϪⲈⲔⲀⲀⲤ [66]. (*Thompson* L ro) ...ϪⲈⲔⲀⲤ ⲈⲀⲚ-ⲔⲰ ⲚⲤⲰⲚ ⲚⲘⲘⲚⲦϢⲀϤⲦⲈ ⲘⲚⲚⲈⲠⲒⲐⲨⲘⲒⲀ ⲚⲔⲞⲤⲘⲒⲔⲞⲚ, ⲚⲦⲚⲰⲚⲌ ⲌⲚ ⲞⲨⲘⲚⲦⲢⲘⲚⲌⲎⲦ ⲘⲚⲞⲨⲘⲚⲦⲈⲨⲤⲈⲂⲎⲤ / (*P* 131[8] 94 ro) ...ϪⲈⲔⲀⲤ ⲈⲢϢⲀⲚⲠⲞⲨⲞⲈⲒϢ ⲚⲚⲈⲨⲬⲢⲎⲘⲀ [.....] ⲚⲦⲈⲦⲈⲔⲢⲒⲤⲒⲤ ⲘⲠⲚⲞⲨⲦⲈ ⲞⲨⲰⲚⲌ ⲈⲂⲞⲖ. (*Ch.* 87.46ff.) ⲀⲖⲖⲀ ⲔⲀⲚ ⲘⲀⲢⲚⲤⲀⲌⲰⲚ ⲈⲂⲞⲖ ⲚⲚⲒⲚⲞϬ ⲚⲚⲞⲂⲈ ϪⲈⲔⲀⲤ ⲔⲀⲚ ⲚⲦⲚ-Ⲧ2ⲎⲨ ⲈⲠⲈⲔⲞⲨⲒ ⲚⲀⲄⲀⲐⲞⲚ ⲈⲦⲚⲚⲀϢϬⲘ-ϬⲞⲘ ⲚⲀⲀϤ is admittedly difficult. Can the conjunctive here be in construction with and adnexal to ⲔⲀⲚ " at least ", to ϪⲈⲔⲀⲤ, or syncategorized by ⲘⲀⲢⲚⲤⲀⲌⲰⲚ (§7.2.1.1.2)?

7.2.6.2 The conjunctive in *action-advancing* (*promotive*) role: ⲀⲨⲰ ⲚⲤⲰϢⲠⲈ (*IV* 52.16, 53.23) ...ⲀⲨⲰ ⲚⲤⲰϢⲠⲈ ⲈⲢϢⲀⲚⲚⲈⲦⲘⲘⲀⲨ Ⲣ-ⲠⲂⲞⲖ ⲚⲚⲈⲦⲞⲨϢⲀⲖⲎⲖ ⲚⲘⲘⲀⲨ ⲘⲈⲨⲈϢϬⲘ-ϬⲞⲘ ⲈϢⲖⲎⲖ / [...] Ⲏ ⲌⲈⲚϢⲈⲈⲢⲈ ϢⲎⲘ Ⲏ ⲌⲈⲚⲌⲖⲖⲞ Ⲏ ⲌⲖⲖⲰ ⲌⲢⲀⲒ ⲚⲌⲎⲦⲚ, ⲀⲨⲰ ⲚⲈⲤϢⲰⲠⲈ (sic) ⲈⲦⲢⲈⲨⲞⲨⲰⲘ ⲚⲤⲞⲠ ⲤⲚⲀⲨ ⲘⲘⲎⲚⲈ... This role, already more or less stereotyped in Late Egyptian [67], is not really established by these exx., since the lacunae may have con-tained a nuclear verb form subcategorizing the conjunctive.

7.2.6.3 Questionable cases. In (*III* 108.12f., collated) ⲈϢϪⲈ-ⲀⲔⲢ-ⲚⲀⲒ ⲚⲀⲚ ⲚⲦⲚϢⲀⲀⲦ ⲚⲦ-ⲚⲞⲨϬⲤ ⲚⲀⲔ, ⲈⲒⲈ-..., -ⲀⲚ should perhaps be added, since the stative ϢⲀⲀⲦ shows the form to be the (circumstantial) negative present.

7.3 THE NON-VERBAL NUCLEUS: ADNEXAL (RHEMATIC) CONJUNCTIVE

Both nucleus and conjunctive are here essential *sentence constituents*, with the conjunctive the ad-nexal (" predicative ") expansion of an element which, in its own extent, constitutes or contains a pre-dicative unit (§7.1.3). With reference to the following conjunctive-rheme, the initial constituent is the-matic (topical), often passing judgment, appreciating, expressing an opinion (about probability, imminence, significance etc.) or attitude.

7.3.1 Nucleus: *predicative modifiers* (predicative - in their own extent).

(1) ⲠⲀⲢⲀ-/ⲈⲦⲒ ⲔⲈⲔⲞⲨⲒ ⲠⲈ + *conjunctive* — a recurring, typical (though by no means exclusively She-noutean [68]) expression, for which we also find the variant ⲠⲀⲢⲀⲔⲈϢⲎⲘ ⲠⲈ: " shortly, nearly, almost... " (ἔτι/παρὰ μικρόν) — affirmative, negated, even converted. (Although strictly speaking ⲔⲈⲔⲞⲨⲒ ⲠⲈ is a

---

[66] Cf. ϪⲈⲔⲀⲤ + *conjunctive* in Bohairic, STERN §§448, 511, MALLON–MALININE §250. For LE and Demotic (*ḏd* + conj.) cf. VOLTEN 1964:67ff., JOHNSON 1974 exx. E526-7.

[67] Cf. LE *mtw.ḫpr* (VOLTEN 1964:63ff., FRANDSEN 1974:165, BORGHOUTS 1979:19f.).

[68] Cf. *Prov.* 5:14 (ⲠⲀⲢⲀⲔⲈϢⲎⲘ + *perf.*), *Ps.* 36:10 (ⲈⲦⲒ ⲔⲈⲔⲞⲨⲒ ⲠⲈ + *conj.*), 72:2 (ⲠⲀⲢⲀⲞⲨⲔⲞⲨⲒ + *perf.*), *Sap.* 15:8 (ⲘⲚⲚ-ⲤⲀⲔⲈⲔⲞⲨⲒ ⲈϤⲚⲀ-), *Is.* 10:25 (ⲈⲦⲒ ⲄⲀⲢ ⲔⲈⲔⲞⲨⲒ ⲠⲈ + *conj.*), 28:10, 13 (ⲈⲦⲒⲔⲈⲔⲞⲨⲒ ⲠⲈ [ϪⲈ ⲈⲨⲈ-]), 29:17 (ⲚⲔⲈⲔⲞⲨⲒ ⲀⲚ ⲠⲈ + *conj.*), *Joh.* 14:19 (ⲈⲦⲒ ⲔⲈⲔⲞⲨⲒ ⲠⲈ + ⲀⲨⲰ + *neg. fut.*), 16:16ff. (ⲔⲈⲔⲞⲨⲒ ⲠⲈ + *conj.*), *Apophth. Patr.* (Chaîne) 101.3 (ⲠⲀⲢⲀⲔⲈⲔⲞⲨⲒ... ⲈⲒⲚⲀ-ⲠⲈ), LEVY 1909:§85.

case of predicative *noun* — §7.3.2 — I suspect this is the modifier predicated by ⲡⲉ, §1.2.1.2; anyway, both are neutralized in this environment). (*RE 11* 15a 7ff.) ⲉⲧⲉⲓ ⲕⲉⲕⲟⲩⲓ ⲡⲉ ⲛⲧⲉⲡⲉⲧⲥⲏⲍ ⲭⲱⲕ ⲉⲃⲟⲗ... / (*A 2* 390) ⲡⲓⲗⲏⲥⲧⲏⲥ ⲉⲧⲉⲡⲁⲣⲁⲕⲉⲕⲟⲩⲓ ⲡⲉ ⲛϥϣⲱⲡⲉ ⲍⲙⲡⲧⲁⲕⲟ ⲙⲡⲉϥϣⲃⲏⲣ / (*ibid.* 140) ⲉⲧⲓ ⲅⲁⲣ ⲕⲉⲕⲟⲩⲓ ⲡⲉ ⲛⲧⲉⲧⲛⲧⲙϣⲱⲡⲉ ⲉⲡⲧⲏⲣϥ / (*ibid.* 113-4) ⲉⲛⲉ-ⲉⲧⲃⲏⲏⲧⲟⲩ, ⲡⲁⲣⲁⲕⲉϣⲏⲙ ⲡⲉ ⲛⲧⲉⲡⲉⲣ-ⲡⲁⲍⲣⲉ ⲉⲣⲟⲛ ⲥⲗⲁⲁⲧⲉ... / (*P* 130⁴ 116 ⲓⲑ) ⲏ ⲕⲉⲕⲟⲩⲓ ⲁⲛ ⲡⲉ ⲛⲥⲉⲕⲣⲓⲛⲉ ⲙⲙⲟⲛ ⲍⲓⲧⲛⲛⲉⲓϣⲁϫⲉ (also *P* 131⁴ 160 vo) / (*P* 131⁵ 79 ⲡⲁ) ⲛⲕⲉⲕⲟⲩⲓ ⲁⲛ ⲡⲉ ⲛⲅⲟⲩⲱϩⲙ ⲟⲩⲃⲉⲡⲣⲉϥⲥⲱⲛⲧ / (*III* 173.28f.) ⲛⲕⲉⲕⲟⲩⲓ ⲁⲛ ⲡⲉ ⲛⲧⲛⲥⲙⲓⲛⲉ ⲛⲁⲛ ⲛⲕⲉⲅⲣⲁⲫⲏ ⲙⲁⲩⲁⲁⲛ / (*IV* 100.2ff.) ⲉϣϫⲉ-ⲡⲁⲣⲁⲕⲉⲕⲟⲩⲓ ⲛⲥⲉⲧⲣⲉⲩⲡⲱϫⲧ-ⲍⲁⲍ ⲛⲥⲛⲟϥ ⲛⲍⲏⲕⲉ ⲉⲃⲟⲗ...

(2) ⲙⲟⲅⲓⲥ " hardly ", " almost... not " (" *kaum, schwerlich* ") with the conjunctive is used as an elegant rhetorical negation, a striking distinctive Shenoutean trait[69]. ⲉⲙⲟⲅⲓⲥ is a circumstantial/relative-converter, syntactically marked alternant[70]. (*IV* 67.21f., parall. *Wess. 9* 125b 3ff.) ⲉⲛⲛⲁⲁⲍⲉⲣⲁⲧⲛ ⲍⲛⲟⲩ-ⲥⲟⲟⲩⲧⲛ ⲍⲛⲟⲩϣⲓ ⲙⲙⲉ ⲁⲩⲱ ⲉⲙⲟⲅⲓⲥ ⲛⲧⲛⲕⲱⲗⲭ ⲛⲧⲛⲛⲁⲍⲃ ⲙⲛⲧⲛⲁⲡⲉ ⲙⲙⲁⲧⲉ ⲙⲡⲥⲟⲡ ⲉⲧⲛⲛⲁⲥⲫⲣⲁⲅⲓⲍⲉ ⲙⲙⲟⲛ / (*Ming.* 84) ⲡⲥⲁⲉⲓⲛ ⲉϣⲁϥⲃⲱⲕ ⲁⲛ ⲉⲣⲁⲧϥ ⲛⲟⲩⲟⲛ ⲛⲓⲙ ⲍⲁⲡⲗⲱⲥ ⲉⲣ-ⲡⲁⲍⲣⲉ ⲉⲣⲟⲟⲩ, ⲙⲟⲅⲓⲥ ⲅⲁⲣ ⲛϥⲃⲱⲕ ⲉⲣⲁⲧϥ ⲙⲡⲁⲣⲭⲱⲛ ⲏ ⲡⲣⲙⲙⲁⲟ (" hardly even to the Governor... ") / (*P* 130⁴ 100 vo) ⲉϣϫⲉ-ⲕⲁⲧⲁⲡⲧⲁϣⲉⲟⲉⲓϣ ⲙⲡⲉⲩⲁⲅⲅⲉⲗⲓⲟⲛ· ⲙⲟⲅⲓⲥ ⲛⲧⲉⲛⲉⲧⲕⲱ ⲛⲥⲱⲟⲩ ⲙⲡⲉⲩⲉⲓⲱⲧ ⲙⲛⲧⲉⲩⲙⲁⲁⲩ... ⲣ-ⲙⲡϣⲁ ⲛⲓⲥ̄, ⲉⲓⲉ... / (*IV* 111.1f.) ⲉϣⲱⲡⲉ ⲇⲉ ⲧⲉⲡⲣⲱ ⲧⲉ, ⲙⲟⲅⲓⲥ ⲛⲥⲉⲉⲣ-ⲧⲉⲩⲁⲡⲣⲏⲧⲉ ⲛⲉⲣ-ⲍⲱⲃ ⲛⲥⲉ+-ⲟⲩⲱ / (*III* 39.9ff.) ⲉϣⲁⲣⲉⲛⲣⲱⲙⲉ ϫⲉ ⲉⲭⲙⲡⲕⲁⲍ ⲉⲧⲃⲉⲑⲟⲧⲉ ⲉⲩϣⲁⲛⲛⲁⲩ ⲉⲣⲟⲟⲩ, ⲉⲙⲟⲅⲓⲥ ⲛⲧⲉⲛⲉⲛⲧⲁⲩⲟⲩⲱⲛⲍ ⲉⲣⲟⲟⲩ ⲧⲁⲭⲣⲟⲟⲩ ⲉⲡⲉⲓⲙⲉⲉⲩⲉ ⲛⲧⲉⲓⲍⲉ — the conjunctive is here in paradigm with the thematic Second Tense, following the focalized ⲙⲟⲅⲓⲥ (consider *III* 24.23 ⲙⲟⲅⲓⲥ ⲛⲧⲁ-ⲧⲉⲧⲛⲟⲡⲟⲩ ⲉⲧⲟⲟⲧⲛ): (*A 1* 51) ⲡⲉⲧϣⲁϫⲉ ⲛⲙⲙⲉ ⲙⲟⲅⲓⲥ ⲛⲧⲉⲡⲛⲟⲩⲧⲉ ⲡⲟⲣⲭϥ ⲉⲣⲟ — "almost", synonymous with (ⲡⲁⲣⲁ-)ⲕⲉⲕⲟⲩⲓ ⲡⲉ (Amélineau: " peu ne s'en est fallu ") / (*ibid.* 165) ⲛⲉⲧⲟ ⲛⲍⲙⲍⲁⲗ ⲛⲧⲁⲕⲁⲑⲁⲣⲥⲓⲁ ⲙⲛ-ⲧⲁⲛⲟⲙⲓⲁ ⲁⲩⲱ ⲉⲙⲟⲅⲓⲥ ⲛⲧⲉⲡⲙⲟⲩ ⲡⲟⲗⲅⲟⲩ ⲉⲃⲟⲗ ⲛⲍⲏⲧⲟⲩ / (*III* 181.15ff.) ...ⲉⲛⲡⲱⲧ ⲣⲱ ⲉⲍⲣⲁⲓ ⲉⲭⲱⲟⲩ ⲛⲍⲉⲛ-ⲙⲟⲟⲩ ⲉⲛⲁϣⲱⲟⲩ, ⲁⲩⲱ ⲙⲟⲅⲓⲥ ⲛⲥⲉϣⲱⲙ ⲛⲟⲩⲕⲟⲩⲓ / (*RE 10* 160b 17f.) (ⲟⲩⲛϭⲟⲙ ⲛⲛⲁⲓ ⲉⲛⲉⲍⲥⲉ... ⲉⲃⲟⲗ ⲍⲙⲡⲍⲓⲛⲏⲃ ⲁⲩⲱ ⲡⲉⲛⲕⲟⲧⲕ) ⲁⲩⲱ ⲙⲟⲅⲓⲥ ⲛⲧⲉⲍⲉⲛⲕⲟⲩⲓ ⲛⲉⲫⲏ / (*Wess. 9* 144d 8ff.) ...ⲙⲟⲅⲓⲥ ⲅⲁⲣ ⲛⲧⲉⲛⲁⲅⲅⲉⲗⲟⲥ ⲡⲁⲍⲧⲟⲩ ⲛⲥⲉ-ⲟⲩⲱϣⲧ ⲛⲁϥ ⲕⲁⲧⲁⲡⲙⲡϣⲁ / (*Miss.* 234) ... ⲉϥⲧⲁⲙⲟ ⲙⲙⲟⲛ ⲙⲡⲁⲓ ϫⲉ-ⲙⲛⲧⲟϣ ⲍⲛⲧⲁⲣⲉⲧⲛ ⲁⲩⲱ ⲙⲟⲅⲓⲥ ⲛⲧⲉⲡⲣⲱⲙⲉ ⲙⲟⲩⲛ ⲉⲃⲟⲗ ⲉϥⲉⲡⲓⲑⲩⲙⲉⲓ ⲉⲣⲟⲥ ⲛⲛⲁⲩ ⲛⲓⲙ. Additional exx.: *III* 149.8f., 200.10 (ⲉⲙⲟⲅⲓⲥ), *IV* 86.4, 109.7. 167.26, 192.11, *A 1* 157, 201, *A 2* 26 (ⲉⲙⲟⲅⲓⲥ), *P* 130² 76 ro etc.

(3) ⲙⲛⲛⲥⲱⲥ, ⲙⲛⲛⲥⲁ- + *conjunctive*[71]. (*A 2* 430, not Sh.) ⲉϥⲉⲓⲛⲉ ⲛⲟⲩⲁ ⲉⲁϥⲧⲥⲓⲟϥ ⲉⲃⲟⲗ ⲍⲛⲟⲩⲉⲃⲓⲱ ⲉⲟⲩⲛ-ⲟⲩⲡⲁⲍⲣⲉ ⲉϥⲧⲁⲕⲏⲩ ⲛⲍⲏⲧϥ ⲍⲛⲟⲩⲙⲛⲧⲗⲁⲙⲁⲍⲧ, ⲙⲛⲛⲥⲱⲥ ⲛⲧⲉⲧⲙⲛⲧⲁⲧⲁⲙⲁⲍⲧⲉ ⲡϣⲱⲛⲉ ⲉⲣⲁⲓ ⲛⲍⲏⲧϥ ⲉⲩⲭⲙⲟⲥ ⲙⲡⲟⲛⲏⲣⲟⲥ — possibly a case of the conjunctive subcategorized by a non-temporal " parabolic " perfect, §7.2.4.1(2) / (*Wess. 9* 138b 3ff.) (ⲙⲏ ⲉϣⲁϥϣⲱⲧ ⲁⲛ ⲙⲙⲟϥ ⲍⲙⲡⲧⲟⲕ) ⲙⲛⲛⲥⲱⲥ ⲛϥⲑⲉⲣⲁⲡⲉⲩⲉ ⲙⲙⲟϥ — the conjunctive expanding ⲉϣⲁϥϣⲱⲧ? / (*IV* 83.22f.) ...ⲙⲛⲛⲥⲱⲥ ⲛⲥⲉⲕϣⲱⲥ ⲙⲙⲟϥ in a preceptive context — conj. subcategorized by ⲉⲩⲛⲁ- ? / (*Ch.* 18.13ff.) ⲛⲑⲉ ⲅⲁⲣ ⲛⲟⲩⲣⲣⲟ ⲛⲇⲓⲕⲁⲓⲟⲥ ⲉⲁϥⲣⲉⲍⲧ-ⲡⲉϥϫⲁϫⲉ... ⲉⲁϥ-ϫⲟⲟⲥ ⲉⲧⲣⲉⲛⲉⲧⲉⲛⲟⲩϥ ⲧⲏⲣⲟⲩ ⲛ-ⲧⲟⲟⲧⲟⲩ ⲉⲭⲱϥ, ⲉϥⲟⲩⲱϣ ⲉⲧⲣⲉⲩϫⲓ-ⲉⲟⲟⲩ ⲧⲏⲣⲟⲩ ⲍⲓⲟⲩⲥⲟⲡ, ⲙⲛⲛⲥⲱⲥ ⲛϥⲕⲧⲟϥ ⲛϥϥⲓ ⲛⲧⲉϥⲁⲡⲉ ⲍⲓϫⲱϥ — the conj. microcoordinated to ⲉⲧⲣⲉ-, or a case of the conj. after the parabolic perf.? / (*IV* 45.22f.) ⲡⲁⲗⲓⲛ ⲟⲛ ⲙⲛⲛⲥⲁⲛⲉⲓⲍⲃⲏⲩⲉ ⲧⲏⲣⲟⲩ ⲛⲥⲉϭⲛ-ⲍⲉⲛⲣⲱⲙⲉ ⲉⲣⲁⲓ ⲛⲍⲏⲧⲛ ⲉⲩⲟ ⲛⲛⲟⲉⲓⲕ ⲉⲧⲉⲩⲯⲩⲭⲏ ⲙⲁⲩⲁⲁⲩ... / (*P* 130¹ 37 ⲡⲛⲍ) ...ⲛⲁⲓ ⲛⲧⲁⲩⲍⲟⲙⲟⲗⲟⲅⲉⲓ ⲙⲡⲍⲱⲃ ⲉⲑⲟⲟⲩ ⲛⲧⲁⲩⲁⲁⲩ ⲁⲩⲱ ⲙⲛⲛⲥⲁⲟⲩⲟⲩⲟⲓϣ ⲛⲥⲉⲁⲣⲛⲁ ⲍⲛⲟⲩⲙⲛⲧ-

---

[69] See §1.3.11.6 with exx. and references. For the " conjunctional syntax " of correspondents in other languages, TOBLER 1912:15ff. (" *à peine si...* "), JESPERSEN 1962:38ff. (" *hardly* "), LÖFSTEDT 1936:48 (" *vix*: Adverbium in konjunktionaler Funktion "). In Irish, the equivalent *ar éigean* usually enters a Cleft Sentence construction as the formal rheme (" *vedette* "), although one suspects that here too it is not focal. The *grammatical* significance of ⲙⲟⲅⲓⲥ lies in the peculiar negation categorization of the conjunctive: ⲙⲟⲅⲓⲥ marks a non-cotextual, " uninduced " negation.

[70] Although ⲙⲟⲅⲓⲥ is not proclitic (witness ⲙⲟⲅⲓⲥ ⲅⲁⲣ ⲛⲧⲉ-, *Wess. 9* 144d 8ff.), it is but rarely separated from its following conjunctive, and is to a degree univerbized with it. This is symptomized by the conversion of the whole complex (the conjunctive cannot of course be converted — probably another reason why ⲙⲟⲅⲓⲥ + *conj.* is so converted). Cf. the double conversion in ⲡⲁⲓ ⲉⲙⲟⲅⲓⲥ ⲉⲣⲉ- (*Luc.* 23:53 Horner codd., ⲡⲁⲓ ⲉⲛⲉⲙⲟⲅⲓⲥ ⲉⲛⲉⲣⲉ- Quecke).

[71] The Coptic conjunctive recalls here the LE " narrative-continuative " (" Clause Conjugation ") *jw.f ḥr sḏm* following *ḥr-ḥr-s3* phrases (HINTZE 1950:14ff., FRANDSEN 1974:91f.).

ϢΟΥϢΟΥ ΜΠΝΡ-ΛΑΑΥ ΝΝΟΒΕ — the conjunctive expanding the protatic ("*fallsetzend*") relative? Compare here too the focalized ΜΝΝϹⲰϹ before the Second Perfect (*III* 210.21)[72].

(4) ΚΑΝ "at least": (*Ch.* 87.49ff.) ΚΑΝ ΜΑΡΝϹΑ2ⲰΝ ΕΒΟΛ ΝΝΙΝΟ6 ΝΝΟΒΕ ΧΕΚΑϹ ΚΑΝ ΝΤΝ+2ΗΥ ΕΠΚΕ-ΚΟΥΙ ΝΑΓΑΘΟΝ... ΕΤΝΝΑϢ6Μ-6ΟΜ ΝΑΑϤ. — see §7.2.6.1 (3) above.

7.3.1.1 CONJUNCTIONAL MODIFIER + CONJUNCTIVE SYNTAGMS. Here the already difficult question of a modifier preceding a non-autonomous verb form to create a new autonomous whole becomes even more critical: here are elements which (I believe) are still bona-fide modifiers, expanded by the conjunctive, but which are nevertheless difficult to envisage as thematic sentence constituents (or, on their own, as predicative). As I see it, three alternative approaches present themselves here. (a) This difficulty stems from ethnocentric prejudice — either because of the status of these elements in Greek or their equivalents in other Indo-European languages; (b) the conjunctive functions here in fact as a "conjunctional" alternant-form of the verbal sentence, or (c) the conjunctive is really integrated in the verbal framework — i.e. it is subcategorized by some verbal element or other preceding the "conjunctions", the latter not entering any dependency with it: this last analysis would account for many, though not all, of the following examples:

(1) 2ⲰϹΤΕ/ΜΗΠⲰϹ, ΜΗΠΟΤΕ "consequently (... not...)", "as a result (... not...)", "so that... (not)/lest" (see footnote 66): (*Wess. 9* 142a 1ff.) ΟΥΝ2Α2 ΝϢΗΡΕ ΕϢΑΥϹΟΥⲰΝΟΥ ΕΒΟΛ ΝΝΕΥΕΙΟΤΕ ΧΕ-ϹΕΕΙΝΕ ΜΜΟΟΥ... 2ⲰϹΤΕ ΝϹΕΤΜΡ-ΒΟΛ ΕΠϢΑΧΕ ΕΤϹΗ2 ΧΕ-ΠΕϹΠΕΡΜΑ ΝΝΟΕΙΚ 2ΙΠΟΡΝΗ / (*Ch.* 85.21ff.) ϹΕΡΑϢΕ ΕΧΝΝΕΤΕΙΡΕ ΜΠΔΙΚΑΙΟΝ 2ⲰϹΤΕ ΝϹΕϹΜΟΥ ΕΡΟΟΥ / (*IV* 23.10ff.) ΤΝϤΙ 2Α2Α2 Ν2ΙϹΕ ϢΑ2ΡΑΙ ΕΝΚΕ2ΒⲞΟΥΕ ΕΤ6ΟΧΒ ΑΥⲰ ΝΚΕΤΡΟΦΗ 2ⲰϹΤΕ ΝΤΝΤΜϹΕ-ΜΟΟΥ ΕϹΕΙ; similarly specifying ("even that...", "namely, that...") *ibid.* 158.2, *III* 21.14f. / (*III* 169.20f.) ΑΜΟΥ ΕΒΟΛ 2ΝΜΠΟΛΙϹ ΝΤΑΝΟΜΙΑ ΜΗΠΟΤΕ ΝϹΕΧΙΤΚ ΝΜΜΑΥ Ε2ΡΑΙ ΕΤΟΟΤϹ ΝΤΟΡΓΗ ΕΤΝΑΕΙ / (*ibid.* 222.4f.) ΚΑΛⲰϹ Ν2ΟΥΟ ΕΝϢΑΝϹΑ2ⲰΝ ΕΒΟΛ ΝΝΕΝΝΟΒΕ ΜΗΠΟΤΕ ΝΤΕΟΥΜΚΑ2 Ν2ΗΤ ϢⲰΠΕ ΝΑΝ ΜΝΟΥΑϢΑ2ΟΜ. The conjunctive after 2ⲰϹΤΕ is in paradigm with Ε- + *infinitive* and the "that"-form ΕΤΡΕϤϹⲰΤΜ (§7.4); the conj. usually expresses an *intended* consequence, whereas ΕΤΡΕϤ- conveys the meaning of a consequence naturally or automatically ensuing, objective, unintentional and even undesirable[73]; consider such a typical instance as (*III* 155.3ff.) ...2ΕΝΡⲰΜΕ ΝΕ ΕΥΤΑΚΟ ΜΠ2ΗΤ Ν2ΕΝΚΟΟΥΕ 2ⲰϹΔΕ (sic) ΕΤΡΕΠϢΑΧΕ ΕΤϹΗ2 ΧⲰΚ ΕΒΟΛ Ε2ΡΑΙ ΕΧⲰΟΥ ΧΕ..., *III* 33.28f., 63.12, 114.23, *IV* 95.21, 156.23, 180.5f., *Ch.* 64.33ff., 127.21f. etc. Note that ΜΗΠⲰϹ + *conjunctive* negatives only 2ⲰϹΤΕ + *conjunctive*; 2ⲰϹΤΕ ΕΤΡΕϤ- is negatived by 2ⲰϹΤΕ ΕΤΜΤΡΕϤ- (*IV* 196.2). The post-2ⲰϹΤΕ slot features also the following constructions, external to the opposition of ΕΤΡΕϤ- and the conjunctive (non-pertinent, suppletive):

2ⲰϹΤΕ	Ø-Nominal Sentence (*IV* 183.2)
	ΜΝΤΑϤ- (*IV* 184.11)
	thematic Sec. Present (*Ch.* 103.53ff., focalizing 2ΜΠϹΗΥ...)
	Ε+adjective-verb (circumstantial, with 2ⲰϹΤΕ a premodifier; *IV* 87.4)

After ΜΗΠⲰϹ we find the thematic Second Perfect (focalizing ΕΠΧΙΝΧΗ: *Wess. 9* 131b 25ff.).

(2) ΕΙΜΗΤΙ "otherwise", "unless", "be it not that..." — the conjunctive affirmative; the conjunctive may be taken here as entering a *protatic* syntagm (§7.2.4). (*III* 138.11f., parall. *Wess. 9* 163-4)

---

[72] This (and ΜΟΓΙϹ above) brings us yet again to the question of the *premodifiers* (considered above, §1.1.2.2). ROSÉN's suggestion (1979:462ff.). that Hebrew pre-*še* adverbials are invariably focal ("logical predicates", in a construction comparable to the Cleft Sentence) is hardly acceptable without further qualification: the (essentially contextual) question of their thematic or rhematic status can only be settled on the basis of (a) contextual (FSP), (b) suprasegmental data. Be that as it may, the Coptic conjunctive is, I believe, a specifically *rhematic* subordination form.

[73] Somewhat like the the Greek opposition of ὥστε + *finite verb* vs. ὥστε + *infinitive* (BLASS–DEBRUNNER §391, MAYSER II/1 298f.).

ЄΙΜΗΤΙ 2ΜΠΑϢΑΙ ΜΠΝΑ ΜΠΧΟΕΙC Ι͞C Ν4ΚΩ ΝΑΙ ΕΒΟΛ ΝΝΑΝΟΒΕ ΤΗΡΟΥ, ΕΜΜΟΝ CΝΑΤΩΜ Ν6ΙΤΑΤΑΠΡΟ / (*K* 933) ΜΝΛΑΑΥ 6Ε ΝΑΡ-ΜΠϢΑ ΜΜΟΚ ΠΝΟΥΤΕ ЄΙΜΗΤΙ ΝΓΡ-2ΝΑΚ / (*Ch.* 158.25ff.) Ν†ΝΑϢΟΥΩΜ ΑΝ ΟΥΤΕ †ΝΑϢCΕ-ΜΟΟΥ ΑΝ ЄΙΜΗΤΙ ΝΤΑ6Ν-ΠΕϢΑΙΟΥΟΜ4 ΑΥΩ ΠΕϢΑΙCΟΟ4 / (*III* 107.8f.) ΟΥ ΓΑΡ ΠΕΤ† ΟΥΒΗΝ ЄΙΜΗΤΙ ΝΤΝ† ΟΥΒΗΝ ΜΑΥΑΑΝ / (*IV* 60.15) (ΝΝΕϢΛΑΑΥ ΝΡΩΜΕ... ΒΩΚ ΕΠCΩΟΥ2...) ЄΙΜΗΤΙ ΝCΕΚΩΛ2 ΝϢΟΡΠ. The paradigm following ЄΙΜΗΤΙ includes the following finite pred. syntagms[74]:

	ΧΕ-	extraposition + Sec. Present (*A 1* 64 ЄΙΟΥϢϢ ΕΤΡΕΡ-ΒΟΛ... ЄΙΜΗΤΙ ΧΕ-ΑΝΟΚ ΑΥΩ ΝΤΟ)
		circumstantial present (ЄΙΜΗΤΙ premodifier, *IV* 61.2)
		Cleft Sentence with nom. *vedette* (*K* 9067)
ЄΙΜΗΤΙ		ΜΕϢΑΚ + Nom. Sentence (*A 2* 75)
		perfect (*A 1* 122f., *A 2* 392, *IV* 36.16)
		present (*Wess. 9* 142d 2ff.)
		(i.e. non-verbal predications, converted/complex syntagms or tense-marked verbal predications)
	Ε-ΤΡΕ4-	(*III* 144.17, 183.1f., *IV* 34.27 etc.)[75]
	conjunctive - tense-unmarked.	

(3) Η (- Η) " alternatively ", " unless "[76]. With the disjunctive Η the difficulty in analysis is acute. The conjunctive may be here a means to give the disjoined term(s) a *marked form* of alternative members in a disjunction framework[77]: (*Leyd.* 328) ...ΧΕ-Η ΝCΕΤϢΟΥΝ ΕΧϢ4 Η Ν4ΤϢΟΥΝ ΕΧϢΟΥ Η ΝCΕϢϢΤ ΜΜΟ4 Η Ν4ϢϢΤ ΜΜΟΟΥ ΝΤΟ4 / (*III* 38.17) ΚΑΝ ΕΚϢΑΝ6Ω, Ν†ΝΑ6Ω ΑΝ Η ΝΓΤΑΜΟΙ " I shall not desist unless you tell me... ".

7.3.2   Nucleus: *Predicative Nouns*

(1) ΚΕΚΟΥΙ ΠΕ + *conjunctive* (" it is a small [matter] that...") : (*IV* 81.25f.) Η ΚΕΚΟΥΙ ΑΝ ΠΕ ΝΤΝΡ-ΤϢΡΕ ΝΝΕΝΟΥΕΡΗΤΕ ΑΥΩ ΝΤΝΧΑΑΧΕ 2ΝΝΕΝ6ΙΧ...

(2) ΟΥΡΙΚΕ ϢΗΜ ΠΕ + *conjunctive* (" it is (but) a small turn whether... ") : (*Ch.* 68.43ff.) ΟΥΡΙΚΕ ϢΗΜ ΠΕ ΝΤΕΠΡΩΜΕ ϢϢΠΕ ΝϢΗΡΕ ΜΠΝΟΥΤΕ Η Ν4ϢϢΠΕ ΝϢΗΡΕ ΝΔΙΑΒΟΛΟC.

(3) ΟΥΜΟΙ2Ε ΤΕ + *conjunctive* (" it is a wonder that... ") : (*III* 156-7) ΜΜΟΝ ΟΥΜΟΕΙ2Ε ΑΝ ΤΕ ΝΤΕΤΕΙ-ϢΟΜΤ ΝCΥΝΑΓΩΓΗ ΜΟΥ2 Ν2ΕΝ2ΒΗΥΕ ΝCΕϢΟΟΠ ΑΝ Η ΝΤΟ4 ΕΥϢΟΟΠ ΝΤΑΤΜΕΙΜΕ ΑΝΟΚ.

(4) ΟΥϢΙΠΕ ΠΕ + *conjunctive* (" it is a shame that... ") : (*P* 131⁵ 76 vo, not Sh. ?) ΟΥϢΙΠΕ ΓΑΡ ΠΕ ΝΟΥΧΡΗC-ΤΙΑΝΟC . Ν4Α2ΕΡΑΤ4 ΕΠΝΟΥΤΕ ΕΡΕΤΕ4ΨΥΧΗ ΜΕ2...
The conjunctive is here in paradigm with the " that "-forms, ΕΤΡΕ4- and ΧΕ- (§7.4). This is striking in an instance such as (*P* 130⁴ 116 Κ) 2ΕΝ2ΒCΩ ΝΔΑΙΜΩΝΙΟΝ (sic) ΝΕ, 2ΕΝϢΑΧΕ ΝΕ ΝΑΙ ΝΤΕ2ΕΝΡΩΜΕ ΧΟΟΥ (and not divine truth). (Read ΝΤΑ-?)

---

[74] For ЄΙΜΗΤΙ Ε+(*pro)noun* (e.g. *III* 45-6, 90.3) in the sense of " except for... ", see §6.1.4.1.2 and Ch. 1, n. 98. In that sense, ЄΙΜΗΤΙ also precedes modifiers (*III* 168.8f.,12, *IV* 120.11).

[75] In most instances ΕΤΡΕ4- may be interpreted as complementing (expanding) a preceding nucleus, not in construction with ЄΙΜΗΤΙ (which is but a premodifier). However, in view of the frequent ЄΙΜΗΤΙ expanded by Ε + (*pro)noun* (preceding note) I think ЄΙΜΗΤΙ ΕΤΡΕ4- too is a case in point. For the construction of ЄΙΜΗΤΙ in the NT and in general, see LEFORT 1948b and JELANSKAJA 1977; for ЄΙΜΗΤΙ as a protasis form, cf. SHISHA-HALEVY 1974:374.

[76] See BLASS-DEBRUNNER §448(8) and reff.; KÜHNER-GERTH II 297f.(4) (ἤ = alioquin) cf. SCHWYZER II 578 n. 3 ἀλλ'ἤ).

[77] Cf. the same dilemma with regard to Hebrew 'o še-: Blau *apud* ROSÉN 1979:464f. (Rosén doubts that the adverbial nature of 'o " or " is sufficiently established by its syntax). See note 72.

7.3.2.1 A few examples raise the question whether the conjunctive can also be adnominal-adnexal (contentualizing) to non-predicative nouns: (*IV* 10.2f.) (I truly wonder that, seeing how much they blasphemed), ⲙⲡⲉⲡⲉⲩⲁⲅⲅⲉⲗⲓⲟⲛ ϭⲱ ⲛⲟⲩⲉⲱⲛⲥⲁϩϥ ⲉⲟⲩⲙⲁⲉⲓⲛ ⲛⲧⲉⲧⲙⲡⲉⲭ̅ⲥ̅ ⲕⲱ ⲛⲁⲩ ⲉⲃⲟⲗ "the Gospel did not remain unwritten, as a sign that Christ (did) not forgive them... " / (*ibid.* 113-4) ⲙⲏⲡⲟⲥ (sic) ⲛⲧⲉⲧⲛⲉⲓ ⲉⲩⲕⲁⲓⲣⲟⲥ ⲛⲧⲉⲛⲉⲧⲁⲣⲭⲉⲓ ⲉϫⲛⲛⲉⲓⲧⲟⲡⲟⲥ... ⲉⲣ-ⲧⲉⲓⲁⲛⲟⲙⲁ / (*ibid.* 121.22f.) ⲉⲱⲡⲉ ⲉϥⲱⲁⲛⲉⲓ ⲛϭⲓⲟⲩⲕⲁⲓⲣⲟⲥ ⲛⲧⲉⲡⲛⲟⲃⲉ ϭⲙ-ϭⲟⲙ ⲉϩⲣⲁⲓ ⲉϫⲛⲛⲉⲧⲟⲩⲏϩ ϩⲙⲡⲉⲓⲙⲁ — here the conjunctive could be *formally* subcategorized by the conditional (§7.2.4).

Here too the conjunctive shares the paradigm with ⲉⲧⲣⲉϥⲥⲱⲧⲙ (§7.4).

7.3.3 Nucleus: *Miscellaneous Predicative Syntagms or Expressions*

(1) ⲙⲉⲱⲁⲕ + *conjunctive*: (*Ch.* 124.54ff.) ⲙⲉⲱⲁⲕ ⲛⲧⲉⲟⲩⲣⲱⲙⲉ ⲛⲛⲁⲏⲧ ϫⲟⲟⲥ ϫⲉ-... / (*Berl.* 1611 5 ⲁⲥ) ⲙⲉⲱⲁⲕ ⲉⲧⲃⲉⲧⲉϥϭⲓⲛⲣ-ϩⲱⲃ ⲙⲡⲟⲛⲏⲣⲟⲛ ⲛⲧⲉⲡⲁⲓ ⲛⲁⲩ... (read ⲛⲧⲁ-?). Add. exx.: *Ch.* 28.40ff., 78.31f., *IV* 160.18, *A 2* 147, etc.

The paradigm after ⲙⲉⲱⲁⲕ includes:

ⲙⲉⲱⲁⲕ	ⲛⲉⲟⲩⲛ- (*P* 131⁴ 86 ⲣⲁ) perfect (*Wess. 9* 164c 26ff., parall. *III* 139.4f.) future (*III* 219.20ff., *IV* 97ff.)	} *tense-marked*
	conjunctive	*tense-unmarked*

Not in opposition with the preceding are:

ⲙⲉⲱⲁ⸗	ϫⲉ- [78] / (Ø-) Nom. Sentence (*A 1* 76, *Ch.* 201.30f.)
	Second Tense (ⲙⲉⲱⲁⲓ ϫⲉ- *Ep.* 66; *Ch.* 188.19ff., *P* 130⁴ 116 ⲓⲑ)
	ⲟⲩⲛ (*IV* 72.16f.)

(2) ⲁⲣⲏⲩ + *conjunctive*: (*III* 117.8) (...ⲉⲉⲓⲙⲉⲧⲁⲛⲟⲉⲓ...) ⲁⲣⲏⲩ ⲛⲧⲉⲟⲩⲛⲁ ⲉⲓ ⲉϫⲱⲉⲓ ⲙⲡⲉⲙⲧⲟ ⲉⲃⲟⲗ ⲙⲡϫⲟⲉⲓⲥ / (*IV* 128.6f.) ⲉϥⲟⲩⲱⲱ ⲛϭⲓⲡϫⲟⲉⲓⲥ ⲉⲧⲣⲉⲛⲱⲁⲁⲧϥ ⲉⲃⲟⲗ ⲙⲙⲟⲛ... ϫⲉ-ⲁⲣⲏⲩ ⲛϥⲣ-ϩⲧⲏϥ. The paradigm after ⲁⲣⲏⲩ includes also the (tense-marked) perfect (*III* 140.30f.), and the (non-pertinent) Second Present (*ibid.* 184.20).

(3) ϩⲁⲙⲟⲓ + *conjunctive*: *negative conjunctive* only — thus in suppletive neutralization with ⲅⲉⲛⲟⲓⲧⲟ + *conj.* (4). (*IV* 96.4f.) ϩⲁⲙⲟⲓ ⲛⲧⲉⲧⲙⲡⲱⲁϫⲉ ⲧⲥⲁⲃⲱⲧⲛ ⲉϩⲉⲛⲕⲉⲥⲕⲓⲙ... / (*ibid.* 164.7f.) ϩⲁⲙⲟⲓ ⲛⲥⲉⲧⲙⲣ-ⲃⲟⲧⲉ ⲙⲡⲛⲟⲩⲧⲉ ⲏ ⲛⲥⲉⲧⲙⲁⲁⲩ ⲛⲃⲟⲧⲉ / (*Ch.* 183.27ff.) ϩⲁⲙⲟⲓ ⲛⲑⲉ ⲉⲧⲉⲙⲉⲥϯ-ⲟⲩⲱ ⲛϩⲉⲛϯ-ⲟⲩⲱ ⲛⲁⲅⲁⲑⲟⲛ... ⲛⲥⲧⲙϯ-ⲟⲩⲱ ⲟⲛ ⲛⲙⲡⲟⲛⲏⲣⲟⲛ / (*P* 130⁴ 139 vo) ϩⲁⲙⲟⲓ ⲛⲧⲉⲧⲙⲛⲉⲛⲧⲁⲩⲕⲟⲧⲟⲩ ⲛⲁⲩ ⲣ-ϭⲣⲱϩ / (*Wess. 9* 117a 15ff.) ϩⲁⲙⲟⲉⲓ ⲛⲥⲉⲧⲙϥⲓ ⲛⲧⲉⲛⲯⲩⲭⲏ ⲛϩⲏⲧⲛ ϩⲛⲟⲩⲟⲣⲅⲏ. Also *Ch.* 113.14ff. After ϩⲁⲙⲟⲓ, the conjunctive is in paradigm with ⲉⲛⲉ- (ⲛⲁ)- (*Wess. 9* 120b 16ff., *III* 173.26, *P* 131⁸ 94 ro) and ⲉⲣⲉ- ⲛⲁ- (*IV* 116.23f.); ⲛⲉ + Nom. Sentence is a non-pertinent member (*IV* 92.18).

(4) ⲅⲉⲛⲟⲓⲧⲟ (ϭⲉ/ⲇⲉ) + *conjunctive*: (*III* 112.16ff.) ⲅⲉⲛⲟⲓⲧⲟ ϭⲉ ⲛⲑⲉ ⲛⲧⲁⲡⲛⲟⲩⲧⲉ ⲛⲁϩⲙⲉⲛ ⲛⲅⲉⲛⲟⲥ ⲛⲓⲙ ⲛⲣⲱⲙⲉ ⲛϥϯ-ϭⲟⲙ ⲛⲁⲛ ⲟⲛ ⲛⲧⲛⲧⲁⲉⲓⲟϥ / (*Wess. 9* 124a 12ff.) ⲅⲉⲛⲟⲓⲧⲟ ⲇⲉ ⲛⲧⲉⲧⲛⲧⲣⲉⲟⲩⲥⲙⲓⲛⲉ ⲱⲱⲡⲉ ⲙⲛⲛⲉⲧⲉⲣⲏⲩ ⲛⲧⲉⲡⲁϩⲏⲧ ⲙⲧⲟⲛ / (*Ch.* 118.31f.) ⲅⲉⲛⲟⲓⲧⲟ ϭⲉ ⲛⲧⲛϭⲛ-ⲟⲩⲛⲁ ⲙⲡⲉϥⲙⲧⲟ ⲉⲃⲟⲗ ⲙⲡⲉϩⲟⲟⲩ ⲙⲡϫⲁⲡ. ⲙⲏ ⲅⲉⲛⲟⲓⲧⲟ " God forbid " is construed with ⲉⲧⲣⲉϥ- (*III* 29.16f., 41.15, *IV* 15.4).

(5) ⲁⲗⲗⲟ [79] + *conjunctive*: (*IV* 85-6) ⲁⲗⲗⲟ-ⲛⲧⲉⲧⲙⲡϩⲏⲧ ϫⲓ-ⲗⲁⲁⲩ ϫⲉ-ϥⲱⲱⲛⲉ, ⲁⲗⲗⲟ-ⲧⲣⲉⲕⲁⲛⲁⲅⲕⲁⲍⲉ ⲙⲙⲟⲕ ⲡⲁⲣⲁⲛⲉⲛⲧⲁⲡⲉⲕϩⲏⲧ ⲱⲟⲡⲟⲩ. One cannot say which (if any) of the differences between the conjunctive and the " that "-form ⲧⲣⲉ- here (neg.:affirm., nom.:pronom. actor, non-reflexive:reflexive object) is

---

[78] ϫⲉ- appears to be the valency-rection of the verbal lexemic component -ⲱ- in ⲙⲉⲱⲁ⸗, this analyzability significantly coinciding with *conjugability*: ⲙⲉⲱⲉ ϫⲉ- (*A 1* 76), ⲙⲉⲱⲁⲓ ϫⲉ- (*Ep.* 66): " you / I do not know that... ".

[79] Not in the NT (yet cf. *I Cor.* 15:39). See Blass–Debrunner §127(1), Preisigke 59, Mayser II/3:16f.

responsible for the selection of either form. ⲀⲖⲖⲞ- is elsewhere followed by a noun(-equivalent): *IV* 3.2, *A 1* 161-2, 191, *A 2* 52, 391, 411 (note the position of ⲀⲚ in Ⲏ ⲀⲖⲖⲞ + *noun* ⲀⲚ... ⲀⲖⲖⲞ...) etc. I doubt that ⲀⲖⲖⲞ in Coptic is by itself predicative; it is probably (like ⲞⲨⲈⲦ- in the synonymous ⲞⲨⲈⲦ— ⲞⲨⲈⲦ—, a favourite Shenoutean constellation which does not contain the conjunctive, *Dictionary* 495-6) a *predicative-frame* (ⲀⲖⲖⲞ - ⲀⲖⲖⲞ -) component.

(6) (ⲚⲈ)ⲚⲀⲚⲞⲨⲤ (ⲠⲈ) + *conjunctive*: (*Wess. 9* 158b 24ff.) ⲚⲚⲀⲚⲞⲨⲤ ⲀⲚ ⲚⲦⲚⲢ-ⲞⲨⲌⲞⲞⲨ Ⲏ ⲤⲚⲀⲨ Ⲏ ⲞⲨⲈⲂⲞⲦ Ⲏ ⲞⲨⲢⲞⲘⲠⲈ... ⲈⲚ;Ⲓ ⲈⲌⲢⲀⲒ ⲌⲀⲌⲈⲚⲂⲀⲤⲀⲚⲞⲤ — note the Ⲛ- ⲀⲚ negation / (*P* 130¹ 37 ⲠⲚⲌ) ⲚⲈⲚⲀⲚⲞⲨⲤ ⲠⲈ ⲚⲚⲈⲦⲘⲘⲀⲨ ⲚⲤⲈⲬⲞⲞⲤ ⲬⲈ-. The conjunctive here is in paradigm with the non-rhematic (adjunctal) (Ⲉ)-ⲦⲢⲈ;-, cataphorically heralded by -Ⲥ- (§5.2.2.1).

7.4 Eхсursus: the conjunctive and " that "-forms in functional assignment

In certain environments, the conjunctive is in substitution not only with specifically adjunctal, modifier verb-forms but also with such as display elsewhere a typically *nominal* syntax: " that "-forms. The question whether or not the conjunctive itself is an adjunctal " that "-form is *per se* irrelevant. What is significant is that the conjunctive contracts extensive substitution relationships with two Coptic " that "-forms: the prospective ⲈⲦⲢⲈ;ⲤⲰⲦⲘ and ⲬⲈ-, nominalizing tense-marked verbal predications, Nominal-Sentence patterns, ⲞⲨⲚ-/ⲘⲚ-, adjective-verbs and various focalization patterns. These (conj./ⲈⲦⲢⲈ-) paradigms are defined by the following environments:

(a) *adnominal*: ⲈⲠⲘⲀ ⲈⲦⲢⲈ;- (*III* 146.15, 163.19f., 186.15, *IV* 68.19; *Mich. 158* 17b; *Ch.* 130.11f. [80]); after *predicative nouns*: pred. time expressions [81]: ⲠⲈⲞⲨⲞⲈⲒ; ⲠⲈ ⲈⲦⲢⲈ- (*III* 224.20), ⲠⲔⲀⲒⲢⲞⲤ ⲠⲈ ⲈⲦⲢⲈ- (*Ch.* 167.47ff., parall. *III* 74.14), ⲠⲚⲀⲨ ⲠⲈ ⲠⲀⲒ ⲈⲦⲢⲈ- (*IV* 29.26); ⲠⲘⲀ ⲠⲈ ⲠⲀⲒ ⲈⲦⲢⲈ- (*Mich. 158* 14a 6); cf. *IV* 33.20f. (ⲠⲈⲤⲘⲞⲦ...), 51.7 (Ⲡ;ⲀⲨ Ⲛ;ⲞⲘⲦⲈ ⲚⲞⲨⲚⲞⲨ).

(b) *ad-modifier*: ⲈⲒⲘⲎⲦⲒ, ⲌⲰⲤⲦⲈ ⲈⲦⲢⲈ- (§7.3.1.1); ⲈⲦⲒⲔⲈⲔⲞⲨⲒ ⲠⲈ ⲈⲦⲢⲈ- (*Rossi 2/3* 90).

(c) *adverbal*, after ⲤⲚⲀ;ⲰⲠⲈ, ⲈⲤ;ⲀⲚ;ⲰⲠⲈ, ⲚⲀⲚⲞⲨⲤ (§§7.2,, 7.2.4, 7.3.3, see §5.2.2.1); after ⲘⲎ ⲄⲈⲚⲞⲒⲦⲞ (*III* 29.16f.).

This substitution must be pointed out, even if we cannot at present isolate a real functional difference between ⲈⲦⲢⲈ;- and the conjunctive in those environments; note that in case (a), it is at times impossible to distinguish between adnominal and *ad-pattern* status of ⲈⲦⲢⲈ;-.

The following table is a display of functional domains of " that "-forms (finite verb nominalizations, " abstract relative " forms or syntagms), for Shenoutean Sahidic and (for a comparative-contrastive rather than diachronic view) two earlier stages of Egyptian [82]. This issue awaits yet special monographic study, for every dialect and stage of the language (in Coptic, the difference between Sahidic and Bohairic is very

---

[80] In (*III* 82.18f., parall. *Ch.* 45.4ff.) ⲈⲠⲘⲀ ⲚⲦⲢⲈⲨⲢ-ⲌⲎⲂⲈ... ⲀⲦⲈⲚⲦⲢⲈⲨⲈ;-ⲖⲞⲨⲖⲀⲒ, ⲦⲢⲈ- is fully causative.

[81] A nominal time-expression displays the broadest paradigmatic spectrum of adnominal expansion in Coptic:

ⲠⲚⲀⲨ, ⲠⲔⲀⲒⲢⲞⲤ	*circumstantial*: adnexal, contentualizing (*IV* 102.15 cod. C)
	relative, no anaphora: attributive (*III* 68.2f., 83.12, *IV* 94.25f., 102.15 codd. A, B)
	relative, with anaphora: attributive (*III* 21.1, 189.20f., *IV* 87.7, 179.1)
ⲠⲚⲀⲨ/ⲠⲔⲀⲒⲢⲞⲤ ⲠⲈ	ⲈⲦⲢⲈ;: prospective, contentualizing (*III* 74.14, 224.20, *IV* 29.26)
ⲞⲨⲔⲀⲒⲢⲞⲤ	*circumstantial*: adnexal + attributive, neutr. (*III* 181.10f.,23f.)
	conjunctive: adnexal, contentualizing (*IV* 113-4, 121.22).

[82] I am here merely collecting together and sometimes rearranging material to be found in the following studies: (ME/OE) Polotsky 1969:470-4, 1964:269ff., 275ff. (= *CP* 54ff., 60ff.), 1976:§§2.2-7; Callender 1975 (esp. §4.4); de Cenival 1972; Frandsen 1975; Vernus 1980; Schenkel 1981; Edel *passim*, esp. §§511-531; Gardiner *passim*, esp. §§156, 187, 192, 223, 233, 237, 329. (LE) Erman 1933 esp. §425 Anm., 409-440, 795; Groll 1970 esp. 178-191; Frandsen 1974 esp. 109ff., 153-170; Černý-Groll, esp. 188f., 491ff.

striking); the picture needs further resolution in Coptic no less than in pre-Coptic Egyptian [83]. The thematic function (in focalization patterns) has, for obvious research-historical reasons, been overplayed to an extent at the expense of others. Note that the presentation below is schematic and incomplete, not taking into account (a) " concrete " nominalizations — participles, relative forms; (b) the infinitive with no actor in immediate syntagm; (c) the *negatived* " that "-forms (incl. " that "-forms after negators of existence), not necessarily coextensive with affirmative ones. The exclusion of these important elements cannot but distort the picture. Furthermore, some less central functional categories are omitted as well: " that "-forms as headings (superscriptions) [84]; in initial (protatic) " *casus adverbialis* " status [85]; in apposition to an anaphoric or cataphoric pronoun.

	COPTIC	LATE EGYPTIAN	MIDDLE/OLD EGYPTIAN
theme-topic in focalization patterns	(Ch. 2) *Second Tense/relative; circumstantial*	$j.jr.f$ sdm / $j.sdm.f$ *circumstantial* [86]	$mrr.f$ / $sdmw.f/sdm.n.(tw).f$
subject = theme in Nominal Sentence	ЄТРЄ- [87] ХЄ- [88]	$p3y.f$ sdm / $p3$ sdm $j.jr.f$	$mrr.f$
(grammatical) subject of verb/adjective	(Є)ТРЄ- [89]	$p3y.f$ sdm / $p3$ sdm $j.jr.f$	$mrr.f$
predicate of Nominal Sentence	ХЄ- (gloss, after ПЄ [90]) (Є)ТРЄ- [91]	$p3y.f$ sdm / $p3$ sdm $j.jr.f$	$mrr.f$, $sdm.n.(tw).f$, (passive $sdmw.f$?)
" *Wechselsatz* " (" balanced construction ")	ЄЧ- (§2.7.1.1)	?	$mrr.f$ / $sdmw.f$ / $sdm.n.f$
object of verb	(Є)ТРЄ- (prosp.) ХЄ- (non prosp.)	$p3y.f$ sdm / $p3$ sdm $j.jr.f$; r-dd; prosp. $sdm.f$ (lex. valency distr.)	$mrr.f$ / prosp. $sdm.f$, $sdmw.f$, ($sdm.n.f$); ntt-/wnt- (lexeme valency/sentence-form distribution)

[83] In ME/OE, for instance, the distribution of $sdmw.f$ and its relationship with $mrr.f$ and the non-" emphatic " prospective are far from clear; so are the distributional schemes of ntt-/wnt-, and of $mrr.f/sdm.n.f$ (" emphatic ") outside focalization patterns. For Demotic, almost all of the assignment work awaits to be done.

[84] ME: $mrr.f$; LE: infinitive + $jr.n.$? Coptic: ЄТРЄЧ-? (cf. *III* 218.14), ХЄ- (*Ch.* 153.5ff.).

[85] Cf. SHISHA–HALEVY 1974 (see §2.8.3 here for the Sec. Tense as a " that "-form outside focalization patterns).

[86] Cf. SHISHA–HALEVY 1978.

[87] *III* 26.4, *Ch.* 155.44ff.

[88] *III* 26.4, *Ch.* 47.42.

[89] *III* 29.16f., 105.14, *IV* 85-6, *Ch.* 197.19f.

[90] *III* 214.17, *Ch.* 122.18ff., 137.30ff., 142.11f.

[91] Also after ЄТЄПАІ ПЄ (*Ch.* 160.14f.); after the copular ПЄ: *III* 184.7,8, 224.20f.

	Coptic	Late egyptian	Middle/old egyptian
governed by prepositions, expanding modifiers	ⲧⲣⲉ- (ⲉ-, ⲛ-, ⲛⲥⲁ-, ⲁⲛⲧⲓ-, ϩⲓⲧⲛ-, ⲙⲛⲛⲥⲁ-) ⲭⲉ- (ⲉⲧⲃⲉ-, ⲉⲃⲟⲗ) (conjunctive)	$p3y.f$ $s\underline{d}m$ / $p3$ $s\underline{d}m$ $j.jr.f$; prosp. $s\underline{d}m.f$ (after $m\text{-}\underline{d}r\text{-}$, $m\text{-}\underline{h}t\text{-}$) [92]	$mrr.f$ / prosp. $s\underline{d}m.f$, $(s\underline{d}mw.f.)$, $(s\underline{d}m.n.f)$ / $s\underline{d}m.t.f$; $ntt\text{-}$ (lexeme valency/sentence-form distribution)
in initial modal role: jussive-optative-hortative	Second Future (ⲉϥⲛⲁ-) (§2.1.3) (ⲉⲧⲣⲉ-, n. 63)	prospective $s\underline{d}m.f$	prospective $s\underline{d}m.f$, $mrr.f$ (?) [95]
adnominal	(ⲉ)ⲧⲣⲉ- [93] ⲭⲉ- [94] (conjunctive)	$(n\text{-})$ $(p3)$ $s\underline{d}m$ $j.jr.f$ / $p3y.f$ $s\underline{d}m$	$(n\text{-})mrr.f$, $(s\underline{d}m.f$, $s\underline{d}m.n.f)$

---

[92] Not analyzable synchronically, according to Groll 1970:409ff.

[93] *III* 218.14 (ⲟⲩⲗⲟⲅⲟⲥ), *IV* 118.24 (ⲧⲉⲭⲣⲉⲓⲁ), 61.24f. (ⲧϭⲓⲛϣⲁϩⲁ), see above §7.4 (a), and note 81; exx. in Rudnitzky 1956: 131ff.

[94] See Rudnitzky 1956:132, Shisha–Halevy 1972:97.

[95] See De Cenival, *RdE* 24:42f. (1972); Junge 1978.

TEXTUAL SOURCES CONSTITUTING THE CORPUS

Observations on editions follow the bibliographical information. For reasons of space, I have limited cross-references to a minimum (parallels between *A*, *Ch.*, *L* and *Wess.*, also with numerous unpublished fragments, are not specified here, neither are codicological interrelationships. The following is not a bibliography of Shenoutean philology, the need for which is met elsewhere (*Bibl.* = P. J. Frandsen and E. Richter-Aerøe, "Shenoute: A Bibliography", in: D. W. Young [ed.] 1981:147-176). For some surveys of editions, see R. McL. Wilson, *ed.* 1978:21 n. 122 (Krause), 156f. (Orlandi).

A. Editions of Published Manuscripts
(arranged in alphabetic order of abbreviations or reference codes)

A 1, 2	E. C. AMÉLINEAU, *Œuvres de Schenoudi*, Paris, Leroux, 1907-1914. (*Bibl.* No. 1). Quoted by page. *A 2* 268-285 is by Besa (Kuhn, CSCO 157/copt. 21 [1956] p. X f.), 530-2 by Basilius (Lucchesi, *Analecta Bollandiana* 99:78 [1981]). Amélineau's fragment XXI (*A 2* 415ff.) has now been identified as a translation (at first sight, expert and faithful) of some of Gregory of Nyssa's homilies on Ecclesiastes: Orlandi, *Vetera Christianorum* 18:337f. (1981). In special cases, quotations from this fragment have been retained, marked as "not Sh.". — This, the first extensive edition of Shenoute's works, is on the whole negligent and not always reliable. Wherever possible, I have collated Amélineau's more suspect readings with the Naples MSS and, when necessary, emended them; sometimes I quote the MS in preference to Amélineau's text. Reviews and critical remarks by Nau, Leipoldt, von Lemm and others.
Berl. Sitz.	L. Th. LEFORT in *Anhang* to Bang - von Gabain, "Türkische Turfantexte, II. Manichaica", *Berliner Akad. Sitzungsberichte* 1929:430. Edition of *P* 131^4 158 ro. (Not in *Bibl.*).
BKU	*Ägyptische Urkunden aus den Königlichen Museen zu Berlin: Koptische Urkunden* (Berlin, Weidemann, 1904): No. 180^2 (*Ostr. Or.* 8710 vo). (*Bibl.* No. 6).
BMCat.	W. E. CRUM, *Catalogue of the Coptic MSS in the British Museum* (London, The British Museum, 1905): see below for fragments described and/or edited here). (Not in *Bibl.*).
Cat.	L.-Th. LEFORT, "Catéchèse christologique de Chenoute", *ZÄS* 80:40-45 (1955). (*Bibl.* No. 71).
Ch.	E. CHASSINAT, *Le quatrième livre des entretiens et épîtres de Shenouti* (MIFAO 23, Le Caire 1911). (*Bibl.* No. 19). Parallels with *A 1*, *BMCat.*, *L III*, *Wess.* and unpublished MSS. Part translations, commentaries, glossaries etc. by Du Bourguet, Barns, Koschorke-Timm-Wisse and Cherix. The attribution of *Ch.* 200-209 (206.56-208.22 is paralleled in Kahle, *Bala'izah*, No. 50) is problematic: the authorship of "Liberius" is historically impossible, and in my opinion the Shenoutean authorship is still a pos-

sibility (a commented edition and translation has been prepared by F. Wisse). Quoted by page and line.

CO W. E. CRUM, *Coptic Ostraca from the Collections of the Egypt Exploration Fund, the Cairo Museum and others* (London, The Egypt Exploration Fund, 1902): No. 13 (Ostr. Cairo 8113). (*Bibl.* No. 26).

(*Gol.*) *Jelanskaja* A. I. JELANSKAJA, " Fragment sotryvkom iz sočinenija Šenute ", *Pigulevskaja Volume* (*Ellinističeskij Bližnij Vostok, Vizantija i Iran*, Moscow, Nauka, 1967) 48-51 (formerly MSS Gol. Copt. 40). (*Bibl.* No. 39).

Ench. A. SHISHA-HALEVY, " Unpublished Shenoutiana in the British Library ", *Enchoria* 5:53-108 (1975), with plates 9-30. (*Bibl.* No. 123). Quoted by page and column.

Ep. CRUM-WINLOCK-EVELYN-WHITE, *The Monastery of Epiphanius at Thebes*, II (New York, The Metropolitan Museum, 1926) Nos. 56, 57, 58, 66. (*Bibl.* No. 35).

(*L*) *III, IV* J. LEIPOLDT, *Sinuthii Archimandritae Vita et Opera Omnia*, III (CSCO 42/copt. [ser. 2] 4, Paris 1908) and IV (CSCO 73/copt. [ser. 2] 5, Paris 1913). The best extensive critical edition to date. (*Bibl.* No. 80, see the index of references, p. 175f.). Reviewed by Spiegelberg and Junker. Numerous observations by von Lemm, Jernstedt and others. Translation by H. Wiesemann (CSCO 96/copt. 8, 1931, and CSCO 108/copt. 12, 1936), partial translation (of No. 20-22) by Leipoldt himself (in *Festschrift Barnikol*, Berlin 1964, 52-56). Parallels in *A, Ch., Wess.* etc. (some noted by Leipoldt, with many additions), also in unpubl. or recently published fragments (e.g. Leipoldt's No. 22 - *III* 76.16-77.10 - in *ViK* 922; No. 32 in *B.L.Or.* 8664, see *Or.* below; Nos. 71, 74: see *Lucchesi* below; others are noted above, following relevant quotations). Leipoldt's No. 76 (*IV* 129-153) is not by Shenoute (see *IV* pp. x-xiii; LEIPOLDT 1903:11ff., with various indications of non-Shenoutean composition; Lefort, *Œuvres de S. Pachôme* [CSCO 159/copt. 23] xxiif.). Among other linguistic phenomena betraying non-Shenoutean authorship, observe the frequent *jussive* ⲉⲧⲣⲉϥ- (e.g. 133.20, 136.13, 145.12), extensive non-rhetorical use of ⲙⲁⲣⲉϥ- (e.g. 129.22, 131.20, 135.4); peculiar use of the conjunctive, esp. the conj. continuing or relieving ⲉⲧⲣⲉϥ- at a distance (e.g. 130.7, 131.8, 133.8, 141.22f., 147.19f. etc.): the conjunctive supplies the details in a framework of ⲉⲧⲣⲉ- preceptive jussive. Way of expression different from the Shenoutean: 132.26f., 140.12, 143.5; a special use of -ϭⲉ-, 131.27, 136.11, 138.12,24, 143.5, 145.4; different sentence structure, with frequent anacoluthia, which is unusual in *preceptive* Shenoutean texts. For *III* p. 244 (Gregory of Nyssa) see above, on Amélineau fgt. XXI. — Quoted only by volume (*III, IV*), page and line.

Lemm O. VON LEMM, " Koptische Miscellen, No. CXXIV " (VON LEMM 1972b:413ff.): P. Gol. 38. (*Bibl.* No. 91).

Leyd. PLEYTE-BOESER, *Manuscrits coptes du Musée d'antiquités des Pays-Bas à Leide* (Leiden, Brill, 1897): *Sh.* Nos. 57, 58, 61, 63-5, 67, 72, 73, 75-7, 79-81, 84, 89; *Sh.?* Nos. 60, 68, 69, 89, 90. (Not in *Bibl.*). See *Crum Papers* XI 54, also observations in VON LEMM 1972b:44ff., 1972a:401.

Lucchesi E. LUCCHESI, " Deux feuillets coptes inédits de Shenouté ", *Mus* 91:171-8 (1978): *P copte* 130² 115, 122, 131 (partly parallel to *L* Nos. 71 and 74). (*Bibl.* No. 98).

Ming. G. L. MINGARELLI, *Aegyptiorum codicum reliquiae...* (Bologna, Typis Laelii a Vulpe, 1785): Nos. IV, V, XIII, XIV (according to Gabrielli, *Manoscritti e carte orientali* p. 56, " Marciani 9, 10, già orientali 192-3 "). (Not in *Bibl.*).

Miss.   E. C. AMÉLINEAU, *Monuments pour servir à l'histoire de l'Égypte chrétienne aux IVe*, *V^e*, *VIe et VIIe siècles* (Mém. de la Mission Archéol. Française 4/1, Paris 1888) 277-287 (" Fragmentum ", ΝΓ - ΞΔ, see p. xlvii); pp. 229-236, although somewhat unusual in genre for Shenoute, is nevertheless Shenoutean in style. (Not in *Bibl.*).

Mun.   H. MUNIER, *Manuscrits coptes* (*Catalogue général des antiquités égyptiennes du Musée du Caire* Nos. 99201-9304; Le Caire, IFAO, 1916): *Sh.* Nos. 9257, 9262, 9266-9, 9281, 9282, 9291, 9292, 9298; *Sh.?* 9289, (??) 9255. (*Bibl.* No. 103). Quoted by page.

Or.   A. SHISHA-HALEVY, " Two New Shenoute Texts from the British Library ", *Orientalia* 44:149-185 (1975), with plates IX-X. (*Bibl.* No. 121). New parallels: *VIK* 9292 parallels *B.L.Or.* 8664, here publ., from ΛϾ 34 to ΛΖ 46; *P* 131^6 72 parallels ΜΒ 17 to ΜΔ 20. Prof. B. Layton informs me that the originals for *B.L.Or.* 7561 have been located; that fragments CIII, CIV, CV and CVII cannot have belonged to the main MS (pp. ϤΘ-ΡΔ), also that CI is parallelled by the fragment of Crum, *Papyruscodex*, Appendix. It would therefore seem that the Shenoutean authorship of all fragments on pp. 172-5 is at best doubtful. Quoted by page and line.

Quot.   QUOTATIONS FROM SHENOUTE: (1) In Besa (*ed.* Kuhn, CSCO 157/copt. 21, Louvain 1956), 7.16f.,19ff., 32.33 (see p. 141-2); (2) in Sahidic " Lives of Shenoute ": ed. Amélineau in *Miss.* (1888) 240.3ff., (1895) 640.2f.; ed. Shore, *JEA* 65:143 (1979), p. 138. (3) In the unpublished MS *B.L.Or.* 8811 (formerly Curzon 110), quotations edited by the present writer in *BASP* 17:167-172 (1980); see *Ryl.Cat.* 29f.; one quoted passage parallels *Wess.* 9 91a-b, No. 30b. (4) In *BMCat.* 94 (No. 214).

RE 10, 11   H. GUÉRIN, " Sermons inédits de Senouti ", *Revue égyptologique* 10:148-164 (1902), 11:15-34 (1904), publ. separately in 1903 (Paris, Leroux): Louvre 10.162. (*Bibl.* No. 49). The worst edition of Shenoute: see criticism and corrections by VON LEMM 1972a:405-419. Parallel in part: *BMCat.*, No. 253 (unpubl., see below). Quoted by page and line.

Rossi   F. ROSSI, *I Papiri copti del Museo egizio di Torino* (Torino Accad. Memorie 41-2, Torino, Loescher, 1887-1892): *2/3* (1891) 4-90 (" Pap. Peyron IV ", Ιθ-ΡϤϾ), *2/4* (1892) 44-45 (17 fgts.). (*Bibl.* No. 113). See Orlandi, *Mus* 87:122 (1974). Critical observations, emendations, reconstruction and reedition in part by VON LEMM 1972b:27f., 1972a:350-398. Quoted by fascicle and page.

Rudnitzky   G. RUDNITZKY, " Ein Sermon aus dem Schatzkästlein unseres Vaters Apa Schenute ", *Festgabe C. Wehmer* (Amsterdam 1963) 13-18 (Cod. Heidelb. 63). (*Bibl.* No. 115).

Ryl.Cat.   W. E. CRUM, *Catalogue of the Coptic MSS in the John Rylands Library* (Manchester, The University Press, 1909): Nos. 67-70. (*Bibl.* No. 30). Quoted by page.

Teza   E. TEZA, " Frammenti inediti di un sermone di Scenuti in dialetto sahidico ", *Accad. Nazionale dei Lincei, Rendiconti*, ser. 5 degli Atti, v. 1 (1892) 682-97. (*Bibl.* No. 137). Critical observations etc. by VON LEMM 1972a:298-400.

Wess. 9   C. WESSELY, *Studien zur Paläographie und Papyruskunde* IX (= *Griechische und koptische Texte* I, Leipzig, Haessel, 1909): *Sh.* Nos. 29-32, 35, 36, 38, 41, 42, 44-49, 50-54 (No. 50 is an incipit catalogue of Shenoutean works, to be published and translated, with identifications and additional incipits, by F. Wisse); *Sh.?* 37, 39, 43. (*Bibl.* No. 144). Parallels in some editions and unedited fragments. Textual observations etc. by VON LEMM 1972b:217. Quoted by page, column and line.

Wess. 18   C. WESSELY, *Studien zur Paläographie und Papyruskunde* XVIII (= *Griechische und koptische Texte* V, Leipzig, Haessel, 1917): *Sh.* No. 287; *Sh.?* No. 281. (*Bibl.* No. 145). Quoted by page, column and line.

Young	D. W. YOUNG, " A Monastic Invective against Egyptian Hieroglyphs ", in D. W. YOUNG ed. 1981:348-360 (Mich. 158.13 a-d).
Z, Zoega	G. ZOEGA, *Catalogus codicum copticorum manuscriptorum qui in Museo Borgiano Velitris adservantur* (Roma 1810). (Not in *Bibl.*). Forty-eight Borgian codd. are attributable, with greater or lesser certainty, to Shenoute. Of these 15 were edited in *A* and *L*; 17 in *L* (two in *L* alone), 27 in *A* alone (No. 230, Leipoldt's No. 76, is not by Shenoute: see above). Nos. 301 (*IB* 15, 474 - a copy of 300), 233* (*IB* 9, 408, copy of 233), and 287-8 (*Sh.*?? *IB* 14, 461) have not been edited to date. I quote *Zoega*, where applicable, in lieu of the unreliable *A*.

B. Unpublished Fragments

This list is not meant as a check list or repertory of unedited sources of Shenoute's writings, but as a reference listing of all MSS actually scanned and utilized in the present work. A few words on the procedure of sifting out unedited Shenoute fragments: I have relied heavily on CRUM's opinion, in his *Dictionary*, Catalogues and Papers (Large blue " *S* "; XI 14, XI 54 are here especially relevant). His opinion is used as an authoritative starting point for further examination, never as a last word. I have not as a rule touched upon the question of *codex assignment* of fragments. This important project (of which the main proponent is Prof. Tito Orlandi of Rome) should be undertaken by competent palaeographers, with all the material before their eyes, and should be combined with the compilation of such a repertory as is mentioned above (see §0.1).

ENGLAND

LONDON, *The British Library*,
Dept. of Oriental MSS and Printed Books

Fragments (in *BMCat.* numbering):
Sh. (*B.L.Or.* 3580A) 144 (publ. in *BMCat.*)
    (*B.L.Or.* 3581A) — all (partly = ᴾ) published in *BMCat.* —
            192ᴾ, 194ᴾ, 195ᴾ, 196ᴾ, 198ᴾ, 199, 201, 202ᴾ, 203ᴾ, 205, 206, 209ᴾ, 210ᴾ, 211ᴾ,
            212, 232ᴾ, 253ᴾ (parallel to *RE 10* 159a 1-24), 991, 992ᴾ.
    B.L.Or. 6954 (12) vo, one of the " Horner fragments "; I have used a copy made by Prof. Layton.
Sh.? (*B.L.Or.* 3581A) 215 (partly publ. in *BMCat.*), 251. *Sh.*?? 252.
No. 214 contains a Shenoute quotation (VON LEMM 1972b:27f.).

MANCHESTER, *The John Rylands University Library*

Nos. 67-70 (partially publ. in *Ryl.Cat.*; No. 67 is included in *L*, No. 22, cod. D, where however Leipoldt merely reprinted the *Ryl.Cat.* text). I have used photographs and Crum's copies (*Crum Papers* II 10).

CAMBRIDGE, *University Library*

Or. 16/1699 (H. Thompson's MSS [" Thompson ", " HT "], presented in 1939), fragments *E* (1f.), *F* (1f.), *G* (1f.), *H* (4ff.), *J* (2ff.), *K* (4ff.), *L* (1f.), *X* (1f.). This is part of a collection of approx. 80 fragments, previously in the possession of Hyvernat. Some Shenoutean ones (*A, C, D, E*) have been published. A large box (Or. 16/1700) contains various items, including the paper and envelopes which previously held these fragments, slips with Thompson's transcripts, notes regarding the fragments, correspondence, etc. Thompson seems to have paid special attention to the Shenoutean texts, to judge by his notes on parallel MSS, Biblical quotations and a detailed list of the Shenouteana of the collection.

OXFORD, *The Bodleian Library*

(Volume b 4) *Sh. Cl.Pr.* 22, 36; *Sh.?* *Cl.Pr.* 33. The " b 4 " fragments, originally Woide's, were bought following his death for the Clarendon Press, then deposited in the Bodleian. Abbé Hyvernat's handwritten catalogue of 1887 is very detailed in the description of the fragments. For further information on this collection, see *Crum Papers* II 1; *PSBA* 30:231f. (1908); *RdE* 1:106 n. 2 (1933). (*Cl.Pr.* 39 is " Pseudo-Shenoute ".)

FRANCE

PARIS, *Bibliothèque Nationale*

Fonde copte (I have used microfilms):

130^1: ff. 14-19, 35-7, 124-142 (ff. 14-16 were edited in P. Cauwenbergh, *Étude sur les moines d'Égypte*, Paris 1914, p. 176f.; other isolated passages have been edited elsewhere).

130^2: *Sh.* ff. 1-11, 24, 25, 44-8, 49-64, 65-74, 75-6, 78, 80-1, 89-96, 97-100, 103-4, 105, 109-111, 112, 115, 116, 117-9, 123, 124, 126, 128, 130, 132; *Sh.?* ff. 32-7, 38-43, 106-8, 120.

130^4: *Sh.* ff. 90, 93-4, 95-6, 97-8, 100-5, 107, 110-111, 115-130, 139-142 ro (" Florilegium Sinuthianum "), 155-160 (" Florilegium Sinuthianum "); *Sh.?* ff. 84-9, 99, 114.

130^5: *Sh.* ff. 15-7, 18, 19, 20, 21-2, 23-4, 27, 37-9, 48-9, 52, 55, 56, 57, 58, 59, 61, 64, 65, 66, 67, 69, 70, 80, 81, 83, 86, 87, 88, 90, 92, 93, 94-5, 97-8, 100, 101, 103, 105, 106, 108, 111, 112, 113, 115-9, 121, 125, 128; *Sh.?* ff. 33-4, 50, 51, 96, 99, 133.

130^8: f. 153.

131^1: ff. 37, 75.

131^4: ff. 86-93, 140-7, 150-3, 154-8, 160, 161.

131^5: *Sh.* ff. 4-6, 8, 19, 20, 47, 52, 56, 65, 67, 118, 126, 128, 133-5, 144, 149; *Sh.?* ff. 13, 16, 17, 22, 28, 42, 43, 64, 79-82.

131^6: *Sh.* ff. 13, 14-5, 16, 23, 29, 30, 31, 32, 44, 56-7, 66-7, 80, 81, 105, 117; *Sh.?* ff. 20, 21, 28, 42-3, 64, 71, 90, 110.

131^7: *Sh.* ff. 32, 39, 40, 45, 46, 57, 65, 71; *Sh.?* ff. 11, 25.

131^8: *Sh.* ff. 84, 94, 109; *Sh.?* ff. 91, 92, 105, 119.

(NB: there is a wide margin of error in including or excluding fragments in this list.)

AUSTRIA

VIENNA, *Nationalbibliothek*

ViK: Sh. 912, 913, 918, 920, 921, 924, 926, 927, 928, 933, 940, 9006, 9028, 9040, 9099, 9291, 9292, 9293, 9294, 9298, 9315, 9316, 9320; *Sh.?* 929, 9066. (Crum, who identified in *Dictionary* as Shenoutean also Nos. 919, 9100, 9343, 9598, 9764, 9868, was well aware of the existence in Vienna of unedited Shenouteana. See also Till in *Or.* 41:388 [1935] and *ZDMG* 95:169 [1941].) I have used microfilms.

GERMANY

BERLIN (WEST), *Staatsbibliothek Preussischer Kulturbesitz*

MS Or. 2° 1611.5-7, 1613.1-7 (microfilms and copies).

UNITED STATES

NEW YORK, *Columbia University Library*

Parchment (# 25), photograph in *Crum Papers* I 101.

ANN ARBOR, *University of Michigan Library*

Mich. Ms. 158 (Crum's " 550 "), 14a, 17 (D. W. Young's copies), 15, 16, 18, 19 (quoted from *Dictionary*). The Michigan Shenouteana are being edited by D. W. Young. See *Young* p. 348 and now YOUNG 1982.

DURHAM (*North Carolina*), *Duke University Library*

Duke Univ. Coptic MS (unnumbered), 2ff. (in the Perkins Rare Books Room), kindly copied by Mr. D. Spanel. Possibly Shenoute.

REPUBLIC OF EGYPT

CAIRO, *Egyptian Museum*

No. 8007 (photographs).

CAIRO, *Institut Français d'Archéologie Orientale (IF)*

Cod. 1, quoted from *Dictionary*.

BIBLIOGRAPHICAL REFERENCES

ABBREVIATIONS (OF PERIODICALS AND SERIALS)

ASAE	Annales du Service des Antiquités de l'Égypte
BASP	Bulletin of the American Society of Papyrologists
BIFAO	Bulletin de l'Institut français d'Archéologie orientale (Le Caire)
BO	Bibliotheca Orientalis
BSAC	Bulletin de la Société d'Archéologie Copte
BSL	Bulletin de la Société de Linguistique de Paris
BSOAS	Bulletin of the School of Oriental and African Studies
CdE	Chronique d'Égypte
CFS	Cahiers Ferdinand de Saussure
CSCO	Corpus Scriptorum Christianorum Orientalium
FL	Folia Linguistica
GGA	Göttingische gelehrte Anzeigen
GLECS	Groupe linguistique d'Études chamito-sémitiques
GM	Göttinger Miszellen
IF	Indogermanische Forschungen
IJAL	International Journal of American Linguistics
IOS	Israel Oriental Studies
JAOS	Journal of the American Oriental Society
JEA	Journal of Egyptian Archaeology
JL	Journal of Linguistics
JNES	Journal of Near Eastern Studies
JPs	Journal de Psychologie
Lg	Language
MDAIK	Mitteilungen des Deutschen Archäologischen Instituts, Abteilung Kairo
MH	Museum Helveticum
MIFAO	Mémoires de l'Institut français d'Archéologie orientale
MIO	Mitteilungen des Instituts für Orientforschung
MLR	Modern Language Review
Mus	Le Muséon
OLP	Orientalia Lovanensia Periodica
OLZ	Orientalistische Literaturzeitung
Or	Orientalia
PICL	Proceedings of the International Congress of Linguists
PSBA	Proceedings of the Society for Biblical Archeology
RdE	Revue d'Égyptologie
RE	Revue égyptologique
RT	Recueil de travaux relatifs à la philologie et à l'archéologie égyptiennes et assyriennes
SL	Studia Linguistica

TCLP	Travaux du Circle linguistique de Prague	
TLP	Travaux linguistiques de Prague	
TUGAL	Texte und Untersuchungen zur Geschichte der altchristlichen Literatur	
VR	Vox Romanica	
WZKM	Wiener Zeitschrift für die Kunde des Morgenlandes	
ZÄS	Zeitschrift für ägyptische Sprache und Altertumskunde	
ZcPh	Zeitschrift für celtische Philologie	
ZDMG	Zeitschrift der Deutschen Morgenländischen Gesellschaft	
ZPh	Zeitschrift für Phonetik und allgemeine Sprachwissenschaft	
ZRPh	Zeitschrift für romanische Philologie	
ZV	Zeitschrift für Völkerpsychologie und Sprachwissenschaft	

BOOKS AND ARTICLES

Abel, K. — 1876-7 — *Koptische Untersuchungen*, Berlin: Dümler, Harrwitz u. Gossmann

Ahlman, E. — 1938 — " Über Adverbien ", *Studia Fennica* 2:19-44

Allerton, D. J. — 1978 — " The Notion of ' Givenness ' and its Relations to Presupposition and to Theme ", *Lingua* 44:133-168

Ammann, H. — 1920 — " Von doppelten Sinn der sprachlichen Formen ", *Sitzungsber. Heidelb. Akad., philos.-hist.*, IX, Abh. 12

Andersson, E. — 1904 — *Ausgewählte Bemerkungen über den bohairischen Dialect im Pentateuch koptisch*, Uppsala: Almquist and Wiksell

Bally, Ch. — 1950 — *Linguistique générale et linguistique française*, Berne: Francke

Barri, N. — 1975a — " Nucleus and Satellite in Nominal Syntagmatics ", *Linguistics* 157:67-85

— 1975b — " Adjectifs antéposés et adjectifs postposés comme signes linguistiques différents ", *FL* 7:209-220

— 1977 — " Giving up Word-Formation ", *FL* 11:13-38

— 1978 — " Theme and Rheme as Immediate Constituents ", *FL* 12:253-365

— 1979 — " Giving up Neutralization ", *CFS* 33:7-20

Baum, R. — 1976 — *Dependenzgrammatik*, Tübingen: Niemeyer

Bazell, C. E. — 1949 — " Syntactic Relations and Linguistic Typology ", *CFS* 8:5-20

— 1954 — " The Choice of Criteria in Structural Linguistics ", in: U. Weinreich – A. Martinet, *Linguistics Today*, New York: Publications of the Linguistic Circle of New York, 6-15

Becker, C. F. — 1836 — *Ausführliche deutsche Grammatik*, Frankfurt a. M.: Hermann

— 1841 — *Organism der Sprache²*, Frankfurt a. M.: Kettembeil

Beckman, N. — 1934 — " Västeuropeisk Syntax: Några Nybildningar i Nordiska och andra västeuropeiska Språk ", *Göteborgs Högskolas Arsskrift* XL, 4

Beneš, E. — 1968 — " On Two Aspects of Functional Sentence Perspective ", *TLP* 3:267-274

Bergson, L. — 1960 — *Zur Stellung des Adjektivs in der älteren griechischen Prosa*, Uppsala: Almquist and Wiksell

Blass, Fr. — 1960 — *Der Ausdruck der zeitlichen Unmittelbarkeit* (= Romanica Helvetica, 68) Bern: Francke

Blass–Debrunner: — Fr. Blass – A. Debrunner, *Grammatik des neutestamentlichen Griechisch* [12], Göttingen: Vandenhoek and Ruprecht, 1965

Blomqvist, J. — 1969 — *Greek Particles in Hellenistic Prose*, Lund: Gleerup

Bloomfield, L.	1926	" A Set of Postulates for the Science of Language ", *Lg* 2:153-164
	1935	*Language²*, London: Allen & Unwin
Blümel, R.	1914	*Einführung in die Syntax*, Heidelberg: C. Winter
Böhlig, A.	1973	" Zu einer ungewöhnlichen Verwendung des Qualitativs im Koptischen ", *GM* 8:7-9
	1977	" Zu N im Koptischen ", *GM* 23:11-23
	1979	" Zur Stellung des adjektivischen Attributs im Koptischen ", in: *Festschrift Elmar Edel* (= *Ägypten und Altes Testament*, Bd. 1), Bamberg, 42-45
Böhlig, G.	1956	*Untersuchungen zum rhetorischen Sprachgebrauch der Byzantiner* (= Berliner byzant. Arbeiten, 2), Berlin: Akademie-Verlag
Bolinger, D. L.	1972	" Linear Modification ", in: *Syntactic Theory*, I. *Structuralist*, ed. F. W. Householder, Penguin Books, 31-50
Borghouts, J. F.	1979	" A New Approach to the Late Egyptian Conjunctive ", *ZÄS* 106:14-24
Brinker, K.	1972	*Konstituentenstrukturgrammatik und operationale Satzgliedanalyse*, Frankfurt a. M.: Athenäum
Brøndal, V.	1943	*Essais de linguistique générale*, Copenhagen: Einar Munksgaard
Browne, G. M.	1976	" Notes on Coptic Texts ", *CdE* 50:231-2
	1978a	" Notes on Coptic Literary Texts ", *Enchoria* 8 (Sonderband):7(53)-10(56)
	1978b	" Ad CG II 7, 139:20 ", *BASP* 15:191-3
	1979a	*Michigan Coptic Texts* (= Studia et Textus, 7), Barcelona: Papyrologica Castroctaviana
	1979b	" The Sahidic P Palau Rib. Gospel of Luke ", *CdE* 53:199-202
	1979c	" Notes on Coptic Texts ", *BASP* 16:169-173
Busse, W.	1974	*Klasse, Transitivität, Valenz: transitive Klassen des Verbs im Französischen* (= Intern. Bibliothek für allgem. Linguistik, 36), München: Fink
Callender, J. B.	1970	*Coptic Nominal Sentences and Related Constructions*, University of Chicago Dissertation, mimeographed
	1971	" Notes on Constructions with *jn* ", *Studies in African Linguistics* (UCLA) 2:1-21
	1973a	" Grammatical Models in Egyptology ", *Or* 42 (Gelb Volume): 47-77
	1973b	" Coptic Locative Constructions ", *JEA* 59:190-8
	1975	*Middle Egyptian* (= Afroasiatic Dialects, 2), Malibu: Undena Publications
Cardona, G.	1973	" Indian Grammarians on Adverbs ", in: *Issues in Linguistics*, Papers in Honor of H. and R. Kahane, ed. B. B. Kachru *et al.*, Urbana: Univ. of Illinois Press, 85-98
de Cénival, J. L.	1972	" Sur la forme *sḏm.f* à redoublement ou *mrr.f* ", *RdE* 24:40-5
Černý, J.	1976	*Coptic Etymological Dictionary*, Cambridge: Cambridge Univ. Press
Chafe, W. L.	1976	" Givenness, Contrastiveness, Definiteness, Subjects, Topics and Point of View ", in Ch. N. Li (ed.), *Subject and Topic*, New York/London: Academic Press, 25-55
Chaîne, M.	1933	*Éléments de grammaire dialectale copte*, Paris: Geuthner
Cherix, P.	1979	*Étude de lexicographie copte: Chenouté, Le discours en présence de Flavien* (*Les noms et les verbes*) (= Cahiers de la Révue Biblique, 18), Paris: Gabalda
Coseriu, E.	1969	*Einführung in die strukturelle Linguistik*, Tübingen: Fotodruck Präzis
	1971	*Sprache: Strukturen und Funktionen* (= Tübinger Beiträge zur Linguistik, 2), Tübingen

| | 1975 | *Sprachtheorie und allgemeine Sprachwissenschaft* (= Intern. Bibliothek für allgem. Linguistik, 2), München: Fink |

Coyaud, M.   1979   " Les modes d'expression de l'emphase dans divers langues ", in: *Actes des colloques: Relations Prédicat-Actant(s) dans les langues de types divers*, Paris: SELAF (LACITO-documents), 109-122

Crönert, W.   1903   *Memoria Graeca Herculanensis*, Leipzig: Teubner

Crum, W. E.   1939   *Coptic Dictionary*, Oxford: The Clarendon Press (referred to as *Dictionary*)

Crum, W. E. –
    Evelyn-White, H.G.   1926   *The Monastery of Epiphanius at Thebes*, vols. I, II, New York: The Metropolitan Museum of Art

Crum Papers, kept at the Griffith Institute, The Ashmolean Museum, Oxford

Czermak, W.   1928   " Rhythmus und Umbildung im Agyptisch-Koptischen ", *ZÄS* 63:78-89

    1931   *Der Rhythmus der koptischen Sprache...*, Wien: Hölder–Pichler–Tempsky (Sitzungsberichte d. Akad. d. Wissenschaften Wien, philos.-histor., 213/2)

Dahl, Ö.   1974   " Topic-Comment Structure Revisited ", in: Ö. Dahl (ed.), *Topic and Comment, Contextual Boundness and Focus* (= Papiere zur Textlinguistik, 6), Hamburg: Buske, 1-24

Damourette, J. – Pichon, E., *Des mots à la pensée: essai de grammaire de la langue française*, 1932-1951, Paris: Éditions d'Artrey, 1911-49

Daneš, F. (ed.)   1974   *Papers on Functional Sentence Perspective* (Janua Linguarum, s. minor 147), The Hague: Mouton

    1970   " Zur linguistische Analyse der Textstruktur ", *FL* 4:72-9

Daumas, F.   1952   *Les moyens d'expression du grec et de l'égyptien comparés dans les décrets de Canope et de Memphis* (= Supplément de l'ASAE, Cah. 16), Le Caire: Imprimerie de l'IFAO

Denniston, J. D.   1966   *The Greek Particles*[2], Oxford: The Clarendon Press

Dik, S. C.   1972   *Coordination: Its Implications for the Theory of General Linguistics*, Amsterdam: North-Holland Publ. Company

Drescher, J.   1969   " Graeco-Coptica ", *Mus* 82:85-100

    1970   " Graeco-Coptica II ", *Mus* 83:139-155

Dressler, W.   1968   *Studien zur verbalen Pluralität* (= Sitzungsber. österreich. Akad., philos.-histor., 259/1)

    1973   *Einführung in die Textlinguistik*[2] (= Konzepte d. Sprach- und Literaturwissenschaft, 13), Tübingen: Niemeyer

    1978   *Current Trends in Text-Linguistics*, Berlin/New York: W. De Gruyter

Dressler, W. –
    Schmidt, S. J.   1973   *Textlinguistik: Kommentierte Bibliographie*, München: Fink

Dubois, J.   1965   *Grammaire structurale du français: nom et pronom*, Paris: Larousse

Ebeling, G.   1905   *Probleme der romanischen Syntax*, Halle a.S.: Niemeyer

Edel, E.   1959   " Die Herkunft des neuägyptisch-koptischen Personalsuffixes des 3. Person Plural *-w* ", *ZÄS* 84:17-38

    1956-1964   *Altägyptische Grammatik* (= Analecta Orientalia, 34/39), Rome: Pontificium Institutum Biblicum

Edgerton, W. F.   1935   " On the Origin of Certain Coptic Verbal Forms ", *JAOS* 55:257-267

Emmel, S.   1981   " Proclitic Forms of the Verb + in Coptic ", in: Young (ed.) 1981, 131-146

Erman, A.	1915	" Unterschiede zwischen den koptischen Dialekten bei der Wortverbindung ", *Sitzungsber. preuss. Akad.* 1915/1, 180-8
	1933	*Neuägyptische Grammatik²* (written by W. Erichsen), Leipzig: Engelmann
Fecht, G.	1964	" Die Wiedergewinnung der altägyptischen Verskunst ", *MDAIK* 19:54-96
Fehling, D.	1969	*Die Wiederholungsfiguren und ihr Gebrauch bei den Griechen vor Gorgias*, Berlin: W. de Gruyter
Firbas, J.	1964	" On Defining the Theme in Functional Sentence Analysis ", *TLP* 1: 267-280
Fodor, I.	1959	" The Origin of Grammatical Gender ", *Lingua* 8:1-41, 186-214
Fraenkel, E.	1964a	" Kolon und Satz: Beobachtungen zur Gliederung des antiken Satzes, I ", in: E. Fraenkel, *Kleine Beiträge zur klassischen Philologie*, Rome: Edizioni di storia e letteratura, 73-92
	1964b	" Kolon und Satz, II ", in: *Kleine Beiträge...* 93-130
	1964c	" Nachträge zu Kolon und Satz II ", in: *Kleine Beiträge...* 131-9
	1965	*Noch einmal Kolon und Satz* (= Sitzungsber. bayer. Akad., philos.-histor., 2), München: Beck
Fraenkel, J. J.	1947	" A Question in Connection with Greek Particles ", *Mnemosyne* III/ 13:183-201
Frandsen, P. J.	1974	*An Outline of the Late Egyptian Verbal System*, Copenhagen: Akademisk Forlag
	1975	*At-Former*, Aegyptologisk Institut, Københavns Universitet
Frei, H.	1956	" Charactérisation, indication, spécification ", in: *For Roman Jacobson* (edd. Halle, Lunt et al.), The Hague: Mouton, 161-8
	1961	" Désaccords ", *CFS* 18:35-51
	1966	" Modes de réduction des syntagmes ", *CFS* 22:41-51
	1968	" Syntaxe et méthode en linguistique synchronique ", in: *Methoden der Sprachwissenschaft* (edd. Frei, Robins, Schnelle *et al.*), München/Wien: Oldenbourg, 39-63
Fries, Ch. C.	1957	*The Structure of English*, London: Longman, Green
Frobeen, C.	1898	*Zur Lehre vom Prädikativum*, Königsberg: Hartung
Funk, W.-P.	1976	" ' Blind ' oder ' unsichtbar '? Zur Bedeutungsstruktur deverbaler negativer Adjektive im Koptischen ", paper delivered in the *IV. Koptologische Arbeitskonferenz*, Halle (Sale), 15-17 Nov. 1976; I have used a typescript kindly put at my disposal by the author.
	1977	" Zur Syntax des koptischen Qualitativs ", *ZÄS* 104:25-39
	1978a	" Towards a Synchronic Morphology of Coptic ", in: Wilson (ed.) 1978, 104-124
	1978b	" Zur Syntax des koptischen Qualitativs (II) ", *ZÄS* 105:94-114
	1981	" Beiträge des mittelägyptischen Dialekts zum koptischen Konjugationssystem ", in: Young (ed.) 1981, 177-210
von der Gabelentz, G.	1869	" Ideen zur einer vergleichenden Syntax ", *ZV* 6:376-384
	1875	" Weiteres zur vergleichenden Syntax ", *ZV* 8:129-165
	1901	*Die Sprachwissenschaft: ihre Aufgaben, Methoden und bisherigen Ergebnisse*, Leipzig: Tauchnitz
Gamillscheg, E.	1930	" Zur Einwirkung des Affekts auf den Sprachbau ", *Neuphilologische Monatsschrift* 1:14-34

Gardiner, A. H.	1957	*Egyptian Grammar*³, London: Oxford University Press
Garvin, P. L.	1954	Review of Hjelmslev's *Prolegomena to a Theory of Language* (tr. Whitfield, 1953), *Lg* 30:69-96
	1958	" Syntactic Units and Operations ", *Proceedings of the Eighth International Congress of Linguistics* (Oslo, 1958) 626-633
Gerber, G.	1885	*Die Sprache als Kunst*², Berlin: R. Gärtners Verlagsbuchhandlung
Godel, R.	1945	" Formes et emplois du redoublement en turc et en arménien moderne ", *CFS* 5:5-16
	1954	" Notes inédites de F. de Saussure ", *CFS* 12:49-71
Goldenberg, G.	1971	" Tautological Infinitive ", *Israel Oriental Studies* 1:36-85
Gonda, J.	1957	" The Use of the Particle *ca* ", *Vâk* 5:1-73
Goodwyn, W. W.	1965	*Syntax of the Moods and Tenses of the Greek Verb*, London/New York: Macmillan
Gossen, C. Th.	1951	" Quelques aspects de la mise en relief d'une idée en français et en italien ", *ZRPh* 67:147-8
Greenbaum, S.	1969	*Studies in English Adverbial Usage*, London: Longman
Gregorius, Anba	1981	" Greek Loan-Words in Coptic ", *BSAC* 23:199-222
Grimes, J. E.	1975	*The Thread of Discourse* (= Janua Linguarum, s. minor 207), The Hague: Mouton
Groll, S. I.	1970	*The Negative Verbal System of Late Egyptian*, London: Oxford University Press
Gülich, E. – Heger, K. – Raible, W.	1974	*Linguistische Textanalyse* (= Papiere zur Textlinguistik, 8), München: Fink
Gülich, E.–Raible, W.	1975	*Textsorten: Differenzierungskriterien aus linguistischer Sicht*², Wiesbaden: Athenaion
Guillaume, G.	1919	*Le problème de l'article et sa solution dans la langue française*, Paris: Hachette
Gunn, B.	1924	*Studies in Egyptian Syntax*, Paris: Geuthner
Hall, R. A. Jr.	1965	" Fact and Fiction in Grammatical Analysis ", *Foundations of Language* 1:337-345
Halliday, M. A. K.	1961	" Categories of the Theory of Grammar ", *Word* 17:241-292
	1967	" Notes on Transitivity and Theme in English, 1-2 ", *JL* 3:37-81, 199-244
	1968	" Notes on Transitivity and Theme in English, 3 ", *JL* 4:179-215
	1972	" Language Structure and Language Function ", in: J. Lyons (ed.), *New Horizons in Linguistics*, 140-165
Halliday, M. A. K. – Hasan, R.	1976	*Cohesion in English*, London: Longman
Harris, R.	1972	" Performative Paradigms ", *Transactions of the Philological Society* 1972:44-58
Harris, Z. S.	1951	*Methods in Structural Linguistics*, Chicago: University of Chicago Press
	1952	" Discourse Analysis ", *Lg* 28:1-30
Hartmann, P.	1971	" Texte als linguistisches Objekt ", in: W.-D. Stempel (ed.), *Beiträge zur Textlinguistik*, München: Fink, 9-29
	1975	" Textlinguistische Tendenzen in der Sprachwissenschaft ", *FL* 8:1-49
Haselbach, G.	1966	*Grammatik und Sprachstruktur: Karl Ferdinand Beckers Beitrag zur allgemeinen Sprachwissenschaft in historischer und systematischer Sicht*, Berlin: W. de Gruyter

Havers, W.	1931	*Handbuch der erklärenden Syntax*, Heidelberg: C. Winter
Hausenblas, K.	1966	" Über die Bedeutung sprachlicher Einheiten und Texte ", *TLP* 2:59-69
	1964	" On the Characterization and Classification of Discourses ", *TLP* 1: 67-83
Helbig, G.	1971	" Theoretische und praktische Aspekte eines Valenzmodels ", in: G. Helbig (ed.), *Beiträge zur Valenztheorie*, The Hague: Mouton, 31-49
Hellwig, A.	1974	" Zur Funktion und Bedeutung der griechischen Partikeln ", *Glotta* 52: 145-171
Hintze, F.	1950-1952	*Untersuchungen zu Stil und Sprache neuägyptischer Erzählungen* (= Veröffentlichungen d. deutschen Akad. d. Wissenschaften z. Berlin, Institut für Orientforschung, 2, 6), Berlin: Akademie-Verlag
Hjelmslev, L.	1939	" Notes sur les oppositions supprimables ", *TCLP* 8:51-7
	(1943)	*Omkring Sprogteoriens Grundlaeggse*,
	1961	translated[2] by Whitfield as: *Prolegomena to a Theory of Language*, Madison: University of Wisconsin Press.
	1947	" Structural Analysis of Language ", *SL* 1:69-78
Hockett, Ch. F.	1967	" Where the Tongue Slips, There Slip I ", in: *To Honor Roman Jakobson* (The Hague: Mouton) II, 910-936
Hofmann, E.	1936	*Ausdrucksverstärkung: Untersuchungen zur etymologischen Verstärkung und zum Gebrauch der Steigerungsadverbia...* (= Ergänzungshefte d. Zeitschr. f. vergl. Sprachforschung, 9), Göttingen: Vandenhoek & Ruprecht
Horn, J.	1980	" *'innamā* und die Zweiten Tempora oder: Wie man Polotsky nicht beikommen kann ", *GM* 39:61-88
Householder, F. W.	1952	Review of Harris (1951), *IJAL* 18:260-8
	1971	*Linguistic Speculations*, Cambridge: Cambridge University Press

International Congress of Linguists, Proceedings (*PICL*):

6 (1949)	Paris: Klincksiek
8 (1958)	Oslo: University Press
9 (1964)	The Hague: Mouton
10 (1969)	Bucarest: Éditions de l'Académie
11 (1974)	Bologna: Il Mulino

Isačenko, A. V.	1954	*Grammatičeskij stroj russkogo jazyka...*, Bratislava: Isdat. Slov. Akad. Nauk
Jacobson, S.	1964	*Adverbial Positions in English*, Stockholm: AB Studentbok
Jacobsson, B.	1977	" Adverbs, Prepositions and Conjunctions in English: A Study in Gradience ", *SL* 31:38-64
Jannaris, A. N.	(1897)	*An Historical Greek Grammar, Chiefly of the Attic Dialect. ..*, 1968, Hildesheim: Olms (reprint of 1897, London)
Jelanskaja, A. I.	1965	*Koptskij Jazyk*, Moscow: Nauka
	1966	" Osnovn'e osobennosti sintaksisa složnopodčinennyx predloženij v koptskom jazyke ", *Jazyky Afriki* 309:183-204
	1967	" Slučaj nesoglasovanija podxvatyvajuščego mestoimenija s antecedentom opredelitel'nogo predloženija v koptskom jazyke ", in: *Drevnij Egipet i Drevnjaja Afrika*, Moscow: Nauka, 27-29
	1970	" Razgadka zakona Šterna-Jernstedta ", in: *Pismenn'e Pamjatniki i Problemy Istorii i kultury Narodov Vostoka...*, Moscow: Nauka, 145-6
	1977	" ⲭⲉ en tant qu'indice d'irréalité en copte ", in: *Ägypten und Kusch* (*F. Hintze Anniversary Volume*) (= Schriften z. Geschichte u. Kultur d. alten Orients, 13), Berlin: Akademie-Verlag, 139-142

Jernstedt, P. V.   1925   "Zum Gebrauch des koptischen Qualitativs", *Doklady Akad. Nauk SSSR*, ser. B, 74-7

1927   "Das koptische Praesens und die Anknüpfungsarten des näheren Objekts", *Doklady Akad. Nauk SSSR* 1927, 69-74

1929   "Graeco-Coptica", *ZÄS* 64:122-135

1949   "K determinacii v koptskom jazyke", *Sovetskoje Vostokovedenije* 6:52-62 (I refer to P. Nagel's German translation, with paragraph division and notes, "Zur Determination im Koptischen", in: *Wissenschaftliche Zeitschrift der Martin-Luther-Universität Halle-Wittenberg*, Gesellsch.- u. sprachwiss. Reihe 27, Heft 3:95-106 (1978)

1959a   *Koptskie Texty Gosudarstvennogo Muzeja...*, Moscow/Leningrad: Akad. Nauk SSSR

1959b   *Koptskie Texty Gosudarstevennogo Ermitaža...*, Leningrad/Moscow: Akad. Nauk SSSR

1967   "Egipetskie privativn'e prilegatel'n'e-istočnik grečeskix slovarnyx novšestv", in: *Ellinističeskij Bližnij Vostok, Vizantija i Iran...* (Pigulevskaja Volume), Moscow: Nauka, 44-5

Jespersen, O.   1937   *Analytic Syntax*, London: Allen and Unwin

1948   *Modern English Grammar*, II: *Syntax*, Copenhagen: E. Munksgaard

1949   (by N. Hailsund), *Modern English Grammar*, VII: *Syntax*, Copenhagen: E. Munksgaard

1962   *Selected Writings*, London: Allen and Unwin

Johnson, J. R.   1976   *The Demotic Verbal System* (= Studies in Ancient Oriental Civilization, 38), Chicago: The Oriental Institute

Jones, L. K.   1977   *Theme in English Expository Discourse* (= Edward Sapir Monograph Series, 2), Lake Bluff, Illinois: Jupiter Press

Junge, F.   1972   "Mehrfache adverbielle Bestimmungen nach zweiten Tempora", *ZDMG* Supplement II (Vorträge d. XVII. deutschen Orientalistentages) 33-41

1974   "Linguistik und Ägyptologie", *GM* 10:59-75

1978   *Syntax der mittelägyptischen Literatursprache: Grundlagen einer Strukturtheorie*, Mainz a. Rhein: Philipp von Zabern

Kahle, P. E.   1954   *Bala'izah: Coptic Texts from Deir el-Bala'izah in Upper Egypt*, Oxford: Oxford University Press

Karcevskij, S.   1936   "Sur la nature de l'adverbe", *TCLP* 6:107-111

Kasser, R.   1965   "Comment séparer les mots en copte?", *Mus* 78:307-312

Kern, F.   1888   *Die deutsche Satzlehre: eine Untersuchung ihrer Grundlagen²*, Berlin: Nicolai

Kickasola, J. N.   1975   *Sahidic Coptic (ⲛ) ... ⲁⲛ Negation Patterns: A Morpho-Syntactic Description of Sequences and Adjuncts*, Brandeis Univ. Dissertation, Ann Arbor: University Microfilms

Klum, A.   1961   *Verbe et adverbe* (= Acta Univ. Upsaliensis, Studia Romanica Upsal., 1), Stockholm: Almquist and Wiksell

Koschmieder, E.   1965   *Beiträge zur allgemeinen Syntax*, Heidelberg: C. Winter

Krámský, J.   1972   *The Article and the Concept of Definiteness in Language* (= Janua Linguarum, s. minor 125), The Hague: Mouton

Kühner, R. – Gerth, B., *Ausführliche Grammatik der griechischen Sprache: Satzlehre⁴*, 1955, Leverkusen: Gottschalk

Kuryłowicz, J.	1936	" Dérivation lexicale et dérivation syntaxique ", *BSL* 37:79-92
	1960	" La position linguistique du nom propre ", in: J. Kuryłowicz, *Esquisses linguistiques*, Wroclaw-Kraków: Zaklad Polsk. Akad. Nauk, 182-192
	1964	*The Inflectional Categories of Indo-European*, Heidelberg: C. Winter
Lauer, S.	1959	*Zur Wortstellung bei Pindar* (Inaugural-Dissertation philos.-histor. Fakultät Univ. Bern), Winterthur: Keller
Layton, B.	1979	*The Gnostic Treatise on Resurrection from Nag Hammadi* (= Harvard Dissertations in Religion, 12), Missoula: Scholars Press
	1981	" Compound Prepositions in Sahidic Coptic ", in: D. W. Young (ed.) 1981, 239-268
Lefort, L. Th.	1948a	" ⲭⲉⲕⲁⲥ dans le NT sahidique ", *Mus* 61:65-73
	1948b	" ⲉⲓⲙⲏⲧⲓ dans le NT sahidique ", *Mus* 61:153-170
	1950	" Gréco-copte ", in: *Coptic Studies in Honor of W. E. Crum*, Boston: The Byzantine Institute, 65-71
Leipoldt, J.	1903	*Schenute von Atripe und die Entstehung des nationalägyptischen Christenthums* (= TUGAL, 25), Leipzig: Hinrichs
von Lemm, O.	1972a	(ed. P. Nagel), *Kleine koptische Studien* (= Subsidia Byzantina, X), Leipzig: Zentralantiquariat der DDR
	1972b	(ed. P. Nagel), *Koptische Miscellen* (= Subsidia Byzantina, XI), Leipzig: Zentralantiquariat der DDR
Lepschy, G. C.	1972	*A Survey of Structural Linguistics*, London: Faber and Faber
Levy, A.	1909	*Die Syntax der koptischen Apophthegmata Patrum Aegyptiorum* (Inaugural-Dissertation), Berlin: Gröschel
Lichtheim, M.	1964	" Notes on the Late-Egyptian Conjunctive ", in: *Studies in Egyptology and Linguistics in Honour of H. J. Polotsky*, Jerusalem: The Israel Exploration Society, 1-8
Löfstedt, B.	1966	" Die Konstruktion *c'est lui qui l'a fait* im Lateinischen ", *IF* 71:253-277
Löfstedt, E.	1936	*Vermischte Studien zur lateinischen Sprachkunde*, Lund: Gleerup
	1956	*Syntactica: Studien und Beiträge zur historischen Syntax des Lateins*, II: *Syntaktisch-stilistische Gesichtspunkte und Probleme*, Lund: Gleerup
Löpfe, A.	1940	*Die Wortstellung im griechischen Sprechsatz, erklärt an Stücken aus Plato und Menander*, Freiburg i. d. Schweiz: Paulusdruckerei
Lohmann, J.	1965	*Philosophie und Sprachwissenschaft* (= Erfahrung und Denken, 15), Berlin: Duncker und Humblot
Longacre, R. E.	1976	" Discourse ", in: *Trends in Linguistics, Studies and Monographs*, 1: *Tagmemics*, vol. 1 (edd. Brend-Pike), The Hague: Mouton, 1-44
Lyons, J.	1966	" Towards a ' Notional ' Theory of the ' Parts of Speech ' ", *JL* 2:209-236
	1968	*Introduction to Theoretical Linguistics*, Cambridge: Cambridge University Press
MacCana, P.	1973	" On Celtic Word Order and the Welsh ' Abnormal Sentence ' ", *Ériu* 24:90-120
Malkiel, Y.	1959	" Irreversible Binomials ", *Lingua* 8:113-160
Mallon, A. – Malinine, M.,		*Grammaire copte*⁴, 1956, Beyrouth: Imprimerie catholique
Martinet, A.	1949	" About Structural Sketches ", *Word* 5:13-35
	1965	*La linguistique synchronique, études et recherches*, Paris: Presses Universitaires

Mathesius, V.   1941   " Základní fonce poradku slov v čestine " (" The Fundamental Functions of Word-Order in Czech "), *Slovo a Slovenost* 7:169-180

Mathesius, V. –
Vachek, J.   1975   *A Functional Analysis of Present-Day English on a General Linguistic Basis*, The Hague: Mouton – Prague: Academia

Matthews, P. H.   1974   *Morphology: An Introduction to the Theory of Word-Structure*, Cambridge: Cambridge University Press

Mayser, E., *Grammatik der griechischen Papyri aus der Ptolemäerzeit...*, 1926-1938, Berlin: W. de Gruyter

Meier, G. F.   1961   *Das Zero-Problem in der Linguistik* (= Schriften zur Phonetik, Sprachwissenschaft und Kommunikationsforschung, 2), Berlin: Akademie-Verlag

Mingarelli, A., *Aegyptiorum codicum reliquiae Venetiis in bibliotheca Naniana asservatae*, Bologna 1785

Mink, G.   1978   " Allgemeine Sprachwissenschaft und Koptologie ", in: Wilson (ed.) 1978:71-103

Misteli, F.   1882   Review of Stern, *Koptische Grammatik*, *ZV* 13:428-455

Mohrmann, C. *et al.* 1961   *Trends in European and American Linguistics, 1930-1960. Edited on Occasion of the 9th International Congress of Linguists...*, Utrecht: Spectrum

Moorhouse, A. C.   1959   *Studies in the Greek Negatives*, Cardiff: University of Wales Press

Morenz, S.   1952   " Die Nϭⲓ-Konstruktion als sprachliche und stilistische Erscheinung des Koptischen ", *ASAE* 52:1-15

Müller, C. D. G.   1956   " Koptische Redekunst und griechische Rhetorik ", *Mus* 69:53-72

Müller-Hauser, M. L.   1943   *La mise en relief d'une idée en français moderne* (= Romanica Helvetica, 21), Herlenbach-Zürich: Rentch

Nagel, P.   1964   *Untersuchungen zur Grammatik des subachmimischen Dialekts* (dissertation, mimeographed), Halle a. Saale

                       1969   " Grammatische Untersuchungen zu Nag Hammadi Codex II ", in: Altheim-Stiehl (edd.), *Die Araber in der alten Welt*, Berlin: W. de Gruyter, V/2 393-469

                       1973a   " Marginalia Coptica I: ' Die Wolke neben ihm ' ", *Wissenschaftl. Zeitschr. d. Martin-Luther-Univ. Halle-Wittenberg*, Gesellsch.- u. sprachwiss. Reihe 22, Heft 6:111-115.

                       1973b   " Marginalia Coptica II: Zum substantivierten Relativsatz ", *ibid.* 117-121

                       1980   " Die Determination des Subjektsnomen im Präsens I und das Problem der Satztypen des Koptischen ", *Hallesche Beiträge zur Orientforschung* 2:77-93 (= Martin-Luther-Univ. Halle-Wittenberg Wissenschaftl. Beiträge 1980/8 [I 11])

Otto, E.   1965   *Stand und Aufgabe der allgemeinen Sprachwissenschaft*[2], Berlin: W. de Gruyter

Palek, B.   1968   *Cross Reference: A Study from Hyper-Syntax* (= Acta Univ. Carolinae. Philologica. Monographica, 21), Prague: Univ. Karlova

Parker, R. A.   1961   " The Durative Tenses in P. Rylands IX ", *JNES* 20:180-7

Paul, H.   1920   *Prinzipien der Sprachgeschichte*[5], Halle a. Saale: Niemeyer

Peyron, V. A.   1841   *Grammatica Linguae Copticae*, Taurini: ex Regio Typographeo

Piehl, K.   1902   " Etudes coptes III ", *Sphinx* 5:89-92

Pinkster, H.   1972   *On Latin Adverbs*, Amsterdam: North-Holland Publishing Company

Poch, M.   1959   " Procédés de mise en relief. La phrase segmentée dans quelques oeuvres d'Albert Camus ", *Orbis* 8:161-8

Polotsky, H. J.	1930	Review of De Vis, *Homélies coptes de la Vaticane*, *OLZ* 33: 871-881 (= *CP* 342-7)
	1933	Review of Erichsen, *Fajumische Fragmente der Reden des Agathonicus...*, *OLZ* 36:417-9
	1934	Review of Till, *Koptische Dialektgrammatik*, *GGA* 196:58-67 (= *CP* 363-372)
	1937	" Deux verbes auxiliaires méconnus du copte ", *GLECS* 3:1-3 (= *CP* 99-101)
	1939	Review of Crum, *Coptic Dictionary* (fasc. 2-5), *JEA* 25:113 (= *CP* 373-377)
	1940	" Une règle concernant l'emploi des formes verbales dans la phrase interrogative en néo-égyptien ", *ASAE* 40:241-5 (= *CP* 33-7)
	1944	*Études de syntaxe copte*, Le Caire: Publications de la SAC (= *CP* 102-207)
	1949	" Une question d'orthographe bohairique ", *BSAC* 12:25-35 (= *CP* 378-388)
	1950	" Modes grecs en copte? ", in: *Coptic Studies in Honor of W. E. Crum*, Boston: The Byzantine Institute, 73-90 (= *CP* 208-225)
	1957a	Review of Till, *Koptische Grammatik*, *OLZ* 52:219-234 (= *CP* 226-233)
	1957b	" The Emphatic *sḏm.n.f* Form ", *RdE* 11:109-117 (= *CP* 43-51)
	1957c	" Zu den koptischen literarischen Texten aus Balaizah ", *Or* 26:347-9 (= *CP* 389-391)
	1959	" Zur Neugestaltung der koptischen Grammatik ", *OLZ* 54:453-460 (= *CP* 234-7)
	1960a	" The Coptic Conjugation System ", *Or* 29:392-422 (= *CP* 238-268)
	1960b	Review of Böhlig, *Der achmimische Proverbientext*, *OLZ* 55:23-7 (= *CP* 395-7)
	1961	" Zur koptischen Wortstellung ", *Or* 30:294-313 (= *CP* 398-417)
	1962a	" Nominalsatz und Cleft Sentence im Koptischen ", *Or* 31:413-430 (= *CP* 418-435)
	1962b	Review of Till, *Koptische Grammatik*², *OLZ* 57:478-481 (= *CP* 269-271)
	1964	" Ägyptische Verbalformen und ihre Vokalisation ", *Or* 33:267-285 (= *CP* 52-70)
	1965	*Egyptian Tenses*, Proceedings of the Israel Academy of Sciences and Humanities, II, 5 (= *CP* 71-96)
	1969	" Zur altägyptischen Grammatik ", *Or* 38:465-481
	1970	" Coptic ", in: Th. A. Sebeok (ed.), *Current Trends in Linguistics*, 6: *Linguistics in South West Asia and North Africa*, The Hague: Mouton, 558-570
	1971	*Collected Papers*, Jerusalem: The Magnes Press, The Hebrew University (*CP*)
	1973	" Notre connaisance du néo-égyptien ", in: *Textes et langages de l'Égypte pharaonique: Hommage à Jean-François Champollion*, Le Caire: IFAO, 133-141
	1976	" Les transpositions du verbe en égyptien classique ', *IOS* 5:1-50
Prätorius, J.	1881	Review of Stern, *Koptische Grammatik*, *ZDMG* 35:750-761
Quecke, H.	1962	" Eine mißbräuchliche Verwendung des Qualitativs im Koptischen ", *Mus* 75:291-300

| | 1970 | *Untersuchungen zum koptischen Stundengebet* (= Publications, 3), Louvain: Institut Orientaliste |

1970   *Untersuchungen zum koptischen Stundengebet* (= Publications, 3), Louvain: Institut Orientaliste

1972   *Das Markusevangelium saïdisch* (= Papyrologica Castroctaviana, 4), Barcelona: Papyrologica Castroctaviana

1975/6   "Zu Schenutes Gebrauch des Qualitativs", *OLP* 6/7 (*Miscellanea in honorem Josephi Vergote*) 479-486

1977a   *Das Lukasevangelium saïdisch* (= Papyrologica Castroctaviana, 6), Barcelona: Papyrologica Castroctaviana

1977b   "Eine neue koptische Bibelhandschrift, II ", *Or* 46:300-303

1978   "Das saïdische Jak-Fragment in Heidelberg und London (S 25) ", *Or* 47:238-251

1979   Review of Janet H. Johnson, *The Demotic Verbal System*, *Or* 48:435-448

1981   Review of B. Layton, *The Gnostic Treatise on Resurrection from Nag Hammadi*, *Or* 50:259-263

Forthcoming: "Zum substantivischen Relativsatz im Koptischen ", to appear in: *Proceedings of the Second Congress of the International Association for Coptic Studies* (held in Rome, 1980)

1982   Review of P. Cherix, *Étude de lexicographie copte*, *Or* 51:284-288

Regula, M.   1951   *Grundlegung und Grundprobleme der Syntax* (= Bibliothek der allgemeinen Sprachwissenschaft, Reihe 2), Heidelberg: C. Winter

1966   "Espèces et formes de la mise en relief et de l'anticipation ", *CFS* 23: 121-138

Reiner, E.   1968   *La place de l'adjectif épithète en français: théories traditionnelles et essai de solution* (= Wiener romanistische Arbeiten, 7), Wien/Stuttgart: Braumüller

Robins, R. H.   1966   "The Development of the Word Class System of the European Grammatical Tradition ", *FL* 2:3-19

1970   *Diversions of Bloomsbury: Selected Writings on Linguistics*, Amsterdam: North-Holland Publishing Company

Rosén, H. B.   1957   "Die 'zweiten' Tempora des Griechischen: zum Prädikatsausdruck beim griechischen Verbum ", *MH* 14:133-154

1964   "Outlines of a General Theory of Juncture ", in: *Studies in Egyptology and Linguistics in Honour of H. J. Polotsky*, Jerusalem: The Israel Exploration Society, 153-189

1968   "Die Grammatik des Unbelegten ", *Lingua* 21:359-381

1970   "Les successivités ", in: *Mélanges M. Cohen*, The Hague: Mouton, 113-129

1977   *Contemporary Hebrew* (= Trends in Linguistics, State of the Art Reports, 11), The Hague: Mouton

1979   Review of J. Blau, *An Adverbial Construction in Hebrew and Arabic*, *BSL* 74:459-465

Rothenberg, M.   1970   "Quelques remarques sur les relations syntaxiques de l'adjectif qualificatif en français contemporain", *FL* 4:229-268

1971   "Les propositions relatives à antécedent explicite introduites par un présentatif ", *Études de Linguistique Appliquée* (n. s.) 2:102-117

Rudnitzky, G.   1956   "Zum Sprachgebrauch Schenutes, I, II ", *ZÄS* 81:48-58, 129-139

Säve-Söderbergh, T.   1949   *Studies in the Coptic Manichaean Psalm-Book: Prosody and Mandaean Parallels* (= Arbeten utg. med understöd av Vilhelm Ekmans universitetsfond, 55), Uppsala: Almqvist and Wiksell

Sandmann, M.   1939   " Substantiv, Adjektiv-Adverb und Verb als sprachliche Formen ", *IF* 57:81-112

                      1956   " On Neuter Adjectives Determining Verbs ", *MLR* 41:24-34

                      1954   *Subject and Predicate: A Contribution to the Theory of Syntax* (= Edinburgh University Publications, Language and Literature, 5), Edinburgh: The University Press

Satzinger, H.   1976   *Neuägyptische Studien: Die Partikel* ir. *Das Tempussystem* (= Beihefte zur WZKM, 6), Wien: Verlag des Verbandes der wissenschaftlichen Gesellschaften Österreichs

Saussure, F. de   1949   *Cours de linguistique générale*[4], Paris: Payot

Sauvageot, A.   1950   " La catégorie de l'objet ", *JPs* 43:157-170

Schenkel, W.   1966a   " Die Konversion, ein Epiphänomen des Kemischen (Ägyptisch-koptischen) ", *MDAIK* 21:123-132

                      1966b   " Das Präpositional- und Adverbialattribut des älteren Ägyptisch, eine Apokoinou-Konstruktion ", *JEA* 52:53-8

                      1967a   " Adversarien zum Attribut, Apposition und Genitiv-Relation des Ägyptischen ", *MDAIK* 22:71-83

                      1967b   " Antizipation innerhalb der Wortgruppe und die sog. Badalapposition im Ägyptischen ", *JNES* 26:113-120

                      1972   " Neue linguistische Methoden und arbeitstechnische Verfahren in der Erschließung der ägyptischen Grammatik ", in: *Textes et Langages de l'Égypte pharaonique*, I, Le Caire: IFAO, 167-176

                      1978   " Infinitiv und Qualitativ des Koptischen als Verbaladverbien, oder: Die Jernstedtsche Regel und die Satzarten des Koptischen ", *Enchoria* 8:13-15

                      1981   " *Sḏm=f* und *sḏm.w=f* als Prospektivformen ", in: Young (ed.) 1981, 506-527

Schmidt, K. H.   1973   " Transitiv und Intransitiv ", in: *Akten der IV. Fachtagung der indogermanischen Gesellschaft*, Wiesbaden: Reichert, 107-124

                      1974   " Zur formalen Verkettung von Determinans und Determinatum ", in: *PICL* 11:445-451

Schmidt, R.   1839   *Stoicorum Grammatica*, Halle (reprinted 1967, Amsterdam: Hakkert)

Schoemann, G. F.   1862   *Die Lehre von den Redetheilen nach den Alten*, Berlin: Hertz

Schuchardt, H.   1905/6 " Über den aktivischen und passivischen Charakter des Transitivs ", *IF* 18:528-531

Schuchardt-Brevier: see Spitzer 1928

Schwarze, M. G. – Steinthal, H., *Koptische Grammatik*, 1850, Berlin: Dümmler

Schwyzer, E. (with Debrunner, A.), *Griechische Grammatik*[3], II (*Syntax und syntaktische Stilistik*), 1950, München: Beck

Sebeok, Th. A. (ed.) 1975   *Current Trends in Linguistics*, 13 (*Historiography of Linguistics*), The Hague: Mouton

Sechehaye, A.   1950   *Essai sur la structure logique de la phrase*, Paris: Champion

Seiler, H. J.   1952   " Negation, den Begriff des Prädikats betonend ", *SL* 6:79-91

                      1960   *Relativsatz, Attribut und Apposition*, Wiesbaden: Harrassowitz

                      1967   " On Paradigmatic and Syntagmatic Similarity ", *Lingua* 18:35-79

| | 1968 | " Probleme der Verbsubkategorisierung, mit Bezug auf Bestimmungen des Ortes und der Zeit ", *Lingua* 20:337-367 |

Sethe, K.   1916   *Der Nominalsatz im Ägyptischen und Koptischen* (= Abh. königl. sächs. Gesellschaft d. Wissenschaften, philologisch-histor. Kl., 33/3), Leipzig: Teubner

Sgall, P.   1974   " Focus and Contextual Boundness ", in: Dahl (ed.) *Topic and Comment, Contextual Boundness and Focus*, Hamburg: Buske, 25-51

Shisha-Halevy, A.   1972   *The Circumstantial Sentence in Shenoute's Coptic*, Jerusalem (Hebrew University Dissertation, mimeographed)

                       1973   " Apodotic ЄЧСШТМ: A hitherto Unnoticed Late Coptic, Tripartite Conjugation Form and its Diachronic Perspective ", *Mus* 86:455-466

                       1974   " Protatic ЄЧСШТМ: A hitherto Unnoticed Coptic Tripartite Conjugation-Form and Its Diachronic Connections ", *Or* 43:369-381

                       1975   " Two New Shenoute-Texts from the British Library, II (Commentary) ", *Or* 44:469-484

                       1976a " Commentary on Unpublished Shenoutiana in the British Library ", *Enchoria* 6:29-60

                       1976b " Akhmîmoid Features in Shenoute's Idiolect ", *Mus* 89:353-366

                       1976c " The Circumstantial Present as an Antecedent-less (i.e. Substantival) Relative in Coptic ", *JEA* 62:134-7

                       1978   " Quelques thématisations marginales du verbe en néo-égyptien ", *OLP* 9:51-67

                       1981   " Bohairic - Late Egyptian Diaglosses ", in: Young (ed.) 1981, 314-338

Siertsema, B.   1965   *A Study of Glossematics: Critical Survey of its Fundamental Concepts*[2], The Hague: Nijhoff

Spiegelberg, W.   1909a Review of Leipoldt, *Sinuthii Archimandritae Vita et Opera Omnia* III, *OLZ* 12:439-441

                       1909b " Koptische Miszellen ", *RT* 31:153-161

                       1912   " Koptische Miscellen ", *RT* 34:152-163

                       1925   *Demotische Grammatik*, Heidelberg: C. Winter

Spitzer, L. (ed.)   1928   *Hugo-Schuchardt-Brevier: ein Vademecum der allgemeinen Sprachwissenschaft*[2], Halle: Niemeyer

Steindorff, G.   1904   *Koptische Grammatik*[2], Berlin: Reuther & Reichard

                       1951   *Lehrbuch der koptischen Grammatik*, Chicago: University of Chicago Press

Steinitz, R.   1969   *Adverbialsyntax* (with E. Lang) (= Studia Grammatica, 10), Berlin: Akademie-Verlag

Steinitz-Schädlich, R. 1970   " Probleme der adverbialen Subkategorisierung ", in: *PICL* 10, II 977-984

Steinthal, H.   1847   *De pronomine relativo commentatio philosophico-philologica cum excursu de nominativi particula*, dissertation reprinted in: *Kleine sprachtheoretische Schriften* (ed. Bumann, 1970), 3-113

                       1890   *Geschichte der Sprachwissenschaft bei den Griechen und Römern*[2], Berlin: Dümmler

Steinthal, H. -
    Misteli, F.   1893   *Charakteristik der hauptsächlichsten Typen des Sprachbaues*, Berlin: Dümmler

Stempel, W. D. (ed.)   1971   *Beiträge zur Textlinguistik*, München: Fink

Stern, L.		*Koptische Grammatik*, 1880, Leipzig: Weigel
	1886	" Versuch über eine gleichmäßige Worttrennung im Koptischen ", *ZÄS* 24:56-73
Tesnière, L.	1965	*Éléments de syntaxe structurale*[2] (ed. J. Fourquet), Paris: Klincksiek
Thesleff, H.	1955	*Studies on Intensification in Early and Classical Greek* (Commentationes hum. Litterarum, Soc. Scientiarum Fennica, 21/1), Helsingfors
Till, W.	1928	*Achmîmisch-koptische Grammatik*, Leipzig: Hinrichs
	1941	" Zur Worttrennung im Koptischen ", *ZÄS* 77:48-52
	1954	" Die Satzarten im Koptischen ", *MIO* 2:378-402
	1960	" La séparation des mots en copte ", *BIFAO* 60:151-170
	1961	*Koptische Grammatik (saïdischer Dialekt)*[2], Leipzig: VEB Verlag Enzyklopädie
Tobler, A.	1886	*Vermischte Beiträge zur französischen Grammatik*, I
	1894	*Vermischte Beiträge zur französischen Grammatik*, II
	1899	*Vermischte Beiträge zur französischen Grammatik*, III
	1908	*Vermischte Beiträge zur französischen Grammatik*, IV, Leipzig: Hirzel
Trubetzkoy, N. S.	1936	" Die Aufhebung der phonologischen Gegensätze ", TCLP 6:29-45
	1939a	*Grundzüge der Phonologie* (= TCLP, 7), Prague
	1939b	" Le rapport entre le déterminé, le détérminant et le défini ", in: *Mélanges de linguistique offerts à Charles Bally* (Genève), 52-75
Tuki, R.	1778	*Rudimenta Linguae Coptae sive Aegyptiacae*, Roma
Vernus, P.	1981	" Formes ' emphatiques ' en fonction non ' emphatique ' dans la protase d'un système corrélatif ", *GM* 43:73-88
Volten, A.	1964	" The Late Egyptian Conjunctive ", in: *Studies in Egyptology and Linguistics in Honour of H. J. Polotsky* (Jerusalem), 54-80
Wackernagel, J.	1892	" Über ein Gesetz der indogermanischen Worstellung ", *IF* 1:333-436
Weil, H.	1879	*De l'ordre des mots dans les langues anciennes comparées aux langues modernes: question de grammaire générale*[3], Paris: Vieweg
Weinrich, H.	1966	" La place de l'adjectif en français ", *VR* 25:82-9
	1977	*Tempus: besprochene und erzählte Welt*[3], Stuttgart: Kohlhammer
Weiss, H. F.	1968	" Beobachtungen zur Frage der griechischen Komponente in der Sprache des Schenute ", in: *Probleme der koptischen Literatur* (ed. Nagel, Wissenschaftliche Beiträge d. Martin-Luther-Universität Halle-Wittenberg, 1968/1) 173-185
	1972	" Zum Problem der Einwirkung des Griechischen auf die Sprachen des byzantinischen Orients ", in: *Von Nag Hammadi bis Zypern*, 28-34
Wente, E. F.	1959	*The Syntax of the Verbs of Motion in Egyptian*, Chicago (Univ. of Chicago dissertation, photographic reproduction)
Werlich, E.	1975	*Typologie der Texte*, Heidelberg: Quelle & Meyer
Wiesmann, H.	1914	" Miszellen ", *ZÄS* 52:128-130
	1917	" Miszellen ", *ZÄS* 53:146-7
	1927	" Miszellen ", *ZÄS* 62:66-8
Wilson, M. R.	1970	*Coptic Future Tenses* (= Janua Linguarum, s. practica 64), The Hague: Mouton
Wilson, R. McL. (ed.)	1978	*The Future of Coptic Studies*, Leiden: Brill
Worrell, W. H.	1945	*A Short Account of the Copts*, Ann Arbor: Univ. of Michigan Press (the Henry Russel Lecture for 1941-2)

Young, W. D.   1969   " Unfulfilled Conditions in Shenoute's Dialect ", *JAOS* 89:399-407

                      1961   " On Shenoute's Use of Present I ", *JNES* 20:115-9

              (ed.)   1981   *Studies Presented to Hans Jakob Polotsky*, Beacon Hill: Pirtle & Polson

                      1982   " Unpublished Shenoutiana in the University of Michigan Library ",
                              in: *Egyptological Studies* (ed. S. Israelit-Groll; Scripta Hierosolymitana,
                              28), Jerusalem, 251-267

Zoega, G.   1810   *Catalogus codicum copticorum manuscriptorum qui in Museo Borgiano
                              Velitris adservantur*, Roma: Typis Sacrae Congregationis de Propaganda
                              Fide

ADDITIONAL REMARKS AND REFERENCES

§0.0.1 My investigation, analytic (not synthetic), microscopic (not macroscopic or panoramic), aims at a description of (sub-)systemic structure, not language structure. However, this work does not constitute a monography in the strictest sense, or claim the last word on any of the issues treated therein. As a matter of fact, it embodies a compromise between the need for a broad basis and for a charting as detailed as possible.

§1.1.2.1 B2 (p. 27) and p. 36 n. 75: ЄIC + *temporal expression*. ЄIC is here not a preposition but a focussing element. A series of work-notes by the author on the syntax of ЄIC, ЄIC ZHHTЄ and various existential clauses in the Sahidic New Testament, published in the *Göttinger Miszellen* (77:67ff., 1984), suggests that ЄIC- is a *hic-et-nunc*-deictic member in the existential-statement paradigm.

§1.2.1.1, spec. obs. (1): On " inalienable " possession, see Lévy-Bruhl's classic study, " L'expression de la possession dans les langues mélanésiennes ", *MSL* 19:96-104 (1914); also H. B. Rosén, "Die Ausdrucksform für 'veräusserlichen' und 'unveräusserlichen Besitz' im homerischen Griechisch", *Lingua* 8:264-293 (1959), reprinted in *Strukturalgrammatische Beiträge zum Verständnis Homers*, Amsterdam 1967; *idem*, " Sur quelques catégories à expression adnominale en hébreu-israélien ", *BSL* 53:316-342 (1958). Lévy-Bruhl's term is not satisfactory, since many of the items intimately related or belonging to their owner can nevertheless be "alienated" from him — note the rather extreme and macabre example of limbs being severed from the body (e. g. in martyrological context; in the Bohairic Martyrologies they then cease in fact to be grammatically treated as existing in a special relationship with their owner).

The predication of possession is of course a more comprehensive issue. Observe that, beside OYN-syntagms, Coptic employs for this purpose the Nominal Sentence predicating the pronominalized *possessum* [with a pronominal possessor: (*III* 90.19f.) ПШК ПЄ ПNOYB, ПШК ПЄ ПZAT, TШK TЄ TOIKOYMЄNH; nominal possessor: (*ibid.* 47.20) ПA-NЄΘHPION AN ПЄ].

§2.0.2.1 (Thematization): A germane question not treated here is the determination of the actor noun in the verbal topic, more specifically the correlation of prominent thematization with the *definite* or *referential* actor.

§2.0.2.4, §2.8: The possible correlation of complement placement with relative rhematicity is a direction worth pursuing. A hypothesis: cases of conditioned/non-pertinent placement excepted, the further in the clause an element is placed, the more rhematic it is.

§4.2.2: It appears aften all viable to integrate the phenomenon of " Affective Placement " in a general theory of the information-functional structure of the text; that is to say, placement or paradigm " β ", ППONHPOC NPШMЄ, signals a higher degree of Communicative Dynamism than placement " α ", ПPШMЄ МПONHPOC, this opposition in information weight being in either case mapped onto the basic attributive dependence.

§5.1.1.0.1: A general theory of Coptic determination — of noun definiteness, indefiniteness, specificity, genericity, in relation to such discourse-oriented phenomena as reference and indication — is yet a distant goal. Particular constituents of this theory will be the functional definition of *zero-determination* (different zeroes, according to the various commutations and paradigm extent) and *proper names*.

§5.3 n. 42: A. Schleicher's study was published as Mém. Acad. St.-Pétersbourg, ser. VII, 1859, I No. 7.

§6.0.1.1 (Frontal extraposition): The significance of " definitization " of the fronted noun must be correlated with topicalization in the framework of a general theory of discourse-oriented determination. It appears that all grades of formal determination are represented in this status, although zero determination is very rare; ⲀⲚⲀϢ ⲘⲈⲚ ⲘⲠⲞⲨⲈⲓⲢⲈ (*III* 18.15 f., cf. §3.1.1.1.0.1) is instructive: the noun is the lexical component of a compound verb, and here is the only way of *focalizing* this component, with the zero resumption completing an idiomatic native equivalent of the "tautological infinitive" (GOLDENBERG 1971).

§6.0.2 (Links and delimitations): Another link:delimitation opposition is symptomized by the non-syllabic:syllabic status of the plural definite article before the initial vowel of a noun lexeme, regular (inside the noun syntagm) at least with native lexemes (Ⲛ̄ⲰⲚⲈ, Ⲛ̄ⲒⲞⲨⲆⲀⲒ *vs.* ⲚⲈⲢϢⲞⲨ, ⲚⲈⲬⲎⲨ). With lexemes of Greek origin, we find (in Chassinat's edition) both Ⲛ̄ⲀⲢⲬⲎ and ⲚⲀⲢⲬⲎ, Ⲛ̄ⲀⲠⲞⲤⲦⲞⲖⲞⲤ and ⲚⲀⲠⲞⲤⲦⲞⲖⲞⲤ, and so on; it is my impression that these cases too may be accounted for as conditioned by factors outside the noun syntagm, e.g. sandhi with the preceding word. (See Polotsky, *OLZ* 59:253 n. 1, 1964 - note omitted by error in *CP*.) See now, for the " Middle Egyptian " dialect, *CdE* 58/115-6, p. 316.

§6.0.2.3: Generally speaking, two lexemes join in relatively open juncture, unless one contains an active grammeme (the case of ⲤⲈⲦⲠ-ⲠⲢⲰⲘⲈ), whereas grammemes and mixed grammeme-lexeme syntagms join in relatively close juncture.

§6.1.1.2.1 (d), ad *RE 10* 161a 27ff.: The augens may have a special standing when the referate is a noun syntagm in address (" vocative ") status: here the definite article is situation-conditioned, hence (like a proper name) not really (i.e. pertinently) " definite ".

§6.1.3, §6.2.1: The prominence of personal indication marked by the augens *may* overlap and coincide with thematic prominence, especially in the case of coincidence with a different marking of topicalization; consider (*III* 137.27) ⲈⲒⲚⲀϢϢⲠⲈ ⲀⲚⲞⲔ ⲘⲠⲒⲤⲦⲞⲤ ⲬⲈ-, sim. *Ch.* 156.1f. or (*Cat.* 42.14, 43.8) ⲚⲦⲔ-ⲚⲒⲘ ⲚⲦⲞⲔ.

§7.1.3.1 (The conjunctive base and the *nota relationis*): See also Schleicher, "Zur Morphologie der Sprache " (reference in add. to §5.3, above), p. 24.

§7.2.1.1.5.1: See now M. Green, " The ⲦⲀⲠⲈ Pattern in Coptic Non-Biblical Texts ", *ZÄS* 110 (1983) 132-143, arriving at very similar conclusions regarding the rhetorical role of this form.

§7.2.3.2, ad *IV* 162.2ff.: Compare the variant text in *K* 9223 p. 67, where the same effect of vivid, dramatic action is achieved by the juxtaposition of perfect forms: ⲚⲌⲞⲤⲞⲚ ⲀⲠⲀⲒ ⲈⲒ ⲈⲂⲞⲖ ⲀⲠⲀⲒ ⳨-ⲦⲈ̇ⳍⲚⲀⲌⲂ ⲈⲌⲞⲨⲚ ⲚⲌⲞⲤⲞⲚ ⲀⲠⲀⲒ ⳨-ⲦⲰⳍ ⲈⲌⲞⲨⲚ ⲀⲠⲀⲒ ⲈⲒ ⲈⲂⲞⲖ.

§7.3.1.1 with n. 73 and **§7.4**: The distinction of *factive* and *non-factive* introduced by P. and C. Kiparsky in *Progress in Linguistics* (edd. Bierwisch and Heidolph, The Hague 1970) 143-173, applies to Coptic " that "-forms: ⲬⲈ- factive or unmarked, ⲈⲦⲠⲈ- marked non-factive, the conjunctive a marginal non-factive form. (Consider the variation of ⲦⲠⲈ- and conjunctive after ⲘⲚⲚⲤⲀ- in Ruth 2:11 (Shier), although ⲦⲠⲈ- does not share the markedness for non-factivity of ⲈⲦⲠⲈ-.)

INDEX OF SUBJECTS DISCUSSED

(The references are to chapters, paragraphs or pages. The index is selective.)

—, of augens: §6.1.0.2 ff.

—, of modifiers: §1.3.1 ff. *passim*

—, of Nominal Sentence patterns: 34f., 161[36]

Protasis: 100, 201ff.

Protatic "*fallsetzend*" forms, followed by conjunctive: §§7.2.3.5, 7.2.4

Protatic forms, followed by conjunctive: §7.2.4

Pro-verbs, conjugation bases: §5.3; *Addenda* ad §5.3

—, conjunctive "base" not one: 191f.

Punctuation: 98[138], 164

Quantifiers: 143f.

Questions, multiple: 90; *see also* Rhetorical questions

Quotation, topicalization of (figure): §2.7.2.4

Quotations in Shenoute: 4, 198

—, topic and focalization-pattern selection: 88ff.

—, ⲦⲀⲢⲈϤ-: §7.2.1.1.5.1

Rection: §4.2.2.1.4; 5, 24ff., 108, 144f.

Relative conversion: 6[14], 19, 68f.

Relative, substantivized (determinated): §5.2.3.1; 83f., 114, 152[38]

—, as object: two distinct syntagms: §3.1.1.2.1

—, of future tense, followed by conjunctive: §7.2.3.5

—, of present tense, followed by conjunctive: §7.2.4.1

"Relief": 65[14], 72

Resumption as junctural symptom: 94f., 162; *see also* Zero, resumption of

Rheme: 69ff., *see also* Focus

Rhetorical apodosis, eventual role of conjunctive in: §7.2.6.1

Rhetorical dialogue: §0.2.5.2.1

Rhetorical figures and schemes: 9[41]; *see also under* Figures

Rhetorical focalization/topicalization figures: §2.7.1-2

Rhetorical narrative: 10[46]; *see also* Perfect, non-narrative

Rhetorical questions, Second Tenses and focalization patterns: §2.1.2; 76f., 89, 90, 94

—, apodosis of (ⲦⲀⲢⲈϤ- and conjunctive): 196

—, and particle placement: 171

Rhetoricity: §0.2.5.2.1

Rhythmic factors regulating object construction: §3.1.3.3.2; 121

—, and placement of rear extraposition: 99

Rosén, H.B.: 8, 160[22]

Second Tenses: Ch. 2; 8[34], 10[46], 183, 191

—, autofocal: §2.1

—, and Basic Tenses: §2.7.3.1; 65[16]

—, circumstantial conversion of: §2.0.1.1.2

—, conjunctional uses of: 100

—, constituents of Bipartite Pattern: 62ff.

—, and converters: §2.0.1.1

—, coordination + disjunction of, with Basic Tenses: §2.7.3.1

Transitive/intransitive verb lexemes in Coptic: 106[4]
Transitivity/intransitivity: §3.0.1.1-2
Tripartite Conjugation bases, pro-verbs: §5.3
Tripartite Conjugation pattern, IC-analysis of: §5.3; 124, 191f.

" Unique morpheme ": §1.3.1.1

Valency: §§3.0.1.1-2, 3.1.2.0.1; 24ff.
" Vedette ": *see* Cleft Sentence, Focus
Verb lexeme, marked as focal: 76ff.
—, morphology of: §3.0.2.1
Verbal predicate, durative/non-durative, homonymous: §3.1.2.1.1
Verboid of possession: 113
Verbs of incomplete predication, object construction of: §3.1.1.2.3
" *Verstärker* ": *see* Augens

" *Wechselsatz* ": §2.7.1.1; 33, 81, 161[36]
Word in Coptic: §6.0.2.3; 6, 7[25], 9
Word order: §§2.8.2, 6.0.1.3; 14 and *passim*

Zero: 6
—, anaphora: §3.1.1.1.0.1; 133
—, cataphora: 151
Zero article: Ch. 5 *passim* (esp. 142ff.)
—, resumption of: Ch. 5 *passim* (esp. 146ff.); 109
Zero determination: *see* Zero article
—, incompatibility with N- in object construction: §3.1.1.2.1
—, pronominal object anaphoric to: §3.1.1.1.0.1
Zero-marked nouns in modifier status: §1.3.2
Zero morpheme (2nd person sgl. feminine) in juncture contour: 162[37]
Zero subject of predicative modifier: §1.2.1.3.3; 151
Zeroing, anaphoric: 112f.

COPTIC MORPHS AND WORDS

I. OF GREEK ORIGIN

ⲀⲖⲎⲐⲰⲤ: §1.3.11.1.2
ⲀⲖⲖⲀ: §1.3.11.6
ⲀⲖⲖⲞ: §7.3.3
ⲀⲚⲦⲒ: §1.3.11.5
(ⲌⲀⲠⲀⲌ) ⲌⲀⲠⲖⲰⲤ: §1.3.11.1.7
ⲀⲢⲀ: 76[74]
ⲀⲢⲬⲀⲒⲞⲤ: 136

ⲄⲀⲢ: *see* Greek particles, Enclitics
ⲄⲈⲚⲞⲒⲦⲞ: §7.3.3

ⲆⲈ: *see* Greek particles, Enclitics
ⲆⲒⲔⲀⲒⲰⲤ: §1.3.11.1.7

ⲈⲒⲘⲎⲦⲒ: §§1.3.11.6, 7.3.1.1
ⲈⲔⲘⲈⲢⲞⲨⲤ: §1.3.11.6
(ⲞⲨⲔ)ⲈⲦⲒ: §1.3.11.6
ⲈⲨⲦⲀⲌⲒⲀ (εὐταξία): §1.3.11.6

Ⲏ (– Ⲏ): §7.3.1.1

ⲔⲀⲔⲰⲤ: §1.3.11.1.3
ⲔⲀⲖⲰⲤ: §1.3.11.1.3; 72[57], 85
ⲔⲀⲚ: §1.3.11.6, 7.3.1
ⲔⲀⲦⲀ: §1.3.11.5

ⲖⲞⲒⲠⲞⲚ: §1.3.11.2.4

ⲘⲀⲖⲒⲤⲦⲀ: §1.3.11.2.5.1
ⲘⲀⲖⲖⲞⲚ: §1.3.11.2.5
ⲘⲈⲚ: *see* Greek particles, Enclitics
ⲘⲎ... ⲀⲚ: 101[56]

ⲘⲞⲄⲒⲤ: §1.3.11.6; 52, 70, 72[57], 84, 208
(ⲞⲨ) ⲘⲞⲚⲞⲚ: §1.3.11.2.1

ⲌⲞⲘⲞⲒⲰⲤ: §1.3.11.1.4
ⲌⲞⲘⲰⲤ: §1.3.11.1.4
-ⲞⲚ-marked modifiers: §1.3.11.2
ⲞⲚⲦⲰⲤ: §1.3.11.1.6
-ⲞⲤ, -ⲞⲚ, concord in adjectives of Greek origin:
   4.2.2.1
ⲌⲞⲤⲞⲚ, ⲈⲚ-, ⲈⲪⲞⲤⲞⲚ: §1.3.11.6
ⲌⲞⲦⲀⲚ: §1.3.11.6

ⲠⲀⲖⲒⲚ ⲞⲚ: §1.3.11.3
(ⲞⲨ) ⲠⲀⲚⲦⲰⲤ: §1.3.11.1.5
ⲠⲀⲢⲀ: §1.3.11.5
ⲠⲖⲎⲚ: §1.3.11.6
ⲠⲞⲖⲖⲀⲔⲒⲤ: §1.3.11.6
ⲠⲢⲞⲤ: §1.3.11.5

ⲤⲬⲈⲆⲞⲚ: §1.3.11.2.3

ⲦⲀⲬⲀ: §1.3.11.6
ⲦⲀⲬⲨ: §1.3.11.4
ⲦⲞⲦⲈ: §1.3.11.6

ⲪⲀⲚⲈⲢⲞⲚ: §1.3.11.2.2

ⲬⲰⲢⲒⲤ: §1.3.11.5
-ⲰⲤ-marked modifiers: §1.3.11.1; 81

ⲌⲰⲤ: §1.3.11.5; 59, 80
ⲌⲰⲤⲦⲈ: §§1.3.11.6, 7.3.1.1

II. OF NATIVE COPTIC ORIGIN

ⲀⲚ, Ⲛ- ⲀⲚ: §§2.9., 6.0.3.3; 63[7], 69

ⲀⲢⲎⲨ: 211

ⲀⲦ-: §3.4.2

ⲀⲨⲰ, and enclitics: 165

—, coordinating modifiers: 35

—, a modifier: §1.3.10

ⲀⲨⲰ vs. zero, coordinating the conjunctive: 188f.

Ⲉ-, preposition in adnominal status: 21

ⲈⲀϤ-: 10[42], 82, 86

ⲈⲂⲞⲖ ⲀⲚ ⲬⲈ-: 78, 102[160]

ⲈⲒⲈ: 98

ⲈⲘⲀⲦⲈ: §1.3.1.1

ⲈⲚⲈ, converter vs. interrogative marker, juncturally distinct: 163[42]

ⲈⲚⲈ, interrogative marker: 66[26]

ⲈⲚⲈⲌ: §1.3.6; 23

ⲈⲠ-marked modifiers: §1.3.7

ⲈⲠ- + infinitive: §1.3.7.6

ⲈⲠⲦⲎⲢϤ: §1.3.7.2

ⲈⲠⲌⲀⲈ: §1.3.7.1

ⲈⲠⲈⲌⲞⲨⲞ: §1.3.7.4

ⲈⲠⲬⲒⲚⲬⲎ: §1.3.7.3.1

ⲈⲢⲞ⸗, predicative: 38

ⲈⲦⲢⲈϤ- as "that"-form: §7.4

—, as topic: 91

—, jussive: 205[63]

—, with conjunctive: §7.2.5.2

ⲈⲰϪⲈ-, topicalizing: §2.7.2.1.1

(ⲌⲰⳠ) ⲈⲰϪⲈ-: 78f.

ⲈⲌⲞⲨⲚ Ⲉ-: 19[22]

ⲈⲌⲢⲀⲒ, "up/down": 29f.

ⲈⲬⲚ-, predicative: 38

ⲈⲒⲠⲈ, with Ⲛ- + iterated noun as predicative complement: §1.3.3.2

  Ⲟ Ⲛ-: §1.2.1.3.1

  Ⲡ-, object of: §3.1.1.2.3

  Ⲡ-/Ⲟ Ⲛ-, allomorphs of "intransitive" Ⲡ-: 106[4]

  Ⲡ-, + modifier: §1.2.1.3.2

  Ⲡ-, with Second Tense: 80

  ⲢⲠⲔⲈ-: see Conjugation mediators

  ⲢⲌⲞⲨⲞ/Ⲉ-: see Conjugation mediators

ⲈⲒⲤ + time expression: 85, Addenda ad §1.1.2.1 B

ⲈⲒⲤ + (Nom. Sentence + modifier): 36[75]

ⲔⲈ-/ⳠⲈ-: 143ff., 146ff.; see Determinators

ⲔⲞⲨⲒ, ⲈⲦⲒⲔⲈⲔⲞⲨⲒ ⲠⲈ: §7.3.1

ⲔⲞⲨⲒ, Ϣ⎻Ⲙ: 134

ⲘⲈ, ⲌⲚⲞⲨⲘⲈ: §1.3.5.2

ⲘⲘⲎⲚⲈ: §1.3.1.1

ⲘⲘⲒⲚ ⲘⲘⲞ⸗: §6.1.4.2

ⲘⲘⲀⲦⲈ: §1.3.1.1

ⲘⲘⲀⲨ: §1.3.1.1

ⲘⲚ-, preposition, in adnominal status: 21, 36

—, coordinating modifiers: 36

ⲚⲘⲘⲀ⸗, coordinating a second pronominal rectum of a prepositional phrase: 36

ⲘⲒⲚⲈ: 137[28], 143[9]

ⲘⲚⲚⲤⲀ-: §7.3.1

ⲘⲀⲨⲀⲀ⸗: §6.1.4.1

—, and ⲘⲘⲀⲦⲈ: §6.2; 43

ⲘⲈϢⲀⲔ: §7.3.3

ⲘⲞⲈⲒⲌⲈ ⲈⲬⲚⲘⲞⲈⲒⲌⲈ: 38, 143[9]

Ⲛ-, conjugation "base" of conjunctive: §§7.1.1, 7.1.3

Ⲛ-, "nota relationis": §1.0.1-2; 6[19], 131[12] and passim; Addenda ad §7.1.3.1

—, adnominal: Ch. 4 passim (esp. §4.0.1 ff.); 20f., 131f.

—, adverbal: Ch. 3 passim; 27, 29, 81

Ⲛ-modifiers: §§1.0.1.2, 1.3.1; 2, 11f.

Ⲛ-/ⲘⲘⲞ⸗, predicated in Bipartite Pattern: 36f.

—, identity and homonymy issues: §3.1.2.0.1

—, rection: Ch. 3 passim (esp. §§3.0.1.1, 3.1.2)

—, "belongs" to the verb, not the governed noun: 17[13], 107[5]

ⲚⲀ⸗, preposition: §6.1.5

—, predicated: 37f.

-ⲚⲀ-, future characteristic, bracketing: 161[33]

ⲚⲈ-, converter: see Preterite converter

ⲚⲀⲘⲈ: §1.3.5.1

ⲚⲒⲘ, determinator: 143f., 144[16], 146ff.

—, Ø-...ⲚⲒⲘ, as object: §3.1.1.2.1

ⲚⲒⲘ ⲈⲚⲈⲌ, "whoever": §1.3.6.1; 83

ⲚⲀⲚⲞⲨ⸗: 150

ⲚⲚⲀⲌⲠⲚ-: 35

ⲚⲦⲀ-/ⲦⲀ-, conjunctive, 1st person sgl.: §7.0.2

ⲚⲦⲀϤ-/ⲈⲚⲦⲀϤ-, Second/relative perfect: 68f.

—, circumstantial + Second Perfect: 67

Thompson (Cambridge)		ViK (Vienna) (K)					
D 59	45	913	24	9028	78, 133, 134	9298	18[19], 151
H 1 ro	46	926	79	9040	115	9315	78
2 vo	46	927	22	9068	85	9316	65, 99
3 ro	47	928	52, 202	9100	106[4]	9317	95
K 3 vo	137, 196	933	95, 112, 210	9223	Add.		
L ro	207	934	19	9291	22		
				9292	107[6]		
				9294	24, 25, 125		

DATE DUE
